# Alaska at War

# Alaska at War 1941–1945

## THE FORGOTTEN WAR REMEMBERED

EDITED BY FERN CHANDONNET

University of Alaska Press

Fairbanks

University of Alaska Press
P.O. Box 756240
Fairbanks, AK  99775-6240

Originally published in 1995 by the Alaska at War Committee, Anchorage, Alaska.

ISBN 13: 978-1-60223-013-2
ISBN 10: 1-60223-013-7


Library of Congress Cataloging-in-Publication Data

Alaska at War Symposium (1993 : Anchorage, Alaska)
Alaska at war, 1941–1945 : the forgotten war remembered / edited by Fern Chandonnet.
     p. cm.
Originally published: Anchorage, Alaska :  Alaska at War Committee, c1995.
A collection of papers from the Alaska at War Symposium, Anchorage, Alaska, November 11–13, 1993
Includes bibliographical references and index.
ISBN 978-1-60223-013-2 (pbk. : alk. paper)
1.  World War, 1939–1945—Campaigns—Alaska. 2.  World War, 1939–1945—Campaigns—Alaska—Aleutian Islands. 3. Alaska—History—1867–1959. 4.  Aleutian Islands (Alaska)—History—20th century.
I. Chandonnet, Fern. II. Title.
  D769.87.A4A425 1993a
  940.54'28—dc22                                          2007014821


Cover design by Dixon Jones, Rasmuson Library Graphics

This publication was printed on acid-free paper that meets the minimum requirements for ANSI / NISO Z39.48–1992 (R2002) (Permanence of Paper for Printed Library Materials).

# Table of Contents

## ALASKA AT WAR

Georgeanne L. Reynolds ———————————————————————— ix
*Introduction and Acknowledgements*

## KEYNOTE ADDRESSES

Dean C. Allard ——————————————————————————————— 3
*Naval Views on the North Pacific before and during World War II*

William A. Jacobs ——————————————————————————— 13
*American National Strategy in the Asian and Pacific War*

M.V. Bezeau ————————————————————————————————— 19
*Strategic Cooperation: The Canadian Commitment to the Defense of Alaska in the Second World War*

Brian Garfield ————————————————————————————— 27
*The Thousand-Mile War: World War II in Alaska and the Aleutians*

Hisashi Takahashi ——————————————————————————— 33
*The Japanese Campaign in Alaska*

Alvin D. Coox ———————————————————————————————— 39
*Reflecting on the Alaska Theater in Pacific War Operations, 1942-1945*

Buck Delkettie———————————————————————————————— 43
*An Alaskan Scout Remembers*

William Draper————————————————————————————————— 47
*A Brush with War*

George F. Earle ——————————————————————————————— 53
*Painting with the Tenth Mountain*

## WAR IN THE NORTH PACIFIC

B.B. Talley and Virginia M. Talley——————————————————— 59
*Building Alaska's Defenses in World War II*

Admiral James Russell————————————————————————————— 67
*Recollections of Dutch Harbor, Attu, and Kiska in World War II*

William S. Hanable ——————————————————————————————— 75
*Theobald Revisited*

Fern Chandonnet ——————————————————————————————— 81
*The Recapture of Attu*

Alastair Neely ——————————————————————————————————— 87
*The First Special Service Force and Canadian Involvement at Kiska*

Galen R. Perras ——————————————————————————————— 97
*Canada's Greenlight Force and the Invasion of Kiska, 1943*

George F. Earle ——————————————————————————————— 103
*Kiska: Birth of a Division*

Teruo Nishijima ——————————————————————————— 109
  *Recalling the Battle of Attu*
Gary J. Candelaria ———————————————————————— 113
  *Tin Can at War: The USS "Monaghan" and the War in Alaska*
Karl Kaoru Kasukabe————————————————————— 121
  *The Escape of the Japanese Garrison from Kiska*
M. Joseph Leahy ———————————————————————— 125
  *The Coast Guard at War in Alaska*
Ralph M. Bartholomew ——————————————————— 131
  *The Tenth Emergency Rescue Boat Squadron, Eleventh Army Air Force*
Joseph M. May and Harold Steinhoff ————————————— 135
  *Life on Adak, 1942-1944*
Stephen M. Morrisette ———————————————————— 141
  *The Story of Three B-24s, Fairbanks, 1942*
  *The Man who Walked out of Charley River* ———————————— 143

## DEFENDING THE TERRITORY

Zachary Irwin ——————————————————————————— 149
  *Search and Rescue in the Air Transport Command, 1943-1945*
Chris Wooley and Mike Martz————————————————— 155
  *The Tundra Army: Patriots of Arctic Alaska*
Ray Hudson ——————————————————————————— 161
  *Aleuts in Defense of their Homeland*

## THE ALASKA HIGHWAY

Heath Twichell ——————————————————————————— 167
  *The Wartime Alaska Highway: Boon or Boondoggle?*
William R. Hunt and Alex Hunt ———————————————— 173
  *The Wrong Route: Donald MacDonald and the Alaska Highway*
Norman Bush ——————————————————————————— 179
  *The Alcan Saga, 1942-1943*
Harry Yost———————————————————————————— 185
  *Snapshots from a Soldier's Scrapbook*
Jane Haigh———————————————————————————— 189
  *Roadside Development along the Alaska Highway: The Impact of World War II on Military Construction on the Alaska Highway Corridor*

## WAR'S IMPACT ON THE HOME FRONT

David A. Hales ——————————————————————————— 197
  *World War II in Alaska: A View from the Diaries of Ernest Gruening*
Stephen W. Haycox ————————————————————————— 203
  *Mining the Federal Government: The War and the All-America City*
Bob King ———————————————————————————— 211
  *The Salmon Industry at War*
Michael Burwell ——————————————————————————— 219
  *The SS "Northwestern": The Ship that Always Came Back*

Frank Norris ————————————————————————————————— 227
    *Hollywood, Alaska, and Politics: The Impact of World War II on Films about the North Country*
W. Conner Sorensen ————————————————————————————— 235
    *The Civilian Conservation Corps in Alaska and National Preparedness*
Helen Butcher ——————————————————————————————— 241
    *My Alaska War Years, 1941-1946*
Gaye L. Goerig ——————————————————————————————— 245
    *The Civilian Population—Seldovia*
Timothy Rawson ——————————————————————————————— 253
    *World War II through "The Alaska Sportsman" Magazine*
Ronald K. Inouye ——————————————————————————————— 259
    *For Immediate Sale: Tokyo Bathhouse—How World War II Affected Alaska's Japanese Civilians*
Nancy Yaw Davis——————————————————————————————— 265
    *Childhood Memories of the War: Sitka*

## MINORITIES IN ALASKA'S MILITARY

Lael Morgan ———————————————————————————————— 271
    *Race Relations and the Contributions of Minority Troops in Alaska*
Charles Hendricks ——————————————————————————————— 277
    *A Challenge to the Status Quo?*
Sylvia K. Kobayashi——————————————————————————————— 285
    *I Remember What I Want to Forget*

## ALEUT RELOCATION AND RESTITUTION

Dean Kohlhoff——————————————————————————————— 291
    *'It Only Makes My Heart Want to Cry': How Aleuts Faced the Pain of Evacuation*
    *The Politics of Restitution*——————————————————————— 297
Henry Stewart——————————————————————————————— 301
    *Aleuts in Japan, 1942-1945*
Marie Matsuno Nash, Office of Sen. Stevens ————————————————— 305
    *An Alaskan Who Was Interned Introduces Remarks by Senator Ted Stevens*
Flore Lekanof Sr.——————————————————————————————— 307
    *Aleut Evacuation: Effects on the People*

## LEND-LEASE

Baker B. Beard——————————————————————————————— 311
    *The Bradley Mission: The Evolution of the Alaska-Siberia Air Route*
Daniel L. Haulman——————————————————————————————— 319
    *The Northwest Staging Route*
Tat'iana Kosheleva——————————————————————————————— 327
    *The Construction and Use of the Fairbanks-Krasnoiarsk Air Route, 1942-1945*
Alexander B. Dolitsky ————————————————————————————— 333
    *Alaska-Siberia Lend Lease to Russia*
David S. Raisman ——————————————————————————————— 341
    *The Alaska-Siberia Friendship Route*

Richard A. Russell ———————————————————————————— 345
    *The Hula Operation*

## HISTORIC PRESERVATION

Larry Murphy and Daniel Lenihan ————————————————— 353
    *Underwater Archaeology of the World War II Aleutian Campaign*
Charles E. Diters———————————————————————————— 359
    *Attu and Kiska, 2043: How Much of the Past Can the Present Save for the Future?*
Linda Cook ————————————————————————————————— 365
    *The Landscape of a Landmark: Strategies for Preservation*
Barbara S. Smith ——————————————————————————————— 371
    *Making it Right: Restitution for Aleut Churches Damaged in World War II*
Jack E. Sinclair——————————————————————————————— 377
    *Turning the Forgotten into the Remembered: The making of Caines Head State Recreation Area*
R. Bruce Parham ——————————————————————————————— 383
    *Right Before your Eyes: Finding Alaska's World War II Records in the National Archives*

## THE WAR'S AFTERMATH

John H. Cloe ————————————————————————————————— 393
    *The Legacy of the War*
John T. Farquhar——————————————————————————————— 399
    *Northern Shield and Drawn Arrow: Alaska's Role in Air Force Reconnaissance Efforts, 1946-1948*
Janice Reeve Ogle———————————————————————————————— 407
    *The Air Route Nobody Wanted: Reeve Aleutian Airways*
Leo J. Hannan ———————————————————————————————— 411
    *A Legacy of World War II: Alaska Territorial Guard/Alaska State Guard*
Gwynneth Gminder Wilson ————————————————————— 413
    *A Well-Kept Secret*
John Cloe, Elmer Freeman, and Lael Morgan ———————————— 415
    *Writing about the War*

R. Bruce Parham——————————————————————————————— 421
    *Selected bibliography*

    *Index* ——————————————————————————————————— 443

# Introduction

ALASKA WAS CHANGED FOREVER BY WORLD WAR II. The Japanese invasion of the Aleutians brought to the territory a military buildup and subsequent peacetime population surge which continue to shape the face of the state today. The construction of military bases and of the accompanying support facilities—accomplished in the most inhospitable of climates and in the country's most remote regions—was one of the largest and most rapid undertakings in modern military history.

During the course of the war, the U.S. War Department spent nearly three billion dollars on military construction and operations in Alaska. It also sent some 300,000 military personnel to a territory that in 1940 had harbored barely more than 73,000 residents, 500 of whom were military.[1] More than fifty years later, physical reminders of World War II dot the Alaska landscape. The mark of the war on Alaska is indelible.

In 1938, as part of a simultaneous American base buildup underway throughout the Pacific, the U.S. military began planning for the construction of army, army air, and navy bases in Alaska for Sitka, Kodiak, and Dutch Harbor. The effort was touted as an important defensive barrier against a possible Japanese attack on the continental United States via the Aleutians.[2]

Many airports, harbors, communications facilities, roads and highways were built on the Alaska mainland to facilitate the movement of the military throughout the territory. The war also gave Alaska its first road link to the rest of the United States—the Alaska or "Alcan" (Alaska Canadian Military) Highway, along with a new internal network of roads. These as well as other improvements, in addition to large amounts of surplus equipment, were left after the war and radically improved Alaska's infrastructure, thus forming the basis for considerable postwar economic growth. By 1950 the territory's population had grown to more than 128,000, twice that of the pre-war period.[3] The war also proved Alaska's strategic importance and assured a large military presence after 1945.[4]

In June 1942, as part of a strategy to anchor a defensive perimeter around its possessions and conquests in the northern and central Pacific, Japan launched an assault on Alaska. Two aircraft carriers, the *Junyo* and *Ryujo*, launched attacks on Dutch Harbor on June 3 and 4. Another force captured two western Aleutian islands—Kiska and Attu—on June 6 and 7.

The Japanese Imperial High Command used this opportunity to protect its northern flank from attack, suspecting that Lieutenant Colonel Jimmy Doolittle's April 1942 raid on Tokyo had been launched from the outer Aleutians.[5] The attack on the Aleutians was also a diver-

I would like to thank R. Bruce Parham, Assistant Director, National Archives-Alaska Region, for writing the historical narrative on the Aleutian Campaign and the significance of World War II in Alaska on pages three and four of the introduction. I would also like to express my appreciation for his editorial comments.

[1] Alden Rollins, comp., *Census Alaska: Numbers of Inhabitants, 1792-1970* (Anchorage: University of Alaska Anchorage Library, 1970), 1940-3.

[2] Joan M. Antonson and William S. Hanable, *Alaska's Heritage*, vol. 2, *Unit 4-Human History: 1867 to Present*, Alaska Historical Commission Studies in History No. 133 (Anchorage: Alaska Historical Society for the Alaska Historical Commission, 1985), p. 309.

[3] Rollins, comp., *Census Alaska*, 1950-2.

[4] Antonson and Hanable, *Alaska's Heritage*, vol. 2, p. 318.

[5] After the war ended, the Japanese learned that Doolittle's raid had been launched from aircraft carriers under the command of Admiral "Bull" Halsey from the central Pacific. Brian Garfield, *The Thousand-Mile War: World War II in Alaska and the Aleutians* (Garden City, N.Y.: Doubleday & Company, Inc., 1969; reprint, New York: Bantam Books, 1982), p. 8.

sionary move in conjunction with the planned invasion of Midway Island. Admiral Isoroko Yamamoto, Commander in Chief of the combined Japanese fleet, used the Aleutians as bait to force the weakened American carriers out of Pearl Harbor into battle and, presumably, to their destruction. Because of the Aleutian operation, the Japanese at the crucial Battle of Midway did not have the superiority in air carriers that they might have had. The *Junyo* and *Ryujo* were too far away to be recalled to help the main striking force. If Yamamoto's plan had succeeded, Japan would have gained undisputed control of the central and western Pacific.[6]

In the North Pacific theater, American and Canadian forces occupied Adak and Amchitka in January 1943. After a month of bitter fighting, on May 30, 1943, an American force of 15,000 troops destroyed the Japanese force of about 2,500 on Attu at a cost of 550 killed and more than 1,100 wounded. On July 28, the remaining 5,000 Japanese troops left on Kiska managed a brilliant escape under cover of fog. Three weeks later, on August 15, nearly 35,000 U.S. and Canadian troops made unopposed landings to reoccupy Kiska. They were as astonished as they were relieved to find the Japanese gone.[7] After the recapture of Attu and Kiska, many of the American military forces in Alaska were transferred to other theaters of operation in the Pacific or in Europe. The remaining North Pacific forces became a tactical threat for staging offensive operations against the Kuriles and ultimately the northern island of Hokkaido, tying down thousands of Japanese soldiers who might have been sent elsewhere.

After the retaking of Attu and Kiska, the Aleutians were to become a backwater. Still, Alaska was to continue to exert some influence in the North Pacific Theater. From the Aleutians, the Eleventh Air Force launched bombing raids on Japanese bases in the Kuriles. These were the first attacks on the Japanese home islands by shore-based aircraft.

Large construction projects continued throughout the territory. The construction of the Alaska Highway, Northwest Staging Route, Canol (Canadian Oil) project, as well as other large-scale endeavors provided support for the lend-lease route for ferrying aircraft, supplies, and equipment to the Soviet Union.

Due in large part to the area's remarkably inhospitable climate and topography, the North Pacific did not develop as a major theater of operations. This reality was manifested with the Japanese decision to abandon Kiska Island after the annihilation of its garrison on Attu. Japan chose to concentrate on the defense of its positions in the central and southwest Pacific.

After American forces retook Attu and Kiska, the Aleutian front became one of the loneliest and least-remembered theaters of operations. The war had moved elsewhere and took a sense of purpose with it. Assignments to the Aleutians were looked upon with dread as they often meant enduring foul weather, long periods of darkness, grinding boredom, food shortages, no one-year rotational policy, the feeling of uselessness, and worst of all, very few women.[8] For years, the Aleutian Campaign has been called the "Forgotten War."

In November 1993, as part of a commemoration of the war, an international conference on World War II in Alaska, northwest Canada, and the North Pacific region was hosted in Anchorage by Alaska at War. Formed in May 1992, this nonprofit association grew out of the Alaskan Command's World War II Commemoration Committee on Elmendorf Air Force Base. The symposium brought an international and inter-disciplinary group of scholars, historians, American and Japanese soldiers, civilian evacuees, Alaska civilians, government officials, and even descendants of prisoners of war together to reflect on the issues, personalities, and effects of the war within the microcosm of the Alaska theater. The symposium has shed light on a mix of obscure and well-known aspects of American, Canadian, Soviet, and Japanese military involvement in Alaska during World War II; on Allied and Japanese defense strategies; on the adverse effects of wartime conditions on the Aleuts and Alaskan Japanese civilians; on the economic, social, and psychological impact of the war in reshaping Alaska and northwest Canada; and on the legacy of the war.

A nineteen-member steering committee worked for eighteen months to bring together a careful mix of seventy speakers from all nations involved in World War II in Alaska. Papers on the Japanese campaign in the Aleutians were presented by Japanese scholars and by Japanese soldiers who had been stationed on Attu and Kiska. Russian and Canadian military historians offered their perspectives on lend-lease and other topics. One account of the devastating Aleut evacuation and relocation in June 1942 was presented by one of its victims. A survivor of the United States' internment of Japanese-Americans related her experiences at the War Relocation Authority's camps at Puyallup, Washington, and Minidoka, Idaho.

The three-day symposium was the focal point of a week-long conference which included a film series, an art

---

[6] U.S., Army, Department of Naval Intelligence, *The Aleutian Campaign, June 1942-August 1943* (Washington, D.C.: Office of Naval Intelligence, 1945; reprint, Washington, D.C.: Department of the Navy, Naval Historical Center, 1993), pp. 1-2; and Gerhard L. Weinberg, *A World at Arms: A Global History of World War II* (New York: Cambridge University Press, 1994), pp. 335-336.

[7] Weinberg, *A World at Arms*, p. 633.

[8] John Haile Cloe with Michael F. Monaghan, *Top Cover for America: The 11th Air Force in Alaska, 1920-1983* (Missoula, Mont.: Pictorial Histories Publishing Co. for the Air Force Association, Anchorage Chapter, 1991), p. 128.

exhibit, a tour of Elmendorf Air Force Base, several receptions, and a USO-style dance with a '40s theme. The Anchorage Museum of History and Art hosted the opening reception in conjunction with the exhibit, *"A Brush with War: World War II Art from the Alaska Campaign."* Two of the artists featured, William Draper, a professional artist sent by the army to record the war, and soldier-artist George Earle, who painted pictures of Kiska small enough to fit into his pack, gave a joint presentation at the museum. The museum also displayed *"Faces of War,"* an exhibit that showed the human side of war with captured photographs of Japanese soldiers in the Aleutians, images of American airmen, Aleut refugees, and USO entertainers. The exhibit was jointly presented by the Air Force, National Park Service, Aleutian/Pribilof Islands Association, and the museum.

Although the conference focused principally on Alaska, many papers addressed the profound and permanent impact that World War II had on northwest Canada and the North Pacific. The papers touch upon the significance of the war with such diverse themes as military history, Alaska politics, the treatment of Native peoples, and the reshaping of northern society.

Drawing on the perspective of half a century, informed by the wealth of sources now available, and taking into account changing interpretations that have emerged in the light of developments over the years, the symposium provided a forum for the reconsideration of the region's role in the war effort, the performance of the military forces on both the Allied and Japanese sides, the contributions of Alaskans, and the political, economic, social, and psychological impact and after-effects of the war. The symposium and, therefore, these proceedings will no doubt promote new research, reexamine familiar themes, and stimulate further analysis of World War II in the northern Pacific.

The papers are presented in ten sections: (1) "Keynote Addresses," (2) "War in the North Pacific," (3) "Defending the Territory," (4) "The Alaska Highway," (5) "Minorities in Alaska's Military," (6) "Aleut Relocation and Restitution," (7) "War's Impact on the Home Front," (8) "Lend-Lease," (9) "Historic Preservation," and (10) "The War's Aftermath."

Section 1, "Keynote Addresses," presents the views of a distinguished group of speakers on a variety of topics, primarily covering how Allied and Japanese war plans and air, sea, and land strategy developed prior to the outbreak of war in 1941, and how these concepts were implemented by both sides in the North Pacific.

Dean C. Allard, Chief of Naval History, U.S. Department of the Navy, opens the volume with a keynote address on naval views on the North Pacific before and during World War II. Allard analyzes the concepts of naval planners in the 1920s and 1930s and shows how

Brigadier General (Ret.) Benjamin B. Talley, left, Chairperson Georgeanne L. Reynolds, and Admiral (Ret.) James Russell at the Alaska at War Conference in Anchorage. *(Photograph by Jim Stuhler, U.S. Army Alaska, Public Affairs, Fort Richardson, Alaska)*

these concepts evolved during the war. His examination also provides an incisive glimpse of the role the North Pacific played in the Orange and Rainbow war plans, and how the strategy of the Battle of Midway was similar to or different from pre-war concepts. He also assesses the strategic implications of lend-lease operations in support of the Soviet Union and examines the final naval surface and air campaign against Japan.

William A. Jacobs, a professor of political science and history at the University of Alaska Anchorage, offers an assessment of American national strategy in plans for an Asian and Pacific war against Japan. Jacobs argues that the fundamental pattern of U.S. military operations against Japan was well established in American strategic planning long before the outbreak of hostilities in 1941. While there were many disagreements about specific plans, America assumed that Japan would possess the initiative in the beginning and that the United States would, accordingly, be forced on the defensive. In the middle stages of the conflict, the United States would fight to gain the strategic position from which the final phase could be launched: a strategic "siege" of the Japanese home islands. With few exceptions, prewar planners did not expect Alaska or the North Pacific to play a decisive role in any part of these operations. Jacobs concludes that although events proved them right, Alaska and the North Pacific made important contributions to the war in Europe through the transport of lend-lease aid to the Soviet Union.

M.V. Bezeau, the Director of Ceremonial, National Defence Headquarters, Canadian Department of National

Defence, is responsible for traditions and heritage programs within Canada's military. Bezeau offers a much needed perspective on the Canadian commitment to the defense of Alaska during World War II. He explains how strategic cooperation between Canada and the United States, based on the mutual defense of North America, encompassed the provision and protection of American lines of communication to Alaska and support for Canadian-American forces in the Aleutian theater.

Brian Garfield, the author of *The Thousand-Mile War: World War II in Alaska and the Aleutians* (1969), was the featured banquet speaker at the symposium. He provides a fascinating account of many of the characters, adventures, and red tape he encountered while conducting research for his book. Garfield also offers a plausible explanation for the famous "Battle of the Pips" (radar blips), the phantom encounter that briefly diverted the U.S. Navy ships screening Kiska, thus allowing the Japanese to evacuate the island.

Hisashi Takahashi, professor of military and diplomatic history at the National Institute for Defense Studies in Tokyo, examines the Japanese campaign in Alaska. Takahashi also offers a fresh perspective on the Japanese mindset as an international rivalry and arms race goaded Japan from 1935 onward to prepare for possible war with the United States and the Soviet Union. He explains how the planned attack on Midway evolved in an atmosphere of profound disagreement between factions in the army and navy.

Alvin Coox, director of the Japan Studies Institute at San Diego State University, examines the Aleutian Campaign from both Japanese and American viewpoints. Citing Samuel Eliot Morison, Coox describes the area as a "theater of military frustration" to illustrate that service in the Aleutians constituted "hard time" for soldiers and, often, a place for commanders who were bound for anonymity.

Next, Buck Delkettie presents his luncheon talk, "An Alaskan Scout Remembers." Delkettie, formerly of the 297th Infantry, Fort Richardson, Alaska, was transferred to the Alaskan Scouts in 1942, where he served until his discharge in late 1945. During his tour of duty he served as a radio operator and boat operator. He was also responsible for training new infantry groups, no mean task when one considers the constraints of Alaska's harsh terrain and weather. Delkettie leads the reader on a roller-coaster tour of experience and perception that includes viewing enemy-held Kiska from the belly of a B-24.

In the final essays in this section, artists William Draper and George Earle discuss World War II combat art and their experiences in the Aleutians. Draper was an official combat artist, whereas Earle was a soldier who painted scenes of Kiska while stationed there with the Eighty-Seventh Mountain Infantry.

Section 2, "War in the North Pacific," offers a variety of perspectives on the land, sea, and air war in the North Pacific. Among the fifteen papers presented in this session, several offer assessments of pre-war and wartime naval strategy; reminiscences of Dutch Harbor, Attu, and Kiska; HULA-2 training operations of Soviet naval personnel at Cold Bay; the Canadian-American military invasion of Kiska; the Battle of the Komandorski Islands; and the legacy of the war. Other essays flesh out images of Rear Admiral Robert A. Theobald in his role as commander of the North Pacific Force (May 1942 to January 1943); the Coast Guard at war in Alaska; the life of the soldier on Adak; and the Tenth Emergency Rescue Boat Squadron of the Eleventh Army Air Force.

Four fascinating first-hand accounts—in addition to that of soldier-artist George Earle—add to the breadth and originality of this session. Admiral James Russell, who commanded Navy Patrol Squadron 42 in Alaska during the war, offers an analysis of military developments in the North Pacific from the perspective of both a field commander and an eminent strategist. Russell's talk is modeled along the lines of a summary report on the Aleutian Campaign that he prepared for the three-volume work, *The Campaigns of the Pacific War*. General Benjamin B. Talley and Virginia Talley recount General Talley's experiences as resident engineer in charge of military construction in Alaska on projects including Yakutat Airfield, Fort Abercrombie (Kodiak Island), Fort Glenn (Umnak Island), Fort Mears (Unalaska Island), and major fortifications on Amchitka and Shemya. What emerges is a greater appreciation of the logistical challenge facing the engineers, soldiers, and construction workers during the military buildup in the Aleutians and on mainland Alaska. Karl Kaoru Kasukabe, a Japanese intelligence officer on Attu and Kiska, discusses how the Japanese garrison slipped away from Kiska without being detected. Joe May, a first lieutenant with an antiaircraft battalion that landed on Adak in 1942, provides perspective on the lives of soldiers stationed there from 1942 to 1944.

Galen R. Perras, an instructor of history at the Royal Military College of Canada, examines Canada's Greenlight Force: its conceptualization, the politics—international and provincial—that determined its formation, its initially chaotic organization, and finally its disappointing deployment to Kiska. The major difficulties were with Canada, as the army, stung by accusations that poorly-trained troops had been sent to their doom in Hong Kong and Dieppe, spent much more time and effort to ensure there would be no grounds for such criticism again. Perras also provides an incisive glimpse into how Canadian troops, under American command and organization for the first time in their history, tolerated and overcame operational difficulties.

Section 3, "Defending the Territory," features an essay

by Zachary Irwin, Associate Professor of Political Science at Pennsylvania State University, which describes the sled-dog rescue of downed airmen, especially those ferrying lend-lease aircraft along the Northwest Route from Montana to Nome. By war's end, the development of the helicopter and the use of other methods would render this form of rescue obsolete. Nevertheless, the ingenious experiments with harnesses, parachutes, and the sizes of teams (of both men and dogs) constituted valuable experience for U.S. troops. In another essay, Chris Wooley and Mike Martz discuss the Tundra Army and the role played by Major Marvin "Muktuk" Marston in its development. In the final essay in this section, Ray Hudson provides an account of the Aleuts who served in the armed forces as scouts, infantrymen, and seamen.

Section 4, "The Alaska Highway," offers several essays, including Heath Twichell's assessment of early critics who had said that the Alaska Highway was in the wrong place and that it would take too long to build. Some even charged that the undertaking had been of so little military value that it should never have been built at all. Dr. Twichell assesses the Alaska Highway's contribution to Allied victory in light of these misgivings. William R. Hunt, Professor Emeritus of History at the University of Alaska Fairbanks, discusses several aspects of the Alaska Highway's construction and concludes that the route was not needed as much as had been thought, but that it was nevertheless a successful exercise of American-Canadian cooperation. Jane Haigh's essay explores the development and growth of towns along the Alaska Highway after the end of construction. Harry Yost's recollections are those of a soldier who helped build the Alaska Highway and who, as a truck driver, then hauled supplies the length of the road.

Section 5, "War's Impact on the Home Front," looks at life in Alaska during the war. University of Alaska Fairbanks professor David A. Hales offers a glimpse into the work and thought of territorial governor Ernest Gruening. Among the problems Gruening faced during the war years were the federal government's proposed immigration plans, a territory appallingly unprepared for war, bombardment by the Japanese, racism among civilians, the establishment of price controls, and rationing and shortages. The essay by W. Conner Sorensen looks at the role of the Civilian Conservation Corps in the war effort. Focusing on the salmon industry at war, Bob King lends needed perspective on how the war affected the salmon canners, then the largest industry in the territory. Michael Burwell provides a suspenseful account of the SS *Northwestern*, a steamer with a long and checkered history in Alaska.

Frank Norris, a historian with the National Park Service, Alaska Region, offers a fascinating study of how Hollywood treated wartime Alaska on film. Equally interesting are Steve Haycox' examination of the development of Anchorage from its sleepy pre-war days to its status today as the state's bustling financial and population center, and Timothy Rawson's history of *The Alaska Sportsman*—the forerunner of today's *Alaska* magazine. The periodical presents a special view of the territory's politics, preparedness, and propaganda during the war years. The section would be incomplete without several personal recollections—Nancy Yaw Davis' vignettes about her childhood in wartime Sitka, including one about the appearance of what must surely have been a Japanese submarine (although her mother said it was a rock and not a sub at all), and Gaye L. Goerig's story of how her father, an engineer with the Tenth Army Air Force Emergency Rescue Squadron, met her mother, an employee of Cook Inlet Packing Company in Seldovia.

Section 6, "Minorities in Alaska's Military," examines American government attitudes toward the African American and Native American troops working on various northern defense projects. Lael Morgan, a professor of journalism at the University of Alaska Fairbanks, and Charles Hendricks, a historian with the U.S. Army Corps of Engineers, examine in separate essays the views of army leaders during World War II with respect to the employment of minorities as soldiers, the missions they accomplished, working conditions, and the impact of their efforts on northern defense projects. Both present new research on the experiences of the African-American regiments who worked on the Alaska Highway, in the Aleutians, and on the CANOL project. Morgan also presents a compelling account of Native-American troops in Alaska's Territorial Guard. Hendricks focuses on the running debate in official circles over the use of minority troops in Alaska. Ronald Inouye of the University of Alaska Fairbanks discusses the internment of both Aleuts and Japanese-Americans in Alaska. Inouye illustrates his essay with personal stories gleaned from Alaska's Japanese Pioneers History Project.

In Section 7, "Aleut Relocation and Restitution," the emphasis on minorities broadens to include the tragic story of the Aleuts, who were evacuated and relocated to southeast Alaska or shipped by the Japanese to Otaru, Japan. Flore Lekanof, of the Aleutian/Pribilof Islands Association, relates the wrenching experience which the evacuation from their homes was to the Aleuts living in the Pribilofs. They were allowed to take with them little more than what they wore—along with a sackful of personal items—and were then left to suffer the ravages of exposure and disease in Funter Bay, in Southeastern Alaska.

Dean Kohlhoff, a professor of history at Valparaiso University, addresses Aleut survival strategies in the U.S. camps, while Henry Stewart, who teaches at Mejiro Women's College and Waseda University, recounts their treatment in Japan. A second essay by Dr. Kohlhoff discusses the 1988 legislation that authorized monetary restitution to the Aleuts. Finally, Marie Matsuno Nash, of Senator Ted Stevens' office, tells of the senator's efforts to bring attention to Aleut and Japanese-American issues and his crusade to appropriate restitution funding for the Aleuts.

Section 8, "Lend-Lease," features the essays of two Russian scholars, David Raisman, a journalist and historian from Magadan, and Tatiana Kosheleva, curator of history at the Irkutsk Regional Studies Museum. Raisman discusses the development of the Alaska-Siberia Air Route (ALSIB), not only in terms of the international give and take involved at its conception, but in the human toll its construction and use exacted from Americans and Russians alike. Kosheleva examines the participation of the Siberians in the lend-lease program and chronicles the construction of the air base at Kirensk, Siberia, a destination of lend-lease fighter planes leaving Alaska.

Baker B. Beard, a cadet at the U.S. Air Force Academy, discusses the establishment of ALSIB and the role of Major General Follett Bradley in negotiating and implementing the transcontinental air route across Siberia. The U.S. Air Force Historical Research Agency's Daniel L. Haulman describes the air route and then considers its construction, its benefit to the Eleventh Air Force in Alaska, and its operation as a lend-lease instrument. Alexander Dolitsky follows the development of lend-lease, from President Roosevelt's initial expressions of concern about *Wehrmacht* successes against the Soviets, to the establishment of the ALSIB route and the eventual transfer of thousands of U.S. aircraft to the Russian military effort on the Eastern Front.

In Section 9, "Historic Preservation," the physical remains of World War II in Alaska are acknowledged and the real issue of saving the past for the future is explored. Linda Cook, a historian with the National Park Service, Alaska Region, defines the importance of the National Historic Landmarks program and demonstrates how physical remains can provide a window to the past. The relics on such battlegrounds as Dutch Harbor, Attu, and Kiska honor the troops deployed there more than fifty years ago, as well as Aleuts taken from their homeland, and the returning families of fallen Japanese soldiers. Larry Murphy and Daniel Lenihan, also with the National Park Service, describe the results of the survey of Kiska Harbor by the service's Submerged Cultural Resources Unit and the U.S. Navy, which revealed many underwater sites and materials associated with American-Japanese combat in the Aleutians.

Charles E. Diters, of the U.S. Fish and Wildlife Service, Alaska Regional Office, describes World War II remains on Attu and Kiska, and ponders to what extent they can be preserved in place for the future, given the islands' remoteness. Barbara Sweetland Smith presents a compelling portrayal of the damage done to Russian Orthodox churches and liturgical art, and the prospects for restoration. Finally, Jack E. Sinclair, of Alaska State Parks, discusses the military buildup of Resurrection Bay and the Seward area, and the recent designation of Caines Head as a State Historical Park.

Section 10, "The War's Aftermath," looks at various post-war events and developments. U.S. Air Force Academy historian John T. Farquhar presents a tense account of the post-war reassessment of U.S.-Soviet relations and the perceived need to keep Alaska at the ready. Janice Reeve Ogle relates the story of Reeve Aleutian Airways' civilian support of the war effort, the airline's subsequent growth, and its present role as the mainstay for travel to the Aleutians, the Alaska Peninsula, and the Pribilof Islands. Gwynneth Gminder Wilson presents a short essay on the U.S. Navy's cryptography work which led to the deciphering of German and Japanese codes. Finally, three historians—John Cloe, Elmer Freeman, and Lael Morgan—discuss writing about the war.

These essays—so diverse and multifaceted—capture in print the World War II experience in Alaska, and in the Aleutians particularly. This publication, then, represents the final and perhaps the best part of Alaska at War, because it is a permanent contribution to the commemoration and understanding of the North Pacific Campaign. This volume is a gift to the men and women who fought the war and, at the same time, to the generations to come. It is hoped that our work will help ensure that the "Forgotten War" will be remembered.

*Georgeanne L. Reynolds*
*Conference Chair*

# Acknowledgements

DEVELOPING A CONFERENCE AND SEEING THE PROJECT through can be an overwhelming experience. None of the members of the Alaska at War Steering Committee had ever undertaken a task of this magnitude. Nevertheless, with a measure of elbow grease, not a little ingenuity, and a good sense of humor, the committee met each challenge head on and forged ahead. The dedicated and hard-working members of the committee are:

Georgeanne L. Reynolds, Chair
Sandra L. Faulkner, Vice-Chair
R. Bruce Parham, Secretary-Treasurer
Joan M. Antonson
Chief Kevin Baker, USN
Captain Robert E. Baratko, USN (Ret.)
Carol Burkhart
Janet F. Clemens
John H. Cloe
Kurtis Hawk
Charlie Hawkes
Monty Henninger
Gary Hoff
Michele Hope
Sylvia Kobayashi
Frank Norris
Russ Sackett
Jim Stuhler
Teresa Fullenkamp
Tom Wiltsey

The following federal and state agencies and local organizations are represented by the committee: Army Corps of Engineers, Alaska District; National Park Service, Alaska Regional Office; National Archives and Records Administration—Alaska Region; Alaska Department of Natural Resources, Office of History and Archaeology; U.S. Navy; Alaskan Command History Office; U.S. Army Alaska; Minerals Management Service, Alaska Outer Continental Shelf Region; Alaska Public Lands Information Center; Alaska Association for Historic Preservation; Cook Inlet Historical Society; and the Sheraton Anchorage Hotel.

These organizations employ many of us and it is through the generosity and understanding of our respective offices that we were able to play such a large part in organizing the conference. Special thanks are due to the Anchorage Museum of History and Art and its director, Patricia B. Wolf. The museum hosted the opening reception, the World War II film series, and the luncheon with artists William Draper and George Earle—all of it done in the polished and professional manner that Anchorage has grown accustomed to. The museum also worked diligently with the committee to mount a major exhibit of World War II art, *A Brush with War: World War II Art from the Aleutian Campaign*, which included paintings and drawings by Mr. Earle and Mr. Draper.

Other cooperating agencies and individuals who assisted with the art exhibit include Mary Lou Gjernes and Joan Thomas of the U.S. Army Art Collection, Center for Military History, Washington, D.C.; John D. Barnett and Gale Munro of the U.S. Navy Art Center, Washington, D.C.; the Alaska Air National Guard, Kulis Air National Guard Base, Anchorage; Marty Murray and Persenia Whittern of the Unalaska Historic Preservation Commission, City of Unalaska; Rear Admiral Roger Rufe and Lieutenant Ray Massey of the U.S. Coast Guard, Seventeenth District, Juneau; Walter Van Horn and Janelle Matz of the Anchorage Museum of History and Art; Barbara Walton of the Denver Public Library,

Western History Department; Gary Hoff, Alaskan Command; and Carol Burkhart of the National Park Service. A special thanks must go to William Draper and George Earle for their strong encouragement and assistance with this effort.

Agencies and individuals who helped with the film series include the Alaska Historical Commission; the Alaska Public Lands Information Center; the Aleutian /Pribilof Islands Association, Inc.; the Anchorage Museum of History and Art; Bill Blakefield, National Archives and Records Administration, Washington, D.C.; the National Archives—Alaska Region; the Cook Inlet Historical Society; Michael and Mary Jo Thill, Gaff Rigged Productions, Girdwood, Alaska; Mike Martz, Executive Producer, KYUK Bethel Broadcasting, Inc.; and the Anchorage Municipal Libraries, Z.J. Loussac Library.

The Alaska at War Conference and the publication of the proceedings have been possible due to generous grants and matching funds from the U.S. Department of Defense, Legacy Program; the Quest for Truth Foundation, Seattle; the Alaska Humanities Forum; and the Japan Foundation's Center for Global Partnership.

Special thanks are due to Captain Robert E. Baratko, USN (Ret.), who was an integral part of the committee prior to his retirement and even after departing for a new career in Juneau. He consistently had solutions for any problem we encountered. Dr. Yuichi Inouye, Deputy Consul, Consulate of Japan, Anchorage, took a keen interest in the conference very early on, as he has in other World War II commemorative events in Alaska. He directed us to the Japan Foundation, which, in turn, provided funding for the four Japanese speakers, a generosity for which we are most grateful. Mina Jacobs, of the Anchorage Museum of History and Art, and Katerina Solovjova, of the National Park Service, Alaska Regional Office, were of immeasurable help in making the Russian participants feel welcome.

Thanks also to Senator Ted Stevens for his interest in the Aleut relocation and restitution session. A special thanks to Michael and Mary Jo Thill of Gaff Rigged Productions for presenting their poignant documentary film, *Aleut Evacuation: The Untold War Story*, featuring Aleut survivors of the relocation. The film has been shown on public television stations throughout the United States and is now available on videocassette from the Aleutian/Pribilof Islands Association, Inc., in Anchorage. I only regret that it cannot be included in this publication.

To edit this work, we were extremely fortunate to have found Ann and Fern Chandonnet of Chandonnet Editing and Research of Anchorage. The Alaska at War Publication Committee, in particular, wishes to express its gratitude to Fern Chandonnet for doing a masterful job of giving this work much of its coherence and in preparing this manuscript for publication. All of the maps were produced by Debbie Dubac, of Dubac Designs of Anchorage, who painstakingly worked long hours to produce them.

The staffs of the Anchorage Museum of History and Art; Department of Archives and Manuscripts of the University of Alaska Anchorage Consortium Library; Historical Section of the Alaska State Library; National Archives—Alaska Region; University of Alaska Fairbanks Elmer E. Rasmuson Library; the Historian's Office of the Alaskan Command; National Park Service, Alaska Regional Office; Office of History and Archaeol-ogy; the U.S. Forest Service, Alaska Region, Juneau; and the Yukon Archives were especially helpful in our search for World War II photographs. M. Diane Brenner and Mina Jacobs of the Anchorage Museum of History and Art, India Spartz of the Alaska Historical Library, Marge Naylor-Heath of the Alaska and Polar Regions Department of the Elmer E. Rasmuson Library, Dennis Walle of the Consortium Library, and John Cloe of the Alaskan Command provided invaluable assistance in locating photographs to support the text. Fred Pernell of the Still Picture Branch at the National Archives at College Park was also very helpful. The staff of the U.S. Navy Art Center were prompt and cooperative in providing duplicate color negatives for the Draper and Earle artwork reproduced here. We would also like to express our appreciation to the authors of these papers, many of whom generously provided us with the use of their photographs for this volume.

We would like, finally, to acknowledge two individuals who deserve special mention. They were featured guests at the Alaska at War Conference and contributions from both are included in this volume. The two men who will always be remembered for their larger-than-life roles in "The Forgotten War" are Rear Admiral James A. Russell, USN (Ret.), the ranking naval officer in the Aleutians when the Japanese attacked Dutch Harbor, and Brigadier General Benjamin B. Talley, USA (Ret.), the architect of the military buildup in the Aleutians.

*Georgeanne L. Reynolds*
*Conference Chair*

*Alaska*
*May 1995*

The papers presented at the Alaska at War Symposium in 1993 and published in this volume are the products of a wide range of individual research and experience.

In many cases the authors availed themselves of archival and other resources of governmental agencies and of the various branches of the military.

The representations of the historical record in this book may at times seem in line with the policies and dictates of the United States government, and of other governments, during the period under discussion. Nevertheless, in no way do the authors wish to convey the impression that theirs is the official version of government policy or that their presentations and conclusions have been either authorized or mandated by any government agency.

The papers presented here are the products of individual scholarship and effort, and the conclusions drawn are the authors' own.

# Keynote
# Addresses

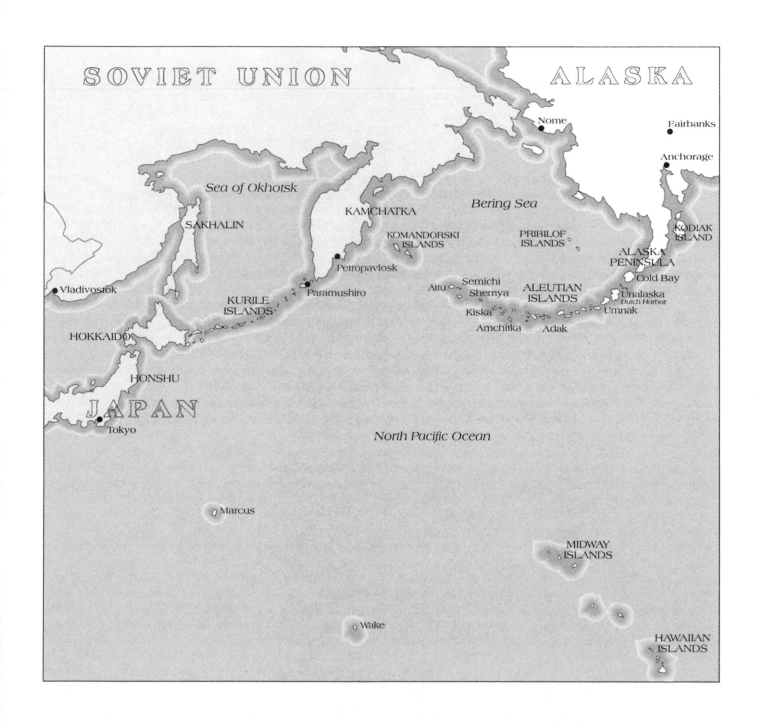

# The North Pacific Campaign in Perspective

*Dean C. Allard*

FROM THE EARLIEST YEARS OF THIS CENTURY, AMERICAN military planners focused their attention on the possibility of a conflict with Japan. It was primarily within that context that Alaska and the North Pacific region in general became important elements in the nation's strategic thinking.[1]

The American scenario for a war with Japan anticipated that Japan would open hostilities with an attack on the U.S. territory of the Philippines. Our response would be an American counteroffensive featuring either a slow or rapid advance across the Pacific, followed by a decisive fleet action in which the main force of the Imperial Japanese Navy, it was hoped, would be defeated. Finally, the U.S. fleet would impose a crushing maritime blockade on Japan's home islands. The focus of these operations was the Central Pacific. But military doctrine demanded that the vital flanks of that region, including the North Pacific, be defended or used to the maximum extent possible to further American war aims.

Interest in the North Pacific was heightened by other considerations. One was geography. The shortest distance between the United States and Japan, via the great circle route, lay astride the Aleutian Chain. The westernmost island in that chain, Attu, was only 650 miles from the major Japanese military base at Paramushiro at the northern end of the Kurile Islands. But it also was recognized that naval operations in Alaska, particularly in the strategic Aleutians, would be impacted by the incredibly bad weather found in that region. There was one further restraint. Although Japan's Kurile Islands were within easy striking range from the Aleutians, the Kuriles

themselves were far removed from Japan's all-important economic areas in Honshu. The distance from Paramushiro to Tokyo, for example, was almost 1,300 miles. The vital sea lanes used to bring oil, iron ore, and other essential commodities to Japan from the resource-rich areas in south Asia were even more remote.

If it is essential to stress that any war with Imperial Japan was likely to include operations in the North Pacific, then it must also be acknowledged that additional strategic considerations were involved. I have pointed out the proximity of the Japanese Kurile Islands to the Aleutians. But the other major power in the North Pacific, the Soviet Union, was equally close to Alaska. If the Soviets were allied with the United States, the vital Pacific route across which supplies and American military forces could reach Russia's maritime provinces was in the northern sea lanes terminating at Petropavlovsk on the Kamchatka Peninsula or farther south at the port of Vladivostok. In the event of Soviet-American enmity, such as the cold war that occupied the world's attention for four decades after World War II, the proximity to the Soviet Union demanded that strenuous defense efforts be made in the Alaska region.

One further factor deserves mention. To a considerable extent, the thinking of our Pacific strategists was dominated by the need to defend the U.S. territory in the Philippines.

Obviously, the same requirement existed for the Territory of Alaska. That task was reflected in the concept of a defense triangle demarcated by lines connecting Alaska, Hawaii, and the Panama Canal that the army's

---

[1] See Edward S. Miller, *War Plan Orange: The U.S. Strategy to Defeat Japan, 1897-1945* (Annapolis: Naval Institute Press, 1991).

planners advanced in the 1930s as the basis for the nation's strategy in the Pacific. For the navy, the need to defend Alaska was underscored by its rich natural resources, including the coal and, later, the petroleum required by American warships.[2]

To return to the connection between the North Pacific and a possible conflict with Japan, it is interesting to note that as early as 1911 Alfred Thayer Mahan argued that the best chance for a speedy American victory lay in concentrating the U.S. fleet at Kiska. Mahan felt that the simple presence of this force on the northern flank would lead the Japanese fleet to withdraw from their presumed conquest of Hawaii at the outset of a war with the United States. From Kiska our fleet also could fall upon Japanese positions located to the west of Hawaii.

Other naval strategists, however, vigorously rebutted Mahan's view. They agreed that it was important to safeguard the Northern Pacific.[3] But, in their view, major fleet operations in the Aleutians were not feasible because of that area's severe climatic conditions and poorly charted waters,[4] the inadequacy of Kiska's harbor, and the remoteness of the Aleutian island chain from Japan's most important economic targets. In the face of these arguments Mahan soon abandoned his advocacy of a northern strategy.[5]

In the years leading up to World War II, American war planners generally did not see the North Pacific as a major theater of war. There was one notable exception. General Billy Mitchell, the famed prophet of air power, emphasized in the 1920s the value of using the Aleutians as a base for a bombing campaign against Japan. Despite the meteorological problems involved in air operations in the area, Mitchell was impressed by the strategic significance of the North Pacific as the area where the spheres of interest of Japan, Russia, and the United States intersected. He was convinced that an American bombing capability in that area could deter war with Japan, or, if necessary, win a quick and decisive American victory.[6]

More typical of military thinking in this period were plans for relatively minor military activities typical of warfare on the flanks of a major battlefield. In this tradition, planners recognized the possibility that the Japanese might seize positions in the Aleutians for use as bases for raiders, other light naval forces, or for intelligence-gathering purposes.[7] In response to that threat and in order to allow our own use of this strategic area, American planners recommended that bases for smaller naval units be established in the area.[8] These facilities offered an opportunity for strategic diversions that might force the enemy to withdraw units from the more important areas in the Central Pacific.[9] Another indication of U.S. interest in the North Pacific came in 1935 and 1937 when the American Navy's annual fleet problems were conducted, in part, in Alaska waters. These exercises involved simulations of major fleet engagements as well as the capture or defense of advanced bases.[10]

Almost two decades earlier, the U.S. Navy's attention also was drawn to the need to operate in another area of the Northern Pacific when it provided support through the port of Vladivostok for U.S. Army operations in Siberia. The purpose of America's military intervention in Russia from 1918 to 1920 was to thwart any effort by the Japanese, whose forces also were in Siberia, from permanently seizing territory at a time when the Russians were locked in a bloody civil war.[11] This operation was a reminder that Asia's North Pacific coast was a potential area of operations for the United States. That possibility was echoed in 1937 when naval strategists, including Admiral Harry Yarnell, the commander of the U.S. Asiatic Fleet, recognized the desirability of enlisting the Soviet Union in an alliance opposed to Japanese aggression in Asia.[12]

In the 1930s, as the United States began to prepare for possible involvement in another world war, and as the Washington arms limitation treaty restraints on the construction of bases in the Aleutians expired, naval leaders gave increasing attention to the need for facilities that would allow the permanent stationing of forces in the Alaska region. In 1932 and 1933, surveys by the navy identified potential base sites in the Aleutians at Dutch Harbor and Adak for seaplanes and ships. In the event

---

[2] William R. Braisted, *The United States Navy in the Pacific, 1909-1922* (Austin: University of Texas Press, 1971), pp. 37-38; Commander in Chief, U.S. Pacific Fleet, "Administrative History of the North Pacific," 27 November 1945 (ms. in Navy Department Library, Washington, D.C.), p. 11.

[3] Miller, *War Plan Orange*, p. 100.

[4] Braisted, *USN in the Pacific*, p. 33.

[5] Miller, *War Plan Orange*, p. 93.

[6] Russell F. Weigley, *The American Way of War* (New York: Macmillan, 1973), pp. 230-33.

[7] Braisted, *USN in the Pacific*, pp. 128, 149.

[8] Ibid., pp. 143, 482; Miller, *War Plan Orange*, pp. 41-43; Pacific Fleet, *Administrative History of the North Pacific*, p. 12.

[9] Miller, *War Plan Orange*, p. 170.

[10] U.S. National Archives, *Records Relating to USN Fleet Problems* (Washington: National Archives, 1975), pp. 10-11.

[11] See Betty M. Unterberger, *America's Siberian Expedition, 1918-1920* (New York: Greenwood Press, 1969).

[12] Robert W. Love Jr., *History of the U.S. Navy*, vol. 1 (Harrisburg, Pa.: Stackpole Books, 1992), pp. 597-98, 602.

Before World War II, U.S. military planners did not view the North Pacific as a major theater of war. Correspondingly, the largest ship in Alaska waters—until the bombing of Dutch Harbor—was the two-thousand-ton-displacement gun boat USS *Charleston.* (*U.S. Navy photograph, courtesy of Command Historian's Office, Alaskan Command.*)

of war with Japan, according to a 1936 proposal by the commandant of the Thirteenth Naval District (the Seattle-based command that had naval jurisdiction over Alaska), the navy should deploy four seaplane squadrons, ten submarines, and fifteen patrol vessels as a first step in defending the region. In 1937, Ernest J. King, then the commander of the air component of the fleet's Base Force, and later the navy's senior uniformed leader during World War II, urged that Sitka be developed as a seaplane base. By this time King and other leaders concluded that Kodiak should be another major base area. In the first part of 1938, temporary deployments to Kodiak of submarines and amphibian patrol aircraft tested its suitability.[13]

These activities culminated in the worldwide study of naval base needs that Admiral Arthur J. Hepburn submitted to Congress in December 1938. Consistent with the flank strategy that was typical of naval thinking with regard to the North Pacific, Hepburn did not recommend a major fleet base for this area. But he did call for three aviation facilities from which amphibious patrol aircraft could aid in the defense of Alaska and the Pacific Northwest. One of these was at Dutch Harbor, which, because of its location in the Aleutians, was considered to have the greatest strategic value. Nevertheless, because of the severe weather in the Aleutians, Hepburn

chose Kodiak instead of Dutch Harbor as the site for the largest seaplane base in Alaska. The third facility chosen as an airdrome was Sitka, in Alaska's Southeast. Admiral Hepburn's committee also recommended that Kodiak and Dutch Harbor be developed for use by submarines. Once again, due to Dutch Harbor's advanced location in the Aleutians, the admiral especially identified that location as having "vital importance in time of war...."[14] By the fall of 1941, work was completed at Dutch Harbor, Kodiak, and Sitka and these sites became capable of supporting operations by seaplanes and smaller combatant ships.[15]

Strategic developments during the more than two years between 1939 and 1941, before the United States became directly engaged in World War II, continued earlier trends. The possible use of the North Pacific for diversionary operations was revealed once again in a scheme put forth by President Roosevelt in August 1939. At that time it seemed virtually certain that German aggression would lead to a general European war. In order to deter the Japanese from aiding Hitler by attacking European possessions in Asia, FDR called for deploying a major naval force in the western Aleutians. Through its presence and radio deception techniques, that squadron could suggest to the Japanese that major American operations were in the offing. Roosevelt

---

[13] Pacific Fleet, *Administrative History of North Pacific*, pp. 13-19.

[14] 76th Congress, 1st Session, "Report on Need for Additional Naval Bases" (hereafter cited as "Hepburn Report"), House of Representatives Report 65 (Washington: Government Printing Office, 1938), pp. 20-22, 31.

[15] See base histories in Paolo Coletta, ed., *United States Navy and Marine Corps Bases, Domestic* (Westport, Conn.: Greenwood Books, 1985); Pacific Fleet, *Administrative History of North Pacific*, p. 23.

hoped this threat would make the Japanese "jittery" and "keep them guessing." The President's naval advisors cautioned against such a provocative course of action, however, and it did not materialize.[16]

In this short-of-war period, there also were reminders of the Soviet Union's status as a major North Pacific power. Within a few months of the outbreak of the Russian-German war in June 1941, the Soviets became the recipients of American lend-lease supplies and equipment. One of the principal routes used was in the North Pacific, where Vladivostok was the main receiving port and American-built ships operating under Soviet flags provided most of the lift. In addition, under the lend-lease program almost 8,000 U.S. aircraft were flown to Fairbanks, Alaska, where they were transferred to Soviet crews for the long ferry flight across Russia to the Eastern Front. In comparison to other lend-lease routes, the North Pacific area was relatively safe. In fact, throughout the rest of the war the Japanese honored the nonaggression treaty they had signed with Russia in April 1941. But, despite that situation, the United States consistently sought to achieve a fundamental shift in the balance of Pacific power by enlisting the USSR in an anti-Japanese coalition. Joseph Stalin, however, was embroiled in a life-and-death struggle with Germany and was no more willing than Japan to expand hostilities by opening a new front in the North Pacific.[17]

These prewar preparations were indispensable when war actually came to the shores of Alaska after December 1941. Nevertheless, despite the existence of a base structure and of well-developed strategic plans, the navy had only minuscule forces in the area when the Japanese launched their attack on Pearl Harbor. In comparison to the 22,000 army personnel in Alaska, the navy could count fewer than 600 personnel at its main bases in Dutch Harbor, Kodiak, and Sitka. In terms of units, the navy operated only six PBY aircraft, a 2,000-ton gunboat, two old destroyers, two large Coast Guard cutters, plus minor patrol and yard craft.[18] Fortunately, in case of an emergency, the United States could count on the assistance of a Canadian Pacific naval squadron comprised of three cruisers, seven corvettes, and a number of smaller ships.[19]

Early in the war, Admiral King and other American strategists explored the possibility of obtaining Soviet bases in Siberia to support an aerial assault on Japan's home islands or amphibious operations against the Kuriles. But the Soviet Union, which was fighting for its life against Hitler's Germany, continued to reject involvement in a war with Japan. Since there was no prospect of opening a major front in the North Pacific in 1942, the hard-pressed U.S. Navy sent only minor reinforcements to the North Pacific during the initial months of that year.[20] But this situation changed in May 1942 when American intelligence picked up information on Japanese plans for an operation to seize the island of Midway, from which location the enemy could threaten Hawaii. More fundamentally, Admiral Yamamoto, the Japanese fleet commander, hoped that an invasion of Midway would force the United States Navy to accept a major naval engagement that would inflict ruinous American losses. The stratagem of seeking to divert the United States from the main point of attack by launching a lesser operation on its flank also was part of Yamamoto's plan. It is not surprising that Japan chose the Aleutians as the site for this diversionary operation.

For the North Pacific phase of his campaign, Yamamoto organized an attack force formed around two light carriers, under the overall command of Admiral Boshiro Hosogaya, with orders to attack U.S. bases in the Aleutians and to seize positions in the western Aleutians. In addition to drawing away U.S. forces from the critical Midway area, the Japanese goal was to preempt an anticipated invasion of the Kurile Islands by the United States, a course of action that we now know was rejected by American military leaders in 1942. Professor Takahashi points out that the Japanese also were motivated by fears that we would use the Aleutians to launch a bombing campaign against their home islands.[21]

Admiral Nimitz, well aware of Japanese strategic intentions from his intelligence sources, did not send his major strength to Alaska waters. Instead he concentrated the three U.S. carrier task forces then available in the Pacific for the famous ambush of Japan's attack force off Midway on the morning of June 4, 1942. The eventual loss of four of the enemy's first-line carriers at Midway changed the entire course of the Pacific War. But, at the

---

[16] B. Mitchell Simpson III, *Admiral Harold R. Stark: Architect of Victory, 1939-1945* (Columbia, S.C.: University of South Carolina Press, 1989), pp. 5-6.

[17] Miller, *War Plan Orange*, pp. 334-35.

[18] Brian Garfield, *The Thousand-Mile War: World War II in Alaska and the Aleutians* (Garden City, N.Y.: Doubleday, 1969), p. 59; Samuel E. Morison, *History of United States Naval Operations in World War II*, vol. 4 (Boston: Little, Brown, 1947-1962), p. 165.

[19] Morison, *History of USN*, vol. 4, p. 165 footnote.

[20] Grace P. Hayes, *The History of the Joint Chiefs of Staff in World War II: The War Against Japan* (Annapolis, Md.: Naval Institute Press, 1982), pp. 131-35.

[21] Morison, *History of USN*, vol. 4, pp. 161-62; Hisashi Takahashi, "Japanese Campaign in Alaska," paper read at Alaska At War Conference, Anchorage, Alaska, 13 November 1993.

same time, Nimitz was able to spare some naval reinforcements for Alaska. Under the command of Rear Admiral Robert A. Theobald, the North Pacific Force included five cruisers, fourteen destroyers, and six submarines by early June 1942. Theobald also controlled more than a hundred army air force and navy aircraft based in Alaska. The Admiral did not command American ground forces, but he was expected to establish a cooperative relationship with his army counterpart, Brigadier General Simon B. Buckner. Unfortunately, from the time Theobald arrived at his headquarters at Kodiak in late May 1942, he displayed a capacity to create discord rather than good will in the navy's relationship with its sister service.[22]

During the enemy's offensive in June 1942, Theobald largely ignored the enemy's capabilities and made an assumption that proved to be mistaken when he concluded that Japan's intent was to seize Dutch Harbor. He also has been faulted by historians for deciding to establish his headquarters afloat where, because of the need for radio silence, he was unable to exercise effective command of his assigned naval and army air force units.[23]

Other papers in this volume will provide details on the dramatic events in June 1942 when the Japanese launched their attacks in the Aleutians. That campaign was neither the first nor the last time in which the incredibly bad weather in the Aleutians played a major role. When the North Pacific fogs lifted, it became evident that Dutch Harbor had been hit by three raids launched from Admiral Hosogaya's carriers on June 3 and 4. But in comparison to the strikes made at Pearl Harbor seven months earlier, the enemy had limited success. The base at Dutch Harbor continued to be operational despite the fact that some damage was inflicted to its facilities and forty-three American lives were lost. On the other hand, counterattacks by American aircraft against Admiral Hosogaya's carrier force were completely ineffective.[24]

On 10 June 1942, American officials learned of the results of the amphibious phase of the Japanese thrust into the North Pacific. To Admiral Theobald's surprise,

the objective was not Dutch Harbor. Instead, on June 7, 1,200 Japanese troops landed without opposition at Attu. On the previous day, a comparable force had seized Kiska, another undefended position. Attu and Kiska were remote from the rest of Alaska and even further removed from the United States. Hence, strategists might argue that the wisest policy would have been to bypass Attu and Kiska, as we did later with many Japanese-held islands elsewhere in the Pacific. But several factors forced the United States to accept the challenge of reconquering these positions. One was the psychological effect of the enemy's seizure of American territory. Another was the need to maintain sea and air lines of communication across the North Pacific between the United States and our Soviet allies, especially in order to allow the continued flow of the lend-lease supplies that were of considerable significance to the Russian war effort.[25] In addition, Admiral King and other naval leaders were determined to wage an offensive strategy in the Pacific. Finally, since a major amphibious offensive was not scheduled to begin in the central Pacific until late in 1943, forces were available for an effort to return Attu and Kiska to American control.[26]

To prepare for these landings, the North Pacific Force, including its army air force components, undertook a systematic campaign of aerial and naval gunfire bombardment against Japanese positions on Attu and Kiska. The United States also used its surface ships, submarines, and aircraft for an interdiction campaign that was almost entirely successful—after the fall of 1942—in halting Japanese movements to the two islands. In all, the enemy's attempts to reinforce Attu and Kiska resulted in the loss of no fewer than three Japanese destroyers, three submarines, and nine merchant ships.[27] In these operations American naval and air forces were undertaking one of their classic roles in a maritime campaign—the isolation of the battlefield from outside support. The essential character of this campaign was comparable to the prolonged and bloody Solomons Campaign in the South Pacific, also being waged in 1942-1943, in which Japanese and American forces bitterly contested the control of the sea and airspace around

[22] Morison, *History of USN*, vol. 4, pp. 163-71.

[23] Ibid, pp. 165-80.

[24] Sources on this campaign include ibid., pp. 175-84; Garfield, *Thousand-Mile War*, pp. 24-44; John H. Cloe, *The Aleutian Warriors: A History of the 11th Air Force and Fleet Air Wing 4* (Missoula, Mont.: Pictorial Histories Publishing Company), pp. 75-143; Elmer Freeman, *Those Navy Guys and Their PBYs: The Aleutian Solution* (Spokane, Wash.: Kedging Publishing Co., 1992), pp. 72-117; and Frederick D. Parker, *A Priceless Advantage: U.S. Navy Communications Intelligence and the Battle of the Coral Sea, Midway, and the Aleutians* (Fort Meade, Md.: National Security Agency, 1993).

[25] Hayes, *History of JCS*, pp. 131,172-73; for the importance of the lend-lease program, see Robert H. Jones, *The Roads to Russia: United States Lend-Lease to the Soviet Union* (Norman, Ok.: University of Oklahoma Press, 1969).

[26] Morison, *History of USN*, vol. 7, pp. 8-9; Gerald E. Wheeler, "Thomas C. Kinkaid," ms. in Naval Historical Center, Washington, D.C. Chapter 12 of this comprehensive biography, published in 1994 by the Naval Historical Center, covers the admiral's tour as the North Pacific Commander.

[27] Morison, *History of USN*, vol. 7, p. 65; Clay Blair, *Silent Victory: The U.S. Submarine War Against Japan* (Philadelphia: Lippincott, 1975), pp. 416-21.

insular positions. Upon that control depended the ability of a nation to attack its enemy ashore or, alternatively, to land, supply, reinforce, or evacuate its own forces.

The theories of maritime support and blockade are simple. But their execution in the Aleutians was greatly complicated by the extraordinarily poor meteorological and oceanographic conditions in the area. Writers on the North Pacific campaign, including Brian Garfield and Samuel Morison, seem to vie with each other to find ever more graphic words to describe the heavy and sudden fogs, the williwaw winds, the raging seas, and the uncharted hazards to navigation found in the Aleutians.

Many tons of gunfire rounds and of bombs dropped by army and navy aircraft rained down on Attu and Kiska over the months following June 1942. But, because of the severe operational limitations resulting from poor visibility, other environmental conditions, and the enemy's ability to develop well-protected defensive positions in the spongy tundra of the Aleutians, relatively minor damage was inflicted.

At the same time, the Japanese were equally ineffective in attacking our ships and planes. Operational hazards associated with meteorological or oceanographic conditions inflicted greater damage and losses to American units than did enemy fire. John Cloe points out, for example, that out of the total of 225 Allied aircraft destroyed in the Aleutians campaign, no fewer than 184 were operational losses, with weather being the "prime culprit."[28]

There were happier aspects of the Aleutian amphibious campaign. By their joint nature, amphibious operations demand the type of cooperation between the navy and the army that often was absent while Rear Admiral Theobald served as the North Pacific commander. That was the reason Admirals Nimitz and King replaced Theobald with Rear Admiral Thomas C. Kinkaid in January 1943. Kinkaid met King's test of being offensive-minded, having previously served as an effective carrier task force commander in the Solomons. He also was fully capable of establishing harmonious and productive relations with the army.

One of Kinkaid's first steps after assuming his new position was to confirm Theobald's earlier decision to move his headquarters from Kodiak to Adak, a thousand miles west of Kodiak and only 250 miles east of Kiska. Here Kinkaid established a joint headquarters and mess with General Buckner and developed a close professional and personal relationship with that notable leader of the army in Alaska.[29]

Under Admiral Kinkaid there occurred the most

famous single chapter in the campaign to prevent the enemy from supporting its troops in the Aleutians. This was the Battle of the Komandorski Islands, fought on March 26, 1943, about 180 miles west of Attu. On that day an American force of two cruisers and four destroyers, under Rear Admiral Charles H. McMorris, intercepted Admiral Hosogaya's squadron, comprised of four cruisers and five destroyers. Those ships escorted three transports carrying reinforcements and supplies from Paramushiro to Attu. Over the next three-and-a-half hours the Japanese and the Americans traded more than five thousand rounds of gunfire at ranges of eight to twelve miles. Hits were scored by both sides but, amazingly, no ships were sunk. Both commanders called for air support during the engagement, but neither Japanese nor American aircraft were able to reach the scene of battle. The dramatic climax in this grueling naval surface action came when battle damage caused the cruiser *Salt Lake City* to go dead in the water for several minutes, while her accompanying destroyers sought to protect the crippled ship by counterattacking the greatly superior enemy with torpedoes. It was at this time that Hosogaya, unaware of *Salt Lake City's* condition, elected to break off the action and return to Paramushiro, hence admitting failure in his mission of supporting Attu.[30]

Considering the staunch defense that the Japanese offered when amphibious forces from the army's Seventh Division landed at Attu on May 11, 1943, the inability of the Japanese to move major reinforcements to that island was all the more important. The Attu expedition included a landing force of eleven thousand men and a flotilla of twenty-nine ships commanded by Rear Admiral Francis W. Rockwell. Three old battleships and an escort carrier were part of this force. Their heavy guns and aircraft supported the forces ashore and, if necessary, were ready to repel any attempt by the Japanese Navy to interfere with the operation. Attu was assaulted before Kiska because it was believed to be less extensively defended. But American troops faced a very tough fight against the twenty-five hundred Attu defenders, virtually all of whom fought to their deaths. Attu was secured by May 29, by which time the United States counted six hundred dead and twelve hundred wounded.[31] Brian Garfield notes that as a percentage of the total force involved, this was second only to Iwo Jima as the most costly Pacific campaign. But Garfield also observes that Attu "by its very mistakes and failures ... led to later successes in the Pacific...."[32]

Sobered by the bloody nature of the Attu campaign,

---

[28] See, Wheeler, chap. 12 of "Thomas C. Kinkaid,"; Morison, *History of USN*, vol. 7, pp. 9-21, 37-66; Cloe, *Aleutian Warriors*, p. 322 and passim.

[29] Wheeler, "Thomas C. Kinkaid", Chapter 12.

[30] Morison, *History of USN*, vol. 7, pp. 22-36; Garfield, *Thousand-Mile War*, pp. 171-79.

[31] Morison, *History. of USN*, vol. 7, pp. 37-51.

[32] Garfield, *Thousand-Mile War*, pp. 256, 299.

the United States prepared a stronger force for the seizure of Kiska in August 1943. The enemy also learned from his experience in the Aleutians. Unable to adequately supply and reinforce Kiska, the Japanese decided to abandon that position. On July 28 their forces, demonstrating typical skill in using the Aleutian fogs for concealment, evacuated the entire Japanese garrison on Kiska, a force that consisted of more than five thousand individuals.[33]

Perhaps it would only have been possible in the Aleutians, with their incredibly thick weather, that this withdrawal remained unknown to the United States. In addition to its skillful use of the Aleutian environment, the enemy took advantage of the temporary withdrawal of U.S. ships for refueling and replenishment following the phantom July 26 naval action that we know as the Battle of the Pips. One must acknowledge that there was growing suspicion among some American officers that the Japanese had left the island. Nevertheless, Admiral Kinkaid decided to proceed with the operation. A flotilla of nearly a hundred ships landed a force of thirty-four thousand American and Canadian troops at Kiska on August 15, 1943, fully expecting to meet another fanatical Japanese defense force. It was a week before the enemy's complete absence was confirmed. In the meantime, offering stark evidence that operations were never easy in the Aleutians, twenty-five troops died from friendly fire, while seventy naval men lost their lives when a Japanese sea mine severely damaged the destroyer *Abner Read*.[34]

Although Admiral Nimitz refused to send his carrier forces to the North Pacific during the Midway Campaign and thereby ignored the Japanese bait, it can be argued that in the longer run the Japanese mounted a successful deception campaign in the Aleutians. Samuel Eliot Morison notes that for more than a year about ten thousand Japanese troops tied down an American and Canadian army that reached a peak strength of 100,000 in August 1943.[35] With the complete elimination of the Japanese from the Aleutians, however, American strategists reexamined the wisdom of continuing a major campaign in the North Pacific. They soon concluded that it was essential to redeploy many of the forces in the North Pacific to other regions of the Pacific and eventually to the Atlantic for other major amphibious operations that were being planned. In October 1943,

Admiral Kinkaid himself was detached and ordered to the Southwest Pacific Theater where he became the highly successful naval commander for General Douglas MacArthur. In June 1944, General Buckner left the North Pacific for Hawaii, where he took command of the Tenth Army.

The Joint Chiefs of Staff did recognize that at a later date it might be desirable to seize positions in the Paramushiro area using support bases on the Kamchatka Peninsula. Also discussed was the option of obtaining the air facilities in the Soviet maritime provinces that would be essential for the type of strategic bombing campaign against Japan that Billy Mitchell had championed in the 1920s.[36] As had always been the case, the precondition to either of these courses of action was the Soviet Union's willingness to engage actively in the war against Japan. But this fundamental change in the strategic balance of power in the North Pacific would not occur until after the Russians and their Western allies completely defeated Germany.[37]

In the meantime, the United States made preparations for the possible reinstatement of the North Pacific as a major theater of war. As had been true earlier, Admiral King, the navy's senior officer, was a special champion of this strategy.[38] Specific actions for this eventuality included the construction of bases in the western Aleutians for a long-range bombing campaign by B-29s against Japan's home islands. Earlier in the war, base development was the responsibility of army engineers commanded by army colonel Benjamin B. Talley. But, after the spring of 1943, naval construction battalions were the primary developers of facilities in the Aleutians. As was true for their army counterparts, the Seabees were entirely successful in overcoming the formidable problems of weather and terrain and completed their assigned tasks.[39] Although B-29s did not actually deploy to the Aleutians, other aircraft of the Eleventh Army Air Force and the navy's Fleet Air Wing Four (including B-17 Flying Fortresses, B-24 Liberators, and the navy's PV-I Venturas and PV-2 Harpoons) launched more than fifteen hundred attack sorties against Japanese bases in the Kuriles from 1943 until the end of the war. Starting in February 1944, a naval surface force consisting of light cruisers and destroyers, also operating out of the Aleutians, undertook approximately fifteen shore bombardment and anti-shipping

---

[33] Morison, *History of the USN*, vol. 7, pp. 56-61.

[34] Ibid., pp. 61-65.

[35] Ibid., pp. 64-66.

[36] Hayes, *History of the JCS*, pp. 482-84, 496.

[37] See Nimitz letter to Commander, North Pacific, 7 January 1944, in *Pacific Fleet, Administrative History of North Pacific*, pp. 138-40.

[38] Hayes, *History of the JCS*, pp. 484-86, 493, 496, 672-76.

[39] U.S. Navy, *Building the Navy's Bases in World War II*, vol. 2 (Washington: GPO, 1947), pp. 163-90.

missions against Paramushiro and other positions in the Kuriles, as well as in the Sea of Okhotsk.[40] American submarine attacks, aimed at isolating the Kuriles by destroying the shipping that provided these island positions with support, also were underway at this time. The Japanese could only respond with occasional, ineffective air strikes against the Aleutians. One of the major reasons the United States undertook its aerial and surface operations was to deceive the Japanese into believing that an amphibious assault on the Kuriles was imminent, hence causing them to station a disproportionate defense force in that area. The ruse worked. Japan did retain up to eighty thousand men and five hundred combat aircraft in the Kuriles that could have been used with much more deadly effect on other Pacific battlefields.[41]

At the Yalta Conference in February 1945, the Soviets finally confirmed their intention to enter the war against Japan after Germany's final defeat. One of the major concessions made by Franklin Roosevelt in return for this long-desired event was agreement that Russia could take possession of the Kurile Islands. In 1945 the United States also prepared for the opening of the new front by stepping up the flow of lend-lease aid across the North Pacific. As Richard Russell points out in his paper, that effort included the transfer of hundreds of smaller naval amphibious, minesweeping, and patrol ships and the training of their Soviet crews. These preparations clearly foresaw an amphibious assault on the Kuriles. In fact, many of these resources appear to have been used during the Soviet occupation of the Kuriles during the latter part of August 1945. In addition, plans were developed to maintain sea and air communications in the Pacific when the Russians became full partners in the war against Japan.[42] But the long-standing hope of establishing American bases on Soviet Far Eastern territory was met with suspicion by our Russian allies. The only concrete step taken in this direction was the establishment in September 1945 of two U.S. naval weather stations, one at Petropavlovsk and the other on the Siberian mainland.[43] How the United States and the Soviets might actually have cooperated in waging a combined amphibious and aerial campaign against Japan in the North Pacific remains speculation, since the Russians

actually fought Japan for such a short time before that nation capitulated.

The North Pacific campaign sketched in this talk is too often forgotten. In part this is because these operations are dismissed as having little strategic consequence. Edward Miller, an authority on U.S. strategy in the Pacific, expresses this view by referring to the "evils" of the North Pacific route to Japan, which included "weather, topography, logistics, remoteness from vital objectives." For these reasons, as well as Stalin's refusal to fight Japan until Hitler was defeated, Miller states that "the north remained a strategic backwater."[44] Samuel Eliot Morison expressed the same view and added that "sailors, soldiers and aviators alike regarded an assignment to [the Aleutians] region of almost perpetual mist and snow as little better than penal servitude."[45]

These authorities make valid points. But there is more to the story. The importance of warfare on the flanks is reflected in the use of the North Pacific by both Japan and the United States for strategic diversions and deception. The North Pacific also was a vital route for the flow of lend-lease supplies to Russia. In fact more tonnage went to the Soviets via this route than through the North Russian and Persian Gulf corridors combined.[46] This material support was of considerable importance in the Russian victory over Germany. A joint U.S.-Soviet air and amphibious campaign against Japanese targets in the North Pacific had great potential significance and was a contingency for which the United States needed to be prepared. The basic requirement that a sovereign nation defend its own territory was honored by the United States.

Finally, the human dimension of warfare needs to be taken into account. Everyone who experienced the North Pacific campaign—military and civilian alike—felt the profound effect of armed conflict. It is fitting on this Veterans Day, therefore, to remember the congratulatory message that Admiral Frank Jack Fletcher, the North Pacific commander in August 1945, issued at the end of the war. Fletcher reminded his people that their

part in bringing Japan to her knees has been an important one. Ours has not been a spectacular job but all those who helped drive the invader from

---

[40] See Naval Historical Center, *U.S. Naval Experience in the North Pacific During World War II: Selected Documents* (Washington: Naval Historical Center, 1989), pp. 44-75; Otis Hays Jr., *Home From Siberia: The Secret Odysseys of Interned American Airmen in World War II* (College Station, Texas: Texas A and M University Press, 1990), pp. 97-117; David Rees, *The Soviet Seizure of the Kuriles* (New York: Praeger, 1985), pp. 46-47.

[41] Katherine L. Herbig, "American Strategic Deception in the Pacific, 1942-44," in Michael I. Handel, ed., *Strategic and Operational Deception in the Second World War* (London: Frank Cass and Co., 1987), pp. 264-81.

[42] Rees, *Soviet Seizure of the Kuriles*, pp. 61-62, 72-73, 78-82; Hayes, *History of the JCS*, pp. 672-76, 684-85; Jones, *Roads to Russia*, pp. x-xi.

[43] G. Patrick March, "Yanks in Siberia: U.S. Navy Weather Stations in Soviet East Asia, 1945," *Pacific Historical Review*, 1988, pp. 327-42.

[44] Miller, *War Plan Orange*, pp. 334-35.

[45] Morison, *History of USN*, vol. 7, p. 3.

[46] Jones, *Roads to Russia*, p. 290.

the Aleutians, hammered from sea and air at his Kuriles outposts, or worked in the williwaws to prepare for future blows now happily unneeded can well be proud participants in today's victory. Let us celebrate this day not in triumph but with thanksgiving and gratitude. Let us not forget our comrades who cannot share it. The world is now at peace. Let us face the problems that will now con-front us with the same spirit [that] has won this terrible war.[47]

*Dean C. Allard is the Chief of Naval History, a position he has held since 1989. He manages the Naval Historical Center and, as a staff member of the Office of Chief of Naval Operations, he oversees other historical and museum activities of the navy.*

---

[47] Quoted in *Pacific Fleet, Administrative History of North Pacific*, p. 302.

# American National Strategy in the East Asian and Pacific War: The North Pacific

*William A. Jacobs*

D R. DEAN ALLARD OPENED THIS CONFERENCE WITH A fine keynote address in which he set out the framework of American strategy in the Pacific in the Second World War. I intend to restate some of the main themes in that address, to elaborate on some of them, and to set events in the North Pacific in the larger context of Allied strategy as a whole. In particular, I want to suggest that events in Alaska and the North Pacific were ultimately more significant for the European theater of the war than for the Asian and Pacific.

Let me begin with some of Dr. Allard's most important points. First, so far as active military operations were concerned, the North Pacific was a strategic backwater. This was primarily the result of an ambivalent strategic geography. The Aleutians lay on or near the great circle route from the West Coast of the United States to Japan, a position that appeared to offer strategic opportunities for either power. From the American perspective, the westernmost of the islands were within raiding range of the Japanese-held Kuriles, but they were too far away from any of the worthwhile central objectives in the Japanese home islands. This was true even when B-29 aircraft—very long range bombers—became available for American operations in 1944. These aircraft could not be brought within range of profitable targets in the home islands without seizing bases in the Kuriles from the Japanese or obtaining the right to operate from bases in the Soviet Far East.[1]

Apart from geographic position, the wretched weather was a fundamental obstacle to air and surface operations. Large-scale military efforts limited to dumb iron and high explosives require mass and persistence to be effective. Big forces must be used over an extended period of time to achieve decisive results. This could not be done from Aleutian bases. All of the difficulties involved in air, sea, and ground operations in the region were amply demonstrated when the Japanese seized two islands in the Aleutian Chain in 1942, and the Americans—with Canadian assistance—drove them out in 1943.

Dr. Allard rightly emphasized that the only thing that could have fundamentally altered the strategic importance of the Aleutians as an area of operations was the outbreak of war between Japan and the Soviet Union. In 1941 and 1942, Washington thought that Japan might repudiate the Japan-USSR Neutrality Pact and move north from Manchuria and Korea. The Japanese government considered and rejected this option in mid-1941. Some American authorities thought that the landings on Attu and Kiska in 1942 were intended to screen the strategic flank of such an adventure. The Soviets might have entered the war at any time by simply allowing American forces to use their territory. But this would have closed one of their most important lines of supply with little or no offsetting benefit. As it turned out, the Soviet Union did not become a belligerent in Asia until the summer of 1945, after the Neutrality Pact had expired.

Dr. Allard also underlined the importance of American lend-lease aid to the Soviet Union and pointed in

[1] Wesley Frank Craven and James Lea Cate, *The Army Air Forces in World War II*, vol. 5 (Chicago: University of Chicago Press, 1953, reprint USAF Office of Air Force History, 1983), map on p. 5.

Admiral Thomas Kinkaid, center, confers with commanders during a planning session for retaking Kiska. To his left are Generals Charles Corlett, Simon Buckner, William Butler, and G.R. Pearkes (Canada). To his right are Admiral Francis Rockwell (head bowed) and General John DeWitt. *(Acc. No. 70-11-77, Hanna Call Collection, Rasmuson Library, University of Alaska Fairbanks)*

particular to the flow of very large tonnages across the North Pacific and through Japanese home waters to the Soviet Far East port of Vladivostok. The Grand Alliance was able to exploit this important line of communications precisely because the Japan-USSR Neutrality Pact remained intact until the very last phase of the war.

To identify and attempt to measure the significance of Alaska and the North Pacific in the Second World War, one has to recognize the serious weaknesses under which the United States and its allies labored in the early and middle phases of the conflict.

When Japan attacked Pearl Harbor on 7 December 1941 and Hitler declared war on the United States four days later, the American strategic position was very weak and was, for a time, to grow considerably weaker. The U.S. rearmament program was in its earliest stages; neither the economy nor the armed forces were ready for a global struggle. They would not reach their peak strength for another two years at least. At the outset, the Axis held the initiative and either possessed or were soon to gain powerful strategical positions. In Europe, the United States found itself in a situation radically different from that which it enjoyed in 1917 when it had entered a war behind a relatively secure front held by

the powerful armies of France and Great Britain. In 1941, the United States had to face the prospect of clawing its way, in the company of its Canadian and British allies, back on the European continent. In western Europe, the Allies did not fully regain the strategic position they had enjoyed throughout the Great War until June of 1944.[2]

In Asia and the Pacific, after the fall of the Philippines, the Netherlands East Indies, Burma, Malaya, and Singapore, the Allies held no strategic position from which to bring any form of destructive power to bear directly on the Japanese homeland. The Americans, with their Australian, British, Indian, Chinese, and Canadian allies, were forced into a prolonged struggle for position, first to contain the Japanese, then to push back the strategic perimeter. The Allies did not gain the Pacific bases from which to attack the Japanese home islands at long range, persistently and in strength, until the summer of 1944.

From their position of weakness, the American and British governments drew three conclusions that governed their strategy in the early and middle stages of the war:

1. They put first priority on the defeat of Hitler.

---

[2] I have been greatly influenced in my understanding of the Allied position in the early years of the war by the work of Gerhard Weinberg, particularly his *World in the Balance: Behind the Scenes of World War II* (Hanover and London: University Press of New England, 1981), pp. 27-52.

They reckoned Nazi Germany to be a far more dangerous state than Japan, especially considering the modern economic resources that had come under its control as a result of the disasters of 1940.

2. They had to preserve as much of the position they now possessed as they could. In short, they were committed to the strategic defensive supplemented by peripheral offensive operations in Asia and the Pacific. In Europe, as much as they would have liked to attack Hitler directly, they would have to be content with offensives on the margin for a considerable time.

3. They correctly appreciated that their fortunes depended overwhelmingly on the ability of the Red Army and Air Force to survive the German onslaught and to continue to fight. Second only to their own preparations and operations, they would provide major support to the Soviet Union.

At the first Washington Conference in December 1941, still unsure of the Soviet prospects for survival, the Allied Combined Chiefs of Staff (CCS) told President Roosevelt and Prime Minister Churchill that it was "essential to afford the Russians assistance to enable them to maintain their hold on Leningrad, Moscow, and the oil fields of the Caucasus, and to continue their war effort."[3] Slightly more than a year later, as the Red Army was drawing the noose ever more tightly around Stalingrad, the CCS recommended that "the Soviet forces must be sustained by the greatest volume of supplies that can be transported to Russia without prohibitive cost in shipping."[4] Lend-lease support of the Red Army and Air Force was, for some time, the most visible application of the Europe-first policy.

Among the many problems involved in carrying out this policy, three were most important: the difficulty of arranging anything of consequence with Soviet officials, the allocation of production of war material between the growing needs of the western Allies themselves and Soviets, and the obstacles in the way of actually getting the supplies to the territory of the Soviet Union. The last of these brings us back to Alaska and the North Pacific.

The Allies initially placed great hopes in the North Atlantic sea route to Britain and thence around the North Cape to Archangel and Murmansk. But ice, the

*Kriegsmarine*, and the *Luftwaffe* made this so hazardous that convoys along this approach were temporarily suspended in the summer of 1942. Their attention then shifted toward a more rapid development of two other sea routes: one leading from the American East Coast around the Cape of Good Hope across the Indian Ocean to the Persian Gulf; the other from the West Coast of the United States across the Pacific to Vladivostok along the great circle route.

From the beginning of Soviet aid in 1941 to the end of lend-lease in 1945, about 17.5 million long tons of supplies and equipment, carried in some 2,803 ships, went from the Western Hemisphere to the Soviet Union.[5] Almost 48 percent of this tonnage made its way in Soviet-registered ships across the North Pacific. Just over half a million tons went via the Bering Sea into the Soviet Arctic during the short summer shipping period, to be landed at the mouths of the Kolyma, Lena, and Yenisei Rivers.[6] The vast majority of the traffic passed through Japanese waters to land at Vladivostok at the far eastern terminus of the Siberian Railway.

Under the terms of the Treaty of Portsmouth, which ended the Russo-Japanese War in 1906, La Perouse Strait—between Hokkaido and southern Sakhalin—was to be kept open for navigation. The same was true of Tartarski Strait to the north, lying between Sakhalin and the Soviet mainland. The Japan-Soviet Neutrality Pact committed each party to the maintenance of the status quo and thence to the principle of free passage through La Perouse.

There were difficulties, however. Ice made the going dangerous in late winter, and the Japanese interfered with shipping. They objected in particular to the practice of reflagging American freighters to provide the Soviet Union with Pacific shipping. The dangers of the North Cape route and the delays encountered in developing the Persian Gulf infrastructure put more demands on the North Pacific than the pre-war Soviet Far East merchant fleet could handle. It was simply too small. Consequently, the U.S. transferred a large number of vessels to Soviet registry. After the Soviet victories over the Germans in mid-summer 1943, the Japanese were eager for better relations and their interference eased.

To avoid losing the route to Japanese interdiction, the Allies had to limit their cargoes to so-called non-military goods. About 60 percent of the railroad equipment, 75 percent of the petroleum products, and slightly less than half of all the food sent by the United States to the Sovi-

---

[3] "Memorandum by the United States and British Chiefs of Staff (WWII)," printed as Appendix I in Michael Howard, *Grand Strategy* (London: H.M.S.O., 1972).

[4] CCS, "Conduct of the War in 1943," C.C.S. 155/1, 19 Jan 43. Printed as Appendix III(D) in Howard.

[5] T.H. Vail Motter, *The Persian Corridor and Aid to Russia* (Washington, G.P.O., 1952), p. 4.

[6] Robert Huhn Jones, *The Roads to Russia* (Norman: University of Oklahoma Press, 1969), p. 211, table 1; Motter, Appendix A. There is a difference of about 50,000 tons between Jones and Motter.

ets during the war went via Vladivostok.[7]

The second important dimension of lend-lease for which the North Pacific was significant was the supply of combat aircraft. Shortly before the United States entered the war, the Joint Board, the predecessor of the Joint Chiefs of Staff, suggested that aircraft might be delivered to the Soviet Union by air if Japan cut the line of sea communications. The hazards of the North Cape route and the logistical problems experienced in Iran led the Americans to concentrate the shipment of lend-lease combat aircraft via northwest Canada and Alaska. A second consideration of great importance to the army air forces was the possibility of operating American heavy bombers from Soviet Far Eastern bases. To that end they proposed to ferry lend-lease aircraft to the Soviet Union in the hope of gaining information about airfields and the operational infrastructure of Soviet forces in the region. They intended nothing hostile in this; they simply wanted information that the Soviets were not volunteering about the areas in which the U.S. might have to operate should Japan and the USSR go to war.

Initially, Stalin refused to permit anything of this kind. He refused to allow American pilots or survey parties into the region, no doubt realizing that in addition to intelligence-gathering he would be playing fast and loose with the Neutrality Pact. By mid-summer 1942, however, it became clear that neither the northern route, nor the Persian Gulf could bring in enough aircraft, so Stalin consented to use the Alaska route, the Americans having dropped their proposal to use American pilots.

The Alaska-Siberia (ALSIB) route, supported by the Alcan Highway, became the route of choice in 1943. The planes were flown by American ferry pilots from Great Falls, Montana, to Fairbanks, Alaska, using supporting airfields along the Alaska-Canada highway, newly constructed for the purpose. Red Air Force pilots took over in Fairbanks, flying the machines to Nome and thence to

Williwaw winds whipping in off the Bering Sea lifted and twisted this heavy steel matting off a frozen, snow-covered hardstand at the edge of an Amchitka runway in October 1944. The wind rolled up approximately thirty-five hundred square feet of matting—weighing eight tons. *(Command Historian's Office, Alaskan Command.)*

a series of airfields in Siberia. All in all, the United States delivered about eight thousand aircraft along this route.[8]

The North Pacific played one other significant role in the Second World War which has yet to make its way into general accounts—largely because of the long delay in declassifying certain documents.[9] From the spring of 1944 to the end of the war, the Americans ran the first and arguably the largest and most complex of their strategic deception operations in the Pacific from the Aleutians. Apart from the tactical deceptions carried out in the theaters, the Americans were slow to adopt strategic deception for the Pacific War. Following the expulsion of the Japanese forces from their toehold in the Aleutians, Joint Security Control, the American organization in Washington charged with coordination of deception activities, prepared a draft deception plan which was sent to Lieutenant General Simon B. Buckner, the senior army officer in Alaska. Buckner returned his amended version in January 1944. In his turn, Admiral Chester Nimitz, the C-in-C of the Central Pacific Theater, weighed in with further modifications. In March 1944, the Americans finally began a major radio deception operation from the Aleutians.

The Americans hoped the radio game, supplemented by occasional small air raids and photo-reconnaissance operations over the Kuriles, would convince the Japanese of the imminence of a five-division assault on two points in the Kuriles. These deceptions supported the Japanese decision—taken in early 1944—to reinforce the northern area and to maintain large forces there. Total Japanese troop strength increased from twenty-five thousand in January 1944 to some seventy thousand in June. They also increased the air forces from a mere thirty-eight aircraft to some 589 (with later withdrawals to a much lower number). Japanese intelligence estimated that American forces in Alaska and the Aleutians had quadrupled from 100,000 to 400,000 in the first six months of 1944. In

---

[7] Computed from Jones, table 1.

[8] Craven and Cate, chap. 6 of *The Army Air Forces in World War II*, vol. 7 (Chicago: University of Chicago Press, 1983). On ALSIB, see also Richard C. Lukas, *Eagles East: The Army Air Forces and the Soviet Union, 1941-45* (Tallahassee: Florida State University Press, 1970).

[9] Katherine L. Herbig, "American Strategic Deception in the Pacific: 1942-44," *Intelligence and National Security* 2:3 (1987), pp. 260-300.

fact, the Americans had reduced their establishment by more than 30 percent.

To what degree were Alaska and the North Pacific region important in shaping the character, the length, and the outcome of the two great wars that made up the Second World War? It is clear that weather and the geography of basing discouraged both the Japanese and Americans from using the Aleutians as the platform for major offensive operations. Each made token commitments to guard against the possibility that the other might violate the rules of strategic common sense. Each succeeded for a time in diverting large enemy forces to the region, forces which might have been more profitably employed elsewhere. These actions produced brief and nasty fighting but no decisive strategic result. Only war between Japan and the Soviet Union would have changed this situation and made the North Pacific a major theater of operations.

Because that did not happen, the fundamental strategic importance of Alaska and the North Pacific lay in the assistance given to the Soviet Union. Judging the impact of lend-lease in general, and that portion of it that crossed the Pacific in particular, is a difficult task. This is one of the most important unsettled problems in the historiography of the Second World War and the opportunities for new research in the archives of the Russian Federation may produce a more definitive judgment than can now be made. In the meantime, a few generalizations can safely be advanced. First of all, lend-lease aid to the Soviet Union, whether it came over the Atlantic, through the Persian Gulf, across the North Pacific, or through Canadian and Alaska skies, contributed primarily to the defeat of the Axis in Europe. The physical impact of food, material, and weapons shipped in 1941 was modest at best. The Soviet Union could probably have survived Operation Barbarossa without it. The same might be said about Germany's 1942 offensive in the south, but by this time it is clear that Allied aid was arriving in large quantities. About 1.5 million tons—mostly food, petroleum, and raw materials—landed in the first six months of 1942. About 2,300 aircraft were delivered in that year, most of them coming in through the northern route or the Persian Gulf.

As a recent writer puts it:

Lend-Lease alone did not enable the Soviet Union to launch Operation Uranus [the Stalingrad counter-offensive], nor would its absence have prevented the attack. On the other hand, although the direct contribution to Soviet operations seems modest, aid arrived at a time when the Soviet margin of military superiority was thin or nonexistent, stockpiles of food and petrol were barely adequate, and transport, communications, and coordination of large forces were handicapped by lack of equipment. In this environment of scarcity, Lend-Lease certainly aided in the buildup of the Soviet forces and, perhaps, their offensive success.[10]

In 1943 and 1944 the whole strategic situation in the Soviet Union turned around. The Red Army and Air Force gained the initiative and, from the summer of 1943, subjected the German armed forces to a relentless series of sophisticated and savage offensives. These ground up the German army and threw it out of European Russia, pushed it back into Germany, and, with the armed forces of the Western Allies, ultimately forced it to unconditional surrender. It is difficult to be certain on the point, but the best judgment seems to be that sooner or later the Red Army would have been able to go over to the offensive without lend-lease. However, it would not have been able to inflict so much destruction, to operate so relentlessly, to shift its line of advance so regularly, without the air support, vehicles, communications equipment, logistics support, and petroleum provided by lend-lease.[11]

Thus, Alaska and the North Pacific contributed to a quicker and more decisive defeat of Nazi Germany with fewer casualties to the armies of Great Britain, Canada, and the United States.

*William A. Jacobs, a professor of political science and history, joined the University of Alaska Anchorage faculty in 1973. He has written about air support and superiority during 1944, strategic bombing in World War II, and on civil and military relations in the United Kingdom.*

---

[10] Hubert P. Van Tuyll, *Feeding the Bear: American Aid to the Soviet Union, 1941-45* (Westport: Greenwood Press, 1989), p. 56.

[11] Here I am closely following van Tuyll's argument.

# Strategic Cooperation:
# The Canadian Commitment to the Defense of Alaska in the Second World War

*M.V. Bezeau*

ALASKA IS NOW ONLY A FEW HOURS BY AIR FROM THE rest of the continent. It was more isolated in 1942. Then, Eight (Bomber-Reconnaissance) Squadron, Royal Canadian Air Force (RCAF), found itself staging north in short hops, dogged by bad weather, which soon scattered its aircraft from Yakutat to Anchorage. Fourteen (Fighter) Squadron, RCAF, took an entire month early the next year to crawl painfully up the coast from Vancouver to Umnak Island. What were they doing there at all, far from their own territory, helping a more powerful neighbor with defense? In total war, the realities of power are not always simple.

Canada had regarded Japan as the most likely enemy in the inter-war years, but turned its attention to Europe when war began with Germany in September 1939. The threat seemed nearer after the collapse of France in the spring of 1940. Prime Minister Mackenzie King of Canada and President Roosevelt of the United States met and, on 18 August, issued the Ogdensburg Declaration, which announced the establishment of a Permanent Joint Board on Defense (PJBD) for military cooperation in North America.[1] The new Board quickly prepared a "Joint Canadian-United States Basic Defense Plan—1940," based on the assumption of the destruction or neutralization of British Forces, allowing Ger-

many and Italy free rein, possibly in conjunction with a hostile Japan. The plan provided for the joint defense of Canada, Newfoundland—then still a British colony—and the United States. Canada was to concentrate forces in British Columbia for the initial support of United States garrisons in Alaska, if required, and provide facilities to aid American air and water movement there. These facilities included not only coastal installations, but also the North-West Air Route, planned in the late 1930s as a great circle—that is, shortest distance—civil aviation staging route to the Orient, and then under construction.[2]

Fear of British collapse was unjustified, however, and, in early 1941, the British and Americans held secret conversations to coordinate the defeat of Germany and her allies if the United States felt "compelled" to go to war. The conversations concluded in staff agreements which considered Germany the predominant Axis member and the Atlantic and European areas the decisive theaters. War in Europe was to take precedence over any with Japan. Two combined principles were accepted: unity of command in each theater, and the integrity of national forces.[3] Canada and the United States then updated their existing plan, naming the replacement the Joint Canadian-United States Basic

---

[1] C.P. Stacey, *Arms, Men and Governments: The War Policies of Canada, 1939-1945* (Ottawa: Queen's Printer, 1970), p. 339.

[2] S.W. Dziuban, *Military Relations Between the United States and Canada, 1939-1945* (United States Army in World War II; Special Studies; Washington: U.S. Govt. Printing Office, 1959), pp, 33, 86-90, 100, 366-369; M.V. Bezeau, "The Realities of Strategic Planning: The Decision to build the Alaska Highway," in Kenneth Coates, *The Alaska Highway: Papers of the 40th Anniversary Symposium* (Vancouver: University of British Columbia Press, 1985), p. 26.

[3] S.E. Morison, *History of United States Naval Operations in World War II*, vol. 1: *The Battle of the Atlantic, September 1939-May 1943*, (Boston: Little, Brown, 1947), pp. 45-46; W.F. Craven and J.L. Cate, eds., *The Army Air Forces in World War II*, vol. 1: *Plans and Early Operations, January 1939 to August 1942* (Chicago: University of Chicago Press, 1948), pp. 136-139.

Defense Plan 2, short-titled ABC-22. Work on a subordinate west coast plan had barely begun when, on 7 December 1941, Japan struck Pearl Harbor. The next day both countries put ABC-22 into effect against the new enemy.[4]

Just before the strike, Lieutenant General John L. DeWitt, the commanding general of the American Western Defense Command, suggested a combined meeting to draw up a tentative area defense plan based on ABC-22. An American draft was forwarded shortly, quickly accepted, and detailed work began on the Joint Canadian-United States Pacific Coastal Frontier Plan No. 2, or ABC-Pacific-22, formally approved by all Allied west coast commanders on 23 January 1942. One shared task committed Canadians to "support the defense of Alaska" and "associated naval operations," although they scarcely visualized a future demand for support far from their own borders.[5]

The first American requirement was to secure their lines of communications to Alaska. They had already negotiated access to the airfields and corridors of the North-West Staging Route through the Joint Board in late 1940 and continued to press for the route's completion over the following years. Now they turned their attention to two more infrastructure projects: the Alaska Highway and the use of the northern British Columbian port of Prince Rupert.

Americans had long wanted a land route to Alaska, and saw this as an opportune time to gain Canadian approval because of the Japanese threat. Canadians thought the highway's proposal and its military justification "a most dubious egg" since its planned completion date was so far in the future as to be of no practical military benefit. American insistence on the road's construction was so strong, however, that Canada felt it could not stand in its way. A route following the line of the North-West Staging Route was chosen, in part to service the airfields. The survey started in the spring of 1942, and construction shortly thereafter. The pioneer road was completed late that year, but, as the Canadians had predicted, made no real strategic difference to the war.[6]

Not so the use of Prince Rupert, which also led to direct Canadian involvement in Alaska. Even before the Pearl Harbor attack, the United States build-up in its advanced Pacific posts had strained Seattle and more southerly ports, and Americans had shown an early interest in the use of Canadian facilities. An American survey in early 1941 had found Prince Rupert potentially able to supply all of Southeastern Alaska and part of western Alaska. A return trip to the Anchorage area was 1,000 miles less than from Seattle, an important difference when shipping was scarce. As a result, ABC-Pacific-22 specifically authorized the United States Army "to establish such facilities as may be required at Prince Rupert for the supply of U.S. Troops in Alaska." An American sub-embarkation port was opened there in April 1942. The United States quickly expanded the port's capacity, creating a nearby personnel staging area with its own port facilities and an ammunition storage dump.[7]

Canadian air defense of Prince Rupert was weak, however. The lack of suitable land for a runway restricted the air force to a seaplane base just north of the port. Without a runway, there was no fighter protection. Allied cooperation now provided a solution to this long-standing problem. The Americans had built a sparse airfield on Annette Island, about sixty miles away, but could spare no air combat units for it.[8] Now the two countries' requirements came together. Canadians tentatively suggested in March that it might be possible to deploy an RCAF fighter squadron to Annette until an American one was available, and Americans welcomed this reinforcement. No. 115 (Fighter) Squadron was selected and was complete on Annette by 5 May, with responsibility for the "fighter defense of Prince Rupert and its approaches." It was the first Canadian force ever based in U.S. territory to directly assist in American defense. Small Canadian Army detachments were added later to protect the squadron.[9]

The military deployment went smoothly, with no significant local problems. However, although the new arrivals knew nothing about it, the movement of Canadian units to Alaska raised the problem of American

---

[4] Dziuban, *Relations*, pp. 48n, 73, 104-108; COS Committee to Ministers, 17 December 1941, DHist 193.009(D3).

[5] Minutes of Joint Services Committee (Pacific Coast), 19 December 1941, DHist 193.009 (D3); Freeman to Canadian western regional commanders, 18 December 1941, DeWitt to Canadian commanders, 21 December 1941, telephone message from Beech, 22 December 1941, Alexander to Secretary, DND, 23 December 1941, (MD11 HQS 638-1-1-20-2), DHist 169.009 (D138); ABC-Pacific-22, 23 January 1942, DHist 112.3M2 (D500).

[6] Bezeau, "Strategic Planning," in Coates, *Highway*, pp. 25-35.

[7] Dziuban, *Relations*, pp. 238-240; COS to Minister, 16 January 1942, DHist 193.009 (D3); ABC-Pacific-22, Annex IV, Section III, 23 January 1942, DHist 112.3M2 (D500); Journal of Discussions and Decisions of PJBD 26th Meeting, 25-26 February 1942, W.L.M. King papers, PAC MG 26 J4, vol. 319, file 3369.

[8] "R.C.A.F. in the Aleutians," chap. 2, p. 4, DHist 74/3, vol. 1; United States, Eleventh Air Force, "History of the Eleventh Army Air Force," n.d., pp. 14, 53, 68, DHist 80/176.

[9] Ibid., p. 34; "Report of Meeting," 6 March 1942, DHist 193.009 (D5); AOC WAC to AFHQ, 27 May 1942, C.G. Power papers, box 69, file D2019, Queen's University Archives; "R.C.A.F. in the Aleutians", chap 2, p. 4, DHist 74/3, Vol. 1; Clarke Interview, 25 October 1979, H.P. Clarke biographical file, DHist; Stacey, *Arms*, p. 388; Dziuban, *Relations*, p. 252.

customs duties on their equipment and supplies. Even in war, the mills of civilian bureaucracy grind exceedingly fine. U.S. Secretary of State Cordell Hull solved the problem by designating all unit personnel as "distinguished foreign visitors" and so granted free entry of goods.[10]

From an American viewpoint, the Annette Island force provided one piece in long-neglected Alaska defenses. Army planners had acknowledged the Japanese threat since the 1930s, but, since the bulk of U.S. Navy strength was in the Pacific after 1937, more concern had been shown about Atlantic defense and Germany.[11] Serious Alaska preparations only started in 1939. The navy had overall strategic responsibility. The army's role was to support and defend those places where coastal installations required protection. Army plans placed heavy reliance on air power in spite of the shortage of aircraft and the fact that, due to distance and weather, Alaska was not easy to reinforce quickly. The general plan in the fall of 1941, re-confirmed on 6 December—the day before the Pearl Harbor attack— was to base defense on selected main airfields, such as Annette Island, manned by a composite group of fighters and bombers. After Pearl Harbor, defense priorities focussed on seven key areas: first, Anchorage; second, Kodiak; third, the naval installation at Dutch Harbor and the new airfield being built on Umnak Island; fourth and fifth, Yakutat and Annette Island; last, Naknek and Cold Bay. In theory, if these were defended successfully, Alaska as a whole was reasonably safe. Some limited aerial reinforcement was carried out in the new year, in spite of the hazards of winter flights along the imperfectly-developed airways. Fair-weather initial operating capability on the North-West Staging Route had only been achieved the previous fall, and winter flying was hazardous. Little more could be done. Global demands prevented the expansion of the Eleventh Army Air Force in Alaska beyond the five combat units already there, although plans called for more than three times as many.[12]

Meanwhile, after rapid success and light losses in their initial operations to conquer an enlarged empire of Greater East Asia, the Japanese embarked on plans to expand the defensive perimeter around the new gains. Strategic points in the Aleutians, Midway Island, and on the line from Hawaii to Australia would be seized.

The outer Aleutian Islands and Midway Island would be taken first and simultaneously, though the Aleutian strike would come earliest, as a diversion. The Midway operation was expected to force a decisive fleet action with the U.S. Navy which, if successful, would allow Japanese control of the central and western Pacific. The Japanese Imperial General Headquarters issued the order for both invasions on 5 May 1942. Americans intercepted and decoded most of it, and redeployed forces to meet the threat. Most American naval strength was committed to the defense of Midway. In Alaska, army and navy forces were placed under unified command.[13] Air reinforcements were urgently needed, but the United States had only limited resources available. For further support, they now looked to Canada.

ABC-22 and its subordinate Pacific plan had committed Canada to a supporting role in Alaska, but the two countries had very different views of what this role entailed. The Canadian west coast commanders appreciated that Alaska was the "easiest and most attractive objective" if Japan attacked North America, but felt that increased Canadian commitments would center on the protection of American convoys and make the defense of Prince Rupert "of prime importance."[14]

American ideas differed. On 1 April 1942, President Roosevelt had implied that Canada should take a larger role in Pacific defense, especially for Alaska and the Aleutian Islands, and that Canadian forces might be stationed in Alaska territory. Since this was coincident with the agreement to base a fighter squadron on Annette Island, Canadians placed little importance on the statement. However, Americans on the Permanent Joint Board on Defense noted that the RCAF should have plans ready for the further air reinforcement of Alaska. After considerable discussion, the Board agreed that prudent local planning should be carried out. On 12 May, the Canadian Western Air Command was ordered to comply, although with misgivings. The Canadian Chiefs of Staff's opinions were shaped by a west coast appreciation which confirmed that Prince Rupert's defense was Canada's first concern if Alaska was attacked. The Joint Board now appeared to place the onus on Canada to provide air reinforcements further north instead. Alaska's defenses were weak, but RCAF west coast strength was adequate for Canadian needs only if the Americans were strong. There was no

---

[10] Ibid., p. 254; correspondence, July 1942 (AFHQ 035-11-1, vol. 1), PAC RG 24, vol. 17,634; Clarke interview, 25 October 1979, H.P. Clarke biographical file, DHist; letter, 29 November 1979, J.Y. Scallon biographical file, DHist.

[11] Stetson Conn, R.C. Engleman, and Byron Fairchild, *Guarding the United States and Its Outposts* (United States Army in World War II; The Western Hemisphere; Washington: Department of the Army, 1964), p. 5.

[12] Craven and Cate, vol 1, *Plans*, pp. 167, 276, 303; United States, Eleventh Air Force, "History of the Eleventh Army Air Force," n.d., pp. 64-66, 83-84, 91-93, 107, 111, 118, 121-124, 128-129, 131, DHist 80/176.

[13] Ibid., p. 191; Craven and Cate, vol1, *Plans*, p. 464.

[14] Joint Service Committee—Pacific, "Appreciation of the Situation," 1 April 1942, DHist 193.009 (D6).

reserve "to assume major commitments in Alaska." Defense there had to remain the concern of the United States, with Canadian reinforcements "limited to local support in the Panhandle." However, Western Air Command complied with its direction. Subject to the situation, it would send a fighter and a bomber-reconnaissance squadron to Whitehorse for onward dispatch (what is now called "maritime patrol," with either amphibious or land planes, the latter of which comprise all the units mentioned in this paper). These plans were discussed with local American air staff in Alaska. When the Permanent Joint Board met again on 26-27 May to discuss the problem further, events had outrun the Board's deliberations.[15]

The earliest American wireless interceptions were not passed to Canada. Ottawa was finally informed by its west coast commanders on 21 May that they had received word from the United States the day before that Japan was about to attack Midway Island and the Aleutians. Western Air Command passed on this information, along with the warning from the army's Pacific Command General Staff that "should this situation develop it is possible that action might be taken against Prince Rupert." Since Canada was committed to assist in Alaska's defense only to the extent consistent with maintaining its own, Western Air Command recommended sending a bomber-reconnaissance squadron to join the fighter unit on Annette Island, but recommended against moving more fighters to Alaska until the American fighter defense of the Seattle area improved.[16]

However, Americans now believed that a request for two squadrons beyond the Annette Island force would be approved. In Alaska, all spare combat aircraft were moved forward to meet the threat. To help cover the gap, the expected RCAF squadrons were asked to proceed to Yakutat, halfway between Annette and Anchorage. The Canadian Chiefs of Staff discussed this request on 29 May. They agreed the request would weaken Canadian defenses, but felt this could be accepted under the circumstances. However they continued to be concerned about Prince Rupert. Therefore they decided to reinforce Annette Island with a bomber-reconnaissance and a fighter squadron, and bring more fighters from eastern Canada. Two of the Annette Island squadrons were to be prepared to move further north if necessary, with follow-on reinforcement to Annette. This plan seemed to cover all possibilities for a raid which, to those in Ottawa, was "about to be made on Alaska and probably on our Pacific coast."[17]

When the Americans heard of these plans, they immediately requested that the incoming squadrons go directly to Yakutat, with approval for moves to Kodiak, Anchorage, Cordova, or Cold Bay if required. The Canadian Army's Chief of the General Staff, then on the west coast, was adamant that the squadrons should not go beyond Annette Island and leave Canadian areas unprotected. Air Force Headquarters assured him that no move would take place until the situation was clearer and reinforcing squadrons reached the coast.[18]

That caused consternation among the Americans, and the reaction was immediate. When DeWitt found that the squadrons were unavailable, he telephoned the War Department in Washington and asked it to intercede with Ottawa and arrange the squadrons' release. The complaint that "Ottawa" had "vetoed" local west coast agreements was passed on immediately, with a formal request for the move to Yakutat until at least 8 June, the first that Canadian headquarters had heard of a time limit on the request. Its possible effects on Prince Rupert defenses were discussed, and all three services agreed that the RCAF should comply. The orders were on their way within a few hours.[19]

Eight (Bomber-Reconnaissance) Squadron moved first. Although maps had been requested on receipt of the warning order, none had arrived, and no one knew the route or had even seen an air navigation map north of Prince Rupert. Admiralty charts were obtained —fewer than the number of aircraft—but they were small scale and lacked coastline details or land contours. Still, they had to do. On 2 June, the squadron's Bolingbroke aircraft departed for their destination via

---

[15] Wrong to Robertson, 1 April 1942, Under-Secretary of State for External Affairs to Prime Minister, 6 April 1942 (DEA/23-As), Department of External Affairs (DEA); Journal of Discussions and Decisions of PJBD Meetings, 7 and 27 April, 27 May 1942, W.L.M. King papers, PAC MG 26 J4, vol. 319, file 3369; "R.C.A.F. in the Aleutians," chap.3, pl, DHist 74/3, vol. 1; Minutes of the 157th and 158th Meetings of the COS Committee, 5, 12 May 1942, DHist 193.009 (D53); Extracts from Minutes of the Cabinet War Committee, 14 May 1942, PCO files. DEA; Macdonald interview, 7 February 1980, 17, JKF Macdonald biographical file. DHist.

[16] C.P. Stacey, *Official History of the Canadian Army in the Second World War*, vol. I: *Six Years of War: The Army in Canada, Britain and the Pacific* (Ottawa: Queen's Printer, 1966), p. 173; AOC WAC to AFHQ, 21 and 27 May 1942, C.G. Power papers, box 69, file D-2019, Queen's University Archives.

[17] Johnston to Minister, CAS to C-in-C West Coast Defenses, 29 May 1942, ibid.; W.L.M. King diary, 30 May 1942, PAC MG 26 J13; Minutes of the 161st Meeting of the COS Committee, 29 May 1942, DHist 193.009 (D53).

[18] AOC WAC to AFHQ (A63 and A465), "Memorandum of Telephone Call," 30 May 1942, C.G. Power papers, box 69, file D-2019, Queen's University Archives.

[19] "Report of Telephone Conversation," "Diary of Action by DCAS in Respect of Alaskan Situation," CAS to C-in-C West Coast Defenses, 1 June 1942, ibid.; Dziuban, *Relations*, p. 253..

Annette Island and Juneau. At the latter, the last leg's route was traced off local maps before the aircraft flew on to arrive at Yakutat on 3 June, the day the Japanese attacked Dutch Harbor. One Bolingbroke immediately carried out a short patrol, the first operational mission in support of Alaska Defense Command. The next day, Eight (BR) was told of enemy contact and ordered to have all aircraft stand by armed with bombs. The armorers soon discovered that the bomb shackle adapter rings—designed in Canada to take U.S. ordnance —would fit the only sized American bomb not stocked in Alaska. New adapter rings were made hurriedly and flown north to the squadron.[20]

Enemy carrier aircraft struck Dutch Harbor on 3 and 4 June, but the crushing Japanese defeat at Midway completely overshadowed this success and made impractical any major offensive beyond the original conquest perimeter. There was now little strategic reason to continue the Aleutian operation, but, after some hesitation, the commander of the force was ordered to continue as planned. A Japanese force landed on Kiska on 6 June and Attu on the 7th.

Alaska Defense Command could now redeploy its resources to match the threat and its location. The Canadian squadrons comprised one quarter of the Eleventh Air Force's combat units, even though American reinforcements were on their way north. In late June, after most of these had arrived, the Canadians were still one-eighth of the combat strength, so it was important to move them forward. On 5 June, the squadrons at Yakutat were ordered to move at once to Anchorage. The Canadian commander, Wing Commander G.R. McGregor, immediately signalled Western Air Command for authority to comply. If the wing was to get into battle, he explained, it would have to advance. Permission was granted, and the squadron started north to reassemble at Elmendorf on the 7th. Meanwhile, fighter squadron No. 111, still struggling north through the Canadian interior, had its destination changed, continuing north in packets to complete its strength in Alaska on the 24th. The last group,

equipped with belly tanks, flew the coastal route through Annette Island and Yakutat.[21]

There were few illusions about the chance for action at Anchorage or more active employment elsewhere. When forces were sent to Nome as a precaution against enemy incursions, the Canadians were alerted for duty, then told they would probably not be needed. McGregor had already decided his squadrons were seen essentially as a convenient rear-area security force, and this incident confirmed his opinion. He recognized the usefulness of freeing American units from Anchorage's defense, but wondered if this use of two scarce Home War Establishment squadrons was in Canada's best interests.[22]

After hearing these feelings, the Americans expressed a willingness to allow a chance to meet the enemy. No. 111's pilots and selected ground crew—more than half the unit—would go forward to Umnak Island, the most advanced American base, to relieve an equivalent number of personnel from the American Eleventh Fighter Squadron, equipped with the same aircraft: P-40s or, as Canadians called them, Kittyhawks.[23]

On 13 July 1942, Wing Commander McGregor and the first group of six pilots started west. It was an unlucky trip. One aircraft was accidentally lost and another damaged on the first leg. Replacement fighters were brought forward and the last two legs began on the 16th, but tragedy struck shortly after the planes passed Dutch Harbor. They ran into bad weather and McGregor ordered them to turn back. As the other aircraft followed him in the turn, they lost contact and five crashed in the fog. McGregor himself later narrowly missed a rocky ledge as he circled low on the fog's edge for half an hour calling them. Only one answered, a fighter which continued on to Umnak and landed through the only available break in the cloud cover.[24]

Replacement pilots arrived a month later. Replacement aircraft were harder to find. Canada's allotment of American-built aircraft was limited and none were available for shipment north. But McGregor found a

---

[20] No. 8 Squadron ORB Daily Diary, 1-5 June 1942, DHist; RCAF Wing, Elmendorf, ORB Daily Diary, 8 and 30 June 1942, DHist; "Historical Summary," 5, R.E. Morrow biographical file, DHist; Watkins interview, 16 August 1979, Smith to Bezeau, 22 October 1979, Tingley to Bezeau, 16 November 1979, E.J. Watkins, W.J. Smith, and S.A. Tingley biographical files, DHist.

[21] "11 AF Assigned and Attached Units," DHist 80/176, file 2; Courtney to CO XI Bomber Command, 12 June 1943, ibid., file 4; RCAF Wing, Elmendorf, ORB Daily Diary, pp. 5-6, 27 June 1942, DHist; Johnson to AMAS, WAC to AFHQ and minute, CAS to C-in-C West Coast Defences, "Memorandum for Record," 5 June 1942, C.G. Power papers, box 69, file D-2019, Queen's University Archives; 8 Squadron ORB Daily Diary, 5-7 June 1942, DHist; "Historical Summary," pp. 5-6, R.E. Morrow biographical file, DHist; 111 Squadron ORB Daily Diary, June 1942, DHist.

[22] No. 8 Squadron ORB Daily Diary, 11 June 1942, DHist; RCAF Wing, Elmendorf, ORB Daily Diary, 18-20, 27 June 1942, DHist; McGregor to AOC WAC, 30 June 1942, in ibid.; Courtney to HQ Eleventh Air Force, 3 December 1942, DHist 80/176, file 4; "11 AF Assigned and Attached Units," ibid., file 2.

[23] "Report by the Minister for Air to the Cabinet War Committee," 11 July 1942, C.G. Power papers, box 63, file D-1078, Queen's University Archives; RCAF Wing, Elmendorf, ORB Daily Diary, 4-8 July 1942, DHist.

[24] No. 111 Squadron ORB Daily Diary, 13-17, 22 July and 17 September 1942, DHist; Eskil's "Report of Events ...," 18 July 1942, RCAF Wing Daily Diary file, DHist; RCAF Wing, Elmendorf, ORB Daily Diary, 13-16 July 1942, DHist.

local solution. In accordance with a previous directive on transferring equipment, new P-40Ks could be loaned by XI Fighter Command, and a simple signature on a shipping voucher would acknowledge their sale to Canada, an approach in stark contrast to the bureaucracy experienced earlier at Annette. McGregor could thus obtain replacement aircraft without going through the Washington subcommittee which allocated such resources and, hopefully, without reducing the Canadian allotment. He asked permission to do so, quietly, without informing Washington. Authorization soon arrived, but with a note that final accounting would be made through regular channels.[25]

Eight (BR) Squadron also sent a detachment forward that summer. On 12 July it was ordered to send three aircraft to Nome for patrols over Norton Sound and the Bering Sea. Nome was becoming a staging post for American lend-lease aircraft being ferried to the Soviet Union up the North-West Staging Route through Canada, and Canadian airmen saw their first two Soviet aircraft land in mid-August. Only a few months later, however, on 21 October, the Nome patrols were ordered discontinued for the winter, and the aircraft withdrawn again to Alaska's southern coast.[26]

Meanwhile, it had become clear that there was no danger of a further Japanese offensive in the Aleutians. Instead of committing sufficient forces to drive the enemy out, however, the Joint Chiefs of Staff decided to seize the initiative in the southern Pacific. Alaska operations were thus limited to the forces already available, plus any DeWitt could spare from resources under his command. To the Allied supreme command, the minor Japanese incursions in Alaska were of little importance. With Rommel threatening Alexandria, Roosevelt wanting an offensive against Germany, and the need to stop the Japanese in the Solomons and New Guinea, the Combined Chiefs saw the North Pacific as strictly a defensive theater.[27]

Under the circumstances, Lieutenant General DeWitt submitted a modest plan for continued joint operations. Using only the forces available, among which was a small group of Royal Canadian Navy ships—three armed merchant cruisers, essentially merchant vessels fitted with guns for convoy escort, and two corvettes serving under USN command—he proposed to advance down the Aleutian Chain as a step toward Kiska. The chosen target was Adak, where an airstrip was built with amazing speed. The first Adak-Kiska mission was flown on 14 September. Bad weather then prevented further attacks for ten days. In the interval, fighter reinforcements from Umnak, including four Canadians, flew in for the first P-40 raid on the Japanese.[28]

At approximately 1000 hours on 25 September, the Canadians, as part of a large force of bombers and fighters, swept low across Little Kiska Island toward the North Head of Kiska Harbor. There they struck gun positions and then the main Japanese camp area and radar installations. Coming back for a second pass, they met two Rufes—the seaplane version of the Zero fighter—which had taken off to meet the attack. After a brief and over-confident display of aerobatics, the enemy leader struck at an American P-40, only to be hit in turn by Squadron Leader Boomer of 111 Squadron. "I climbed to a stall practically, pulled up right under him. I just poured it into him from underneath. He flamed up and went down." Shortly after, Major Chennault of the sister American Eleventh Fighter Squadron downed another Rufe.[29]

After this brief taste of action, the Canadian fighter squadron withdrew from its advanced deployment. Three American fighter squadrons would soon be lost from the theater, and this necessitated redeploying the remainder. In October, 111 (Fighter) Squadron was transferred to Kodiak for the defense of that naval base.[30]

Winter weather prevented any amphibious assault to clear the Aleutians until spring. In the interim, American forces stepped down the Aleutian Chain to Amchit-

---

[25] Ibid., 20 August to 3 September 1942.

[26] No. 8 Squadron ORB Daily Diary, 12 July to 25 September, 1-23 November 1942, DHist; United States, Eleventh Air Force, "History of the Eleventh Army Air Force," n.d., p. 194, DHist 80/176; RCAF Wing, Elmendorf, ORB Daily Diary, 21 October 1942, DHist.

[27] Conn, *Guarding*, pp. 264-266; S.E. Morison, *History of United States Naval Operations in World War II*, vol. 4, *Coral Sea, Midway and Submarine Operations, May 1942-August 1942* (Boston: Little, Brown, 1949), pp. 259-263; W.F. Craven and J.L. Cate, eds, *The Army Air Forces in World War II*, vol. 4, *The Pacific: Guadalcanal to Saipan, August 1942 to July 1944* (Chicago: University of Chicago Press, 1950), p. 368.

[28] Stacey, *Government*, pp. 321, 390-1; United States, Eleventh Air Force, "History of the Eleventh Army Air Force," n.d., pp. 173-186, 195-196, 203, DHist 80/176; United States, 11th Fighter Squadron, "History of Eleventh Fighter Squadron" [June 1944], pp. 47-49, 136, documents 56, 58, ibid.; Conn, *Guarding*, pp. 270-272; S.E. Morison, *History of United States Naval Operations in World War II*, vol. 7, *Aleutians, Gilberts and Marshalls, June 1942-April 1944* (Boston: Little, Brown, 1951) pp. 12-13; Craven and Cate, vol. 4, *Guadalcanal*, pp. 369-371, vol. 7, *Services Around the World* (Chicago: University of Chicago Press, 1958), pp. 294; 111 Squadron ORB Daily, 18, 21 September 1942, DHist.

[29] Ibid., Appendices 3 and 4, 25 September 1942, DHist; United States, 11th Fighter Squadron, "History of Eleventh Fighter Squadron" [June 1944], pp. 48-49, DHist 80/176; K.A. Boomer and H.O. Gooding biographical files, DHist.

[30] United States, Eleventh Air Force, "History of the Eleventh Army Air Force," n.d., pp. 187, 212-214, DHist 80/176; "11 AF Assigned and Attached Units," ibid., p. 2; RCAF Wing, Elmendorf, ORB Daily Diary, 16-24 September, 12 October, 1942, DHist; 111 Squadron ORB Daily Diary, 19 and 22 September, 8, 10-13 October 1942, DHist.

ka Island, just over fifty miles from the Japanese and close enough to exploit momentary breaks in the weather.[31]

During this quiet period, the Canadian contribution to the Eleventh Air Force changed. The usefulness of Eight (BR) Squadron had been questioned for some time. It was equipped with the British Bolingbroke, always subject to severe supply problems, and there were no targets within its limited range. With American fighter strength running down, it seemed best to replace No. Eight with a fighter squadron, that is, if the Canadians stayed at all. It was clear that they had little likelihood of offensive action; the limited airfield space in the Aleutians was already occupied by more suitable American aircraft types. However, the Canadian western air commander received assurances that the squadrons were indeed needed for several more months, after which it was hoped that they could be relieved by American units. On this basis, after months of hesitation, Canada agreed to maintain two fighter squadrons in northern Alaska until the next May.[32]

Eight Squadron left for Canada in February 1943. At the same time, Fourteen (Fighter) Squadron headed north along the coast. Winter weather intervened, as it did so often in this campaign, and the squadron staggered forward, airstrip by airstrip, to finally reach Umnak Island on 18 March. The ground party quickly turned out to watch as "the whole Squadron of fifteen Kittyhawks arrived over the aerodrome."[33] The air trip had taken over a month. By then, plans for the spring offensive were getting underway.

With no extra resources available, Alaska commanders singled out Attu Island, rather than the nearer Kiska, as the easier target, one which could be taken with the smaller forces already under command. The operation was set for 7 May.[34] Canadians had pressed to have their squadrons participate if possible. The crowded fighter strip on Amchitka could not take any more aircraft, but Americans agreed to accept a "pilots only" flight forward. Monthly tours would alternate between the two Canadian squadrons. Fourteen Squadron got the opportunity first, its pilots flying forward by air transport. The first RCAF sorties over Kiska, in American planes, were on 18 April, and continued routinely thereafter.[35]

Eleven thousand American troops gathered for the Attu assault. It was assumed that it would take three days to secure the island. It took just short of three weeks. The fighting was severe, and this lesson was not forgotten when attention turned to Kiska.[36]

In order to free the large forces tied up in the North Pacific, the Combined Chiefs of Staff approved the clearing of Japanese from the Aleutians at the Washington TRIDENT Conference in May. The target date for the assault was 15 August, with final selection left to the local commander. As a result of Attu experience and enemy strength estimates, the assault force was doubled. Americans had tentatively suggested the inclusion of Canadian Army troops in May. Canada had two under-strength home defense divisions on the west coast, patently wasted in their current role. A formal request for a brigade followed, and the troops assigned. By the end of July, the allied land forces assembled numbered more than thirty-four thousand, including the Canadian Thirteenth Infantry Brigade Group and seven hundred Canadians in the First Special Service Force, a combined American-Canadian unit.[37] A very hard fight was expected. But, in secret, the Japanese withdrew in late July. Although American commanders gradually sensed the change on Kiska, a full assault was ordered, just in case. It was not needed, and served only as an anti-climax to the whole, frustrating campaign.

With the Japanese gone, Canadian withdrawal from Alaska was rapid. The Special Service Force left immediately, and the two fighter squadrons in August and September. Canadian Army troops of the Thirteenth Infantry Brigade Group were less fortunate. They did not start back until November, with the last shipload leaving Kiska in January 1944.[38]

[31] United States, Eleventh Air Force, "History of the Eleventh Army Air Force," n.d., pp. 221, 247, DHist 80/176; Louis Morton, *Strategy and Command: the First Two Years* (United States Army in World War II; The War in the Pacific; Washington: Department of the Army, 1962), pp. 424-425, 427; Morison, vol. 7, *Aleutians*, p. 17.

[32] RCAF Wing, Elmendorf, ORB Daily Diary, 2 August, 14 October 1942, DHist; Butler to AOC WAC, 17 October 1942, Stevenson to AFHQ, 19 December 1942, Stevenson to Secretary, DND for Air, 9 February 1943, DHist 181.002 (D433).

[33] No. 8 Squadron ORB Daily Diary, 28 January, 4 February to 15 March 1943, DHist; 14 Squadron ORB Daily Diary, 5 February to 18 March 1943, DHist.

[34] Craven and Cate, vol. 4, *Guadalcanal*, p. 379; United States, Eleventh Air Force, "History of the Eleventh Army Air Force," n.d., pp. 257-258, DHist 80/176; Conn, *Guarding*, pp. 279-280.

[35] DeWitt to CG ADC, to Stevenson, 16 February 1943 (WAC S201-8-1), DHist 181.002 (D433); Morrow to Bezeau, 29 February 1980, "Historical Summary," pp. 21-22, R.E. Morrow biographical file, DHist; No. 14 Squadron ORB Daily Diary, 31 March, 1-17 April, and ORB Operations Record, 18 April-6 May 1943, DHist.

[36] Morison, vol. 7, *Aleutians*, p. 50; Conn, *Guarding*, pp. 284, 294-295.

[37] Ibid., p. 296; Stacey, *Government*, pp. 48, 391; Stacey, *Six Years*, pp. 497, 500, 502.

[38] Ibid., p. 505; 111 Squadron ORB Daily Diary, 12-22 July and 1-20 August 1943, DHist; AFHQ to WAC, 14 July 1943 (WAC S201-8-1, vol 1), DHist 181.002 (D433); 14 Squadron ORB Daily Diary, 5-29 September, 5 October 1943, DHist.

This left only the two squadrons and protecting army troops on Annette Island, where deployment had never been fully satisfactory. The RCAF had welcomed the airfield's use in 1942 because no Canadian alternative was available, but facilities had remained below standard. Now, with a new airfield under development at Terrace, B.C., and the recent construction of emergency landing strips elsewhere, it was time to leave. Redeployment was substantially complete by 20 November. Except for the army troops still awaiting transport in the Aleutians, the Canadian commitment to Alaska's defense had ended.[39]

That commitment had been one of strategic cooperation for the mutual defense of North America. It encompassed the provision and protection of American lines of communication to Alaska, and then, after the Japanese landings, air, sea and finally land reinforcements to the combat forces.

Logistically, this support was very important, for it simplified the shipment of men and material, including land-base aircraft to the Soviet Union. Operationally, however, the campaign was a sideshow in a total, world-wide conflict. To those in the theater, the problems were no less real for all that. Human enemies were few, but persistent. The hardest enemy, except during the intense battle on Attu, had been distance, weather, and isolation.

The campaign remains interesting for another reason. Canadians think of Americans as having adequate resources to handle virtually any task. This campaign showed the limits of power which exist for us all. In a global war, everyone's resources are stretched to the limit, and no one country can act alone. Allies are needed, and faithful friends stand by each other in adversity.

*M.V. Bezeau is Director of Ceremonial, National Defence Headquarters, and is responsible for tradition and heritage programs within the Canadian armed forces.*

---

[39] RCAF Wing, Elmendorf, ORB Daily Diary, 29 December 1942, DHist; correspondence, 13 October to 20 November 1943 (WAC S202-1-1, vol. 1) DHist 181.002 (D421); Stacey, *Arms*, p. 388.

# The Thousand-Mile War:
# World War II in Alaska and the Aleutians

*Brian Garfield*

IT HAS TAKEN US SEVERAL YEARS TO MAKE THIS TRIP. WE started out for Alaska one summer three years, four years ago, but my friend up here warned us off that particular summer. He said he was in his cabin and these two six-foot mosquitos walked in. And one of them said to the other, "Should we eat him here or take him down to the river?" And the other one said, "Let's eat him here. If we take him down to the river the big mosquitos will take him away from us." So my friend high-tailed it out of there. He got over to Elmendorf and he tried to hitch a ride out on a flight. And this thing came in for a landing and they pumped ten thousand gallons of high octane into it before they realized it, too, was a mosquito. Okay, enough Alaska jokes, I'm sorry.

I feel a bit phony, I must say. I feel I'm here under false pretenses because when Dutch Harbor underwent its first action, I was dive-bombing my parents' victory garden in upstate New York. And when the campaign in the Aleutians came to its end, I had grown to be four-and-a-half. That's years old, not feet tall. By the time I went into the service, the war had been over for a dozen years or more. So I'm probably the least qualified person you can imagine to talk about it.

I'm not an Aleutian warrior, unless you count a flight out there and some visits to various islands aboard the Reeve Aleutian Airways as warfare, which I think is not too far a stretch. But, basically, I'm not a soldier; I'm just a storyteller. And originally I didn't set out to write a history of the war in Alaska. I had nothing that ambitious in mind. I had a plot in mind for a story about some guys in an isolated bomber unit, and I was looking for a place to set the story, and I was sick and tired of all of the Eighth Air Force stories that were set in England. So I picked up a copy of Edward Jablonski's book, *B-17 Flying Fortress*, which is a great book. And I saw his single paragraph about B-17 service in the Aleutians. I had never heard of the war in the Aleutians—this was about 1966, I believe. It sounded new and different, so I went to the New York Public Library to look it up. And I'm sure most of you know what I found; next to nothing. The little bit I did find was tantalizing. It looked like a story that might have scope and size, it certainly had a beginning, a middle and an end. It overflowed with both tragedy and triumph. It had heart. It had laughs. It had the best and the brightest. It also had thick-headed idiots for a little comic relief.

So I deep-sixed the idea of doing a novel, a work of fiction, because from the point of view of a storyteller the actual events of the campaign in the Aleutian Islands of Alaska formed a perfect classical dramatic structure. I don't think even Aristotle could have improved on it. You had three acts, each divined by a dominant and heroic personality center stage—in this case, Buckner, Eareckson, and Kinkaid. You had an exciting opening to hook the reader, that was the mini-battle at Dutch Harbor, of course. And then you had a splendid buildup of adventure and suspense that escalated and led to the spectacular dramatic climax, which was the Battle for Attu. Complete with that awesomely magnificent charge of a light brigade on the part of a hopelessly outnumbered, but super-humanly valiant Colonel Yasuyo Yamasaki and his men. And then there was the coda: the anticlimax and the irony at Kiska. And all of this had never really been told in any comprehensive way. Along the way the story seemed to highlight a very long honor roll of people whose heroism in the face of unspeakably atrocious conditions was a stunning example of the very best of what human beings can be.

I had the privilege of corresponding or spending time in the company of some of these people. There isn't time to recite their names, you can find them in the alphabetical indexes of John Cloe's book or mine and half a dozen others. But they were those without whom the book couldn't have been written. And they are more its authors than I am, in many ways.

All this was the good news. The bad news was: Where was I supposed to start? There was very little available in 1966. I was like all the people who came up here during the war. They stumbled innocently in here and had no idea what they were getting into. Well, first I went to Washington, but it turned out that quite a few of the records that I wanted to see were classified. And remember we're talking about the '60s. We're talking about records from events that have taken place twenty-five years earlier than my request to examine them. I couldn't imagine a need for security at that late date. But all the records were still kept in locked file cabinets in Alexandria, in what used to be a torpedo factory on the waterfront. And they were not willing to unlock those cabinets for me.

Brian Garfield (*Aaron Jones Studio, Santa Fe, New Mexico*)

The reason they were held in a classified archive apparently was that nobody had ever asked to look at them. So I went over to the Pentagon to the book and magazine division. And the Pentagon says, no problem, we'll give you a clearance and you can look at anything you want. But I wasn't crazy about that idea. If you get a clearance before you look at classified materials, you can't publish anything without the government's permission. In effect, the government assumes the right to censor your work before you print it. I had no particular desire to give away sensitive secrets, but I also didn't want to write the official authorized whitewash. I wanted to write the real story, whatever it might be. I didn't even know what it was yet. But I'd seen pieces of it. I'd seen inklings. And I knew they might be firm, they might be embarrassing, they might be painful, but I was selfish and I wanted to exercise my own discretion. So I

did not apply for a security clearance. I asked instead that the records be declassified, that the padlocks be taken off the file cabinets so that I and any other ordinary citizen could see them.

That was my own personal battle of the Alaska War, and I very nearly lost it. It was 1967, a time of anti-war demonstrations. I had already published a novel about Viet Nam that had one or two skeptical sarcasms in it. And up at the Pentagon— I'm fairly well convinced— a few colonels had convinced themselves that I was either a peacenik or a spy.

I would have lost the battle had it not been for the intervention of Senator Ernest Gruening. Gruening was an amazing diplomat. He had this indescribable and marvelous way of making bureaucrats see exactly how silly the official position was, without causing any of them to take personal offense. He was one of only two senators who had voted against the Gulf of Tonkin Resolution. But from what I saw he was held in warm and genuine respect by the military, partly because he was a great wit but also because he had been a great warrior as governor of Alaska during the ocean campaign. So he was the front-line warrior in my personal little war to unlock those security cabinets in Alexandria, where they had the North Pacific war records. And those led me to dozens and then hundreds of veterans that served in this theater. I met some really magnificent people, and they made this a very happy job.

After all that huffing and puffing, we had blown down the walls of censorship and it turned out that there really wasn't anything particularly embarrassing in those files. As I remember, the one thing that the officers at the Pentagon then were afraid of—not afraid of, they were nervous about—was discussing the relief of command from General Albert Brown during the midst of the Battle of Attu. When I looked into the records of that, I was able to persuade both General Brown and his successor, General Landrum, as well as Admiral Kinkaid—who had relieved Brown of his command—to discuss the issue with me and to send me their records and whatever files they had on the issue. And I believe that as I presented it in the book, it's as balanced an account as any of us will find, and I don't think it brings any sort of disrespect on any of those three gentlemen. I think the problem was one of time and communication. Landrum was quite serious when he said that all he did was complete the action that his predecessor had started. He didn't change the plan at all.

The other things that the Pentagon feared most were things that you and I, I believe, would see as trivial. For example, the United States delivered all that lend-lease material to the Soviets by way of Alaska. Red Army personnel came to Alaska to pick up aircraft and other material, took it back to Siberia and, as we now know after some of the discussions here this week, some of that lend-lease stuff was part of an effort to seduce or bribe Stalin into joining the war against Japan. And I don't think the Pentagon was embarrassed by this effort itself, I think they were embarrassed by its failure. The Soviets did not go to war until after the bombs had been dropped on Hiroshima and Nagasaki. Then the Russians jumped in and grabbed as much territory as they could, including the Kurile Islands.

But it seems to me that these facts do not make the American commanders out to be idiots. The Americans took a calculated risk, it failed. But the facts only make Stalin out to be a shabby scavenger, which should not come as a blinding surprise to anybody twenty-five years later. Nevertheless, the Pentagon was very nervous about releasing anything about this matter.

The irony is that when the army suspected somebody in the United States of Communist leanings—Dashiell Hammett is a case in point—they immediately shipped such people off to Alaska, which of course was the only theater of the war in which these dangerous characters could make regular contact with the Russians.

Anyhow, an extraordinary number of people—Hammett was just one of many—who were very, very witty served in the North Pacific. Their outrageous humor made this job fun. Even in their darkest trials they displayed an astonishing ability to laugh at the most serious things and at the most serious of times.

I'm jumping around a bit but I don't want to make this too long. So forgive my transitions; they're not too clean. But I've received a lot of information over the past twenty-five years from veterans, some of whom I believe take too much glee out of correcting the mistakes in my book. But I have to admit that the book makes a very easy target. You don't have to wade through a lot of pages to start weeding out mistakes. They start right at the top of the first page. That's where I said that one of the carriers that attacked Dutch Harbor was avenging damage that had been imposed on it by the Doolittle raid over Tokyo. The carrier that attacked Dutch Harbor was the *Ryujo*,

that's R-y-u-j-o in the Western alphabet. The *Ryuho*, R-y-u-h-o, is the carrier that was bombed by Doolittle. The two ships were not the same. But, hey, I come from Arizona. Spanish is our second language and if the letters H and J are indistinguishable in Spanish.... Fortunately John Cloe and Stan Cohen—who unfortunately isn't here—and several other excellent writer-historians have corrected some of the errors that I committed. And I think we all benefit from the precision of their research.

One example that I particularly enjoyed is that my book restated a common belief that Japan's attack on Dutch Harbor was launched as kind of a retaliation for the Doolittle raid. But John Cloe and Admiral Jim Russell did some excellent detective work, and John was able to report in his book, *The Aleutian Warriors*, that the decision to attack Dutch Harbor was on Japan's planning board before the Doolittle raid. But still, I betcha that some of those Japanese flyers, when they dropped their bombs on Dutch Harbor, must have been saying something like, "Here's one for you, Jimmy Doolittle."

About the items that the symposium's organizers have kindly left on your table—those typewritten slips of paper: For those of you who are doing research that might be helped by looking through any of the material (memoirs, letters, and so forth) that I have received from veterans over the years, they are at the University of Oregon at the Knight Library and the address is on that slip if you'd like to copy it down.

And also I should mention that the collection of Larry Reneke's files and memoirs and photographs is also at the Knight Library at the University of Oregon in Eugene. Larry Reneke, as some of you probably know, was an intelligence officer who compiled incredible amounts of material just on day-to-day operations, including his own personal photographs and diaries and so forth. He now lives in New York State and sells insurance, and still takes an active interest in Eleventh Air Force history.

By the way, the reason why these files are at the University of Oregon rather than here is not an intentional insult to Alaska. It's just that when I was young the University of Oregon asked me if they could be the repository for my papers—all the papers, manuscripts, all that sort of thing—and I said sure. And rather than divide up that collection, I just send everything to Oregon.

Back from the aside, if you don't mind. The Alaska theater made unique demands on people. In some ways it shaped their whole lives. Take my friend Lucian Warnick, a bomber pilot from the Eleventh Air Force and now a retired math professor. I first met Lucian through Larry Reneke while I was doing research for *The Thousand-Mile War*. If any of you knew him way back then—I think Admiral Russell knew him—be assured that Lucian has not changed a bit. He is still just as outrageous as ever. He's seventy-whatever, I don't know exactly. But I know that only a few years ago he was blasting through mountains of grease on a motorcycle that he had rented, and took a tumble all the way down a mountainside. But he's fine. He's indestructible. You can find various references of him to him in *The Thousand-Mile War*. He was on, I think, both of the Paramushiro raids. I don't think Lucian has to take a back seat to anybody when it comes to heroism. He soared in the bomber command up here for years. As most of you probably know, there was no rotation policy for air crews here because it wasn't an overseas theater. So I think Lucian actually logged something like ten thousand combat hours at the controls of B-17s and B-24s.

He swore to his men that they were safe with him, and he kept his word. He lost I'm not sure how many airplanes, either three or four, in the campaign, but he never lost the life of a single crew member or passenger. But he did spend so much time in those loud four-engine boiler factories that he lost most of his hearing. He's one of the guys that went up to Nome and drank their Russian counterparts under the table that memorable night in 1942. I don't think that the Russians believed that the Americans knew how to hold their liquor until then. Lucian was probably one of the finest combat pilots ever from the Aleutians.

Anyway, the day the war ended, and this is the point I was getting at about the effect of the war, Lucian said, "I know when the party's over. I've had my share of good luck." He has never piloted an airplane since then. He flies in airplanes as a passenger to visit his grandchildren, takes vacation trips all over the world, and especially to fly all over the place to bridge tournaments. He manages a couple of card clubs on the side and he's become a bridge master. And that all started because up here in the Aleutians for months on end those guys had nothing to do but play cards. I count one of my personal great triumphs as the time I finally beat Lucian Warnick at backgammon. I still can't beat him at poker.

There really isn't time to talk any more of the terrific people who helped me put the book together. But while we are on the subject of very special people, I do feel obliged to mention two gentlemen that it has been my great pleasure to talk with at this conference, one of whom I had not met before—General Benjamin Talley, who built practically everything in Alaska. And the other I feel obliged to mention, and I also feel it's a great privilege to mention, the man who stands head and shoulders above us all, a gentleman, gentle man in every good sense, who personifies the qualities that make up the greatness in a human being in war or in peace. Whole key sections of my book would not have been written without his generous help. He took me in, he and Gerry took me in as their house guests, let me pore over the files, and yet my book, I think, is the least of it. Few

human beings have touched so many lives in such fine ways. I expect half the people in the known world are his friends, and that includes a great many Japanese flag officers, his opposite numbers who used to be enemies. Of course, I'm talking about Admiral James S. Russell, Jim Russell. A man whose accomplishments are exceeded only by his modesty. Four stars, the highest ranking flying officer in the United States Navy.

During the war the Aleutians campaign got more thoughtful coverage in the *National Geographic* magazine than it did in most newspapers and news magazines. I believe that the mostly freelance photographers and reporters who provided material for *National Geographic* were mistaken for insignificant naturalists by our eagle-eyed censors, so their copy and even their photographs sometimes got passed right through where all others were blocked. One thing that the *National Geographic* did not cover any better than the rest of us was the events that took place on Monday, July the 26th, 1943.

I would like at this point to try and make a small contribution to the gathering of this convocation by offering a solution to the mystery of the Battle of the Pips.

Allied forces had retaken Attu out there at the end of the Chain. So the Japanese troops on Kiska were trapped between enemy islands. United States intelligence knew that a Japanese task force had been launched toward Kiska, either to reinforce it or to evacuate it. We didn't know which. A big American fleet went out looking for the Japanese force. A patrolling PBY Catalina, one of Jim Russell's, reported seven Japanese ships south of the Aleutians on course for Kiska. So the American fleet changed course to intercept them. In due course seven radar blips were picked up by the American task force, which consisted of three battleships, five cruisers, and eleven destroyers. This was a major force. They went to flank speed, they opened fire on the seven radar pips, or "blips" as we call them nowadays. Big guns and torpedoes at ranges up to twelve miles. The attack lasted more than an hour. The entire Pacific seemed to be exploding. One by one the seven pips vanished from the radar screens. It looked good, seven enemy vessels sunk. But when the sun came up, the only wreckage that could be found was on board the American ships, the concussions from their own broadside had disabled quite a bit of hardware and done quite a bit of damage, destroyed three or four float planes, I think. They had expended vast amounts of fuel and ammunition, so the fleet had to retire to refuel and rearm.

Japanese radar on top of Mount Kiska saw the Allied fleet retiring. It signaled the all-clear for the untouched task force, which was far out to sea, nowhere near those blips that had been seen on the radar. Unopposed, the Japanese force evacuated every last person from Kiska—5,183 people, to be exact—and got them home to Japan without a single casualty.

Meanwhile, right behind them, the American task force returned and established an unbreakable blockade around Kiska. For weeks thereafter, as we know, Kiska was bombed and shelled. Allied commanders at Adak believed the enemy was dug deep into tunnels waiting for glorious battle. So at vast expense and in expectation of brutal combat, such as had been endured on Attu, Kiska was invaded by an amphibious force of nearly thirty-five thousand men, of whom at least ninety-nine American and Canadian troops and sailors were killed by booby traps, mines, and friendly fire.

But, of course, there were no Japanese forces on Kiska. So a lot of ridicule took place and naturally there ensued a mountain of analysis and rationalization and detective work. The seven pips had pulled the American task force away from station just long enough for the enemy to extract its troops from Kiska. And nobody in the United States knew when and how that evacuation had taken place until quite some time after the war when Admiral Russell found out as a result of his investigations in Japan.

The seven pips must have been a Japanese ruse, a trick. That was the prevailing opinion of most of the American commanders at first. But they felt the mystery had to be explained. Various theories were then put forth. Some folks I talked to to this day are convinced that those seven radar blips were big decoy targets that were being pulled by Japanese submarines. But that idea has been set aside by the Japanese veterans who were in a position to know. Other folks favored the idea that Japan had turned loose weather balloons to fool American radar. And you also can find scattered theories of all kinds: whales, northern lights, ghosts, mass hallucination, hysteria. I can tell you it was not any of those things. The seven images were picked up independently by the American radars on almost all the ships in that fleet. The only ones that didn't pick them up were the ones that were below the horizon. If you triangulate the logs of those ships, you place the same seven objects at the same spot at the same time, moving at the same speed on the same heading. Whatever it was, it was real, it was tangible. It was seven objects; large, large objects.

The navy was now faced with a dilemma. It was very hard to believe that this thing could have been a complete coincidence, given the timing of it. It was very hard to believe that perhaps the Japanese had had nothing to do with the mysterious pips. But finally the navy gave up and in 1944 published its conclusion. Peculiar cloud conditions had caused the temporary bending of radar beams that reflected images of seven islands from somewhere beyond the horizon. To this day, I believe, that is still the official version, even though it's not merely implausible, but scientifically impossible. Radar doesn't work that way.

In the last few years I have received a couple of letters from a gentleman named George Fulton, who may someday go down as one of the unsung heros of this campaign, even though he wasn't in it. George Fulton is a long-time captain in the Aleutian fishing fleet. He's the author of the book *Good Morning Captain*; he's been a commercial fisherman for at least forty years; spent part of his career fishing for crab in the western Aleutians; and is still alive and navigating, which means that he's a pretty sound skipper. He's also an expert in shipboard radar. On his first ship he bought some navy surplus radar equipment, which was essentially the same equipment that was used by the force during the Battle of the Pips, and since then he has constantly updated, until now he's got the most sophisticated new GPS color type of radar. But he knows radar. He also knows the Aleutians.

Captain George Fulton wrote to me as follows, and I'll quote now:

When I first read your book, the part about the Battle of the Pips, I checked with three other captains who had also read it and they all had arrived at the same conclusion. So during July 1991, I crossed North Head on Akutan Island and with your book in hand, duplicated the Battle of the Pips using color radar. Sure enough there were blips on the tube and their density changed from red to orange to yellow and finally to black, providing an exact replication of the Battle of the Pips. What you described fits exactly the life-like pattern of dense flocks of mutton birds or dusky shearwaters, which is their correct name. The shearwaters migrate annually between New Zealand and Alaska. Arriving in the Aleutians in late May, spending the summer and departing in September/October. Also known as fulmars, these birds are one to two feet long, with wing spans up to four feet. They're subarctic sea birds. They're members of the albatross family. They travel in enormous flocks. The females lay one egg a year. They feed on plankton, and when they fly low they appear to shear the water with their wings. Practically every summer morning in the vicinity of Unamak Pass, these birds sleep in massive racks. The dusky shearwater is dull brown in color and very hard to see visually at night. And even a huge flock would be impossible to see with the naked eye from the distances of eight to twelve miles that the fleet was scanning in 1943. Today with our new radar we can see them all the time and avoid them, since when startled they will fly directly into our bright lights and land on deck by the thousands.

As mutton birds fly they veer left and right. This accounts for the zigzagging that was reported on the radar logs. Once they have decided that they have found an interesting feeding area, the hundreds of thousands of birds that you're looking at on your screen thin out into groups of mere thousands, settle to the water and start diving for food and disappear totally off your radar scope. Because of its design, a World War II radar would see those zigzaging racks of birds as mass single blocks if they were airborne and navigating to a new feeding ground at night. The first bearing in your book gives a course that would be consistent with the logical course these birds use to search for plankton. It is exactly how modern factory trawlers find massive pollock schools. In fact, we use the mutton birds as a clue during the summer months when pollack feed on the same plankton.

The letter has quite a few more details, but you get the idea. It's the only explanation that I have heard in twenty-five years that accounts plausibly for every detail of this historical oddity. Captain George Fulton deserves full credit for solving it, and I hope he won't be too mad at me for having stolen his thunder by reporting it here. But I did feel obliged to bring something new to this conference.

Thank you. And finally, I'd like to express both personal and, I expect, on behalf of all of us, gratitude and admiration for the twenty people who have put on this extremely rewarding conference; Georgeie Reynolds and the nineteen associates whom she listed just a few minutes ago, who have steered the proceedings along such a challenging Iditarod of an expedition.

## Question/Answer

Okay, time's up. It's your turn to throw things at me. I hope you don't have too many vegetables and fruit left, but please feel free to ask any questions that come to mind. But be forewarned that I may not have answers. My ignorance is even bigger than one of those mosquitoes. If there aren't any, we can all leave. Anyone? No questions. Yes, questions?

*QUESTION*: What are you working on now?

*ANSWER*: What am I working on now? I just had a book published called *Suspended Sentences*. It's a collection of stories. I just finished writing a novel that I hope will be published next year. I'm not sure whether they'll keep my title. My title is *Smoke*. They just finished filming *Death Wish 5*. We love it when they film these horrible sequels and they have to send us a check. And they did *Stepfather 3* last year, same thing. And I'm starting work on a new book in the next couple of months.

*QUESTION*: (Indiscernible—not near microphone)

*ANSWER*: I think that's what we're going to be talking about on the panel tomorrow afternoon. I have some oddball things about it, but they're not that different from anybody else's. I think that during the Aleutian Campaign itself, this theater was regarded as having considerable importance or potential importance, by both sides. It was only after the war that hindsight made it look as if it had been either a wasted effort or an insignificant effort. In fact, any theater that involves about a half million people and the great number of actions and catastrophes that occurred up here is not minor. But I think at the time when it was taking place, American soil had been invaded and that made it rather sensitive to our government, if not our press. The press did report what they could about what was going on in the Aleutians. But it seems that almost every action that took place up here happened to coincide with a bitter action that was taking place somewhere else in the world. The Battle of Midway, or North African landings or whatever, stole the headlines, and this made page twenty.

When I was in New York about a week and a half ago, when half of Southern California was on fire, and I picked up a copy of the New York Times, the only piece they had on the fires in California was on page twenty. They'd had elections that day, you know. They had a new mayor; there was a new governor in New Jersey; there was a lot of news that seemed a lot more important to the New York Times than the fact that twenty-five thousand people had been thrown out of their homes in California. And I think that the Aleutians and Alaska suffered a very similar fate during the war. There were always bigger things going on somewhere else.

*QUESTION*: (Partially indiscernible) ... diaries, he was told on December the 7th, when Pearl Harbor was bombed, that the Japanese planned on coming to the Aleutians at that time except for the weather. Do you have any evidence that that was true?

*ANSWER*: From what I've heard since I wrote the book, mostly from Admiral Russell, the subject of simultaneous attacks on Dutch Harbor and Pearl Harbor had been discussed at considerable length amid the Japanese planning officers. And they had discarded it in favor of massing as much force as they could, as many first-rate pilots and as many aircraft as they could, on Pearl Harbor alone. So I don't think it was the weather that discouraged it. I think it was a strategic decision.

*Brian Garfield is the author of more than sixty books and fourteen motion pictures and is one of the world's most popular creators of suspense fiction and films. More than twenty million copies of his books have been sold around the world. His first published novel was written when he was eighteen. "The Thousand-Mile War: World War II in Alaska and the Aleutians" was first published in 1969 and is still in print.*

# The Japanese Campaign in Alaska as Seen from the Strategic Perspective

*Hisashi Takahashi*

IN THE EYES OF THE IMPERIAL JAPANESE NAVY (IJN), THE northern theater of naval operations, which included the Aleutians and the Kurile Islands, had long been of very little strategic significance, especially because the terribly bad climate and barren and rocky land made an air base technically almost impossible. This was in spite of the fact that—in terms of sheer distance—the long chain of the Aleutians was fairly close to the Japanese-owned Kurile Islands.

However, strategic necessities arising from a fierce arms race and the international powers' political rivalry gradually led the IJN to reassess the importance of the northern theater. From around 1935 on, the IJN launched a task to build airstrips on the Kuriles in preparation for possible war with the United States and the Soviet Union. By the end of 1938 the IJN completed such construction on Paramushiro, Matua, and Etorofu (or Iturup) islands. But there was neither a hangar on these airstrips nor appropriate military facilities to accommodate troops, and their use was largely limited to emergency landings in summertime. In addition, intelligence activities with a focus on Alaska and the Aleutians remained dormant.

The outbreak of an entirely new war on the Eastern Front between Nazi Germany and the Soviet Union in June 1941 alerted the Kwantung Army in Manchuria and the Northern District Army in Hokkaido to be ready for a possible armed confrontation with the Russians. But even then the IJN showed little interest in such preparation. A month later, however, the Fifth Fleet was formed—with two light cruisers as its nucleus. The fleet's major task was to study and prepare for a war with Russia.

Then, after the twists and turns of events that followed, at the time of the Pearl Harbor attack Combined Fleet Command assigned the Fifth Fleet an extremely low-key mission to patrol north of the Bonin Islands for the safety of Admiral Nagumo's task force. So the Twenty-First Squadron, under Fleet Commander Boshiro Hosogaya, assisted the return trip of the task force, while the Twenty-Second patrolled east of Kamchatka. In the meantime, the North Pacific theater for a while remained calm and peaceful.

Much to the surprise of Japanese Naval Command, a smashing victory at Pearl Harbor wiped out the Pacific Fleet of the United States—with the exception of two aircraft carriers which remained intact and, ever ominously, threatened Japan's home islands.

The first stage of assault operations immediately following the Pearl Harbor attack was closely coordinated in the Philippines, Hong Kong, Malaya, and the Dutch East Indies, and they proved almost no trouble. A series of victorious campaigns came so fast and with so few losses during the early stages of the war that the Japanese people were overjoyed and stood firm behind the sacred slogan of the Great East Asian War. Among the rank and file of Japanese troops, feelings of relief became quickly pervasive, while the top brass tended to be puffed with conceit, at least for the moment.

The so-called "victory disease" had set in. Even the usually sensible, well-balanced, and cool-headed IJN willy-nilly took a heavy dose of such euphoria. So it was quite understandable that the operations division of the Naval General Staff quite wrongly estimated that the

Allied counteroffensive would be launched with Australia as its base and that it would not be earlier than the spring of 1943.

However, Admiral Isoroku Yamamoto, commander in chief of the Combined Fleet and the mastermind of the surprise attack on Pearl Harbor, remained unperturbed in the midst of national excitement. In his letter to one of his friends, dated January 9, 1942, Yamamoto wrote:

A military man can scarcely pride himself on having "smitten a sleeping enemy;" it is more a matter of shame, simply, for the one smitten. I would rather you made your appraisal after seeing what the enemy does, since it is certain that, angered and outraged, he will soon launch a determined counterattack, whether it be a full-scale engagement on the sea, air raids on Japan itself, or a strong attack against the main units of our fleet.

Yamamoto added elsewhere that he "felt intolerably embarrassed at the way the achievements in the battle of those under me and of the young rank and file have made me a star overnight."

Admiral Yamamoto's ever-growing concern was the threat of American aircraft carriers. About one-and-a-half months before Pearl Harbor, Yamamoto wrote to Navy Minister Shigetaro Shimada one of his most revealing letters:

Based on my close observation of Admiral Kimmel's character and of today's American naval strategy, I do not think that Americans will necessarily resort to the "gradual" orthodox approach of naval fighting.

At the time when our assault operations in Southeast Asia are in progress, and they turn out to be successful, what if all of a sudden enemy planes come down from the skies and launch air raids on Tokyo and Osaka and burn them to ashes overnight, and even though the damages are slight? When I come to think about such a possibility, I can easily guess the reactions of Japanese people towards the Navy. I cannot help but remember with much bitterness the time of the Russo-Japanese War.

Rear Admiral Matome Ugaki, Yamamoto's chief of staff, wrote the following in his diaries on December 26, 1941: "If only we could destroy the American Task Force!! We must do it by all means! We must not let them carry out an air raid on Tokyo. I consider this mission to be most vital."

On the other hand, the Naval General Staff was little concerned about such air raids. For example, the Operations Section chief, Captain Sadatoshi Tomioka, recalled that in those days he had wondered why Commander-in-Chief Yamamoto was so much worried about air raids on the homeland, and that only after the end of war could he fully understand the real reasons for such concern.

Yamamoto's fears were realized much too soon. The Americans' lethal weapon subsequently was made visible on February 1, 1942, when they quickly moved in on the Marshall Islands. This first successful counteroffensive by the Americans after the Pearl Harbor debacle was followed by the air raids on Wake later that month (the 24th), and on Minami-Tori Jima in early March (the 4th).

In order to meet such exigencies the Fifth Fleet carried out a patrolling mission east of Japan's home islands. However, most of its patrol boats were unarmed fishing boats. Each boat carried fourteen members on board, half of whom were naval officers. As of late February, 1942, they had seventy-six such boats.

In the meantime, Japanese victories outpaced the planning of the Imperial General Headquarters, and the time from January to mid-April 1942 was spent in research and tentative planning for the second stage of new operations. In this process serious disagreements within and between the army and navy came to surface and often disrupted negotiations, which in turn resulted in mealymouthed bureaucratic compromise and haphazard planning, thus overshadowing the course of the war.

Four alternative plans were put forward: Whether Japan should press on to Australia or to India, or launch an attack on Hawaii, or possibly make a preemptive strike against the Soviet Union. The last two plans were rather quickly put aside because of fierce opposition. The army was not in favor of another Hawaii operation, while the navy was suspicious of the army's grand traditional plan of attacking the Soviets' maritime provinces.

The army wanted to capture Port Moresby as a stepping-stone for a Japanese occupation of northern Australia, because Australia was considered to be a home base for counteroffensive operations led by General MacArthur.

Another plan—an attack into the Indian Ocean—was put forward by Combined Fleet command. Their aim was to deliver a fatal blow at Great Britain and India by attacking Ceylon with a force of five army divisions, by luring out and destroying the British Far Eastern Fleet, and then by linking up with German forces as they advanced from the Caucasus into the Middle East. However, the army offered head-on opposition. And so this plan was eventually abandoned, which made way for

Highly intelligent and blunt of speech, Admiral Isoroku Yamamoto, the commander of the Japanese Combined Fleet and mastermind of the surprise attack on Pearl Harbor, was the ablest of Japanese war leaders. He led the Japanese in a war he did not approve of. *(Photo No. 80-JO-79462, National Archives, College Park, Md.)*

the third plan by the IJN—the most grandiose of them all.

The new plan put forward by Admiral Yamamoto aimed at neutralizing Australia by cutting off the American-Australian lines of communication, that is, by capturing New Caledonia, Samoa, and the Fijis. The plan was subsequently named the "FS Operation." The key to this plan was a surprise attack and occupation of Midway at least by early June of 1942, at the same time occupying vital points in the Aleutians as a diversionary operation—thus expanding Japan's sea and air defenses two thousand nautical miles to the east. As part of this impressive scenario, Yamamoto concurrently wanted to lure American aircraft carriers out onto the ocean to be crushed once and for all.

In this sense, even Admiral Yamamoto was not immune to the old-fashioned, nostalgic, fixed idea of a replay of the Battle of Tsushima during the Russo-Japanese War—the spectacular, decisive confrontation of great fleets on the high seas. However, one can detect behind this grand scheme Yamamoto's hidden attempt at an early peace settlement with the United States. However naive Yamamoto had been, he seriously thought that another smashing victory—this time at Midway—would give Japan a most favorable chance for peace.

After a bureaucratic tug of war, the MI Operation—the operation against Midway—was finally approved on April 5, 1942. The plan included a raid on Dutch Harbor and the occupation of Kiska and Attu in the Aleutians. However, the army opposed the dispatch of troops, while the Naval General Staff was not convinced of the effectiveness of aerial reconnaissance using Midway, an isolated island, as a base of operations.

The Naval General Staff in general, and the operations section in particular, were also doubtful about the feasibility of conducting patrols by large aircraft in the western Aleutians, primarily because of the bad climate. For example, Commander Tatsukichi Miyo, chief of air operations of the operations section, considered the cutting off of communications lines between the United States and the Soviet Union more vital by far if the Japanese were to prevent the Americans from using Siberia as a base of aerial operations against the Japanese homeland.

Then a totally unexpected event overtook and shook up the Japanese. On April 18, in broad daylight, Tokyo was raided by American B-25 bombers from the USS *Hornet*. The damage done by the Doolittle raid was not very great, and the Japanese punningly remarked that this daring attempt was a "do-nothing" rather than "do-little" affair. However, its psychological effect was far-reaching and far from negligible.

This was exactly the nightmare Yamamoto had long been possessed by. He wrote in a letter to Admiral Koga:

About the raid ... one has the embarrassing feeling of having been caught napping just when one was feeling confident and in charge of things. Even though there wasn't much damage, it's a disgrace that the skies over the imperial capital should have been defiled without a single enemy plane being shot down. It provides a regrettably graphic illustration of the saying that a bungling attack is better than the most skillful defense.

Immediately after the Doolittle raid, letters of protest rushed in to Yamamoto's headquarters. Writing in his diary on April 27, one of his operations staff expressed his bitter indignation, "How can we call these lowly creatures 'real Japanese'?"

Following this surprise raid, the date for the Midway Operation was brought forward, quickly overcoming the army's persistent opposition to the dispatch of troops as well as the Naval General Staff's opposition to both the MI and AL Operations. Nagumo's task force was again assigned this extremely important job—this in spite of the fact that his fleet had just completed its operations in the Indian Ocean, after spending four-and-a-half months at sea since Pearl Harbor, and was badly in need of adequate rest and recuperation. It had sailed a total of fifty thousand nautical miles, going south to raid Rabaul and Port Darwin, advancing into the Central Pacific to pursue the enemy task force that had raided the Marshall Islands in February, and then stretching its area of operation to the west into the Indian Ocean by raiding Colombo and Trincomalee in Ceylon.

There will be no need here to narrate what transpired at Midway. Suffice to mention that, compared with Pearl Harbor, when luck was all on the Japanese side, everything that could possibly go wrong actually went wrong at Midway. Its traumatic disaster—that is, the loss of four heavy carriers, *Akagi, Kaga, Soryu,* and *Kiryu,* in addition to hundreds of first-rate veteran pilots who could not easily be replaced—abruptly turned the tide of the war and doomed Japan to ultimate surrender. In the words of Admiral King, "This was the most decisive defeat tasted by Japanese naval forces since the days of Toyotomi Hideyoshi."

The Midway Operation was immediately scrapped by Yamamoto and, to make matters worse, the supposedly coordinated operation in the North Pacific theater became entirely isolated and ended up as a misadventure.

So far I have come a long way in order to put the Aleutians Operation in a proper strategic perspective of the IJN.

Now let me draw your attention to the strategic objective of the Aleutians, or AL Operation.

In this country this operation is understood by the majority of military historians as essentially a "diversionary action." However, the Japanese side of the story is a little more complicated. In brief, there was considerable confusion as to the strategic objectives of this operation.

The Naval General Staff side wanted to make this operation into a diversionary and supportive action for the sake of the Midway Operation. On the other hand, the thinking of Combined Fleet Command was to preempt the enemy's attempt to advance its outpost of large aircraft into the western Aleutians in preparation for aerial attacks against the Japanese home islands. So, to their mind, a diversionary action in support of the Midway Operation was never brought into consideration.

Moreover, the Fifth Fleet, the prime actor in the operation, had its own independent thinking. Because of the low-key status assigned to it by Combined Fleet command, the Fifth Fleet wanted to boost up its morale by launching an assault operation into the North Pacific. It also wanted to extend its outposts for patrolling activities.

The confusion of strategic objectives was further complicated by the Japanese Army's own thinking and its interests. Although as a result of the Doolittle raid the army willy-nilly recognized the need to advance the outpost for patrolling into Midway and the Aleutians, it did not want to keep its troops in such far-out places for too long. So the army finally agreed to send its troops on the sole condition that they would be returned home as soon as possible.

Now, let me explain the strategic impact of the defeat at Midway on the outcome of the Aleutians operations. I will try to be very brief and just mention the outlines.

First, because of the defeat at Midway, the occupation of Attu and Kiska islands immediately lost its significance. Second, the operation failed to distract Admiral Nimitz from Midway, thus defeating the original purpose. Whether it caused an element of uncertainty and consternation on the part of Americans is still debatable.

The AL Operation was commanded by Vice Admiral Boshiro Hosogaya, Commander in Chief of the Fifth Fleet, who had under him the heavy cruiser *Nachi* and two destroyers as a support force. His chief of staff was Captain Tasuku Nakazawa, who had earlier studied at Stanford University and had long kept his interest in the northern theater. Vice Admiral Kakuji Kakuta was commander in chief of the Second Strike Force and had two light carriers (*Ryujo* and *Junyo*), two heavy cruisers (*Takao* and *Maya*), and three destroyers.

The AL Operation went more or less according to plan, with the exception of an attack and occupation of Adak Island, which was immediately canceled after Midway on June 5. Dutch Harbor was raided on June 4. The reason why the IJN was interested in striking Dutch Harbor was that they thought there were a large number of airplanes and ships which might later pose a threat to the Japanese. Kiska and Attu were occupied on June 7 and 8 respectively, without resistance. But their occupation gained Japan almost nothing.

What, then, was the real purpose of such an occupation? The Japanese had three objectives: First, to prevent the Americans from using these small islands as airfields; second, to advance the patrol perimeter against the American task force; and, third, to cut U.S.-Soviet lines of communication.

Originally the occupation was expected to last until winter. However, the debacle of the MI Operation made the second objective almost meaningless. The third objective was from the very beginning out of the question. Combined Fleet Command considered the first objective to be critically important, and decided to hold the two islands as long as possible. However, no additional planning was immediately available for reinforcement of the defense of these islands. Originally, a group of destroyers and six seaplanes was set aside to assist the defense, in addition to garrison troops. A little later, six seaplane fighters and six midget submarines were dispatched to Kiska.

American response to the occupation of Attu and Kiska was much quicker and more deadly than had been anticipated. American forces immediately launched raids and, in July, started to use submarines to strike Japanese destroyers and transport ships. Under such circumstances, Combined Fleet Command clung to the idea of holding the islands with only the garrison forces, while strongly opposing the dispatch of ground-based fighters and bombers for defensive operations. On the other hand, the Fifth Fleet strongly demanded such dispatch and the construction of airfields.

When Kiska was exposed to naval bombardment by Americans, the Imperial General Headquarters ordered the garrison troops on Attu to advance to Kiska. This they did on September 18. In the meantime Kiska was attacked from the skies. As the American aerial offensive intensified, the damage on the Japanese defenses quickly increased, resulting in the destruction of the facilities and the sinking of ships. In the midst of formidable raids the Japanese garrisons worked hard to build airfields, but there was little likelihood of obtaining any planes from outside.

Then, on November 1, a new policy was established in Tokyo to reoccupy Attu, in order to strengthen the defenses on Attu and Kiska, and to newly occupy Semichi. What followed afterwards until the bitter end of fighting on Attu on May 29, 1943—and with the miraculous evacuation of more than five thousand garrison troops from Kiska on July 28—was a sheer waste of ships, men, and vital supplies that could have been better used elsewhere rather than on this near-arctic wasteland.

*Hisashi Takahashi is a professor of Military and Diplomatic History at the National Institute for Defense Studies in Tokyo. He has been a Fulbright Senior Research Fellow at the Department of History, San Diego State University.*

# Reflecting on the Alaska Theater in Pacific War Operations, 1942-1945

*Alvin D. Coox*

RETALIATION BEGETS RETALIATION IN WAR. THE Doolittle raid on Japan in 1942, itself a response to the Japanese attack on Pearl Harbor four months earlier, shook the high command of the Japanese Navy, especially the Combined Fleet Commander, Admiral Isoroku Yamamoto. As a result, offensive planning against the Midway sector (known as Operation MI) was stepped up, and it was agreed that this campaign would proceed before the envisaged thrusts against Fiji and Samoa. In a closely related compromise between the Japanese Navy and the Japanese Army, a simultaneous invasion of the Aleutians was planned. Although the Soviet Union appeared to the Japanese to pose no threat as long as this offensive (known as Operation AL) did not violate Russian territory, brief but intensive study was addressed to limiting the scope of the action.

The Japanese Imperial General Headquarters (IGHQ) opted to conduct only a diversionary occupation of the islands rather than a protracted campaign of destruction. Bases along the great circle (the shortest route from North America to the heart of Japan) that had the potential for enemy offensive use were to be seized. Thus, the new U.S. Navy submarine and air station at Dutch Harbor on Unalaska in the eastern Aleutians was to be raided, while three islands in the westernmost part of the chain would be occupied: Attu in the Near Islands; Kiska in the Rat Islands, more than two hundred statute miles east of Attu; and Adak in the Andreanof Islands, more than two hundred statute miles farther east of Kiska. This plan typified Japanese naval strategy of the time, which had already been demonstrated in the Philippines and the Dutch East Indies. Successful invasions of these islands had been characterized by preliminary neutralization of defenses, wide distribution of military objectives, and multidirectional angles of attack. Because of limited Japanese Navy sea support capabilities, wretched terrain, few harbors, and chronic bad weather—gales, snow, fog, and biting cold—large-scale mobile ground action in the Aleutians would not have been possible. In addition, the optimum months of operation were few.

On May 5, 1942, the jittery IGHQ directed Yamamoto to implement operations MI and AL in conjunction with the Japanese Army. The Japanese Navy committed its Fifth Fleet under Vice Admiral Boshiro Hosogaya, including Rear Admiral Kakuji Kakuta's carrier strike force, which centered on two light carriers and a seaplane carrier. The Army's *Hokkai* (Northern Seas) Detachment, commanded by Major Matsutoshi Hozumi, consisted of little more than one infantry battalion. Two transports (one for Attu, the other for Adak) were to carry one thousand to twelve hundred army troops of the Attu occupation force (Operation AQ) under the command of Rear Admiral Sentaro Omori. Another six transports, with 550 Maizuru special naval landing troops (comparable to U.S. Marines) plus a construction crew, all to be landed in Operation AOB, were the responsibility of Navy captain Takeji Ono's Kiska occupation force. Hosogaya held his own small unit as a support force for fueling and standby beyond Paramushiro in the northern Kurile chain, twelve hundred miles north of Tokyo and 650 miles west of Attu. Kakuta sortied from Ominato in northern Honshu on May 25, followed by the Kiska invasion detachment on May 27, and the Attu force heading directly northeast for its objective on the next day.

U.S. Navy defense of the Alaska sector was the assignment of Rear Admiral Robert A. Theobald's new Task Force Eight, later called the North Pacific Force, with USN and Army Alaskan Defense Command air support, all on CINCPAC-ordered "fleet opposed invasion" alert status. But although U.S. intelligence possessed considerable detail concerning Operation MI, far less was known about the Japanese drive against the Aleutians. Theobald and his associates believed that the enemy amphibious groups were not really bound for Kiska and Attu (as was reported by intelligence on May 28) but would probably strike at the Dutch Harbor region. Therefore Task Force Eight was deployed mainly south of Kodiak to cover mainland Alaska and the eastern Aleutians, some five hundred miles from Kakuta's true objective. The U.S. task force never made contact with the enemy during Operation AL, however.

In the early hours of June 3, from a point about 180 miles southwest of Dutch Harbor, Kakuta launched his strike planes, undetected by U.S. Navy pickets or search aircraft. The carrier *Junyo's* attack planes could not find the target, but twelve aircraft from *Ryujo* located Dutch Harbor and hit the oil-tank farm, army barracks, hospital, radio station, and PBY reconnaissance planes in the anchorage. Antiaircraft fire brought down one bomber during the twenty-minute raid. Following up soon afterward on the morning of June 3, Kakuta sent forty-five planes against five U.S. destroyers that had been sighted at Makushin Bay on Unalaska. This time the target was obscured and the raiders returned to their carriers, having lost one Zero escort to P-40 fighters.

Yamamoto then gave orders to commence pre-invasion bombardment of Adak, but the worsening weather slowed strike-force speed to nine knots and caused Kakuta to decide on a second attack at Dutch Harbor, where visibility was reportedly good. (The minor Adak mission was suspended by Hosogaya and eventually canceled for good on June 25.) On the afternoon of June 5, Kakuta launched thirty-one aircraft in a second raid on Dutch Harbor, something Vice Admiral Chichi Magma had not attempted on Pearl Harbor. Among other targets, the oil tanks were finished off. Thirty-two Americans died in the two raids. U.S. bombers, which finally caught up with Kakuta's empty carriers, scored no hits, and two American planes were lost. The Japanese pilots returned to their carriers, having lost only one fighter.

The unopposed Japanese landings on Attu (June 5) and on Kiska (June 7) proceeded according to plan, despite or because of Japanese intelligence's overestimates of the defenses. On Attu a small Aleut village was

taken and two American missionaries were seized; on Kiska, ten unarmed U.S. weathermen were captured. Not until June 10 did a U.S. flying boat bring word of enemy ships at Kiska and tents on Attu. Admiral Chester Nimitz, however, resisted the temptation to divert aircraft carriers to the North Pacific after his Midway victory, while Hosogaya's greatly reinforced flotilla plied the waters southwest of Kiska unopposed until steaming away on June 24.

In the next stage, the Japanese strove to retain the pair of bleak islands, while the Americans undertook to suppress and then eliminate the invaders. From mid-June till month's end, two U.S. Navy and U.S. Army Air Force air offensives were launched against Kiska. (Attu was beyond range.) The scale of the effort and its results were modest. On June 30 Hosogaya shepherded twelve hundred troop reinforcements and six midget submarines into Kiska under cover of a powerful task force. During the next month American submarines mauled enemy destroyers and subchasers between Agattu and Kiska until the requirements of the Guadalcanal operation forced the withdrawal of all fleet submarines. Hosogaya's battle force was also depleted by Combined Fleet priorities. Thereupon he worked to develop bases for Japanese land-based bombers. Hampered by wretched terrain and weather conditions, Japanese offensive bombing efforts proved costly and chimerical.

Pressed to act, Theobald twice set out to bombard Kiska in July but was forced back each time by weather. On August 7 his subordinate, Rear Admiral W.W. Smith, carried out a naval bombardment for less than an hour, hitting barracks, barges, and flying boats but striking no warships and killing few enemy personnel. At the end of the month, U.S. Army engineers landed on Adak and within a fortnight had prepared an airstrip suitable for fighter and bomber use, bringing Kiska within closer flying range in September and October. The Japanese did not discover the Adak base until early October.

Meanwhile, IGHQ had decided to give up Attu and concentrate on building up and defending Kiska. In successful evacuation operations, for which the Japanese Navy was to become famous, transports and destroyers ferried the entire army garrison to Kiska in three unscathed stages between August 27 and September 16, under the protection of Hosogaya's reduced fleet. On October 24, IGHQ ordered Attu reoccupied and in early December reinforced the *Hokkai* Detachment with eleven hundred more men (originally intended for Shemya Island), renaming it the Garrison Unit. Major General Junichiro Minoki now commanded a combat force of three infantry battalions.

In early 1943, Theobald was relieved by Rear Admiral Thomas C. Kinkaid, and Rear Admiral Charles H.

McMorris replaced W.W. Smith as commander of the cruiser-destroyer force. Toward the middle of the month the Americans came even closer to Kiska by occupying and developing air facilities on uninhabited Amchitka, only sixty miles away—an action that, although highly appropriate, had contributed to Theobald's relief because of interservice disagreement.

IGHQ decided on February 5 to cling to the western Aleutians "at all costs." Hosogaya did his best to construct airfields on Kiska and at Holtz Bay on Attu, but his resources were skimpy and the going was unsatisfactory. McMorris tried to interfere, with a direct-fire bombardment of Attu on February 18; damage was negligible. The Americans continued their anti-shipping patrols, while U.S. Army and Navy air squadrons pounded Kiska and Attu. On March 9 the Japanese ran the gauntlet, bringing in badly needed supplies and munitions. In another attempt on March 26, Hosogaya was intercepted by McMorris's much smaller task group. In a strictly ship-to-ship action, fought at long range for nearly four hours, the two forces engaged in a traditional but inconclusive battle off Attu—the Battle of the Komandorski Islands. Concerned about the two large *Maru* merchant-cruiser transports and freighter he was convoying, Hosogaya waged a very cautious but ineffective operation and eventually turned back.

McMorris had fought a bold offensive-defensive action that prevented the Japanese reinforcements from getting through. Hosogaya was retired from service the next month.

Because of the lack of logistics, sealift, and manpower available for a major invasion of Kiska and because Kiska's defenses were stronger than Attu's, Admiral Kinkaid and Major General John L. DeWitt had recommended on March 3 that Attu be assaulted first. Submitted through Nimitz, the proposal was approved by the Joint Chiefs of Staff on March 18. D-Day was set for May 7. Rear Admiral Francis W. Rockwell was named amphibious force commander and given three old battleships to buttress his firepower and an escort carrier to supply close air support for the first time in the Pacific Theater. Kinkaid also had three heavy and three light cruisers, nineteen destroyers, five transports, and various support craft. The landing force was to be made up of the U.S. Army's Seventh Infantry Division, which had undergone amphibious training in California.

Although Japanese IGHQ warned the new Fifth Fleet commander, Vice Admiral Ohiro Kawase, that the defense of Attu should now be accorded priority, Kawase deferred a major reinforcement of the island until, from his standpoint, the time would be more propitious, at the end of May. Throughout late April, USAAF planes hammered Kiska; Attu was accorded little attention. The wide-ranging U.S. naval and aerial pickets, however, missed at least one minor Japanese Navy evasion of the Aleutians blockade: a *Maru* transport bringing several scout planes to Attu around May 7, in weather so foul that Rockwell's own invasion force of twenty-nine ships was forced to delay its assault until May 11.

The Seventh Division came ashore unopposed in Operation Landcrab on the north shore of Attu around Holtz Bay and on the south shore at Massacre Bay. Colonel Yasuyo Yamasaki had only coastal guns and a dozen antiaircraft cannon to support the defense of the island by his 2,630 troops. Although not surprised by the invasion, he had not responded to the softening-up air strikes, a battleship bombardment, or the landing assault. Yamasaki instead tried to wage an inland defense of the valley between the bays on an island fifteen miles wide by thirty-five miles long. Kawase deployed his meager naval and air resources from Paramushiro. Admiral Mineichi Koga, the new commander of the Combined Fleet after Yamamoto's death on April 18, shifted strong formations from Truk to Tokyo Bay but was deterred from close intervention by bad weather and reports of the U.S. battleships and carriers operating offshore. Minor Japanese submarine and air counterattacks did nothing to take pressure off Yamasaki's isolated command, which put up a stubborn fight against the green Seventh Division. Indeed, the U.S. ground-force commander, a major general, had been relieved on May 16 after he was heard to lament that six months would be needed to take Attu.

Yamasaki's men clawed their way back to the last high ground between Chichagof and Sarana bays. At dawn on May 29, realizing that the inevitable defeat was near, Yamasaki launched a human-wave banzai charge of what the Americans described as "a howling mob a thousand strong" that overran a medical station and two command posts before being checked. By next morning all Japanese who had not been killed committed suicide with grenades. A total of 2,351 Japanese were recorded in the "body count." Only twenty-eight prisoners were taken—a ratio replicated constantly in the Pacific War. Of the eleven thousand American assault troops, approximately six hundred had been killed and twelve hundred wounded (as well as fifteen hundred incapacitated by illness). At the last minute, IGHQ had prepared to evacuate the remnants of the Attu garrison, but events overtook them, and Kiska commanded subsequent attention.

At the Imperial Palace in Tokyo, a high-level army-navy conference had been called on May 20 to reevaluate the deteriorating situation in the Aleutians. It was now admitted that island operations lacking Japanese air and sea supremacy were foredoomed. The conferees made the embarrassing decision to evacuate Kiska, whose garrison was twice as large as the one on Attu. Lieutenant General Kiichiro Higuchi, commanding the Northern Army, was ordered immediately to remove the troops on Kiska to the Kuriles. I-class submarines, which began the process on May 26, had by June brought out 820 wounded and sick soldiers and civilians. But the evacuation was proceeding too slowly, and seven of thirteen submarines had already been lost. Thereupon a destroyer squadron commander, Rear Admiral Masatomi Kimura, cleverly exploited fog cover, raced into shrouded Kiska on July 28, and extricated 5,183 men aboard six destroyers and two cruisers in a mere fifty-five minutes. The evacuation was aided greatly by the U.S. fleet's engagement, on the night of July 26, of a phantom flotilla that drew a thousand real rounds in the "Battle of the Pips," caused by American radar and intelligence mistakes.

In one of the weirdest episodes in the Pacific War, the Americans failed to detect the evacuation of Kiska for more than two weeks after the last Japanese had departed, although during that time the island had been blockaded and worked over by sea and air bombardment. Conflicting or misinterpreted data from U.S. intelligence or operational sources were regarded as inconclusive or even attempts at deception. The Americans accordingly took no chances with Kiska. At Adak, Rockwell massed almost a hundred ships and more than thirty-four thousand well-equipped troops, including fifty-three hundred Canadians, all under U.S. Army major general Charles H. Corlett. Learning from earlier amphibious mistakes and displaying impressive levels of new leadership, the Allied army began landing on Kiska on August 13 after a softening-up bombardment of the shore defenses. The island was eerily silent, and the only troop casualties (fifty-six killed or wounded) were caused by fire-fights between friendly patrols operating in the mist. The search of empty Kiska went on until August 18; the only living things found were a few stray dogs.

Many have argued that the Japanese never should have bothered with the desolate Aleutians and that the Americans, too, should have ignored the unimportant invasion. At the time, however, IGHQ regarded the island chain as a threat to the Kuriles and even to the homeland, particularly in the event of Soviet Russian-American military collaboration. After the Japanese Navy's setback at Midway, there was some thought of diverting attention from the central to the North Pacific. A number of Americans did ponder possibilities of striking at Japan through the Aleutian aerial corridor—an unrealistic proposition, as the 1942-43 campaign

demonstrated. But from the Americans' standpoint, the need for ousting the Japanese from the Aleutians—U.S. soil within the Territory of Alaska—was undoubtedly psychological, symbolic, and keenly felt. General George Marshall advised General Douglas MacArthur on August 10, 1942: "You should be aware that the pressures to meet the growing dangers of the situation in the Aleutians ... make our problem exceedingly difficult and complex." Some Americans honestly but wrongly feared that mainland Alaska itself was in danger of invasion from the Aleutian stepping-stones; yet on September 25, 1942, MacArthur warned USAAF General Henry H. Arnold that the Japanese "move into the Aleutians is part of the general move into Siberia."

A force of ten thousand Japanese troops, with fluctuating but generally minor naval and air assistance, eventually diverted as many as one hundred thousand Allied fighting men supported by sizeable naval forces and air power. Still, the Japanese squandered the whole Attu garrison, eighteen vessels, and precious logistical and ordnance stores. Referring to Attu, Vice Admiral Takijiro Onishi admitted: "We took a foolish liking to the place and poured in too much material and unnecessary personnel, making it impossible to leave. There are ... many islands like that in the south." Added Onishi: "We should have just pounded Attu and withdrawn from there." More importantly, Combined Fleet warships were deployed as backup at times when they were more needed to block U.S. operations at locations such as Guadalcanal. Additionally, the Kuriles and even Hokkaido had to be reinforced after the Japanese were ousted from the Aleutians.

Whereas the Japanese revealed great skill in evacuating endangered garrisons, their enemy was developing a more significant capability in conducting amphibious operations and leapfrogging Japanese-occupied islands, whose isolated garrisons were left to wither. Service in the Aleutians constituted "hard time" for soldiers and sailors and airmen of both sides. Many commanders lost or tarnished their reputations or at best were relegated to anonymity. IGHQ certainly earned no luster for its conduct of Operation AL. Despite the cost in men, material, time, and effort, the Aleutians campaign exerted scant influence on the Pacific Theater as a whole, from either the Japanese or the Allied point of view. The American naval historian Samuel Eliot Morison called it the "theater of military frustration."

*Alvin D. Coox is a professor of history and the director of the Japan Studies Institute at San Diego University.*

# An Alaskan Scout Remembers

*Buck Delkettie*

GOOD AFTERNOON, EVERYONE. IT'S A PLEASURE TO BE here today. For many years I didn't know what Veterans Day meant. Even during the war, I didn't think much about it. It seems that as I am getting older, it seems to me we hardly meet one another, especially us old veterans who have been around for many years and there's so many of them that are gone. There's still a few of us around and able to sort of talk to you. I see a few of them here who were with the Alaskan Scouts when I was in. And I know they can check me out if I'm wrong on any of the stuff I'm going to say.

I'd like to tell you first, I was there back in 1941. The leaders of the Alaskan Scouts were Colonel Lawrence Castner, Colonel William Verbeck, and Captain Bob Thompson, who was a lieutenant at the time. He made captain during the war, in battle. And, finally, there was Lt. Verlakelum. Those were the officers who kept us little Indians intact, sometimes kept us from running away.

And then there were the regular army people: Sgt. Hank Farrington, Arnold Spalding, Edgar Walker, James Radford, Sam Bates. And Norton Holzhauser, who trained us differently. He taught us how to recognize things and write the information down in a book or on a piece of paper, maybe a day later. For example, we would go down Fourth Avenue and walk down one side of the street and back up the other side. Afterward, we'd write down what we observed, what we saw. And you'd be surprised what many of us came up with. Some saw a lot of whiskey bottles, beer bottles, different things like that. We weren't trained for anything like that. But the sergeant kept it up, and so we learned to

find and view things that were important in our work.

We also had radio operator instructors—Woodrow Page and Vincent Herdum. They taught us how to operate a radio. Not mechanical work, but mostly Morse Code, and real light maintenance. And then we had John Highland who was our map instructor. He taught us what a map was for, how to read it; he taught us how to find tunnels, bridges, swamps, mud flats, glaciers, sand, the contours of the map, and just generally how to read them.

So we were busy from January of '42 until June of that year. Then we had boat building, sled building. And mostly doing carpentry work. That was Mel Tilden, Jake Jacobson, and Billy Bart. They were the leaders in training us how to take care of this stuff, how to build things, make snowshoes. And Arnold Lakard was good at that. He was good at cutting rawhide into different sizes and different lengths. He showed us how to cut it out, and how to stretch it and preserve it.

And then we had Arthur Upickson, who was the mechanic on all of our outboard motors. We had I think around fourteen outboard motors that we took care of. And on different trips we went from Nenana down the Yukon to Unalakleet. And Arthur Upickson was with us; Billy Westall was our riverboat navigator. So any time our motor broke down, Arthur was there to fix it. He was a wonderful mechanic.

And then we had our doctor, old Doc Philip Kendrick. He was the medic that was with us all the time. And the last I heard, he's down in Waterville, Washington.

As for the rest of us, there were many names. I can

remember days when the sergeant would get up and talk to us about our rifles, how to be soldiers in the army. But in about a year we had him pretty well trained to our group. We taught him how to do things our way. How to take bear out of the woods, how to make our own snowshoes, how to go into the woods and catch your own food, how to just plain survive in the woods.

Eagle River was a good place to go, same way with Eklutna Lake. We learned a lot up in those areas. We used to go to Goose Bay and then walk from there up into Big Lake. And there we taught many of them how to survive in the woods.

Myself and maybe four other guys did not know much about school. My last grade in the school was the fourth grade. When I was eleven years old and going in the fifth grade, they moved the school at old Iliamna, so there was no more school. They moved the school, the post office and everything. They left us nothing.

So when I got into the army, I found it was a good place to learn something. After May of 1942, the colonel figured we had enough training, I guess. So he shipped us down to Ugashik, where we landed at Old Woodley Airways. From there we walked from Ugashik down to Port Moller; it was 237 miles. And the first day out, my little tally machine broke, so I couldn't count our strides any more. So I had to walk and count my strides and mark them down as I went. We made that trip in forty days and I counted every step of the way. During the daytime I had to keep my mouth shut and concentrate on my counting.

There was Arnie Lakard, Joe Kelly, James Radford, and the radio operator and myself that went down. We had some wonderful times. There was a lot of rain down in that country. There were days we walked only four miles, and sometimes we walked ten or twelve miles. It was a wonderful trip going down the peninsula. When we got to Port Moller, Woodley Airways picked us up and took us back to Iliamna.

Before we left here in May, Colonel Castner had told us the Japanese were going hit the Aleutian Islands in June, the second and fourth of June. He told us to really be careful. At that time, there were bombs falling more than once down in Dutch Harbor. And they got a little taste of bombing down there.

After we got back, we started on the Chain, the Aleutian Islands. I think it was in the first part of August, when we left here, took the *Cavanaugh*. I happened to be one of them that was aboard the *Cavanaugh*. It was a beautiful yacht. We went from here to Kodiak. And from Kodiak, I was with a group that went aboard the old *Moonlight Maid*, another yacht taken over by the navy. It was an old boat and it stank from diesel oil. It was dirty. We made it to Dutch Harbor on that little boat. Then in Dutch Harbor we all got together again and got aboard two subs—the *Triton* and the *Tuna*. We had build two umiaks [skin boats] at Fort Richardson. A guy named McNells taught us how to do it. These were attached to the sub. Anyway, during a storm things got pretty bad and we submerged, which broke up the umiaks.

So we had to use little rubber rafts to go ashore on Adak. There was Arnie Lakard, myself, and Col. Castner. And all we had to move the little rubber rafts with was a little oar about three feet long. We had a rough time going ashore. Offshore wind, cold. It was in August, around the twenty-third.

I'd like to tell a little story about Walker and Robert Church. They were getting aboard one of the little life rafts, and I don't know if it was Walker or Church, but one of them had a knife in a sheath that had a hole in it. And he jumped into the raft and punctured the raft. The submarine was going to tow them back to Dutch Harbor. That was a scary night. They said to us that they could hear the captain shout, "The moon is coming out, I'm taking her down. You boys better get going."

But it was hard to scramble, especially out there. We didn't know how deep it was or how far it was to shore. When we got to shore we were all soaking wet. We stayed five days on that island before the main troop came in.

That first night we were there, we all sat watch for two hours on and four off, I believe it was.

One man, Peridike, was on watch, and Col. Castner was lying down a little ways from us. When it was time for Peridike's relief, he goes over and kicks this guy and says, "Hey, who do you think you are, George Washington? Come on, get up!"

Anyway, the guy he kicked got up and it was old Col. Castner.

"Oh, no! No! Lie down," says Peridike.

The colonel refused and he took his turn on watch.

That's just the type of people we were. It was a great group. We worked together, loved one another, and obeyed orders from one another. Rank didn't really mean much. We took orders from whoever was in charge, whether it was in the boat or on the radio, or on the map, whether we were going on a trip. It was a wonderful thing.

One scary part of being on Adak was when the main troop arrived. We were all on the beach when they came, and nobody knew we were there except the intelligence crew. And the only way we could let them know we were there and who we were was by flashlights and lanterns.

The troops came running ashore with fixed bayonets and here we were trying to stop them. Which was scary, real scary. We just sat up there and hollered, "Hey, hey,

hey!" You lose your voice, you forget everything, because you see this guy coming at you with a fixed bayonet. You know he's going to get you. And we were waving our lights. But everything turned out all right and there were no casualties.

We stayed until the runway was finished. And then, of course, they started running bombers over to Kiska.

Then Bob Thompson—I believe at the time he was still a lieutenant—says, "Let's go on a reconnaissance trip. Let's see if we can get a a ride on one of these planes." So he walked up to this first commander or pilot and says, "Can we get aboard and do some observing?"

They talked for quite a while and I guess he said "Yes," because he ran me up there to the lead plane, a B-24. I jumped in. There I was, no parachute, no nothing. Thompson got in the plane down on the end, a B-17.

And away we went. It seemed like we were just right above the water, rolling up and down with the waves. We flew to Kiska and came right over the hill, dropped our bombs, and then just kept flying. After we got up high, the pilot started circling and it looked like the whole island was burning up. I asked the gunner alongside me, "Boy, did they get everything on the island?"

He said, "Oh, no. It's just smoke."

So we made a couple of rounds with all the rest of the planes—B-24s, B-26s, B-17s. And there were fighters, too—the P-40s and P-38s.

One P-38 was knocked down while I was there. So we came down lower, dropped a life raft, and then climbed back up again. You could see these old shore guns shooting at the life raft and the water fly up—it looked like twenty feet. We climbed still higher and got away from the flak. And here comes an old PBY. He came gliding along and landed and picked up the life raft. Then we went on home.

When we got back to Igagik, we saw we had a big hole in our plane. I said to the gunner, "When this plane starts going down, I'm hanging onto you."

That's one experience I'll never forget. As we went through and dropped the bombs and flew around again, I observed six landing craft, one sunken ship, and two broken airplanes.

I went back and made the report and we were called on the carpet for making a trip without permission. But we talked our way out of that one. It was a great trip, really.

While I was there I also got to go aboard a PT boat. We got acquainted with the PT commander during our ptarmigan hunts on the island. The Scouts and some of the army groups had permission to go up in the hills and shoot ptarmigan for dinner, which we did until somebody got drunk and shot a hole through the general's stovepipe. No more hunting for ptarmigan.

Then we got in good with the navy, who *were* allowed to go hunting. This one fellow, a machine gunner, got sick, and the commander asked Captain Thompson if I could take his place for a few days. Bob said it was okay. So I got to stay on a torpedo boat for about a week, which was a lot of fun. They took me out and ran around the islands. And those things can travel! I don't remember what the speed was—it seemed like seventy miles an hour. But those waves bounce you around and you'd better hang on and keep your shirt tied on tight and stay steady. There was no stopping that boat; they slow down for nothing.

Once we were staying in a little cabin on Amchitka. And one night the Japanese came over in one of their planes, and we heard this roar so we all jumped up and out of the cabin and ran around the corner. That day I had been out fishing and had caught a bunch of little bass for supper. I had laid the fish behind the building. Anyway, as I came running around the building, here was this big old fluorescent flare that had been dropped. So I just grabbed my rifle and, boom, let them have it. After that they always pointed me out as the Indian who shot his own fish.

The Japanese came over every morning at ten and every evening at six, and you could set your watch by them. They were always on time. If you were playing pinochle, you had to stop at about five minutes to six, because the Japanese were coming.

We lost quite a few men there when the bombs buried them in their foxholes. We were going down the east end of Amchitka one time, where it's pretty flat, and we got caught out by some Zeros. They hit us and got one man.

The Scouts were pretty lucky, actually. We only lost one man in the whole campaign of the Aleutians. Two men got shot up—Ken Hill and Liv Peters. I believe it was Liv Peters who got twelve bullets on the right side of his body. Ken got a bullet right through his jaw. Last I heard, he was still alive.

Amchitka was quite a place to explore. We'd go from the north end to the East Cape. One time there was Philip Otrick, Arthur Upickson, and Billy Westall. And we stopped at one broad area where you could crawl into your little things and sleep. And Arthur Upickson got in there and threw his sleeping bag down where there was a pile of bones on a bed. Arthur said, "You'd better get out of the way, 'cause I'm going to bed." And he scraped off all the bones and he laid down.

Those are some of the stories about the things we did. A lot of them good, a lot of them fun. A lot of things were sad, too. We also had some miserable times down there. Weather and fierce winds blowing. It's very hard to climb over a mountain when the wind is coming from the east. And sometimes you had to fill your pack up with rocks to climb over the top, just so you wouldn't get knocked down.

When the invasion came for Attu, there was a group of us that were on reserve. We were sent to Shemya Island. That's the Semichi Group, where there are three little islands. Norbert Church and myself strung lines from one island to another. And each time a big storm came up, our communication was cut off.

After we came back from the Aleutian Chain, that winter Nels Hedlun and I took a trip. Nels, myself, and Joseph Rosenhauer, made a trip from Naknek—down here by King Salmon—by dogsled. We flew our dogs down. We had knockdown sleds that we put back together every time we came to a place. We started off in King Salmon or Naknek and drove all the way to Nunivak Island. The first trip we made was from Naknek and we went first by Copper Creek, next stop was Levelock. From Levelock we went up into the hills and then to Dillingham. We stayed there about three weeks recuperating, dancing, and having fun. And then we left there and went to a little village called Copeland, where Rosenhauer had his first taste of good Indian Eskimo living. Nels and I got in there and we ate the Native food. But Rosenhauer couldn't do it. He had to start his little gas stove and cook his own meal. But we stayed there and Rosenhauer brought his little army cot in and set it up and slept on that. Nels and I threw our sleeping bags up on the bank with the rest of the people.

We went from there over into Togiak, from Togiak to Good News Bay, from Good News Bay to Glenhawk, and from there into Bethel. At Bethel we stayed another week. From there we took off again and went down the coast, were we took a plane and flew across to Nunivak Island. I never measured how many miles that is, but it must be at least eight hundred miles that we traveled by dog team. We had a plane that stored our stuff at Good News Bay, Bethel, Nunivak Island, and Dillingham.

After that trip, which took us over two months, the Scouts came back here to Anchorage. This was in the spring. So we started another trip, this time with Bill Duggan.

We built a scow, which I think measured about fifteen by thirty. Walter was probably one of the group that worked on it. We took the scow up to Nenana. We had twenty-five-horsepower outboard motors. From Nenana we went down the Yukon River. When we got down to Tanana we hit the ice and so had to stay and follow the ice as it went out the Yukon. There were many floods in that area at that time. Galena was flooded. The army air force there was flooded out. And we went down to Nulato; most of those homes there had two feet of water in them. And it was sad. And we kept on going and followed the ice to the mouth of the

Yukon. From there we went to headquarters at Unalakleet.

I headed from Unalakleet to Shag Village. Another group headed from Unalakleet up to Moses Point. Still another group went down the Yukon towards Stratum Bay or that area. These were possible landing areas for our amphibious groups, possible landing fields for the airplanes, and possible camp sites and trails that we could go over. We had a wonderful time there at Unalakleet; we were there from June until November.

One memory I have is of a place where Frank Harrington was standing on the beach and we were making supper. He had a small movie camera and was taking pictures of the mosquitos that were swarming around the camp fire. I've never seen so many mosquitos in my life. If we made tea or coffee you had to scrape them off the top. They were that thick. And so one man and I went up the Unalakleet River, about thirty miles, I think. And we camped at night. Next morning I heard him out there making coffee. And I could hear this noise that sounded like a motor coming up the river. I said, "Hey, who's that coming up the river?"

He said, "Nobody. Look at your tent."

I looked at the little white tent and they were just dark along the edges with mosquitos. I mean, thick. I never have seen mosquitos so thick in my life.

One time Pat Moore, who was with the map-making group, said we had to go to Unalakleet.

I said, "Okay, but the weather's gonna be rough."

"That's all right," he said, "we'll make it."

So I took a boy with me that I had been training with, Johnny Sevetlee. I said, "Johnny, you come along, I know you can handle the boat real well."

So I put him in the boat with me and I told him, "Now you handle the oars in case this motor quits. You'll have to fight it some way to get back into the bay."

As we went out that harbor, Pat said he was seeing the seven seas all at one time. It was that rough. After we got out past the river and into the ocean it wasn't too bad, although it was rough. But going into the Unalakleet River was something else. Some of the boys said they didn't know how I did it.

I said, "I don't either."

It was just white from the mouth of the river into the bay. You couldn't tell where the streams were, and you couldn't tell where the channel was, but we got in there.

Well, we thank you very much. I'm glad I was here.

*Buck Delkettie was drafted into the 297th Infantry at Fort Richardson on 12 November 1941. He was transferred to the Alaskan Scouts in January 1942, where he served until his discharge in late 1945. During his tour of duty, Delkettie served as a radio operator and boat operator.*

# A Brush with War

*William Draper*

I'D LIKE TO SAY HOW HONORED I AM TO BE HERE WITH THE Alaska at War Conference and to have my paintings on the walls here. It's a great honor to me.

Now I'll start out telling you how I was a combat artist for the United States Navy, an official one. I was twenty-eight when the war started. My draft status was 3A and I wore glasses, which didn't help me get in. So I decided to volunteer my services at 150 Causeway Street, in Boston, which is where a part of the navy was situated.

I went in and said, "Can I do anything to help? I'm an artist."

And they said that I could help as a civilian.

And so I was assigned to draw the wakes of submarines going under water. I would see photographs of it and try to interpret the shapes of the wakes, in order to show how far ahead the submarine was as they bombed. I did that for about two months.

I had permission at that time to go into the navy yard. So I decided I'd go in and paint some pictures there, which I did. I painted five and sent them down to Washington with some other work of mine, and I was picked as one of the official combat artists.

There were five of us: Griffith Bilcoe, Dwight Shepler, Mitchell Jamison, Al Merriam, and me. And so I got into the navy as a lieutenant (jg) and I was sent to Harvard for a sixty-day-wonder course. The course started on a Monday and I was suddenly called to the front office. They told me I was being withdrawn from school.

I thought, "My God, what have I done already?"

I found out that they wanted me at 150 Causeway Street again to do cartoons of submarines thumbing their nose at planes. And so I did that and never did get any training. I didn't know the floor from the deck or the bulkhead or anything such as permission to come aboard and salute. I was lost.

After two months of doing that I went down to Washington and was a line officer. My first assignment was the Aleutians. (Later I was sent to Bougainville. I landed with the Marines there and then went on to Saipan and Guam. I landed with the assault ships at Guam and was with Task Force Fifty-Eight for a month. But that's another story.)

I'm talking about the Aleutians. My first assignment, I flew up to Seattle and then took a boat across to Kodiak. At Kodiak I went to the officers' BOQ and got a bunk and slept there. And I had my paints and my canvases, so the next morning I was very anxious to get started. I went out with my paints and set up the easel. Right away I saw a wonderful blue glass thing. I think the picture is right here, and I started painting that.

These two MPs came up and arrested me and said, "Don't you know that's secret?"

I didn't know anything about it and so I was brought over to Admiral Reeves and reported. After everything was explained I was told I could paint it.

I was there in Kodiak, painting, oh, maybe three weeks or a month. I did about eight pictures of planes coming in. One time I was painting Womens Bay on one side and Pyramid Mountain on the other, and between there was just empty space. Suddenly this plane came in and landed and a little truck came out and refueled it. I finished the painting and showed it to the guys there.

They said, "There's no plane like that. The propellers

have four blades instead of three."

I told them these propellers had four blades. And they continued to maintain that I was wrong. Anyway, it turned out that the plane was a B-26 and they had never seen one before.

After that I was to go to Dutch Harbor. I got into a PBY and we started off and went for quite a time. The fog was terrible and so we turned around and came back. The next day we started out again, and had to turn back yet again. On the fifth day we went out and made a forced landing at Cold Bay. I finally got to Dutch Harbor the next day. The weather was really terrible. My Lord, the williwaws! I had my canvas out there painting and the williwaw came and blew all these stacks of wood and everything else, blew the stuff about a hundred yards away. My pallet fell over. I chased the canvas, which got covered with a lot of dust and everything, and which I tried to scrape away. I finally put a lot of white paint all over it and smudged it around. It turned out to be one of my best paintings.

This was in Dutch Harbor in November. I climbed up on the mountainside and I found violets growing there, in bloom in November, which I think is quite extraordinary.

Then I went on to Umnak by boat, a DE, a destroyer escort. There was a guy named Grady Cochran who was captain. Well, I've never seen such terrible waves and wind. We were out there fifty-five degrees and everybody on the boat—on the ship, I suppose I'm supposed to say—was sick, except for the captain and me. Really I didn't get sick. But there were a lot of others who were. We got into Umnak and I was put up with some army pilots there.

As bad as the weather was, sometimes it would clear off and I would get out and paint. And I'd paint tents. It's awfully hard to describe. It's much better if you can look at them on the walls here.

But I was there until Christmas. And the week before Christmas the pilots and myself were all really snowbound in a Quonset hut. We couldn't get out. We got somebody to bring in sandwiches somehow. And I painted them all in the hut there that week. I had them all posing and the painting finally appeared in the *National Geographic*.

I went on to Adak in a small boat with army personnel, about sixty of them, and they were all sick. It was the most awful three days getting to Adak. I got there and reported to the executive officer, who turned out to be Sam Hammel, a friend of my brother's. He asked that I move in with him, which I did, and which turned out to be great.

I got a lot of boards made for me to paint on. Sam advised me that we were going to Amchitka in a few days on the *Arthur Middleton*. And so we took off and wound up in the worst storm ever. I don't understand why they tried to land there that day. This was January 12 and I was trying to paint a jeep being brought up from the hold. But I didn't get very far on that because a destroyer was breaking apart on the rocks over there and people were all in the water, trying to rescue the crew of the destroyer. After five minutes in that water they were dead. And then the ship that I was on, the *Arthur Middleton*, went aground. The wind was so strong that we just went in and went aground in Constantine Bay. And then the landing boats—we had to abandon ship, except of course for those who were told to stay.

I was climbing over to the cargo net and getting ready to climb down when this lieutenant colonel came up and asked, "What have you got there?"

I said, "It's a paint box; I'm painting for the historical record."

He said, "My God! What next!" and ran down the deck.

And so we got ashore. There were only about fourteen navy guys there, including me. I moved in with the head of the Seabees. There was a Captain McKinnon there, a wonderful man, and Sam Hammel built his tent and lit the stove, on what he thought was nice hard ground. After the stove had been going for a while the ground got terrible—muddier and muddier. Finally, we were in a foot of mud in the tent and we had a terrible time getting boards to put down there because the lumber was being used to build piers. This lumber had all been thrown overboard, with the expectation that it would float ashore. Instead the boards all went out to sea with the tide.

And dead sea otters. My God, it was awful! And even some money along the shore where some of the landing boats had broken apart.

And then soldiers would go by Aleutian graves with their beautiful stones and beautiful wooden crosses. The soldiers pulled a lot of them down and burnt them to make little fires. I have one picture of them sitting around a little fire with a Russian Orthodox grave behind.

Anyway, one day they were draining a lake down below, and I was watching them do it and painting the scene. Suddenly it got very dark. It got darker and darker. I wondered what was going on. Some of the men thought there was supposed to be an eclipse of the sun tomorrow. I told them it must be today, I was sure of it. Turned out I was right.

On Amchitka the planes came over every day. On Adak we had cover—air cover—most of the day. But on Amchitka, early in the morning and after six at night, Pontoon Joe, as he was called, would fly over. There were a couple of planes with pontoons that would fly in and drop these bombs. A few bombs would come down and thud into the tundra and nobody was hurt. And we all sort of waited for Pontoon Joe to come over.

Finally the airfield was finished and some of our planes came over from Adak and settled down for the night. The next day some Pontoon Joes came over. Our planes flew up—the Japanese of course didn't expect any American planes—and we shot them all down. Which was very exciting.

We went back to Adak. By this time I'd grown a beard. When I came in to report to the new executive officer he grabbed me by the beard and said, "Don't you know you should be clean shaven here in Adak?"

I said, "I just came back from Amchitka."

He had these little pig eyes. I'd been a boxer when I was younger, and I wanted to hit him. I couldn't do it because he was a lieutenant commander and I was only a jg. But when he pulled my beard, if I had known what I could have learned in that Harvard sixty-day-wonder course, I could have hit him and nothing would have come of it. Or maybe it would've. He was a nasty piece of work.

Finally, I was ordered back to Washington. I'd heard from the captain of the port that there was a big transport being refueled by tanker out in the Bering Sea, twelve miles out. I went to the exec and told him I had orders to go back. Could he send a boat out with me?

He said, "Certainly not. Who told you there was a tanker out there?"

I said, "The captain of the port."

He told me to wait for the mail boat. Finally I got on the mail boat and we went out the twelve miles to the tanker. The sea was calm but there was a big swell. We came alongside the tanker and here I had heavy winter gear, liners and boots and all. And so they threw over a little rope ladder over the side of the transport and I was in this mail boat and grabbed a hold. I knew nothing about ladders. And it was pathetic because I could never chin myself with all the weight I was carrying. I grabbed the last rung of the ladder and there I was hanging onto the edge over the transport and the boat disappeared from underneath me. I thought, this is it. I looked over and kept looking down and hoping, because I knew if I went in the water it would be the end, because it was February and this was the Bering Sea. I hung there and finally saw the boat under me again. I let go and dropped about ten feet into the boat. Then suddenly this great cargo net came out and down and I just stuck myself through it and was zoomed up to the deck of the tanker.

Grady Cochran, who had been the captain of the DE, was on board, said, "Draper what in hell are you doing coming over like that?"

I said, "Don't talk to me now. I have a terrible headache."

Finally, my gear came up and my paintings and all the stuff, in another cargo net. I was able to relax then and talk to Grady.

And so I got back to Washington, which was the end of my Aleutian experience. And it was a great experience, I'll tell you that.

Thank you.

I want to tell you also that I was very flattered to have been commissioned by the One Percent for Art Program through Ray Hudson and Gertrude Svarny. I have a painting of the Church of the Holy Ascension of the Russian Orthodox Church in Unalaska. And I'm very happy that it's there.

*William Draper has been teaching at the Art Students League in New York. During World War II, he was awarded the Bronze Star for meritorious achievement as a combat artist in the Pacific Theater. After the war he concentrated on portraiture.*

*Kodiak —Cooperation,* by William Draper. *(Courtesy of the U.S. Navy Art Collection)*

*Arctic Vigil,* by William Draper. *(Courtesy of the Navy Art Collection)*

Troops of the Eighty-Seventh Mountain Infantry train at Camp Hale, Colorado, 1942, by George F. Earle. *(From the author's collection)*

Quisling Cove on the afternoon of D-day, west coast, Kiska, by George F. Earle. "Quisling" was an arbitrary name applied to the cove by the military. *(From the author's collection)*

# Painting with the Tenth Mountain

*George F. Earle*

BILL DRAPER'S AND MY INITIATIONS INTO THE SERVICE were somewhat different. But there's a similarity to them, too, I think, certainly in some of the early confusion.

I was a painter with at least some ambition at the time of Pearl Harbor. The day after the attack on Pearl Harbor I was down at No. 1 Church Street in New York City trying to enlist in navy intelligence. I had heard that if you had a Snipe [a small sailboat—ed.] there in Long Island Sound, as I did, you were very eligible for naval intelligence. Parenthetically, painters are said to be kind of emotional, and I've always been told that my failure as a painter—if that's the word—is because I wasn't emotional enough. But I was down there signing up the day after Pearl Harbor.

Anyway, in the next line, beside mine, was an early skier friend who said, "Hey, George, you're in the wrong line!"

And quick as a flash I jumped from the line for naval intelligence into the ski line, which was probably a very good move on my part.

From the standpoint of the history, the beginning of the mountain troops is amazing. Early on they were called "ski troops" and attracted a great many skiers, mountaineers, timber cruisers [men hired to scout wilderness areas for timber companies—ed.], a few cowboys, and some mule skinners.

The whole idea of this unusual army, initially a regiment of three thousand men, was put across to the powers that were, the military minds in Washington that took care of such things, by a rather amazing fellow nicknamed "Minny" Dole. Dole was an earlier skier. He had started the National Ski Patrol, which those of you who ski today know as a nation-wide and very important part of skiing. Minny Dole had witnessed an early ski accident in New England and as an insurance broker he was, I guess, golden-tongued enough to take the idea of the ski patrol and put it on a national basis. Then came the Finnish War—as we called it—when Russia moved into Finland and thought that they would take the country over in three days. The Russians were greatly embarrassed by Finland's white-clad ski troops, and were in fact treated to a few near-disasters.

Minny Dole took his idea to Washington to see if he could convince the military minds that a special ski troop or mountain or winter warfare unit should be formed in the U.S. Army. He sold them on the idea. And the unit first assembled at Fort Lewis, outside of Seattle—I think it was the day before Pearl Harbor.

Meanwhile, I was being embarrassed back in Stamford, Connecticut, because the army, as you might guess—early on, right after Pearl Harbor—*were* somewhat overwhelmed with paperwork and my orders simply didn't come through. In the little town of Stamford, where I had a small art school while I was also doing courses for a master's degree at nearby Yale, the little town was putting on all these farewell dinners for me. And every morning after the dinner I was still there. This went on for some weeks.

Finally the orders came and I was very proud of them. They sent me up to Fort Devens, outside of Boston. I got on the train at Stratford with the orders, and through the car (this was a civilian train, of course) an old peacetime sergeant came in and with a gravelly voice said, "Are there any would-be military personnel on this train?" Of course we were all in civilian clothes.

There were three of us. He leaned over and looked at the orders of the other two. Then he came down to me. I had a "V" in front of my number because I was a volunteer and I was very proud of it. He said, "What the (bleep) is this 'V'?" Whereupon he took his big fountain pen and scratched it out. I never saw the "V" again.

At Devens they kept me long enough so that I learned to make a bed right. The idea was that all the ski-troop recruits had been approved around the country by the National Ski Patrol—part of Minny Dole's idea—and we were supposed to have a letter from Minny Dole himself. In my case, the letter saved me from being sent to field artillery. What happened was they asked for my educational qualifications. And I had a BFA. The sergeant at the desk said, "Must be Field Artillery, no doubt." So I almost wound up at Fort Knox.

But I flashed this letter from Minny with its ski patrol heading on it and they kept me in Devens until five other similarly-aimed guys arrived, also going to the ski troops. So we went out together in a civilian train, the Super Chief. And the nation's near hysteria about patriotism at that time, a month after Pearl Harbor, meant that we were wined and dined all the way across the country. They tried to present a military menu to us at the first meal that we had. And a group of high school history teachers that happened to be on the train almost killed the steward who was presenting this very limited military menu. From that time on he offered us nothing but the best steaks on the train.

I'm sure I would have remained a private if my name had not been George Earle, which was also the name of the governor of Pennsylvania at that time. Of course I was in no way related to the governor and was scarcely aware that he shared my name. Anyway, I was stuck into a company of Pennsylvania coal miners, young guys, most of whom were at least semi-illiterate. I wrote their letters for them, and I read their letters to them, and when the company commander came around and asked, "Who do you guys feel is leader enough to go to officer candidate school?" They said, "Of course, the guv! The guv should go!"

I think that was the reason I got anywhere in the army, and had the time to paint, which I would not have had as an enlisted man, I'm sure.

Of course, Bill Draper was officially authorized to do his paintings. I wasn't; I stole the time. At a recent alumni meeting at Vail, Colorado, celebrating the foundation of the Tenth Mountain Division, they had enlarged some of these little paintings, reproduced them, and passed them out to the veterans. I was called up on the stage and one guy in the audience called out, "Hey, when did you do any fighting?" All because this was stolen time

that I was able to manage as an infantry officer in the Tenth Mountain Division.

Let me be a little more informative about the Tenth Mountain. I think that the adventure on Kiska was very important to its later success. I hope that some of you did hear my paper on that part of it. So I'm going to skip mention of that right now. But the real military value of the Tenth Mountain Division was not that the men could ski, although a very large percentage of the men did learn to ski and to take part in the weekend races between snowshoers and skiers. (By the way, we found that the mule skinners were absolutely impossible to teach skiing to. They were as stubborn about it as the mules would have been. And, yes, somebody did try to put snowshoes on the mules as an experiment, which didn't work out either.) Anyway, it wasn't the skiing and it wasn't the snowshoeing.

A special camp was built for us in Colorado—Camp Hale—where we had trained in advance of Kiska as a regiment. The skiing parts of this three-thousand-man regiment on Kiska were brought back early—we were only on the island for two months—to cadre and help train a light division of twelve thousand men. This is the division that went on to Italy and fought with distinction as the spearhead elements of the spring offensive of the combined American and British armies in Italy. This was a very successful drive that we spearheaded—getting ahead of our support. We were given flat out credit for shortening the war in Italy because of our fast drive from a position in the Apennines just north of Florence up into the foothills of the Alps, all in just nineteen days.

The real difference, though, as I started to say, besides the fact that the division was in excellent condition and used to climbing hills and so forth, the real advantage was that we were self-sufficient as far as supplying ourselves went. We were not tied by an umbilical cord to the road nets and trucks and support vehicles. We had mules and the snow-weasel—the T-15 or M-29, as it was called earlier—a light, full-track vehicle which was the forerunner of the snowmobile.

We took the weasels along the ridges. As forward liaison officer for the regiment I used to sit in on some of the interrogations that we had in the spring of '45, as the drive went on, and I found some of the German prisoners indignant, as though we had played unfairly, because we had come into their positions from the ridge instead of across their prepared fields of fire leading up from the valleys. They wished that we could straighten this thing out and play by the rules from then on.

The skis actually did not work out in Italy at all, even though the ground was snow-covered when we first arrived there. The skis were, surprisingly, too noisy. The Italian snow was corn snow, from all that sunlight. If we'd had nice powder, I'm sure we could have made use of them for patrol work. The debate about how many ski-patrols actually were tried out in Italy is still raging amongst our alumni groups. But there unquestionably were two or three, and all of them had to withdraw quickly as far as any night patrol work was concerned because the Germans could hear them coming. The sound of the skis on the corn snow was quite loud.

I notice on the tags on the paintings in this exhibit that I am supposed to have been working with tempera, and that is not true. I would like to explain a little bit about the fact that I had my little cigar box full of these little tiny oil paints that you can buy in art stores still. And a little jar of turpentine, which very soon became gasoline—there was very little turpentine available on Kiska Island. The real secret of being able to do it so easily out of your pocket was that I had these five-by-seven watercolor pads. And the watercolor paper was thick enough to soak the oil out of the oil paint so that I wouldn't have to wait for the oil to dry; I could fold a paper across the top immediately and it was all finished. And I had one beautiful, big, fat brush with a wonderful point on the end of it. I wish I could find as good a brush today. And that was it.

I want to share something with you, from a diary that I kept on Kiska Island. In part it explains the environment of the first painting that I did on Kiska. I wish the painting were here now. It isn't, but I do have it on a slide which I will be showing later this afternoon.

The scene is the first landing on Kiska, at Quisling Cove, by the Eighty-Seventh Mountain Infantry. And here it starts: This diary was written five days after the actual landing:

> Sunday, A.M., I was to go ashore in command of the first boat of the second wave. Saturday night we had sung a lot and were a bit sillier than usual in our general horsing around in the compartment. A few of us wrote final letters, heroically, against the tide of banter. We were in bed by eleven.
>
> First wave up at five o'clock; second at six. Showered, shaved, breakfasted. And then, as the first wave was still leaving at seven, I went out on deck and painted a picture. I can't believe it. It seems incredible.

Of course we expected the first wave was going to be decimated and we were going to push on through them. We had no inkling at all that the enemy had left the island two-and-a-half weeks earlier. But let me continue with the diary:

> There were loud explosions on shore that later proved to be aerial and naval bombardments on the other side of the island. The island seemed to be jumping up and down, as a matter of fact. I had just finished the painting of the low clouds and the morning sunlight, when the loudspeaker announced my boat. And I had to hurry. At the time I remembered noting that the tensest moment of all was while I was painting. And that I had been more nervous before important high school football games, which sure surprised me.

I think Bill Draper will agree with me that the whole painting thing was so natural to us that it was a calming influence, even in the tensest times, and it was reassuring in a way to just do your thing under any circumstances.

Some fellow officers were interested in the Kiska paintings and in 1944, before we were sent to Italy, they helped finance reproductions of eight of them by a company in Chicago. Sometime in the 1980s a widow of one soldier donated these paintings to the Museum of Western History, in Denver, and at about that time I saw a little box in the Tenth Mountain Division Foundation's quarterly newspaper with the query, "Who is the artist?" I knew instantly that these reproductions were of my paintings. So I got in touch with the museum. But first I went out into my garage and got the sixty-four paintings out of a steel box that had been in my garage for forty years. The museum now has the entire collection.

So I hadn't really ever imagined that these paintings would wind up in a show like this and in an exhibit with Bill Draper—who I knew to be a much-envied official painter of the navy—and [army air forces artist Ogden] Pleissner, over here, another painter whose work I admired. It's really wonderful, to me, to have this kind of honor. Even though I had been trained as a painter, I never imagined that these little paintings which I was doing as an infantry officer would be honored in this fashion.

Thank you very much.

*George F. Earle is retired from teaching at Syracuse University, School of Architecture, and the State University of New York. Earle painted while serving for four years of combat duty with the Tenth Mountain Division, 1942-1946.*

# War
# in the
# North Pacific

Troops come ashore on Attu, May 1943.
*(Photograph courtesy Command Historian's Office, Alaskan Command)*

# Building Alaska's Defenses in World War II

*Benjamin B. Talley*[1]
*and Virginia M. Talley*

THE TREMENDOUS MILITARY CONSTRUCTION PROGRAM in Alaska during World War II had its inception with the work of a board of officers of the army, navy, and Army Air Corps. They made an inspection of Alaska in the early summer of 1939, as a result of which they recommended construction of bases at Annette Island, Yakutat, Sitka, Kodiak, Dutch Harbor, and Nome. Ladd Field, near Fairbanks, was already an Army Air Corps cold-weather testing station, and its enlargement was recommended.

Construction authorization followed on the heels of the board's report. The navy would be responsible for construction at Sitka, Kodiak, and Dutch Harbor, the Army Corps of Engineers at Annette Island and Yakutat. The Construction Quartermaster of the Army would handle the remainder. Originally, the Civil Aeronautics Administration (CAA) was responsible for construction of a large number of airfields in the Interior.

In 1940, the Territory of Alaska, which is about one-fifth the size of the contiguous forty-eight states, had little infrastructure and a small population of perhaps seventy-five thousand spread over an area of 486,400 square miles. If imposed over a map of the lower forty-eight states, Alaska would stretch from the coast of Georgia north to the Canada-Minnesota boundary and west to the area of San Diego, California. The largest town was Fairbanks, with a population of about twelve thousand. Anchorage had less than three thousand. Except for the railroad between Seward and Fairbanks, transportation was primarily by use of waterways or bush planes. Outside the territory, little was known of its geology, climate, and geography or of the various regions of the territory with their vastly differing conditions.[2]

In September 1940, then-captain[3] Benjamin B. Talley became resident engineer in charge of construction of a field at Yakutat, a field which at the time had been neither designed nor located.

On September 11, Talley flew to Yakutat by way of Juneau. There he paid his respects to the territorial governor, Ernest Gruening. Talley chartered a plane from Alaska Coastal Airlines to go to Yakutat. Governor Gruening accompanied him on the flight, as it gave the governor an opportunity to go in that direction, and money for travel was scarce in those days.

In Yakutat, Talley slept in a bunk in the warehouse provided by the Libby, McNeil, Libby Cannery. He went to the field site on the cannery speeder on their Yakutat

---

[1] This paper is based on documents in the possession of Brig. Gen. Benjamin B. Talley, USA-Ret., including a "Daily Log" of some 300 single-spaced typewritten pages reporting to the District Engineer in Seattle on Talley's activities in Alaska during World War II; oral histories compiled by John Haile Cloe, Command Historian, Alaskan Command, and by Dr. Charles Hendricks, Historian, Historical Division, Office of the Chief of Engineers, U.S. Army Corps of Engineers; and a "Narrative Report of Alaska Construction 1941-1944," by Col. James D. Bush Jr., published by the U.S. Army Engineer District, Alaska.

[2] See the introduction in Col. James D. Bush Jr., *Narrative Report of Alaska Construction 1941-1944* (U.S. Army Engineer District Alaska), which outlines in more detail the geography, geology, climate, and existing social developments in 1940—from the engineer's viewpoint.

[3] Talley was promoted through grades from Captain to Colonel by the end of October 1942. He gave up promotion to Brigadier General when he left Alaska in 1943, after the Battle of Attu, to go to the European Theatre of Operations.

and Southern Railway, which the army leased, along with the cannery dock and warehouse. Incidentally, after Talley had become president of the Yakutat and Southern, Colonel Otto F. Ohlsen, then the president of the Alaska Railroad, issued a pass to Talley on the Alaska Railroad in exchange for one on the two-mile Yakutat and Southern.

Talley visited the site for the field, decided where the runways were to be located, the types of runways, and how they would be built. He submitted a list of initial equipment to start construction. The message was transmitted on the cannery radio at Yakutat.

Before returning to Seattle, Talley visited Anchorage and Fairbanks along with the division engineer, Colonel (later LTG) John C.H. Lee, and the Seattle district engineer, Colonel (later BG) Beverly C. Dunn. At that time the principal industry in Anchorage was the Alaska Railroad, which had its shops located there. Troops were just arriving at Fort Richardson (today Elmendorf Air Force Base) and were living in tents in the mud, for it had been a very rainy fall that year.

In October, Talley boarded a ship in Seattle to go to Yakutat. The ship was loaded with the organization equipment needed to maintain a company detachment or post at Yakutat, along with preliminary construction equipment which could be obtained on short notice. A company from an aviation battalion which had been at work on Annette Island where Major (later MG) George J. Nold was building an airfield was made available for the Yakutat project. The troops with their equipment boarded the ship at Ketchikan.

When the ship docked at Yakutat, the skipper was concerned that unloading the ship would take a very long time. Talley said that if the troops could live aboard while they unloaded, the job would be finished in three or four days. Usually, once a ship is in port, passengers don't live aboard. Talley forbade any soldier to leave the

The intrepid Col. B.B. Talley takes a break while on reconnaissance on Amchitka, 1942. *(Command Historian's Office, Alaskan Command.)*

dock until the ship was unloaded, and the task took only about two days.

Construction began immediately. Talley's instructions had been to complete the project by July of the following year. He soon notified the district and division, however, that by Thanksgiving work would have proceeded sufficiently so that planes could land on the Yakutat field and the passengers could join in Thanksgiving dinner. The division and district engineers arrived in Yakutat as invited and had dinner in one end of the dining room while troops under Lieutenant (later Colonel) John W. Baum were finishing installation of the roof on the far end of it.

By year's end, all barracks at Yakutat had been constructed to the point of beneficial occupancy. The finishing grade was being made on the runway, and equipment for paving was being assembled.

In January 1941, army construction, including Army Air Corps military construction, was transferred from the construction quartermaster to the Corps of Engineers. Talley transferred to Anchorage and was given responsibility for all army and air corps construction on the mainland of Alaska and elsewhere—except Annette Island and army construction on naval bases. His orders were contained in a letter which said, essentially, that he was to take over construction. As a second lieutenant he had studied the manual for the construction of pontoon bridges, where the captain marched the troops to the bridge site and commanded: "Sergeant: Build the bridge!" He felt like that sergeant, but those were all the orders he needed and all that he ever received.

Major Nold continued construction at Annette Island under Seattle. Talley's responsibilities eventually included twenty-eight of a total of thirty-nine wartime projects scattered throughout the mainland and the Aleutians.[4] To do the necessary reconnaissances and supervision of

---

[4] See Bush, op cit., footnote 2, Preface, for a listing of all the wartime Corps of Engineers projects.

construction, he spent two-thirds of his time in the field.

Before leaving Yakutat, Talley arranged for a civilian construction man who was already working for the Corps to transfer to Yakutat from Anchorage to be responsible for completing the runway construction.

On January 7, 1941, at about 2:00 A.M., Talley arrived at Seward by way of a Coast Guard boat from Yakutat. Colonel Ohlsen, manager of the Alaska Railroad, met him with the Alaska Railroad speeder, and they drove to Anchorage through a night illuminated by spectacular northern lights.

The existing timetable for construction of Fort Richardson, including Elmendorf Field, was two years.[5] Talley was convinced that the United States would soon be at war. He made a fundamental and very basic decision that all paving at Elmendorf Field, the first two hangars, and the gasoline system would be installed during one working season. Until then, essentially all construction other than in emergencies halted during the winter months.

There were objections: it was the middle of winter, work could not be done until the ground thawed; there was no aggregate; it would be impossible to stockpile it in the necessary quantities even to get work done in the summer; cement in the necessary quantities could not be obtained. Finally, there would not be enough time in the construction season to do the job. These objections were overcome by breaking the ground and gravel pits with jackhammers and thereafter keeping ahead of the frost. Warehouses were built to stockpile cement, and two complete "paving spreads"—rather than one—were put to work.

Much of the steel in the arch hangars at Elmendorf was put up at temperatures colder than fifteen degrees below zero, and the workers erected steel at Fairbanks until the temperature reached twenty-five degrees below zero. Carpenter work was stopped only when the wood froze and a nail couldn't be driven into it. Concrete was poured at minus fifteen degrees, heating both the aggregate and the water and keeping a hot flame going inside the mixer while concrete was mixed. The concrete was warmed with steam boilers after it was poured. (Oh, what it cost! But preparation for war was essential!)

As a result, by October 1941, two paved runways five thousand feet long were in place, two parking areas four hundred by four thousand feet were completed, and two hangars were erected. An aqua-gasoline system was installed. In addition, the troops were in barracks. Similarly, a large runway was paved at Ladd Field.

In November 1941, General Buckner asked Talley to go to see General John L. DeWitt in San Francisco and from there to go to see the army chief of staff in Washington, General George Marshall. Talley was to ask for three things: approval of construction of a base on Umnak Island; authorization for troops to garrison a base at Nome; and acquisition of a squadron of transport planes. General Marshall was so busy that he was unable to see Talley for almost a week, but eventually he was available just after he had been called to the White House to see President Roosevelt about the dangerous situation in the Pacific. General Marshall arranged for a meeting with a number of top officers, including General Leonard T. Gerow, G3 of the army, and General Arnold, chief of the Army Air Corps. The garrison at Nome and construction of Umnak were approved.

Talley returned to Alaska on December 6 and learned of the Japanese attack on Pearl Harbor the following morning. At that time, he changed from civilian to military attire.

In January 1942, the troops from Yakutat moved to Umnak, and a supply base was established at Chernofsky Bay on Unalaska Island, since there was no good harbor on Umnak. On Umnak, for the first time under field conditions, the runways were constructed using Marston mat—interlocking pierced steel planks. By the time of the Battle of Attu in the summer of 1943, soldiers and other workmen could lay a runway five thousand feet long in a week.

The exposed position of Pustoi Bay on Umnak Island required that materials and equipment be brought by barge from Chernofsky Harbor on Unalaska Island. As a result, everything had to be handled five times, using ship cable slings and cranes, so that there was excessive breakage. Breakage of shiplap and one-inch lumber ran as high as 45 percent. Due to storms and rough seas, many barges loaded with materials and equipment were lost. Barge and ship's docks were wrecked by storms several times.

The Umnak base was built in secrecy, using the Blair Packing Company, a fictitious cannery, as the cover, and when the Japanese attacked Dutch Harbor in June 1942, they knew nothing of it and were surprised by land-based planes coming out of the west.

Talley had made a bet of a case of champagne with navy personnel on Kodiak that the base would be ready by April 1, 1942, the date on which he and Captain (later Colonel) Carlin Whitesel, who was project engineer in charge, had agreed. On March 31, a plane with Brigadier General William O. Butler, commanding general of the

---

[5] After the end of the war, when the air force became an entity separate from the army, Fort Richardson, which was primarily an air base, was turned over to the air force and was renamed Elmendorf Air Force Base. The air force paid for building what is now Fort Richardson for the army.

Eleventh Air Force, Colonel Richard Park, division engineer from Portland, and Talley on board, landed at Umnak, and Talley sent a radio message in the clear to Commodore Parker on Kodiak: "Make mine Moet. Talley." The duty officers couldn't decode the message, so they eventually awakened Commodore Parker who immediately recognized the message to mean: "Umnak is operational." Talley asserts that one way to be sure that an air base project will be finished on time is to tell the men working on it that on such and such a date a plane carrying several high-ranking officers will arrive. One of the men stationed on Umnak drew a cartoon showing a plane landing on one end of the field while soldiers were laying pierced steel plank at the other end.

Immediately following Pearl Harbor, the strength of all garrisons increased and construction expanded accordingly. The civilian labor force grew to about fourteen thousand, and Army Corps of Engineer units were sent to Alaska as fast as they could be mobilized. Ultimately they numbered about nine thousand. The decision to complete the Elmendorf project in one season paid off, and air strength increased rapidly. The base was ready for the planes as fast as they could be flown to Alaska.

As officer in charge of construction, Talley was charged with responsibility to determine the feasibility of constructing air strips on the several islands of the Aleutian Chain and elsewhere. After Umnak came construction on Adak, Atka, Amchitka, and, later, Attu and Shemya. In addition, numerous airfields were built across the mainland, down the peninsula and on many other islands of the Aleutian Chain. To prepare for later construction, this meant going out on armed personal reconnaissances, preparing beach maps and laying out the fields. Every island of substantial size in the Aleutian Chain was examined, either from the ground or from the air, to determine the possibility of using it for a base or airfield or for an auxiliary air strip to be available in emergencies.

Very reluctantly, the navy would furnish airlift for the party in flying boats (PBYs). Parties usually consisted of two or three technical personnel and six to eight Alaskan Scouts. The navy would fly them out, land their PBYs in some protected bay or cove, put the party in rubber life rafts, and take off. The party would go ashore, hide the boats, and play cops and robbers with the Japanese reconnaissance planes (and in one case on Amchitka, with a Japanese patrol), while surveying the area and picking suitable landing places and field sites—if they existed. For security, members of the party remained some distance from each other. Everyone was instructed that if he heard a plane approaching, he should fall to the ground and, if possible, lie in a fetal position curled around a clump of grass.

After the Japanese occupation of Kiska and Attu, it became necessary to have an air base within a shorter distance from those targets. Talley led reconnaissance parties to both Tanaga and Adak. Tanaga was closer to Kiska, and it would have been quicker and easier to build an air base on Tanaga. Adak, however, had a much larger harbor, better from the standpoint of the navy. As a result, the major construction was on Adak. It is the second largest island of the Aleutians, located approximately four hundred miles west of Umnak Island and two hundred miles east of Kiska.

Because of mountainous terrain on Adak, location of a suitable site for an airfield was a problem. However, there was a shallow tidal lagoon, a large marshy area which was flooded at high tide but substantially drained at low tide. By diverting creeks and establishing a system of dikes and tidal gates, it became possible to construct two runways. Because of the natural possibilities for runway construction afforded by the level bed of the lagoon, the dike was finished, a dam to keep out the tides was in place, and aircraft, including heavy bombers, could land within ten days after start of construction.[6]

Talley needed to be present when the troops came ashore on Adak to start construction. A navy PBY was to take him from Dutch Harbor. Captain Leslie E. Gehres was also a passenger. The sea was so rough at Adak that Captain Gehres refused to permit the pilot to land, on the basis that although they could have landed, the PBY could not have taken off. The plane therefore went to Atka where it landed, again in very rough water, and the passengers went aboard the seaplane tender *Casco*. During dinner, Talley made such a fuss about his needing to get to Adak that Captain Gehres finally ordered a navy destroyer—which had been standing by in the harbor to guard the *Casco*—to take Talley and Lieutenant Colonel Leon B. "Slim" De Long, who accompanied him, to Adak. During the night, the captain of the destroyer notified Talley that the *Casco* had been torpedoed by a Japanese submarine which had been on the bottom of the harbor at Atka but had surfaced after the destroyer departed. Fortunately, there was such a strong wind that the *Casco* had blown ashore.

As a result of this incident, Talley's standing with the navy sank very low, and it wasn't helped by the fact that he sent one of his tugs, the *Moonlight Maid*[7] (a name

---

[6] See Bush, op cit., footnote 2, "Airfields," p. 230.

[7] The *Moonlight Maid* had formerly been the pleasure yacht of a Mr. Fleischmann, of the margarine dynasty.

which the navy deplored, but which he had refused to change), to tow the *Casco* to Sitka.[8]

One reason that the airfields, bases, and other projects could be built so quickly was that Talley was given broad authority in many fields. He had authority to obligate a million dollars without request of higher authority. In Seattle, a $17 million revolving fund provided a stockpile of materials. As soon as materials were drawn, they would be replaced. Eventually he had overseen construction of more than $300 million, $150 million of it during the spring of 1943, at a rate of almost a million dollars a day. He could purchase or design and build a fleet of boats, tugs, barges, and landing craft, and eventually had 254 boats large enough to need Coast Guard registry. That was more boats than the navy had in Alaska.

Talley had been designated superintendent of the Army Transport Service for Alaska. This particular duty was withdrawn from him when he diverted a ship to Umnak in order to be sure that necessary supplies and heavy equipment for the air corps were on hand. The decision to divert the ship turned out to be a good one, since the base on Umnak was ready when the Japanese attacked Dutch Harbor.

Almost all travel to Alaska in those days was by steamer. As Talley's office was the largest employer in Alaska, he was also made the representative of the U.S. Department of Labor in Alaska for the purpose of determining wage scales. To keep employees from changing from one job to another, travel was restricted in Alaska. Most employees had to obtain clearance from the Corps office before they could buy a ticket at the railroad station.

Projects were going forward on many fronts. Originally, Seward was the port for all of Southcentral Alaska. There was a large wooden trestle on the Alaska Rail-

road between Anchorage and Seward. Had this been destroyed, Southcentral would have been cut off from most shipping. Whittier was closer to Anchorage, and it was decided to construct an extension of the railroad from Portage to Whittier.

Opening Whittier involved digging two tunnels, one nearly a mile in length, the other nearly three miles long.

Troops unload strips of Marston mat for construction of an airbase runway on Amchitka, October 1943. *(Command Historian's Office, Alaskan Command)*

The longer one is through a single boulder. After surveys, the tunnels were dug, and dock facilities were built quickly. West Construction Company of Boston, later acquired by the Morrison-Knudsen Company, was the prime contractor.

Some of the contractual negotiations were, of necessity, informal. Fortunately we had and still have the finest civilian construction organization in the world, headed largely by men of honor and integrity. For example, it was necessary to extend the CAA airfield at Juneau to meet military requirements, and to construct bunkers for aircraft safety. Morrison-Knudsen was completing its work for the CAA at Juneau and was ready to move its equipment. Talley and another engineer went to Juneau and met with the M-K representatives. They outlined what was to be done, asked M-K to go ahead with construction, and stated that the Corps would follow with a

---

[8] A navy tug came to Sitka to tow the *Casco* to Seattle for repairs.

letter of intent and later with a formal contract.

Some months later, an M-K official came to Talley's office in Anchorage and told him that the Juneau work was about completed—but what about the letter of intent and contract? After a short discussion, the parties agreed they would base cost of the contract on the actual cost of the job. M-K turned over their books to the military auditors, who worked with the M-K accountants to arrive at a mutually satisfactory cost figure.

In the Aleutians, still more airfields and bases were needed. Amchitka was closer to Kiska and Attu than Adak. Lights and smoke from fires on Kiska could be seen from Amchitka. A reconnaissance party went there in December 1942, following an aerial reconnaissance earlier. They found that suitable airfield sites existed, that harbor sites were available for landing operations, and that there was an ample water supply for garrison use.[9] The Japanese had previously been on Amchitka and had dug some test pits; and there was evidence that at least a small party of Japanese was still on the island.

Before going to Amchitka, Talley had received instructions that he was to submit his report directly to the Western Defense Command at San Francisco, with a copy to General Buckner at Kodiak. If the report was favorable, troops to build at Amchitka would begin loading at once. The report was favorable, and Talley started for Kodiak in a PBY which was returning for overhaul.

About seventy-five miles from Kodiak, the plane lost one engine, and the other could not keep it in the air. The pilot, navy lieutenant Ewing, made a forced landing in very rough sea, popping rivets from the hull of the plane and severely damaging one sponson. The pilot notified Kodiak of the predicament. Seven hours later a picket boat arrived to pick up the passengers. Meanwhile, the plane was kept afloat only by constant bailing with buckets. After the passengers were off, the plane sank.

After reporting to General Buckner in Kodiak, Talley flew to Anchorage, arriving on Christmas Eve, and began lining up personnel and equipment to off-load the ships when they arrived in Constantine Harbor at Amchitka.

Troops landed early in January, and a flight strip was ready in less than two weeks.

In March, Talley made an air reconnaissance of Shemya, sketching the layout of the field from the nose of a B-24. The plane flew over Massacre Bay at Attu and strafed a Japanese landing craft.

For the Attu operation—against the advice of those who knew the Aleutians—the War Department assigned the invasion to the Seventh Motorized Division, which had been training in the California desert for service in North Africa. Talley offered the commanding general of the Seventh Division, Major General Albert E. Brown, three of his best engineers, men who were familiar with the Aleutians, to serve for Brown, and not under Talley's control. Those three included Major (later Colonel) James D. Bush Jr. In addition, Whitesel and engineers from Adak and Umnak were sent to Attu. They built a runway paved with pierced steel plank near Massacre Bay in eleven days. General Butler staged his planes at Adak to land on the field at Attu on the twelfth day. Meanwhile, the Japanese banzai charge was fought on Engineer Hill where Major Bush had insisted on fortifying his camp for the protection of his men. He and his men were able to stop the charge, ending the Battle of Attu.

The previous day, Talley took a survey party to Shemya to make ready for the arrival of the Eighteenth Engineers, who had worked on the Alaska Highway. He remained with them until they started work. He was privileged and pleased to return to Shemya fifty years later for the renaming of Eareckson Air Force Station[10] in honor of Colonel William O. Eareckson, the innovative and dynamic leader who had been head of the Bomber Command of the Air Corps in Alaska in World War II.

After the Battle of Attu, Talley requested transfer to the European Theatre to take part in the liberation of Europe. The final report, dated June 13, 1943, from the "Daily Log"[11] which he kept from 20 October, 1940, to June 13, 1943, reads in part:

> [T]omorrow night ... will be the last time I shall probably meet many of those with whom I have worked so closely and whom I have come to admire so greatly. Together we have done a fine work—one in which we take a great deal of pride, and we believe it to be a valuable contribution to the War effort.
>
> ... I should mention that I have seen many changes, have seen men and women rise to outstanding greatness. I have seen many with whom I

[9] Bush, op cit., footnote 2, "Reconnaissance and Surveys," p. 429.

[10] Toward the end of "Shemya AFB's Final Dining Out," 18 May 1993, at Shemya AFB, Mrs. Sally Eareckson Kennerly, the daughter of Colonel Eareckson, was the honored guest. She was asked to make a few remarks, whereupon she graciously paid tribute to Talley for his work in building the airfields which made possible the conduct of the air war. She then gave him a bottle of Moet champagne. It had taken fifty years for him to collect, since the navy personnel had not paid off on their bet.

[11] Benjamin B. Talley, "Daily Log." The original of this document is in the archives of the University of Alaska Anchorage.

have rubbed elbows give their utmost to the War effort and break their health in so doing.

The changes in Alaska perhaps have been no greater than the changes in many of us up here—myself included. From this experience, I have gathered a broadened understanding of people...

I have one of the finest organizations that an officer has ever been privileged to head, and to the combined efforts of these fine people, the support of the Commanding General, the untiring assis-tance of the District Engineer and the people of the Seattle District goes the credit for the successes which together we have attained.

*From January 1941 to June 1943, Benjamin B. Talley was Officer in Charge of U.S. Army and Air Corps construction in Alaska. This involved an outlay of more than $300 million for construction of bases throughout mainland Alaska and the Aleutian Chain. General Talley has been a resident of Alaska since 1964.*

# The Aleutian Campaign

*James S. Russell*

## Preliminary Events and Planning

Success at Pearl Harbor went beyond Japanese expectations. The United States Pacific Fleet was immobilized by a sudden stroke of Japanese naval air power and a comparatively easy and rapid expansion to the south took place. Japanese planners realized that inevitably the war must turn to the defensive. When this occurred, a strong outer perimeter of air bases from which to conduct air reconnaissance and attack, backed by a powerful fleet operating on interior lines with its own concentrated carrier-borne air power, would make the war so expensive for America that she would tire of it. Then a peace could be secured which would gain for Japan the needed resources in lands to the south, the control of China, and a strong and dominating position in East Asia.

The first United States air attack against the home islands of Japan occurred on 18 April 1942, when the planes of the Doolittle Raid took off from a carrier six hundred miles east of Honshu. This token attack directed Japanese attention to the east and northeast. It added point to the argument of those Japanese planners who advocated taking advantage of the favorable situation created by the success of current operations to extend the defensive perimeter of the empire. In 1942 the American territory nearest to the Japanese homeland was that in the Aleutian Islands. Japan's perimeter, originally conceived to pass through the Kuriles, Wake, Marshalls, Bismarck Archipelago, Timor, Java, Sumatra, Malaya, and Burma, was intended to be moved outward to include the western Aleutians, Midway, Samoa, Fiji, New Caledonia, and Port Moresby.

The plan for the Midway and Aleutian Campaign was prepared on a staff level below that of the Imperial Headquarters. It was presented in completed form to that headquarters, to the Naval General Staff, and to the Commander in Chief, Combined Fleet. The Commander in Chief, Combined Fleet, approved the plan and was anxious to carry it out. The Chief of the Naval General Staff initially opposed the plan, but gave way to the enthusiasm of the Commander in Chief, Combined Fleet, and ultimately approved it. The agreement of the army was then secured in Imperial Headquarters and the plan became a scheduled operation.

The Aleutian and the Midway operations were intimately related. The main strength of the Japanese Fleet was to be employed in the seizure of Midway and would offer battle to the United States Pacific Fleet under one of three tactical plans, the choice of which would depend upon developments. In the north a small but relatively powerful part of the Japanese Fleet, the Second Mobile Force, composed of two aircraft carriers, two heavy cruisers, and three destroyers, would strike Dutch Harbor a paralyzing blow, while, at the other end of the Aleutian Chain, the islands of Adak, Kiska, and Attu would be seized by other forces regularly attached to the Japanese Fifth Fleet.

The mission of the Fifth Fleet up to this time had been twofold: (1) "The defense and patrol of assigned area;" and (2) "Anti-Soviet security." The "assigned area" embraced the eastern seaboard of Japan, including Marcus Island, Ogasawara Islands, Hokkaido, and the Kurile Islands. That "anti-Soviet security" was regarded seriously was evidenced by the fact that float planes of the *Kimikawa Maru* made an extensive photo reconnaissance of Kamchatka in January 1941. On 11 May (east longitude date), from a position 150 miles south of Kiska, the *Kimikawa Maru*, supported by the light cruiser *Kiso*, used her float planes to make a photo reconnaissance of Adak and Kiska. This was quite successful in the case of Adak, but thwarted by weather in the case of Kiska.

Apparently the Japanese overrated, rather than underrated the severity of weather in the Aleutians. It is believed that this is attributable to their experience in the Kuriles, the proximity of which to the Asian mainland gives them a far greater range of temperature and more severe winter weather than that experienced in the Aleutians. However, the Japanese fishing boats for a long time had been depleting areas of Bristol Bay of fish by their thorough methods, and these, along with the seal and sea otter harvesting in the southern Bering Sea, must have amassed for Japan very considerable meteorological and geographic information.

At any rate, the Aleutian campaign was first planned as a reconnaissance in force. Adak was to be occupied, any United States military installations there destroyed, its harbors mined, and then the occupying force withdrawn to land on Attu. The job ashore on these two islands was to be done by the army. Kiska was to be occupied by a naval landing force. Kiska and Attu were to be held until fall and then the occupying forces withdrawn before the onset of severe winter weather. Meanwhile the Japanese expected confirmation of their belief that these northern islands, so like their own Kuriles, were unfit as bases for sustained air operations. An advantage to be derived from the seizure of islands in the western Aleutians was that a base there would allow flying boats to cover the northern half of the fourteen hundred miles between Adak and Midway. The barrier air patrol thus established would prevent a surprise penetration of the United States Pacific Fleet beyond the contemplated Japanese base at Midway towards the Empire. And, incidentally, further carrier raids of the Doolittle variety would be made much more difficult.

The first blow in the Aleutians, the Japanese carrier attack against Dutch Harbor, was timed to be one day earlier than the carrier attack against Midway, thus to confuse the enemy and throw off his timing.

## The Japanese Occupation

The Second Mobile Force, the principal elements of which were the two carriers *Ryujo* and *Junyo*, launched their attack against Dutch Harbor on schedule on 3 June (west longitude date). It was not considered a success by them, however, since about two-thirds of the planes turned back due to weather. Only six fighters and thirteen carrier attack planes, all from *Ryujo*, reached the

target. The force retired, refueled destroyers, and attempted to carry out the plan for the second day which called for a reconnaissance and air attack on Atka and Adak. While visibility had been the principal difficulty the first day, they found that wind and sea conditions, as well as visibility, were a bar to flight operations the second day. They therefore steamed towards Dutch Harbor and as wind and sea improved they launched two weather scouts. Late in the afternoon they launched against Dutch Harbor a single attack of about thirty-two planes flown by pilots selected for their experience. This flight reached the target and did considerable damage. The surface units of the Second Mobile Force were scouted throughout most of the second day by PBYs, and alarming attacks by B-17s and B-26s developed which, since they were handicapped by unfavorable weather, did them no damage. Returning from the attack, the *Junyo* planes chose a rendezvous point off Umnak Island which turned out to be almost directly over a United States airfield—regarding the existence of which the Japanese had hitherto obtained no intelligence. Here they lost four planes to defending United States fighters.

The Second Mobile Force retired to cruise in a support area about four hundred miles south of Kiska. It had no further contacts with United States forces. A planned interception of United States air raids against Kiska was cancelled due to weather, but two carrier scout planes reached and reconnoitered the Komandorski Islands on 13 June (east longitude date).

On the day of the second attack on Dutch Harbor, which was the day of the main engagement at Midway, two occupation forces moved up to positions from which to run in to their objectives. The first of these forces was the so-called Adak-Attu Occupation Force, and the second, the Kiska Occupation Force.

As a result of the Japanese defeat at Midway, the occupation of the western Aleutians was cancelled by the Commander in Chief, Combined Fleet. However, within about an hour this order was countermanded and these two forces were ordered to proceed with their operations. Shortly thereafter a message was received indicating a further change in plan. The Adak occupation was cancelled and the Adak-Attu Occupation Force was directed to seize only Attu. The Kiska Occupation Force landed a battalion of naval landing force at Reynard Cove on Kiska at 1500, 6 June (150th meridian west longitude, zone plus 10, time and date). The Adak-Attu Occupation Force landed a battalion of army troops on Attu at about 0300, 7 June (zone plus 10, time and date).

The reasoning of the Japanese Fleet commanders which occasioned the rapid cancellation, reinstatement, and ultimate modification of the plan for the occupation of the western Aleutians is not clear. Some credence may be given to one account which states that the Commander in Chief, Combined Fleet, Admiral Yamamoto, decided against the Aleutian occupation immediately upon learning of the destruction of the major carrier force at Midway, but thereafter gave way to the recommendation of the Commander in Chief, Fifth Fleet, Vice Admiral Hosogaya, and ordered the occupation of just the two westernmost islands, dropping from the plan Adak, which is only three hundred miles west of Dutch Harbor, but retaining Kiska, which is six hundred miles west. Certainly there would be a great temptation to save something from the debacle at Midway and the story in the Japanese newspapers that some American territory had been occupied would detract from any leak of the sad information on the loss of carriers in the larger battle.

It is quite evident that the Japanese High Command was concerned over the possible intervention of the United States Pacific Fleet in this token occupation of American soil, for the carrier *Zuiho* was detached from the defeated Midway force and sent up to reinforce the Second Mobile Force as the latter stood by at a discreet distance in support of Kiska. When this force returned for a rapid replenishment at Ominato during the period 22-29 June, it sortied—reinforced by a fourth carrier, the *Zuikaku*—and remained in a support position until 6 July. By this time the Japanese were apparently convinced that the Americans would not accept a carrier duel in the bad visibility of summer in the Aleutians, or that the aircraft carriers of the Pacific Fleet were deploying elsewhere.

Due both to the vagaries of weather and the extreme demand for search from the Dutch Harbor area, United States air reconnaissance did not discover that an occupation of Kiska and Attu was taking place until four days after it had begun. The PBYs led off in the bombing of Kiska, followed by B-17s and the longer range B-24s as soon as these could be concentrated at the strip on Umnak Island. Initially this strip could be used only as a staging point, but it was expanded as rapidly as possible to the proportions of an air base. Ironically, no suitable airfield site could be found on Unalaska Island, which has two harbors but impossible terrain for a airfield. As a result the good terrain on Umnak was utilized and was served by lightering material to an indifferent beach on that island.

The initial Japanese landings on Attu and Kiska were made with combat and labor troops totalling about twelve hundred men at each location. At the end of June the Kiska garrison was doubled. Anti-aircraft and communication personnel were added as well as submarine base personnel and six midget submarines. On about 6 September 1942, the army troops on Attu were all moved to Kiska, leaving Attu unoccupied—except for a small naval communications unit—until 30 October 1942, when the so-called Second Attu Invasion Force of Japanese Army troops was landed. Little by little the garrisons on these two islands were built up—although with extreme difficulty—as the United States air and sea blockade tightened, until on Attu, at the time of the United States assault, May 1943, there were twenty-five hundred troops and, on the same date at Kiska, about fifty-four hundred.

A meeting of commanders at Kodiak Naval Air Station, spring 1942: left to right, Capt. Leslie Gehres, Commander, Patrol Air Wing Four; Lt. Charles Perkins, Executive Officer, VP-42; Lt. Cmdr. James S. Russell, Commander VP-42; and Capt. Russell Cone, Commander, Thirty-Sixth Bombardment Squadron. *(James S. Russell photo, Command Historian's Office, Alaskan Command)*

Japanese air activities from their acquired bases in the western Aleutians were beset with difficulties from the start. Fog and the swell in the Kiska harbor were found to be great operational hazards. Additionally the lightly armed and unarmored float planes were no match for United States bombers and fighters. A unit of six Kawanishi type 97 flying boats was moved in on 8 June, but the surviving planes, only half the original number, were flown out on 15 August when it was decided that the long-range aerial reconnaissance was impractical because of enemy attacks, sea, and weather at the base. Float planes continued to be brought in, however. The seaplane carriers soon found the harbor of Kiska untenable due to United States bombing and, after being attacked even at outlying anchorages, thereafter limited their activities to flying off planes to land at Kiska or Attu from distances offshore, or to quick dashes into port with hasty unloading in darkness or bad weather.

PBY-5s of Squadron VP-45 taxi at Casco Cove, Attu, May 1943. An airfield was later built at the base of the mountain. *(Alaska Aviation and Historical Museum, Anchorage)*

## Expulsion of the Japanese

Having successfully seized bases in the western Aleutians, the Japanese decided during the fall of 1942 to hold and reinforce their Aleutian outposts rather than to withdraw from that area as was originally planned. A Japanese Imperial Headquarters directive of 1 November 1942 implemented that decision with orders for the moving up of troops, the construction of defense works, and the building of airfields on Kiska and an island of the Semichi group adjacent to Attu. The then-firm intention of the Japanese to hold the northern anchor of their defensive perimeter in the Aleutians was evident from the fact that the date of February 1943 was set for the completion of the tasks contained in the directive.

That the Japanese had come to the Aleutians to stay was also evident from United States reconnaissance. As United States strength was gradually built up, the action against the Japanese grew from operations of attrition—principally by air and submarine, but with a surface ship bombardment of Kiska on 7 August 1942 thrown

in—to an advance down the Aleutian Chain to secure bases closer to the Japanese. The island of Adak was occupied on 30 August 1942 and an airfield was in operation there by 13 September 1942; the island of Amchitka was occupied on 12 January 1943 and fighters operated from there on 17 February. With this extension of bases to the westward and the control of the air thus assured, United States naval surface forces augmented the blockade in early February 1943. On 19 February the United States heavy cruiser *Indianapolis* and two destroyers intercepted and sank the thirty-one-hundred-ton *Akagane Maru*, en route to Attu loaded with a platoon of troops, stores, and materials for an airstrip.

With the sinking of the *Akagane Maru*, the Japanese began a series of operations in which the entire strength of the Fifth Fleet—two heavy cruisers, two light cruisers, and six destroyers—was used to escort supply ships to Attu. The first convoy run was successfully completed when the ships discharged in Holtz Bay on 10 March (east longitude date). The second convoy run was intercepted off the Komandorski Islands on 27 March 1943 (east longitude date) by a much weaker United States force of one heavy cruiser, one light cruiser, and four destroyers. In the ensuing battle, although the United States heavy cruiser and one destroyer were heavily damaged, a successful delaying action was fought and the Japanese force finally withdrew because of radio intelligence of impending air attack. While supply ships had been precariously running the air blockade into Kiska and Attu under the cover of weather and darkness, the Komandorski action ended all surface ship supply to these bases.

The successful American assault and occupation of Attu against the fanatical resistance of the Japanese Army garrison took place during the period of 12-28 May 1943. During the progress of this action ashore, the Japanese made three unsuccessful air raids and attempted but gave up an evacuation, first by destroyer, then by submarine. Japanese air sorties against the United States amphibious forces at Attu were made on 14, 23, and 24 May (east longitude dates). The first two sorties were made by nineteen—the last by seventeen—twin-engined naval land-based attack planes from Paramushiro. The first sortie did not reach the target due to weather; the second dropped torpedoes but made no hits; and the last was intercepted by P-38s and driven off.

The United States amphibious assault on Attu caused a very considerable reaction in the Japanese Fleet. A concentration of major units began in Tokyo Bay about mid-May in preparation for a sortie against the United States forces at Attu. Before the fleet sailed, however, Colonel Yamasaki, in command of the Attu garrison, announced on 28 May that he would make his final charge. With Attu in United States hands, and the relatively heavy concentration of United States air strength in the Aleutians, Japanese fleet operations in the north were cancelled as being of no promise.

The situation confronting the Japanese was an unhappy one. Kiska, the strong point at the north end of the Japanese perimeter, was bypassed and could no longer be supplied. Moreover, the assault and occupation of Attu might presage a further amphibious advance from the north towards Japan, and the defenses of the Kuriles were weak. The Japanese therefore decided to withdraw the Kiska garrison and absorb it in the defenses of the Kuriles. The defense of the Kuriles was to be greatly augmented.

An Imperial Headquarters directive of 21 May 1943 read, in part:

The Kiska Garrison Force will evacuate in successive stages, chiefly by submarine, as expeditiously as possible. Also, with due regard for fog conditions, and after ascertaining the enemy situation, transports and destroyers are to be used in con-

junction with this movement if circumstances are favorable. Defenses of the Kuriles, Hokkaido and Karafuto are to be strengthened expeditiously. Garrison units for the Northern and Central Kuriles, now standing by in Hokkaido, as well as Hokkaido garrison units, will be moved up and deployed in the northern and Central Kuriles. Furthermore, particular attention will be given to the strengthening of antiaircraft and coastal batteries in the Northern Kuriles. Army and Navy air forces will be deployed immediately in the island chain to act as the backbone of defense. All air and shipping base installations will be put in order and strengthened immediately.

The army air strength to be deployed was "the major part of the First Air Division," and the navy, "the major part of the Twelfth Air Fleet"—eighty-eight and 146 airplanes, respectively.

After a costly attempt to evacuate the Kiska garrison by submarine, in which three of the large undersea craft were sunk, it was decided to employ light cruisers and destroyers, utilizing the thick fog of the summer as cover to prevent the detection and destruction of the evacuating force. Accordingly, light units of the Japanese Fifth Fleet sortied from Paramushiro on 7 July 1943 and stood by about four hundred miles southwest of Kiska awaiting favorable weather until they were forced by lack of fuel to return to Paramushiro, where they arrived on 18 July. The Japanese sortied again on 22 July and made a successful dash into Kiska Harbor on 29 July (east longitude date) with two light cruisers and ten destroyers. After a brief visual landfall at the southwest end of Kiska Island at 1105 (Tokyo time), this force circumnavigated the north end of the island at high speed in thick fog. Hugging the shoreline, the navigation was by soundings, radio bearings, and indifferent radar information. The force anchored at 1350, embarked approximately 5,100 troops, got underway at 1435 and, dividing into two groups, departed by approximately the same route they had followed coming in. Outbound, the light cruiser *Abukuma*, leading one of the groups, sighted a submarine off the northwest coast of Kiska. This was the only contact with United States forces made by any of the Japanese ships.

The day on which the Japanese evacuated the Kiska garrison, a strong United States task group was absent from its patrol southwest of Kiska Island as it engaged in fueling. A close-in patrol by submarine was in effect. A single destroyer patrol on a radius of forty miles from the island had been removed on 24 July (east longitude date) and was not again activated until 30 July. Air searches were in effect, but were hampered by fog. Ashore the Japanese preparations for evacuation were interpreted as a redeployment for defense. United States air and surface ship bombardments were continued after the Japanese evacuation. On 16 August (east longitude date) an assault landing was made on Kiska by elements of United States and Canadian troops, comprising thirty-four thousand men. The Japanese had escaped from Kiska.

## Pressure on the Kuriles

With Kiska occupied by the United States, the war in the north settled down to one of attrition by submarine against the Japanese, minor air raids, air reconnaissance, and minor surface ship raids against shipping and Japanese bases in the Kuriles.

On 5 August 1943, the Japanese Northeast Area Fleet was organized, comprised of the Fifth Fleet and Twelfth Air Fleet. The Commander in Chief, Northeast Area Fleet, was charged with the defense of the Kuriles area and given tactical command of local base forces. An Imperial Headquarters Directive of 30 September 1943 stated, "The object of Northeast Area Operations is to smash the oncoming enemy and to defend the Kuriles, Hokkaido, and other integral parts of the Empire. Simultaneously, and insofar as possible, enemy strength in the Aleutians is to be whittled down."

Despite the last statement, Japan was on the defensive in the Kuriles, and desperately concerned over an amphibious advance from that direction against the empire. In November 1943 an estimated 262 airplanes were in Hokkaido and the Kuriles, in about equal numbers for the army and navy. Air activity was confined to defensive fighter patrols and antisubmarine patrols except for a few Attu reconnaissance missions. Also one attack mission against Attu was conducted on 10 October 1943 by naval twin-engined land-based attack planes. Air strength in the Hokkaido-Kuriles Area in the summer of 1944 was approximately five hundred planes. By the spring of 1945 practically all air strength had been withdrawn from the Kuriles except for about eighteen army fighter planes on Paramushiro and twelve navy dive-bombers divided between Shimushu and Etorofu.

The importance which Japan attached to the defense of the Kuriles is indicated in the number of army troops deployed there. From 14,200 men in late 1943, the garrisons were increased to a total of forty-one thousand men in mid-1944, and decreased to twenty-seven thousand men in 1945. These men were Japan's answer to the threat of United States invasion from the north via the Aleutians. The men were not in action, except in defense against harassing air raids, or against sporadic shore bombardment by light United States naval forces. However, they were required to maintain their defensive positions and hence were unavailable for combat assignment elsewhere. Moreover, their supply and movement afforded excellent shipping targets for aggressive United States submarines. This resulted in a heavy loss of ships to Japan as well as a loss at sea of about 10 percent of the total personnel deployed to the islands.

## Comments and Conclusion

The Aleutian campaign in its two phases, consisting first of the Japanese expansion into and expulsion from the western Aleutians, and second of the operations of holding and attrition against the forces in the Kuriles, was in true perspective a minor part in the war against Japan. However, it had results, both tangible and intangible, which deserve to be recorded.

Foremost among the tangible results was the direct loss to Japan of ships, aircraft, personnel, equipment, and materials. This loss was relatively small, but not insignificant to a nation which had to fight an economical war. Japan salvaged nothing from what she put ashore in Attu and Kiska except approximately fifty-one hundred men—less their equipment from the latter island. In western Aleutian operations she lost three destroyers sunk and four heavily damaged, five submarines sunk, and nine cargo transport ships sunk. Of these, air attack accounted for one destroyer sunk, two severely damaged, two submarines sunk, and seven cargo transport ships sunk. Nothing has been found to date upon which an accurate report of Japanese air losses can be based. Estimates indicate seven planes lost in the carrier raid on Dutch Harbor, sixty from those water-based at Kiska and Attu during the Japanese period of occupation, and an undetermined number in the Kuriles. Equally vague is the information on personnel killed. Of particular interest in this study were those killed in air raids on Kiska. From interrogations this is estimated to be between 5 and 7 percent of the garrison over the period of occupation of one year and two months, a disappointing total in view of the United States attempt to bomb the Japanese out.

Another, less evident, tangible result was the absorption in the northern theater of operations of parts of the military strengths of the opposing powers, a commitment of forces to this theater which prevented their use elsewhere. Covered by a short initial effort involving a part of the Japanese Fleet, represented by the employment of two aircraft carriers in early June, four by the end of that month, and terminating with the withdrawal of fleet support on 7 July 1942, the Japanese put ashore garrisons on Kiska and Attu. The maximum combined strength of these garrisons at any time was about eighty-five hundred men, yet the United States gathered together a landing force of 34,500 men by July 1943, in order to expel the Japanese from their holdings. Such is the disproportion of forces required to wrest the initiative from a small but aggressive nation which has made quick early gains against a powerful but unprepared opponent. When Japan fell back upon the Kuriles, this disparity of forces was no longer in her favor. She then had to deploy a far greater fraction of her total men under arms against the threat of invasion from the north than did the United States to hold a reestablished frontier and to conduct sufficient operations to ensure the semblance of threat. Compounding the ill effect upon Japan, the highly trained United States amphibious troops, experienced and hardened in the Aleutians, were employed in the Central Pacific to speed the advance toward the heart of the empire over an alternate route, the choice of which lay with the side having the initiative. The air situation was analogous.

The chief intangible result of the Aleutian Campaign may be said to have been its effect upon national morale and the lessons afforded to the military. The shortest distance between the United States and Japan is through the Aleutian Islands. The great circle route from Seattle to Tokyo is twelve hundred miles shorter than that from San Francisco through Honolulu to Tokyo. The seizure of American territory in Attu and Kiska was given great emphasis in the Japanese press. It colored Japanese propaganda, where it was flaunted as an example of the prowess of Japanese arms and of the uselessness of attempting to interfere with Japan's assumption of her sphere of influence in Asia. In the American press the attack against Dutch Harbor was compared to that against Pearl Harbor and an immediate and complete public release of damage was demanded. Japanese expansion into the Aleutians gave rise to popular clamor in the United States for their expulsion at all cost. American rejoicing over the victory at Midway was tempered by dark foreboding over the possibility of an invasion of Alaska. It may be said, however, that in overall effect on the course of the Pacific War, Japan's initial successes in the Aleutians served only to heighten the resolve of the American people and to further mislead public opinion and generate false confidence within Japan.

Another intangible result of the Aleutian Campaign was its effect upon the probable participation of Russia in the Pacific War. Russia was an ally of the United States in Europe and a potential ally in the Pacific. The probability of Russia's commencing hostilities against Japan depended in some degree upon the possibility of assistance reaching her by seaborne transport. An air route via Nome was in operation and over it was ferried a large number of lend-lease aircraft. The water route passed through the Aleutians and the Kuriles. In order to facilitate a future entry of Russia into the war against Japan it was necessary to secure this water route, which was done to the extent of expelling the Japanese from the Aleutians and weakening and con-taining their forces in the Kuriles.

The military lessons of the Aleutian campaign were of considerable moment. The paucity of United States naval forces in June 1942 caused orders to be given to the task force commander to operate cautiously, under the concept of calculated risk; he was not to hazard his surface fleet unless assured of a disproportionately large return in damage to the enemy. These were difficult orders indeed. He elected to deploy the major portion of his destroyers to hiding places in the fjords of islands around Dutch Harbor so that they might execute a night torpedo attack if the opportunity offered. The principal U.S. naval surface ship strength was held in waters south of Kodiak, almost certainly out of reach of the Japanese but equally beyond range of any promising quarry. The defense of the Aleutians and Alaska was entrusted to air, for which there was the Eleventh Army Air Force of six heavy bombers, twenty medium bombers, and thirty-two fighters, and a navy patrol wing of twenty amphibious flying boats. At the time of the Dutch Harbor raid the Japanese Second Mobile Force was found and attacked, but no damage done to any surface ships. When the occupation of Kiska was discovered, orders were given to bomb the Japanese out. The impracticability of this effort was evident from the course of subsequent events. With thrice the original air strength and two air bases as close as sixty and two hundred miles, respectively, from Kiska, air effort alone did not suffice to drive the Japanese from their honeycomb defense. Although blockaded by air and sea, the Japanese held their much-bombed island outpost, Kiska, until it was outflanked by the amphibious assault and capture of Attu.

Early experience in the Aleutian campaign also developed clearly the disadvantages of the northern short route to Japan. The prevalence of fog in the summer and great storms in the winter was known, but the effect on air operations was not fully appreciated. Significant was the ratio of total theater loss to combat loss in aircraft of the Eleventh Air Force. This ratio was 6.5 to 1, as against 3 to 1 for an average of all Pacific theaters. Reflected in it were unusual hazards due to weather—visibility at base, icing, storm damage, poor maintenance, condition of the runways—and the hazard of operating from a sparse number of airfields strung along a single line of islands which paralleled the direction of the target. Significant also was the number of days upon which successful bombing missions could be flown: for a period of nineteen days—11-30 June 1942—during the early attempt to bomb the Japanese out of Kiska, only six successful heavy bombing missions were completed. Likewise in the critical period of the Attu occupation, weather permitted air bombardment and support on only nine out of twenty days.

Much was learned in the art of building airfields. In an atmosphere of secrecy and urgency, two airfields were built in the vicinity of Dutch Harbor in late winter of 1941-42, and spring of 1942. Completed in four months' time by army engineers, these fields were used to great advantage when the Japanese attacked. However, in the move to Adak, a field was made on this barren island in only fifteen days. In the dead of winter on the island of Amchitka, a fighter strip was in operation a little over a month after the initial landing. Certainly the Aleutians ranked high as a school for the rapid building of air fields.

With prevailing bad visibility the Aleutians early became an experimental and proving ground for airborne search radar. The British ASV equipment, hastily manufactured in the United States, was installed in the search planes of Fleet Air Wing Four beginning in March 1942. By the date of the Japanese attack on Dutch Harbor all the flying boats of that wing were equipped with it. Assisted by this device, search planes were able to locate the Japanese Second Mobile Force and, in at least one instance, to avoid contact with the Japanese fighter patrols. It enabled the weakly armed flying boats to conduct aerial search in darkness and poor visibility, conditions favorable to their defense. Also, in an area so poorly equipped with radio aids, the importance of radar in providing navigational fixes and in permitting instrument letdowns cannot be overemphasized. Without radar the effectiveness of air search would have been reduced to practically nothing. Without it the Japanese gave up as ineffective their flying-boat searches from Kiska. Later in the campaign, radar was made to serve yet another purpose when Ventura search land planes led blind bombing attacks over Kiska.

Unique in the naval history of the Pacific war, the Aleutian campaign provided at the Komandorski battle the only conventional daylight gun duel between opposing surface forces in which air attack was not made. The Japanese had airborne at the scene of the battle one ship-based reconnaissance plane; the United States none. Yet, with victory almost in their hands and a United States heavy cruiser seriously damaged and at one time stopped dead in the water, the Japanese broke off the action for an important, if not governing, reason: fear of imminent air attack. Failure to conduct an air attack is a dark chapter in the United States air effort. The bombers, both heavy and medium, were delayed several hours because they found it necessary to change their bomb load from one of demolition against Kiska to one appropriate for employment against warships. When they arrived at the scene of battle, the Japanese surface fleet had withdrawn and was beyond range.

Despite the fact that the area is one of the most unsuitable in the world for air operations, due to the weather and terrain, aircraft played a dominant role in the North Pacific as they did in all theaters of the war against Japan. The opening blow of the campaign was struck against Dutch Harbor by carrier aircraft of the Japanese Fleet. The first counterblow against the occupation of Kiska was struck by United States flying boats and bombers. The first amphibious moves to the westward were for the purpose of securing airfields so that added pressure from the air might be applied against Japanese holdings. In later stages of the war aircraft maintained a steady though relatively small effort against the Kuriles in order to maintain, in conjunction with submarine patrols and surface ship sweeps, an attrition of shipping and a threat to Japan from the north.[1]

*Admiral Russell graduated from the U.S. Naval Academy in 1926. During World War II he commanded Navy Patrol Squadron 42 in Alaska, a quiet theater until the Japanese hit Dutch Harbor—the day before they hit Midway. Russell retired from the navy in 1965 as a four-star admiral but was recalled to active duty in 1967 and 1968. He was named to the National Museum of Naval Aviation Hall of Honor in 1990.*

---

[1] This paper initially appeared, in substance, as chap. 6, "The Aleutian Campaign," in *The Campaigns of the Pacific War* (Washington, D.C.: Government Printing Office, 1946).

# Theobald Revisited

*William S. Hanable*

## Introduction

REAR ADMIRAL ROBERT A. THEOBALD, UNITED STATES Navy, at worst is cast as the "Colonel Blimp" of World War II in Alaska, a caricature of a military officer—rigid, pompous, incompetent and inflated with self-importance. At best he is cast as an unfortunate, sent to a remote theater with scanty resources to do a difficult job, a man hampered by his own personality and by inter-service rivalries.

The purpose of this paper is to illuminate our view of Theobald. This effort is based on papers Theobald chose to preserve regarding his service in Alaska waters. They are preserved in the archives of the Hoover Institution on War, Revolution, and Peace at Stanford University. That he chose to preserve them is remarkable in that neither his official biography nor his obituary mentions the months in 1942 when he was Commander, Task Force Eight (later called the North Pacific Force), and responsible for the defense of Alaska.[1] This should have been, or could have been, a highlight of his career. Instead it ended that career.

This paper examines the circumstances that brought Theobald to Alaska, the instructions he received and the resources he had to carry those instructions out, his thoughts and actions during his service in Alaska, and his retrospective consideration of his service in Alaska after he had been relieved of command.

## Theobald's First Battle

Robert A. Theobald, born in 1884, began his naval career by graduating from the Naval Academy in the top 10 percent of his class in 1907. This was six years after the academy graduation of Admiral Ernest J. King, who commanded the entire United States Navy in World War II, and two years after the academy graduation of Admiral Chester W. Nimitz, who was Theobald's immediate superior during his tenure as commander of Task Force Eight. These men would ultimately decide Theobald's professional fate.

After graduation Theobald did the things that led him and others to high command during World War II. He was a destroyer captain and battleship gunnery officer, executive officer, and captain. During World War I he saw service on the Atlantic as gunnery officer of the battleship *New York*. His shore tours included student and faculty appointments at the Naval War College, a tour as head of the Naval Post Graduate School, and service in the Chief of Naval Operations' War Plans Division (OP-12). He wrote articles for the *Proceedings* of the U.S. Naval Institute, on subjects such as "Handling Men" and "Loyal Initiative." When the Japanese attacked Pearl Harbor on December 7, 1941, Theobald was type commander for destroyers in the United States Pacific Fleet.[2]

On December 7, 1941, during the Japanese raid, he

---

[1] Theobald's service as Commander, North Pacific Force, is listed in "Transcript of the Author's Naval Career," in his *The Final Secret of Pearl Harbor: the Washington Contribution to the Japanese Attack* (Old Greenwich, Conn.: The Devin-Adair Company, 1954). In that book Theobald suggests that President Franklin Delano Roosevelt withheld information about the pending Japanese attack in order to gain public support for war with Japan.

[2] John Haile Cloe, *The Aleutian Warriors, A History of the 11th Air Force and Fleet Air Wing Four* (Missoula, Mont.: Pictorial Histories Publishing Co., Inc., 1991), pp. 89-90; *U.S. Naval Institute Proceedings Cumulative Index 1874-1977* (Annapolis, Md.: Naval Institute Press, 1982), p. 337.

was in the port of Pearl Harbor.[3]

In April 1942, U.S. Naval Intelligence intercepted radio messages to Toyko from Japanese naval forces concentrating in the western Pacific. The messages requested charts of coastal Alaska waters as far east as Kodiak Island. By early May, references to Attu, Kiska, and Dutch Harbor were appearing in Japanese naval radio traffic. On May 20, naval intelligence intercepted and almost immediately identified the entire Japanese operations order for planned attacks on Midway Island and the Aleutians. A few days later about 90 percent of the intercept was decrypted.[4]

Even before the Japanese operations order for the Midway and Aleutian attacks was intercepted, Nimitz ordered Theobald to the Aleutians as Commander, Task Force Eight. Theobald's charge was, in coordination with the army, to oppose the advance of the enemy in the Aleutians-Alaska area, taking advantage of every favorable opportunity to inflict strong attrition.[5] Theobald started for Alaska on the destroyer *Reid* (DD-369) on May 22, 1942.[6]

When he arrived in Alaska, Theobald was fifty-eight years old. According to a contemporary observer, he was "a jolly old sea-dog type of warrior. A ruddy-faced, gray-haired barrel-chested man, he has an explosive laugh, a quick wit, a broad culture and a voice that booms forth like an organ."[7] Two photographs taken during his Alaska service offer a stark contrast. One, taken ashore, shows a glaring admiral drawn up in front of a chart of the North Pacific. The other, taken aboard ship, shows an affable admiral—hands in pockets—comfortable on the deck of his flagship.

Immediately after arriving at the newly-established Kodiak Naval Base on May 27, Theobald conferred with his army counterpart, Major General Simon Bolivar Buckner, commander of the Alaska Defense Command; Brigadier General William O. Butler, commander of the Eleventh Air Force and (under Theobald) commander of the air component of Task Force Eight; and Captain Leslie E. Gehres, commander of Naval Patrol Wing Four. The four officers discussed Theobald's "estimate of the situation, functions of command, and matériel matters."

This meeting was Theobald's first with the army commander with whom he was to cooperate and with the air officers who were to command Task Force Eight's air components. From this point on he would squabble constantly with the two army generals until he was relieved of his command in December 1942.[9]

Theobald's situation was not impossible. Although the Japanese naval forces that were going to attack the Aleutians were superior to his naval forces, Theobald had land-based air power under his command and knowledge of the enemy's intentions.

The Japanese forces that Theobald faced included two carriers with a combined complement of forty fighters, twenty-one torpedo bombers, and twenty-one dive bombers; three heavy cruisers; and five destroyers. The Japanese also had two light cruisers and five destroyers in the far western Aleutians. These ships were escorting landing parties that would seize Attu and Kiska islands.[10]

To counter the Japanese forces, Theobald had an air striking group that included seventy-five fighters and thirty-one army bombers strung out between Anchorage and Umnak (twelve P-40 fighters at Umnak; twenty-one P-40s and twelve B-26 bombers at Cold Bay; seventeen P-40s, twelve F4F fighters, and five B-17 heavy bombers at Kodiak; and twenty-five P-38 fighters and fourteen B-26s at Anchorage). This group was supplemented by an air search group that included twenty-three navy PBYs, two army B17s, and two army LB-30s (the naval version of the B-24 heavy bomber). While assigned to the air search group, these aircraft could be, and some were, used in an attack role. Also available to Theobald were a Canadian fighter squadron and a Canadian reconnaissance squadron at Yakutat.[11]

Theobald's naval warships included the heavy cruis-

---

[3] Information on Theobald's presence at Pearl Harbor is given in Rear Admiral Husband E. Kimmel's introduction to *The Final Secret of Pearl Harbor*, p. vi.

[4] W.J. Holmes, *Doubled-Edged Secrets: U.S. Naval Intelligence Operations in the Pacific During World War II* (Annapolis, Md.: Naval Institute Press, 1979), pp. 88-89.

[5] CINCPACFLT Operation Order 28-42, May 11, 1942, p. 2, in the Theobald Papers, Hoover Institution on War, Revolution, and Peace (hereafter Theobald Papers).

[6] "A War Diary, Commander North Pacific Force, Task Force Eight, United States Pacific Fleet" (hereafter War Diary), May 22-May 31, 1942, in Box 7, Theobald Papers.

[7] Joseph Driscoll, *War Discovers Alaska* (Philadelphia: J.B. Lippincott Company, 1944), p. 99.

[8] War Diary, May 27, 1942; Letter, June 16, 1942, Theobald to Nimitz, in Theobald Papers.

[9] Brian Garfield, *The Thousand-Mile War, World War II in Alaska and the Aleutians* (New York: Doubleday & Company, Inc., 1969); Cloe, *The Aleutian Warriors*; William S. Hannable, "The Struggle for Control of Air Power in the North Pacific, 1942," paper presented at the Eleventh Naval History Symposium, United States Naval Academy (Annapolis, Md.: October 1993).

[10] Mitsu Fuchida and Masatake Okumiya, *Midway, The Battle That Doomed Japan, The Japanese Navy's Story* (Annapolis, Md.: Naval Institute Press, 1955), p. 82.

[11] Commander, North Pacific Force and Area, *Administrative History of the North Pacific Area, 1 August 1940-14 August 1945*, pp. 103-104 (here-

Vice Admiral Charles S. Freeman, right, Commander, Pacific Northern Naval Coastal Frontier, greets Rear Admiral Robert A. Theobald, Commander, Task Force Eight, at the Kodiak Naval Air Station in August 1942. *(Photo No. 80-G-24997, National Archives, College Park, Md.)*

ers *Indianapolis* and *Louisville*; the light cruisers *Nashville*, *St. Louis*, and *Honolulu*; the modern destroyers *Case*, *Reid, Gridley*, and *McCall*; and the old destroyers *Sands*, *Kant, Dent, Humphreys, Gilmer*, and *Talbot*. He also had at his disposal six "S" class submarines, twenty-one light surface craft grouped into a surface search group, and two oilers in a tanker group.[12]

On balance, Theobald had the resources to inflict punishing attrition on the Japanese. To be successful in this he had to employ his forces properly. He also had to hope that the "friction" of warfare did not work in favor of the Japanese.

What did happen was that Theobald, provided with detailed information about Japanese plans, chose to suspect that information. The operation plan he drafted while en route to Alaska and issued after his meeting with Buckner, Butler, and Gehres, assumed that the

Japanese intended to seize bases in the Umnak-Dutch Harbor-Cold Bay area to prevent bombing of their homeland and as prelude to further operations in Alaska. Umnak (to the west of Dutch Harbor) or Cold Bay (to the east of Dutch Harbor) would be seized first, according to Theobald. Once one of these areas was taken, the Japanese would then attack Dutch Harbor and the area not initially attacked.[13] Theobald's operations plan rejected the intelligence he had received indicating that the Japanese planned to attack Dutch Harbor and to occupy Adak, Attu, or Kiska.[14]

Theobald's rationale for ignoring the intelligence he received was explained in a May 29, 1942, memorandum to the group commanders in his task force. The Japanese, he wrote,

have been issuing radio orders and instructions

---

after *Administrative History*). This history is available in hard copy at the Navy Department Library, Washington, D.C., and on microfiche as vol. 156, *United States Naval Administrative Histories of World War II*.

[12] *Administrative History*, pp. 103-104.

[13] Commander Task Force Eight (CTF 8) Operation Plan 1-42, pp. 3-4, in Box 7, Theobald Papers.

[14] Rear Admiral Robert A. Theobald, Memorandum, May 29, 1942, "For Task Group Commanders Present at Kodiak," in War Diary, May 22-May 31, 1942, Box 7, Theobald Collection.

concerning composition and objectives of a Japanese force destined for operations in Alaska.... The continued repetition of the messages by radio transmission leads to the inevitable conclusion that the Japanese desire certain information to reach us in the event that we are breaking their codes.[15]

His analysis went on to point out that "Having used two weeks of radio transmissions to bring our naval forces into the Alaskan theater, they [the Japanese] now appear to desire the presence of that force well to the westward." This was intended either to divert American forces from the true Japanese objective or to lure the American forces "into an area where they could be trapped between two strong Japanese Forces."[16]

This was not a new position for the admiral. Four months earlier he had written an appreciation on intelligence for his own files. In it he justified his skepticism toward radio intercept intelligence by citing the attack on Pearl Harbor. On December 1, 1941, he wrote, naval intelligence had placed most if not all of the Japanese carriers in their home waters or in the southwestern Pacific. "This deduction is now a matter of history. These carriers must have been halfway between Japan and Hawaii on December 1, 1941."[17]

This also was not a position that the admiral would readily abandon. On June 10, after the Japanese attack on Dutch Harbor and the occupation of Attu and Kiska had proved the assumptions in his operation order to be wrong, he issued Annex F to that order. In the annex he restated his belief that the Japanese activity in the western Aleutians was designed to draw his naval forces to the west where they could be trapped and destroyed.[18]

Having convinced himself that much of the intelligence he received was intended to deceive, Theobald concluded that the Umnak-Dutch Harbor-Cold Bay area was the probable primary objective of the impending Japanese attack. This, he wrote, gave greater strength to the possibility of a Japanese attack in the Kodiak-Kenai Peninsula area.[19]

Deriving his disposition of his forces from his assessment of true Japanese intentions, Theobald placed the main body of his naval task force in the approaches to Kodiak and the Alaska Peninsula at 51 degrees 5 minutes North, 151 degrees 20 minutes West on June 3, 1942. On the one hand, this located them away from Kodiak, where the Japanese might find them at anchor, and in position to steam toward the enemy task force once it was located. On the other hand, this placed the cruisers, his only heavy naval force, hundreds of miles from the announced intended location of the Japanese attack in the Aleutians. The cruisers were to "exploit favorable opportunity to deliver attrition attacks on enemy forces."[20]

Since Theobald chose to go to sea in his flagship, the Nashville, this also placed him hundreds of miles away from his headquarters, his air search and striking groups, and the scene of the Japanese attack that did occur. As he radioed to Nimitz just before his departure, "Hereafter cannot communicate without breaking radio silence from sea which I desire to avoid if possible."[21]

Theobald placed his "Destroyer Striking Group" in Makushkin Bay on the west coast of Unalaska Island.[22] He ordered the commanding officer of the destroyer striking group to attack the Japanese force if it was located, although knowing that such an attack would probably result in the loss of most if not all of the destroyers. In justifying this decision he noted that he was asking a great deal of Patrol Wing Four and had insisted that as many army aircraft as possible be based at Cold Bay and Umnak. "It seemed essential to me that I use every weapon of attrition which I had." On the other hand, he wrote later, "There was nothing I could do with the cruiser force in the face of enemy carriers." Army and navy bombers would have to sink or heavily damage the enemy carriers before Theobald's cruisers could join the fight.[23]

His submarine group was to station two boats in the southern approach to Umnak Pass, two boats north of Umnak Island, and two in the approaches to Cold Bay.[24]

By June 1, one B-17, six B-26s, and seventeen P-40s were in place at Umnak, positioned to defend Dutch Harbor. There were also eight radar-equipped PBYs located in or around Dutch Harbor. An additional six B-

[15] Theobald, Memorandum, May 29, 1942, "For Task Group Commanders Present at Kodiak," in Box 7, Theobald Collection, p. 1.

[16] Theobald, May 29, 1942, p. 5.

[17] Theobald, "Intelligence," January 1942, in "War Estimates File," Box 12, Theobald Collection.

[18] Annex F to Commander Task Force Eight, North Pacific Force, Operation Plan No. 442, "Appreciation of Alaskan Situation as of June 10, 1942," in Box 7, Theobald Collection.

[19] Theobald, May 29, 1942, p. 5.

[20] CTF 8 Operations Plan 3-42, May 31, 1942.

[21] Theobald, radio, 012103 June 1942, in War Diary, June 1, 1942-June 30, 1942.

[22] The Case, Reid, Sands, Kane, and Dent. Theobald kept the Humphreys with his main body, which included the Nashville, St. Louis, Honolulu, Indianapolis, Louisville, Gridley, McCall, Gilmer, and Talbot.

[23] Theobald, letter, June 16, 1942, to Admiral Nimitz, in Box 7, Theobald Collection.

[24] CTF 8 Operations Plan No. 142, pp. 4-8 and CTF8 to Commander, Destroyer Striking Group, radio, May 31, 1942, in Box 7, Theobald Collection.

26s and sixteen P-40s and more PBYs were at Cold Bay.[25] His operation plan also said that as soon as the expected enemy task force was located, additional army bombers would be sent from Anchorage and Kodiak to Cold Bay and Umnak.[26]

The critical test of Theobald's operation plan came on June 3, 1942. Although expected and searched for, the attacking Japanese force was able to approach Dutch Harbor without detection—due to weather and garbled transmission from the one navy patrol aircraft that did sight them. On the morning of that day Japanese aircraft from the carriers *Junyo* and *Ryujo* bombed Dutch Harbor and Unalaska. When Dutch Harbor reported the bombing, army fighters to the east at Cold Bay scrambled. Army fighters at Umnak—to the west of Dutch Harbor and Unalaska—did not receive word of the attack in progress due to poor communications.[27]

The Japanese renewed their attack on Dutch Harbor on June 4. As the carrier aircraft returned to their ships, army P-40s based at Umnak rose to attack them and destroyed several. At the same time, navy PBYs from Cold Bay and Dutch Harbor and army bombers from Cold Bay and Umnak attempted to attack the Japanese carriers. Hampered by weather, opposed by Japanese fighters, and hindered by improvised weaponry (navy torpedoes slung under army aircraft), the bombers did little damage to the Japanese task force despite their aggressive and brave aircrews.

The destroyer striking group in Makushkin Bay, for reasons that are still not clear, remained anchored there. Japanese planes returning from the June 3 attack on Dutch Harbor sighted them. Twenty-four aircraft from the Japanese ships returned to attack them but were foiled by bad weather.[28]

Theobald found his inability to communicate while aboard his flagship to be intolerable. First he sent the destroyer *Humphreys* into Kodiak with a memorandum to Butler, Gehres, and navy captain Ralph Parker, commander of the Alaska sector of the Northwest Sea Frontier. In it he complained of Butler's decision not to send planes from Kodiak to Cold Bay after the Japanese carriers and their escorts had been located, "unless other-wise directed." Theobald, at sea and under radio silence, was of course in no position to respond to Butler's message.[29]

The admiral would later cite three reasons for his decision to take his headquarters to sea: (1) There was no flag officer available to whom he could entrust the command of his cruiser task group. (2) Just before Theobald had left for the North Pacific, Vice Admiral Leary in the South Pacific had been rebuked for establishing his headquarters on shore. (3) "Prior to this war no one had ever envisaged the exercise of command of sea-going units from headquarters ashore."[30]

When the air attacks on the Japanese carriers and their accompanying cruisers appeared to be ineffective, Theobald himself went to Kodiak in the *Nashville*. He arrived there on the morning of June 5 and met with Butler. He asked Butler to direct his air units not to await specific orders before attacking enemy ships within range from Cold Bay and Umnak, and also to order concentrated, rather than isolated, attacks. Back aboard the *Nashville*, Theobald then rejoined his other cruisers in the North Pacific.[31]

Theobald's operation plan, his decision to take his flag to sea where he was incommunicado, and the ineffective response to the Japanese attacks on Dutch Harbor on June 3 and 4 drew criticism at the highest levels of naval command. Serious consideration was given to relieving him immediately. Admiral Freeman, who came north to inspect the Alaska Sector, Northwest Sea Frontier, was warned that he should stand by to replace Theobald. Only after Freeman returned to Seattle and filed a positive report about Theobald were plans to relieve him shelved.[32]

His relief, however, was only a few months away. The squabbling with army generals eventually demanded the attention of Army Chief of Staff General George C. Marshall, and Navy Commander-in-Chief Admiral Ernest J. King. Along with lackluster performance, these factors resulted in Theobald's banishment to a shore establishment in December 1942.

A December 8, 1942, letter from Nimitz relieved him. From Alaska Theobald went to the Boston Navy Yard

---

[25] Stetson Conn, with Rose C. Engelman and Bryon Fairchild, *The United States Army in World War II, The Western Hemisphere, Guarding the United States and Its Outposts* (Washington, D.C.: Office of the Chief of Military History, Department of the Army, 1964), p. 261.

[26] Paragraph 3(c), CTF Operation Plan No. 142, in War Diary, May 22-May 31, 1942, in Box 7, Theobald Collection.

[27] See Cloe, *The Aleutian Warriors*, pp. 118-134, for a detailed account of the Japanese attack and the American response to it.

[28] Fuchida and Okumiya, *The Battle That Doomed Japan*, pp. 140-141.

[29] Theobald, memorandum, "Notes on Operation of Task Force EIGHT," June 3, 1942, to Brigadier General Butler, U.S. Army; Captain R.C. Parker, U.S. Navy; Captain L.E. Gehres, U.S. Navy, attached to War Diary, June 4, 1942, in Box 7, Theobald Collection.

[30] Theobald, "Written But Never Sent," November 6, 1942, in "Navy Department Correspondence and Orders, 1940-1949," in Box 10, Theobald Collection.

[31] Theobald, letter to Admiral Nimitz, June 16, 1942.

[32] Admiral E.J. King, Commander-in-Chief, United States Fleet, letter, September 28, 1942, to Rear Admiral R.A. Theobald, in "Navy Department Correspondence and Orders 1940-1949," Box 10, Theobald Collection.

where he served as Commandant, First Naval District. Two years later the chief of naval personnel advised him that a naval retiring board had determined "that you are incapacitated for active duty by reason of physical disability incurred in line of duty. Retirement will be effective 1 February 1945."[33] Theobald died in 1957.

## A Retrospective Assessment

Historians, like other people, are sometimes influenced in their assessments by the likability of historical figures. Theobald, whatever his persona during his lifetime, has not left an appealing record. His plans and estimates all too often seem to have been written to demonstrate his own brilliance. His correspondence to his subordinates is frequently acerbic. His correspondence to his superiors is frequently defensive.

Despite these characteristics, there are some things to admire about Rear Admiral Robert A. Theobald. There can be no question of his personal or moral courage, both attributes required of a military leader. Although his decision to go to sea before the Japanese attacked Dutch Harbor in June 1942 can, and has been, criticized on other grounds, it reflected the instinct of a naval officer who knew his place in war to be at sea. His pre-attack insistence on aggressive air attacks and orders for a possibly suicidal destroyer attack on the Japanese reflected the moral courage required of someone who has to send others into risky situations.

Even Theobald's operation plan, although it did not achieve the desired result, had merit—despite its intricate and ultimately flawed assessment of the intelligence with which he had been provided. He was the one who insisted on concentration of air assets as far to the west as possible; the one who positioned his destroyers where they might have attacked the Japanese carriers and cruisers; and the one who positioned his own cruisers where they were not likely to be surprised by Japanese aircraft but could intervene to protect either Kodiak or Dutch Harbor.

Where Theobald failed in his first battle was to provide leadership when required. Although he would later rationalize it, his decision to go to sea and effectively abdicate his role as commander, was a bad one. Had he kept his headquarters ashore he might have speeded additional air assets to Cold Bay and Umnak. He might also have launched the projected destroyer attack on the enemy carriers, something that might have succeeded, in view of the poor visibility and the availability of land-based air cover for the destroyers. He might also have been able to direct his cruisers toward the enemy if he had had a clearer picture of what was going on, something he could not obtain at sea in radio silence.

*William S. Hanable is the deputy director of the Joint Federal-State Commission on Policies and Programs Affecting Alaska Natives. He was Deputy Command Historian for the Eleventh Air Force/Alaskan Air Command from 1989 to 1992.*

---

[33] Chief of Naval Personnel, letter to Rear Admiral Robert A. Theobald, October 11, 1945, in "Navy Department Correspondence and Orders 1940-1949," Box 10, Theobald Papers.

# The Recapture of Attu

*Fern Chandonnet*

JUST BEFORE DAWN ON MAY 11, 1943, TROOPS OF THE Seventh Scout Company of the Seventh Infantry Division paddled inflatable rafts away from their submarines and toward Beach Scarlet, on Attu Island. Thus began the first island amphibious assault by the U.S. Army in World War II.

The scouts landed some nine miles northwest of the mission's ultimate objective, the main Japanese base at Chichagof Harbor. Their arrival was unopposed. But if the soldiers imagined that the eerie quiet that met them was an augur of the course of events to come, they were soon disabused of the notion: As they slogged inland through boggy tundra with their hundred-pound packs, they turned to watch their own warplanes mistakenly strafe the landing craft they had left behind on the beach.

The War Department had called on the Seventh Infantry Division to recapture Attu. The unit, based in California and under the command of Major General Albert Brown, was a motorized division and desert-trained. After undergoing amphibious training in April 1943, the Seventh left San Francisco on troop transports.

Early intelligence reports estimated Japanese strength on Attu to be five hundred second-rate troops. Just prior to the American landing operation, however, intelligence revised the figure to fifteen hundred. And the Japanese soldiers themselves would eventually force a revision of the qualitative assessment.

By midday on May 11 the division's reconnaissance troop stepped off its transport at Scarlet Beach and marched inland to join the scouts as a provisional battalion. Four miles east, at Holtz Bay, the First Battalion

came ashore at Beach Red. And the Second and Third battalions of the Seventeenth Regiment arrived for the main attack six miles south of Chichagof Harbor at Massacre Bay—designated Beaches Blue and Yellow.

At 1800 hours the southbound First Battalion was stopped short of a hill objective by enemy fire.

An hour later the main force was compelled to halt as well, pinned down by a fusillade from the sharp ridges in front of them. Japanese soldiers had dug themselves into the high ground, their positions further obscured by the Aleutian mist.

The Third Battalion attempted an encircling movement to reach Jarmin Pass to the west, but stopped its thrust after incurring heavy losses.

By the end of D-day, thirty-five hundred American soldiers had landed on Attu: four hundred at Beach Scarlet, eleven hundred at Beach Red, and two thousand at Beaches Blue and Yellow.

Initially, planners had speculated that the mission would take three days to complete. The grim fact was that before U.S. troops could secure Chichagof Harbor, they would have to endure nineteen days of furious combat. The men were to fight a tough, resolute enemy under conditions of wretched weather, unforgiving terrain, and sometimes nonexistent supplies and communications.

Even with reinforcements and naval and air support, U.S. troops failed to achieve Jarmin Pass again on the second day. By evening, a casualty report revealed forty-four Americans dead.

By May 15, Japanese in the northern sector withdrew southward to Moore Ridge. Northern Force troops pur-

Top, a pre-war view of Attu village, on Chichagof Harbor. *(Photograph courtesy Command Historian's Office, Alaskan Command)*
Above, Japanese on Attu. *(Captured Japanese photograph, courtesy Command Historian's Office, Alaskan Command)*
Right, Japanese soldiers on Attu, 1943. *(Captured Japanese photograph, No. B 80-1-44, courtesy Anchorage Museum of History and Art)*

Top, A *maru* lies anchored at Holtz Bay. *(Photograph courtesy Command Historian's Office, Alaskan Command)*

Above, a field piece fires on Japanese positions during the battle for Attu. *(Acc. No. 70-11-41, Hanna Call Collection, Rasmuson Library, University of Alaska Fairbanks)*

Left, U.S. sailors enjoy a hot meal on a beach in the Holtz Bay area, May 29, 1943. *(Acc. 70-11-47N, Hanna Hall Collection, Rasmuson Library, University of Alaska Fairbanks)*

Right, a mop-up squad examines a Japanese gun emplacement on D-day, Attu. The smoke is from just-detonated grenades. *(Acc. No. 70-11-33N, Hanna Call Collection, Rasmuson Library, University of Alaska Fairbanks)*

Far right, American troops fire at Japanese soldiers dug in on a ridge, May 11, 1943. *(Photo No. B 75-90-21, Anchorage Museum of History and Art)*

Below, on May 14, 1943, American troops carry a wounded comrade back to the beach. *(Photo No. B 80-75-30, Anchorage Museum of History and Art)*

sued the retreating enemy but were slowed by fire from their quarry, who again had attained the high ground. Worse, the Americans were stopped abruptly when their own bombers mistakenly hit their advancing line.

On May 16, the Northern Force gained a foothold on the north end of Moore Ridge. The greatly outnumbered Japanese withdrew that night toward Chichagof Harbor.

On the following day, troops from the Seventeenth Regiment, in the southern sector, discovered that the enemy had withdrawn from Jarmin Pass as well. Amer-ican soldiers finally occupied the pass.

The linkup of Northern and Southern Forces on May 18 signalled a change in the fortunes of U.S. troops. Still, it would be another eleven days of hard fighting and heavy casualties before American soldiers drew the noose around the remaining Japanese at Chichagof Harbor. The enemy had retreated, it was true, but they left manned machine-gun and mortar nests on the heights to bedevil the advancing Americans.

On May 29, the remaining Japanese at Chichagof Harbor, about eight hundred strong, mounted a desper-

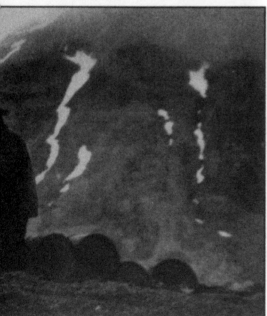

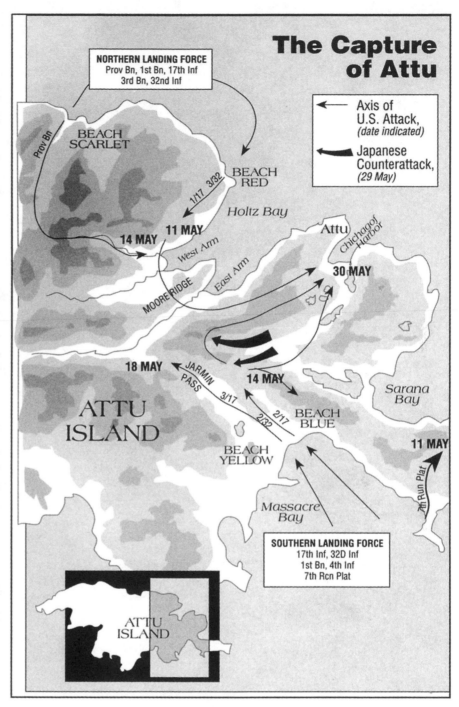

**The Capture of Attu**

NORTHERN LANDING FORCE
Prov Bn, 1st Bn, 17th Inf
3rd Bn, 32nd Inf

→ Axis of U.S. Attack, *(date indicated)*

← Japanese Counterattack, *(29 May)*

BEACH SCARLET

Prov Bn

1/17 3/32

BEACH RED

Holtz Bay

Attu

Chichagof Harbor

14 MAY 11 MAY

West Arm

30 MAY

East Arm

MOORE RIDGE

18 MAY JARMIN PASS 3/17

14 MAY

Sarana Bay

ATTU ISLAND

2/17 2/32

BEACH BLUE

11 MAY

7th Rcn Plat

BEACH YELLOW

Massacre Bay

SOUTHERN LANDING FORCE
17th Inf, 32D Inf
1st Bn, 4th Inf
7th Rcn Plat

ATTU ISLAND

ate counterattack in an effort to break through the encircling American line. The initial thrust succeeded and the Japanese overran two command posts and a medical installation. A hastily organized defense of Engineer Hill halted the offensive. Through the night the Japanese repeatedly attacked the American position and were just as regularly mowed down by the U.S. defenders. By morning, Japanese bodies covered the slopes of the hill. An estimated five hundred of the attackers had committed suicide. The Japanese garrison on Attu was no more.

Of a U.S. force that eventually totaled more than 15,000 men, 549 had been killed, another 1,148 wounded, and some 2,100 were taken out of action by disease—trench foot, mainly—and nonbattle injuries. Most of the latter were exposure cases brought about by bad weather and poor clothing.

Of the Japanese garrison, 28 men lived to surrender. American soldiers counted 2,351 enemy dead. Hundreds more were presumed to have been buried in the hills.

Both sides paid dearly for Attu.

# The First Special Service Force

*Alastair Neely*

*"... the Force never in all its service yielded an inch of ground nor left a battle with an indecisive conclusion. The Force won everything it fought for..."*

The Independent Record
Helena, Montana
Sunday, August 7, 1955

CONCEIVED IN THE DARK DAYS OF 1942, THE FIRST Special Service Force was in existence for only two-and-a-half years, but during that brief period it amassed an illustrious combat record. Starting from scratch, the Canadian and American governments created a multinational force which was trained in commando techniques and which would eventually be deployed in both the Pacific and Mediterranean theatres of operation. During its brief history, the unit participated in two invasions and four major campaigns.

Two books, *The First Special Service Force: A War History of the North Americans, 1942-1944,*[1] and *The Devil's Brigade,*[2] and a major motion picture produced by David L. Wolper, have paid homage to this unit. Unfortunately, the Force's Alaska operations are covered only in short sections in each of these books and are omitted in the feature film. While the unit was in Alaska from July 23 to August 22, 1943, the experience gained as part of the Kiska invasion force provided invaluable lessons and saved many Force members'

lives in future operations.

In order to comprehend the Force's Kiska accomplishments, it is important to understand the unit's original mission. Take three overstrength regiments; add specially designed equipment ("the Weasel"); mix in commando training and exotic locations such as Montana, Norway, northern Italy, and Rumania; add snow; and you have the makings of a great B war movie—or an eccentric plan called Operation Plough. The Force was the end result of a plan devised for establishing a special mobile force that would take part in commando operations in occupied Europe in the "fourth element" of warfare—snow.[3] The plan called for widespread sabotage of enemy installations just prior to the planned invasion of Europe in the spring of 1943. Due to political and practical considerations, the plan was cancelled and, at the time of the planning for the Kiska invasion, the Force was without a mission.

The first mention of the Force's participation in the invasion of Kiska was from the Combined Chiefs of Staff meeting at the Trident Conference, May 12-25, 1943, in Washington, D.C.[4] This conference was under way as the reports of bitter fighting on Attu were beginning to come in. The invasion of Kiska and what to do with the F.S.S.F. were listed as separate items on the agenda. At the conference, on May 24, final approval was given for the invasion of Kiska and Canadian participation was

---

[1] R.D. Burhans, *The First Special Service Force: A War History of the North Americans, 1942-1944,* (Washington: Infantry Journal Press, 1947).

[2] R.H. Adleman and G. Walton, *The Devil's Brigade,* (Philadelphia: Chilton Books, 1966).

[3] D. Lampe, *Pyke: The Unknown Genius,* (London: Evans Brothers Ltd., 1959).

[4] C.P. Stacey, *Official History of the Canadian Army in the Second World War: Six Years of War,* (Ottawa: Queen's Printer, 1966).

sought.[5] This was to be in the form of both a Canadian brigade, and naval and air force support for the invasion forces. In the months leading up to this conference, the Force's mission had been altered three times. First, they were to land in the Caucasus Mountains; second they were to be shipped to New Guinea; and third they were earmarked for the invasion of Sicily, code-name Operation Husky. To assist the Kiska invasion and to give the unit much-needed battle experience, the Americans suggested that it be deployed to the Aleutians. The request for the use of the Force was a separate issue and did not enter into the negotiations with the Canadian and American governments over the participation of the Thirteenth Infantry Brigade in the operation.

As a result of the Canadian content of the unit, permission had to be elicited from the Department of National Defence prior to the unit's being committed to the invasion. In advance of a formal request, on June 11, 1943, the War Committee of the Canadian Cabinet approved the use of the Canadian troops assigned to the Force in the invasion of Kiska.[6]

Orders were issued and the Force transported by three trains from Fort Ethan Allen in Vermont to San Francisco, California, with the first train departing on June 28, 1943. For security purposes, each train took a different route and observed security measures along the way. All trains arrived in San Francisco by Sunday, July 3, and equipment was off-loaded for transport to Camp McDowell on Angel Island, within sight of Alcatraz and the Golden Gate Bridge.[7]

It was here on July 4, 1943, that officers of the regiments received their first detailed briefing about the mission from Major General Charles H. Corlett, commanding officer of Amphibious Training Force Nine. The officers and sergeants were told what was known at that time about Kiska. On the island, there were approximately twelve thousand Japanese troops, who had had almost a year to prepare the defenses. Based on the experience at Attu, the prevailing opinion was that it would be a hard campaign.[8]

The next six days were taken up with replacing and issuing new equipment to the combat regiments and the loading of two Liberty ships—the SS *Nathaniel Wyeth* and the SS *John B. Floyd*—which were to transport them to the Aleutians. Anti-gas clothing was also issued along with new footwear. A medical examination of sorts was given to the troops on July 9 to see if they were fit to go overseas. The exam involved only taking the troops' temperatures (Battalion War Diary, July 1943). While at

United States and Canadian troops disembark at Kiska, August 15, 1943. *(National Archives of Canada, courtesy of Command Historian's Office, Alaskan Command)*

Fort McDowell, no leaves were allowed, for security purposes. As with any unit going overseas, there was a rush to purchase money orders and to buy personal items from the camp store.

On July 11, the Force set sail from San Francisco for the Aleutians as part of a convoy of seven transports and four destroyers and almost immediately it would seem that most of the unit became seasick. Total Force complement going overseas was 2,460. The ratio of Canadians to Americans in the combat regiments was forty to sixty. The service battalion consisted entirely of American personnel except for one Canadian officer and a sergeant who looked after Canadians affairs. Once at sea, a more detailed briefing was held on board for officers, describing the mission and for the first time this information was passed along to the men. On one of the ships—due to the rolling seas—the bunks over a hundred men collapsed. There were no serious injuries (Battalion War Diary, July 1943).

Conditions were poor aboard the ships during the voyage north and there seems to have been concern

[5] Ibid.

[6] Ibid.

[7] *First Canadian Special Services Battalion War Diary* (hereafter cited as Battalion War Diary), July 1942.

[8] Burhans, *A War History*, 1947.

among Force officers, especially Col. Adams, about discipline among the men. Discipline improved with the development of a regular routine after the men had been at sea for several days (Battalion War Diary, July 1943). As a result of the cramped quarters on the Liberty ships, there was no room for exercise. Therefore the meals for the men were cut back to two per day and consisted of a mid-morning snack and supper. By July 15 there were only a few cases of seasickness reported among the troops.

Aboard ship, the men were given instruction on how to identify Japanese ranks, useful phrases, and camouflage, and were able to inspect captured Japanese firearms. On July 19 the convoy duty was taken over by four destroyers from Dutch Harbor, Alaska. Upon entering Alaska waters, men of the Force were posted for submarine and aircraft watches.

At 2200 hours, the convoy dropped anchor at Adak. The ships were still observing blackout procedures, but the men of the Force were amazed that the same regulations were not being applied to the island. Adak originally was going to be the base of operations for the unit until it was discovered that the bivouac area selected was not suitable. Adak Island was the headquarters of the Canadian Thirteenth Infantry Brigade Group, which had recently arrived.[9] During the operations, there was very little contact between the two Canadian groups. Operating as an American unit, the Force reported through their change of command. From there, the Liberty ships pressed on with a destroyer and destroyer escort to Amchitka, 170 miles west. On July 24 the ships entering the Harbor at Amchitka disembarked their troops. From port to their bivouac area was a five-mile march and a large number of the troops dropped out along the way. They were carrying their full field kit and seventy pounds of additional equipment and supplies. The weight of the equipment and the fact they had been confined to ships for fifteen days contributed to the higher-than-average dropout rate (Battalion War Diary, July 1943).

To set up their camp the troops had to dig between one to four feet into the tundra to find solid ground on which to pitch their tents. Each tent slept between five and ten men, with one small stove issued per tent. Fortunately, the two days it took to set up their base were lovely days, bright and warm (Battalion War Diary, July 1943).

The plan was to have the Force get acclimatized to the environment and—it was hoped—to have three weeks of training before the invasion took place. As a result of

their recent amphibious training and the high state of readiness, the Force trained independently of other units.[10] Training objectives prior to the invasion were: (a) improve ability for sustained operation in the field under adverse conditions; (b) improve ability to operate over terrain typical of this locality; (c) improve combat firing techniques; and (d) improve amphibious techniques (Battalion War Diary, July 1943).

On July 27, route marches began to get the men accustomed to walking over the tundra and traversing the landscape. For the next several days, the words "fog," "raw," "occasional drizzles," "heavy rain," and "wind" punctuate the unit's war diary (Battalion War Diary, July - August 1943). As a result of the limited training space, the three regiments were rotated. For example, if a unit was involved in rubber boat and landing craft practice, the other two regiments would be on route marches or the firing range. Since the Force had its own service battalion, a lot of the everyday housekeeping routine could be done by this unit. Thus the regiments were able to do five to six weeks training in three. Their training involved amphibious maneuvers, using both landing craft and rubber boats, weapons practice, shoreline bluff climbing, demolitions, hand-to-hand combat, bayonet, compass, conditioning marches, and first aid.[11]

Three incidents from their training exercises on Amchitka highlight particular problems of fighting in this climate. On July 30, while training with the navy on rubber boat deployment a thousand yards offshore, the ramp of a Landing Craft Transport was lowered to allow the boats to be launched. The ship promptly sank and members of the Force had to be rescued from the water (Battalion War Diary, July 1943). Even though this was the middle of summer, there was always the problem of exposure to the elements. On August 5, the First Regiment started its two-day march carrying full battle equipment in an attempt to simulate combat conditions. The weather turned so foggy and rainy that instead of navigating by compass the regiment returned to camp the next day following the power lines in single file so as not to get lost (Battalion War Diary, August 1943). This helped to teach them about what equipment they should carry, the types of clothing they should take, and how to keep it dry. On August 6, the Second Regiment was scheduled to go on the same type of march, but did not depart that day as 150 of the men were considered medically unfit (Battalion War Diary, August 1943).

On August 9, the regiments received their combat assignments. The First and Third Regiments were

---

[9] D. Hist., File 595.013 [D2].

[10] Burhans, *A War History*, 1947.

[11] D. Hist., File 145.3009 [D7].

assigned the role of leading the invasion forces ashore. Landing five hours before the main force, their role was to mark the beaches, clear obstacles, mark beach exits, and secure a safe landing area. The First Regiment was to land on D-day and the Third Regiment on D-day plus one. The Second Regiment was to act as a mobile reserve and parachute onto Kiska in support of the other two regiments or any unit needing assistance. On August 13, an officer and an NCO made a practice jump to test conditions and equipment. Senior officers were flown over Kiska so that they could see what their objectives were and to familiarize themselves with the terrain (Battalion War Diary, August 1943).

By August 12, all regiments had finished their training and were preparing for the invasion. At this time, the units were joined by observers from the U.S. Navy, Marines, artillery, and sixty-four officers and men from the Alaskan Scouts (Battalion War Diary, August 1943). The Alaskan Scouts were attached to the Force because of their knowledge of the land and to assist in the completion of the mission wherever possible. On August 12th, Radio Tokyo announced the date for the Kiska landing to be August 15, 1943. Since this was the correct date for the invasion, some in the Force worried that information on their landing beaches and plans had been compromised.

The Force planned to travel light and to have supplies parachuted to them. The men carried two-thirds of one Field Ration K and two-thirds of one Field Ration D. Johnson machine guns were substituted in lieu of rocket launchers, and flame throwers were not to be taken. Each man was issued four grenades and each company one package of explosives (Battalion War Diary, August 1943). Other supplies and equipment would be parachuted to them as the invasion continued. Field bags would be limited to mess gear, toilet articles, socks, towel, sleeping pack, sweater, and poncho. No vehicles were assigned to the Force as part of the operation. The Weasel, which had been specially designed to operate in this type of environment, was assigned to other invasion units.[12]

It was understood that casualties would be the responsibility of the medical personnel and supply battalion. As reported in the operational orders, "No soldier will delay the execution of his battle mission to turn aside to assist wounded" (Battalion War Diary, August 1943). The supply battalion had been specially set up for this type of mission and it would be their responsibility to relieve the fighting forces of the day-to-day activities of transporting the wounded, carrying supplies, and preparing meals. This would allow the three combat regiments to concentrate on their mission. The dead were to be removed as quickly as possible from the battle field and buried according to procedures set out by Graves Registration.[13] This is very interesting, given that with the Canadian involvement in the Force no accommodation was made for the return of bodies to the Canadian government. Any Canadian casualties were to be buried alongside the Americans.

At 0900 hours on August 14, the First Regiment set sail from Amchitka and the Third soon followed. Fitted with parachutes, the Second Regiment was ordered to remain on alert. Intelligence provided as to what to expect from the Japanese was very limited. The unit had maps and aerial photographs, but that was all. An S2 Estimate of the Enemy Situation prepared on August 12, 1943, by First Lieutenant Finn W. Roll of the Force draws the following conclusions:

a) The enemy may defend Kiska Island and Little Kiska. The enemy may effect a withdrawal.

b) All indications are that the enemy will defend the island from strongly prepared positions, with the best of his fighting ability. Evacuation or withdrawal from the Island is improbable due to superior United States Naval Forces in the area (Battalion War Diary, August 1943).

The report also stated that over the previous week considerable movement of personnel had been observed and that new trenches and foxholes have been dug. In most attacks, the advantage lies with the defender; however during the assault on Kiska the Force was hoping for foggy weather so that they could infiltrate enemy positions without being seen.

The First Regiment, under the command of Colonel A.C. Marshall, was designated to be among the Allied troops to land. The invasion force consisted of nearly a hundred ships and Assistant Secretary of War John J. McCloy had come to view the invasion. This unit traveled from Amchitka on the Destroyer *Kane* and an LST. At 0030 hours on August 15, the troops started to transfer from the ships to rubber boats. Their orders were to land from rubber boats, move inland, secure the high ground covering the beaches, and mark the beaches so that the main landing force could land. With rubber boats and a night landing it was felt that the element of surprise could be maintained and that the regiment could approach the shore unnoticed. Unfortunately, instead of the hoped-for cloud and fog cover, the weather turned clear and the regiment had to paddle into the

---

[12] Burhans, *A War History*, 1947.

[13] D. Hist., File 322.009 [D527].

Men of Canadian and U.S. forces on the beach at Quisling Cove, Kiska. *(Photo No. 208-AA-7E-8, National Archives, College Park, Md.)*

beaches under bright moonlight.[14] The First Regiment was charged with marking beaches 9 BLUE, 9 YELLOW and 10 SCARLET.

Beach 9 BLUE, located in Quisling Cove at the mouth of Limpid Creek, was to be marked with a six-foot square blue panel and blue signal lights; Beach 9 YELLOW, three hundred yards northwest of Limpid Creek, would be marked with a similar six-foot square yellow panel facing seaward; and Beach 10 SCARLET, at the mouth of Lily Creek, would utilize a red panel (Battalion War Diary, August 1943).

If in the course of the landing the beach-marking party found any beaches unsuitable for use, a two-foot square white panel would be placed below the above-mentioned panel.

It took more than an hour for the first boats to make land and by 0145 hours the First Regiment had sufficient troops ashore to start carrying out its mission. Patrols moved out to secure the high ground and take up defensive positions. The regiment's main objectives were Link Hills, Lawson Hills, Larry Hill, Lasso Hill, and Lame Hill Ridge. These were the high points surrounding the invasion beaches. The troops were to actively patrol this area and capture or destroy any enemy personnel or installations found. Meanwhile other members of the regiment remained on the beaches to clear the rock obstacles which might impede the main landing. In a coded message "Tell Williamson baby needs a new pair of shoes", the First Regiment informed Colonel Adams at Amchitka that the Second Regiment was not needed and the enemy had evacuated the area.[15] With the beachhead secure, the main landing force, consisting of the Eighty-Seventh Mountain Infantry Regiment and 184th Infantry Regiment, landed at 0630 hours.[16] The main mission of the First Regiment was nearly complete and later in the day they withdrew to positions on Link Hills, Lawson Hills, Larry Hill, and the Lame Hill Ridge line. From these positions, the regiment assembled, reorganized, and prepared to assist other troops of the Southern Sector as ordered by the commanding general.

---

[14] Adleman and Walton, *The Devil's Brigade*, 1966.

[15] Burhans, *A War History*, 1947.

[16] S.W. Dzuiban, *Military Relations Between The United States and Canada, 1939-1945*, (Washington: Department of the Army, 1959).

Military units over the course of their history acquire nicknames—some flattering and some not. The First Regiment nicknamed itself "Freddy's Freighters," in honour of all the supplies they had to carry up the mountains to their positions on the first day of the invasion.[17] The second day of the invasion saw them still in reserve, but they had an opportunity to explore and collect souvenirs and war trophies.

With only a small portion of the island explored at the end of the first day, the consensus seems to have been that the Japanese had been evacuated. Nevertheless, the second landing, set for August 16 and involving the Third Regiment and other Allied units, went ahead.

Operating from the LST, the Third Regiment were to land on North Kiska by rubber boats on D-day plus one. This phase of the operation had been changed only a week prior to the invasion as the beach directly in front of Robber Hill, which the regiment was to clear, was too heavily defended.[18] An alternative plan was devised and put into operation. Similar to what happened the day before, their mission was to clear and secure the beaches for the main landing force. Departing from the LST in rubber boats around midnight, they paddled toward shore. As with the day before, the moon appeared and cloud cover was at a minimum. This made paddling to shore easier, but it also made their detection by the enemy easier.[19] The Third Regiment was to mark two beaches: Beach 14 RED, which was located on Broad Beach in Bamboo Bay at the mouth of Rainbow Creek, and Beach 14 GREEN, which was southwest of Beach 14 RED in Bamboo Bay (Battalion War Diary, August 1943).

Similar beach marking procedures were to be used; however, the approach to securing them would be different. Instead of landing directly on the beaches, they were to land further along the coast, cross a small bar or bight, move inland to secure the high ground, and then mark the beaches. The plan called for the regiment to reach the bar separating West Kiska Lake from the Bering Sea no later than 0300 on D-day plus one, cross this rock formation which according to intelligence was only a couple of feet high, and paddle across West Kiska Lake to land at the mouth of Robin Creek.[20] The only problem was that these two-foot high rock and shale formations turned out to be twenty feet high (Battalion War Diary, August 1943). Loaded down with supplies and equipment, the men of the Third Regiment had to climb over these boulders, move their rubber boats over

this terrain, and launch them in West Kiska Lake. Alaskan Scouts covered the movements of the Force over the bight and helped to set up the beach markers on Beach 14. By 0400 hours, the regiment had secured Ranger Hill and patrols were moving toward Riot and Rose hills. By the time the main landing force arrived, all objectives assigned to the regiment were captured. With the objectives secured and the main force landing, the Third Regiment withdrew to reassemble, reorganize, and act as a reserve for the main force (Battalion War Diary, August 1943).

There was no prescribed role for the First and Third regiments after the first day of battle, the reason being that these units were expected not to exist as fighting units. Their assigned mission, if the Japanese contested the invasion, would have led to high casualties among the assault units—projected by planners to be 20 percent on the first day. After one or two days of combat, these units would have ceased as a fighting group. The regiments were given the role of providing security for the area and protecting captured Japanese equipment and records which might provide intelligence information. Elements of the First Regiment, under the command of Major Jack Akehurst, landed on Little Kiska on August 17, 1943, to secure the island and check the defenses. On the same day, Segal Island, north of Kiska, was checked by Colonel Marshall's battalion to see if any Japanese were there. The unit found the remains of two trappers.

The Force consisted of three regiments and, by far, the Second Regiment had one of the toughest jobs to perform in this invasion. They had to wait beside planes on Amchitka and be prepared to land on "any point on Kiska or Little Kiska, as designated, to relieve or exploit an emergency tactical situation" (Battalion War Diary, August 1943). From August 15 to 17, the Second Regiment remained on alert on Amchitka, prepared to parachute on Kiska. Ten C-47 aircraft were allocated to drop the Second Regiment. This group of aircraft could deliver two companies of Force personnel in support of ground troops on Kiska. For six hours on August 16, when the second landing was taking place in North Kiska, members of the regiments waited in their aircraft for the fog to lift and to receive orders. Neither came for this regiment as flying weather continued to be poor and the unit was not needed on Kiska.[21]

On August 18, the Force received orders from the Combined Chiefs of Staff recalling the unit to the United States. The Force had been discussed at the Quebec

---

[17] Adleman and Walton, *The Devil's Brigade*, 1966.

[18] Burhans, *A War History*, 1947.

[19] Adleman and Walton, *The Devil's Brigade*, 1966.

[20] Burhans, *A War History*, 1947.

[21] Ibid.

(First) Conference of August 1943 and a decision made to send them next to Italy.[22] Other American and Canadian units garrisoned the Kiska unit in November 1943. On January 12, 1944, the last remaining Canadians left this island.[23] On August 23, the First and Third regiments departed for San Francisco on board the SS *Bell* and the Second Regiment and supply battalion sailed aboard the SS *Heywood* on the 24th. The trip home was markedly different from the trip to the Aleutians. It was a more relaxed atmosphere as the mission was completed and the men were able to unwind after nearly a month of tension.

On August 30 and September 1, 1943, the men arrived and were taken to Camp Stoneman near San Francisco. There they received back pay and half the Force was given a ten-day leave and told to report to Fort Ethan Allen in Vermont. The other half of the unit traveled by train to Vermont where they received their leave. In less than three months' time, this unit would be in combat in Italy.

Although not a problem during the Kiska Operation, discipline required giving special powers to Canadian officers in the Force. Each Canadian officer had the powers of a detachment commander and the senior Canadian officer could, if the circumstances arose, convene a Field General Courts-Martial.[24] For the purposes of command, American officers were considered to be part of the Canadian forces. These powers did not extend to discipline and punishment.

Promotions were also a problem under this dual command and control structure, with the question arising as to whether officers of one country could be recommended for promotion by a foreign national.

Kiska also proved to be the training ground for Force officers. Frederick and Colonel Williamson, senior Canadian officers in the Force, were able to evaluate their junior officers. As a result, four officers were sent back to Canada after returning from Kiska on September 21, 1943 (Battalion War Diary, September 1943). On the American side, officers were also replaced. These included two Red Cross men and a chaplain who was caught selling communion wine to the troops.[25]

The Force had a unique relationship with the press. Despite the fact that it was a secret military organization, there were many press accounts of the Force's activities while it trained in Montana. One of the conditions of allowing the Force to participate in the invasion was that there be no mention of the unit by name and reporters were not allowed to accompany them on their mission.[26] The first mention that the First Special Service Force was part of the Kiska invasion did not appear in Canadian newspapers until January 1944.

The name "First Special Service Force" also served them well in the Aleutians. It sounded innocent and disguised the true role of the Force. In choosing the name, army officials did not want a title which would identify the Force with any special military group such as the commandos or rangers, since that would tend to underline and point out the unit's main feature.[27] The name sounded harmless enough that throughout the Force's existence it was confused with the "Special Services" entertainment branch of the army and the publishers of *The Yank*, the American military newspaper.

A common trait among elite units was that many tried to make their uniforms distinctive by modifying them. The Force was no exception. Issued with American uniforms, these were soon changed to meet their own requirements. Troops adopted the airborne style of wearing the trousers tucked into their jump boots. They were issued berets with the crossed arrows insignia for officers and spearhead insignia with the CANADA USA logo.

While in the Aleutians, the men were issued special clothing such as arctic jackets, shoe pacs, and rubber suits.[28] Shoe pacs were designed to keep the feet dry but, unfortunately, they did not offer the support that parachute boots did and there were therefore many more foot problems related to blisters than trench foot. In one instance, the Second Regiment had 150 men who were considered medically unfit to participate in a two-day march because of blisters (Battalion War Diary, August 1943). Rubber suits also provided excellent protection from the elements when the troops landed alit from their rubber boats. On the negative side, there was no zipper or fly in the suit, which made going to the washroom a problem. If the Force learned one thing while on Amchitka it is summed up in the August 6 war diary: "The big lesson learned was what equipment and clothing should be taken and how carried" (Battalion War Diary, August 1943). Proper packing, storage of equipment, and what to carry into combat are lessons that can be learned only in the field. When the First and

---

[22] Ibid.

[23] Stacey, *The Canadian Army in the Second World War*, 1966.

[24] R.A. Beaumont, *Military Elites, Special Fighting Units in the Modern World*, (Indianapolis: Bobbs-Merrill, 1974).

[25] Adleman and Walton, *The Devil's Brigade*, 1966.

[26] G.R. Perras, "Canada as a Military Partner: Alliance Politics and the Campaign to Recapture the Aleutian Island of Kiska," *Journal of Military History*, 56, July 1992.

[27] Adleman and Walton, *The Devil's Brigade*, 1966.

[28] Ibid.

Third regiments landed on Kiska, they were carrying the basics. They had arranged in advance that any additional supplies, such as ammunition, food and clothing, would be parachuted to them.

Prior to this operation, the Force received little intelligence information on Kiska. In his book, Burhans—the Force's intelligence officer—discusses at length the operation's intelligence failures. He summed it up as "intelligence of the island enemy proved little better than guesswork".[29]

The Force wanted to land small patrols on the island to scout and identify strong points; however, the navy turned the plan down. Although maps of the island had been updated by aerial photographs, they were based on a 1935 survey and were of poor quality. There seems to have been a conflict between army and navy personnel about whose responsibility it was to collect and distribute information.[30] For example, all photographs taken of Kiska had to be sent to the navy and they decided which ones were released. Therefore, the Force had access to only a small part of the intelligence picture.

There were three intelligence mistakes which directly affected the Force and, if the landing had been opposed, might have led to disaster: (a) the failure to correctly anticipate the strength of the tides and currents surrounding the island; (b) the failure to anticipate the phases of the moon; and (c) the failure to correctly calculate the height of the bight separating West Kiska Lake from the Bering Sea. Instead of being two feet high, the collection of rocks which created this bight ranged from sixteen to twenty feet high.

The Force could move faster and respond to changing situations on Kiska more quickly than other units because of its Service Battalion. The battalion of three companies had been created to allow for the three combat regiments to concentrate on training and on carrying out the mission. In this battalion, there were the Force's communications, records, and administrative sections along with military police, cooks, bakers, parachute packers, barbers, carpenters, repairmen, vehicle mechanics, and drivers. Also, during combat missions these troops would supply and evacuate the wounded. With the Service Battalion in place, the Force was entirely self-contained and therefore did not need the resources and support that other military units required. It could go anywhere and do anything which was required of it and did not need to rely on the military's normal chain of command.[31]

There are only three memorials which I have been able to locate dedicated to this period of the unit's history. The first is located in Helena, Montana, and it was unveiled in August 1947. The second is in Castillon, France, and the date of its unveiling is unknown. The third plaque is in Rome, Italy, and was unveiled on June 2, 1984. No memorial or plaque specifically dealing with the unit's role in the Aleutian campaign has ever been unveiled.

To many people, the Kiska invasion is only a footnote in the history of the F.S.S.F. As one of my colleagues at a museum told me when I mentioned coming to Anchorage to give a paper, nothing really happened; they went up to the Aleutians to stay a month, invaded a deserted island, returned home, and then went to Italy where the real war was going on. The truth is that the lessons learned on Kiska saved lives at Monte la Difensa, Anzio, Mussolini Canal, Rome, and southern France. During the year that the Force was in combat in Italy and southern France, 295 American and 155 Canadian members of the unit were killed in action.[32] If the Japanese had not evacuated the island, I feel that this would have been the first and last mission for the F.S.S.F. Anticipating high casualties and with no future mission planned, I think the Force would have been disbanded and its troops used as replacements for other airborne forces.

The lessons the Force learned at Kiska can be summed up as follows:

• Kiska proved to be the ultimate training exercise. Simulations and training exercises can only go so far. It wasn't until the island was completely searched two days after the invasion that anyone could say with absolute certainty that the Japanese had evacuated. Therefore, for the first forty-eight hours, the unit operated as though it were in a combat zone.

• The Force learned to operate over rugged terrain and under poor weather conditions, which would serve them well in the winter campaigns on the Italian front.

• The Force learned the right and wrong ways to conduct an amphibious landing. These lessons were applied to their invasion of Ile de Port-Cros and Ile du Levant in August 1944.

• The Force learned the importance of training and physical fitness for all ranks. All members of the Force were expected to keep themselves physically fit—officers and enlisted men alike.

• The Force was able to put into practice its infiltration and demolition skills during the invasion.

• The Force learned the necessity of good leadership and initiative on the part of its officers and men, as

---

[29] Burhans, *A War History*, 1947.

[30] Adleman and Walton, *The Devil's Brigade*, 1966.

[31] Burhans, *A War History*, 1947.

[32] Ibid.

well as leadership by example and a willingness to accept responsibility. Poor officers were replaced and new training programs developed as a result of the lessons gleaned at Kiska.

• The Force learned the need for good intelligence. There were further intelligence failures in the history of the Force, but the unit learned and developed its own intelligence gathering system and not to rely solely on the information given by others.

• The Force learned the importance of fire discipline and working with other military units. Until Kiska, the Force had trained independently of other military formations. Kiska allowed the unit to work in a combined operations setting.

The Force took its mission seriously, trained hard, and executed its portion of the mission flawlessly. Even today, the history of this unit can be seen in the Canadian and American military. For Canada, it is the Canadian Airborne Regiment and, for the United States, it is the Green Berets.

Over the years I have talked to veterans of the original Force. Several expressed an interest in returning to Anzio, Rome, or southern France to visit. Interestingly, I have never met one who wanted to return to Kiska.

*Alastair Neely is a librarian at the London Public Library in Ontario and is the Director of the First Hussars Museum.*

Left on Kiska Island by the Japanese, this dog soon found new friends among the American forces. This was a first-day scene outside the Japanese central telephone control shack. Americans found the system in such good condition that they took over and plugged in. *(No. 208 AA-7E-1, National Archives)*

# "When We Got there, the Cupboard Was Bare": Canada's Greenlight Force and the Recapture of Kiska, 1943

*Galen Roger Perras*

IN AUGUST 1943 THE CANADIAN PUBLIC WAS RIVETED BY the exploits of the First Canadian Division as it participated in the conquest of Sicily. But in that same month, half a world away and far from the glare of publicity, fifty-three hundred Canadian soldiers, most members of the Thirteenth Infantry Brigade (or "Greenlight Force"), landed alongside thirty thousand Americans on the Aleutian island of Kiska. Expecting a pitched battle, the invaders discovered instead that the Japanese garrison had departed covertly less than three weeks before. This seeming waste of months of preparation was not well received in Canada. Historian C.P. Stacey described the operation as a "fiasco" and "a ridiculous anti-climax,"[1] while Prime Minister William Lyon Mackenzie King remarked that the "expedition should have never taken place."[2]

Chaos plagued the organization of the brigade. From the moment the Canadian army reported that it had been asked by its American counterpart to aid in the recapture of Kiska, until the day the soldiers actually splashed ashore, Canada's government and its military advisors fought for control of the operation. Fearing a political backlash and demonstrating a marked lack of confidence in its military after the disasters at Hong Kong and Dieppe, the Cabinet, after reluctantly giving its approval, set about to rein in the army and prevent another Hong Kong-style catastrophe. The result was unparalleled civilian interference in such areas as the composition of the brigade, sailing orders, and operational planning.

On the other hand, the army commanders had entered into secret negotiations with the Americans without government approval or knowledge, revealing those discussions only when it became unavoidable. Feeling marginalized within an alliance where decisions were made in Washington, D.C., and London, and in a nation where their civilian masters consulted them infrequently, prominent officers set out to involve themselves and their troops in action wherever it might be found. Kiska proved to be that action.

The immediate origins of Greenlight Force lay in a visit to Vancouver on 19 April 1943, by General John L. DeWitt, commander of the United States' Western Defense Command (WDC), a jurisdiction that included Alaska. On 12 June 1942, only one day after Japanese forces were confirmed on Attu and Kiska, he asked for amphibious forces and aircraft carriers "to clear Kiska and Attu of enemy."[3]

DeWitt soon found an ally in Admiral Chester W. Nimitz, commander in chief of the United States Pacific Fleet. In November 1942 these two men convinced General George C. Marshall, the United States Army Chief

---

[1] C.P. Stacey, *Six Years at War: The Army in Canada, Britain and the Pacific*, vol. 1 of *Official History of the Canadian Army in the Second World War*, (Ottawa, 1955), pp. 500-505.

[2] National Archives of Canada [hereafter NAC], W.L.M. King Papers, Diaries, MG26 J13, entry for 26 October 1943.

[3] United States National Archives [hereafter NA], Dispatches and Records from the Chart Room of the Commander in Chief, U.S. Fleet, Action Dispatches 3 Jan 42 - 15 Nov 1942, RG38, box 89, file Aleutians - Action Dispatches June 3-13, 1942, telegram, no. 121745, DeWitt to Chief of Staff Army, 12 June 1942.

of Staff, to set a target date of 15 May 1943 for the recapture of Kiska.[4] Marshall's reservations accompanied him to the Casablanca Conference in January 1943, where the Anglo-American Allied Combined Chiefs of Staff met to hammer out their strategic direction for 1943 and beyond. The Americans argued for increased effort against Japan; their British counterparts insisted that Germany had to be dealt with first. Britain's view carried the day but only after some concessions were made. Offensive action against Japan was approved including "operations to make the Aleutians as secure as they may be."[5]

When DeWitt arrived in Vancouver on 19 April to meet with Major-General George Pearkes, the General Officer Commander in Chief, Canadian Pacific Command, he obviously was on a fishing trip for troops. Informing Pearkes that an invasion of Attu would occur in early May, DeWitt revealed that there would likely be a second operation directed at Kiska. Catching the hint, Pearkes enthusiastically suggested that Canada might want a part in such a venture and asked to be allowed to send an observer team to Attu. DeWitt, happy that his suggestions had been well-received, approved the despatch of the observers and promised his full cooperation in any shared action in the future.[6]

It should come as no surprise that Pearkes had risen to the bait offered by DeWitt. Before being relieved of his divisional position in Britain, Pearkes had entertained hopes of leading a corps. When told by the commander of the First Canadian Army, General Andrew McNaughton, of the impending change, Pearkes had expressed a desire to stay with his unit in Britain so that he could lead it into combat. Sentenced to what must have seemed a backwater of the war, Pearkes would not allow this opportunity to slip away.

In Ottawa, General Stuart apparently was not as enthusiastic. Pearkes' message generated no response until mid-May after a second telegram—this one from General Maurice Pope—arrived at National Defence Headquarters (NDHQ). Pope, the chair of the Canadian Joint Staff Mission in Washington, had been approached on 8 May by John Hickerson, a senior State Department official and the Secretary of the American Section of the Permanent Joint Board on Defence (PJBD). In Hickerson's opinion, Canada had done little to date in the Pacific and some people wanted the Dominion to dispatch an infantry division to the southwest Pacific. Hickerson had much more in mind than simple garrison duty. He confided that it was only a matter of time before an operation began in the Aleutians. When that happened, Canada should take part.[7]

Hickerson's choice to seek out Pope was a correct one. Maurice Pope, "the best educated and best informed of Canadian generals and the one with the most inquiring mind,"[8] was intrigued. Certain that "we were desirous of associating ourselves in such a project rather than sit quietly awaiting an invitation to do so," Pope relayed the details of his conversation with Hickerson to Stuart and asked permission to discuss the matter with Marshall.[9]

Pearkes did not sit idle while he waited for a response from Ottawa. He asked his staff for reports on the training progress of the units in his jurisdiction. Moreover, in a move that was both cunningly anticipatory and politically dangerous, Pearkes concluded that the authority existed to employ home defence soldiers in the Aleutians.[10]

In a meeting with Pearkes on 24 May, DeWitt put forward two proposals. The first envisioned Canada supplying one infantry battalion and an antiaircraft battery for garrison duty on Amchitka or Attu, ready to move by 15 June. The second suggestion called for a brigade group to be ready by 1 August. The United States would provide transport and logistical support.[11] Pleased with what he had heard, Pearkes happily recommended accepting both options. Pearkes was certain that activity in the Aleutians would raise troop morale and give Canadian soldiers badly needed combat experience. He therefore asked the CGS for authorization to begin concentrating a brigade group and to continue planning with DeWitt.[12]

Stuart now had no choice but to consult Ralston as only the Cabinet had the power to authorize participation in the venture. The memorandum, which Stuart submitted only minutes before Ralston had to attend a War Committee meeting, presented five reasons for

[4] Grace Person Hayes, *The History of the Joint Chiefs of Staff in World War II. The War Against Japan* (Annapolis, 1982), p. 273.

[5] *Foreign Relations of the United States: The Conferences at Washington and Quebec, 1943* (Washington, D.C., 1970), p. 797; Michael Howard, *Grand Strategy, vol. 4, August 1942-September 1943* (London, 1942), pp. 629-30.

[6] NAC, Department of National Defence, RG24, vol. 2921, file HQS 9055-1, report entitled "General Staff Report on Greenlight Force Period from Inception to Dispatch to Adak", July 1943.

[7] NAC, RG24, vol. 2919, file HQS 9055(1), telegram, CAW 305, Pope to Stuart, 10 May 1943.

[8] J.W. Pickersgill, cited in J.L. Granatstein, *The Generals: The Canadian Army's Senior Commanders in the Second World War* (Toronto: 1993), p. 207.

[9] NAC, RG24, vol. 2919, file HQS 9055(1), telegram, CAW 305, Pope to Stuart, 10 May 1943.

[10] D. Hist., file 322.009 (D490), memorandum from Pearkes to his senior officers, 21 May 1943.

[11] D. Hist., file 322.009 (D490), telegram, PCO 2020, Pearkes to Stuart, 25 May 1943.

[12] Ibid.

signing on. First, echoing Pearkes, the CGS argued that the troops involved would gain much-needed combat experience, a commodity in short supply in the Canadian Army. Moving soldiers to an active theater would increase the prestige of the army (and no doubt the government) at home and raise the morale of the home defence conscripts. Third, by employing NRMA draftees in combat, the considerable hostility directed towards the "Zombies" by substantial portions of the Canadian public would be lessened. Stuart was confident too that by acting to help remove enemy forces from American soil Canada would strengthen ties with the United States and demonstrate an intention to play a full part in the Pacific Theater. Finally, participation would be in complete accord with the spirit of plans drawn up by the PJBD and approved by the governments of Canada and the United States.[13]

Having little time to digest the memorandum's contents, Ralston, with Stuart in tow, rushed off to the War Committee meeting. There, after informing his colleagues that the United States had made some enquiries concerning the use of Canadian troops in the Aleutians, Ralston turned the floor over to Stuart, the CGS summarizing the major points of his submission. The War Committee chose to delay a decision until the following day to allow more time for study.[14]

Prime Minister King was disturbed by what had transpired. King realized very quickly that Ralston was virtually ignorant of DeWitt's suggestions, and the prime minister had come away convinced that Stuart had initiated contact with the Americans. King angrily noted in his diary that the "Minister of Defence should have been the one taking, if anything of the kind were contemplated, the initial step in discussion with the War Committee of the Cabinet."[15]

Prime Minister King's comments before the War Committee on 27 May made it quite clear that King believed the use of Canadian soldiers in combat would raise military morale and give the troops valuable experience. King was worried about "the predominant part played by the Americans in our own northwest." Ever cautious though, the prime minister pointed out possible drawbacks. Inevitably Canada's contribution would be small in comparison to its southern neighbor, and King feared that little credit would accrue from a successful outcome while failure would certainly reflect to a disproportionate degree on his government. Having thus referred obliquely to the disaster at Hong Kong and the Royal Commission that had followed,[16] the wily politician took his refuge in a choice not to countenance joining the venture unless the expedition was in accord with the strategic plans of the Allied Combined Chiefs. Thus he preferred to wait until the United States made an official approach to the War Committee.[17]

The War Committee agreed to entertain a proposal for a Canadian role in the Aleutians. However, determined to cut the best deal possible and eager to reassert civilian supremacy, the Committee voted to transfer the matter from military jurisdiction to the ministerial sphere. Before Canada would consider the matter seriously, an invitation to take part would have to come from either President Roosevelt or Secretary of War Henry L. Stimson.[18]

On May 31, the War Committee met. There was little discussion. Ralston, in the absence of King, told his colleagues that the prime minister had approved the dispatch of the force to Kiska. With that endorsement, the ministers quickly assented.[19]

However tortuous the process of getting Greenlight Force included in the campaign to retake Kiska had been, it paled in comparison to the contortions that occurred as the brigade was put together. Pearkes was told on 3 June to begin concentrating a brigade group for special training, the formation to be ready to move to Alaska by 1 August for further drill.[20] While the Canadian troops would carry their own weapons, the United States would furnish special clothing, vehicles, and the bulk of medical and other services.[21]

---

[13] NAC, RG24, vol. 2919, file HQS 9055(1), memorandum, Stuart to J.L. Ralston, 26 May 1943.

[14] NAC, RG2 7c, microfilm reel C-4875, vol. 13, minutes of the Cabinet War Committee, 26 May 1943.

[15] NAC, MG26 J13, diary entry for 26 May 1943.

[16] The loss in December 1941 of two Canadian battalions at Hong Kong prompted charges of government incompetence and claims that many of the soldiers were virtually untrained. A one-man Royal Commission, presided over by Supreme Court Chief Justice Lyman P. Duff, cleared King's government of any substantial wrongdoing in the affair; Canada, Royal Commission on the Expeditionary Force to the Crown Colony of Hong Kong. Report by Sir Lyman P. Duff (Ottawa, 1942), 61 pp. Accounts of the debacle can be found in C.P. Stacey, Six Years of War; and Carl Vincent's flawed No Reason Why: The Canadian Hong Kong Tragedy—An Examination (Stittsville, 1981). The extensive historiography on the subject is reviewed in Galen Roger Perras, "'Defeat Cries Aloud for Explanation:' An Examination of the Historical Literature on the Battle of Hong Kong", unpublished paper presented at the conference "Canada and the Second World War in the Pacific", sponsored by the Canadian Committee for the History of the Second World War, Victoria, 27-29 February 1992.

[17] NAC, RG2 7c, microfilm reel C-4875, vol. 13, minutes of the Cabinet War Committee, 27 May 1943.

[18] Ibid.

[19] NAC, RG2 7c, microfilm reel C-4875, vol. 13, minutes of the Cabinet War Committee, 31 May 1943.

[20] NAC, RG24, vol. 2919, file HQS 9055(1), telegram, CGS 619, Murchie to Pearkes, 3 June 1943.

[21] D. Hist., file 322.009 (D510), minutes of meeting between representatives of Pacific Command and Western Defense Command, 29 May 1943.

By June 2 the brigade's basic order of battle was settled. The core was the Thirteenth Brigade Headquarters, the senior brigade in Pacific Command. The three infantry battalions chosen (the Winnipeg Grenadiers, the Canadian Fusiliers, and the Rocky Mountain Rangers) were the only units in Pacific Command most nearly up to war establishment, and all had been rated by their divisional commanders as prepared for combat operations. Other formations included the Twenty-Fourth Field Regiment, Royal Canadian Artillery, the Twenty-Fourth Field Company, Royal Canadian Engineers, a machine-gun company from the Saint John Fusiliers, and various service detachments.[22]

Pulling the brigade together was a complex task. Exercise Wool, a staff drill concluded on 31 May, revealed that the static Canadian infantry battalion pattern was not well-suited for war in the Aleutians. Specialized sections such as carrier and anti-tank platoons were dropped while mortar platoons were enlarged and anti-aircraft sections added.[23]

On 7 June, Pearkes met in Ottawa with Stuart and Vice Chief Major-General J.C. Murchie. Stuart proposed as well that a francophone unit, Le Regiment de Hull, should be added. Stuart, originally from Trois Rivieres, believed it very desirable to have French Canadian participation, thus ensuring truly transnational representation.[24] No doubt Stuart hoped their inclusion of a francophone formation might soften the harsh criticism levelled at Quebec for its supposed "malingering" and encourage a more active war effort by French Canadians.

The most important, and far-reaching, decision made at the 7 June meeting concerned the eligibility of soldiers to serve in Greenlight Force. One of the most haunting aspects of the Hong Kong debacle had been charges that hundreds of the men sent to that doomed outpost had been badly trained. At Stuart's urging NDHQ's senior officers—a group known as the Military Members—ruled that no soldiers enrolled after 15 February 1943 could be included in Greenlight Force. Additionally, all troops who had failed to complete at least four months' training would not be allowed to embark.[25]

This ruling, when combined with other measures to remove overage and medically unfit personnel, caused considerable difficulties. The Rocky Mountain Rangers had 106 reserve recruits removed on 12 June. Between 12 and 28 June the Winnipeg Grenadiers lost at least fifty-two men while absorbing 196 new soldiers.[26] Very badly hit was Le Regiment de Hull. Twenty of its thirty-nine officers were cashiered, including its commander, second-in-command, and adjutant—the regiment's three most senior officers.

Training was to take place in a very condensed period of time. Canada had been notified in mid-June that the target date for the Kiska invasion had been set for 15 August rather than later in September. This change dictated that Greenlight Force had to be ready to move to Alaska by 10 July so as to ensure a full month's training with the larger American contingent.[27]

All that time would be needed as the units were to be recast on an American pattern. Three of the Canadian infantry battalions would be remodelled into amphibious battalion land groups (BLGs), while Le Regiment de Hull was assigned the duties of an American engineer unit. The francophone troops would form beach combat teams to help unload supplies. DeWitt also revealed the size of the Kiska task force: five battleships with appropriate escorts, including possibly an aircraft carrier; at least 148 aircraft; twelve American combat teams; the joint American-Canadian First Special Service Force; and Greenlight Force; all told, approximately thirty-two thousand troops.[28]

When the soldiers of Greenlight Force began arriving at their concentration bases on Vancouver Island after 18 June, they faced a rigorous drill regime designed to prepare them for the peculiar conditions they would face in the Aleutians. One of the lessons learned from the bitter fighting on Attu was that the rough terrain and peculiar climate of the Aleutians required troops to be in absolutely top-notch physical condition.[29]

On 12 July the brigade boarded its transports and headed to Adak. General Buckner and Rear Admiral Thomas C. Kinkaid, the U.S. Navy's senior officer in Alaska, both expressed favourable opinions about the

[22] NAC, RG24, vol. 13,381, war diary of "Greenlight" General Staff Pacific Command from July 1 to July 31, 1943, reported entitled "General Staff Report on Greenlight Force Period From Inception to Dispatch to Adak", 18 July 1943.

[23] D. Hist., file 322.009 (D510), minutes of meeting concerning Exercise Wool, 31 May 1943.

[24] NAC, RG24, vol. 2919, file HQS 9055(1), minutes of the meeting of the Military Members, 7 June 1943.

[25] Ibid.

[26] NAC, RG24, vol. 15,204, war diary of the Rocky Mountain Rangers, June 1943; and NAC, RG24, vol. 15,292, war diary of the Winnipeg Grenadiers, June 1943.

[27] NAC, RG24, vol. 2919, file HQS 9055(1), letter, Colonel Francis J. Graling, U.S. Military Attache to Stuart, 13 June 1943.

[28] NAC, RG24, vol. 13,831, file May 11 to June 30, 1943, letter, Pearkes to Stuart, 15 June 1943.

[29] This need to have troops in top physical condition was trumpeted in many reports about Attu: D. Hist., file 322.009 (D506), report by Colonel L.V. Castner, Alaska Defense Command, "Lessons Learned From Operations on Attu", 7 June 1943; and NAC, RG24, vol. 13,826, folder 3 War Diary General Staff Operations Pacific Command 1-30 June 1943, report entitled "Lessons Learned From the Attu Operations", 14 June 1943.

appearance and bearing of the Canadians.

Nevertheless, alarming problems threatened the brigade's cohesion. The force was short of specialists, and few of the units outside of the infantry battalions had any experience in battle drill tactics. Most important, Pearkes warned Stuart:

> The discipline in all units left much to be desired. This was exemplified by cases of officers grumbling about conditions in front of their men, cases of men refusing to draw special equipment, reluctance of a sub-unit to go on parade, and numerous cases of absence without leave or desertion.[30]

On Adak, Greenlight Force troops were kept very busy with  marches and individual and sub-unit training, the latter emphasizing battle drill, patrolling tactics and schemes designed to improve the skills of junior officers.[31]

Greenlight Force began splashing ashore on the northwest side of Kiska on 16 August, a day after American troops had landed further south. The brigade's BLGs were to move inland as quickly as possible, as they sought an enemy believed to have withdrawn into the hinterland. Despite heavy fog on both 15 and 16 August, all troops reached and surpassed their initial goals.

The speedy progress stemmed from the fact that there was no enemy opposition. On 16 August, American forces reported contact with a few Japanese riflemen and occupied a trench in which hot coffee reputedly was found.[32] Continued searches located no enemy soldiers but uncovered considerable evidence that the Japanese had hurriedly left Kiska within the past three weeks.

Had the Japanese stayed and fought, the struggle would have been bloody. A July 1943 study asserted that the terrain favoured the defender, "especially in the initial stages of a landing." A report prepared after the island had been occupied confirmed those conclusions. The Japanese garrison, estimated at seventy-eight hundred, had been well-armed and its defences were strong and well-planned. Holding or developing some of the beachheads would have been difficult, perhaps impossible. An estimate of seven thousand Allied casualties out of thirty thousand troops was put forward.[33]

Despite the absence of opposition, the operation was not entirely bloodless. Thick fog made movement and the identification of friendly forces difficult. Jittery nerves, cases of mistaken identity, and Japanese mines and booby-traps took their toll. Twenty-eight soldiers were dead with another fifty injured after the first two days on the island. Only four of the fatalities and several of the wounded fell victim to mines; the rest were shot by their own side, one American lieutenant commenting that "the troops were shooting at anything that moved."[34] An additional sixty-one men were killed or missing when an American destroyer struck a floating mine.[35] Of the total of 313 casualties suffered by the forces on Kiska, the Canadians accounted for four dead and another four wounded. All the Canadian fatalities were the result of encounters with Japanese munitions.[36]

The expressed sentiment in the wake of the anticlimax was  disappointment. Soldiers interviewed on

---

[30] D. Hist., file 595.013 (D4), memorandum written by Pearkes, 20 July 1943. This document was to be included as an appendix in Nicholson s official report but was omitted. Stuart was sent a copy by Sherwood Lett on 21 July; D. Hist., file 322.009 (D486), liaison report no. 29, Lett to Stuart, 21 July 1943.

[31] D. Hist., file 148.9009 (D6), 13 Canadian Infantry Brigade Group Training Directive no. 1, 7 July 1943; and D. Hist., file 595.013 (D4), 13 Canadian Training Operation Order no. 2, 5 August 1943.

[32] D. Hist., file 322.009 (D878), telegram, 160650, unknown origin to Norpacfor, 16 August 1943; and D. Hist., file 181.003 (D2337), United States Army S-2 Periodic Report no. 58, 17 August 1943.

[33] NA, RG407, box 37, file 91-TF2-0.3, Intelligence Memorandum no. 6, "A Study of Enemy Defensive Installations on Kiska Island As Known 5 July 1943", 5 July 1943; D. Hist., 595.023 (D1), report produced by Advance Command Post, Headquarters Alaska Defense Command, "Enemy on Kiska", undated; and D. Hist., file 595.023 (D2), Nicholson report, Appendix 56. Pearkes was expecting some 1,800 Canadian casualties of which 1,300 might require evacuation. Experience at Attu had demonstrated that for every 100 personnel involved, six would die, twelve would become walking wounded, while twelve would be stretcher cases; D. Hist., file 322.009 (D497), telegram, PCA 1038, Pearkes to General H.F.G. Letson, 10 July 1943; and Ibid., memorandum, Major J.H. McIntosh to Pearkes, 14 June 1943.

[34] Lieutenant Colonel Charles R. Shrader, *Amicide: The Problem of Friendly Fire in Modern War, Research Survey No. 1*, Combat Studies Institute, U.S. Army Command and General Staff College (Fort Leavenworth December 1982), p. 91.

[35] USNOY, Combat Narratives, "The Aleutian Campaign June 1942-August 1943", Office of Naval Intelligence, United States Navy (1945), p. 103.

[36] NAC, RG 24, vol. 15,204, war diary of the Rocky Mountain Rangers, entry for 17 August 1943; NAC, RG24, vol. 15,292, war diary of the Winnipeg Grenadiers, entry for 22 August 1943; and NAC, RG24, vol. 15,182, war diary for Le Regiment de Hull, entries for 29 August and 28 September 1943. General Charles H. Corlett, commander of Amphibious Task Force Nine, remarked in an unpublished autobiography that the Canadians "apparently had not been well trained on the subject of booby traps... Our men who had been very thoroughly instructed on these dangers were not hurt." United States Military History Institute, Charles H. Corlett Papers, manuscript autobiography, *One Man's Story: Some of It About War*, 1948.

Kiska or upon their return to Canada said that they felt "let down" by the refusal of the Japanese to stand and fight.[37] This feeling was best stated by Le Regiment de Hull's report on the Kiska operation: "When we got there, the cupboard was bare."[38] But when Pacific Command was expecting up to eighteen hundred casualties in a brigade numbering only five thousand men, surely a great many soldiers privately were very pleased not to have encountered any Japanese.

Although George Pearkes must have been disgruntled by what had transpired at Kiska, he was far too busy to dwell on what might have been. Instead, he was concentrating on what could be: follow-up operations across the Pacific. By early August Pearkes had focused his attention on a potential target: Japan's Kurile Islands. The Kuriles were important strategically because of their proximity to the Aleutians, their position between Hokkaido and Siberia, and the fact that the islands lay along the great circle route, the shortest route between Japan and mainland United States.[39]

Stuart too had been contemplating a new role for Canada in the war. When the War Cabinet met at the end of August, Stuart reported that the United States was considering operations in the north Pacific and that Canada might be asked to take part. Greenlight Force was well suited for such activity.[40]

When the War Committee reconvened a week later, the prime minister demonstrated absolutely no enthusiasm for Stuart's proposals. His patience at an end, King, in a pointed jab at his senior military advisors, bluntly recommended that Canada avoid being put in a position where American requests might force the Dominion into commitments beyond its capacity.

The planning staff of the Joint Chiefs also favoured dropping the idea for the time being. This recommendation was accepted by the Joint Chiefs on 5 October 1943.[41]

One week later the future of Greenlight Force was decided by the War Committee. As the U.S. was about to reduce drastically its Alaska garrison, leaving a token force in the Aleutians would have a negligible effect. It was best to bring the brigade home.

The early return of the brigade was eagerly anticipated by its members. The dismal weather, the bleak treeless terrain, irregular mail service, and primitive living conditions were beginning seriously to damage morale. There was little to do but train and prepare defensive positions.

What the Kiska experience revealed was the substantial divergence of opinion between Canada's civilian authorities and their top army advisers at a critical junction in the war. Canadian troops had gone into action twice before 1943—at Hong Kong in December 1941, and Dieppe in August 1942—and both operations had ended in bloody catastrophe and political recriminations. Given such experiences, it should come as no surprise that King and his ministers were not enthused at the prospect of a third expedition to a remote and dangerous outpost.

*Galen Roger Perras works as a strategic analyst for the Canadian Department of National Defence. He is completing his doctoral program in history at the University of Waterloo in Ontario. The foregoing is a précis of the longer and more comprehensive paper presented at the Alaska at War symposium.*

---

[37] "Kiska Canucks `Let Down' Guelph Officer Reveals", *Toronto Globe and Mail*, 26 August 1943; and "Felt `Let Down' on Kiska, Returned Buddies Say", *Toronto Globe and Mail*, 9 September 1943.

[38] NAC, RG24, vol. 15,183, war diary of Le Regiment de Hull, "Report on Kiska Operations", undated.

[39] D. Hist., file 322.009 (D506), report, "A Study of the Kuriles", prepared by Lieutenant-Colonel B.R. Mullaly, 10 June 1943.

[40] NAC, RG2 7c, microfilm reel C-4875, vol. 13, minutes, Cabinet War committee meeting, 31 August 1943.

[41] NA, RG218, Decimal File 1942-1945, box 194, file CCS 334 Joint Chiefs of Staff (9-14-43), supplementary minutes of 117th meeting of the Joint Chiefs of Staff, 5 October 1943.

# Kiska:
# Birth of a Division

*George F. Earle*

THE STORY OF KISKA IN AUGUST 1943 WAS LONG kicked around and only recently forgotten. Seldom, if ever, has so much ammunition, weaponry, and manpower been expended and thrown into a battle against no enemy. The least that can be said about it is that as wars go it was unique. First it was to be the Battle of Kiska, the early war's best and most widely known secret. And then, as its planning grew into a great and heralded amphibious landing force of thirty-five thousand specialized soldiers, it became the "Kiska Invasion." Finally, somewhat ignominiously, as the trap was sprung and it became "the foe-less battle," it remains as the "Kiska Landing." Of course there really was, as well as there wasn't, an enemy. But the true enemy and the basic cause of the deaths on gray, grim Kiska was Nature—the nature of Kiska herself—the wild juncture of natural forces that gives that tiny mountainous ridge rising from the sea the citation for the worst sea-level weather in the world.

A positive result of the operation was that the three-thousand-man experimental regiment that spearheaded the landings proved the military value of mountain troops trained in climbing, off-road backpacking, and operating under extreme weather conditions. Indeed, they proved their value so convincingly that they were cadred into a "mountain division" that later became an outstanding combat division in Italy, and remains today one of the army's top, first-used combat divisions.

My story of Kiska starts early in World War II with two striking events: One, Japan's unbroken year of victories in the Pacific, with only the Doolittle bomber strike to raise the question that would alarm Yamamoto: "Did they come from the Aleutians?"[1] The other, much earlier, was Russia's near disaster against white-clad ski troops in their 1939 invasion of Finland, a debacle that enraged Stalin. These led to totally dissimilar military plans: Tokyo extended its territorial objectives to Alaska—at the risk of dividing its forces; and Washington authorized an imaginative new kind of combat unit of mountain climbers and skiers. (The first affected the Battle of Midway, which ended Japan's Pacific domination, and the latter contributed directly to the early Allied victory in Italy.) These two unrelated plans produced two military units that seemed drawn to each other in the North Pacific as though fated to cross paths and converge in battle.

So, two untried forces were slated to square off, one a surrounded Japanese garrison desperately maintaining a death-grip on remote U.S. territory, the other an experimental regiment, three thousand selected volunteers assigned to spearhead a large amphibious and climbing assault to break that grip.

This attack, most carefully planned and a secret of the highest priority, soon became World War II's worst kept, best known, military "don't even think it." By late spring of 1943, everyone with a radio and ears in San

---

[1] The Doolittle raid in April of 1942, more disturbing than damaging, was an incredible American effort of swashbuckling heroism and daring ingenuity. Bombers had never before been flown from carriers, and these from more than twice the three-hundred-mile limit of carrier planes—requiring some unorthodox plane modifications and a stiff wind for quick liftoff—so that the Japanese had to assume an Aleutian threat worth diverting vital carriers to.

Francisco, Seattle, and elsewhere knew that for the first time since the War of 1812 an enemy had occupied sacred North American soil, though it was soil they had never heard of: two islands in the Aleutians occupied now for a year. One, Attu by name, had been regained in May—and now the other was to be wrested back by a U.S.-Canadian amphibious force in August.

And as a further embarrassment over this well-traveled "military secret," those invading troops, sweating out their date on the perilous island beaches, were hearing themselves described in detail as mountaineers, told their own unit names, location, and numbers, as well as the size of the assembling fleet, (at Adak), and worst of all, the exact date and hour of their "secret" landing, all this by "Tokyo Rose," as beamed to them from Japan.

By August of 1943, all this advance publicity focused the country's wartime news spotlight on one island named Kiska, an unknown, tiny—five by twenty-two miles—uninhabited, treeless dot, its south shore on the North Pacific, its north on the Bering Sea, part of Alaska but closer to Asia than to the contiguous United States.

At one end was a perfectly shaped steaming volcano, cloud-cushioned, well-wrapped, and, as though publicly shy, her full form rarely revealed; all around were cliff-walled shores and, when visible, a bright green matting of waist-high tundra scrub and deep lush mosses—a great green sponge of slopes rising to a rocky knife-edge crest nearly eight hundred feet above the shore up in the fog, and zigzagging its ridge-line backbone toward the seldom-visible four-thousand-foot cone of the volcano.

The whole vertical form rises out of the sea near the western end of the twelve-hundred-mile Aleutian Chain and is singled out in the *Coast Pilot*, the navigator's bible, as having the world's worst weather: eight clear days a year, against an average of 250 days of rain, and a knock-down deafening wind. The remaining hundred days, black-clouded and threatening, did at times, if begrudgingly, allow bright bands and spotlights of sunshine to electrify the glossy greens of the tundra, or reflect, with dazzling sparkles from roiling patches of sea, sudden breath-taking scenes of beauty when least expected. Even underfoot were unusual ferns and rare alpine flowers—all like some seductive version of Jekyll and Hyde.

In many ways nearby Attu was more deserving of the national attention. Its recovery cost 549 lives—only Iwo Jima would be bloodier—and a horrible suicide charge ended it. But of course for grabbing the spotlight timing is everything. Attu just dropped into place as Act One of the growing drama of Kiska's Act Two, with its heroic and chancy bombing raids; the cat-and-mouse ship and

sub sinkings; and then a grandiose this-will-do-it super blockade—an unprecedented seamless doughnut of ships around the whole fog-bound island. All this building up to Act Three, the Kiska climax.

And the climax? A real media bell-ringer! The world loves a mystery, and Kiska produced a notorious disappearing act—the spooky Case of the Missing Enemy. Not who-done-it? but how-done-it?

For the enemy was suddenly long gone from the island and no one had known it! Neither how nor when! And none more surprised than us! Battleships, planes, and guns all swatting away at empty air—like a whole army or navy of mighty Caseys-at-the-bat! Striking out, and striking out, over and over. Swinging at an enemy who was gone and out of there.

So the world had to know. How did they do it? Cornered and trapped, how can a large Japanese garrison of fifty-eight hundred just vanish? How skip without leaving its very emptiness showing—a nothingness there—a ghost-town look of vacancy, some sign of no one at home.[2] And then those five-thousand-plus escapees sardined below decks, how did they squirm undetected through, over, or under, the seamless ring of ships with their radars and sonars all perking away? And we all the time thinking we knew what was what.

Fifty years later we now do know what was what— how the trapped garrison was rescued. The farfetched facts: some old British radar, farfetched indeed, recovered from the bottom off the Malayan Peninsula, from Britain's sunken battleship, the great *Prince of Wales*, and now in use on Kiska, futilely passing the time, probing the foggy noose of ships around them. There comes a time, though, when the probers jump and come alive, not daring to believe what their screen confirms: there's a huge gap in the doughnut—a big piece gone.

And, true enough, a large segment of our ships— eager for any kind of action—and glad to believe their radar, had actually left, under orders, to go chasing after some alarming radar blips—pips they were called then. A phantom enemy. Possibly a reflected "echo" from some distant island or whatever—maybe perfidious Kiska herself!

Off they went—four battleships, three cruisers, and a covey of destroyers—streaming off to fight what is now called the "Battle of the Pips." No wreckage, debris, nor dead whales were ever found. Nothing but spent ammunition on the bottom. And then off and away to refuel and rearm, leaving the door wide open.

Meanwhile, Presto! The lurking Japanese, a safe distance from blip war and blockade—two light cruisers and eight destroyers—slip easily through the foggy gap,

---

[2] Actually, there were signs observed, but they were considered inconclusive by the high command, and no advance effort was allowed for reconnoitering with scouting parties— normally routine under such circumstances. No word of the evacuation possibility was ever shared below the highest command. "The training would be good for us," was a remembered quote from the top..

skirt the coast and zip into Kiska Harbor. In just fifty-five minutes—unbelievable—the entire garrison of fifty-three hundred men is loaded and evacuated without losing a man. The Japanese left nothing alive but one frantic dog, (or maybe two or three—he kept leaping out of the fog) and some very-much-alive bombs timed to blow, one per day. But fifty-three hundred men in fifty-five minutes! They must have been slid in on slides like coal down a chute.[3]

That was July 28, 1943. On August 15th, before dawn, three one-thousand-man spearheads of mountain troops land—with slow difficulty—one boat at a time. The navy in their reconnoitering, perhaps in heavy fog, seemed to have gotten poor information on the tide. It was out. Exposing a rising garden of volcanic rocks.

Anyway, in time we landed as planned at two coves, on the north—or Bering Sea—side of the island, the side so steep and close to the water as to have been thought unassailable by the enemy. From the rock beaches the mountain troops not only climbed, but cut stair steps for those who would follow, and, as trained, they back-packed all their equipment and support material up to their position objectives along the backbone ridge; and they were there by mid-afternoon of the first day. This was the Eighty-Seventh Mountain Infantry, a regiment of roughly three thousand. Behind them in support were ten times that number, upwards off thirty thousand men, five thousand of them Canadians—most of them regular infantry units and not mountain trained, though trained Special Service Force patrols had also made a landing well before dawn at high tide.

That afternoon and night, up on the high sharp ridge, the real enemy, Kiska, rose in full fury. A tent or shelter was unthinkable. Foxholes, saucer-like, could only be scrunched down into, impossible to dig deeper into the windswept rock. It was discouraging, too, after hard digging, to have positions shifted as the companies and battalions were forced to fill gaps that awaited the support units, units that had not yet arrived and would not for another day.

Visibility wavered like reflections in water—went from blurred to blindness and back to wavering. The volcanic rock piles and a standing soldier struck momentary resemblances as they similarly billowed and rippled like cloth; and a voice would over-shout, quaver, die out, and come back loud in a short-wave sort of way. Orders or report communications were difficult, and had at least once been seriously misunderstood.

That first afternoon I went on a check of our front line positions with the S3, the operations officer, a major, and we came on a wounded lieutenant whom I knew well. He was a few yards below us on the forward slope

and had been shot in the thigh and was unable to climb up to the ridge. He assured us that he had killed the "Jap" who had shot him—he had seen him clearly and close up, and watched him fall—though there was no body that we could find anywhere. We did manage to find in the fog two aid men with stretcher and blankets who got him out of his bloody trousers, which we left weighted down with rocks to mark where the missing "Jap" body might later be found.

In the morning there had been rumors—sightings of helmeted shapes and Oriental faces flitting through the fog. And also unconfirmed exchanges of fire were reported—enough of a drumbeat of reports on the enemy to generate alertness for some kind of counterattack. And since the wound and the blood were certainly not rumors, and the lieutenant was a known reliable fellow, I was surprised, even disconcerted, at my major's suspicious dissatisfaction. He rejected the "fact" of a solitary single-shot "Jap" who fired and fell and then disappeared completely. He was sensing the truth, and well before any of the higher command above us did (or, worse, let on they did). And also before any of the lower rest-of-us could even begin to imagine.

Right then he wanted the two of us to trot down to the "Jap harbor" and prove there was no enemy on the island! I was sure he was crazy. Plumb out of his mind! Though a lowly lieutenant, I braced myself to try to dissuade him, a West Pointer, by some such as: "In combat, Sir, should a staff officer just take off on his own like that?"

He stuck his wet face into mine, our helmets near touching. When he spoke, his words and mouth, I remember, were out of sync.

"Lieutenant," he snapped, "If a staff officer did that he'd be shot. Shot by either the enemy or a court martial firing squad." And, sarcastically, "Isn't that right, Lieutenant?"

Then with a hard smile of acceptance, and facing downhill for a final instant, he turned back and we continued in file along our ridge. But had we obeyed his surge of conviction, however recklessly, precious lives could have been saved.

As to the wounded lieutenant, he recovered to fight another day, back with us in Italy. However, during that night, the inevitable broke out, units had been located in mistakenly reported positions that, because of the zigzag ridge line, were invisibly opposite each other. Firing erupted and counter-fire and counter-attack were called for. Eleven were killed.

From my checking I am satisfied it was eleven, not fifteen, certainly not thirty—figures variously given. The total accidental deaths of all kinds for the regiment were

---

[3] In fact, dozens of cargo nets were strung along the sides of many ships.

twenty-nine—the difference arising from mines and timed bombs; accidental ammunition detonations; skid and roll-over vehicular casualties; unexploded bombs in the tundra; and the insidious booby trap explosions.

Many were the ways to die on Kiska. There were more than three hundred casualties. Seventy-one navy men were killed by an off-harbor mine—against which friendly fire becomes minor. But the eleven stay in mind, in a private Kiska chamber.

I lost two close friends that night in '43: one a young sculptor, Wilford Funk—of the Funk and Wagnalls Dictionary family—who before enlisting had apprenticed to the great Gutzon Borglum and had worked under him on the gigantic presidents' faces at Mount Rushmore, South Dakota. He liked to describe swinging across on a hanging rope from Teddy Roosevelt's mustache to Lincoln's lower protruding lip. He died leading a heroic charge to save that command post that was out of position and mistakenly thought itself being overrun. We were close. I still miss him. He was a friend from the inside out.

The other, Ralph Hamill, I knew less well, though his wife and mine and two others were sharing a house together in Carmel, California. He was a good friend too—very likable—but more from the outside in. The four girls waiting up together heard San Francisco radio at midnight on the 18th announce the great headline: "No Japs on the Island!" Their worries were over! And so, jubilantly they popped the champagne, only in the morning to receive that War Department telegram.

In Italy we saw so much, much more of all kinds of friendly fire mistakes so that we came to accept it as normal—as normal anyway as the harassing 88's. Normal if not too close, or personal—like short rounds from your own artillery, or P-38s diving at your moving jeep with rockets. And yet in Italy there was no covering fog to excuse it. It should have been less acceptable. Instead it was more so. More acceptable because the presence of the enemy was a far better cover than fog or anything else ever could be. It covered everything automatically. And made all the difference.

An old friend of our island, still sensitive over the term "buddy killer," wrote recently about friendly fire killings in Italy:

I killed a soldier during our first fire fight. This was close combat in bad light, smoke, noise and confusion. He suddenly appeared out of the smoke with his machine pistol aimed at my gut. I put him down and, as he went backward downhill and out of sight, I caught a glimpse of an unmistakable O.D. [Olive Drab] American sweater under his mountain parka. I crouched there, frozen in horror, with the thought that I had just killed one of our

own people. When the noise and dust subsided and I could finally move I got to him and looked down into the face of a young German boy wearing one of our sweaters, probably taken from one of our bodies to keep himself warm.

For Kiska, *Time* magazine unsympathetically invented a new word, JANFU (joint army-navy foul-up), to replace the earlier World War II SNAFU (situation normal, all fouled up). There were many more, and all kinds of foul-ups in Italy; but no one blamed us.

Much cleverer than JANFU was our own wordplay: "Optical Aleutian." Optical Aleutian—it carries a certain grace and more than a germ of meaning for, in truth, Kiska's wind and fog produced crowds of optical illusion, and not always bad ones. Illusions however that occasionally drew fire, friendly or imagined, by ships and men, and cost good, good lives. Or as someone put it: "Usually in combat the enemy is the enemy, but on Kiska it was Kiska, and Kiska alone. It fought us and the navy and air corps and often won!"

In any case, the Eighty-Seventh Mountain Infantry, if not born on Kiska, was weaned there, cut its teeth on her cliffs and proved itself on her tundra and fog, on her tough, tough hide and wild foggy scenery. But before winter the regiment was pulled back to its old camp in Colorado to expand, help train, and fit in with the newly forming division; the experimental regiment had come into its majority, became the Tenth Mountain, a light, specially trained division with as unique a military function as the better-understood "airborne" or "armored" divisions, a "mountain" division, the first and only of its kind in the history of our army.

Nobody will say, still, why getting ready for Europe meant assignment to Texas. Washington brass wanted us out of the mountains and onto the flat so they could count us in comfort—that was one theory. Or they hoped to make us more GI. But, anyway, Texas never forgot us. Today there is a "Memorial Tenth Mountain Division Highway" to mark their approval—probably in part from that unforgotten day at high noon when a platoon of rock climbers rappelled all at once out of the top-floor windows of the Hotel Stephen Austin, fifty yodelling men, sailing down the outside walls on climbing ropes, snarling up traffic in down-town Austin for two hours.

But finally it was Italy and back to the mountains—this time the Apennines. First were some unusual assault assignments in the mountains and snow, including a climbing attack up a cliff face on piton-fixed ropes that caught the stunned German defenders with hardly a shot fired. This the much publicized Riva Ridge attack, of the movie, of articles and stories, and in the naming of the famous race horse.

Their final assignment was the division's most costly claim to fame, again spearheading, only this time for the entire Fifth Army's American and British 1945 spring offensive. At times we were as much as thirty miles ahead of all support, and kept going for nineteen days of continuous fighting, capturing, without consolidating to the sides, a long ribbon of territory not much wider than a road, but 108 miles of road—from north of Florence to the Alps—a vulnerably thin line. We passed almost as many prisoners to the rear as we were men marching forward. But by constant pressure we cut through the enemy into rear area headquarters and broke up command and supply systems that kept them from reorganizing and pinching us off. But it meant, "Keep going; no let-up! Tiger by the tail!" So at an average of seven miles a day we had no regular sleep, meals, bathing, laundry, and little chance to even lean against something and sleep standing up. It was just go, go, go, day after day, first through the mountains, then the flat Po valley, and midway a major river crossing—the Po—crossed without air or artillery support and, finally, the Alps and German surrender. It cost almost a thousand men killed, and four times that number in wounded, but it forced an early victory in Italy, and shortened the war in Europe.

From the many commendations sent to us from President Truman and on down, the U.S. commander in chief in Italy, General Mark Clark, made it sound the best: "The Tenth Mountain Division is the finest Army division I have ever seen!"

Sent home early to retrain for a final assault on Japan, the division was disbanded as the war ended, only to be reborn in the '80s. It is a curious coincidence that the original conceiver and midwife of the mountain troop idea was a remarkable civilian, an early skier and insurance broker called "Minnie" Dole, from Connecticut, and that the later instigator for its rebirth who lent his considerable power and influence to bring into being a reactivated Tenth Mountain Division was Senator Bob Dole—who had joined, not as a skier or climber, not in any way related to Minnie, and not from New England, but from pancake-flat Kansas. So a Dole started it and a Dole restored it. But Senator Bob is even otherwise to be honored by the men of the Tenth Mountain. He is one of our seriously wounded veterans, machine-gunned with us in Italy, and still carrying a useless hand. And the strength of his rising above this, to such high personal achievements, reflects the spirit of the Tenth and his indomitable courage and strength.

In conclusion though, I hark back to the division's rugged childhood, when it was just a little, very green regiment on treacherously deceptive soft green Kiska. As we grow and mature, our interests and skills may change, new wrinkles and old character develop, but always be it remembered that the spirit of the Tenth Mountain Division was born and brought up in an unusual and extreme part of the world called Kiska, and that Kiska, in turn, is an unusual part of a most unforgettable part of the world called Alaska. And on behalf of the Eighty-Seventh Mountain Infantry, and its grown up Tenth Mountain Division, we heartily thank you— for our beginnings, our becomings, and our being.

A toast to Alaska and its fiftieth "At War Anniversary!"

*George F. Earle is retired from teaching at Syracuse University, School of Architecture, and the State University of New York. Earle painted while serving for four years of combat duty with the 10th Mountain Division, 1942-1946.*

# Recalling the Battle of Attu

*Teruo Nishijima*

THIS DATE FIFTY YEARS AGO, I WAS IN THE JAPANESE Army, a most unreasonable organization. It happened one night—when the whole division was in bed, except for guards on duty—that one squad of some thirty men drafted in shortly before was awakened by screaming orders, "Get up, get up." They jumped out of their beds, put on uniforms and lined up.

The stupid orders did not come from me, because I was in the line standing at attention. We draftees were wondering what had happened. Then, one of the senior soldiers who woke us beat each of us on the head with a stick. Why did they beat us? Because one of our shoes had a bit of dirt on the sole. Some senior soldier had checked our shoes while we were asleep. Of course, we had cleaned the shoes after the day's training was over, but we had no shoe brushes. In those days, we were short of everything.

Our soldiers had been told that everything was given by the emperor, and it must be used very carefully. Such an unreasonable disciplinary action as I have just mentioned was very common in the Japanese Armed Forces, and it might have happened on Attu as well.

Our people in Japan do not know in detail how their soldiers fought on Attu, because they burnt all the important papers three days after the American landing, and prisoners of war do not like to talk. The messages sent daily from Attu to Kiska were not enough to show us the whole picture.

In June 1942, upon losing the battle of Midway, Admiral Yamamoto ordered his fleet in the Northern Pacific to discontinue Aleutian operations; but soon he withdrew the orders and let them attack Attu and Kiska.

Dr. Samuel Eliot Morison says in his book, *History of United States Naval Operations in World War II*, "The Japanese people, who heard few facts about Midway, were gratified to learn that the Rising Sun was flying over two more American islands."

In September of the same year, the Japanese troops on Attu moved to Kiska, and the following month they recaptured Attu. They took all of the forty-one Aleuts with them when they left Attu. One of them died on the way to Kiska. Without being landed at Kiska, the forty Aleuts were sent to the city of Otaru, in Hokkaido, Japan. In Otaru, sixteen of them died. There, four babies were born and three died.

When the war ended in 1945, all of the 215 Aleuts left the city of Otaru, never to go back to Attu. They went to Seattle through Okinawa and the Philippines. In the Philippines, two of them died. When the Japanese troops occupied Attu in 1942, they found that most of the Aleuts were suffering from tuberculosis.

As to Admiral Yamamoto, some Japanese now say he was no good, because he made a great mistake in attacking Pearl Harbor and he also lost the Battle of Midway. For those two failures, he refused to take the blame. However, it is true that he did not want to attack Pearl Harbor before the declaration of war. It was not his fault, but a failure of the Japanese Embassy in Washington, D.C. They could not submit the papers of declaration to the State Department at the scheduled time, due to clerical inefficiency as it was Sunday.

When referring to dates and times hereafter, I shall use American timing because of the differences imposed by the international date line problems. Colonel

Attu Village on Chichagof Harbor. American bombers destroyed the village after the Japanese evacuated the resident Aleuts to Otaru, in Japan. Note the Japanese installations. *(Official U.S. Air Force photograph)*

Yamazaki arrived at Attu by submarine on April 17, 1943, and took command from Lieutenant Colonel Yoneyama. No boat other than a submarine could approach Attu in those days. The day when Colonel Yamazaki arrived at Attu, Admiral Yamamoto was killed when his plane was shot down by American fighters in the South Pacific. His death was kept secret for some time in Japan, and the American government also kept silent, because they did not want Japan to know that their messages were being decoded. In fact, Japan did not know until the war was over that their messages were being decoded all during the war.

On May 22, General Higuchi, a commander of the Northern Corps, notified Colonel Yamazaki to die with honor, although the army would try to help him as much as possible with the navy. The following day, Emperor Hirohito commended the colonel and his men for their brave actions.

Japanese troops approach Attu Village in June 1942. *(Captured Japanese photo, courtesy Command Historian's Office, Alaskan Command)*

An emperor of Japan has no power—military, political, or commercial. This is why the emperor system has lasted more than a thousand years. In August 1945, Emperor Hirohito stopped the war because his cabinet could not decide whether they should surrender or continue to fight. They asked the emperor for a decision, and he told them to surrender. That was his first and last exercising of power.

Emperor Hirohito was a fine man even though he declared war against your country in 1941, as his cabinet had requested. When he met General MacArthur for the first time on September 26, 1945, in Tokyo, he told MacArthur that he was responsible for all the actions taken by the government and the military. Also he said that he was ready for any punishment and asked MacArthur to save his people. General MacArthur considered the emperor to be a real gentleman. After the meeting, he saw the emperor off at the front door of his headquarters.

On May 28, 1943, Colonel Yamazaki and his men on Attu were surrounded by Americans. The American troops under Major General Landrum were ready to start the last annihilating attack on the following day. Colonel Yamazaki realized the situation and determined to make his final charge ahead of the Americans. He sent a farewell message to Kiska and destroyed the radio equipment. He told the wounded to kill themselves. He told the post office workers to follow behind his soldiers and never to be captured.

Colonel Yamazaki ordered Captain Numata and Lieutenant Commander Emoto, a naval officer, to stay behind and report to the higher headquarters on what had happened on Attu.

Colonel Yamazaki wanted to break through Engineer Hill and go down to Massacre Bay to get to the American guns, ammunition, and food. He might then be able to hold on until re-enforcements arrived.

Colonel Yamazaki wanted to reach Engineer Hill before dawn. But it took too much time getting all his men from scattered positions. So shortly after their arrival at Engineer Hill, the day dawned.

What happened to Captain Numata and Lieutenant Commander Emoto who were ordered not to join the final charge? Nobody knows! On June 2, a Japanese submarine went to Attu. The sea was too rough for it to reach the appointed place. Two days later, they made it, but failed to contact the two officers. On the sixth day the submarine went in again, but the sea was too rough to make contact. Since then the submarine has been missing with Captain Hanabusa and his crew.

In 1953, the Japanese government sent some people to Attu in cooperation with the American government. They found the bodies of Captain Numata and Lieutenant Commander Emoto in a cave. I know why they did not surrender, but now I think they should have done so.

Near Engineer Hill stands a monument dedicated to Colonel Yamazaki. The monument says:

ATTU ISLAND
WORLD WAR II
1943
YAMAZAKI, A COLONEL
IN THE JAPANESE ARMY
WAS KILLED IN ACTION
NEAR THIS POINT, COLONEL
YAMAZAKI COMMANDED
JAPANESE TROOPS ON ATTU

The monument does not record who built it. It just says, "Erected by Order of the Commandant Seventeenth Naval District." I would like to know more about this officer. I respect his courteous action very much.

Most Japanese soldiers did not know about the international treaty concerning treatment of prisoners of war. They were told that to be a P.O.W. brings a great shame on the man as well as his family. All men were expected to commit suicide before being captured. They were told that Americans would butcher them.

One Japanese prisoner of war, who was a doctor, performed an operation on a dying Japanese soldier on board an American ship from Attu. The operation succeeded and the soldier was saved. This doctor told the soldier never to die. When American soldiers diverted their attention, the doctor jumped overboard into the misty waters of the Aleutians. I do not know if this story is true or not. It is said one Japanese P.O.W. heard it from an American MP.

When Colonel Yamazaki and his men perished, the Imperial Headquarters in Tokyo announced that all of the twenty-six hundred soldiers were dead. Three of my friends were among them. After the war, twenty-seven prisoners of war came back to Japan from the U.S.A. Sergeant Iseda, one of them, still thinks he was a better soldier than were the Americans, but he says that Americans are more broad-minded than Japanese. He is still disabled and operates a bed-and-breakfast with his wife. The name of his establishment is "Attu."

Two months after the battle of Attu, American troops landed at Kiska to find no Japanese, but only some dogs. On July 28, all of the 5,219 Japanese soldiers were evacuated from Kiska. Strange to say, the American fleet was not there. It had left to get supplies. Stranger still, the moment the Japanese ships entered a bay, the almost constant mist cleared up and the evacuation was completed in fifty minutes. Lieutenant General Higuchi, commander of the Northern Corps, said later that the spirits of Attu soldiers helped the Kiska troops. It is said

Soldiers pose on snowy Attu Island. *(Captured Japanese photo, Command Historian's Office, Alaskan Command)*

that some soldiers heard shouting when they passed off Attu.

As I said earlier, Higuchi had the unenviable task of informing the troops on Attu that they had to die with honor, but five years before, he saved many lives in Manchuria, where he was stationed as a major general. In March 1938, some twenty thousand Jewish people fled from Germany, and came to the border between Manchuria and Soviet Russia. The government of Manchuria, a puppet government of Japan, did not want to let them in.

Higuchi, then in charge of the border district, was determined to save the Jews. Trains were prepared with doctors, nurses, etc. As a result, most of the Jewish people went safely to the U.S.A. through Shanghai.

Of course, Hitler protested to Japan. Higuchi was ordered to report to Manchurian Army Headquarters, where the chief of staff was Tojo. Higuchi explained to Tojo that Hitler was to blame, not the Jews. Higuchi said later that as far as the Jewish people were concerned, Tojo was right. Without the intervention of Higuchi, the

twenty thousand Jewish people would have frozen to death. The winter on the Russian border is as severe as here in Alaska.

When the war ended in 1945, Russia wanted to arrest Higuchi as a war criminal, but MacArthur's headquarters refused. It is said that the World Jewish Society in New York did not want him to be arrested. In Jerusalem stands a monument called "Golden Book," where the names of those who helped Jewish people are engraved. Among them are the name of General Higuchi, Dr. Einstein, and others.

Fifty years ago, we fought against each other. It does not matter now who won or who lost. The question is: What have we really learned from the war?

Thank you very much for inviting me to your meeting today. I have enjoyed the opportunity of being here.

*Teruo Nishijima is a historian and journalist. He has authored eight books and currently writes a column, "Breakfast Table," for the "Hokkaido Shinbunshu."*

# Tin Can at War:
# The USS *Monaghan* and the War in Alaska

*Gary Candelaria*

**M**ORE THAN FIVE HUNDRED DESTROYERS SERVED IN the United States Navy in World War II.[1] Destroyers were the workhorses of the fleet, performing a multitude of duties. No task force ever had enough destroyers. World War II in Alaska was no different in this aspect of naval warfare, and the destroyers called upon to find and fight the Imperial Japanese Navy in the North Pacific were hard-used and oft-engaged. One "tin can" so employed was the USS *Monaghan* (DD-354).

Farragut-class *Monaghan* was commissioned in 1935.[2] With torpedoes, 5-inch guns, and speed, the eight Farraguts were the first modern U.S. destroyers, vast improvements over the flush-deck, four-stack ships that made up the American destroyer fleet between the wars.

*Monaghan* was no stranger to Alaska, having visited the North Pacific in 1936 and 1938.[3] The designated "duty destroyer" at Pearl Harbor the morning of 7 December 1941, she was already preparing to assist destroyer *Ward* (DD-139) on antisubmarine duty outside the harbor when the attack began. *Monaghan* was quickly underway and out of the harbor during the attack, sinking a midget submarine en route. She fought at Coral Sea and Midway, and thus was a veteran campaigner with four battle stars when ordered to Alaska in July 1942.

Water Tender Joseph C. "Mother" McCrane remembers his first impressions of Alaska on *Monaghan*, where the ship pitched and tossed with seventy-degree rolls:

> When we first went to the Aleutians, we didn't have hardly any foul weather gear at all, nobody had jackets, nobody had anything. The only ones that got coats were the seamen ... we were cold and wet.[4]

*Monaghan* water tender Joseph J. "Candy" Candelaria Jr. describes the Aleutians as "nothing but fog and rough seas, Kiska, Attu, Amchitka and Dutch Harbor, Unalaska, all of that."[5]

*Monaghan's* first Aleutian stay was brief. On 27 July, she collided in fog with destroyer-minesweeper *Long* (DMS-12) off Kiska while maneuvering to bombard the Japanese-held island. Two other destroyer-minesweepers also collided, reducing the task force's minesweeping force to one ship. Unable to sweep the mines thought to be protecting Kiska Harbor, the task force withdrew without accomplishing its mission. The cripples retired to Dutch Harbor where *Monaghan* made emergency repairs.[6] In early August she left Alaska,

---

[1] Calculation based upon figures in M.J. Whitley, *Destroyers in World War Two* (Annapolis, Maryland: Naval Institute Press, 1988).

[2] Sampson Low, Marston and Company, Ltd., *Jane's Fighting Ships, 1943-44* (London: 1943), p. 475.

[3] "Deck Logs, USS *Monaghan*, Volumes I-XIV," volume II, 6 July, 1936, volume IV, 1 July, 1938, U.S. National Archives.

[4] Joseph C. McCrane, personal interview: Clementon, New Jersey, 18 May 1989.

[5] Joseph J. Candelaria Jr., personal Interview: Pico Rivera, California, 28 November, 1987.

[6] Samuel E. Morison, *History of United States Naval Operations in World War II*, vol. 7, *Aleutians, Gilberts, and Marshalls, June, 1942-April, 1944*

escorting a fleet oiler to Pearl Harbor. In September, *Monaghan* entered Mare Island Naval Shipyard to repair a longitudinal beam broken by the pounding Aleutian seas and to permanently repair the Aleutian collision damage.[7]

She went to the South Pacific before returning to Alaska on 21 February 1943. On that same day, she received a new captain, Lieutenant Commander Peter H. Horn.[8] She joined Task Group 16.6 under Rear Admiral Charles Horatio "Soc" (Socrates) McMorris, flying his flag in light cruiser *Richmond* (CL-9). In late March, the task group—heavy cruiser *Salt Lake City* (CA-25), *Richmond*, and destroyers *Bailey* (DD-492), *Coghlan* (DD-606), *Dale* (DD-353), and *Monaghan*—was patrolling near Attu to prevent resupply of the Japanese garrison. A Japanese scout plane spotted the American vessels, and Vice Admiral Boshiro Hosogaya decided to shatter the blockade with a superior naval force while running in a supply convoy to Attu.[9]

At 0730, 26 March, McMorris's squadron was west of Attu. Lead ship *Coghlan* made a five-ship radar contact bearing almost due north. *Richmond* also made contact, but in the dim morning light of the early Aleutian spring, lookouts could not determine what type of ships they were closing on. As the range shortened, more ships came into view, and it was assumed they were merchantmen bound to resupply Attu and Kiska.[10]

Seeing only a light cruiser and a destroyer escorting the convoy, McMorris anticipated a Roman holiday sinking "*marus*." His optimism was shared by the American crews.[11]

Candelaria says: "I remember going up on the deck and across it going down to the fire room. We was going to attack some transports; going to be all over in a few minutes; duck soup."[12]

As the range closed, lookouts began reporting something seriously wrong: first one, then another Japanese heavy cruiser was spotted; a second light cruiser was also seen. Hosogaya indeed had a superior naval force—two heavy and two light cruisers, four destroyers, and two converted, heavily armed merchant cruisers. It was now McMorris who was in danger of becoming duck soup, facing eight warships and two auxiliary cruisers with his six men-of-war.[13]

Hosogaya turned to engage, sending the two troop-carrying merchant cruisers to the northwest with the third *maru*.[14] McMorris radioed for air support and turned to pursue the merchantmen, putting the Japanese fleet to starboard, between him and home.[15] Candelaria continues:

> I went back to my battle station on Gun 4 on the fantail. And as I went, Pharmacist Mate Kresky was at the quarterdeck, and Pace and Johnson, the officers' black mess attendants, were being dragged down to the ammunition lockers. They didn't want to go, they were crying, and I don't blame them, three decks down and dogged-down in the watertight integrity. If a shell hit, it would be the end. Kresky told me, "Look out at them out there, take a look at them," and he was crying. I told him, "You're in one hell of a shape to take care of anybody. You'd better get back there to your station," which was the after head. I didn't see him after that. They later transferred him.[16]

At 0840, the Japanese opened fire on *Richmond* at a range of twenty-one thousand yards, and the Battle of the Komandorski Islands began. McMorris ordered a turn to port, away from the Japanese. He continued turning until he was headed southwest, away from Attu and home, with the Japanese on his port side in hot pursuit.[17] The would-be duck hunters were now the hunted. For the next four hours, the Japanese and American squadrons danced across the North Pacific, firing thousands of 8-, 6-, and 5-inch shells at each other.[18] Komandorski Island was a daylight, surface gun battle, and for much of the fight, it was a stern chase by the Japanese. *Salt Lake City*'s ten 8-inch guns traded heavyweight long-distance blows with the Japanese heavy cruisers,

---

(Boston: Little, Brown and Company, 1952), pp. 9-10.

[7] McCrane reports the damaged beam, *Ship's History, USS "Monaghan,"* (Ships' History Section, Washington, D.C.: United States Navy Department, 1954), p. 4.

[8] "Deck Logs," vol. X, 3 February 1943.

[9] Theodore Roscoe, *United States Destroyer Operations in World War II* (Annapolis, Maryland: Naval Institute Press, 1953), p. 156.

[10] Morison, *Naval Operations*, p. 24.

[11] Ibid.

[12] Candelaria.

[13] Morison, *Naval Operations*, p. 25.

[14] Ibid.

[15] Roscoe, *Destroyer Operations*, pp. 157-158.

[16] Candelaria.

[17] Morison, *Naval Operations*, p. 26.

[18] John A. Lorelli, *The Battle of the Komandorski Islands* (Annapolis, Maryland: Naval Institute Press, 1984), p. 72.

keeping them at bay through most of the battle.[19]

Candelaria recalls the emotion and intensity of the shelling on *Monaghan*:

> I don't remember seeing the actual ships because they were hull-down on the horizon. But their fire was very heavy. I'd see a little "blink!" of light, and then the shells would come overhead and great big geysers of water would go up. Then "blink!" and more shells. We were firing too. Gun 4 would not fire. It had been so hot from firing that the gun would not fire. So Stofford, he was Gunners Mate First, he had to hit the damn thing with a sledgehammer in order to make it fire.[20]

Torpedoman Andrew "Red" Parker was also on *Monaghan*:

> I was on the fantail, and between the depth charge racks was a smoke screen generator, and I was told to stand by it. And I could see the shells from the cruiser hitting in the water, splash!, behind us. And I reported that, and our captain changed course. And the shells went down one side, and we changed, and they went down the other side. And then we made a smoke screen and they stopped shooting at us. And I was thinking then that the next round of shells from that cruiser was going to go right down our ship. I tightened up my life jacket.[21]

*Monaghan* and the other destroyers were in the thick of the fight, moving ahead and astern along the American column, firing as their guns would bear. The shelling was very intense. In only a few minutes after 1000 hours, more than two hundred shells from heavy cruisers *Nachi* and *Maya* fell around *Salt Lake City*, only one of which, a dud, hit.[22]

By 0920, the Americans were running for their lives, towards Japan and the Soviet Union.

"We were scared; a destroyer is only quarter-inch plate," was how Candelaria described the feeling aboard *Monaghan*.[23]

"I remember that as the day I thought I wasn't going to be alive any longer, or anybody else on that ship," recalls Water Tender Russell Friesen.[24]

Parker agrees: "I was scared."[25]

About 22,600 yards separated the American rear—*Bailey*, *Coghlan*, and *Salt Lake City*—from *Nachi*, the van of the Japanese line. At 1013, McMorris ordered a smoke screen.[26] The black oil and acrid white generator smoke did not slow the enemy fire.[27]

*Richmond* was about three thousand yards ahead of *Salt Lake City* when McMorris ordered *Monaghan* and *Dale* to fall back and make smoke with the heavy cruiser and her two destroyers; *Richmond* continued in the lead.[28]

At about 1100, *Monaghan* developed engineering troubles. A reduction gear lost a tooth, which passed through the gear housing with a grinding crash. The engine was slowed to prevent a complete disintegration of the reduction gear. Captain Horn ordered that full speed be resumed, despite potential damage to the ship's propulsion system. The system held together, though it later required extensive repair and was never again quite right.[29]

At the same time, a drama occurred in Number Two fire room. The two small boilers there had been off-line when the battle began. The fire room gang had forced them on-line faster than they should have,[30] causing the boiler casings to heat red-hot and melt the insulating firebrick.[31] The damage was costing *Monaghan* power and speed.

Boilermaker Frank "Killer" Cain was in charge of Number Two fire room when Horn ordered the boiler pressure release safety valves tied down to build up more steam pressure.

Candelaria recalls the scene:

> I remember the chief engineer was running up and down the deck, and Horn ordered him to gag safeties and he (Cain) wouldn't do it. It was against

---

[19] Roscoe, *Destroyer Operations*, p. 159.

[20] Candelaria.

[21] Andrew Parker, personal interview: Gridley, California, 24 April 1992.

[22] Morison, *Naval Operations*, p. 29.

[23] Candelaria.

[24] Russell Friesen, personal interview: Temecula, California, 19 December 1988.

[25] Parker.

[26] Lorelli, *Komandorski Islands*, p. 106.

[27] Ibid., p. 107.

[28] Ibid., p. 108.

[29] Ibid., p. 110. Friesen and Candelaria report that *Monaghan*'s reduction gear was never quite right again after Komandorski.

[30] Lorelli, *Komandorski Islands*, p. 110.

[31] McCrane.

navy regs to gag safeties, and Cain wouldn't do it. Finally, he had to do it.[32]

*Monaghan* remained on station despite her problems, making smoke off *Salt Lake City*'s port side.[33]

"Cain almost got court-martialed for refusing to gag," adds McCrane. "Horn got the Silver Star."[34]

As the battle swirled closer to Soviet Kamchatka and Japanese air bases at Paramushiro,[35] chances of escape dimmed, and internment in a neutral Soviet port loomed.

"We were either going to be sunk or go to Russia," states Candelaria.[36]

At 1103, *Salt Lake City* took a final, telling hit. Taking on water, the ship listed to port five degrees. At 1125, the after fire room went off-line due to oil system damage and speed fell to twenty knots.[37] Three destroyers were ordered to make a torpedo attack to screen the slowing cruiser. The order was cancelled when she regained speed.[38] By this time, the course of the chase had put the Americans south and east of their pursuers. But just when it seemed the Americans would make a run for home and air cover, *Salt Lake City*'s boilers were fouled by seawater. Her fires went out, gushing white smoke from the stacks as they died.[39] She began what must have sounded like a litany of doom: "My speed twenty-two; My speed fourteen; My speed eight; My speed four." At 1154, her yardarm displayed the dismal signal, "My speed zero." Dead in the water,[40] her crew prepared for a last stand.[41]

*Coghlan*, *Bailey*, and *Monaghan* were ordered to protect *Salt Lake City* with a torpedo run; *Dale* was to screen the nearly helpless cruiser with smoke.[42]

Candelaria:

I was down below on the burners in Number One fire room when the order came for the torpedo attack. I turned to Bush (water tender first-class), who was on the blower, and I said to him,

"What is a torpedo run?" He said, "You'll find out; cut 'em in!" because they had run up "Flank Speed Ahead" on the annunciators. Well, when you ring-up "Flank," it just draws that steam off the boilers and you have to start cutting in burners. You really throw the oil in there to attain 30 knots through the water. I was good at that. So that's what I was doing when we went in for the torpedo run.[43]

Friesen was there, too, and he recalls his feelings:

I couldn't see how we could possibly get out of this thing, because we were running from the Japs; they had us on the run and just had everything going for them. It was bad. But when they called for the torpedo run, they said, well, it was going to be a suicide run, just go in and shoot your torpedoes. You're going to get sunk, but at least you'll probably sink one or two of theirs. I says, "Well, it wasn't bad enough to go two hours or so getting shot at constantly, and thinking you're going to get sunk, but they tell you to go straight in!" Well, the bottom really fell out.[44]

"We had all said goodbye to each other," recalls Chief Petty Officer John Richardson.[45]

Machinist Mate Ernest Stahlberg, on the port throttle in Number One engine room, recalls how he got the word:

It was quite an experience. The chief engineer came around and shook hands with everybody when we started making our torpedo run. I was always kidding him about I was going to get off the ship and go to diesel school so I could get a few days back in the states instead of out in the South Pacific for so long. But he just comes around

[32] Candelaria.

[33] Lorelli, *Komandorski Islands*, p. 110.

[34] McCrane.

[35] Morison, *Naval Operations*, pp. 29-30.

[36] Candelaria.

[37] Morison, *Naval Operations*, p. 30.

[38] Roscoe, *Destroyer Operations*, p. 160.

[39] Lorelli, *Komandorski Islands*, p. 122.

[40] Ibid., p. 123.

[41] Ibid., p. 127.

[42] Ibid., p. 129.

[43] Candelaria.

[44] Friesen.

[45] John Richardson, personal interview: Gridley, California, 24 April 1992.

and says, "Well, I guess I should have sent you to the diesel school."[46]

*Monaghan* could see *Richmond* in the distance, underway to the southeast, away from the fight, with the rest of the American squadron between her and the Japanese.[47] *Richmond* looked to be leaving the destroyers and *Salt Lake City* to their fate.

Friesen:

> The *Richmond* had the high-ranking officer (McMorris) on it. And it took off as fast as it could go. We were set to lay the smoke screen and face up to this thing. The *Richmond* was considered to have done a cowardly thing and didn't stay there and help the *Salt Lake City* and take part in this.[48]

Even some of *Richmond*'s officers and men were disturbed by their ship's apparent disinterest and distance from her engaged consorts. *Dale*'s crew had the same feelings.[49] Later, at Dutch Harbor, the men of *Salt Lake City* threw a beer party for their destroyer saviors, but pointedly dis-invited *Richmond*'s crew.[50]

("What ship you from?" was the challenge at the entrance to the beer bust. "*Monaghan!*" "Come on in." "What ship?" "*Richmond*." Over the side they went.[51])

*Monaghan* had to come up *Salt Lake City*'s port side and cut across her bow to form up with *Bailey* and *Coghlan*. By the time she made her transit, she was two thousand yards behind the others, charging the Japanese 18,500 yards away to the northwest.[52]

"We were goners," said Candelaria. "The water was only thirty degrees, you would only last a couple or three minutes in that degree of water."[53]

A forest of splashes sprang up around *Bailey* and *Coghlan*. "I counted over 125 projectiles," says Signalman Frank Andrews, who was on *Monaghan*'s bridge.[54]

*Monaghan*, some distance behind, was not shelled.[55]

"The average lifetime of a destroyer in surface combat is five minutes," opines Candelaria.[56] *Bailey* proved the opinion just about right. Eight-inch shells from *Nachi* and *Maya* found her, and, shortly after 1200, four hits struck the tin can ten thousand yards out from her targets.[57] At ninety-five hundred yards out, *Bailey* fired five torpedoes.[58] All missed, and staggered by her toll of hits, *Bailey* slowed and turned away.

Parker was ready for action on *Monaghan*:

> I had my torpedoes all set. I had the forward (torpedo) mount, and I was sitting there with the binoculars on them, directing them (the aimers) and watching 5-inch shells hit the cruiser. We were trained (aimed), ready to shoot them (the torpedoes).[59]

Firing at *Salt Lake City* slackened as the Japanese shifted attention to the attacking destroyers. The cruiser labored to get her engines back on line, and at 1158, only eight minutes after the fires died, enough steam had been built up to power the screws.[60] The destroyers were still charging the Japanese, and *Bailey* and *Monaghan* were dusting *Nachi* with their 5-inch guns while *Coghlan* took on *Maya*.

At 1203, as *Coghlan* came abreast of damaged and slowing *Bailey*, the Japanese began to turn away to the west. Before *Coghlan* could launch torpedoes, the target angle was too unfavorable to hope for a hit. The range, extreme when *Bailey* launched, was even greater and opening. *Coghlan* held her torpedoes and she and *Bailey* turned back toward *Salt Lake City*.[61] *Monaghan* too, held her torpedoes, and turned away.

"They said, 'Train the tubes in midships and save them,'" says Parker.[62]

Firing ceased at 1212; by 1215, the Japanese were hull

---

[46] Ernest Stahlberg, personal interview: Gridley, California, 24 April 1992.

[47] Lorelli, *Komandorski Islands*, p. 129.

[48] Friesen.

[49] Lorelli, *Komandorski Islands*, p. 137.

[50] Candelaria.

[51] Ibid.

[52] Lorelli, *Komandorski Islands*, pp. 129-130.

[53] Candelaria.

[54] Frank Andrews, personal interview: Gridley, California, 24 April 1992.

[55] Roscoe, *Destroyer Operations*, p. 161.

[56] Candelaria.

[57] Lorelli, *Komandorski Islands*, pp. 133-134.

[58] Ibid., p. 134.

[59] Parker.

[60] Lorelli, *Komandorski Islands*, p. 128.

[61] Ibid., p. 135.

[62] Parker.

down on the horizon, moving away.[63] Two American ships were hurt, but they held the "battlefield."

"They broke up and run," says Friesen. "I don't know why they did that; I mean, they had the battle won."[64]

Candelaria concludes his story:

I don't know, to be truthful, why the Japanese left when they had us. Because there wouldn't have been but wiping up if they'd of kept on; it was all over, they had us. We were heading in the wrong direction, they were chasing us and we were heading towards Paramushiro and Japan, or else to be interned in Russia and the Kamchatka Peninsula. But they broke off the engagement and turned around and left.

They say that they were afraid of planes, but the planes never arrived. They chased us all day long, and they pretty near had us. There was a friend of mine from Bakersfield on the *Dale* named Wimpy Mallard. And they say that, since the Battle of the Komandorski Islands, he has never missed church on Sunday. I don't know if he made some kind of promise, but he's never missed since.[65]

McMorris had won. The Japanese supplies and reinforcements never reached their destination, and he saved his ships to fight another day. Komandorski Islands was the last daylight gun battle between surface fleets without the assistance of combat aircraft or submarines in history (to this point).[66] It lasted four hours; its like will probably never be seen again.

Returning to Dutch Harbor, *Monaghan* had a brief engine failure that slowed her speed. Stahlberg describes what happened:

The fire rooms got a shot of water in the oil fuel system that was supplying the oil to the boilers that were on the line. We lost steam completely, and we had to secure the engines immediately, otherwise we'd have been in a lot of trouble. But as soon as the fire room was able to shift tanks and get their steam back up, well, we resumed our normal operation.[67]

*Monaghan* made reduction gear repairs alongside a destroyer tender in Dutch Harbor and remained on station through the following summer. In May, she joined Task Force Fifty-One for the invasion of Attu,[68] where her role was one of escort and antisubmarine screen and patrol—with little action. She remained on escort duty until 13 June.[69] On 18 June, she and sister *Hull* (DD-350) and *Lansdowne* (DD-486) took up blockade stations off Kiska.[70]

On 20 June, while patrolling two miles off Bukhti Point, *Monaghan* fired on an unidentified surface target. Visibility was only five hundred yards in fog, and the target ran for the beach and was lost as it merged with the radar land echo. *Monaghan*, in return, took fire from Japanese shore batteries at Gertrude Cove, but retired unharmed.[71]

*Monaghan's* last ship-to-ship engagement of the war occurred on 22 June, 1943. At 0135, radar picked up a surface target fourteen thousand yards out; *I-7*, a submarine, was running into Kiska to remove troops of the garrison, per the Japanese decision to evacuate the island.[72] *Monaghan* closed and opened fire at 0230, and the submarine fired back, both ships shooting blind in fog and darkness. The exchange lasted ten minutes before it ended without damage to either side.[73]

At 0310, *Monaghan* resumed fire and the Japanese answered. At 0318, the submarine was hit. The destroyer kept on firing as the submarine fled toward Kiska Harbor. Nearing treacherous rocks, *Monaghan* broke off.[74] *I-7* had been holed in her conning tower by one of *Monaghan's* shots, but made it to harbor where she unloaded supplies. Unable to submerge, there was no point in attempting to evacuate troops. *I-7* may have tried to escape on the surface, but, with the American destroyers on the beat outside, she was intentionally run or accidently ran aground on Twin Rocks, where she was abandoned and scuttled.[75]

---

[63] Morison, *Naval Operations*, p. 33.

[64] Friesen.

[65] Candelaria.

[66] Roscoe, *Destroyer Operations*, p. 156.

[67] Stahlberg.

[68] *Ship's History*, p. 5.

[69] Samuel E. Morison, *The Two-Ocean War: A Short History of the United States Navy in the Second World War* (Boston: Little, Brown and Company, 1963), p. 271.

[70] *Ship's History*, p. 5.

[71] Ibid., p. 5.

[72] Roscoe, *Destroyer Operations*, p. 252.

[73] Ibid., p. 252.

[74] Ibid., p. 252.

[75] Morison, *Two-Ocean War*, p. 272.

*Monaghan* alternated between escort, antisubmarine patrol, and Kiska bombardment and blockade duty. She shelled the island five times between 8 and 20 July.[76] As the U.S. Navy pounded Kiska, the Imperial Japanese Navy planned to evacuate the garrison. On the night of 21-22 July, a large Japanese task force departed Paramushiro. Four days later, it was five hundred miles south southwest of Kiska. *Monaghan* and sister *Aylwin* (DD-355), on Kiska station, were in perfect position to intercept the evacuation fleet—and to be sunk by its three light cruisers and dozen destroyers. They escaped and the Japanese evacuated Kiska without incident because of the Aleutian fog and the fog of the phantom "Battle of the Pips."[77]

Pursuing a suspected Kiska relief convoy two hundred miles southwest of Kiska, seventeen warships moved to intercept. The two Kiska destroyers were recalled to the fleet. Just past midnight on 26 July, the Americans opened fire on radar contacts eighty miles southwest of Kiska. More than a thousand rounds of 14- and 8-inch shells plowed the surface of the North Pacific, aimed at targets that existed only on radar screens. Investigation later determined the radar "targets" were probably return echoes from Amchitka and other islands, 100 to 150 miles away.[78]

Following the "Battle of the Pips," the fleet refueled and rearmed 105 miles southeast of Kiska at 0900, 28 July. The Japanese evacuation fleet slipped into foggy Kiska Harbor at 1840, and one hour later was on its way home with 5,183 troops. The Americans resumed the Kiska bombardment on 30 July, and kept up the shelling until the invasion of the abandoned island on 15 August.[79]

*Monaghan* was with the Kiska invasion fleet, and after the island was secured, she resumed her escort and antisubmarine patrol duties along the Aleutian Chain. The monotony of sea and fog, patrol and bombardment affected the men's nerves. No one liked the cold, rough, foggy Aleutian duty.[80]

Candelaria remembers the Aleutians' rough waters:

You have to be in one of them storms; in the Aleutians, they were bad. We would roll way over, and then come back and roll the other way. And we would pitch way up out of the water, and then come down. And if you were up on deck, going to the mess hall, or going to the fire room, you would hang on to the lifeline. And when she pitched, you'd hang on, and when she rolled, went down, you'd run in order to get to where you were. You'd have to time the pitches and the rolling in order to move up topside.[81]

Friesen worried about drowning:

I thought about it all the time because I wasn't a good swimmer. And where I used to figure, when we were in the Aleutians, it was always foggy and cold. The word would get around if you ever hit the water, you're dead in five minutes, no way you could survive. If the ship sinks for some reason or another, you're dead anyway ... if you didn't die from the explosion, you're going to die from the cold water.[82]

"It was a long, tedious grind up there in the Aleutians," Candelaria remembers.[83]

In September, *Monaghan* escorted a convoy to Pearl Harbor. With little regret, her eight months of Alaska duty were over. When she left Pearl Harbor in early October, it was for the West Coast and then the Central Pacific.[84]

In December, 1944, *Monaghan* sank in Typhoon Cobra off the Philippines. Only six of her crew of 250 survived. During four years of war, DD-354 earned twelve battle stars for Pacific action. Two of these were earned by this tin can at war in the cold waters of the Aleutians—one for the Komandorski Islands and the occupation of Attu, the second for her night engagement with *I-7* off Kiska.[85] Clearly, *Monaghan* did her part to defend and reclaim Alaska for the United States.

*Gary Candelaria is the superintendent for Laramie National Historic Site, Wyoming. His University of Oklahoma graduate thesis was a study of naval destroyers and their role in the Pacific in World War II. The thesis focused on his father's ship, the USS "Monaghan."*

---

[76] Morison, *Naval Operations*, p. 55.

[77] Ibid., pp. 58-59.

[78] Ibid., pp. 60-61.

[79] Ibid., p. 61.

[80] Roscoe, *Destroyer Operations*, p. 252.

[81] Candelaria.

[82] Friesen.

[83] Candelaria.

[84] *Ship's History*, p. 6.

[85] Ibid., pp. 9-10.

# The Escape of the Japanese Garrison from Kiska

*Karl Kaoru Kasukabe*

I HAVE INDEED BEEN LUCKY FOR BEING A MOUNTAINEER! Before the war, among other employees at the Mitsubishi Nagoya Aircraft Works, I climbed three-thousand-meter peaks in the Japan Alps in mid-winter—a natural laboratory for experiments in low-temperature science.

We experienced the effects of high altitude at minus thirty to minus fifty degrees Celsius and gathered experimental data for the pilots of our country's Zeros and Flying Dragons.

My studies in meteorology and the experiences I had with the Chukyo Alpine Club made it possible for me to understand complex weather patterns and, eventually, by taking advantage of thick fog as cover, to help my garrison slip out of Kiska Island without the Americans knowing it.

The Japanese forces on Kiska were ever on the alert, constantly trying to find some way to get out of the Americans' tight encirclement by PBYs, submarines, and coastal torpedo boats escorted by destroyers—in effect, a triple blockade.

From July 24 to 29, 1943, many coded fleet operations telegrams (and many not coded at all) flooded into our communications corps on Kiska. We were aware of the fact that the large American fleet was pulling ships and planes off the blockade and lining up in the waters west of Kiska. The aim, obviously, was to intercept any Japanese rescue fleet. And so both fleets engaged in the game of cat-and-mouse in the foggy Aleutian waters.

American radar operators, perhaps through frustration and nervousness, reported what they thought was radar contact with the Japanese fleet. The result was an all-out attack on "radar blips."

At 1920 hours on 28 July, a Japanese Army sentry on the outpost at Vega Point observed the dim light of the American fleet some one hundred kilometers away, on a compass heading of 160 degrees.

The American force's uncoded messages flooded in and Japanese naval intelligence was thereby able to pinpoint the position of the U.S. fleet. We focused on transmissions from portable telecommunications equipment and took note of the slang spoken among the immigrant rank and file on Amchitka, 134 kilometers away. We were able to determine that PBYs were engaged in refueling operations and that the task force itself was refueling and rearming.

The Japanese were able to determine areas around Kiska where engagement seemed unlikely to occur and to identify a window of from ten to twelve hours when dense fog would most likely provide cover for the rescue operation. Garrison headquarters had to carry out the evacuation operation within that limited amount of time.

After considering the PBYs' three-hundred- to five-hundred-mile-radius patrolling area and their range from bases on Shemya and Amchitka, Kiska headquarters decided to make the attempt.

The approach to Kiska Harbor would take four hours; loading fifty-three hundred men, one hour; and departing from Kiska would take another four hours. Originally, the arrival of the fleet at the Kiska anchorage had been scheduled for 1800 hours. In order to put it four hours ahead, that is, at 1400 hours, Kiska headquarters transmitted the single Japanese Kana-letter code, "Yu, Yu, Yu," at five-minute intervals, ordering the Japanese rescue fleet to approach at the earlier time. This pre-arranged, one-time code was unbreakable. The Japanese rescue fleet anchored at Kiska Harbor at 1340 hours on 19 July, 1943.

Two light cruisers and nine destroyers had replaced their usual cargos of seaplanes and torpedoes with a total of twenty landing craft. These were unloaded at sea and, along with the nineteen boats berthed at the Kiska garrison, made for a formidable armada indeed!

The rope ladders aboard the cruisers and destroyers were hung down, and they covered both sides of the ships. Many landing craft, large and small, sailed right alongside the large vessels as men from the garrison threw their rifles and bayonets into the sea and climbed the ships' rope ladders to safety. The shuttles to and from the rescue fleet, employing thirty-nine landing craft, had made it possible to complete the embarkation of fifty-three hundred men within fifty-five minutes! Thus did the Japanese garrison make its escape from Kiska.

The garrison's radar had been installed on the crater ridge above Kiska Harbor and commanded a 360-degree view. Originally it had been salvaged from the British battleship "Prince of Wales" and in fact had been the first radar seen in Japan. Thanks to British ingenuity, Japanese operators had been able to discern objects as far away from Kiska as three hundred kilometers.

Now, oddly, this example of the very latest in technology would become part of a simple and solemn observance.

At a pre-arranged signal—the explosions signifying the destruction of the radar installation—the whole garrison, now aboard the rescue fleet, prayed silently for those Americans and Japanese who had been killed in action.

From 1942 to 1943, the Aleutian Campaign had consumed as many lives as were now safely aboard the rescue ships: 2,638 Japanese had perished on Attu, and another twenty-five hundred men had died on and around Kiska Island and on the rough waters of the Aleutians. In addition, there were the thousands of American casualties in the Aleutian theater.

The thirty-nine landing craft were scuttled and, along with the rope ladders and weaponry, sent to the bottom of Kiska Harbor. The rescue fleet made for Paramushiro, at the northern edge of the Kuriles, at full speed—thirty knots.

If things had happened differently, we would have butchered each other to the last man on the beaches and,

Japanese soldiers await evacuation from Kiska, July 1943. *(Captured Japanese photograph, courtesy Command Historian's Office, Alaskan Command.)*

in the underground fortress where I sat with others of the intelligence corps, I would have been doomed to die. The dead would have been left on the lonely tundra wilderness forever, the landscape of which is bleakness itself.

The American forces massed for the invasion of Kiska numbered ten thousand and would have faced the Japanese garrison of nearly six thousand. The latter were disciplined troops, poised like rattlesnakes, ready to strike, and well-situated in the fortified holes on the lava ridges around Kiska Harbor.

Very likely that tundra wilderness would have turned scarlet with the blood of fifteen thousand American and Japanese troops.

As a postscript, let me relate to you an example of the wonderful communication that now prevails between our peoples. On June 10, 1943, my barracks, along with me and all my belongings, was buried in a bombing raid, and I was taken to the garrison's first-aid barracks in an unconscious state. When I was evacuated with the others who had been wounded, I thought—because of the loss of the unit's flag—that I had left something of myself behind. As it turned out, Mr. Sherman Smith, originally of the Tenth Mountain Division, had kept the flag in perfect condition for forty-three years! I must say that I will always be deeply grateful to Mr. Sherman Smith, who crossed the Pacific to return to me the Flag of the Rising Sun.

*Karl Kaoru Kasukabe lives in Nagoya, Japan. He served in a noncombatant military intelligence role on Attu and Kiska before the Japanese departure in 1943. He is secretary of the Japan Alpine-ski Soldiers Association.*

# The Coast Guard at War
# in Alaska

*M. Joseph Leahy*

WHEN THE U.S. ENTERED WORLD WAR II, THE Coast Guard had operated continuously in Alaska for more than seventy years. Founded in 1790 as the U.S. Revenue Marine, the service first came to Alaska in 1865 when the territory was still Russian America.

The revenue cutter *Shubrick* came to Sitka—under the command of Captain Charles M. Scammon—in temporary service to the Western Union Telegraph Company for a survey of a telegraph line to Russia. Upon anchoring in the Russian-American port, Scammon learned his was the first U.S. government vessel ever to visit Sitka.

Another Revenue Service officer came to Sitka as the U.S. agent two years later. First Lieutenant George W. Moore began his duties at Sitka in August, 1867, two months before Russian America was transferred to the U.S.

The next year the cutter *Wayanda* cruised to the Pribilof Islands under command of Captain John Wesley White. Assigned to prevent illegal killing of fur seals there, White later recommended the seal islands be set aside as a government reserve.

In 1869, the Service sent the cutter *Reliance* to Sitka, the first U.S. government vessel to be stationed in Alaska. The following year the schooner sailed to Unalaska, the Pribilofs, and beyond to Norton and Kotzebue sounds. In doing so, the *Reliance* became the first U.S. government vessel to pass through the Bering Strait.

The service's work here has been generally humanitarian in nature. However, an exception occurred in 1882 when, under the direction of a naval commander, the revenue cutter *Corwin* bombarded and burned Angoon, a Tlingit Indian village in Southeast Alaska. The incident resulted from a misunderstanding of Tlingit customs and the federal government has since apologized for its actions.

Elsewhere in the 1880s, the Revenue Service explored and mapped Alaska's Interior, enforced salmon fishing regulations, and rescued whalers stranded after arctic ice crushed their vessels. Revenue Service officers also policed restrictions on liquor imports here.

In the 1890s, revenue cutters carried domesticated reindeer from Siberia to Alaska, enforced pelagic sealing laws, and, during the Klondike gold rush, patrolled the Yukon River. In 1912, the service rescued residents of Kodiak and nearby Eskimo [Alutiiq] villages following the volcanic eruption of Mount Katmai.

In 1917, the Revenue Cutter Service absorbed the Lifesaving Service and was renamed the Coast Guard. In Alaska, the service gained a lifeboat station at Nome; however, by this time the Service had already been in the marine rescue business for fifty years in Alaska.

Throughout its history here, the service has provided logistical support for other agencies and organizations. Coast Guard cutters have, in fact, carried everything from mail to missionaries. Their regular passengers included federal judges and their courts, Public Health Service doctors and dentists, territorial governors, visiting congressmen, lighthouse keepers, archaeologists, anthropologists, and even oilmen.

As a result of this marine "taxi service," the Coast Guard's duties have been diverse. For example, Coast Guard cutters escorted the army's Douglas World Cruisers through Alaska on their 1924 around-the-world

A Coast Guard PBY assigned to duty with LORAN construction in the western Aleutians, 1943. *(Photograph courtesy of the U.S. Coast Guard)*

flight. They were there as a safety net for the fliers, but the cutters also carried fuel and supplies, and provided radio communications to keep the world informed of their progress.

In the mid-1930s, the Coast Guard was assigned a task reflecting a growing international concern. In 1935, a presidential order directed the Coast Guard to enforce provisions of the Neutrality Act relating to foreign vessels in U.S. waters.

Significantly, in Alaska this meant documenting and reporting movements of Japanese fishing vessels common to coastal waters here. We know now, of course, that some of these vessels were gathering strategic information as well as Alaska's abundant seafood.

The U.S. had good reason to be nervous about the events in Europe. In 1938, as we know, Germany annexed Austria and, in the following year, moved into Czechoslovakia, Albania, and Poland. In response to Hitler's aggression, on September 3, 1939, France and England declared war on Germany.

Coincidental with Germany's European expansion—though not at all related—the Coast Guard took over the Lighthouse Service. The merger doubled their personnel in Alaska and gave the service its first operating base

here—the former Lighthouse Service depot at Ketchikan.

The Coast Guard also acquired fifteen lighthouses, several buoy tenders, and about nine hundred aids to navigation, including buoys, shore lights, and channel markers. More significant, however, the Coast Guard acquired the Lighthouse Service's intimate familiarity with Southeast Alaska waters. As 1939 progressed, it became increasingly apparent this knowledge would be needed in preparing for the territory's defense.

Aggression in Europe and hostilities in Asia triggered long-awaited appropriations for improvements and additions to Alaska's military defenses. In early 1941, with a Pacific war theater seeming ever more likely, Alaska's military commanders—the army's General Simon Bolivar Buckner and the navy's Captain Ralph C. Parker—began detailed contingency planning; the Coast Guard's newly appointed Alaska District commander, Fredrick A. Zeusler, joined them.

In these strategy meetings, the Joint Chiefs recognized that every scenario for Alaska's defense relied on having a secure corridor for moving military personnel and cargoes to the territory, and if necessary, to evacuate its sixty thousand residents.

The commanders directed the Coast Guard to improve navigation in the Inside Passage from Dixon's Entrance to Icy Strait and to secure the waterway from enemy incursions. Zeusler assigned the task to his district's former Lighthouse Service personnel.

The Inside Passage—a north-south inland waterway extending from Puget Sound to Haines, Alaska—was open to ocean access in many places along its nearly two-thousand-mile length. In Southeast Alaska alone, its course ran through more than a thousand islands, rocks and reefs presenting many potential hazards to mariners and numerous hiding places for enemy watercraft.

To improve navigation in the Inside Passage, the Coast Guard installed new buoys and lights and established safe anchorages for convoys. Lighthouse crews were doubled for round-the-clock lookout duty. In addition, new observation stations were built on Forester Island and other strategic locations. These sites were at the northern and southern entrances to Wrangell Narrows; at Marmion Island at the southern entrance to Juneau's Gastineau Channel; and at the entrance to Seward Harbor.

To further secure the Inside Passage, the Coast Guard began regular surface patrols, giving particular attention to Dixon's Entrance and other ocean-access points. These patrols were augmented by reconnaissance aircraft from the U.S. Army and Navy, the U.S. Wildlife Service, commercial airlines, and from Canadian forces.

Although it was considered "hot" for potential enemy incursion, the Inside Passage contained extensive fisheries and other maritime commerce considered essential to national interests. Enabling these maritime activities to continue in a potential war zone further complicated security planning for the region.

Canneries were identified as likely targets for enemy occupation since they held large quantities of food and fuel; to safeguard these sites, security patrols were planned and procedures established to provide clearance papers for cannery workers.

Additional plans were made to regulate vessel movements and to coordinate radio communications within the Alaska fishing industry. In theory, fishing boats would be told where and when to go and how to get there; they would be required to report their movements via radio but only on assigned frequencies, at specific times, and, using only authorized codes. To insure compliance with security regulations, their radio transmissions would be monitored.

In 1941, security and navigational improvements to the Inside Passage intensified as U.S. relations with Japan deteriorated. In November, the Coast Guard was transferred to the navy—as it had been in every military conflict since 1799. The commander of naval forces in Alaska placed Zeusler in charge of all floating units

from Dixon's Entrance to Seward. By then, many maritime defense strategies had already been implemented or were under development.

A month later, Pearl Harbor was attacked. Captain Zeusler, the District Coast Guard commander, was told of the attack while attending services at Ketchikan's Episcopal church. In bitter irony, contingency plans required Zeusler to detain long-standing members of his church's congregation who were of Japanese extraction.

As planned, military authorities imposed radio silence throughout the territory and communities were ordered to black out their lights. To deny their use to enemy vessels and aircraft, all lighthouses and radio beacons were also discontinued. However, initial confusion between military commands, particularly at Juneau, caused many smaller light buoys to be extinguished hastily by gunfire.

Within a few days, the fear of immediate attack subsided and the Coast Guard began restoring navigation aids to service. A more significant reason for their restoration, however, was an immediate increase in vessel groundings. The lack of navigation aids in Alaska waters was soon understood to be more hazardous to shipping than was the threat of enemy presence.

With war declared, the Coast Guard increased surface and aerial patrols of the region; implemented vessel identification, clearance, and routing procedures; and tightened requirements for entering Alaska ports. As planned, fishing vessel movements and communications came under regulation but, initially, Alaska's stubbornly independent fishermen fell short of military expectations in their compliance.

In fact, they fished where they found fish, moved at will to better grounds, used the radio randomly to report to canneries and to tell their fishing buddies of good sets. And, to confound those monitoring their radio transmissions, they often spoke in their native languages—Norwegian, Swedish, Tlingit, and Haida.

Not surprising, however, their cooperation increased measurably as reports of submarine sightings increased and as other restrictions were implemented. To serve as vessel routing stations, Coast Guard lightships were transferred to Alaska from the Oregon and Washington coasts.

The lightships—from the Columbia River and Swiftsure stations—were positioned near Ketchikan and at Pleasant Island in Icy Strait. Routing officers on board issued clearance papers, gave routing instructions, and assembled convoys. Those bound for Prince William Sound, to Kodiak, and westward to the Aleutians were assembled in Icy Strait for escort by armed vessels.

Convoy escort was performed principally by the Coast Guard, although pitifully few ships were available for this purpose. The escort "fleet" included several patrol boats, several buoy tenders, a handful of commandeered fishing boats, and two World War I navy destroyers.

When ordered to escort duty, most of these vessels were without instructions and publications defining escort procedures; also, many had a difficult time staying ahead of the transport ships they were escorting.

Among these was the cutter *Haida*, a 240-foot patrol boat built after the conclusion of World War I. On one eastbound escort—remembered by crew member Robert Erwin Johnson—the *Haida* steamed straight ahead at about fourteen knots while the steamship being escorted zigzagged back and forth to avoid overtaking her escort.

While supplies and ammunition were being rushed to the westward during 1942, a shortage of fresh fruits, vegetables, and meats occurred throughout the territory. A check of vessel manifests revealed inordinate amounts of cargo space being taken up by liquor. For example, the SS *Aleutian*, arriving at Ketchikan on June 2, 1942, offloaded few groceries for the community; however, 602 cases of whiskey, thirty-seven cases and five half-barrels of wine, and twenty-six cases of ale were landed for distribution in that community. To alleviate future food shortages—and not coincidentally, to reduce liquor-related morale problems—the Coast Guard placed severe restrictions on shipping liquor to Alaska. They also directed that cargo space be reserved on all future northbound vessels for food shipments.

As the war progressed, marine traffic increased, and so did marine casualties. In the air, the situation was the same; the unprecedented amount of military air traffic in the territory resulted in frequent missing and downed aircraft.

One notable aviation casualty occurred in December 1942 when a plane carrying important mail crashed and sank in Juneau's Gastineau Channel. Coast Guard Chief Boatswain Arthur Hook, a commercial diver before the war, smashed through the ice and dived more than a hundred feet to retrieve the pilot's body and the classified mail.

Another crash, two months later, involved a Lockheed Electra flown by Harold Gillam, one of Alaska's most experienced pilots. Owned by the Morrison-Knudson construction company, the twin-engined airplane smashed into a mountain near Ketchikan on January 3, 1943, on an unscheduled flight from Seattle.

The crash resulted from bad weather and the failure of the Electra's left engine—both of which circumstances Gillam reported; however, his reports failed to give his location. From his last reported position, American and Canadian air-sea rescue forces determined Gillam was likely within sixty miles of Annette Island.

Six American and two Canadian vessels—along with two Canadian and five American planes—participated in the search. In addition, several land parties searched the mountainous terrain. The search was discontinued after two weeks during which time no trace was found of the plane or its passengers.

Then, on February 3—a month after the plane disappeared—a patrol vessel spotted two survivors on the beach in Boca de Quadra. The men were taken to Ketchikan for treatment and, despite their weak condition, volunteered to lead rescuers to the mountainside crash site; Chief Boatswain Hook was placed in charge of the search.

Hook's party worked its way through three- to five-foot-deep snow, up heavily wooded slopes, over cliffs, and though rivers and beaver ponds, cutting trees for bridges as they went. At one point, frustrated by their slow progress, Hook wrote a message in the snow using cut boughs to form the words "Send blimp."

Continuing on foot, they arrived at the site on February 5, finding two persons alive, one dead, and pilot Gillam missing. Upon leaving several days later, the rescue party found the trail impassable due to melting snow. Two more weeks passed before the survivors were evacuated and the bodies removed. Gillam's body was found near the shore in Boca de Quadra; he likely died of hypothermia.

Afterward, concluding that future lives might be saved if rescue parties could parachute to crash sites, Zeusler sent Hook and other volunteers to train at the Forest Service's Seely Lake, Montana, Smokejumper School. I believe this was the world's first parachute rescue squad.

Throughout the war, search and rescue was a major responsibility for the Coast Guard. However, the service also took part in combat activities here. One if its cutters, for example, helped defend Dutch Harbor, and others sank a Japanese submarine in Southeastern waters.

On June 3, 1942, when Japanese aircraft first attacked Dutch Harbor, the cutter *Onandaga* was among the eight vessels in port.[1] The first aerial attack on the Dutch Harbor Naval Base was brief; it caused only a few fires and damaged several aircraft. During the time the Japanese planes were in range, the *Onandaga's* gunners shot nearly two thousand rounds of antiaircraft fire at them—in concert with shore batteries and those on other vessels.

---

[1] By coincidence, Zeusler had served his first sea duty on that vessel—appropriately nicknamed the "Rolling O"—thirty years earlier, under the command of Captain J.C. Cantwell. In the 1880s Cantwell served in Alaska's Arctic on the cutter *Corwin* and, in 1898-99, he commanded the *Nunivak*, the service's Yukon River paddlewheeled steamboat.

It is unclear to me how many attacking aircraft there were. One source suggests forty; it is more likely there were fewer than twenty. At any rate, several were shot down and others may have failed to return to their offshore carrier.

Afterward, a navy PBY patrol aircraft located a Japanese surface fleet about eighty miles south of Umnak. The PBY was attacked and crippled by a Japanese Zero before the pilot could return to base. The Coast Guard cutter *Nemeha*, a new sub chaser patrolling the area, rescued the pilot.

The submarine sinking was accomplished through the combined efforts of a Canadian patrol airplane, the Coast Guard cutter *McLane*, and a converted halibut boat commandeered for patrol duty. The action took place in early July after the Japanese attacks on Dutch Harbor and their occupation of Attu and Kiska.

The submarine—identified after war's end as RO-61—was sighted several times near Dixon's Entrance in early June. However, it wasn't located until July 7, when an RCAF Bolingbroke Mark 4 bomber hit it with a 250-pound antisubmarine bomb. The submarine disappeared but was located two days later by the *McLane* and the F/V *Foremost*, a navy-commandeered halibut boat designated YP-251.

The vessels played tag with their underwater adversary for ten hours, during which time depth charges were dropped and at least one torpedo was fired at the surface vessels. The torpedo crossed about twenty-four feet in front of the *McLane* as it was backing away from the *Foremost*, which it had been following. The captains of both vessels watched as the torpedo passed between them.

In the ensuing chase, both vessels dropped depth charges on the submarine and the *Foremost* apparently collided with it while making a hard turn to starboard. The sinking was credited to both vessels; their captains—Lieutenant Ralph "Stormy" Burns on the *McLane* and Lieutenant Niels P. Thomsen on the *Foremost*—were awarded the Legion of Merit for their action.

In the campaign to regain the Aleutian Islands, Coast Guard personnel manned troop transports such as the USS *Arthur Middleton*. Their expertise in landing small boats on rocky Aleutian beaches was particularly helpful in landing troops and supplies at Amchitka and Attu.

The Coast Guard participated with the U.S. Army, Navy, and Canadian forces in other combat activities throughout the theater, particularly in the Aleutian Campaign.

My presentation has been planned to give you an overview of the Coast Guard's role during World War II in Alaska. The few examples I have been able to detail,

Lieutenant Ralph "Stormy" Burns, commander of the Coast Guard cutter *McLane*, watches as a seaman paints a "kill" on the ship's bulkhead in Southeast Alaska, 1942. The *McLane* and the converted fishing vessel *Foremost* had earlier pursued and sunk a Japanese submarine. *(Photograph courtesy of the U.S. Coast Guard)*

however, give only a small sense of their responsibilities. I'd like to take just a few more minutes to list some of the Service's other wartime duties here; for example, the Coast Guard:

• operated the navy post office serving most floating units and stations in Alaska from Ketchikan to Seward;

• operated radio surveillance stations at Ketchikan and Seward;

• maintained the army How beacon on St. Paul Island;

• built, supported and operated radio direction-finder stations;

• built and operated an ANRAC station at Massacre Bay on Adak;

• operated firefighting boats in coastal communities;

- provided diving services for vessel repair and salvage;
- provided weather reporting services to CAA stations in Alaska;
- provided shore protection for all navy bases in Southeast Alaska;
- maintained a library of hydrographic information about Alaska waters;
- transported military personnel on orders or on leave in Alaska;
- transported touring USO entertainers throughout the territory;
- built and maintained emergency anchorage for seaplanes and convoys;
- planned and started construction on five new lighthouses; and
- assisted in the army's Alaska Spruce Program.

The list goes on, but I will stop. Before concluding, however, I want to make note of LORAN construction in Alaska. LORAN—long range navigation—was a new all-weather radio navigation system developed in 1941 and field-tested in 1942 by the Massachusetts Institute of Technology.

Between April 1943 and March 1944, a 140-man Coast Guard construction battalion built and put into operation eight LORAN stations in the western Aleutians and the Bering Sea. The high-priority project cost the lives of more than a dozen men; five disappeared on a boat trip to nearby St. Mathews Island Army Weather Station. A suspicion that they were captured by a Japanese submarine has never been confirmed.

LORAN came to Alaska after hostilities ended here, but the Aleutian Chain was used extensively to guide bombers toward their northern Japanese island targets. The story of LORAN development in Alaska deserves a presentation of its own in some future symposium.

To conclude, we have seen that the Coast Guard was the foremost military service in Alaska from 1865 until World War II. We have also seen that during this time the service provided Alaskans with a variety of humanitarian services and also carried operations burdens for many federal and territorial agencies, including the army and navy.

And we have seen the Coast Guard take on the unglamorous but necessary tasks needed to support military activities and actions during World War II in Alaska.

We have, in fact, seen the Service fulfill the promise of its Latin motto: *Semper Paratus*: Always Ready.

*M. Joseph Leahy is Director, Valdez Museum and Historical Archive, a position he has held since 1984. He serves on the boards of directors for Museums Alaska and the Alaska Historical Society.*

# The Tenth Emergency Rescue Boat Squadron
## Eleventh Army Air Force

*Ralph M. Bartholomew*

THE OFFICIAL WARTIME HISTORY OF THE TENTH Emergency Rescue Boat Squadron was written by First Sergeant Wilson G. Crompton, later Warrant Officer, and is found in microfilmed documents at the Air Force Document Center, Maxwell Air Force Base, Alabama. The history began prior to World War II when, in December 1940, Major Everett S. Davis, Commanding Officer, Elmendorf Air Base, saw the success the Royal Air Force was having in the English Channel with fast heavy-duty small boats as they recovered downed air crews and returned them to fly again.

Lieutenant Gordon R. Donley, later Captain, and then Major, was dispatched to Ketchikan, Alaska, in December 1941, where the Coast Guard had agreed to assist in training small-boat crews. Lt. Donley brought with him a few noncoms on detached service from various Elmendorf squadrons and immediately began recruiting young men in Ketchikan who had been raised in the local fishing fleet and had their basic small-boat training already. The official name of our organization became the "Air Corps Marine Rescue Service," later changed to the "924th QM Boat Sqdn (Avn)," and then to the "Tenth Emergency Rescue Boat Squadron."

As stated in the history, Donley was able to rent the Filipino bunkhouse (vacant because it was wintertime) from the New England Fish Company salmon cannery for use a barracks. Many of his first recruits came from the local Civilian Conservation Corps organization that had been disbanded when the war started. I was number six to enlist as I, too, had spent considerable time in the fishing industry and before that in the Sea Scouts where we had served on a number of cruises on Coast Guard vessels for our early training. New England Fish Company wanted their bunkhouse back as the new salmon season was approaching, and Donley had by then been successful in recruiting enough young men so that the bunkhouse had become too crowded.

We then moved to the abandoned CCC Camp at Ward Lake, some eight miles out the north highway from Ketchikan, which, with just a little cleanup, was both usable and somewhat isolated from the community. That became the "boot camp" for our army training as well as our classroom for the navigation, signaling, and small-boat handling classes. We had by then received two new forty-two-foot Owens twin-screw cabin cruisers, the P-30 and 31, which became our training vessels and later were assigned to air stations as rescue boats.

Not too long after our transfer to the Ward Lake CCC Camp, the military decided to take the Aleuts out of their communities in the Aleutians and move them farther away from the war to Southeastern Alaska points. As our CCC Camp looked like a good place to deposit some of those families, we again had to move, this time to the new Annette Island Army Air Field. I was temporarily assigned to the crash and refueling-ready tent on the runway, and then to the *Nan B.*, an old wood cannery tender taken over by the army. We spent our nights patrolling offshore on the lookout for Japanese submarines, and the days hauling passengers and mail between Annette and Ketchikan, and supplies to outlying overseas communication cable guard posts on Prince of Wales Island.

Lieutenant Donley finally received word that the first

The crew of an eighty-five-foot crash boat gathers on the foredeck, ca. 1943. The skipper, Sergeant Isaac Shadura, is the man holding the Very pistol. Crash-boat commanders, initially almost all NCOs, eventually were promoted to the warrant officer ranks. *(Photograph from the author's collection)*

two of our 104-foot rescue boats were under construction at the Stephens Brothers shipyard in Stockton, California, so he shipped twenty of us to San Francisco for further training in gunnery and celestial navigation with the navy on Treasure Island, engine training at the Hall Scott factory in Berkeley, and weather training at the Stockton Air Base. As we had received yellow fever shots (what did we need those for in the Aleutians?) before leaving Annette, several of our group were hospitalized as the vaccine was found to be unstable. As late as 1988, the government was still checking back on those who had become ill from the vaccine. One of our members spent several months in the Presidio of San Francisco Hospital and nearly died.

When departing for California, we came over to Ketchikan on our own boats, then boarded a U.S. Coast Guard thirty-eight-foot picket boat to go alongside a Standard Oil Company tanker that had slowed down in

the channel for us. We had to climb up a rope netting with our barracks bags, helmets, rifles, gas masks, and sleeping bags, and then sleep on the steel deck in the midship house for the trip to the states. We went back down the netting to a pilot boat at Port Angeles, Washington, then via bus and ferry to Fort Lawton in Seattle where we moved into tents. After a few days we departed via Northern Pacific Railroad chair cars for San Francisco. We first moved into the old Ghirardelli candy factory being used as a temporary barracks, then to tents in Funston Park with an MP detachment.

The boat construction schedule had been delayed, and so it was the fall of 1942 when we finally moved into a barracks in Stockton, California, to help prepare the P-114 and P-115. We assisted in mounting the three .50-caliber machine guns and two 20-millimeter cannons and made such other changes or additions we felt were needed for Alaska service. The P-115 was ready first and

I was assigned as chief radio operator. We departed several weeks ahead of the P-114 downriver for San Francisco where we moored at the foot of Market Street. A young lady-friend of our skipper, Sergeant Don DeSomery, brought Thanksgiving dinner aboard for the crew. (They were later married and returned to Elmendorf Air Force Base together for our 1986 reunion, the first time I had seen them since early in the war.)

An elderly ship pilot, brought out of retirement for the war effort, was assigned to pilot our boat up the Pacific Coast to Seattle. He wanted to travel way offshore to get away from land, and we didn't want to lose sight of land. We stayed within sight of land and took a pretty good beating off the Northern California coast, then went into Coos Bay, Oregon, for refueling. The pilot had us call for a bar pilot from the Coast Guard to enter Coos Bay and they sent out a self-bailing pilot boat that moved at about six knots. We couldn't control our square-stem boat at that speed so finally poured on the power and went in over the bar after passing up the pilot boat. As a result of these problems, we ceased using pilots and moved the boats with our own crews from then on.

After we arrived in Seattle, additional water tanks were installed and the boats proceeded north for assignment—the P-114 to Adak, and the 115 to Cold Bay in the Aleutians. Additional personnel had been shipped to Seattle from Annette Island in the meantime, so a number of re-assignments were made, and I was sent back with others to Stockton for the P-141 through P-146. Prior to going back to Stockton, the squadron obtained two "T" boats—the 33 and 34—for training in Seattle operations, and I served on the T-33.

After adding water tanks in Seattle at the BarBee Shipyard, and with the 141 to 146 traveling together, we went on to our Aleutian base duty stations. I was then aboard the P-142 and assigned to the new air base at Amchitka along with the P-143. We had been delayed

for some hull repair at the Kodiak Seabee ship repair yard after the P-146 had damaged our guards when their engine failed to respond in a landing at Anchorage.

While at the BarBee yard in Seattle, we acquired an eighty-five-foot wood herring seiner type vessel, fitted

Three 104-foot crash boats sail north to Aleutian bases. Each vessel was armed with three .50-caliber machine guns and two 20-millimeter cannon. *(Photograph from the author's collection)*

with a new wheelhouse and a medical dispensary in the hold that was capable of handling twelve patients. The vessel was designated the TP-92 and was stationed in Chernofski Harbor to serve the Umnak area. It was felt that with its fishing vessel lines that it might be able to outperform the higher-speed crash boats. Following the war, this same vessel operated out of Ketchikan as a fish and freight packer, renamed the *Sidney*.

In 1943 we also took delivery at San Francisco of the 158-foot steel vessel, *Col. Joseph C. Morrow*, designated "HA-2" for "hauling auxiliary." The HA-2 was carried on the roster as an aircraft retriever as it was equipped with a thirty-ton jumbo lift boom along with regular cargo booms. The cargo capacity of five hundred measurement tons enabled us to haul priority air force cargos and crash boat parts and supplies to and between all the Aleutian bases from the Tacoma Air Force terminal.

I was transferred from Amchitka to the HA-2 at Adak just after Christmas of 1943 and spent the next two years aboard, variously as the chief radio operator up through mate and executive officer before discharge in November 1945.

The squadron next added six 104-foot crash boats, P-214 through P-217, built by Sagstad Shipyards, Seattle, plus P-219 and 220, constructed in North Bend, Oregon, and powered by three Kermath gas engines. These vessels proved to be underpowered and not as satisfactory as the Stephens Brothers boats with their three Hall Scotts. The 104-foot design was able to operate in extremely tough weather and sea conditions, but was slow when time was of the essence in rescue, so Major Donley obtained five 85-foot PT-style crash boats equipped with 1,350-horsepower Packard engines. Their main problems were that they sweat very badly and had an inadequate heating system for the Aleutians. The eighty-fives were all stationed originally at the Casco Cove PT base in Attu, formerly used by the navy but abandoned after they found the PTs unsuitable for Aleutian use.

The squadron next received eight 104-foot crash boats, P-749 through P-756, modified a great deal from the original design and actually appearing top-heavy. These new vessels allowed some of the older boats to be moved back to mainland stations away from the continued battering of the Aleutian weather. Of these, the P-750 had been built in New York State while the other seven were built in Mississippi and Louisiana. They were powered by the same 1,350-horsepower Packards that had been used in the 85-foot design. Crews reported the workmanship was so bad that they were in the Olson & Winge shipyard in Lake Union, Seattle, for nearly two months repairing, recaulking, and finishing the vessels.

The total number of vessels operated during the period of World War II by the Tenth Emergency Rescue Boat Squadron now totalled forty-one. A review of the available manpower records indicated that more than 520 men were in the organization over that same period.

Very late in 1945 we began returning the vessels from the Alaska and Aleutian bases to Seattle, where most of them were declared surplus and sold to the highest bidders. Some of the eighty-fives became high-speed charter boats and the only other two crash boats that became civilian vessels that I am aware of were the P-115 and the TP-92 mentioned earlier. In 1972, the P-115 showed up in Ketchikan as a salmon troller named the *Shauna* and was identified from records by the Stephens Brothers shipyard. It had been purchased locally from an owner in California who had been using it as a tuna fishing vessel for many years.

The squadron participated in many rescues and life-saving responses, from mountain-climbing and tundra-hiking accidents to transporting seriously ill tugboat crew members to shore hospitals, to emergency calls to outlying weather and radar stations, and aircraft emergency ditching calls. In some cases aircraft had just run out of fuel and needed a tow, since a Kingfisher and other craft had to belly-land on the tundra or beach. Some of the boats had to go out to sea just to provide a radio signal to be used as an approach beacon so aircraft could get down to sea level to find their way into a field.

When a call was received, there wasn't such a thing as checking the weather and planning a trip: we just went out in whatever weather there was. It was amazing that, in the worst weather in the world, and considering the number of boats and personnel that we had, not one person was lost. There were some who asked for a transfer ashore as they just could not avoid being seasick every time out, but they were usually replaced immediately by another who wanted to get out of the mud.

We know we were a successful operation even though it was sometimes a long period between calls, but those things are hard to quantify. When the P38s were called on for experimental fighter cover for the B-24s bombing Paramushiro, they were pushed to the very maximum of endurance. One of their pilots made a comment that put our squadron into perspective. He said, "We knew the chances of being rescued by you guys were slim or none. But one thing we knew for certain was that you would always be out there looking, and that made the difference."

*Ralph M. Bartholomew lives in Ketchikan and is the president of the Eleventh Air Force Association, World War II Veterans of the Aleutian Campaign.*

# Life on Adak, 1942-1944

*Joseph M. May*
*and Harold Steinhoff*

WE LOADED IN SEWARD ABOARD THE NAVY TRANS-port *Bell*. Pretty heavy seas were running at the time. I was talking to a member of the ship's crew. "I understand we're supposed to have an escort," I said.

He replied, "Look across the waves out there. There's a couple of four-stack destroyers there someplace."

We were aboard ship and didn't know where we were going, but headed west. We were called down to the wardroom and the captain of the ship explained that we were going to Adak. We had to anchor well offshore because they had no charts of the waters. We went down rope ladders on the side of the ship and were carried ashore in lifeboats and barges because no landing craft were available then, except a few Higgins boats.

I don't recall much about the landing at Adak. I do recall that our antiaircraft guns came ashore in barges. They blew the bottom out of one of them and were using it as a beaching dock. The guns were on four wheels with double bogies. Our prime movers came in—they weighed ten tons—and they couldn't even move on the beach, but bogged down in the sand. So we finally got some D-8 Cats off and were able to pull our guns to one side.

Equipment was spread out all over the beach. Post Exchange goodies came in. The PX officer wasn't there when his supplies were unloaded. The GI's started helping themselves to the cartons of cigarettes and so these were depleted pretty rapidly.

It was getting late in the day, so General Landrum said, "We better take to the high ground." We spread all the gear out as widely as possible and covered it with tarpaulins to make it look like ten times as much as was really there. We put up blankets and anything else that looked like tents, besides the pup tents we already had up. About five thousand men came in on the landing and General Landrum wanted to make it look like ten thousand, to confuse the Japanese who might overfly or observe from submarines.

They finally decided to move us to the other side of Sweeper's Cove. We set our guns up in the rear of a small hill, at the south end of what would be the runway.

There was no beach discipline. We had no experience at all in amphibious landings. Our gear was spread all over the beach. We could have used "Squeaky" Anderson, who developed quite a reputation as a beach master in other landings in the Aleutians and later in the South Pacific.

I recall a story about Squeaky Anderson. We were unloading runway steel on the dock. The 195th Port Battalion was made up of life-termers from Fort Leavenworth Prison. They had procured some liquor and were drinking. Squeaky came aboard to see why cargo wasn't moving as it should. The men weren't working. He told them he was the beach commander and captain of the port. They didn't pay any attention to him. So he went out and put on his silver oak leaves, said that he was Commander Anderson and they should get to work and get things moving. They told him what he could do with his authority. Squeaky's voice started rising and breaking. So now I knew why they called him Squeaky. He hit high "C" above "C" before it was all over with.

That same outfit, the 195th Port Battalion, had orders

to remain overseas for the duration plus six months. One morning I was down to pick that crew up to take them down to the docks. When I got there they were firing their rifles into one of the huts. It was a long hut, and the company commander and the first sergeant lived in one end, and the supply room was at the other end. The prisoners were shooting into the living quarters end of the hut with their Springfields. We couldn't do anything about stopping that, so I just called up the provost marshal. His name was Lieutenant Fox. I told him, "The 195th men are shooting up the company commander and the first sergeant. You better get down here!" He wanted to know how much ammunition they had. I said, "They got a day's fire." He said, "I'll be down in a couple of hours to see!" So finally he showed up with a few men, and by that time these guys had stopped firing or used up all their ammunition. Luckily the first sergeant and the captain happened to be back in the supply room. So they took the Springfields away from them. I don't know why they had rifles anyway! These men had been known to shoot their feet on the pretense of cleaning their rifles, thinking they would go back to the mainland so their bones could knit. They wouldn't knit, supposedly, out in the Aleutians, it was so damp.

Captain Joe May on Adak, 1943. *(Photograph from the author's collection)*

Finally we got in a black port battalion. They had to work them in separate shifts. They couldn't be at the dock at the same time. They had to move one outfit off the dock before you moved the other one on, because it would have been murder for sure.

Williwaws sometimes came up on the docks, with winds of 100 to 125 miles per hour. We had unloaded a bunch of bridge planks down at one end when a williwaw came up. A sergeant came to me and said, "The planks are blowing away." I said, "What are you taking about?" I thought he was out of his mind because these babies were about three inches thick, and twelve or fourteen inches wide, and twenty-five or thirty feet long. I looked down at the end and sure enough, the planks

were peeling off the stack. So I called up the resident engineer, I think it was Colonel Wetzel, and he thought I'd been on some of the "Aleutian Solution." I said, "No, believe me, the planks are blowing away." So he got some hawser and heaving lines out and some sand bags and bedded the planks down.

When all the ships came in they had sacks of coal in the bottom. Some said they were ballast. Others said they'd soften a torpedo blow. But the bags of coal were then piled up on the beach and rationed out to the men at about seven pounds per day. We never had enough coal, just enough to warm the tent a little at night, and again in the morning to heat some shaving water. So they had to put an armed guard on the coal pile to keep the men from stealing it.

Later on we got Quonset huts and fuel oil burners. Later, spontaneous combustion destroyed the coal pile. You talk about the GI's screaming: they hadn't been allowed to touch the coal before and now it was burning up.

It was amazing to see all that happened as we worked on the dock. They would pull a ship in and put it on the hook in the middle of the harbor. To unload fuel drums they would drop them over the side and let the tide carry them on in. They had something like a steel cargo net laid on the bottom and hooked with cable. Then a D-8 Cat would pull the net and bring in the drums like fish in a net. All the fuel came in fifty-five-gallon drums. We didn't have any tankers. When the mechanics had to fuel the planes they had to hand-pump these drums into the planes. You can imagine how many drums and how long it would take them to fill a B-17 or a B-24. We stacked the drums all up at one end of Sweeper's Cove. There was a revetment of sand between them and the fuel oil drums.

Meanwhile they were unloading runway steel. We had two-and-a-half-ton trucks and it was unbelievable the load we put on them. I'd hesitate to estimate what they weighed. These trucks were probably carrying two or three times what they should be. They would put drivers in them that had very little experience. But they said, "No problem, just get in there, put it in low-low, let the clutch out, keep the motor RPM up, and just stay in the rut in the road." You couldn't get out of it anyway, the rut was so deep in the sand. If a truck went dead they pushed it off to the side with a Cat. Keep the line moving!

I got some experience in laying runway steel. We put

in that airstrip in about a week to ten days. Then we landed a B-17. The runway at times had some water on it. They built a dam at one end. When the tide went out they'd drop the gates. On either side of the runway were dikes or canals. Stationary engines would pump the canals dry but there was at times some water on the runway. I've seen P-38s land that looked like a speedboat coming down.

The food situation was something else. We had C Rations, good old canned C Rations. They were in cans about the size of Campbell's Soup cans. They were pretty darn good food. If you ate too much of it you would break out because they had so many calories in them. It wasn't too long until they started shipping us in B Rations. They were like C Rations except they were in Number Ten cans. We got corned beef in an oblong tin, Spam came in an oblong tin, and Vienna sausage in a Number Ten can. Later on we started getting dehydrated stuff—onions, potatoes, and eggs. If anybody has ever eaten GI dehydrated eggs they will know what I'm talking about. The fellows would almost get ill after having to smell that Spam cooking. Those poor cooks would try every way to disguise that food. They would put onions with it and Spam with Vienna sausage, if you can imagine it. But I have actually seen people get sick to their stomachs when they smelled the Spam. You can wonder why the GI's never wanted to eat Spam after they came home.

Seabees came in not too long after we landed. I understand it was one of the first Seabee outfits to be posted overseas. The first thing the Seabees did was build a mess hall. They didn't do a thing until they got a mess hall. And they built a good one. Our men went down there when they saw the food the Seabees were getting. They had their own refrigerator ships. Any navy ships going back to the states would keep just enough food aboard to get back. They would leave the rest with the navy group and the Seabees. So they had a lot of fresh food. Our guys used to swap some clothing with the Seabees. Some of our clothing was better than theirs for the arctic climate. Our men would get a blue jacket and a stocking cap. Then they would put this gear on and go down to the Seabee chow line. I think a lot of times the Seabees knew who they were but they didn't care because they were glad to see our men get some good food too.

We got a crack at some good food once in a while, not too often. A dentist friend of mine, Captain Martin A. Glyn, knew the navy dentist, Grainger Ewart, who was from the same dental school, the University of Detroit. He was allowed a guest or two about once a month and we would get invited down to the navy mess. Marty was a lot cleaner than I was, because a dentist didn't have to get involved with equipment like I did. I had

Tent life on wartime Adak could be difficult. The coal ration amounted to seven pounds per man per day — about enough to take the chill off the tent at night and to warm shaving water in the morning. An armed guard was assigned to the coal pile on the beach. *(Photograph from the author's collection)*

some diesel fuel and stains on my pants. We had no means of taking baths. Once in a while if we got a little bit of extra white gas we could heat some water and take a bath. We had no showers yet. We left a little bit to be desired for body odor and clothing odor. We had to clean our shirts and pants in leaded gasoline. We couldn't use white gas because that was in very short supply and was needed for the cooking ranges. If we had Coleman lanterns we weren't allowed to use white gas for them because it had to be saved for cooking. So we used candles for light for reading and writing letters at night. But anyway the navy boys were glad to have us and they overlooked our clothing. They had silver service, tablecloths, and busboys. Navy officers were somewhat dressed for dinner. They didn't come in with their heavy parkas on. There seemed to be some discipline about their mess.

They finally built a bar, made up of two Quonset huts. The navy had eight to ten nurses late in 1943. Our navy lieutenant friend would invite us down to the navy officers' club. Marty and I liked to just walk up and down the bar and smell the perfume as we walked by the girls. That was as close as we got to a woman for over two years. The army was still using tech sergeants for nurses. There was quite a difference in the way the different services lived on the island.

Supply ships were infrequent until the Liberty ships. I happened to be working on the docks when the first Liberty ship came in. I was told I could look over the gunwales but couldn't go aboard. It was a Russian ship, and had a load of logs on the deck. It pulled out after a day-and-a-half. The first Liberty ship we saw was Russian—lend-lease! It was well into 1943 before we saw our own first American Liberty ship.

Living conditions on Adak were unbelievable! We'd try to put the tents in a defile or along a hill, just to get them out of the wind. You'd try to dig them in as well as you could. When the wind was blowing heavily it looked like a giant was grabbing it by the top and shaking the whole tent. We had no wood or anything to put on the floor. It was ironic that we used driftwood we picked up on the beach that came in on the Japanese Current—driftwood from Japan. The tent floors otherwise were muddy, and we had only a little heat. For light we used candles, and we had to be careful not to fall asleep with a candle going.

It was a little over a year before we got Quonsets. The hospital got the first Quonsets. Our mess halls were the next to get them. The original mess halls were two or three pyramidal tents stuck together.

Our mess sergeant complained about having to dig a hole each day to bury the garbage. He wanted to know why he couldn't dig one big hole. That day the medical officer was down making an inspection. I asked him if we couldn't dig one big hole. He said, "Sure, why not?" We took our man, Luther, who was on permanent KP, out to the site. The mess sergeant, medical officer, and I staked out an area that would be big enough for a few weeks. It was a pretty good-sized square. This was in the morning after breakfast.

The sergeant told Luther to start digging down and he would tell him when to stop. The medic came back to have chow with us that night. As we walked in the tent I noticed there was somebody missing. I mentioned it to the mess sergeant and both of us at the same time thought of Luther. We looked at each other, then went outside, and sure enough it was dark, and we'd see a spadeful of dirt with a little bit of water coming out of a nice big hole out there. We flashed our lights down in the hole, and Luther said, "Sarge, is she deep enough?" The doctor said, "Is that the fellow you were talking

about, that you wanted to recommend for a Section 8 [a discharge from the military on psychological grounds—ed.]?" We said, "That's it." "Well," he said, "I think I've seen enough. I'll put him in for it." Luther finally got his Section 8, and the doctor told us later on, after the hearing, "He's either the smartest man in the army, or the dumbest." They weren't sure which. But Luther got to go home.

Naturally with the weather the way it was the men were always coming down with colds, not as many

A soldier tends a bomb dump on Adak. (*Army Signal Corps, Command Historian's Office, Alaskan Command*)

though as after we got into Quonset huts with oil heaters. They seemed to dry the air up so we had a lot more respiratory problems.

The GI's would know just when things were happening. They had their own pipeline of information. When the docs got their ration of medical alcohol, the men knew it. They would line up on sick call in the morning, beating their chests for a cough. They would say, "I've got a bad cough, Doc. I need some of that cough medicine." The cough medicine was codeine and alcohol. There were a bunch of dead soldiers (empty bottles) lying outside after the GI's had drunk all the cough syrup. Finally the docs asked them if they would kindly take their bottles with them afterward. They had to ration the alcohol supply for some other uses.

After we got into the Quonsets, the brakes went out on a recon car the men made use of to go to the movies. The motor sergeant asked if he could park it behind my hut, where nobody would bother it. He just wanted to deadline it so nobody would drive it. About midnight I heard a big "boom" and the bulkhead of the Quonset hut was lying almost across my bed. Someone had run that brakeless recon into my hut.

I got up and looked out and here were two individuals running up the hill. James "Ditto" DeTillio was on guard duty that night. I yelled, "Ditto, stop 'em!" So Ditto brought his gun down to port arms and hollered, "Halt! Halt!" They weren't stopping—they were still running—so I slipped my parka on, ran up the hill, grabbed his Springfield, and fired in the air over their heads. They hit the ground. I went up and turned them over and looked at them. Here was a captain and a major—a nurse and a medical officer. They said they wanted to see the regimental commander, Colonel Gleim. I said, "I'm not waking Colonel Gleim up at midnight!" They said, "Oh yes, well what are you going to do?" I said, "Well you're both under arrest." They said, "Oh we've gotta see the colonel. He's a personal friend of ours." So I said, "Well, we'll give it a try. I'll give you the benefit of the doubt." So I called the colonel and he was very upset about it. So he had me bring them up to his hut. He looked at them and said, "What are you going to do with 'em, May?" I said, "Well they're under arrest as far as I'm concerned." He said, "Well, why not? Do you want to call the provost or what's the deal? Or do you want to put them in detention?" We didn't have a guardhouse, but could call the provost marshal to take them in. He said, "You'll have to prefer charges on 'em." So they said, "We'll do anything. Just don't prefer charges. Whatever you need!" He was the supply officer for the hospital. The colonel said that well, he could use a small refrigerator, and a couple of other little items. And I said, "Yeah and I could use a nice little old hospital bed, you know, with a mattress on it," so that I could get rid of my cot. The major said, "You'll have it the first thing in the morning!" Sure enough, we had them, first thing in the morning. The charges were dropped.

I was up to the PX one day and I noticed a whole bunch of the men were lined up at the door. So I went in to the PX officer and said, "What's going on? You got a special deal going here? There's a bunch of GI's, must be fifty or sixty guys lined up." He said, "I don't know what it is. There's something evidently coming in on the ship that they know about, which I don't. I haven't even got the manifest yet!" Sure enough, before long he had his manifest. He got his shipment, and it was Aqua-Velva. The guys were lined up to get their ration, I think it was three or four bottles apiece or something like that. They would step out of line, go outside and drink it, and get back in line again.

We had the same problem with the vanilla extract. (Finally the military started making non-alcoholic vanilla extract.) Everyone was complaining because the desserts—later on when we had desserts—had no flavoring because the vanilla extract would be all gone. Finally the men started making their own brew out of the extra fruit juice they got. They called it the "Aleutian Solution."

This Ditto, the same fellow that was on guard up there that night, had been transferred up from one of the gun batteries. He had been in communications up there and he was working on the switchboard. The colonel called me up one day and said, "You better get on up to the switchboard hut and check on what's going on there. I've been cut off the line a couple of times." So I went on up there and here was Ditto on the board. He said that he had worked these BD-24 boards before, but never anything like they had up here. They had about three or four boards stacked on top of each other. He said that when he came on duty there were all the plugs in there. He just took over from the other guy, who just got up and left. He said, "I didn't know what was what. So I just pulled out all of the plugs and was going to start over afresh."

We had our "A" battery up at the north end of the island up near what we called "Kingfisher Bay." They had the 90-millimeters up there. I think they also had two or three 155-millimeter rifles, old babies from World War I. They were actually on tracks but they used them as seacoast guns. It was the only seacoast equipment we had there, other than the 3-inch and the 90-millimeter guns that were in the regiment. Anyway, they had a problem, the navy did, with a lot of these old Norwegian skippers. Some of them were with the Alaska Steamship Company, and these old boys were pretty stubborn about convoy discipline and regulations. Some of their old ships had trouble keeping up. If they could do twelve or thirteen knots, that was plenty. Some of them had lagged and they came in on their own. Wilkinson was one of the officers in that battery. He said they always had problems with these Norwegian skippers coming in. They would try to contact them on the radio, to ask them to identify. These old boys weren't talking or doing a thing. He would ask them to put on their running lights. These guys were running in the dark. Finally O'Geara, the battery commander, had enough of it. So he loaded up one of these 155's, elevated the barrel a little bit, and fired one. It happened to go right between the pilot house on the back end and some of the forward derrick equipment. Those old babies when they go through the air sound like a railroad train coming down the track. He said, "Boy they lit up everything! They got out the Coleman lanterns, flashlights, candles, whatever they had." I think Squeaky Anderson got in on that one because he was commander of the port. He started laying it on O'Geara for firing on one of our own ships.

I was transferred back with the Canadian Army for temporary duty in mountain warfare, in Terrace, British Columbia. I was supposed to go down to Seattle and back up to Terrace. There was a big williwaw blowing and nothing was moving on the island. So I was a couple of days late in leaving and all of a sudden the airport called up and said, "Get that officer on down here, we've got a transport going out." So I got down there and got aboard the C-47 transport. I was sitting on two or three feet of mailbags. No mail had moved off the island for about three days. I was waiting to leave and pretty soon a carryall pulled up. Here comes Errol Flynn and his crew. They'd been up there on a USO trip. So they loaded aboard and we took off. There were two women in the crew and they kept them up front because they said the only heat was up there. Flynn and the other men were in back with me. It got pretty cold. We had our parkas on and blanket-lined pants. But Flynn broke out two bottles of liqueur. He said it was the only thing he had left. Flynn, and Harry Mendoza who was with him, and I were drinking this liqueur. We didn't notice it too much, it was so darn cold.

We overflew Umnak where we were supposed to drop in and refuel. The crew sergeant said the pilot wanted to go right straight in because he had a tail wind. I asked them how long they had been up in this area. They said about three or four months. I said, "Well I've been up here two years and you don't trust the weather or tail winds." Pretty soon the pilot came back and said they had a little problem now: they were running into headwinds; they couldn't get back into Cold Bay, they would have to go all the way in—but they thought there was enough fuel to make it. So we started letting down into Anchorage, and we started to perspire. The liqueur was working!

When we landed I was the first one off the ship. As I stepped to go down the ladder, my shoe-pacs were slippery, and my head wasn't too clear. So I slid right down on my back, straight out underneath General Buckner, who was standing there to greet Flynn. His aide-de-camp got me out of there fast before Buckner could find out who I was.

When President Roosevelt came to Adak he messed with the Seabees. I believe he was on the *Richmond*, a heavy cruiser. She was in at the T-dock when a williwaw came up (thank God while he was there!) and held them into the dock. So he got a chance to see what this Aleutian weather could be like. When they were ready to leave they couldn't make it because the williwaw had them plastered right against the dock. They tried to move that cruiser with tugs but there was no way they could get it away from the dock. Finally they got loose and started back and got towards Kodiak and found they'd left the president's dog, Fala. They had to send a destroyer back to pick up the dog. That really hit the newspapers.

Roosevelt had noticed the weather on the island and asked how long these troops had been there. They said, "two years." He said, "They will be rotated out as soon as replacement troops can be gotten in." So we were one of the first ones to be on a rotation list.

In August 1944 we were rotated back to the states, by ship. It was snowing the day we left so we had our parkas on. It was cold. We got into Seattle, through the debarkation point, loaded on a train, and went down to Camp Hahn, California. It was about ninety or a hundred degrees when we got down there, practically in our arctic equipment. It took them about a day-and-a-half to cut orders to get us into suntans. We tried to turn in our old equipment. We had brought our guns and everything else back with us. Ordnance just couldn't believe the shipping ticket we had on the weapons because some of our guns were from World War I, although modified. They had never seen anything like this. I had to get my field manual out and show them pictures of the guns so they could determine their nomenclature.

That ended the Adak adventure.

(This is an edited transcript of a cassette audio tape made on 3 June 1993 in Durango, Colorado, by Joseph M. May. He was a captain in the 210th Coast Artillery Group, Ninety-Fourth Gun Battalion, on Adak from August 1942 to August 1944.)

*Joseph M. May is enjoying an active retirement. He has built a biplane and is now building a Kit Fox monoplane. Prior to retirement he owned and operated a guest ranch in the Estes Park area of Colorado.*

*Harold Steinhoff is the president of Four Corners Research Institute in Durango, Colorado. He is a wildlife biologist.*

# A Tale of Two Bombers

*Stephen M. Morrisette*

THERE ARE PROBABLY VERY FEW AIRMEN IN THE FAIR-banks area who do not know how to find the B-24 that is crashed near Wood River Buttes. But I doubt there is more than a handful of men left in Alaska, among them Randy Acord, who know when the big four-engined bomber went down. This is the story of that B-24 and of a second B-24 that crashed near the buttes in the winter of 1943.

In 1943, Ladd Field (now Fort Wainwright) was the home of the Army Cold Weather Test Station. This unit tested everything from motor oil to gun breech heaters to thermal underwear in the arctic environment. On 4 February 1943, Major Ancil D. "Red" Baker was sched-uled to fly a photography mission. His aircraft, B-24D 41-23853, took off at 1400 Alaska War Time (AWT). The mission was scheduled to last only three-and-a-half hours.

On board the aircraft was an unusually large comple-ment. There were fourteen men, counting Red Baker. Their mission was to observe and photograph a solar eclipse.

The flight was routine for the first three hours. Then those countless hours and hours of boredom were inter-rupted by a few of the proverbial moments of stark, rav-ing terror. No. 1 engine sputtered, came back to life, and then died. No. 2 engine didn't bother to sputter—it just died.

Four-engined aircraft can, under certain circum-stances, fly with two engines out on the same wing. One of those circumstances is that the propellers of the offending engines must be feathered. Major Baker was unable to feather either of the dead engines! There was

only one thing Red Baker could do. He pulled the throt-tles back on Nos. 3 and 4 and put the aircraft into a shal-low dive.

The aircraft was flying (gliding) at a descent rate of a thousand feet per minute. In less than ten minutes, Red Baker would run out of altitude beneath him and, as every pilot knows, one of the most useless things in the world is altitude above you. Preparations were made for a forced landing.

The major problem was that a B-24 was not designed to fly with a complement of fourteen. There were not enough ditching stations for everyone. Major Baker directed everyone to strap in who could find a station. The remaining men were placed either in the bomb bay or standing directly behind the pilots. With all possible preparations made, Major Baker banked his aircraft into the wind and prepared to turn it into the world's largest bobsled.

Baker did an exceptional job of landing the big bomber. But B-24s were not noted for good forced land-ings, and this B-24 was no different from the rest. As the aircraft skidded to a stop in the three-foot deep snow, the fuselage crumpled just forward of the leading edge. Part of the nose gear retraction mechanism was forced up through the cabin floor, breaking the legs of the air-men who were standing behind the pilots. However, the aircraft did, literally, stay in one piece. Several men in the bomb bay were also injured and there was one case of frostbite before the fourteen men were rescued.

Mechanics later stripped Major Baker's airplane of all usable parts, and it was then used by the air corps for target practice. Even today, the military still uses the airplane for the same purpose. Today's pilots no longer shoot it—they just "lock onto" it. Today, "858" resembles a colander in the shape of an airplane. It has been filled so full of holes the fuselage no longer supports its own weight. It now lies totally flattened against the tundra. There is not a single salvageable piece left on the aircraft.

One week after the crash, the Cold Weather Test Lab sent up another B-24 to duplicate the conditions which led to Major Baker's crash. On board this B-24 were seven men, including a civilian representative of the Consolidated Aircraft Company.

The pilot, First Lieutenant Clarence Hill, took off from Ladd at 1440 AWT, on 12 February, and proceeded toward the Wood River Buttes area. The plan was to shut both left engines down. During the first test, he was to feather both props. On the second test, he was to allow the props to windmill.

The exact sequence of events during that flight will never be known. Hill's aircraft, B-24D 41-23873, was totally destroyed on impact. The forward fuselage now lies in a crater. Two of the engines are also partially buried in the tundra. The after fuselage is a crumpled tangle of aluminum and steel. Both wings broke away from the fuselage on impact and lie juxtaposed to each other. A post-crash fire consumed the center wing area. The entire aircraft lies in a very small area. These facts, combined with the position of the wings, indicate the aircraft was stalled and spinning when it hit the ground.

Amazingly, there was very little salvaging done to "873." Rusted machine-guns can still be found in the wreckage. Unlike Major Baker's airplane, "873" is very difficult to spot, even when you know where to look. You must fly almost directly over the wreckage and be looking straight down to see it.

Both aircraft lie on the Fort Wainwright Military Reservation. It is probably not this fact but the fact that they lie in the most remote part of the North Star Borough which has protected the sites from looters. Even those pilots who spot the wrecks cannot land their planes nearby. The tundra will not provide a suitable field for an aircraft on wheels or skis.

Eventually, the Cold Weather Test Lab found the reason for the feather pump failures. The oil in the feathering system was congealing in the freezing temperatures. The lab started experimenting with ways to keep the oil fluid, and eventually succeeded. However, success did not come before a third B-24 crashed in 1943.

But that is another story.

*Stephen M. Morrisette is a retired U.S. Air Force captain. He was attached to the Third Wing Group at Elmendorf Air Force Base. He now lives in Eagle River, Alaska.*

# The Man Who Walked Out
# of Charley River

*Stephen M. Morrisette*

IN ANOTHER PAPER, I HAVE TOLD THE STORY OF TWO B-24s that crashed near Eielson Air Force Base in Alaska in the early part of 1943. Several months later, modified aircraft were flown from Ladd Field to check the effectiveness of the corrective actions.

This is the story of one of those test missions—a mission that ended tragically: Another B-24 crashed. Another four airmen died. This time, however, one man survived. This is the story of that man's incredible eighty-four-day survival ordeal during the winter of 1943-44, only three degrees below the Arctic Circle.

The crew began assembling many hours before daybreak. The specially instrumented and equipped B-24D, 42-40910, was standing ready on the Ladd ramp. Second Lieutenand Harold E. "Hos" Hoskins was the pilot. First Lieutenant Leon Crane was the copilot. The flight engineer was Master Sergeant Richard Pompeo, and the radio operator was Sergeant Ralph Wenz. The crew also included a technical engineer who would monitor the test. He was First Lieutenant James B. Seibert.

The preflight was uneventful and at dawn, 0940 Alaska War Time (AWT), Hos Hoskins and Leon Crane pulled back on their yokes and "910" climbed into the cold arctic air. It was four days before Christmas, 1943.

The crew headed east. At ten thousand feet, they strapped on oxygen masks, and Lieutenant Seibert ran his first series of tests. At 1003 AWT, Sergeant Wenz called Big Delta and reported their position as forty miles southeast of Ladd Field (now Fort Wainwright). Another routine radio check was made at 1030, indicating they were over Big Delta.

At fifteen thousand feet, they punched through a thin layer of scud. Hos then leveled off at twenty thousand and Seibert ran a second series of tests—injecting fuel into the oil hopper to see how much fuel was needed to keep the pumps capable of feathering. He was diluting the oil with the fuel, changing the mix at each altitude. With those tests complete, Hos started looking for a hole in a second deck of clouds. At 1100, Wenz made his last radio check with Big Delta. He indicated they were southeast of Big Delta and were flying a random flightpath, staying clear of clouds.

A little before noon, Hos spotted a hole that looked big enought to climb through. He initiated a circling climb within the hole. His goal was to level off above the clouds at thirty thousand feet so Seibert could complete the last series of tests.

It was during this circling climb that things started to go wrong—fast. First, the hole was not as large as Hos thought it was. At or near twenty-three thousand feet, the B-24 entered the clouds. Hos and his copilot were now in IFR conditions. Second, the No. 1 engine failed. Third, the vacuum selector valve froze in the No. 1 position.

To summarize what happened, the crew entered the clouds in a climbing bank, the failed engine distracted the pilots, and more significantly, the failed engine combined with the frozen vacuum selector valve to cause a loss of all vacuum instruments. Results: within seconds, the crew lost situational awareness, and the B-24 entered a spin.

Wenz had time to report an engine had failed and they were in a spin, but did not—or, more probably, could not—report their position. The aircraft broke out of the clouds at about twenty thousand feet. Hos and Crane manhandled the controls and recovered from the spin, but the aircraft immediatley fell off into a secondary spin in the oposite direction. The two pilots managed to stop the spin a second time, but by now the aircraft was in a 300-mile-an-hour nosedive.

Crane screamed at Pompeo to open the bomb-bay doors. During the dive, something snapped in the tail. Crane remembers it sounded like the report of a pistol. The aircraft suddenly whipped into a nose-up attitude, then stalled and fell off into a third spin. Hos screamed, "Bail out!" Crane hit the bailout button. Hos and Crane stayed at the useless controls long enough to give Wenz and Seibert time to get out. Then Hos yelled at Crane and Pompeo, "Get the hell out!" Pompeo was the first to go out of the bomb bay. Crane crawled aft, took off his mittens, strapped on his chute, and fell out of the bomb bay. As he fell into the deadly, cold air, he remembered seeing Hos in the radio compartment.

The last man to leave the aircraft was the pilot, Hos. As Crane descended in his chute, he was able to spot only one other chute, and that was above him. That would have been Hos. He watched as the B-24 continued to spin into the side of a mountain. Hos disappeared on the other side of a ridge. Crane landed on a steep-sided mountain face. He could still make out the burning aircraft on the slope above him. He yelled, trying to locate his fellow airmen, but there was no reply. He was alone. He attempted to hike up the mountain to the crash site, but was unable to because of the steep grade and deep snow. His training had taught him to stay with the wreck, but he could not get to it. Crane had some tough decisions to make. He knew the choices he made would be life-and-death decisions.

Crane took stock of his situation. He knew he was in trouble. He had no food, no sleeping bag, no weapons, and he had left his mittens in the aircraft. The folks at Ladd had no idea where he was and, for that matter, even he didn't know where he was.

On the other hand, he had a lot going for him. Most important was that he had no injuries. He was wearing a new experimental, down-filled flight suit. And as for survival equipment, he had a Boy Scout knife, two books of matches, a letter from his father, and his parachute.

He correctly assumed there was little or no chance of the rescue team's finding him before he died of exposure or starvation. He decided to break with convention and set out to find help for himself and his fellow crewmembers. With that thought, he proceeded downslope to a stream, then downstream. When it got too dark to go any further (at about 1600 hours), he stopped to make camp. He lit a fire, using four of his forty matches and his father's letter. He wrapped himself in his parachute and tried to sleep. Before he fell asleep, he noticed he could still see the glow of his burning aircraft. The plane wasn't the only thing burning that night. Several times he woke up to find his parachute ablaze. Other times he woke up from just plain cold and discomfort.

On the first morning of his ordeal, Crane awoke confident he would find civilization if he continued to work his way downriver. He traveled with great difficulty. He was already suffering from frostbite. His ungloved hands were bleeding and he was dangerously chilled. The snow was hip deep in places. The rocks in the riverbed often reduced his progress to nothing more than controlled stumbling. He spent another restless night wrapped in nothing but his parachute.

The next day brought more pain, hunger, and discomfort. On day three of his ordeal, Crane made a decision that nearly cost him his life. He changed his plans and decided to wait for help. He made camp. He made several vain attempts to kill some tree squirrels but settled instead for some snow and some frozen moss (which he could not swallow).

The fourth day nearly passed before he remembered it was Christmas Day. The thought of Christmas dinner only aggravated his hunger. Crane stayed in place for three more nights. The cold was murderous. The cold, combined with no real food intake, was sapping the strength from his body. He knew he had to move. He spent the seventh night in his makeshift camp. He watched spectacular displays of northern lights while he made plans to move out early the next day.

The next morning broke cold and clear, but Crane's thinking was fuzzy. He made another decision—another change—and, again, it nearly cost him his life. Rather than continuing downstream, he decided to head west and try to find the Alaska-Canada highway. Crane stumbled and crawled up the western slope of the river valley. He continually lost his direction. At midday, Crane could still see the camp he had left earlier that morning. As he sat exhaustedly looking back down his crooked path, he realized he could not possibly make the estimated two hundred miles back to the Alcan Highway. He returned to his camp. He realized he had nearly used up the little strength left in his body. He decided to move downriver again the next morning.

Crane spent the entire ninth day stumbling down the river, always hoping to find a settlement or camp around the next bend. Incredibly, at dusk, he saw a manmade structure. It was a tent standing high above the ground on tall poles. It was what Alaskans call a cache. Crane ran for the cache in the gathering darkness.

As he approached, he saw a small cabin. He entered. It was just large enough to hold a bed, table, and small wood stove. His life had been saved. He tore open several sacks on the table and found the fixings for hot chocolate and bags of dried fruit. He started a fire and melted snow. He was soon drinking hot cocoa and stuffing himself with raisins. He found a ladder for the cache. In it he found a variety of things, including tents, tarps, ropes, tools, and lanterns. He brought the frozen tents into the cabin, laid them on the bunk, wrapped himself up in his chute and tents, and fell asleep.

The next morning, Crane had another breakfast of raisins and hot chocolate. He stuffed his pockets with raisins and set out downstream to find the village he was sure was just around the corner. That assumption would bring him closer to death than he had been so far. He moved downstream all that day and into the night. He couldn't believe such a well-stocked cabin could be so far from a town. By midnight, he realized he was in serious trouble. He estimated the temperature to be minus fifty degrees. His feet and hands were numb. He could not move his fingers to strike a match. He had to make it back upriver to the cabin! As he retraced his steps, he drifted in and out of consciousness. At times, he would awake to find himself wandering away from the streambed. Near noon, on New Year's day, he made it back to the cabin. He managed to light a fire, then slept hard for the next two days.

On the twelfth day of his ordeal, Crane awoke rested but feeling very hungry. He returned to the cache to see if there was anything else up there to eat. In the daylight, Crane found burlap sacks full of flour, jerky, beans, dried soup vegetables, tea, lard, rice, and other foodstuffs. There was clothing, including fur mittens! There was a rifle and even ammunition! On the side of one of the crates of supplies was the name and, presumably, the occupation of his benefactor. The label read "Phil Brail, Woodchopper, Alaska."

For the next week, Crane settled into a rather domestic life. He concentrated on treating his frostbite and rebuilding his strength. He mended his clothes and made inventories. He found a four-year-old calendar and kept track of days by punching the days on the calendar with a nail. One evening, he accidentally knocked the calendar off the wall. As the calendar hit the floor, it fell open to a map of Alaska. Crane was ecstatic! He studied the map for several nights before he found the town of Woodchopper. It was not until then that he realized Woodchopper was where Phil Brail lived, not what he did for a living.

The map was as much a lifesaver as was the food and even the cabin itself. Crane determined he was on a tributary of the Yukon River, probably the Charley River. He also realized that if he was on the Charley River, he was still a very long way from Woodchopper.

Crane decided to make another exploratory trip downstream. This time, he was better equipped and in much better physical condition. He made a backpack from his parachute and carried the rifle.

On the 20th of January, he headed out. On the first day out, Crane discovered a second cabin and a derelict canoe. On the second day, he found a third cabin. In this cabin, he found some old mail, again addressed to Woodchopper, Alaska. He also found a sleeping bag. He would not have to sleep in his silk cocoon again.

The next day Crane continued downstream. On that day, he erroneously concluded he was nearing the Yukon River and returned to Phil Brail's cabin. As he walked back upstream, he estimated he would need a two-week supply of food to make it to Woodchopper. He also decided to wait a few more weeks until the weather improved.

The next several weeks were quite routine (measured by Alaska standards). Crane hunted squirrels and ptarmigan. He chopped a hole in the ice for fresh water daily. He was living the very kind of life Phil Brail would have lived if he were there. There was one major difference—one that depressed him a lot. Leon Crane's thoughts were continually drawn to his family. He realized his parents must have given him up for dead.

Another week passed, and Crane decided not to wait any longer. His ammunition was running low, he had heard the river ice crack several times, his strength had returned, and he felt up to the ordeal. Leon made a sled from some boards and a washtub. He packed it with an estimated two-week supply of provisions and readied himself for the trip that would either save or end his life.

On 12 February, Crane closed the door to Phil Brail's cabin for the last time. He laboriously lugged the crude sled through the snow, sometimes hip deep. The sled was much harder to pull than he had figured. He could not, however, carry the two-weeks' worth of supplies any other way, so he slowly moved downriver.

One day Crane put his foot through some rotten ice. Within a few minutes his mukluk was frozen stiff, but his foot stayed dry. Several days later, he nearly lost his life again. Crane fell through the ice and found himself standing armpit deep in the icy Charley River. Scrambling up the snow-covered bank, Crane knew he had only minutes to live. He reacted quickly. While trembling uncontrollably, he started a fire and stripped to the waist. He started drying his upper garments while stamping around in his frozen mukluks and trousers. Several long, miserable hours later, he donned his upper garments and stripped off his frozen lower garments.

The next day, Crane was moving downriver again. On the fifteenth day of his trek from the Brail cabin, he found another deserted cabin and in it a very small supply of food. He remained there for three days before striking out for the Yukon River again. The temperature during those last weeks of winter was about twenty-five below (about the temperature when the mucus freezes in your nostrils when you inhale sharply).

Sometime during those last days of winter, the ice cracked again. This time, it was the sled that fell through. Without the supplies on that sled, Crane knew he would probably not survive, so he waded into the hip-deep water to recover his supplies and to save the sled. Crane again had to stand naked in front of a fire while his clothes dried. He decided to leave the cumbersome sled and proceed with only a backpack and rifle. It took another eight days to finally reach the Yukon River.

The next day, Crane found a sled dog trail and followed it until he found a cabin with smoke floating above it. There were clothes hanging on a clothesline. There were the sounds of dogs and children and the smell of hot food! As Crane approached the cabin, a rather startled gentleman stepped from the cabin. His name was Albert Ames. Ames took Crane in and introduced him to his wife, Neena, and their three small children.

The man listened to Crane's incredible story and then explained that Crane had walked 120 miles down Charley River, and that he was still thirty miles from Woodchopper. Crane also learned he was 250 miles away from Ladd Field. Ames offered to give him a ride into town on his dogsled and Crane gratefully accepted.

At Woodchopper, a wireless set was used to contact a Wien Airlines bush pilot who was on his way to Circle, a village forty miles further downstream. Two telegrams were also sent, one to his family and one to Ladd Field. Crane also had a chance to meet Phil Brail.

Soon he was in the air again, headed for Ladd. The bush pilot radioed Ladd for permission to land at the military base. When the base asked the reason for his request, the pilot (Bob Rice) answered that he had Lt. Leon Crane on board. After a few moments of silence, in a most unmilitary voice, the operator asked, "Is he alive or dead?"

There was no small stir on base as the word quickly spread that Leon Crane was back—alive! One can only imagine the looks on the faces of Crane's fellow airmen as he walked into Base Ops, eighty-four days after his plane crashed. Crane was taken to the flight surgeon's office for a checkup and was determined to be in great shape. In fact, he had even gained a little weight during his ordeal. There was an emotional reunion with the base commander. During this meeting, the commander arranged for a personal phone call back to the zone of the interior (now known as the Lower 48). Leon spoke to his parents and assured them that, much like Mark Twain, the reports of his death had been greatly exaggerated. He then went to the PX and ordered a chocolate malt.

The very next day, Lieutenant Crane boarded a B-24 and led the rescue team to the crash site. Within a week, ground parties were searching for the other missing crewmen. They found the remains of Lieutenant Seibert and Sergeant Wenz in the wreck of the plane. The two apparently had been unable to get out of the spinning aircraft. There was never a trace found of Master Sergeant Pompeo or of Captain Hoskins.

Building 1001 on Ladd Field was named in honor of Master Sergeant Pompeo. Today, Building 1001 still stands, but there is no evidence the building once bore the name of the fallen aviator. Leon Crane is still alive, as of this writing, and lives in Philadelphia, Pennsylvania.

And so goes the story of the man who walked out of Charley River, an ordinary airman who rose to the ranks of a warrior—a man whose incredible story lives on, if only in the dusty pages of out-of-print books.

*Stephen M. Morrisette is a retired U.S. Air Force captain. He was attached to the Third Wing Group, and stationed at Elmendorf Air Force Base. He now lives in Eagle River, Alaska.*

# Defending
the
Territory

Detail from a war bond solicitation poster by Alaska artist M.C. "Rusty" Heurlin.
*(Photo No. B55.2, courtesy The Anchorage Museum of History and Art)*

# Arctic Search and Rescue: Sled Dogs and Lend-Lease

*Zachary T. Irwin*

THE NORTHWEST AIR ROUTE FROM GREAT FALLS, Montana, through Fairbanks, Alaska, extends some 2,210 statute miles. The route became an essential link in Allied war efforts following Germany's attack on Russia in June 1941, and the Japanese attack on Dutch Harbor almost a year later.[1] Thus, Alaska and the northwest route connected the European front with that of the North Pacific.

In addition to defending North America, armed forces along the route ferried some eight thousand aircraft over three years to Soviet crews in Fairbanks at Ladd Field. The significance of this route extended beyond its ferrying mission and the war's end, for it established the basis for an integrated Canadian-American Air Defense Command and a general re-evaluation of the Arctic's strategic significance.

Search and rescue operations of the Air Transport Command (ATC) were of less far-reaching significance. Parachuting sled dogs and rescue teams in pursuit of crash victims was an effort with popular appeal, yet as early as March 1945 the first R-6 helicopter was placed in rescue service in the Far East.[2] The obsolescence of sled rescue, nevertheless, did not dim the ATC's ingenuity and achievement in pioneering rescue efforts.

Of course the Northwest Route was not the only supply route for lend-lease. More vulnerable routes existed through Iran and around Spitzbergen. Airborne desert sand and distance made the former notoriously hard on aircraft, while the second route was exposed to German attack. This route lay west of Iceland and north around Jan Mayen and Spitzbergen to Murmansk and Archangelsk. After early spring of 1942, German bombers and submarines based in northern Norway had all but cut supplies, and in the summer of that year only five of thirty-five supply ships escaped destruction.[3] Conditions improved after the Allied occupation of Spitzbergen, yet the advantages of the northwest route were considerable, especially from the Allied viewpoint. A series of bases could be used in the war against Japan. Clearly, the obstacles to flight from the continental United States through Alaska and Siberia were varied—in climate, diplomacy, and organization—but throughout 1942 they remained less daunting than those of the European Arctic.

As early as August 1941, Allied leadership had first proposed the delivery of aircraft by way of Alaska. Soviet authorities were not enthusiastic about the prospect of Allied bases linking Russia and North America. Such a route, even outside Siberia, could provide the Japanese with a pretext for renouncing their nonaggression pact with Moscow, if not for immediate attack. General Soviet suspicion of Allied motives was a persistent feature of wartime collaboration. Nevertheless, American pressure and Soviet desperation throughout 1942 eased the objec-

---

[1] For a general history of operations in the area see Stanley Dzuiban, *Military Relations Between the United States and Canada 1939-1945* (Washington, D.C.: Office of the Secretary of Military History, 1959), pp. 199-225.

[2] Capt. Knute Flint, "Rescue by Helicopter," *Saturday Evening Post*, 6 October 1945, p. 34.

[3] Marshal Philip Joubert, "High Latitude Flying by Coastal Command in Support of Convoys to North Russia," *The Geographical Journal*, 108 (1-3) July-September 1946, p. 5.

tions. On August 3, Moscow would give its approval for the route. By the end of September, a mix of more than one hundred A-20s, B-25s, P-39s, and P-40s were flown to Ladd Field.[4] Unexpectedly, Soviet authorities would not accept delivery for another month.

In fact, in March—a few months after the Japanese attack on Dutch Harbor—Northwest and Western airlines had opened the route and operated some nineteen DC-3s to supply the Eleventh Air Force and the Alaska Defense Command. Yet problems were debilitating. Canadian officials were reluctant to authorize the activity of American commercial airlines on Canadian territory and sought the route's militarization.[5] Responsibility for the route was divided among the airline companies, Canadian authorities, and two American services. Morale was hardly better than the inadequate support facilities. Search and rescue operations were rudimentary. In principle, command lay with the Seventh Ferrying Group of the ATC at Great Falls, yet operations at Ladd Field remained with the Eleventh Air Force Command. Recommendations for the route by a Canadian-American Permanent Joint Board on Defense depended on discussions in Ottawa. Matters improved only after mid-October with the creation of an Alaska wing of the ATC under the command of Colonel Thomas L. Mosley, a former commander of the Ferrying Command's Foreign Wing, and his executive, Colonel George E. Gardner, a former vice president of Northwest Airlines. Mosley and General Gaffney, commander of the Alaska Division, ultimately planned for search and rescue operations at Fort Nelson, British Columbia. Gaffney was one of the few reputable experts on arctic flight.[6]

During the extreme winter of 1942-43, Mosley pulled off an astonishing achievement. By spring, more than a hundred aircraft a month were arriving at Ladd Field.[7] Earlier problems in command structure had been resolved. Cooperation with the Canadian Department of Transportation had improved and construction of the Alcan Highway proceeded with a series of bases and landing strips. The extraordinary flow of material and engineering skill intensified throughout the war, exceeding the immediate requirements of lend-lease or the Eleventh Air Force.

## Search and Rescue

The problems of search and rescue in arctic conditions presented an unusual set of circumstances—some obvious, others less so. Obviously, weather conditions, extreme cold, and navigational error were the primary causes of crashes. Survival depended not only on the prompt dispatch of rescue teams but also on the behavior of crash victims. The efforts invested in rescue operations were often a consequence of distance and terrain. An exhaustive analysis of crashes in wartime involving 268 aircraft revealed the following breakdown of locations:[8]

| | |
|---|---|
| Alaska and the Aleutians | 104 |
| Greenland and adjacent areas | 58 |
| Eastern Canada | 38 |
| Western Canada | 24 |
| Labrador | 16 |
| Newfoundland | 6 |
| Maine | 4 |
| Bering Strait | 1 |
| Location uncertain | 17 |

These accidents involved some 617 individuals and an additional twenty-four who were lost from aircraft or parachuted prematurely. Of these, 480 either survived or left information sufficient to reconstruct the circumstances of their death. One hundred and sixty-one either died immediately or remained missing. Some 75 percent of the crashes occurred between December 1 and March 31, and ferrying operations constituted the majority of the incidents.

A smaller share were involved in combat operations against the Japanese, and a few resulted from action against German detachments in Greenland and submarine activity in the North Atlantic and Pacific. The vast majority of crashes were the result of a combination of circumstances: human error compounded by severe weather.[9] Typically, pilots were forced down after losing direction and exhausting fuel. Radio interference was often an aggravating feature of the crash, as was poor visibility—that is, whiteouts and mountain crashes. Mechanical failure was often present but less often a direct source of grounding. A high number of crashes— 10 percent—involved midair collisions. While seldom reported, the lack of maturity of pilots was a certain source.

Two major considerations recommended intense search and rescue: frequent survival of the crash and serious injury. One documented case recorded a pilot's

---

[4] Wesley F. Craven and James L. Cate, eds., *The Army Air Force in World War II*, vol. 7 (University of Chicago Press, 1958), p. 154.

[5] Ibid, p. 156.

[6] Cpt. Richard L. Neuberger, "Wing Commander," *Alaska Life*, May 1944, pp. 42-43.

[7] Craven, et al., *The Army Air Force in World War II*, p. 159.

[8] Richard A. Howard, *Down in the North: An Analysis of Survival Experiences in Arctic Areas* (Maxwell Air Force Base, Alabama: U.S. Arctic, Desert, and Tropic Information Center, 1953), pp. 3-4.

[9] Ibid, p. 5.

survival for 164 days on the Greenland icecap. Yet, in fully 50 percent of the cases, personnel suffered debilitating injury. Initially, a crash site was identified and a team landed such aircraft as the L-1E, capable of operation on short, improvised runways. A team trekked to the site when a plane reported trouble or was declared missing. Yet for all crashes, an average time of five days elapsed before the location was established.[10]

The precise origin of the use of sled dogs in the rescue of downed airmen is not altogether clear. Lieutenant Colonel Norman Vaughn, commander of the ATC base at Goose Bay, and Major Joseph Westover, of the Canadian Sector Search and Rescue Unit, were among the first to apply these concepts, although the full potential of sled dog rescue was not realized until late in 1943.[11]

During the winter of 1942-43, some seventy-nine individuals were rescued, principally by trekking crews. The use of sled dogs appears to have followed the development of bases and ferrying operations along the northwest route during the following year.

Training and operations for search and rescue were centralized at Fort Nelson, British Columbia. The base developed only after the first officers arrived in July 1942 from the 383rd Air Base Squadron in Great Falls. In December, Westover took command of the base. The choice of Fort Nelson flowed from its advantage for ATC ferrying operations. Because of its distance from Edmonton, planes were ready for refueling before they moved on to the next and most hazardous leg of the journey north to Whitehorse and Alaska. Fort Nelson afforded the most logical place to check weather conditions before departure. Nevertheless, the immediate responsibility for search and rescue from Fort Nelson involved a large area east to Fort Smith and nearby waterways, north along the Athabasca to Great Slave Lake, down the Mackenzie past Fort Simpson, and north beyond Whitehorse.[12]

A rescue incident in early winter of 1943 demonstrated the limitations of rescue before the use of sled dogs. A ferried fighter plane was forced down on a frozen lake between Fort Nelson and Watson Lake. An L-1E aircraft took off to rescue the pilot via a nearby landing strip at Smith River, but, just short of the destination, engine failure forced the plane down. A second search located the rescue plane the following day. In the meantime, Westover led a third search for the original fighter plane.[13] Finally, the entire party made its

Lieutenant David Irwin with one of his "parapups," Alaska, 1944. *(Photograph courtesy the author and the Arctic Studies Center, Smithsonian Institution, Washington, D.C.)*

way out to Smith River.

By early 1944, the volume of aircraft and supplies ferried along the route multiplied such incidents. Yet, as of January of that year, only five aircraft capable of short-distance landing were available at Fort Nelson. Why so few were available is not clear, yet the advantages of dogsled rescue were undeniable.

Shortly after this incident, Lieutenant David Irwin led a party by sled overland to the site of a crashed A-20 at the fork of the Fontas and Nelson rivers. The time en route to the site was thirteen days, mainly because of an accident requiring evacuation of two persons on the team by an additional sled.[14] The dogs returned from the crash site in eighteen hours over a distance of more than seventy miles. The entire search and rescue squadron consisted of twenty-one enlisted men and seven officers, including flight surgeons Captain Fallon,

---

[10] Ibid.

[11] C.B. Colby, "Men, Dogs, and Machines," *Popular Science*, October 1945, p. 123.

[12] Lt. Robert V. Fulham, ATC 1460th AAF Base Unit, "Operation and Maintenance Difficulties," 1945 (mimeo), p.3.

[13] Ibid, p. 6.

[14] Lt. Robert V. Fulham, ATC 1460th AAF Base Unit, "History of Flight `B' Search and Rescue."

Captain Torres, and Lieutenants Jamieson, Dean, Lind, and Irwin. Irwin enjoyed the most experience because of his more-than-a-decade spent in the Canadian Arctic. He was well known for his trip of some three thousand miles by sled from Aklavik, near the Alaska border east of Mackenzie Bay, to the Boothia Peninsula.[15] The others had varying experience of arctic conditions, some since the start of the war. From the time of his arrival, Irwin was placed in charge of dog training and ground operations.

When training the dogs, the unit experimented with various harnesses fastened to parachutes, and the dogs were dropped either singly or two at a time. In most cases, a driver, a surgeon, and two enlisted men parachuted close to the crash site. The original kennel of ten dogs was soon supplemented by seven and reached twenty-two by mid-1944. At this time, more than 150 sled dogs were maintained at Fort Richardson near Anchorage, Ladd Field, and Nome for similar land rescue operations.[16] Scout messenger dogs were used on Attu, Adak, and Amchitka Islands.

As early as April 1943, the widely scattered veterinary detachments were grouped into a Veterinary Section, Service Command, Alaska Defense Command. Training for Alaska and western Canada units was centered at Fort Nelson. Throughout all arctic bases, some twenty-nine dog teams were in service by the war's end.

The development of search and rescue depended on flexibility in operations and ease of communication among the several bases in Alaska and Fort Nelson. As mentioned, the dog was dropped in a five-pound canvas harness lined with sheepskin over its back, chest, and belly. Although single dogs were dropped, a pair were more manageable at about fifteen hundred feet with a twenty-eight-foot cargo parachute. At each base, bush trips were carried out with personnel from other units twice monthly, for training purposes. For several days, men lived in a lean-to and were trained in survival techniques. They were subsequently sent into the bush individually.[17] Sleds on wheels were used for summer training. Many of the dogs were trained at war dog reception centers in Great Falls, Montana, and Presque Isle, Maine. Both huskies and St. Bernards were used for packing supplies.

In the event of an actual crash or expected crash, pilots signaled their location and a search party was organized. Flying a grid pattern, the rescue plane ideally determined the crash site and radioed its location to a search party. Emergency supplies and a "Gibson Girl" radio transmitter were often parachuted to the site

A dog awaits assistance out the door of an Army Air Corps C-47 on a flight from Ladd Field. (*Command Historian's Office, Alaskan Command*)

before the arrival of the search party. Problems involved with finding a crash site are hard to exaggerate, especially in the event of heavy snow. It was important to locate a potential runway as close as possible to the crash site because of the rescued pilot's need to be evacuated to a base hospital by aircraft. Often, frozen lakes and level areas were sought at a considerable distance from the site. Recovering a downed but intact plane was the most difficult task, since it required that a runway be created, often with the help of an air-dropped amphibious "weasel" or half-track R-7 tractor. Finally, obtaining reports of crashes or recovered debris from Native peoples was a factor in about 15 percent of searches. All search units sought to maintain good communication with local inhabitants.

Recorded base histories don't indicate a specific share

---

[15] *New York Times*, 28 February 1935, p. 1.

[16] *US Army Veterinary Service in WW II* (Washington, D.C.: Office of the Surgeon General, Department of the Army, 1961), p. 233.

[17] Fulham, p. 6.

of searches initiated as a result of information from indigenous peoples. All base histories, however, refer to such rescue episodes often involving aircraft lost over long periods. Royal Canadian Mounted Police and the French Canadian missionary at Fort Nelson, Father René Leveque, helped alert units about medical emergencies involving Native peoples. One incident recorded in March 1945 involved an unspecified epidemic among members of an Indian settlement fifteen miles south of Coal River and eight miles east of the Alcan Highway.[18] Flight surgeon Captain Jacobs parachuted to the settlement, followed by a dog team led by Irwin. Necessary sulfa drugs reportedly contained the epidemic, while Irwin remained behind for several days to ensure the drug was taken. The rewards of such attention for the mission were common knowledge.

Although the dogs were invaluable in operations involving distance, the Eleventh Air Force Service Command maintained a trekking unit of seven men and a medical office near Ladd Field.[19] At Seldovia, on the Kenai Peninsula, the Tenth Emergency Rescue Boat Squadron maintained a forty-two-foot crash boat that registered ten individual rescues, 139 assists, and seven aircraft recoveries in 1944. The variety of rescue boats and their deployment along the coast indicated a rapid evolution in rescue craft design.[20] The Tenth operated a 150-foot crane retriever vessel for aircraft salvage, and in cooperation with the navy developed a specially fitted eighty-five-foot craft, capable of thirty-five knots and holding a sick bay for seventeen men. The boats' development demonstrated a trend affecting most phases of wartime activity of specialized equipment and matériel in the Arctic.

General Gaffney's Cold Weather Station test facility pioneered the application of materials that would make all aspects of flight and survival less a matter of intuitive skill than of proper equipment. Whereas Vaughn, Westover, and Irwin—among others—taught skills of individual judgment and experience, their type of rescue would become obsolete; nevertheless, both types had worked together smoothly in wartime.

Engineers and armed forces personnel created a legacy of Canadian-American cooperation in which search and rescue was a crucial part. It took place alongside a vast effort that changed the Arctic irreversibly. In addition to the complex of bases, weather stations, and landing strips along the northwestern route, the war left behind the 1,523-mile Alcan Highway, the $130 million Canol refinery and pipeline in Whitehorse, and a permanent telephone connection between Fairbanks and Edmonton. The defense and development of the area would be a joint endeavor of Ottawa and Washington.

Evaluating the trends of success in individual search and rescue missions is difficult, for the outcome not only depended on the skill of the team but also on the circumstances of the crash, the weather, and the victims' behavior. Yet, of the 641 personnel involved in crashes, about 75 percent survived more than twenty-four hours out-of-doors, and the vast majority were rescued from life-threatening situations. A previously cited study compares the survivors with those explorers of earlier times, lauding a common evidence of "fortitude, courage, adaptability, and ingenuity." Surely, the same attributes apply to their rescuers.

*Zachary Irwin is an associate professor in the Department of Political Science at Pennsylvania State University, Behrend College.*

---

[18] Ibid, p. 4.

[19] Lt. C.A. Corvell, "Land Rescue Squad," *Alaska Life*, 7:3, March 1944, pp. 15-17.

[20] Sgt. Allan Merritt, "Crash Boat to the Rescue," *Alaska Life*, 7:9, September 1944, pp. 3-5.

# The Tundra Army:
# Patriots of Arctic Alaska

*Chris Wooley*
*and Mike Martz*

*This presentation is dedicated to the memory of all of the members of the Alaska Territorial Guard now deceased.*

THE ALASKA TERRITORIAL GUARD (ATG), KNOWN locally as the "Tundra Army," was formed in the spring of 1942, following the Japanese bombing of Dutch Harbor and the capture of Attu and Kiska Islands in the Aleutians. The original Alaska National Guard, the 297th Infantry Battalion, was in federal service at the time and the Seventy-Seventh Congress authorized the formation of a territorial militia to assist in the defense of Alaska. Major Marvin "Muktuk" Marston, an Army Air Corps officer assigned to Fort Richardson in Anchorage, was designated one of two military liaison officers for territorial governor Ernest Gruening. Marston's task was the military organization of the predominantly Eskimo villages west of the 154th Parallel along the Bering Sea and Arctic coasts. During the next three years, using surplus World War I weapons and equipment, Marston helped establish a defense force from Barrow to Bristol Bay, comprised almost entirely of Alaska Natives.

The ATG story, as told by Major Marston in his book *Men of the Tundra*, depicts the Eskimos as enthusiastic and capable militia members because their very existence prior to World War II depended on their abilities as hunters and fishermen. Yet, even though Marston was a close friend and advocate of Native people, the Yup'ik and Inupiat were inevitably stereotyped as somewhat primitive. In the 1940s, even the more enlightened non-Natives generally considered Eskimos to be noble, unassuming, and happy conquerors of the forest and tundra—complete masters of the natural world but unable to comprehend or cope on their own with events in the "modern" world.

With the luxury of a historical perspective, and using an anthropological approach, we can see through these stereotypes and appreciate the men and women of the ATG within the context of their unique cultures.

This survey of the Native militia uses archival material and interviews with ATG veterans, and draws upon the authors' experience in Native communities.

Native people in the Arctic and northwest Alaska responded unanimously to the Japanese threat. Initial interactions between army officials and ATG members were sometimes awkward, but patriotism triumphed during this difficult time in arctic village life. Our aim is to put Inupiat and Yup'ik patriotism in context by describing the historical and cultural situation of the villages at the time of the war, and by noting the impact of the ATG on contemporary Alaska Native culture. The devotion to country that patriotism manifests was expressed by the organizers and members of the Tundra Army. That devotion lives on in village Alaska and beyond.

## Introduction

Prior to the arrival of Europeans in northwest and arctic Alaska, warfare was not unknown—Yup'ik and Inupiat oral traditions mention violent conflict with other ethnic groups over trade routes, as well as inter-village conflicts involving rivalries and retribution for social affronts. Evidence of Native conflict includes pre-contact warfare (evidenced by weapons, rod and slat armor, human remains showing trauma-related injuries, and place names recording ancient battles), oral traditions of "bow and arrow wars" on the Yukon-Kuskokwim Delta, and tales of Siberian Yup'ik people who came to arctic Alaska to trade during the nineteenth century and who were killed by Inupiat residents. Media coverage of World War I did reach some villagers; however, prior to World War II, it had only been a few generations since the Inupiat and Yup'ik had been involved in social conflict.

Throughout the eighteenth and nineteenth centuries in arctic and northwest Alaska the Native people participated in trade networks with Siberia; interacted with Euro-American explorers, missionaries, traders, and whalers; and engaged in fur trapping and reindeer herding. Yet, in the 1930s, despite more than a century of acculturation, Inupiat and Yup'ik cultures were portrayed as backward, stone-age primitives in much of the print and motion picture media.

Native people in some cases were unaware that they were the object of such outside interest. While doing oral history research in Barrow, Chris Wooley obtained from the Santa Clara University archives copies of a newsreel documenting a 1930s *umiaq* trip which Father Hubbard, a Jesuit priest, took along the Arctic Coast of Alaska. Native elders who viewed the footage recalled Hubbard's visit and were amused at having been sensationalized on a newsreel. In hindsight, these portrayals are somewhat offensive, yet they remind us how current attitudes toward Alaska Natives—as reflected in the media—have changed.

Marston accomplished a major feat in helping to organize the ATG but was nonetheless a product of his time. He was a staunch advocate of Native rights, yet his portrayals of Native people in print and film are rather sensationalist. Like so many non-Native books about "bush Alaska" popular during that era, his story lacks the local village perspective. History is better synthesized and absorbed by examining multiple versions of the same story. In that spirit we present the words and stories of former members of the ATG.[1]

## "Defend your ground": Forming the ATG

Joining the ATG was a Native response to the very real threat posed by foreigners such as the Japanese. At the time, in the arctic and subarctic coastal villages, there was a growing sense of loss of control of local resources. While reindeer co-operatives and a few small village stores were operating prior to the war, non-local traders were the source of most imported food and supplies. Outside commercial fishing interests in Bristol Bay were seen by some to be elbowing out local Native fishermen. St. Lawrence islanders had watched Japanese fishermen in boats just offshore. During the late 1930s, the Native populations were in the process of rebuilding from the horrible epidemics which struck in the late 1800s and early 1900s, wiping out huge segments of the population and debilitating most of the survivors. Contrary to the popular non-Native image of the people as primitives, Yup'ik and Inupiat people had adjusted to at least a century of intense cultural change prior to Pearl Harbor.

The arctic and Yukon-Kuskokwim Delta regions were not cultural backwaters emerging from the stone age in the 1940s. They were home to rich Native traditions and cultural diversity that, in the years before the war, had adapted to Euro-American industry and values in the North. Yup'ik and Inupiat people who joined the ATG were members of communities which had adjusted to the intense socioeconomic changes brought to their regions by commercial whaling, Christian missionaries, and the advent of schools, commercial fur trapping, village reindeer herding, and scientific and mineral exploration. The frequent cultural contact between Native and non-Native people during the late 1800s and early 1900s provided Inupiat and Yup'ik people with ample knowledge of outsiders.

In rising to face the imminent Japanese threat, ATG units were led initially by an assortment of village leaders, administrators, and churchmen—including non-Native men like Otto Geist in Nome and the Reverend Khlerekoper in Barrow. These men showed bravery and integrity by assisting the militia when a Japanese invasion was thought to be imminent. After the war, as Alaska Native soldiers returned from the Aleutians and elsewhere, local training and leadership became the norm.

The late Patrick Attungana of Point Hope eloquently described the patriotism of his people:

> ... when I think things are too hard for me, I think back on those people who did all the work. Even when they could not read and write the English language, they obeyed, there is a reward laid aside for them... They were our leading men during ATG times... Let's not forget the elders, and the others who without complaint obeyed when our nation called to arms every available man. There I learned again the value of obedience, [men] who without knowing exactly what was required of them,

---

[1] At the Alaska at War Symposium, a short version of this paper accompanied a videotape produced by Mike Martz at KYUK-TV. This included excerpts of interviews with former members of the ATG—many from the Yukon-Kuskokwim area. The authors continue to conduct interviews with surviving members of the ATG for use in a future production, and gratefully acknowledge the assistance of KYUK-TV, the Bethel VFW Post, and the North Slope Borough Commission on Inupiat History, Language, and Culture.

Members of the Alaska Territorial Guard stand in formation at Point Hope. *(Acc. No. 64-98-5138N, Otto Geist Collection, Rasmuson Library, University of Alaska Fairbanks)*

obeyed the national call. Here was a fact that the Inupiaq obeys all that is requested of them.[2]

Laura Beltz Wright of Haycock, Alaska, became the first Alaska territorial guardswoman in 1942 before anyone realized women couldn't belong. Maggie Panigeo Gray (affectionately known to many Alaskans as Magee), was another. Being the school principal at Koyuk and, later, teacher at Wainwright, Magee remembers Billy Mogg and Major Muktuk Marston pulling into Koyuk on a dog sled in December 1942 during the initial ATG recruiting trip on the Seward Peninsula. Coincidentally, Magee was also in Wainwright in the summer of 1943 when Marston arrived in that Arctic Coast village by boat. That supply trip was memorialized in words and sketches in *The Cruise of the "Ada."*[3]

Magee recalls those days:

In 1942 Marston was organizing territorial guards. At the time he was making a trip around Norton Sound. The village corps was starting; it was just beginning a new organization with no rifles, no leadership. They just took somebody like a storekeeper, an FAA headman or somebody who could train a group, you know like a big sergeant... We at Koyuk, being near Nome, realized that we were on the coast and Japan is over here. We were eager to be a part.[4]

Magee described Major Marston: "He's an ornery cuss. He's just like a general. He's very demanding. He's worse than I am. I liked him."

Marston was no stranger to the Arctic. In his younger days he had prospected in northern Canada and, in 1941, came to Nome on a morale-building trip with comedian Joe E. Brown to visit regular army troops stationed there. The resourcefulness and skill of the Native people impressed him, and Marston became obsessed with the task Governor Ernest Gruening assigned him shortly thereafter—organizing the Alaska Territorial Guard.

As Marston related in the colorful *Men of the Tundra*, he fought racism, court-martial attempts, and bureaucratic red tape while helping villagers in the northwest and arctic Alaska successfully organize the ATG. His tales about this episode of Alaska history are an important version of this important story, as are treatments by Nielson, Hendrick, Salisbury, and others. In the villages, local versions of these events survive in the words of the men and women who served in the ATG. These stories complement other versions and are best understood in the context of twentieth-century Native values and world view.

## Local Accounts

Herman Rexford, of Kaktovik on Barter Island, recalled the Marston organization trip, and how vulnerable people felt at the time:

Major Marston arrived in Kaktovik along with Fred Ipalook, and several of us got inducted to the guard right then and there. There was not too many of us right there at Kaktovik. We learned a lot during our encampments.... Another thing included in our training was to learn to drive a vehicle, but above all to defend our country.[5]

---

[2] Patrick Attungana, personal interview, 20 June 1989.

[3] Henry Varnum Poor, *The Cruise of the "Ada"* (Alaska: H.V. Poor, 1945). The abandoned wreck of the *Ada* lies on a beach in Marryat Inlet just outside the village of Point Hope.

[4] Maggie Gray, personal interview, 15 April 1990.

[5] Herman Rexford, personal interview, 11 April 1989.

The late Andrew Oenga recalled Governor Gruening's visit to Barrow with Marston on the initial sign-up in Barrow. This was the first time a territorial governor had toured Native arctic villages—and the first time that many Native people felt they were treated as full-fledged U.S. citizens. Yet, since the governor was not conversant in the local Inupiaq language, he is remembered by some for his limited language skills: "That was when we were first signing up for the Alaska Territorial Guard at the church," said Andrew Oenga, "and he would say in our native tongue, '*Quyanaq*,' [thank you] after we signed up; he could not say anything else."[6]

In the initial recruiting, some official forms and other ATG documents were translated into Inupiaq and Yup'ik.[7] Letters in these collections to and from ATG members are fascinating windows on daily life and issues in the communities, and indicate the strong and lasting ties between outside ATG officials (like Marston and Geist) and local people.

There was widespread church support for the ATG. The Reverend Fred Khlerekoper, of the Barrow Presbyterian Church, recalled:

> We were a strange looking outfit at first. Tall men, short men, snowshirts of all colors and descriptions. The only distinguishing mark was the cobalt blue and gold stars insignia patch of the ATG worn on the left shoulder... We were proud of those patches... But looks were not the whole story. There were not a hundred and ten men anywhere I would rather have anywhere in this area. This was home country to them and rifles and knives were their stock in trade... On the target range, they were better than recruits anywhere.

Villagers took the war threat seriously. They had heard the short-wave radio accounts of nighttime window blackouts along the West Coast, and they followed suit—including those people who still lived in sod-covered houses with skylights. People believed that air raids were imminent, and took every precaution they could. Even the reindeer herders who were out at remote camps were careful with their lights—as these camps were used to store emergency supplies and rations. One Barrow elder noted that villagers went so far as to limit the amount of seal or whale oil put into stoves to avoid visible flare-ups from the stovepipes at night.

## Weapons, Ammunition, and Supplies

Firearms were (and are) an important aspect of life in the villages. Maggie Gray describes the arrival of a batch of Enfield rifles which were issued to train recruits: "And when we were organizing, like the first one at Koyuk, we were shipped something like eighteen to twenty cases of guns and they were all [packed] in Cosmoline."[8]

Anthropologist James Van Stone noted that in the early 1960s in western Alaska, "Many men still own the Model 1917 Springfield .30-06 which was issued during the war to members of the Alaska Territorial Guard."

Patrick Attungana of Point Hope remembered the rifles and recalled: "They were real good. When we at Point Hope were subsistence hunting for big game like walrus and polar bear, we would use them. The shells worked real good."[9]

Historic photographs from the era indicate military equipment, including field telephones, radios, jeeps and clothing, was common in some villages, and it is likely the ATG was the source of some of this material.

## Training

During the war, Barrow's Eddie Hopson, the former president of the Arctic Slope Regional Corporation, had been a squad leader with the army's 208th Infantry. He and a man who later became governor, Bill Egan, had seen mop-up duty in the Aleutians. After the war, Marston picked Eddie Hopson to be one of ten noncommissioned officers to train ATG units:

> It was already organized, and they had been issued shoe pacs, a lambskin coat, and an old Enfield rifle. When I came on, that was in December of 1944, I came to Barrow from Nome. And I stayed on for a year instructing for Alaska Territorial Guard up until June '45... I spent my first six months out in the Nome area—Nome, Golovin, White Mountain and that's about it. Then I served from Barrow to Point Lay.[10]

Local recollections of the training were matter-of-fact. People had a job to do, and they did it with conviction. Some youngsters claimed to be older than they really were in order to belong. One such individual in Barrow recalled how some of the elders would get tired during drills and just stop—and the others would have to march around them. Maggie Gray recalled:

[6] Andrew Oenga, personal interview, 26 July 1989.

[7] Copies of some of these materials are contained in the Otto Geist Collection, University of Alaska Fairbanks Rasmuson Library, and in the Muktuk Marston Collection, Loussac Public Library, Anchorage.

[8] Maggie Gray, personal interview, 15 April 1990.

[9] Patrick Attungana, personal interview, 20 June 1989.

[10] Eddie Hopson, personal interview, 10 April 1989.

We were eager to be a part. Anyone who was eighteen volunteered. You didn't have to know too much. Just learn to handle a rifle, and what to report on when you're on duty. We all took turns day and night in the village. At that time in Koyuk was less that 100 people. We all stood watch. We were taught to recognize American ships. He showed slides of what to look for, and anything that was suspicious.[11]

## Reconnaissance and Reporting

The reconnaissance and intelligence aspects of the ATG had great potential. The sharp eyes and ears of the coastal residents were relied upon for news of any potential invasion, which, as we now know, never came.

But back in the early stages of the war people were extremely vigilant. This reporting backfired somewhat at one point. The presence of a submarine in the Arctic stirred up a lot of excitement during the war, and it was reportedly seen in the Arctic Ocean on three occasions. Only after the army air force was preparing to bomb it did the U.S. Navy admit that the submarine was an American vessel on a secret mission under the ice.

ATG men built and stocked emergency shelter cabins, and built and marked hundreds of miles of trails. Some of the numerous remote reindeer herding camps were to be used as refuge sites in the event of invasion. There were reports of ATG members shooting down Japanese balloon bombs. The units were acknowledged to be exceptional at intelligence gathering.

## The ATG and Racial Issues

Some have wondered why Native people were nearly unanimous in their support of an institution which represented a wider society, one which often viewed Natives as second-class citizens. At that time, Alaska Natives faced discrimination from non-Natives, particularly in towns such as Nome, Juneau, and Anchorage. In Nome, for example, the movie theaters were segregated, and a stir was caused during the mid-1940s by a Native woman who sat in the white seats.

In another infamous example, Governor Ernest Gruening, in Anchorage during the war, reacted to seeing a "No dogs or Natives allowed" sign posted in a downtown window. He went into the restaurant, which was owned by an ethnic European man, and raised the contradiction posed by the sign in a country whose troops were fighting Adolph Hitler and the Nazis. The sign quickly came down.

Although the ATG was an institution which fostered much good will and cooperation between Native and non-Native Alaskans, not all military leaders treated

Major Marvin "Muktuk" Marston pins captain's bars on David Frankson at Point Hope. *(Otto Geist Collection, Rasmuson Library, University of Alaska Fairbanks)*

Natives as equals. For example, General Simon Bolivar Buckner discounted the military worth of the ATG and resisted regularizing the ATG status. In fact, in a letter to General Sturdevant in 1942, Buckner wrote of his opposition to the use of black troops in Alaska because he feared the troops would "remain and settle [in Alaska] after the war, with the natural results that they would interbreed with the Indians and Eskimos and produce an astonishingly objectionable race of mongrels which would be a problem here from now on."

General Buckner's successor, General Emons, ordered an inspection of the ATG units in 1946. One young Native ATG officer was so humiliated at having been falsely accused of dereliction of duty that he committed suicide.

The army questioned the usefulness of the ATG and ordered it disbanded late in 1946. Marston dramatically resigned, and claimed publicly that political pressure from traders, local shippers, and liquor dealers had affected the army's decision. The discrimination which had been evident, Marston claimed, was a result of some of the "exploiters" becoming worried about the business implications of Native people getting organized and gain-

---

[11] Maggie Gray, personal interview, April 15 1990.

ing economic independence. After two years, the Pentagon finally gave in to other Alaska service commanders who lobbied for the continuation of the guard. In 1949, the Alaska National Guard was formed with Muktuk Marston as chief advisor, and the ATG remains a respected institution in many north Alaska communities.

## Social and Political Aspects

The ATG had provided Native people from widely scattered villages and regions a chance to interact with and learn about their more distant neighbors, and to interact with an expanding circle of non-Natives. In addition to the intelligence potential the organization provided, leadership benefits were a significant aspect of the ATG. The ATG helped foster leadership qualities in villagers who became active in village government and business in the 1950s, and whose abilities were instrumental in the early development of ANCSA corporations and Native land claims. Local political involvement by former ATG members was the norm in the 1950s and 60s.[12] The leadership skills, interpersonal contacts, and sense of ethnic identity which the Territorial Guard and, later, National Guard, helped form were important sociopolitical tools which Native people later used to help establish local forms of government and social programs for the citizens of their regions.

The war and the post-war military construction brought an increasing number of Native people to larger towns such as Nome, Fairbanks, and Anchorage. National Guard training camps were also a way for villagers to travel and establish personal ties with people from outside their own region. This may have helped set the stage for recent migrations of Native people to urban Alaska. In the villages, as Worl and Smythe point out, the building of the many National Guard armories had overtones of the ancient institution of the *qargi*—the men's house or communal gathering place. The new social arrangements were often food for laughter:

Kenneth Toovak was out traveling with one of the first white military people he had met. Ken offered to cook breakfast the next morning, and asked the white man, "What would you like?" The man replied, "Cook me two hotcakes and put two eggs on top." The man didn't like his breakfast, but Toovak insisted it wasn't his fault: The man didn't say he wanted the eggs cooked, too.

There were other amusing incidents. There was once an Inupiat drill leader who, just a few days prior, had learned the English versions of drill commands. During exercises out behind the Presbyterian church in Barrow, he forgot the command for halt, and inadvertently marched a portion of his unit halfway into the salt lagoon before he finally gave up trying to remember the English commands and blurted out the Inupiaq word for "stop."

The independence and mobility of some Native people during the 1940s, and the social aspects of the Territorial Guard are apparent in Maggie Gray's story. Maggie served in four ATG units, including Koyuk, Nulato, Tanana, and Wainwright. She explained:

Wherever I went, I went with the guards people for practice or meetings. If you're in the military, you go with a group where there's a branch. Especially in '42 and '45, that was when I was traveling from one school to another, so I would be with an [ATG] group."[13]

## Summary

Some of Alaska's most fascinating residents were at one time associated with the ATG. These veterans experienced episodes of dramatic cultural change, and have seen the Alaska Native village landscape transformed. Warfare is an event guaranteed to change lives and alter landscapes. The ATG made its mark on the cultural landscape of northern Alaska.

In summary, the ATG brought non-Native Alaskans into even more personal contact with Natives than before the war. Native people were forced to prepare for the frightening prospect of war, and were prepared to die defending their homeland. Friendships and new social patterns were formed; racial stereotypes were created, perpetuated, and, in some cases, dashed. The ATG brought Alaska closer together, and the ATG veterans deserve our undying gratitude.

*Since 1990, Chris Wooley has been a consultant to Exxon on archaeological and Native subsistence issues related to the "Exxon Valdez" oil spill.*

*Mike Martz is the executive producer for public television station KYUK in Bethel. He has been with the station since 1982.*

---

[12] For example, a photo of the Point Hope city officers in the 1960s, on file at the Anchorage Museum of History and Art Archives, includes five men—four of whom were ATG members.

[13] Ibid.

# Aleuts in Defense of Their Homeland

*Ray Hudson*

A s members of the American Legion Post, as members of the Orthodox church choir, and as individuals, Aleuts were major participants in the Memorial Day ceremony held by the Coast Guard cutter *Perseus* at Unalaska in 1940.[1] This was not surprising, because the Aleut community contained veterans of military service, including several men who had served in World War I. Physical courage and mental stamina had been characteristics of Aleut people for generations. During the nineteenth century, the Herculean endurance of Aleut hunters braving tumultuous seas over vast distances in skin boats became legendary. Eighteenth-century Aleut warriors were so effective that they eliminated the men who might have recorded their deeds and so, until work by contemporary scholars began to uncover their names and exploits, early Aleuts were mistakenly identified as pacific and nonaggressive. Men such as Itchadaq and Inglagusaq deserve to be better known in the arsenal of American battle history.

When the World War II buildup began in the Aleutians, the population of the Aleutian and Pribilof Islands was just over one thousand. In 1940 there were six viable villages in the Aleutians (excluding False Pass, which had close ties to communities on the Alaska peninsula): Attu, with forty-two people; Atka, with ninety-six; Nikolski, with ninety-eight; Kashega, with forty-three; Unalaska, with 180; and Akutan, with sixty-two. There were two villages that were gravely reduced in population: Biorka, on Sedanka Island, with sixteen people, and Makushin, on Unalaska Island, with only ten. The Pribilof Islands supported two villages: St. George, with 183 people, and St. Paul, with 294. The entire community of Aleuts from Attu to the Alaska Peninsula were engulfed not only by hostile action in or near their home towns but by a military and governmental bureaucracy frequently remote and indifferent—if not actually hostile—to the presence of civilians in a war zone. This paper will consider Aleut involvement in the defense of their homeland by civilians who assisted the military and by Aleut men who saw active duty.

Although thousands and thousands of military and civilian construction personnel had devastating impacts on small residential communities, Aleuts supported what was generally viewed as a necessary wartime activity. Their communities had become part of a national effort. Aleuts took employment with Seims-Drake Construction Company and with other firms supporting or providing services to the military. Aleut homes were opened to care for men wounded in the June 1943 attack on Unalaska/Dutch harbor until military medical facilities were available.[2] The pristine Church of the Holy Ascension at Unalaska, although boarded up for security, was occasionally made available to the military prior to and following the removal of most of the Aleut population in July 1942.

At Unalaska, attempts to cash in on the presence of the military were led by non-Native government employees: The U.S. deputy commissioner and the U.S.

---

[1] National Archives, Record Group 26, Box 611-6641, 1940.

[2] "Bombing of Dutch Harbor, Eyewitness Account by Anfesia Shapsnikoff", November 16, 1972; *The Aleutian Invasion* (by the students of Unalaska High School) (Unalaska, Ak.: Unalaska City School District, 1981), p. 29.

deputy marshal. The city was rapidly incorporated, utilizing a petition signed by virtually all local non-Native residents, about 40 percent of the adult Aleut community, and several temporary residents employed in military construction.[3]

In July 1942, with the exception of a handful of men employed by Seims-Drake, the entire Aleut population of the Aleutian and Pribilof Islands suddenly found themselves cast ashore in Southeastern Alaska. Attitudes among Aleuts differed, of course, but even those who were anxious to leave the scene of immediate fighting were appalled by the depth of indifference with which they were treated and by the poverty and squalor in which they were expected to provide homes for their children and aged. Yet even under these conditions they supported the war effort. Many of those who escaped the camps took jobs in military construction. The Army Corps of Engineers opposed the Fish and Wildlife Service's attempt to remove Pribilof men from defense construction work in Juneau to have them harvest seals for the government. "Many of these men have worked into skilled capacities," the agent of the Fish and Wildlife Service wrote, "and engineers say quote crews cannot spare a man at the present unquote. Engineers also verbally advise a protest being filed through official channels."[4]

And Aleuts, perhaps even more than the rest of the nation, were heartened when in May 1943 they heard the United States was determined to retake the Aleutian Islands captured by the Japanese. Martha Tutiakoff wrote to her sister from the evacuation camp at Burnett Inlet on May 5, 1943:

I mustn't forget. I went over to Aunt Katie and she is fine but more important than that I heard over San Francisco station that the good old U.S. has made up their mind to take the Is. out west. Attu and Kiska. 'Isn't that grand' As soon as the weather permits. Its so foggy now you know, this time of the year. Its the one thing that is stopping them and they refuse to give up the Islands as they

are necessary to the U.S. Gosh I was so happy I could have cried.[5]

This same woman, by the way, provided one of the first public accounts of the attack on Dutch Harbor.[6]

It is not surprising that having lived in the Aleutians for more than eight thousand years Aleuts had extensive knowledge of the islands and especially of the waters that connected and surrounded the islands. For them the Bering Sea and the North Pacific were extensions of the land, a natural continuation of their habitat. M.D. Teben'kov, a governor of Russian America, had employed Mikhail Kadin, an Aleut born in Atka, and Koz'ma Terent'ev, probably of Koniag descent, in the 1850s in the preparation of his superb atlas of the territory.[7] In the 1870s, William Healy Dall had found Aleuts very knowledgeable about the topography of their islands and secured hand-drawn maps of several islands.[8] By 1940 numerous Aleuts had extensive knowledge of various parts of the Chain. This was due, in part, to the fox trapping that had dominated the economy in the 1920s and 1930s and which took men—and occasionally women—to diverse sections of the island chain.

The American military drew on the expert knowledge Aleuts had of the islands. On Unalaska, trail systems were used by the military linking various bays with Unalaska Bay. The trails to several bays followed routes that historical and contemporary Aleuts had used: Kalekta Bay trail had been used by John Golodoff and Vasilii Shaishnikoff as routes to their fish camps at Kalekta and English bays. People from Biorka Village on Sedanka Island used the trail leading from Ugadaga Bay into Unalaska. Similarly, trails Aleuts had developed from Unalaska Village to Makushin Bay, Agamgik Bay, and other bays were adopted by the military.

A war among islands necessitated extensive knowledge of tides, passes, and safe harbors in contrary winds. Aleuts, of course, had this knowledge and none more than Henry Swanson of Unalaska. A veteran of World War I, Henry had extensive knowledge of the Aleutian Islands, much of it gathered from John Gard-

---

[3] Comparison of the August 18, 1941, Petition for the Incorporation of the City of Unalaska with Native Family Record Cards, prepared January 20, 1940.

[4] John R. Stacy, Agent, to E.C. Johnston, March 20, 1943. Fish and Wildlife Service Records, St. Paul, quoted in Dorothy M. Jones, *A Century of Servitude: Pribilof Aleuts under U.S. Rule* (Lanham, Md.: University Press of America, 1980), p. 113.

[5] Letter, Martha Tutiakoff to Katherine Tutiakoff, Burnett Inlet, May 5, 1943. Masami Sugiyama has recorded two instances in which people taken from Attu to Otaru, Japan, expressed their continued loyalty to the United States. After an American plane flew over Otaru on July 14, 1945, an Aleut told a nurse from the tuberculosis sanatorium, "American planes come to help us." Again, when two Aleut children were scolded by a Japanese doctor they replied, "Defeat in the war and No Food." "He was very disappointed to hear that Japan would be defeated because he was taking care of them so much. He could not believe they had that kind of idea." Masami Sugiyama, "On the Trail of the Picture, A Trip to the Aleutians," translated by Hiro Kunsunaki, 1987, copy obtained from the Aleutian/Pribilof Islands Association.

[6] *The Alaska Woman*, August 1942, pp. 4-5.

[7] Richard A. Pierce, *Russian America: A Biographical Dictionary* (Fairbanks, Ak: Limestone Press, 1990), pp. 209, 505.

[8] William Healy Dall, "Geographical Notes in Alaska," *Bulletin of the American Geographical Society*, (1896) 28:1, pp. 5-7.

ner, an Aleut with ties to False Pass and Atka. Among Henry's contributions were these: patrolling Unalaska Bay; transporting a mapping crew around Unalaska Island in the days before the bombing; assisting in selection of sites for outposts in Unalaska and Adak islands; tending outposts on Unalaska and Adak; and piloting vessels delivering supplies for the Battle of Attu. Carl "Squeaky" Anderson, who became port commander for Adak, had first been taken through the Aleutians by Henry in the 1930s. (John Nevzoroff of Atka had also "navigated the Aleutian waters with the late Squeaky Anderson.")[9] When an order came down saying that only GI's were to work on army boats, Henry tried to enlist, but he discovered that he was too old:

> Well, I told them, "Goodbye. See you after the war." But they told me, "Oh, no. You could stay just the way you are." Which was okay. In fact, I was glad later when I disobeyed orders, foolish orders from colonels and this and that. If I was a G.I. I'd have to obey those orders. But I was a civilian, so I'd tell them, "No. You can't do that!" Like ramming the boat ashore amongst the rocks so an officer could land. Things like that when it wasn't necessary, you know.[10]

There were several Aleut men younger than Henry, however, who were of an age to enlist or be drafted. Simeon Pletnikoff of Nikolski Village on Umnak enlisted in November 1941 at Fort Mears, Dutch Harbor. Widespread induction of Aleut men did not occur until after the evacuation of Aleuts to camps in Southeastern Alaska, when men were registered with draft boards in Juneau and other nearby towns.

Numerous Aleut men did not wait for the draft but enlisted in the services. Throughout World War Two, Aleuts from across the Chain served with distinction in the military forces, as did Aleut men from villages on the peninsula. Paul Gundersen from Nelson Lagoon enlisted at Cold Bay on December 19, 1942. He served in the Alaska Scouts at Attu and Shemya.[11] Chester Bereskin of Unalaska served in the Scouts, as did Simeon Pletnikoff of Nikolski. Luke Shelikof, of Akutan, the last

traditional chief of an Aleutian village, was stationed in the Pribilof Islands (and there began to make the bone "butterflies" for which he was later known).[12] Ralph Prokopeuff of Atka was drafted and served at Adak and Anchorage. Herbert and Bill Hope from Unalaska served in the navy. George Fox of Unalaska was killed in action in Italy in 1944.[13]

Although he was Yupik, the pianist and author Simeon Oliver had been raised at Unalaska and considered the Aleutians his home. Even though he was thirty-nine years old he was able to talk himself into the military and was stationed at Fort Richardson, working behind the lines with the Alaskan Scouts. Among his contributions was the pamphlet, "Emergency Foods in the Aleutians", which he prepared for soldiers stranded on the islands. Vincent Tutiakoff of Unalaska also provided hands-on experience for military personnel in ways in surviving off the land. In addition, because of his knowledge of tides and passes, he assisted navigation around Adak, Attu, and Kiska.[14]

Although the military frequently recognized the unique knowledge possessed by many of these men, Aleuts occasionally found themselves mistaken for the enemy. Simeon Pletnikoff recalled a time on Attu, "I had a heck of a time. Out on the front line the Americans would get a hold of me and want to kill me and all that. They tried to take me to the Provost Marshal for impersonating a U.S. soldier. 'What's the matter with you guys? I'm an Aleut.'"[15]

As with the general history of the Aleuts in the nineteenth and twentieth centuries, Pribilof Island Aleuts lived under circumstances radically different from those experienced by Aleuts residing on the Chain. Long under the domination of the Fish and Wildlife Service, Pribilof men had been denied the opportunity to enlist as the Fish and Wildlife Service considered them "wards of the government" and thus, for some reason, ineligible. This kept the men on the islands for their labor and restricted their knowledge of the outside world. During the summer of 1943, the Juneau draft board attempted to register men for the draft against the protestations of the fisheries officials.[16] The draft, of course, won, and on January 15, 1943, nine men left the Funter Bay camp for Juneau.[17] By March, seventeen Pribilof men had been

---

[9] Lael Morgan, *And the Land Provides* (Garden City, N.Y.: Anchor Press, 1974), p. 159.

[10] Henry Swanson, *The Unknown Islands*, 1982, p. 155.

[11] Aleutian Regional School District, *Taniisix*, vol 2. (1981), pp. 44-45.

[12] Ibid. p. 6.

[13] Letter, Charles H. Hope at Unalaska to Alice Hope at Burnett Inlet, July 2, 1944.

[14] Personal conversation with his sister, Martha Herrick, September 13, 1992.

[15] Simeon Pletnikoff, interview conducted for the Unalaska Historical Commission and the National Park Service, June 3, 1992.

[16] Jones, *A Century of Servitude*, p. 110.

[17] Funter Bay Log, Fish and Wildlife Service, January 25, 1943.

inducted and four more were subject to immediate induction.[18] The draft continued to drain the work force of the Funter Bay Camp but the FWS were able to get Aleuts in the military furloughed and others deferred to participate in the harvesting of fur seals in the summer of 1943. That year the labor of about eighty-seven Pribilof Aleuts and thirteen Aleuts from other parts of the Chain resulted in $1.58 million in fur and seal byproducts. Following the fur seal harvest, the Aleuts on active military duty returned to their duty stations.

The military activities of Aleut men were, of course, limited because of their very small numbers. However, Aleuts who served with the military and saw duty in the Aleutian Islands performed a unique service to the Aleut people. For more than eight thousand years Aleuts had survived the torrents of weather, the disappearance of an ice age, volcanic eruptions which created new islands, wars with distant people, and wars among themselves to see the arrival of Europeans in the mid-eighteenth century with a population now between eight and ten thousand people.[19] Over the next two hundred years, although gravely reduced in numbers,

they survived as the dominant population. They were the only people capable of sustaining generations in these austere yet remarkably rich islands and despite the repressive edicts of two governments. They had survived, but now, in the mid-twentieth century, their age-long residence on the Chain was threatened as Americans ordered their removal and the Japanese captured and deported the people of Attu. The Aleuts who served in the Aleutians maintained an Aleut presence in their ancestral homeland and kept unbroken an inhabitation of the islands which had begun millennia before.

As the waves of troops gradually departed at the end of the war, these Aleut soldiers and sailors, together with their families, returned to dramatically altered communities and began the slow and difficult rebuilding that would last the rest of their lives.

*Ray Hudson taught for the Unalaska City School District from 1964 to 1992. Classes he supervised produced ten volumes of local history. One, entitled "The Aleutian Invasion," is about World War II.*

---

[18] *Personal Justice Denied, Report of the Commission on Wartime Relocation and Internment of Civilians*, 1982, p. 343.

[19] Rosa G. Liapunova, "The Aleuts before Contact with the Russians: Some Demographic and Cultural Aspects," *Pacifica* (1990), p. 10.

# The Alaska Highway

Soldiers of the Ninety-Fifth General Service Regiment begin work on the Sikanni
Chief River bridge on the Alaska Highway in British Columbia.
*(Photo No. 111-SC-139940, National Archives, College Park, Md.)*

# The Wartime Alaska Highway:
# Boon or Boondoggle?

*Heath Twichell*

FIFTY YEARS AGO, MOST AMERICANS SAW THE ALASKA Highway, Canol, and the Northwest Staging Route as three separate projects. Today, it is easier to see them as a single enterprise, an attempt to ensure that vital wartime supplies could reach Alaska despite the Japanese threat to the sea lanes of the North Pacific. At a time when skilled workmen made $1.50 an hour, this vast effort cost U.S. and Canadian taxpayers more than $500 million. It was the most expensive construction project of the war—and the most controversial. Early critics said the highway was in the wrong place and would take too long to build; later detractors focused on Canol's wasteful cost. Some even charged that the whole huge undertaking had been of so little military value that it should never have been built at all.

To help prevent Japan's threatened dominance of the northern Pacific in the wake of the naval disaster at Pearl Harbor on December 7, 1941, a secure overland supply line to the unfinished airfields of the Northwest Staging Route and our military bases in Alaska was urgently needed. To meet that need, seven regiments of U.S. Army engineers began bulldozing a trail to Fairbanks across a remote stretch of the Canadian Rockies in April 1942. Open as an emergency route less than eight months later, and substantially upgraded during 1943 by a follow-up work force of fourteen thousand civilian contractors, the fifteen-hundred-mile Alaska Highway (GI's called it the Alcan) was hailed as an epic feat of engineering. Given the incredibly difficult conditions under which it was built, it was certainly that. But it was also the most controversial construction project of World War II. And one of the most expensive.

The U.S. and Canadian politicians and businessmen of the Pacific Northwest who had lobbied before the war for a coastal route to Alaska were outraged by the army's decision to build the road farther inland, along the path of the partially completed Northwest Staging Route but far from the region's population centers. Donald MacDonald, a senior engineer with the Alaska Road Commission and the father of the coastal route proposal, was their most vociferous spokesman. Others, like Alaska's Governor Ernest Gruening, angrily predicted that the largely unsurveyed inland route would take far too long to build, leaving the territory vulnerable in the meanwhile.[1]

Later, when "add-on" projects such as Canol kept raising the overall cost of the Alcan—despite the ebbing Japanese threat—critics with twenty-twenty hindsight began saying that the whole $500 million effort had been of so little military value that it should never have been undertaken. Perhaps the highway's most notable critic was a once-obscure Missouri senator named Harry S Truman, whose hard-nosed investigations of fraud, waste, and mismanagement as chairman of the Senate's Special Committee Investigating the National Defense Program had made him a power to reckon with in Washington.

By the summer of 1943, Truman's committee had completed more than twenty carefully documented investigations. Among the better publicized: mismanage-

---

[1] Copy of Memo, Gruening to Interior Secretary Harold Ickes, Feb. 27, 1942, in Control Division Report to CG, Army Service Forces, (May 1945), Exhibits Section, pp. 168-69.

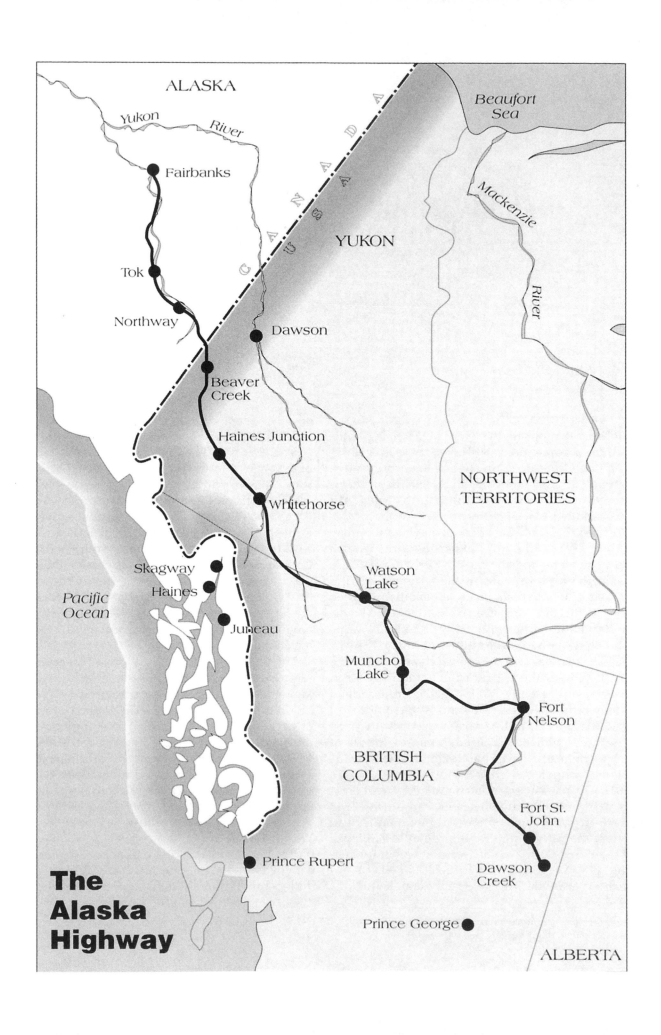

**The Alaska Highway**

ment in the construction of military camps, wasteful practices in the production of aluminum and rubber, fraudulent tests of armor plate, and criminal negligence in the manufacture of defective aircraft engines.[2] As the "watchdog of the war effort," Truman decided it was time to take a look at the army's Brobdingnagian construction program in Northwest Canada and Alaska.

With the Alaska Highway by then a *fait accompli*, Truman's main focus was on delays and cost overruns in the Canol project, which was supposed to supply fuel and lubricants for all the trucks and aircraft using the highway and staging route. But his investigators could hardly ignore the disparity between the public's image of the Alcan and the reality. Long stretches of what magazine writers liked to call "Our Glory Road to Tokyo" were, in fact, not open to through traffic for most of the year following the official ceremony "opening" the highway on November 20, 1942. Winter ice buildups, spring washouts and mud slides, and a summer-long rebuilding program halted all but local traffic for much of that time. Had the Japanese succeeded in cutting the sea lines of communication to Alaska during this period, the territory's citizens and their defenders would soon have faced shortages of food and ammunition. And, as the army's own figures showed, even the rebuilt and reopened highway could only handle a small fraction of the logistical needs of an active theater of war.[3]

Released in January 1944, the Truman committee's report on Canol was a scathing indictment of the project's futility and waste. (It ultimately produced only 311,145 barrels of gasoline and diesel fuel—at a cost of $7.72 per gallon—before it was shut down in 1945.) It was clear, however, that the senator regarded the Alaska Highway as a comparable boondoggle. Said his report: "If the CANOL and ALCAN Highway projects could be reviewed from their inception, the Committee would be of the opinion that the entire Alaska Highway project should be examined most carefully for the purpose of ascertaining whether it should be constructed."[4]

Nevertheless, conspicuously absent among the wartime critics of the Alaska Highway were the pilots who flew the two-thousand-mile Northwest Staging Route between Edmonton and Fairbanks. After a U.S.-Canadian agreement in mid-1940 to cooperate in the defense of North America, construction or upgrading be-

gan on the seven airfields that were to comprise the intermediate stops on the staging route: Grande Prairie, Fort St. John, Fort Nelson, Watson Lake, and Whitehorse in Canada; Northway and Big Delta in Alaska. Hindered by low priorities, the remoteness of the sites, and a weather-shortened construction season, progress on these bases was slow until the shock of Pearl Harbor put Alaska in a new strategic perspective. But even with the Alaska Highway routed so as to link up the airfields and help speed their completion, the staging route was not operating at full capacity until late 1943.[5]

Although the Staging Route was *never* a milk run, with the highway finally open all the way to Fairbanks pilots taking off from Edmonton had few worries about finding fuel, repair parts, a hot meal, or a clean cot at any of the major bases on the two-day flight. Every airfield was also equipped with radio homing beacons; but the most reliable aid to navigation—when visibility was good—was the highway itself. If an in-flight emergency precluded reaching one of the major bases, pilots could put down on one of the dozen rudimentary roadside strips conveniently located at intervals between them. And as a last resort, a pilot in really serious trouble could almost always find a level stretch of gravel road to land on.

The increasing air traffic to Fairbanks had little to do with combat operations against the Japanese—at least after the successful conclusion of the Aleutian Campaign in mid-1943. By then, U.S. strategy had evolved into a two-pronged, island-hopping offensive across the central and South Pacific. But Alaska never fully reverted to its prewar status as a military backwater. From a global perspective it now played an important strategic role in the war on Germany. Starting in September 1942, Ladd Field in Fairbanks became the crossroads airfield on the Alaska-Siberia (ALSIB) ferry route.

One year earlier, taking the position that "our enemy's enemy is our friend," President Roosevelt had persuaded Congress to authorize shipments of lend-lease war matériel to the Soviet Union, whose army had been taken by surprise that June and which was still in full retreat before the German blitzkrieg. Stalin's emissaries came shopping for equipment of all kinds, but their most desperate need was for combat aircraft. German and Russian sources differ somewhat as to the extent of

[2] Roger E. Willson, "The Truman Committee," Ph.D. dissertation (Harvard University), pp. 393-401.

[3] Theodore A. Huntley and R.E. Royall, *Construction of the Alaska Highway* (Washington: Public Roads Administration, 1945), pp. 27-30, 35-40; "Alaska Highway—Problems in Roadway Design," *Western Construction News* (March 1943), pp. 108-09; *Control Division Report*, Exhibits Section, pp. 279-83.

[4] U.S. Senate Committee Investigating the National Defense Pro-gram, 78th Congress, 1st Session, Report No. 10, part 14: *The CANOL Project* (Washington: GPO, 1944), pp. 30-31.

[5] Edwin R. Carr, "Great Falls to Nome: The Inland Air Route to Alaska, 1940-1945," Ph.D. dissertation (University of Minnesota, 1946), pp. 71-78, 106-26; Stanley W. Dziuban, *U.S. Army in World War II: Military Relations Between the United States and Canada, 1939-1945* (Washington: GPO, 1959), pp. 205-15.

the damage inflicted by the *Luftwaffe* on the Soviet Air Force during Operation Barbarossa, but splitting the difference results in a figure of around fifty-five hundred aircraft of all types (roughly 50 percent of the Soviet inventory) destroyed in the air or on the ground—in just the first two weeks of fighting.[6]

Some American planes were soon on their way on ships making the hazardous Murmansk run, or being flown by way of South America-Africa-Iran, but it was not enough. Under the terms of a fall 1942 lend-lease protocol, fighters and bombers from U.S. factories began flying north, via Great Falls, Montana, to Ladd Field; from there they were flown by Soviet pilots over the Bering Strait and on across Siberia to bases within striking distance of Hitler's armies on the Eastern Front. In the three years of ALSIB's existence, the Russians received 7,926 lend-lease aircraft at Ladd Field.

Although lend-lease aircraft bound for the Soviet Union were by no means the only planes headed north from Edmonton, they made up a growing percentage of the military traffic as the war progressed. The tables below give the bottom line of the ALSIB story:[7]

*(Command Historian's Office, Alaskan Command)*

## ALSIB Totals

| Year | Number of Planes Delivered |
|------|---------------------------:|
| 1942 (4 months) | 129 |
| 1943 | 2,497 |
| 1944 | 3,156 |
| 1945 (8 months) | 2,144 |
| Total: | 7,926 |

## ALSIB Totals, by Type of Aircraft[8]

| Fighters | | | Bombers | | Cargo | Other |
|------|------|------|------|------|------|------|
| P-39 | P-40 | P-63 | A-20 | B-25 | C-47 | |
| 2,618 | 48 | 2,397 | 1,363 | 732 | 710 | 58 |

Because of the hazards of the 2,500-mile flight from

Great Falls and the unsophisticated navigational equipment of that era's single-engine planes, fighters being ferried over the staging route were supposed to travel in formation with a "mother ship"—usually a twin-engine C-47 transport. In addition to possessing better electronics, every mother ship also carried spare parts for its "flock"—as well as lend-lease cargo bound for the Soviet Union. Rare was the C-47 that landed in Fairbanks with its formation of fighters intact, however. Delayed by any of a thousand possible mechanical and weather problems, the stragglers came limping into Ladd Field hours, days, or sometimes weeks later.

Even without the hazards on the ALSIB run, some crashes and fatalities were inevitable in an operation of this magnitude. The air force was prepared to accept an overall loss rate of 5 percent—one airplane in twenty. In fact, only about one in every sixty aircraft crashed on the way north to Fairbanks, fewer than half of them (sixty-three) after leaving Great Falls. Along the staging route, most of the pilots bailed out close enough to the highway to walk to safety or be found by search parties. According to the unofficial historian of the USAAF's Seventh Ferry Group, only fifteen Americans lost their lives on the ALSIB run. (What is known for certain about comparable Soviet losses is that thirteen Russian aviators died on U.S. soil and were buried at Fort Richardson, just outside Anchorage. Post-glasnost Russian sources state that another 112 died in crashes en route to the Eastern Front.)[9]

Just as it is hard to get a handle on Soviet combat losses, so is it difficult to estimate how much difference the massive amounts of lend-lease supplies—from shoes and Spam to trucks and planes—actually made in the final Soviet victory on the Eastern Front. Only rarely did Stalin allow public mention or acknowledgement of such U.S. help in the Soviet media. Besides, it was mid-1943, months after the turning-point battle of Stalingrad, before much of the promised equipment arrived in

[6] Richard C. Lukas, *Eagles East: The Army Air Force and the Soviet Union, 1941-1945* (Tallahassee: Florida State University Press, 1970), pp. 9-11.

[7] Dziuban, *Military Relations*, p. 216.

[8] An additional 6,092 lend-lease aircraft were delivered to the Soviet Union via all other routes.

[9] John H. Cloe, *Top Cover for America: The Air Force in Alaska, 1920-1983* (Missoula, Mont.: Pictorial Histories Publishing Co., 1984), p. 154; telephone interview with Brynes Ellender, Bil-lings, Mont., March 29, 1992; Ivan Negenblya, article in Yakutin Youth quoted in Yukon Anniversaries Commission Newsletter (Oct. 26, 1990), p. 3.

quantities large enough to make a noticeable difference along a two-thousand-mile front that stretched from the Arctic Ocean to the Black Sea.

Another Soviet complaint during this period was that our equipment, particularly our airplanes, lacked the rugged simplicity of theirs. The first U.S. warplane to win the hearts of Russian pilots was the P-39 Airacobra, which began to arrive in quantity via ALSIB in the winter of 1943 and which was much admired by them for its speed, maneuverability and durability. The P-39 quickly earned the affectionate nickname "Cobrushka"—"Dear Little Cobra." The last word on all this came from Stalin himself. At the closing banquet of the Teheran Conference, in early 1944, he offered a toast to American aircraft production, without which, he said, the war would have been lost.[10] No doubt Stalin meant to recognize how that production had benefited the Allied cause worldwide, but in his oblique and ambiguous way he was also saying, "Thank you for all those airplanes."

In one respect, ALSIB may have worked too well. Although some items on the Soviet Union's wartime "shopping list" had no conceivable military value (13,328 sets of false teeth, for example), others were of such great importance that they could only be obtained by espionage. Americans could only guess at the contents of the black suitcases, shipped through Great Falls in batches of fifty under diplomatic seal by the Russian embassy in Washington, but an army major claimed after the war to have opened several on his own initiative and found various highly classified documents not meant for foreign eyes. It has also been alleged (though never proved) that ALSIB was one of the channels for stolen U.S. atomic secrets.[11]

Finally, with the Alaska Highway providing an extra margin of safety, ALSIB became the fastest and least dangerous way for high-ranking officials to travel between Washington and Moscow. Vice President Henry Wallace, Soviet Foreign Minister Vyacheslav Molotov, and Ambassador Andrei Gromyko were among the many VIP's who repeatedly used the route.[12]

In assessing the wartime importance of the Alaska Highway, the complaint of Alaska's Governor Gruening about the purpose of the highway's inland location now seems closer to the truth than the War Department would then admit. "What appears to be sought by the army is not a highway at all," said Gruening, "but a kind of leading string for the young flyers."[13]

But in weighing the combined contribution of the staging route and the Alaska Highway to the outcome of World War II, even critics like Gruening could not deny that the nearly eight thousand lend-lease fighters and bombers delivered via ALSIB made a difference—and perhaps a decisive one—against the Germans on the Eastern Front.

No military man appreciated the Alaska Highway more during World War II than General Henry H. "Hap" Arnold, commander of the USAAF. Back in 1934, as a lieutenant colonel, he had flown the lead ship in a pioneering cross-country flight of ten B-10 bombers from Washington, D.C., to Fairbanks. The leg over the Canadian Rockies was particularly dangerous; ground-based navigational aids were then nonexistent, and places to land nearly so. Nine years later, on an inspection of the staging route and the ALSIB operation, General Arnold could see firsthand how much safer flying in the "high granite country" had become. "Never in the history of aviation," he said on a stopover in Edmonton, "has a road been so important to airmen."[14]

Economics supplies another way to gain perspective on the question of the value of the Alaska Highway to the war effort. If the total dollar cost of World War II to U.S. taxpayers is divided by the number of days between Pearl Harbor and V-J Day, the daily average cost of the war comes to about $268 million.[15] At that rate it took less than two days to pay for the highway—wasteful extras and all. Although the fortunes of war dictated (luckily) that it would never serve as Alaska's main supply line, I submit the Alaska Highway was still a bargain: as an insurance policy that gave peace of mind to both the citizens and the defenders of Alaska during a tense and uncertain time; as a combination low-tech navigational aid and fifteen-hundred-mile-long emergency landing strip for the "young flyers" Governor Gruening worried about; and, finally, as the backbone of the U.S. half of the ALSIB operation—the conduit for war matériel of vital military and psychological importance to a beleaguered (if not always appreciative) ally.

And I haven't yet said a word about the highway's

---

[10] George C. Herring Jr., *Aid to Russia: Strategy, Diplomacy, The Origins of the Cold War* (New York: Columbia University Press, 1973), pp. 75-76, 115-20.

[11] Stan Cohen, *The Forgotten War: A Pictorial History of World War II in Alaska and Northwestern Canada* (Missoula, Mont.: Pictorial Histories Publishing Co., 1981), p. 46. Cohen's source is *From Major Jordan's Diaries* (New York: Harcourt Brace, 1952)..

[12] Cloe, *Top Cover*, p. 154.

[13] Control Division Report, Exhibits Section, p. 174.

[14] Statement by Gen. Arnold in Edmonton Bulletin, May 26, 1942.

[15] Cost to U.S for WW II was $360 billion and the war lasted 1,337 days; average cost: $268 million per day. Data from Statistical Abstract of the United States (Washington: GPO, 1990).

postwar role in the economic development of the region it serves. But that's a subject for another conference.

*Heath Twichell has had three careers: as a U.S. Army in-* *fantry officer, as a college professor, and, currently, as an independent scholar. His most recent book is "Northwest Epic: The Building of the Alaska Highway," published in 1992.*

# Wrong Road

*William R. Hunt
and Alex Hunt*

IN CELEBRATING THE GOLDEN ANNIVERSARY OF THE Alaska Highway's construction we have lavishly praised the builders. Certainly the highway was a project of gigantic scale, one to capture the imagination and inflame the patriotism of war-beleaguered Americans, especially if the achievement was presented positively.

At the official opening on November 20, 1942, the flags flew, the band played, and the speakers boasted of the accomplishment; critical evaluation of the project did not lie in anyone's interest.

The celebrants on that proud occasion did not include Alaska engineer Donald MacDonald, the man who had long advocated a highway to Alaska. He conceived the project in the 1920s and was the inspiration for and a member of the Alaska International Highway Commission appointed by President Roosevelt in 1936. But the army, not concerned with highway pioneers, did not invite MacDonald to their ceremony. It was probably just as well: his anger might have affected morale. Who would want to see him shaking his head over the astounding costs of an impassable road built over the worst possible route?

MacDonald had promoted a coastal route, later referred to as Route A. It started from Prince George in central British Columbia, keeping just east of the coastal range and following the old Telegraph Trail to Atlin and Whitehorse. Builders would have no trouble pushing a highway through this well-known country and branches would link Southeast Alaska towns.

But the army built over Route C, from Dawson Creek northwest to Fort Nelson, Watson Lake, and Whitehorse. The route was over unknown country and proved to be difficult. Other routes considered were Route B, following the Rocky Mountain trench—too rugged for much consideration; and Route D, from Winnipeg, following the Mackenzie river system to Norman, thence to the Yukon River—a route advocated by polar explorer Vilhjalmar Stefansson.

The army liked Route C because airfields had been recently built at Watson Lake, Fort Nelson, and Fort St. John. Why the air fields attracted the army mystified MacDonald and Stefansson. The fields did not need a road and they would not help road builders very much. Why should the army build a highway to support arbitrarily located fields which might be readily duplicated anywhere?

Another strategic consideration concerned the threat of Japanese aircraft. Presumably the Japanese could disrupt traffic on Route A much easier than on Route C, if they had reason to do so and had command of the air.

Stefansson saw no sense to strategic objections to his route and thought Route C a terrible choice that had been lobbied by Edmonton merchants. MacDonald, too, believed that Canadian economic interests determined the route. He complained that the highway was "conceived by the Canadian Pacific Railroad in unconscious intercourse with the Joint Defense Board."[1]

MacDonald and Alaska's political leaders had presented their case for Route A in Washington prior to

---

[1] Donald MacDonald to Furth, August 7, 1943, MacDonald Papers, University of Alaska Fairbanks Archives.

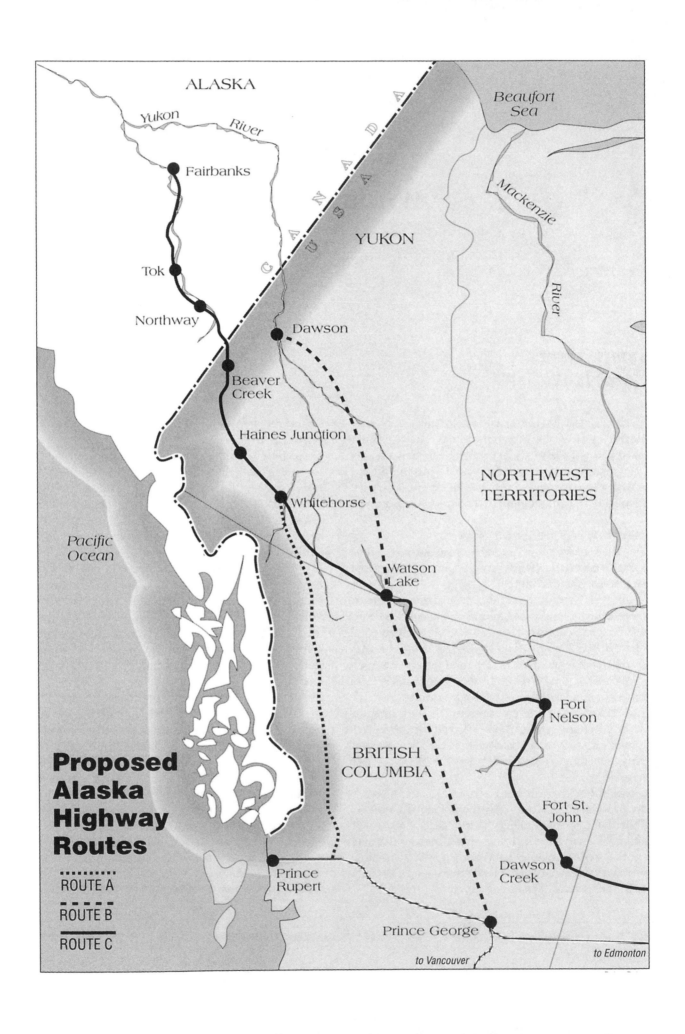

ALASKA

*Yukon River*

Fairbanks

Tok

Northway

*Pacific Ocean*

**Proposed Alaska Highway Routes**

ROUTE A

ROUTE B

ROUTE C

*Beaufort Sea*

YUKON

*Mackenzie River*

Dawson

Beaver Creek

Haines Junction

Whitehorse

NORTHWEST TERRITORIES

Watson Lake

BRITISH COLUMBIA

Prince Rupert

Fort Nelson

Fort St. John

Dawson Creek

Prince George

*to Vancouver*

*to Edmonton*

construction, but authorities refused to second-guess a military decision. Perhaps Washington bureaucrats believed that the Alaskans were motivated by provincial interests. But MacDonald did his best to show that Route C was a bad choice from a highway engineer's viewpoint. "The army engineers," he argued, "no matter how loyal and efficient, no matter what force they had, could never build a supply line to Alaska from Dawson Creek."[2]

In August 1943, ten months after the opening ceremony, MacDonald observed that his doleful forecast had been confirmed. Despite the labors of thousands of workers, there were no trucks moving on the Alcan. The so-called completed highway, he noted, "resembles its parents. It is crooked as hell." Why call it a highway? "Actually it is a belated abortion ... a misbegotten thing."[3]

Donald MacDonald was not unpatriotic in sneering at the highway. He thought it "a tragic thing that my predictions (based upon the obvious) have been sustained. The much trumpeted highway is not at present in operation, and won't be until the October freeze-up. It is officially estimated at being only 38 percent completed."[4] He had seen a senior officer's letter to his superior, warning "that if it requires millions to complete a highway that is already announced as completed, you and I will have to do a lot of explaining.... I am quite certain that by this time that we will all agree, and this includes the Corps of Engineers and the Public Roads Administration, that the Alcan Highway is not and never will become the main supply road to Alaska. To use it as a highway we would have to build an additional 500 miles from Edmonton to Dawson Creek."[5]

MacDonald deplored "a sabotaged, inoperable highway ... 271 miles longer than my route.... A mile of road costs $10,000 a year to maintain it and operate for 1000 tons a day.... As far as Seattle is concerned and the whole Pacific Coast, the Alcan is so economically remote as to be impossible. It is littered with broken-down tractors operated by untrained men, " he said. "The worst thing is that people will accept the army's rationalization that no one can build roads in the north. The fine

Donald MacDonald *(Photo No. 01-4040, Early Prints Collection, Alaska State Library, Juneau)*

road to Alaska will never be built. The mislocated abortion will not be used in peacetime."[6]

He described the tortuous freight route the army was using in the summer of 1943:

Because the road from Whitehorse to Fairbanks cannot be operated at present, commodities are now being shipped from White-horse, the terminal of the White Pass and Yukon RR, to Circle on the Yukon, a distance of 752 miles by river, thence 163 miles by a little truck road [the Steese highway] I built in 1927 (for $6,000 a mile or a total of $978,000) to Fairbanks. As the army is hauling oil pipe for this fool idea, an oil supply from Ft. Norman, this little $6,000 road is carrying an immense burden and is standing up under it. Where the army had ten men to the unit on the Alcan and all the machinery in the world we on this Circle Road had one man to 10 units, 3 tractors, 3 horse graders and picks and shovels. There is something to having men who know the country and what they are doing. No amount of misdirected effort can offset that.[7]

The American public did not know about the Alcan's closure nor that the highway never did serve its intended purpose. The U.S. military did not need the highway once it became evident that the Japanese attack on the Aleutians was only a diversion. And, as the sea lanes to Alaska were never disrupted, an alternative overland supply route was not needed.

We can see why MacDonald was so disappointed in the Alcan. He came to Alaska in 1913 as a young man, worked as a locating engineer for the Alaska Railroad, then joined the Alaska Road Commission in 1924. By 1929 he had established a good reputation for his engineering work, which included construction of the Steese Highway from Fairbanks to Circle and preliminary studies for the Eklutna power project north of Anchorage.

[2] Ibid.

[3] Ibid.

[4] Ibid.

[5] Ibid.

[6] *Alaska Weekly*, October 25, 1929.

[7] Ibid.

But in taking up the advocacy of a long highway that would connect northern Alaska to the states, MacDonald joined the ranks of Alaska's transportation visionaries, a line of scheming zealots extending back to fanciful cartographers of the Northwest Passage and continuing into the present with Alaska's governor, Wally Hickel.

Visionaries usually enjoy telling of the origin of their obsessions and MacDonald was no exception. He told a friend:

It's funny how an idea will come to one. I was amusing myself one winter evening up in Fairbanks—December 1928, it was—poring over maps. Idly I drew a lead pencil line on the map from Hazelton, B.C., north along the old Telegraph Trail to Atlin, thence to Whitehorse. I was hardly thinking of what I was doing. It was almost a subconscious action—but all at once like a flash of inspiration—came the idea of a Fairbanks-Seattle highway. Right away I was impressed with the feasibility and possibility of such a route. There were at least 20 million automobiles whose owners were all quite naturally road enthusiasts looking for new worlds to conquer. I realized there would be tremendous economic force behind such a project. Alaska alone would have little influence, but the "outside" world, practically all on wheels, would furnish the motive force which would result in the consummation of the project.[8]

MacDonald started lobbying for an international highway association. Friends in Juneau got a legislative resolution calling upon Congress to appoint a commission with Canada. With an appropriation of $1,500 for publicity, MacDonald was off and running about the territory organizing support.

He assured everyone that the highway was not too formidable a task:

There are only 750 miles of new road to construct, routed through a country which contains no great engineering obstacles. Many states would undertake projects of more mileage and with far more money involved in a single year ... the time was ripe. The idea itself was as old as the ninety-eighters. We have a good neighbor in Canada. It is indeed fitting that we should work shoulder to shoulder in our battle to subdue nature as we once before battled against a common enemy.[9]

In actuality MacDonald's scheme was impractical because it did not really have the "powerful economic force behind it" that he imagined. North American motorists were far more interested in getting good roads built in southern Canada and the states than in funding a northern highway. Unless Alaska and the Yukon had another gold rush—or a war emergency—wide-scale support for a highway was unlikely.

In promoting his vision, MacDonald often told folks about earlier transportation projects such as the trans-Alaska-Bering Strait-Siberian railroad promoted by Johnny Healy, an old Alaska merchant and hustler. MacDonald believed that if Healy's railroad had been built during the early years of the century when it was being seriously considered, there would have been no war with Japan.

But visionary Johnny Healy failed to build this great continent-linking railroad and visionary Donald MacDonald was shattered when the army chose another route in 1942. He blamed the Canadian Pacific Railroad for deceiving the military:

The CPR did not want a highway that would interfere with the status quo. Couldn't stop it so they sank it. Their PR man, passed off as a northern expert, convinced the powers that the Alaska Highway Commission was a bunch of Chamber of Commerce boosters, and pushed importance of the wind fields put in by bush pilots at Watson Lake, Ft. Nelson, and Ft. St. John. The mislocated fields determined the highway location. Representative Halvorsen of North Dakota slicked Alaska delegate Tony Dimond and got his presentation before the House committee on roads. Halvorsen knew nothing but unscrupulously claimed the prairie extended from Dawson Creek to Fairbanks, using a fake "great circle" route map. Claimed our route was impossible to construct because of snow and rain; and 1200 miles longer from Chicago.[10]

By the time MacDonald got to speak—last—the damage was done.

The army engineers had to obey the general staff and "all of them were great liars."[11] And the weather bureau joined in the deception by inventing facts, relying upon, as MacDonald put it, "a species of scientific semantics delivered with an occult air of scientific finality. All hokum, of course. This, plus the mystic unsupported

---

[8] Ibid.
[9] Ibid.
[10] Op cit., MacDonald to Furth, August 7, 1943.
[11] Ibid.

statement by the army that the route selection was based on 'strategic reasons' had us stymied."[12]

MacDonald credited Thomas MacDonald of the Public Roads Administration with "the most amazingly ignorant or mendacious statement" of all, including assertions that the Alaska coast range was only two thousand feet high, which purportedly allowed the moisture-laden winds to sweep over the low coast range to dump two hundred inches of rain and forty feet of snow on MacDonald's route.[13]

Actually the coastal mountains rise to seven and eight thousand feet and much of the Route A area is semiarid. MacDonald complained to Senator Langer of North Dakota about this misinformation but Langer refused to cross-examine the PRA expert, explaining, according to MacDonald, "Why that man controls all the US road appropriations. If I ridiculed him, North Dakota would get no money."[14]

Of all the players involved, MacDonald found only General Sturdevant of the army engineers honest. Although Sturdevant admitted that there was not even a reconnaissance sketch of the route in existence, he believed, "being divinely inspired," that it would be 1300 miles from Dawson Creek to Fairbanks. "I warned him it would be greater than 1500," MacDonald said, "and it turned out to be 1650 miles."[15]

After the army's decision, MacDonald, who had been toiling for the highway "at no real salary outside of my expenses" for five years, took a job with the army engineers.[16] He directed the survey of a railroad route from Prince George, B.C., to Teller on the Seward Peninsula—the wartime renewal of the old Healy scheme of a trans-Alaska, trans-Siberia railroad. Mac was proud to report that his twenty-five locating parties completed the 2,130 miles, "the longest single railroad survey" ever made, in one year.[17] However, by 1943 the army had abandoned the railroad scheme, thus defeating what MacDonald called the third effort to built an inter-continental route.

We feel MacDonald's disappointment as he reflected on his efforts in 1943: "After 15 years of unpaid and devoted work I am just an office stiff, doing now nothing of importance. I could have saved a hundred million on the construction and operation of the Alaskan highway.

Any sound engineer, given a free rein, could. It was a good fight, my conscience is clear."[18]

Two years later, in 1945, Washington officials rubbed salt into his wounds. A congressional committee on roads made a hurried investigation of roads in Alaska and criticized the Alaska Road Commission for "inadequate engineering knowledge" in work on the Richardson Highway.[19]

MacDonald, who had served the Alaska Road Commission for many years, defended their work, pointing out that the Public Roads Administration, which always had limitless funds at its disposal for work in the states, had no notion of the Alaska Road Commission's meager funding.[20] A Fairbanks newspaper editor also blasted the congressional subcommittee report. The committee, "chaperoned by the head of the Public Roads Administration," should have investigated and exposed the extravagance and waste by the Public Roads Administration on the Alcan, but picked on the Alaska Road Commission work in Keystone Canyon. "It was a wonderful example of whitewashing a scandal and diverting attention," the editor concluded.[21]

Since the army spent $17.5 million on the Alcan and the Public Road Administration another $83,000 per mile by 1945, the Alaska Road Commission's work was an odd place to look for waste and extravagance. The Truman Committee of the U.S. Senate did expose the waste incurred by the Canol project, because its folly was so obvious. But the Alcan and its builders escaped censure.

From today's perspective we can easily agree with MacDonald that the U.S. Army might have been better off with Route A, and peacetime Alaska and the Pacific Northwest certainly would have profited more from a route closer to the coast. The highway was a military failure and neither has it been an effective peacetime spur to the economic development of the North that Route A might have been.

The route dispute is usually mentioned as a footnote to the Alaska Highway story—and rightly so—but the old controversy derives additional interest in the context of northern transportation history. Alaskans have persistently argued that better transportation was the key to

---

[12] Ibid.

[13] Ibid.

[14] Ibid.

[15] Ibid.

[16] Ibid.

[17] Ibid.

[18] Ibid.

[19] Claus-M. Naske, *Paving Alaska's Trails* (New York: University Press of America, 1986), p. 222.

[20] Ibid., p. 223.

[21] Ibid.

economic development, but history suggests that transportation promoters have expected and promised too much. Alaskans have often discovered that particular roads did not accelerate economic development substantially.

Perhaps MacDonald would have been disappointed with his highway if it had been built. But, in any event, I find it pleasant to think about MacDonald and his highway, especially in connection with Governor Hickel. Hickel has proved to be as persistent and controversial a road promoter as any of the visionaries of the past. We shall never forget the icy Hickel Highway to the North Slope. And if his Cordova highway is built, we hope it will be named for Donald MacDonald.

*William Hunt is a writer and historian, and Professor of History Emeritus of the University of Alaska Fairbanks. He is a contributing editor to "Alaska" magazine.*

*Alex Hunt researched and co-authored this paper.*

# The Alcan Saga, 1942-1943

*Norman Bush*

*This is written in memory of the 341st Engineers and the young men who lost their lives during the construction of the Alaska Highway. Among them was Private Wasley, the youngest member of Company D. While on fire duty, Private Wasley was killed by a dynamite explosion during the 1943 Dawson Creek fire.*

ON MAY 2, 1942, THE 341ST U.S. ARMY ENGINEERS, along with their pitifully inadequate equipment, arrived in Dawson Creek, British Columbia, to build the southern sector of the Alaska Highway.

There was no welcoming committee or band to herald our arrival, only mud, rain, and gray skies. We assembled in an area on the north edge of town, where each company received rations, and were assigned vehicles and other miscellaneous equipment. By May 6 we established base camp next to Charlie Lake, Mile 0, just north of Fort St. John.

Because of rains that lasted through May and most of June, true to the predictions of the British Columbians, the 341st was bogged down only a few miles north of base camp. During this time pontoon boats used to move men and supplies up Charlie Lake never reached their destination, and a volunteer search party was called for. Although I was a strong believer in not volunteering for anything, in this case it did not seem to apply. That evening I was among ten volunteers who found cigarettes and partially filled drums of oil that had drifted to shore. Soon after starting a signal fire, Colonel Lane, our regimental commander, and a trapper from across the lake arrived by motorized pontoon boat.

It was then, while Colonel Lane stood silent, that the trapper told how he watched helplessly as the overloaded pontoon boats capsized in the gusty wind, and twelve young men from the 341st Engineers drowned in the icy cold water of Charlie Lake. On the way back to camp by boat, the eerie northern lights reflected on the black water as we passed over where the tragedy occurred.

The next day charges were dropped into the lake to bring the bodies to the surface. I will always remember my buddies and the sound of their stiff, statue-like bodies thumping into the recovery boats. I was lucky on that unforgettable day that I wasn't one of them.

Building the first twenty-five miles of the highway was a process of trial and error. Rain, mud, and swarms of hungry mosquitoes made it the most memorable, frustrating, difficult part of the three hundred miles assigned to us.

By this time I had long since dismissed the idea of shaving, bathing, or changing into clean, dry clothes. In order to travel light our company commander ordered us to leave our extra clothing and shoes at base camp (Charlie Lake), saying they'd catch up with us in about a week. They never did. It's difficult now to believe that I didn't change the clothes I was wearing until nearly four months later. I remember itching a bit, but what bothered me most was when the soles of my shoes disintegrated from getting them too close to the fire too often, in attempts to get them dry.

The highlight of this particular period was when my buddy Joe Schneider and I heard the roaring and rumbling of something (big for sure) coming from the south.

It turned out to be our first Caterpillar D-8 bulldozer clearing everything in its path, and behind were four more. I remember Joe remarking, "The goddamn road will go through now!" And us, a couple of GIs from Company D, cheering and being splattered with mud as each one rumbled by. That was the turning point. Instead of each company using its own equipment and doing its own thing, a special "Cat camp" was formed to blaze trail and set the pace for the line companies who were ditching and building culverts. By the Fourth of July we were camped at Mile 48, north of Charlie Lake. There was still a long way to go, but at least we were now making progress.

That Fourth of July was memorable. Before leaving base camp we all chipped in for a two-quart ration of beer. The intended delivery date was to be the Fourth of July. On the morning of the Fourth the sky was clearing after a couple of days of heavy rain. The road behind us was a sea of mud, and the prospect of supplies of any kind reaching us within the next few days seemed very remote. We were lined up and about to move out when in the distance we heard a Cat headed our way. Soon a flying wall of mud came into view and behind it was a D-8, driven by a farm boy from Kansas and pulling a trailer with our long-talked-about beer. Needless to say, when he rumbled into our washed-out camp and cut the throttle there was much yelling and jubilation. Only the whites of his eyes were showing under a heavy coating of mud. He said at times the mud nearly covered the cat tracks. He had indeed delivered our beer against incredible odds.

After we shoveled the mud from the wooden barrels containing our quart bottles of beer, we formed that memorable beer line on the Fourth of July, 1942. Soon there was harmonica music, singing, and time for thoughts of home. When I got around to shaking hands with the hero of the day and told him we didn't think he'd make it, his only reply was, "I had to. It's the Fourth of July."

There was more to come that day to boost our morale. As we were drinking our beer, a couple of bombers that were headed north flew just above the treetops and dipped their wings to say "Hello." Late in the afternoon when we set up camp at the fifty-mile marker it seemed to us to be a symbol with special meaning. If we could go fifty miles, we could go a hundred, and if we could go a hundred, we could go all the way! That night, a long way from Hometown, U.S.A., we were proud, but very lonesome.

Because of the long northern daylight hours, time during the next two weeks seemed to lose all meaning for us. Rest was wherever and whenever we could get a couple of hours along the side of the road. Food was mostly C rations, Broadcast Brand Chili, orange mar- malade, biscuits, and coffee.

When we reached the Buckinghorse River, Company D was assigned to build a 150-foot bridge over the river's cold, swift-running water. The bridge was completed in the record time of two weeks, but at the cost of one young man's life. He died of pneumonia. I'm sure he would have lived if he had received adequate medical care.

While we were building the bridge, rations arrived and were left by the side of the road near the field kitchen. Late the next night it was a little rainy and quite dark. Joe and I heard what appeared to be a civilian contractor truck growl up the road and stop near our rations. Next, as Joe and I lay holed up in the bush, we witnessed a person, well known to us all, trade several cases of our rations for liquor. When the truck pulled away, he stood quietly for quite a long time, then slowly returned to his quarters.

The night before we moved from the Buckinghorse River, Joe and I sat huddled around a small fire on a hill overlooking the bridge. We talked of home, which seemed like such a long time ago and so very far away. For two months now we had been sleeping in the mud, rain, and brush and had not changed our clothes. We joked about Joe's shoes. They were worse than mine. He was able to stick his toes out the bottoms. As the fire died down we sat alone with our thoughts, watching a truck and some equipment going over the bridge built by Company D of the 341st Engineers.

In the morning we were loaded onto trucks and moved out to rejoin the regiment several miles north. As we were about to leave, the driver advised the truck wasn't safe as he had to pump the brakes to make them hold. Our commander's only reply was, "Use gears."

Much of the way had sharp curves and in some places sheer drop offs where I couldn't see bottom. On the way I moved back to the tailgate. I figured I would have a better chance if I had to jump. Fortunately, there was no need.

We stayed at our new camp site for about a week, repairing culverts and building new ones. The night before we moved, our commander got drunk in the privacy of his quarters. He knocked down the tent center pole and the tent collapsed on him. Luckily, his lieutenant arrived on the scene. Many of us, myself included, had clubs and were intent on beating anything that moved under the canvas. His lieutenant played the officer role quite well. He stayed aloof, quartered by himself, and performed according to orders without question.

About a week later and several miles further north, torrential rains mired us in the mud. Nothing was moving north or south. During this time we ran out of food. Even the C rations were gone, and we were ordered to remain in our tents to conserve our energy until food ar-

A bridge built by the men of Company "D," 34th Engineers, spans the Buckinghorse River along the Alaska Highway in 1942. *(Photograph from the author's collection)*

rived. As Joe and I holed up for the next two days, we shared our last few Hershey bars and talked of the things we'd eat when we got back home.

In the afternoon of the third day, rations arrived on a wagon pulled by a D-8. Then an incredible thing happened. Our commander ordered rifles and ammunition issued to the noncoms to guard the food from his own men. I was ordered up on the wagon to hand the cases to a line formed to pass them along. Joe was at the end of the line, inside the kitchen tent. When I came to a wet carton of pineapple I managed to kick it open without being noticed. The cans were then passed along, one at a time. I knew if there was a way, Joe would get one for us. Actually, he managed to get three. However, the following night at the bottom of a steep hill in back of the kitchen tent, we were only able to find two.

A couple of days later I was assigned to temporary duty with the maintenance crew of the Cat camp at the head of the road. Why me, I never knew, except it had to be someone. As Joe would say, "I broke lucky." The sergeant in charge of the crew managed to get me a pair of shoes. They were pretty beat up and much too large, but at least they had soles. I remember lacing them up

tight so my feet wouldn't slide around so much. I went on duty about 8:00 P.M. and worked until 5:00 A.M. During these hours we fueled the bulldozers, checked and changed the oil if necessary, cleaned the tracks, and took care of other general maintenance. Changing the oil was the worst part. When the bottom plug was unscrewed from the last thread of the crankcase, the hot oil came gushing out. There wasn't any way to keep from getting splattered.

In the morning when the first shift of Cat skinners arrived we were hauled back to the Cat camp field kitchen, which was already being loaded to move up. Breakfast was cold pancakes (the first ones cooked), coffee dregs, and orange marmalade. After the usual morning fare, I'd sack out until about two in the afternoon. Then I'd have a can of C rations and hitch a ride up to the new Cat camp kitchen for supper. It usually was Vienna sausages, biscuits, and diced beets or carrots. After catching up on the latest rumors, I'd go on duty.

On the morning of August 24, word spread that the Muskwa River was only a few miles ahead and there was a possibility that we might reach it that day. This particular morning I sacked out in the brush near the side of the road and was awakened about noon by the sounds of much activity and excitement. For as far as I could see, the road south was jammed with trucks and equipment. Colonel Lane was directing a Cat skinner to block the road with a large tree, stopping all traffic from going further. I was then ordered up on the kitchen truck. Colonel Lane was holding up the regiment so those who led the way in the Cat camp would be first to reach the river. That afternoon, as the kitchen truck bumped and rattled out onto the Alaska Highway, the colonel waved us by. We saluted, and, with a grin, he snapped to attention and returned the salute. Once on the road we stopped and waited while the road was cleared and the Cat that Colonel Lane was now riding pulled in front to lead the way to the river, our destination and the end of three hundred unforgettable miles. At this point there was more than one GI whose emotions were showing as the long-talked-about and rumored Muskwa River came into view.

When the kitchen truck reached the river and ground to a stop, I jumped off and made my way to a point about a half-mile back up the road to wait for Company D, and to wave to the dirty, jubilant young men of the 341st as their limping, beat-up trucks and equipment growled slowly by. When Company D passed by, Joe reached out, grabbed my hand and pulled me up on the side of the truck to join him and the rest of my buddies in their triumphant experience of going the last half-mile.

Good things were still to come that unforgettable day. The company clerk had mail for me, including a package from my folks. After reading the letters, beginning with the oldest first, Joe and I had a party with the goodies from Clifton, New Jersey.

During the festivities I noticed Joe was wearing a pretty good pair of shoes. I inquired as to where he got them. He smiled and told me the story. According to Joe, on a particularly dark night he checked out our commander's foot locker, which had been left in the back of a jeep. He found a pair of shoes just his size and exchanged them for the ones he had on.

When I asked what he meant by "exchanged," he told me he put his old ones back in the "bastard's goddamn footlocker." As Joe smiled and saluted his shoes, it's the only time I can remember tears and my sides aching, both from laughter.

In the evening a brigadier general arrived with a radio-equipped command car, and his driver managed to tune in a station from Edmonton. Although it faded a bit, we were able to hear strains of Glenn Miller's "Moonlight Serenade." As I listened, my thoughts drifted back to the previous summer and a new maroon Chevy convertible with red leather upholstery.

Circulating among us was a member of the 341st who had boarded our troop train and joined up somewhere between Edmonton and Dawson Creek. He had no special breeding or rank, just a sort of collie mix with mud-caked fur who affectionately responded to the name of Muskeg. He never attached himself to any one person or outfit, nor was he intimidated or impressed with rank. All of us were his family. Sometimes he'd be seen riding

The author poses with the Buckinghorse River bridge behind him, 1942. *(Photograph from the author's collection)*

in a jeep with the brass, and sometimes on the back of a truck, or even on a bulldozer. Most of the time, though, he'd be tagging alongside an outfit moving up the line. Muskeg was loved by all of us and to many he seemed to bring home a little closer. The last time I saw him, he was crossing the Muskwa River bridge on the back of a trailer. Destination: Fairbanks, Alaska.

At the Muskwa River I rejoined Company D. A couple of days later we moved several miles north to service and improve a section of the highway, which was now said to be passable from Dawson Creek, British Columbia, to Fairbanks, Alaska.

During this time the 447th, a quartermaster regiment newly arrived from the states whose commission was to haul food and supplies, delivered two cases of frozen steaks to Company D. Our commander commandeered the steaks for an officers' party and morale in Company D hit a new all-time low.

A few days later, I was in an isolated squad when the driver of a 447th Quartermaster truck had to stop until the road was cleared. We learned that he was part of a convoy that was pretty well strung out. Among other supplies, they were hauling eggs and meat. It was decided then and there that if any meat was on the next truck, we'd unload it. After posting a man at a sharp bend about a half-mile down the road to signal when the next truck was coming, we blocked the road with a couple of trees and waited. About twenty minutes later we got the signal, and a quartermaster truck growled around the bend. It pulled up to our road block and stopped. For the first time, I was glad the wind was blowing and gusting because it muffled the sound of Joe inventorying the truck. A couple of boys engaged the driver in conversation while others cleared the road and helped distract the driver. As I waited, I wondered what Joe might find. He soon stuck his head out from under the rear flap and, with a big smile, handed me a case of eggs. Before our lookout signaled frantically that another truck was coming, the eggs were followed by two cases of frozen steaks, a case of Crisco, four cases of canned fruit, and a twenty-five-pound box of hard candy for dessert.

It was all stacked and covered with brush as the hijacked truck proceeded on its way and the driver of the second waved as he rolled by. When the day ended we were a jubilant group of young men as we made our way toward camp, carrying the groceries, singing typical army songs, and enjoying the heady feeling of executing such a successful operation. That night, about a quarter of a mile from camp, there was a party for the enlisted men! All the steak they could eat, topped off with canned fruit of their choice and hard candy. We divided up the eggs for breakfast. As the evening festivities continued, our commander's curiosity was roused to the point of putting in an appearance. Without speaking to anyone, he made his way over to the edge of a deep ravine where a buddy and I were sitting with the remainder of the steaks, about a quarter of a case. As he glared down at us it became apparent that he intended to have it taken to company quarters. However, this did not happen. To show his contempt, my buddy shoved it over the edge of the ravine with his foot. As it rumbled and bounced down out of sight, our leader whirled around and returned to his quarters. There never was any question or mention of how, or where, our windfall was acquired.

Late in September I received orders from regimental headquarters to proceed to Fort Nelson on special assignment, under the command of a Major Heitt—one of the reasons I was not with Company D when they eventually cleared mine fields in France and Germany on their way to Berlin. The next morning I stood by the side of the Alaska Highway and said goodbye to the finest group of young men I've ever known. Joe and I didn't speak, just shook hands. I saluted his shoes and we laughed.

On the truck transporting me to Fort Nelson there were five other men from various companies who were also assigned to Major Heitt. After two dusty, bumpy days we finally arrived at our destination at about midnight. I spent the remainder of the night in one of several tents left by a previous regiment that had used the hill behind them for a garbage dump. I was awakened early in the morning by a large rat crawling over my face. It and the rest of its buddies seemed unafraid and quite friendly. However, after being intimidated with a shoe, they all elected to leave. Since washing, shaving, and dressing were now only a memory, getting up was just a matter of crawling out from under a couple of O.D. blankets. The closest they had come to being washed was during the spring rainy season.

As I made my wary to the field kitchen for breakfast a major in his mid-forties, wearing a shiny new uniform and driving a command car, pulled alongside and stopped. I saluted, which seemed to embarrass him. He smiled, nodded, and introduced himself as Major Heitt and asked if I was assigned to help him. When I told him I was, and introduced myself as Private Norman Bush, he not only shook my hand, but also ate breakfast with me and the five other boys. The major kept insisting the mess sergeant bring us more hot biscuits, bacon, eggs, and juice, choice items we hadn't had in a long time, even though at Fort Nelson they seemed to be abundant.

During breakfast we learned the major had been employed by the Caterpillar Tractor Company. He was commissioned as a major from his civilian employment to establish a parts warehouse at Fort Nelson and at Dawson Creek. Since the leaves had already turned and there was a brisk nip in the air, the major's first priority was to get his boys a new issue of warm clothes and quartered in tents near the large circus-type tent known as the "parts warehouse."

By November first we were experiencing sub-zero temperatures, and by Thanksgiving Day there was a low of forty degrees below zero. Our light was from a Coleman lantern and we received some warmth from a wood-burning, thin-gauge metal stove in the middle of the tent. The stove would glow red hot as long as we were able to stuff it with our nightly supply of dry wood. About all it was really good for was melting the ice in our canteens and thawing the food in our mess kits. These became partially frozen, even if carried only a short distance from the field kitchen.

Our duties until mid-December entailed inventorying and moving spare parts to a warehouse closer to the highway. Since daylight hours were short and the temperatures averaged between fifty and sixty below zero, progress was slow.

At night I'd zip my sleeping bag over my head, leaving only a small opening to breath through. However, my breath would condense and freeze around my nose, and I'd have to rub it to get the feeling and circulation back. My closest encounter with the "all-embracing cold that kills softly and quickly" was the night a buddy who drove the mail truck from Whitehorse to Dawson Creek arrived with a couple of bottles of liquor. I drank too much and then decided to take the major a drink. On the way, the last thing I remember is peacefully and pleasantly sinking down into the snow. The temperature was fifty below zero. I was lucky that the driver of the last truck to arrive that night saw me. The part I remember most is the pain of thawing out. The winter of '42 was one of the coldest on record.

To keep vehicles from becoming deadlined during the extreme cold, motors were left idling and smudge pots were placed under the transmission, differentials, and axles.

During this time, some authoritative idiot was instrumental in having twenty horses transported to our small unit for the purpose of pulling deadlined vehicles and equipment. Someone had to feed and water them. My buddy Ruben Wertzel and I were elected. Feeding them from the accompanying bales of hay was easy, but getting them water in a liquid state at sixty below was a problem—although not for long: They soon froze to death.

At about the middle of December Major Heitt left Fort Nelson to set up the spare parts warehouse near the railhead at Dawson Creek. Before leaving he arranged for us to move from the tents into a Nissen hut. It was fairly well insulated and had a wood floor, two large wood-burning stoves—one at either end—and electric lights from a portable generator. The Major also gave us the news that names would be drawn to determine when we'd be scheduled to leave on a two-week furlough. The drawing was tense and emotional. One of the first two picked to be home for Christmas was a quiet, very religious boy; it almost made a believer of me. My name was drawn to leave February first, almost a year to the day from when I was inducted at Fort Dix, New Jersey.

Soon after, I was assigned to drive over the sector built by the 341st, hauling scrap iron and parts of deadlined equipment from Fort Nelson to Dawson Creek and, on the return trip, spare parts and miscellaneous supplies. The trip I remember most was when I stopped where a truck had rolled over a steep embankment. The driver was sitting against a nearby tree. He didn't respond when I called. He had frozen to death.

I always thought of my buddies as I eased over the Buckinghorse bridge, wondering if it would hold. When I passed the fifty-mile marker, I occasionally thought of a third can of pineapple. Mostly though, I thought about February first when I'd board the Great Northern Train at Dawson Creek to go home.

Perhaps during this year's fiftieth anniversary of the building of the Alaska Highway, a gray-haired old guy (never shot at or a war hero) will return with memories of a great dog named Muskeg, the strains of Glenn Miller's "Moonlight Serenade," and the young men of Company D, 341st Engineers.

*Norman Bush was a member of the 341st Engineers, Company D, from 1942 to 1945. He now lives in Prescott, Arizona.*

# A Soldier's Scrapbook

*Harry Yost*

THE CONSTRUCTION OF THE ALASKA HIGHWAY DURING the summer of 1942 has arguably been ranked as one of the greatest engineering feats of all time. While hardheaded engineers, politicians, and visionaries argue about whether "it was the wrong road, built in the wrong place, for the wrong reasons," or a major step toward the vision of an overland link between Europe and North America, no one can detract from the actual work done by soldiers who punched a pioneer road through the Canadian wilderness literally by brute force.

One of those soldiers was Dolph Schuler. Early in the Great Depression, Dolph's family had emigrated to Canada, as his father put it, "with a covered wagon and a dark night." They lived and worked in and around the oil fields in Alberta. When World War II started in 1939, Mr. Schuler decided it was time to move back to the United States "because he didn't raise three sons to fight the King's war."

Dolph was drafted into the U.S. Army in 1941, during the peacetime buildup, and assigned to the 340th Engineers. Early in 1942 they were sent, via railroad, to Fort St. John, British Columbia. Their task was simple: build a road north from Fort St. John until they met with another army engineer group building south from Whitehorse. This was accomplished by early fall, when the two groups met at Contact Creek, approximately 560 miles north of Dawson Creek, British Columbia.

Dawson Creek had been selected as the southern terminus of the Alaska Highway, even though the railroad hauled all the equipment and troops to its own terminus at Fort St. John. And so all distances were measured from Dawson Creek. Where the road began or ended was of little significance to the soldiers who did the actual work.

The first military crews lived in temporary tent camps, even in forty-below weather. The mess facilities were out in the open, the food served up into the awkward mess kits (only slightly improved since the Civil War, according to some) that had been issued in basic training.

The tents were "heated" by wood, cut by hand using Swede saws, crosscut saws, and double-bitted axes. Yes, chain saws were in existence then, but they were 150-pound monsters requiring two men to operate, and were used only on very large trees. The lodgepole pine and small birch found in the country were what fitted into the stoves, and that is what they used.

An anecdote from that time is about the quandary some officers found themselves in when trying to decide how much wood was needed to get through a winter. The colonel assigned a lieutenant to set up a wood-cutting detail. He dispatched the men under the command of a trusty sergeant who, after a short time, returned with a question as to how much wood was needed. The officer pondered this, conferred with the sergeant, and finally came up with the idea of asking one of the local Natives just how bad the coming winter was going to be. They found an elderly Native resting outside the door of his cabin and put the question to him.

Squinting into the distance, he asserted, "Be very bad winter, much cold!"

The lieutenant was satisfied, but the sergeant, perhaps because he would be directly responsible for the job, was skeptical. "How do you know?" he asked.

The Native pondered a moment, then, looking direct-

Soldiers build a bridge across a gully at Mile 560, between Fort St. John and Contact Creek, British Columbia. Engineers used portable sawmills and local timber to build the necessary structures as the road moved north. *(Photograph by Dolph Schuler, courtesy of Harry Yost)*

ly at the soldier gave his irrefutable answer: "I see signs," he intoned. "Be very bad winter. Much cold."

The sergeant wasn't reassured. "What signs?" he demanded. "Do the animals have thicker fur? Did the geese leave earlier? What signs? Tell me, so I can understand."

The Native studied the white man for a moment, then shook his head sadly as if he couldn't believe such ignorance. "See many white men cutting much wood," he pronounced firmly. "Be very bad winter."

Though they had bulldozers to push stumps and such out of the way, most of the preliminary clearing was done by the soldiers, by hand, with the same tools they used to cut firewood.

A lot of the timber cleared from the right of way was put right back into it. Bridges and even some culverts were constructed from poles. More were used to "corduroy" soft spots so the trucks and other equipment wouldn't sink out of sight. (Several hundred pieces of equipment did, but that's another story.)

Despite being constructed from the materials at

Dolph Schuler transports a tire during the summer of 1942, somewhere on the first five hundred miles of the Alaska Highway. *(Photograph by Dolph Schuler, courtesy of Harry Yost)*

hand—pine and spruce poles—the bridges were quite sturdy. Bulldozers weighing thirty-five thousand pounds were safely driven across them, and some of the log culverts were still in use well into the 1980s.

When the pioneer road was done, and the ground frozen hard enough to handle traffic, Dolph was assigned to drive a truck, hauling supplies north into Alaska. As the weather got colder, another minor glitch occurred. The trucks weren't designed for extreme cold, and the cabs were uncomfortable, to say the least. On top of that, with the coming of snow the roads became very slick. (And the military tires, designed for soft snow and mud, didn't help any.) Trucks regularly slid into the ditch. Dolph counted more than twenty-eight hundred trucks in the ditch during one trip north.

At the beginning of the winter, the military authorities laid down the law: anyone who ditched a truck would receive five days KP (kitchen police duty) as punishment. By this time, the mess facilities were in buildings, which, as the weather got colder, were warm havens for the men. With the prospect of five days in a warm kitchen as against driving a truck in minus-thirty- or minus-forty-degree weather, soon there were more drivers in the kitchens than on the road.

The rules were changed slightly. Henceforth if a driver ditched a truck, he was to get it back on the road as soon as possible and continue his trip. No more KP.

Dolph drove a truck during the winter of 1942-43. When breakup came and the road was impassable, he was reassigned back to California. After a period of "retraining," he was shipped to the British Isles. Dolph Schuler died on D-day, June 6, 1944, when the ship transporting his unit was sunk in the English Channel.

Politicians, engineers, and philosophers still argue the worth of the Alaska Highway. No matter what they may

A casualty of the first winter on the Alaska Highway. Trucks began hauling supplies north to Alaska as soon as the road froze. The first order given was "If you go into the ditch, it's five days on KP." With temperatures well below zero and with poor heaters in the trucks—when there were any heaters at all—there soon were more soldiers on KP than were driving trucks. A subsequent order was more prudently phrased. *(Photograph by Dolph Schuler, courtesy of Harry Yost)*

ultimately decide, their arguments pale beside the accomplishments of the men who simply saluted, said, "Yes, Sir!" and, literally, with their bare hands, punched it through in a single northern construction season. Men like Dolph Schuler simply thought of it as a job to be done, and did it!

*Harry Yost is curator of the Museum of Alaska Transportation and Industry in Wasilla. He has been a freelance writer for about twenty-five years.*

# Roadside Development along the Alaska Highway: The Impact of World War II Military Construction on the Alaska Highway Corridor

## Jane Haigh

THE ALASKA HIGHWAY WAS BUILT IN 1942 AND 1943 by the U.S. Army Corps of Engineers, together with the Public Roads Administration and numerous civilian subcontractors. After years of lobbying for a highway to promote economic development, the road was finally built as a military emergency project with a route chosen to provide support for the Northwest Staging Route. This was a series of airfields which defined an air route from the Midwest through northwest Canada to Alaska.

Just as its original boosters had envisioned, the road did bring development to the region. This report is meant as a road map—a guide to the beginning of an investigation of the regional development in the Alaska Highway corridor, and its impact on people, landscape, and geography.

The military surveyors of 1942, in choosing a route to connect Dawson Creek with the Richardson Highway near Big Delta, unalterably changed our perception of the landscape of northern British Columbia, southern Yukon Territory, and central Alaska. A landscape viewed and experienced only over a period of weeks or months—or a lifetime by river travel, dog team, or by walking—became a road, a linear experience, a continuous travel route. Over the course of one summer the landscape resolved into a series of memorable way stations connected by the thin thread of a wilderness track, often impassible to the trucks it was built to serve.

The road traversed the territory of a variety of Indian groups. While army officials and the public perception may have imagined the small Indian bands as scattered and widely separated, in fact Alaska and Yukon Native

people traveled and traded widely in the regions traversed by the highway corridor. Taking advantage of this local knowledge, Natives were hired as guides to the surveyors blazing the official route. The route followed many miles of traditional trails.

In addition, there were a few segments of existing wagon road. These included the route from Dawson Creek to Fort St. John, and a wagon road from Whitehorse to Kluane Lake, servicing mining camps at Silver City and the trading center at Burwash Landing.

In addition to Native settlements, there were a few scattered white settlements and trading posts. Existing towns and villages along the route included Dawson Creek and Fairbanks, as well as Fort St. John, Fort Nelson, Watson Lake, and Whitehorse. Where the highway alignment followed existing roads and trails, highway workers and contractors took advantage of existing service facilities and army officials took advantage of the residents' local knowledge of conditions.

Thousands of men camped on the shores of Kluane Lake at Burwash Landing. McIntosh's roadhouse is frequently mentioned by both highway surveyors and later travelers. Near Fort Nelson, two old trappers had a cabin on the highway alignment. They did a good business making sourdough pancakes for the first highway crews. Later they expanded to become one of the landmark stops—Lum 'n Abner's. In Alaska, the phones and facilities of Rika's Roadhouse and Bert and Mary's at Big Delta were used by the army for logistical support. Many units reported encampments at Rika's Roadhouse on arriving in the district or between assignments. The headquarters for the Lytle and Green Co., the Public

Roads Administration's main contractor for the Alaska section, was located in existing facilities at Gulkana. Many acres were covered with PRA equipment, maintenance facilities, and support camps.

By 1943, a mimeographed guide (found in the Anthony Dimond collection)[1] listed nearly 350 named camp and bridge locations. By the end of the summer of 1942, these included Northwest Staging Route airfields, military construction camps, civilian construction camps, telecommunications sites, sawmill sites, bridge construction camps, and CANOL camps.

The Dimond list of sites refers to all camps by milepost. However, anyone who has delved into this knows that the milepost references were changed a number of times in 1942 and 1943, due to road re-alignments. Many sites are photographed, and anecdotal references exist in a variety of published and unpublished diaries and personal reminiscences. To my knowledge, no site-by-site impact study has been done. Most troubling are anecdotal reports from local residents of streamside camps where equipment—including fuel barrels—was dumped into streambeds and buried.

The original deal with the Canadians provided for American military maintenance of the highway until the end of the war. At the beginning of 1946, therefore, the Canadian portion of the road was turned over to the Canadians, who maintained it with their military services with headquarters in Whitehorse. The Canadians took over established U.S. military maintenance stations. With few public services available, the Canadians did not open the road to the public until 1948.

The first to travel the road were workers. Travel was restricted to army personnel, or anyone connected with the war effort. In wartime Alaska, this included just about every resident of the territory. The route was served by service-related buses. A variety of materials including bus schedules, travelers' diaries, and personal photograph collections document the travels of passengers from 1943 to 1947. The accommodations were in the early roadhouses, and hotels in the major towns which catered to traveling service people.

The earliest independent highway travelers, from 1946 to 1948, reported camping in abandoned construction camps and clearings. Photographs show encampments of travelers in tents and trailers by the banks of swollen rivers in the spring, waiting for bridges to be rebuilt.

As early as April 1943—while the road was still an unimproved muddy track through the wilderness—the press was already noting the potential for tourist traffic. Morris McDougall began an article in the *Christian Science Monitor*:

> Shortly after completion of the Alcan Highway—that circuitous route cutting through North America's wildest lands—a swashbuckling prospector drove claiming stakes into ground which he later said would be his location for a filling station and tourist cabins for post war traffic.

He goes on to assert, "Canada and the United States are extremely interested in developing postwar tourist travel to this region, which may well become North America's new frontier."[2]

Further development of facilities reflects the general boom and bust eras in the north. With few existing facilities along the road corridor at first, the number quickly rose, reflecting the general optimism and hype about the economic development the road promised. While numbers of people opened roadhouses and other facilities along the route, general traffic could not support all of them. The actual lists of facilities show great turnover in the specific places, even as numbers declined or leveled off.

While the official lists include the more stable places, the reports of the Yukon sanitary inspector for 1949, for example, contain colorful details of other more transient places.

Heath Twichell cites a prediction by Governor Gruening prior to construction of the highway. After stating his objections to the inland route, he predicted:

> that it will be a highly unsatisfactory road when "completed;" that its theoretical completion will precede its actual serviceability by many years; and that what will be called "maintenance" for several years thereafter will in effect be continuous construction and reconstruction.[3]

He could not have been more right. In fact, the continuous construction and reconstruction provided much of the business for the elongated highway community of roadhouses, trading posts, cafes, and gas stations—the stopping places on the highway.

The Alaska Highway corridor was gradually, in fits and starts, developed into a linear service economy. Fragile settlements existed to service the road and its travelers, and depended on the road as their lifeline to

---

[1] Anthony Dimond Collection, University of Alaska Fairbanks APR.

[2] Morris McDougall, "The Highway to Russia," *Christian Science Monitor*, April 3, 1943.

[3] Heath Twichell, *Northwest Epic, The Building of the Alaska Highway* (New York: St. Martin's Press, 1992), p. 95.

The Gulkana Roadhouse exemplified the traditional two-story log roadhouse style. With access to tidewater via Valdez, the area was a center for post-war military and civilian road construction. *(Acc. No. 91-123N, R. Christensen Collection, Rasmuson Library, University of Alaska Fairbanks)*

civilization. A 1947 Canadian government publication[4] listed "accommodation and roadside facilities available on the Alaska Highway." Of thirty-one listings, six were already towns or villages, and seven were existing trading posts or traditional roadhouses. Two listings indicated the Canada-Alaska boundary and Canadian Customs at Snag. Two new junctions listed with store, meals, gas, and oil were Tok Junction and Haines Road Junction. Delta Junction was not listed at all. The remaining fourteen listings must have been new facilities. Most derived from construction camp sites, frequently—but not always—near a river or stream crossing, where prolonged construction required a semi-permanent camp. This 1947 list must be viewed as conservative. By 1948, highway facilities were proliferating. Mrs. Walter Hodges, traveling in 1948, noted, "We have noticed that there are many more accommodations along the route than are shown on our 1948 folder. Apparently lodges and gas stations are springing up fast."[5]

All of these northern truck stops functioned as gas stations, general stores, and tourist stops, including cafes and rooms, either as hotel-roadhouses or as cabins. In the larger towns, such as Tok and Delta Junction, these functions might be in different businesses—hotels that were, for example, separate from gas stations.

A *New York Times* article mentioned "swank hunting and tourist lodges are going up along the highway." The anonymous author also added, "We saw ample evidence of 'boom time' touristic plans in the form of luxurious log hunting lodges, new hotels, tourist cabins, restaurants, stores and military barracks that you'll never recognize when they get through fixing them up."[6]

Roadhouse proprietors along the many remote sections of the highway often combined the service facility with a wilderness lifestyle. Mrs. Hodges describes one such couple and their establishment:

Marsh Lake Lodge, where we are spending the night, is owned by Mike and Mary Nolan, and is a place with atmosphere. The buildings are all of log

---

[4] "General Information Concerning The Alaska Highway-Canadian Section," Bureau of Northwest Territories and Yukon Affairs, Lands, Parks and Forests Branch, Department of Mines and Resources, Ottawa, Canada, August 15, 1947.

[5] Walter Hodge, diary transcript.

[6] "Canada Opens a Highway Built by the United States," *New York Times*, Oct. 8, 1946.

construction, and furnished attractively. We have a cabin-"Sourdough Shack." Accommodations are not of the Waldorf Astoria type, of course, but we are comfortable. There is a trek which must be taken, and there is no running water, but the view of the lake is superb! Mike is a former Mountie, and Mary was a servicewoman during the war. In the winter, when time permits, they visit their trapline, a dog team trip of 5 days. The lodge is open the year round—catering to hunting and fishing parties. Last winter it was written up by Shep Shepherd in one of the sportsman magazines.[7]

An analysis of the distances between stopping places shows a gradual evolution in the development of the highway corridor. Many new facilities developed after the highway opened for tourist travel, resulting in an average decrease in the distance between stops through the 1950s. After 1960, the distances between rose. While there might be similar numbers of facilities, these began to be concentrated at nodes along the highway. Frank Duerden notes from his field work in the Yukon in 1978, "It was evident from the number of abandoned commercial complexes on the highway that while the nodal locations are growing intervening locations are stagnating or dying." Duerden goes on to express his conclusion:

As highway conditions improve, so tourists drive further in a day and rely less on highway services. Thus viable transient oriented enterprises are located at focal points in the territorial road system which are approximately a comfortable days [sic] driving time apart—Watson Lake and Whitehorse, and ... Haines Junction.[8]

However, these generalizations do not tell the whole story. Development of each section of the road really responded to localized economic conditions. Development in British Columbia, Yukon Territory, and in Alaska differed.

Ten years after the completion of the Alaska Highway, and only four years after its opening to the public, Alaska boosters got their longed-for road connection to the west coast courtesy of the British Columbia provincial road-building program. The John Hart Highway was completed in 1952, connecting Dawson Creek with the provincial road system via Prince George. Dawson Creek became the supply center for the North East Coal development,

and also grew as a regional center. Area-wide population in 1986 was about sixty thousand.[9]

Natural gas was discovered in Fort St. John in 1955, leading to a gas boom in the early 1960s, and an area-wide population of fifty thousand by 1986. A Petro Canada gas-processing plant and several refineries are now located at Taylor, thirty-five miles from Dawson Creek and twelve miles from Fort St. John, with a population of 850.

This increase in population base in northern British Columbia, and relative proximity to population centers in southern British Columbia, resulted in increased tourism at scenic sites in the Rockies, such as Summit Lake, Muncho Lake, Teslin Lake, etc. A look through the current *Milepost Guide* reveals that many facilities are tourist oriented rather than the roadside services of the old days.

In the Yukon the transportation system has been developed—built by the Canadian government as part of its "Roads to Resources" initiative. After World War II, the Yukon Government was moved from Dawson City to Whitehorse, and an all-weather road was constructed from Whitehorse to Dawson as a sort of compensation to the Klondike. This provided road access to the silver-lead mines at Keno, Elsa, and Mayo. The new town of Faro was created in the late 1960s to serve the development of the Anvil lead-zinc mine, but was shut down in 1985. With a population of sixteen hundred in 1978, Faro was then second-largest community in the Yukon.[10] While the northern CANOL road has been abandoned, the Robert Campbell Highway from Watson Lake through Ross River to Carmacks on the Alaska Highway serves the mines at Faro and was completed in 1968. Additional roads built as part of the Alaska Highway development serve Carcross and Atlin, B.C., from Whitehorse. The road connection to Skagway is the most recently completed segment. With approximately eighteen thousand people, Whitehorse has nearly two-thirds of the population of the whole territory (approximately twenty-five thousand).

Prior to the completion of the Alaska Highway, the segment of highway from Whitehorse to Kluane Lake was an existing road, with a series of roadhouses and facilities. Many of these facilities were maintained, originally. However, available services are now concentrated in Whitehorse, Watson Lake, Beaver Creek, and Haines Junction. By 1980, the ninety-four-mile segment between Whitehorse and Haines Junction had no facilities whatever.

The region traversed by the Alaska Highway corridor in Alaska is neither a resource-development area nor a

---

[7] Mrs. Walter Hodges, diary transcript, Walter Hodges collection, UAF Archives.

[8] Frank Duerden, *The Development and Structure of the Settlement System in the Yukon* (Whitehorse: Department of Library and Information Resources, 1981), p. 139.

[9] *Milepost Guide* (Anchorage: Alaska Northwest Publishing, 1986).

[10] Duerden, *Development and Structure*, 1981.

tourist destination. Prior to highway construction, this area was accessible only by boat, plane, or dog team. Facilities in this area are concentrated at two new highway communities, which are both a product of the highway construction—Tok and Delta Junction. Tok is the junction of the main highway and a spur to Anchorage; the Tok Cutoff was established in 1942. Construction worker Ray Haman observed in June 1943, "Three or four barracks and a corner with three big roads branching from it was all that comprised the place known as Tok Junction." However, when he returned in late July he noted,

> Tok Junction in the last 50 days had made a great change. I hardly knew the place. It was now a small town with a deep well, a water system, machine shops, warehouses, garages, a bakery, a store, a hospital, office barracks, blacksmith shop, a large mess hall, etc.[11]

The business of Tok is nearly entirely oriented towards tourism, although it is a center for some regional services, and headquarters for a wildlife refuge.

Delta Junction, first called Buffalo Junction, was a construction camp of CCC buildings at the junction of the Alaska Highway and the Richardson Highway, the oldest highway in the state. Both Delta and Tok can be perceived as World War II ghost towns. Military construction and a steady program of road improvements created a diversified economy in the late '40s and early '50s, including military jobs, Alaska Communications Systems, the eight-inch army pipeline built in 1954-55 with the pump station near Tok, and the construction of

After World War II, lunch counters along the Alaska Highway typically were furnished with surplus and castoffs from army mess halls. Behind the counter were the dry goods and foodstuffs of the general store. *(Acc. No. 73-75-1154, Fred Machetanz Collection, Rasmuson Library, University of Alaska Fairbanks)*

the Taylor Highway. During the '50s, the Richardson Highway between Delta and Delta Junction supported fourteen bars in fourteen miles. Work crews, homesteaders, tourists, and trucking added to the diversity of the economy.

Over the years the highway route was improved continuously. A major paving program for the Canadian portion was undertaken in the 1960s. Increased speeds have meant decreased need for services. New highway alignments have even cut the actual length of the road. For while services were originally an average of twenty-nine miles apart, the completion of a new highway alignment in the late 1980s—which cut off the traditional stop at Trutch—left a segment of seventy-one miles between facilities at one point, and sixty-two miles at another, in the Fort Nelson vicinity. "For a while we were an automatic stop," said Dale Young, a business owner in Tok. "One day's travel from Whitehorse, and the road was so bad, by the time you got here, you were ready to stop. We got complacent and rested on our laurels," he said.

Some travelers today make the trip from Watson Lake to Fairbanks in one day. Six hundred miles is a typical cross-country run in the states, but previously unthinkable on the Alaska Highway. Speed has changed the landscape geography of the Alaska Highway and diminished the importance of the landmark stops.

When the road was constructed, Native Americans were not even officially enumerated in Canada or in Alaska. After 1952, the Yukon Indian Agency afforded recognition to sixteen legal bands, some of which were—in whole or in part—resident in northern British Columbia. The officially recognized band names indi-

---

[11] Ray C. Haman, "Adventure in the Alcan (Alaska) Highway," 1945, APR Alaska Highway collection.

cate that bands at Lower Post, Watson Lake, Upper Liard, Atlin, Teslin, Carcross, Lake Laberge, Champagne, Aishihik, Burwash Landing, and Beaver Creek were original occupants of the lands traversed by the highway corridor.[12]

In Alaska, the situation was similar, with road construction impacting lands used by Native bands at Tanacross, Northway, and Mentasta Lake. No Native land claims were recognized at the time in Alaska, the Yukon, or B.C. Natives in both Canada and Alaska have testified that often they did not even know about the highway plan until the bulldozers showed up.[13] Other testimony has indicated that the army routed the construction through existing settlements, such as Canyon, in the Yukon, while soldiers pilfered burial items from grave sites.

The road created employment, transportation and commercial opportunities for Yukon Indians, at the same time that hunting pressure by newcomers depleted traditional food resources. By the early '50s, many traditional village sites had been abandoned in favor of new communities along the highway.[14]

Northway, and Tanacross were, additionally, sites for Northwest Staging Route airfields. At Tanacross and Northway, original airstrips had been built by the Natives themselves. The community and vicinity of Northway has managed to maintain at least one tourist facility since 1950. Facilities are now owned and operated by the Native corporation.

Residents of Tanacross describe building an airstrip in 1935 with picks, shovels, and wheelbarrows under the direction of trader John Hajduckovich. By mid-1942, a thousand GI's were quartered at the Tanacross airstrip and spent frantic days busily scurrying around the army infrastructure of barracks, warehouses, and maintenance facilities directly across the river from the Native village. The army enlarged and paved the strip. A year previously there had been only a few hundred villagers. Ironically, perhaps, today the modern village of Tanacross has moved across the river for better road access, to a site originally developed as a highway construction camp and then abandoned. The Native leaders understood that the airfield would eventually revert to them when military use ceased. This has never happened, and is a documented area of contention to this day.

*Jane Haigh is completing a graduate degree in northern studies at the University of Alaska Fairbanks. She was guest curator for the Alaska Highway's fiftieth anniversary exhibit, "Alaska or Bust," at the University of Alaska Museum.*

---

[12] Catharine McClellan, Lucie Bickel, et al., *Part of the Land, Part of the Water: A History of the Yukon Indians* (Vancouver: Douglas & McIntyre, 1987), p. 94.

[13] Residents of Tanacross, personal communication; testimony of participants, YMHA conference on the Highway, Whitehorse 1992; William Simeone, "Identity, History, and the Northern Athabaskan Potlatch," (doctoral dissertation, McMaster University, 1990).

[14] Julie Cruikshank, "The Gravel Magnet," in Coates, ed., *The Alaska Highway: Papers of the 40th Anniversary Symposium* (Vancouver: UBC Press, 1985).

# War's Impact on the Home Front

Canadians parade in Juneau during World War II.
*(Photograph courtesy National Archives of Canada)*

# World War II in Alaska:
# A View from the Diaries of Ernest L. Gruening

*David A. Hales*

## Introduction

ERNEST L. GRUENING SERVED ALASKA AS TERRITORIAL governor from 1939 to 1953, and in the U.S. Senate from 1956 to 1968. Born in New York City in 1887, he graduated from Harvard College and Harvard Medical School in 1912. Instead of practicing medicine, he pursued a career in journalism and became known for his editorship of a succession of Boston and New York newspapers, including *The Nation*, a liberal journal.[1]

The purpose of this paper is to provide some insights into the activities of World War II as recorded by Gruening through excerpts from his diaries. It is not meant to be analytical or to debate the accuracy of the activities or events as perceived and recorded by Gruening in his diaries. He was an avid believer in the importance of keeping a diary and was fairly consistent in keeping one from 1930 to 1970. These diaries and his papers are on deposit at the Alaska and Polar Regions Department Archives at Elmer E. Rasmuson Library, University of Alaska Fairbanks.

Many of the diaries were typed, but a large portion were available only in Gruening's own handwriting. He wrote very small and often used small notebooks. In some cases he covered every possible inch of the page, including the margins. Because his handwriting is difficult to read, some researchers decided not to use the diaries. Because of the continued interest by researchers, and through funding from the Alaska Humanities Forum and the Rasmuson Library, the diaries were tran-scribed. Mrs. Judy Grahek had worked for C.W. Snedden, publisher of the *Fairbanks Daily News-Miner* and good friend of Governor Gruening. She had often read Gruening's handwriting and was hired to assume the transcribing project.

## Gruening as Governor

On September 2, 1939, just a day after the outbreak of war in Europe, President Franklin D. Roosevelt announced that John Troy had resigned from the territorial governorship because of ill health and that Ernest Gruening would take his place. Gruening's diaries do not give us any clue as to why he accepted the position. On August 8, 1939, he recorded that Harold Ickes told him that Roosevelt was going to appoint a new governor for Alaska and had asked Gruening:

> "How would you like the job?"
> I said, "I wouldn't care for it."
> He said, "I think you would like it. We are all going to be through here when Roosevelt is and this is more salary and a title."
> I said to him, "Well, I am not particularly interested in titles and I think that the work you do here is more important. Besides, I think the Governor of Alaska should be a resident of Alaska, one who has been in the Territory and expects to live there. I think Bunnell would be the desirable person, or Dimond, or somebody of that kind."

---

[1] Sherwood Ross, *Gruening of Alaska* (New York: Best Books, 1960), pp. 23-58.

Ickes replied, "That is just the type we don't want. The best Governors of Alaska have been those who have come from the outside."

Not wishing to get into a controversy and wanting to have time to reflect over the significance of that offer I said, "Well, I will think it over."

He said, "Well, I want a quick decision on it." I told him I would think about it.

Discussed the matter with Oscar who came to the same conclusion—that it was not desirable to accept.

Gruening did not make any diary entries for approximately ten weeks. On October 23, 1939, he recorded the events of a vacation in New England, and wrote:

This period was punctuated with the excitement of the war news. We found ourselves very grateful to Peter for his insistence that no car was complete without a radio—a sentiment of which we had been rather scornful. We found ourselves hanging on the radio at all times and getting the thrilling and tragic news of the embroilment of Europe in war.

While driving toward the Roewer's house early on Saturday afternoon, September 2nd, a news flash boomed out as follows: "Washington: President Roosevelt today appointed Ernest Gruening Director of the Division of Territories and Island Possession, as Governor of Alaska. Gov. Troy resigned on the grounds of ill health."

It was a surprise to me that the resignation had been secured so quickly. This being on a Saturday afternoon of the Labor Day weekend, and what with all the war news relatively few people heard of it. We decided not to tell the Roewers anything about it and hoped it would be broadcast while we were listening during the evening. We kept turning the radio to all the news broadcasts, but without success.

Governor Ernest Gruening in Barrow, 1942. (*Acc. No. 77-158-178N, Fred G. Klerekoper Collection, Rasmuson Library, University of Alaska Fairbanks*)

## Alaska in World War II

Gruening rapidly brought his affairs in Washington, D.C., to closure and rushed off to Alaska. He arrived in December 1939 and delivered his inaugural address on December 5. He was quite familiar with Alaska as he had visited in 1936 and within two weeks traveled approximately four thousand miles to familiarize himself with the North. He was well aware of Alaska's strategic location and lack of military defense.

At the outbreak of war in Europe, Alaska's only military establishment consisted of the old Fort Seward, renamed Chilkoot Barracks in 1922. Eleven officers and approximately three hundred men armed with Springfield rifles manned the post. This was the sad state of affairs, although as early as 1931 George A. Parks, then territorial governor, reminded the secretary of the Interior of Alaska's strategic position as the most feasible air route to Asia. The governor recommended that the Army Air Corps build a station in Alaska, if only to train pilots for flying conditions in northern latitudes. The pleas fell on deaf ears.[2]

In 1934, Japan denounced the fire-power naval treaty of 1922, under which the United States had agreed not to fortify the Aleutians. Anthony Dimond, Alaska's delegate, pleaded for bases at Anchorage or Fairbanks, and also in the Aleutians: "I say to you, defend the United States by defending Alaska."[3]

Year after year Dimond warned his congressional colleagues of the potential danger from Japan. Yet when the Japanese struck Pearl Harbor without warning, Alaska was hopelessly unprepared for war. Major General Buckner stated, "We're not even the second team up here—we're a sand lot club."[4]

Two years after his inauguration, Gruening was preparing for a trip to Washington, D.C. On the morning of December 7, 1941, he telephoned the steamship company at 9:30 A.M. and was informed that the boat would not leave until the next day. He was not disappointed as he yet had much to do. Gruening was not officially notified about the bombing of Pearl Harbor. He first learned of the events from a call from an individual who had heard the news on the radio.

At 10:30 the phone rang and the voice which identified itself as Tom Gardiner said that he had been listening to the broadcast from KIRO (radio) out on the highway and that the Japanese had attacked the Hawaiian Islands and Manila in force by air, with many civilians killed, and much damage done in Pearl Harbor and to our Army defenses.

It seemed hard to believe. But it seemed equally hard not to believe that these incredible facts were true. I called up KINY (radio) which had heard nothing. I then called Carle, manager of the station, at his home, and suggested that he get to his office immediately and see what could be found. I then called up the signal corps and found that they were hearing similar reports from station WLW (radio), Cincinnati. There could be no question about its truth.

I called Frank Metcalf, Director of civilian defense, and told him to organize a meeting of the defense committee immediately and to make all possible preparations for the emergency. I likewise called up Bob Bartlett, Stell and Harry Lucas, all of whom were most incredulous. About 12:30, KINY came on the air with confirmation; the attack apparently caught the Navy and Army napping and damage appears to have been extensive.

One thing is certain: this action, however damaging to our defense, is probably worth all the battleships, planes and personnel that we have lost in welding the country.

A meeting at Juneau's city hall developed local civil defense plans. That evening a trial blackout ensued between 7:00 and 10:00. Then a siren was sounded and a permanent blackout for the night was effected at the request of Commander J.R. Tate of Sitka.[5]

On December 8, Gruening recorded:

The President called Congress, asked for a declaration of state of war, and received an 88 to 0 vote in the Senate and 372 to 1 in the House, Jeannette Rankin alone dissenting. Forty-three minutes after the President had requested it. Received a message from Hinckley asking me to arrange protection for airports. Called in Seeley, and with Ike Taylor and Hesse, went over all airports in Territory, sending out instructions on all those where there is any gas or supplies and where an enemy plane might land.

The days were filled with turmoil, tension, and activity for Gruening. On December 9 he was bombarded with the fact that the blackouts were having a serious economic effect on the residents of Juneau, because it meant closing one shift which then threw workers out of employment.[6]

Added to the stress of the threat of attack and the fact that the United States had declared war on Japan, the Gruenings were faced with personal tragedy. On December 11, Mrs. Gruening received a telegram noti-

[2] Claus-M. Naske and Herman E. Slotnick, *Alaska: History of the 49th State* (Grand Rapids, Michigan: William B. Eerdmans Pub. Co., 1979), p. 110.

[3] Naske, *Alaska*, p. 111.

[4] Naske, *Alaska*, p. 113.

[5] *Diary*, Dec. 7, 1941.

[6] *Diary*, Dec. 9, 1941.

fying her that her father had died, the result of an automobile accident. The notice of the accident, ten days prior to his death, had never reached the Gruenings.[7]

Besides the depressing news received on the radio, Gruening was visited by Major Verbeck of G2 Anchorage. Major Verbeck had recently returned to the United States. He had four years of Japanese military service and had spent part of his childhood in Japan.

Probably as well informed on Japs as any military man, since he served in their Army. Says he knew Japs would fight and has been telling Army men so right along. Says they are much better than our Army and Navy give them credit for and they will give us a stiff battle. Says that plans included raiding of Alaska bases and that aircraft carriers were off the coast but weather was so terrible that it probably prevented planes from leaving carriers (may or may not be true.)[8]

Problems multiplied. It was determined that three schools at Ruby, Naknek, and Paloff Harbor—funded by $68,000 appropriated by the last legislature—could not be built because of priorities and other difficulties incidental to war.[9]

Word was received that certain banks in the states were refusing to honor Alaska checks.[10]

Gruening was also discouraged by the news he received on Dec. 23 as he hosted a party for his office staff and the officers of the ship *Perseus*. Although the *Perseus* was supposed to guard Icy Strait, one of the two important entrances to Southeastern Alaska waters, it had no antiaircraft guns. It had lots of antiaircraft ammunition, and no apparatus for throwing depth charges, but plenty of depth charges.

As he pointed out it is pretty dangerous to throw these charges overboard because you are not sure of getting away fast enough so they don't blow up under you and they are likely to be swept back under you either by tide or wave. The fact is that Alaska is wholly unprepared and if the Japs were to come over here now they could probably take any one of our bases. Sitka has only two planes. Fortunately the weather is against them; they are probably too busy in the southwestern

Pacific, and let us hope that if they do get around to us, we are ready.[11]

And then Tom Dyer, of Standard Oil, reported the serious shortage of oil throughout the territory and the lack of storage facilities near airports. His largest truck carried a thousand gallons of fuel, whereas the capacity of a single bomber is eighteen hundred gallons. A flight of six bombers would require ten round-trips from Juneau to the airport, a total of 180 miles. He further told Gruening that the military authorities had been remiss in not providing covered storage.

Described Sitka situation as such that one hit would destroy the base's entire oil and gas supply. He says one tank is covered but only concealed thereby and not protected against bombs, but next to it in plain sight are two huge fuel tanks—any one of which hit would set off all the others.[12]

In spite of all the pressures, Gruening did take some time for recreation, for he also recorded:
"Went to see Joan Crawford in *A Woman's Face in the Evening*, very good."[13]

Gruening's diary of January 8, 1942, included some interesting information regarding his conversation with Commander J.R. Tate. He told Gruening that the Japanese could easily have taken Dutch Harbor as well as Pearl Harbor if weather had permitted. (See Verbeck's comment earlier in this paper.)

He said we haven't even got ramps out there for our planes. At Sitka the hangars are completed and he could house 24 bombers but all he has are three poor planes only for patrol duty. The amphibian, on which I flew, had a bunch of bombs in the rear which would have to be dumped out of the rear door by hand if an enemy submarine is sighted. None of his planes have any guns... At Kodiak there are only 4 planes. Capt. Park incidentally has gone ashore there. The inadequacy of our present defenses is further indicated by the fact that Tate not only has to patrol all of southeastern Alaska with his three planes, but is supposed to supply convoys for which he has no adequate boats.

---

[7] *Diary*, Dec. 11, 1941.

[8] *Diary*, Dec. 15, 1941.

[9] *Diary*, Dec. 18, 1941.

[10] *Diary*, Dec. 22, 1941.

[11] *Diary*, Dec. 23, 1941.

[12] *Diary*, Dec. 27, 1941.

[13] *Diary*, Dec. 21, 1941.

Along with everything else, many new rules and regulations were instigated. On December 20, Gruening received a wire from Frank Bane of the Office of Price Administration instructing him to institute a tire rationing system: "The wire was as follows: `Due to the impending shortage of rubber supplies the OPA as you know has frozen the sale of all new automobile tires.'"

Rationing and shortages were to become the way of life during World War II. Some directives caused more discontent than others. Gruening was an inveterate tennis player, and his diary the next month indicates his upset: "Got word that automobiles should be frozen, and that no new tennis balls or golf balls will be produced. I can view golf balls with equanimity, but not tennis balls."[14]

The diaries continue with other issues such as his personal visits to communities enlisting local citizens in defense and the establishment of the Alaska Territorial Guard; the problems of returning Alaska residents who were Outside at the outbreak of the war; the censoring of the mail to Alaskans; and many other issues of the time. Unfortunately, Gruening did not continue his diary for a very important period of the war—June 26, 1943, to January 20, 1946. On Jan. 20, 1946, he wrote, "Resuming my diary after a lapse of some years. Various things have brought home to me how extremely useful a diary is."

Fortunately for us he did keep a diary for many of the war years, although he often recorded the events after the fact. These diaries provide us with a record, perspective, and view of Alaska during World War II, through the eyes of its governor, Ernest Gruening.

*David A. Hales is Professor of Library Science and head of the Alaska and Polar Regions Department, Elmer E. Rasmuson Library, University of Alaska Fairbanks.*

---

[14] *Diary*, Jan. 21, 1942.

# Mining the Federal Government: The War and the All-America City

*Stephen Haycox*

THE IMPACT OF WORLD WAR II ON THE WESTERN United States has been much studied by historians. Most have concluded that the effect of the war was enormous, remaking not only the economic, but also the social and political character of the American West. Before the war, the West was economically isolated and underdeveloped, and colonially dependent; it was heavily reliant on natural resource production and there was little industrial development. The war generated considerable economic diversity, and significant self-sufficiency. Not only did mobilization accelerate extractive industries, but it also stimulated new enterprises, including electronics and aerospace—which spawned a host of new service industries in their wake. The principal scholar of this phenomenon, Gerald Nash, of the University of New Mexico, has argued that World War II brought the American West into the twentieth century.[1]

The impact of World War II in Alaska is well known and is related to the war's impact in the West, though because Alaska was even less developed than the West, the impact here was in some ways different. In addition to others, John Nielson, formerly of the University of Alaska in Fairbanks, has compiled this statistical profile: 150,000 troops in the territory by May of 1943, 300,000 different personnel serving in the territory at various times during the war, 300 separate military installations of one kind or another constructed across Alaska (some

of them to be decommissioned literally within months of completion), expenditures totalling at least $300 million for the duration of the war, 67 million acres of land withdrawn in temporary, emergency military reservations.

It is widely understood that in many ways the war changed Alaska forever. The population increase, the expansion of commercial opportunities, the vastly increased reliance on federal spending and the significantly raised level of federal regulation all were recognized at the time and have become the context for the standard interpretation of the war's consequences. As an old-timer told the journalist Joe Driscoll, who was writing dispatches from Alaska in 1943, "The old Alaska is gone; she's wrecked." It was, he said, as bad as being invaded by the enemy.[2]

A study of some aspects of what happened in the town of Anchorage can perhaps provide some insight into the consequences of the war for Alaska. Before World War II, Anchorage was a sleepy little village flung out on the northern frontier of America. Numbering perhaps thirty-five hundred people in 1940, the town was, as it had always been, dependent on the Alaska Railroad. Many had come to Anchorage during the construction of the railroad from other locations in Alaska, many from gold camps which had dried up or had never taken off in the first place. Railroad construction and the government's anticipated development of the

---

[1] See Gerald D. Nash, *The American West Transformed: The Impact of the Second World War* (Bloomington: Indiana University Press, 1985); for Alaska, see John Nielson, *The Military in Alaska's Past* (Westport: Greenwood Press, 1988).

[2] Joseph Driscoll, *War discovers Alaska* (Philadelphia: J.B. Lippincott Co., 1943), p. 122.

Wishbone Hill coal deposits represented jobs and business opportunities. Like many prospects in Alaska, the coal turned out not to be the bonanza it was supposed to be, although some coal was always mined at Eska and Jonesville in the 1920s and 1930s.[3] Mining was the Alaskan thing to do, however, and during this period there was a continuing hope that gold properties in the Crow Creek area to the south and the Hatcher Pass area to the northeast would substitute for Wishbone Hill, a hope which proved futile.

But Anchorage was ideally suited as a service center for Southcentral Alaska, and when it became clear that airplanes would be more than toys of the rich and adventurous, aviation became an important if nascent economic player in the community. Still, the federal government provided the town with the railroad, supplying a monthly payroll that supported many people directly, and trickled down through the commercial sector to many others.[4]

During the Great Depression the government provided new economic support for the town. First, there was the Matanuska colony, a rural rehabilitation project which may have cost the government $200 million by 1942, some small portion of which found its way into Anchorage.[5] Then, in 1936, Public Works Administration loans helped to build a new city hall, a handsome, art deco building which was one of the first major poured-concrete structures in a community that up to that time had been all framed wood and pioneer logs (and that, miraculously, had never burned down). More PWA loans helped fund the paving of some of the downtown streets. The Civilian Conservation Corps—the three Cs—also provided some limited employment. Also, in 1936, the seat of the Third Judicial District was transferred to Anchorage from Valdez, bringing the judge, marshall, clerks of the court, and the district attorney, and a lot of judicial business. Then, in 1939, the government authorized a major federal building which, with a federal jail, would nearly fill an entire city block. And in the same year the Civil Aeronautics Administration established an Alaska division with headquarters in the town.[6]

Socially, Anchorage was ostensibly a classless community. The town was small in population, remote, somewhat isolated, and many people felt that they knew just about everyone else. Many of those who did not take leadership roles were quite aware of those who did, but living in the remote, sometimes harsh, environment created a shared experience and it was on the whole a friendly place.[7] It did not have a lot of money. Unlike most white towns in Alaska, there were very few Natives in the community, and though the Eklutna Indian School was nearby (after 1925), the students there did not get into town often. The town was remarkably unicultural.

A small cadre of businessmen—among them the banker, the druggist, the hosteler, a couple of the principal merchants, the lawyer, and, by the end of the 1930s, the newspaper publisher—provided most of the community leadership and spent a good deal of time trying to think up ways to advance the town.[8] They were dedicated to creating on this frontier as complete a replica of American material and institutional culture as they could, complete with sales outlets for durables and perishables, commercial and nonprofit amenities, including movie theaters and soda shops, a little theater group and a choral society, all the schools, churches, hospitals and fraternal organizations a small town might need, and the playgrounds and summer picnics, too. They had invested in an airplane company in the mid-1920s; they owned the electric generating plant; they had started a golf course on the cleared land which served as combination park strip and landing field, all in hopes of promoting Anchorage as a tourist Mecca; and they encouraged several Alaska wilderness guide ventures for the same reason. Then, in 1940, the U.S. Army handed this group the bonanza they had all been searching for for two decades: it designated Anchorage the headquarters of the militarization of Alaska.

Of course, it was not clear in 1940 just how great a bonanza this decision was going to be. No one knew there would be a Pacific war of the dimension wrought by Japanese expansion. All anyone knew in 1940 was that the Japanese had publicly abrogated the 1921 naval

---

[3] Vincent W. Ponko Jr., "The Alaskan Coal Commission: 1920-1922," *Alaska Journal*, Spring, 1978; William H. Wilson, *Railroad in the Clouds: The Alaska Railroad in the Age of Steam, 1914-1945* (Boulder: Pruett Publishing Co., 1977); "Federal Town Building on the Northern Frontier," *Pacific Northwest Quarterly*, July, 1967; "The Alaska Railroad and Coal," *Pacific Northwest Quarterly*, April, 1982.

[4] Lee J. Cuba, "A Moveable Frontier: Frontier Images in Contemporary Alaska" (doctoral dissertation, Yale University, 1981); a version was published by Temple University Press in 1987.

[5] Orlando W. Miller, *The Frontier in Alaska and the Matanuska Colony* (New Haven: Yale University Press, 1975).

[6] An adequate history of Anchorage remains to be written, though Evangeline Atwood's *Anchorage: All-America City* (Portland: Binford and Mort, 1957) is a useful and important effort. Also very useful is Michael Carberry, *Patterns of the Past: An Inventory of Anchorage's Heritage Resources* (Anchorage: Municipality of Anchorage, 1979). See also transcripts of interviews in *Anchorage Pioneers Oral History Project*, University of Alaska archives in Fairbanks and Anchorage, esp. Robert Atwood and Steve McCutcheon.

[7] *Anchorage Pioneers Oral History Project* (APOHP), memoir of John Bagoy.

[8] Atwood, *Anchorage*, APOHP, memoir of Robert Atwood.

The U.S. Chamber of Commerce named Anchorage an All-America city in 1956. The banner appeared in virtually every photograph and article on Alaska as the territory campaigned for statehood. The title was conferred again in 1965 and 1985. *(RG 77, National Archives Alaska Region)*

disarmament treaty, and that they had made clear their intentions in China, Manchuria, and Korea. That, and the invasion of Poland, though, were enough for Congress to heed the remonstrances of military strategists and to authorize the beginning of Alaska's defense. At least one surviving member of Anchorage's leadership elite takes credit today for Anchorage's being selected as the army headquarters. When army surveyors visited the community, he relates, the town rolled out the welcome mat and outdid themselves in selling Anchorage's civic and strategic attractions.[9] Anchorage was indeed the most logical site: it was the central air location in the territory; it was reasonably close to port facilities (Whittier, Seward) and had some port potential of its own; communication from there to the states was relatively easy; and it was the central logistic location for the northern Pacific rim which had at least a few of the amenities which the officer corps, and perhaps even some of the enlisted personnel, might appreciate. And the townspeople were an eager and likeable lot. Had they not been, the army still likely would have picked Anchorage, but these things are never certain until they are done.

The first troops arrived in Seward in the summer of 1940, and a comfortably gradual, if slow, construction of the military establishment began. Anchorage basked in its new role as army town and the payroll that came with it. Businesses thrived, and the social elite had a new round of contacts to entertain and befriend. Not all the changes were easy. A number of the military kids in the school did not perform well, and some thought they served as a bad influence.[10] General Simon Buckner, the defense commander, endeared himself to the city leadership by challenging federal fish and wildlife officials on the issue of resident hunting licenses for his men, and by demanding that the prostitute's "line" along Ninth Avenue east of C Street be dispersed (which it was, right into the community). But, generally speaking, all was optimism.[11]

This pleasant picture was shattered, of course, on December 7, 1941. The war in Alaska divides into three rather distinct phases. The first lasted from December 1941 to June 1942, and was characterized by a great deal of panic. Military planners had to make a military bas-

tion where there had been none. There was not enough of anything, and there was a sense that everything had to be done at once. Most of the three hundred installations built in Alaska during the war were constructed, or at least begun, in this short seven-month period. They included not only the headquarters and staging bases, but forward bases, supply depots, reconnaissance facilities, and even contingency installations for emergencies. There were, for example, garrisoned airfields built not only in such places as Galena and Nome, but also at Tanacross and Gulkana, deep in the Interior.[12]

The second phase was the planning for the reconquest of the Aleutian Islands. After June 1942 and the failure of the Japanese at Midway, it was clear that Japan's Aleutian campaign was both a diversion and an overreach. The threat of harassing air strikes was real enough, but the army and navy had done their jobs well, and by June of 1942, as much as the Japanese actually did was as much as they could do. The American victory in the Battle of the Komandorski Islands in March of 1943 sealed the doom of the Japanese force in Alaska, and, after the very bloody battle of Attu, the Alaska theater settled down in abject boredom to wait for the end of the war.[13]

The third phase was demobilization, which began in 1944 (in time for General Buckner to get to Okinawa, where he was killed).

Safe but exotic, Alaska was a great venue for the USO. There was plenty of time to cultivate one's affinities, as Dashiell Hammett demonstrated by publishing the Alaska edition of *Stars and Stripes*, and Gore Vidal by penning his first novel, *Williwaw.*

Anchorage, of course, was overwhelmed by the war. Men—and some women—and matériel poured into town as water from a flooding torrent. By mid-1943, according to military sources, the Anchorage area population was more than twenty-five thousand, a phenomenal growth in eighteen months. Activity was frenetic as the town burst its seams for good. Predictably, shortages were chronic. Housing for both people and goods was a nightmare. Townspeople were naturally, instantly and wholeheartedly patriotic. The mayor's wife and a number of other wives dutifully fled the territory at the

---

[9] APOHP, memoir of Robert Atwood.

[10] APOHP, memoirs of Lorene Harrison, Lucy McDannel Whitehead, and Charles and Molly Tryck.

[11] Buckner's challenge to USF&WS (and its notion of the limitations on the Alaska environment) is covered in Morgan Sherwood, *Big Game in Alaska: A History of Wildlife and People* (New Haven: Yale University Press, 1981); the existence of prostitution in the community was apparently widely known and accepted as a fact of the community's life, if not an expression of its moral aspiration; see APOHP, memoirs of Steve McCutcheon, John Bagoy, and Frank Paul.

[12] James Bush, Colonel (CE), *Military Installations in Alaska* (n.pl.: US Army Corps of Engineers, 1944).

[13] In addition to Nielson, *The Military in Alaska's Past,* see Brian Garfield, *The Thousand-Mile War: World War II in Alaska and the Aleutians* (New York: Doubleday & Co., 1969').

army's urging.[14] Those who stayed, and there were many, cooperated with blackouts and accepted what little rationing there was stoically. The social elite tried to ease the tension felt by officers who were over-frustrated with having to do too much too fast with too little, and the women who stayed behind helped to ease the frustration of the enlisted men by staffing the USO club and boosting morale.[15]

As the war progressed, however, Anchorage businessmen realized that they had succeeded beyond their wildest dreams, for war brought many more of the earmarks of the western culture that would allow the townspeople to think of themselves as fully modern and up-to-date. The water, light, telephone, and sewage systems were upgraded; the War Labor Board ran an employment bureau; newspaper circulation climbed beyond the capacity of the outdated

Troops march through downtown Anchorage during the Fourth of July Parade in 1940. *(Russ Dow Collection, Command Historian's Office, Alaskan Command)*

press. Everywhere there was an abundance of what the townspeople had learned to call progress, for the money flowed like rain. Civilian retailers could not get many of the goods they wanted, to be sure, but sold everything they had as fast as they could get it. Everything was for sale, and all of it went for premium prices—so much so that Buckner had to call a meeting of the leading economic elite to remind them not to "slay the golden goose." The urge to make a killing while the market was hot was more than most people could resist, naturally.[16] The Office of Price Administration even had to step in and establish a fee schedule in the relocated "hook shops," where prewar prices prevailed for pre-war regulars—prices that quadrupled for new arrivals.[17] Everyone, it seems, had struck gold. Those Anchorage pioneers who bet their grubstakes on the federal government had guessed right, or had just lucked out. It was an El Dorado the likes of which had never been seen in the Great Land before.

Astonishingly, prosperity continued after the war. At first there was some anxiety. The population in 1946 was probably about fifteen thousand. The first demobilization in 1944 had barely been felt, partly because some goods which had been unavailable suddenly began to come through, and there was a lot of pent-up cash in the city. But with war's end, people held their breath to see what would happen. Remarkably, it was nothing. Government largesse continued to flow, with only the briefest hesitation. Some men who left the territory at war's end were called back within several months.[18] The military moved immediately to shift from a war-time, emergency basis to a permanent defensive profile, a change which was well underway when the War Department was reorganized in 1947. By then, too, the Cold War had begun. Alaska would be central to strategic defense from 1949, when the Soviet Union became an atomic power, until sometime in the 1960s, when missile and satellite technology superseded the long-range bomber as America's principal defensive weapon. The population of the Anchorage bowl would approach thirty thousand by 1950, at the outbreak of the Korean War. Anchorage soon acquired its B-36 runway, and while many smaller army installations were decommissioned, the larger ones underwent major expansion. At the same time, numerous federal agencies upgraded their Alaska operations. These included the B.I.A., the C.A.A., the U.S. Forest Service, the National Park Service, and, of course, the Alaska Railroad. The money continued to flow.[19]

Anchorage's economic and social elite could take little credit for the federal government's commitment to Anchorage; it was in reality a function of raised perceptions about Alaska and a growing sense that a new period in the territory's development was at hand.[20] But city fathers and mothers moved quickly to take advantage of it. Already during the war a utility district had been established, and in September 1945 the South

[14] APOHP, memoir of William and Lillie Stolt; Stolt was mayor of Anchorage in 1942.

[15] APOHP, memoirs of Lorene Harrison, Robert Atwood, and Molly Tryck.

[16] Driscoll, *War Discovers Alaska.*

[17] APOHP, memoir of Steve McCutcheon.

[18] APOHP, memoir of John Zappa.

[19] See Wilson, *Railroad in the Clouds.*

Addition became the city's first annexation. Fairview and Mountain View grew like Topsy after the war, and a number of people who would be major players in the next stage of the town's development, among them Walter J. Hickel, got their start in the postwar boom—Mr. Hickel by building duplexes in what became Fairview.[21] Not long after the war, homesteads were opened with a veterans' preference, and to the southwest of the town, Colonel Marvin "Muktuk" Marston acquired land which he would develop into a residential suburbia, betting that the federal pocketbook would continue to pour.[22] In the spring of 1946 the town voted in a city-manager form of local government and in the summer the city council adopted the first set of zoning ordinances. The town was big enough now that regular air service was begun between Anchorage and Minneapolis in 1947, and the international airport, another federal program, opened in 1951.

From 1950 to 1953 the Korean War brought still more boom times to Anchorage, as did all the construction associated with the Cold War, including the Distant Early Warning radar net and the White Alice troposphere communications radar system, two stories which have been told many times. Remarkably, and surely unpredictably, the merry-go-round continued. By 1960, area population was close to seventy thousand.

Not all the impact was positive, certainly, for despite having hired a city planner, the town could not keep up with its growth. Housing was a continuing problem,

and government agencies, most notably the new Federal Aviation Administration, built their own. The problem of "juvenile delinquency" was so great that federal hearings were held on the matter in the mid-1950s.[23] At the same time, the territorial police, the F.B.I., and the municipal constabulary formed a crime task force to combat the high incidence of alcohol abuse, drug sales, fights

Fourth Avenue, Anchorage, ca. 1941. *(Frank Boyd Collection, Command Historian's Office, Alaskan Command)*

and muggings in the Eastchester area, where most of the night clubs were positioned, just south of the city limits.[24]

But clearly World War II and then its aftermath had accomplished for Anchorage what its early elite had only dreamed of, a permanent, large, and thriving city which would replicate all the cultural attributes of mainstream America. In 1954, a committee of the chamber of commerce began a drive to demonstrate that Anchorage was as good as any other American town—a quest to be

[20] The National Resources Planning Council published a major report on Alaska in 1938. In 1941 the Interior Department embarked on a major planning effort for Alaska, one of the first major aspects of which was the determination of Native land claims; see David S. Case, *American Natives and American Laws* (Fairbanks: University of Alaska Press, 1984); see also Stephen W. Haycox, "Economic Development and Indian Land Rights in Modern Alaska: The 1947 Tongass Timber Act," *Western Historical Quarterly*, February, 1990.

[21] APOHP, memoirs of John Bagoy and Charles Brewster. Emil Pfiel was the first contractor to begin building in Fairview after World War II; Hickel, to whom he offered a partnership, soon outstripped him in the quantity and diversity of his enterprises.

[22] Marston's experiences in World War II are told in his autobiography, *Men of the Tundra: Eskimos at War* (New York: October House, 1969).

[23] U.S. Congress, Senate, "Juvenile Delinquency in Alaska," Senate Report 2774, 84th Cong., 2nd Sess., 1956.

[24] Gerald O. Williams, *Alaska State Troopers: 50 Years of History* (Anchorage: Alaska State Troopers Golden Anniversary Committee, 1991), pp. 37 fol.

named by the U.S. Chamber of Commerce as an All-America City. In the application, Evangeline Atwood included a historical profile of the town which she would later embellish in her book *Anchorage: All-America City.*

By the time the book was published, Anchorage had an automatic telephone system, home mail delivery, a new high school, a community college, a commitment to build a private four-year college, and a host of other amenities which made Anchorage appear in text to be just like all of small-town America: wholesome, progressive, safe, growing, and confident. The coveted All-American banner was awarded the town in 1956 and hung over Fourth Avenue downtown for two years, thus appearing in virtually every photograph which accompanied any article on Alaska and its campaign for statehood, which surfaced in the later 1950s.

Alaskans pride themselves on their self-reliance, their independent spirit, their rugged individualism, and they make something of a fetish of proclaiming their ability to provide for themselves and to manage their own affairs, and of their distrust of government, especially the federal government. It is their greater independence of spirit, many would argue, which makes them unique—better, really, than most folks elsewhere, Outside, where few Alaskans would profess to wish to live. Yet if Alaska is unique, and if its people are more independent and distrustful of the federal government, a proclamation which many Anchorageites are quick to make, whether they have lived in the city fifty years or fifty days, it would be hard to prove their uniqueness or their greater independence by tracing the history of their town. For Anchorage was born of the federal government, weaned and nurtured by it, grew to maturity at its table, and found its economic and civil "takeoff" in the Second World War, along with most of the rest of the western U.S. And all the while, Anchorageites complained as loudly as other Alaskans about the inhibiting and limiting effects of federal power, but—while complaining—learning to mine the federal treasury for the town's livelihood and progress, and to welcome each new federal establishment as a stepping stone on the way to a brighter future. Only after 1968 did Anchorage cozy up to the new guy in town, Mr. P.,[25] and raise to a new level its continuing wail about the federal presence in Alaska's affairs, a presence which made it possible for Anchorage, at least, to realize its dearest aspirations, a re-creation on this frontier of the material and cultural heartbeat of America.[26]

There is a marvelous incongruity, then, between the mythology of Anchorage independence, at least, and the reality of historic reliance on federal largesse, an incongruity which is only one of the things that makes Anchorage such a fascinating place to be.

*Stephen Haycox has taught history at the University of Alaska in Anchorage for twenty-four years. His interests are the history of Alaska and the American West. He has published widely in professional journals and has won awards for social and political commentary on Anchorage public radio.*

---

[25] The story of petroleum development is told in John Strohmeyer, *Extreme Conditions: Big Oil and the Transformation of Alaska* (New York: Simon and Schuster, 1993); an important environmental history of the Alaska pipeline is Peter A. Coates' *The Trans-Alaska Pipeline Controversy: Technology, Conservation, and the Frontier* (Bethlehem: Lehigh University Press, 1991).

[26] On the general topic of the romanticizing of Alaska history, see Stephen Haycox, "Unmasking the Dead Hero: Myth and Alaska History," in Sharon Araji, ed., *Sociology: An Alaskan Reader* (New York: Kendall-Hall, 1994).

# The Salmon Industry
# at War

*Bob King*

DURING WORLD WAR II THE ALASKA SALMON industry found itself positioned next to a major theater of war. The conflict not only hindered the salmon canners, then the largest industry in the territory, but increased wartime demand for food and also provided a needed, but short-term, financial boost to a depressed industry. Ultimately, the war contributed to the growth and modernization of the industry and prompted significant changes in regional employment patterns. But the war also contributed to a general decline in the industry by exacerbating existing weaknesses in fishery management, which in turn contributed to a decline in salmon production.

In 1942, federal fishery biologist Joseph Barnaby was counting salmon swimming toward their spawning streams in Bristol Bay while overhead he watched P-38s, P-40s, and giant Douglas bombers thundering toward the Aleutians.

"There is, of course, a certain amount of inconvenience," Barnaby wrote of the fighting just a few hundred miles away, "but that is to be expected. As for the war itself, no one seems to be very excited about it, at least insofar as the possibility of our being bombed or

invaded. The possibility of air raids seems somewhat improbable to me."[1]

Many who were employed in the Alaska fishing industry during World War II tend to understate those years. Perhaps understandably so. Though the war came as close as the Aleutians, the fighting never directly affected the industry. Though there were, as Barnaby noted, certain inconveniences, they were trivial compared to those involved in the full fury of the conflict. Still, World War II was an event that touched everyone's lives and the conflict had major impacts on the fishing industry, both direct and indirect. World War II would prove to be, in the words of one, a "distinctive epoch in salmon history."[2]

In the 1930s, the canned salmon industry was to Alaska what the oil industry is today. Commercial fishing— mainly salmon canning—was the largest employer in Alaska, operating from the Southeast Panhandle to Bristol Bay. The fishing industry also contributed 81 percent of the territory's tax revenues.[3]

Yet the industry was also at a standstill. Canneries, many of which dated back to the turn of the century, still operated using the same methods and equipment as before. In Bristol Bay, the territory's premier fishing

---

[1] Joseph Barnaby, Associate to Aquatic Biologist, in a letter to Frank W. Hynes, Deputy Fishery Management Agent, dated Bristol Bay, July 20, 1942, U.S. Archives, Anchorage, Fish and Wildlife Service RG-22-5. Barnaby's identification of the bombers as Douglas's may have been incorrect.

[2] Ralph Silliman, 1962, "Problems of the North Pacific Fisheries," U.S. Fish and Wildlife Service Archives, RG-22-5/64, p. 2. This document is a briefing paper on the political and economic problems facing the domestic fishing industry from foreign high seas exploitation of salmon.

[3] "Where Alaska Gets its Revenues," *Pacific Fisherman*, April, 1933. The figure is attributed to Governor George A. Parks in a message to the territorial legislature. Most of the revenues came from a case tax on the canner's pack, an excise tax on earnings, plus various levies on fishing boats and gear.

area, fishermen still worked from sailboats. A decade of depression had left the industry financially weakened. The trade journal *Pacific Fisherman* noted:

> Costs continuing on a relatively high plane, combined with declining prices, made 1938 a year of little profit in the canned salmon industry and losses to a great many; while more difficulties and vexations arose in relation to labor than in any previous year.... Because of this there is considerable discouragement among the packers and a rather drastic retrenchment on the part of the industry at large is looked upon as a distinct possibility.[4]

The malaise that had beset the salmon industry was evident even in their 1939 generic marketing campaign, which included banners proclaiming, "Hooray for Lent!"[5]

In the later thirties, however, the salmon industry was awakened by the drumbeats of the impending Pacific war. In 1937, the Japanese shocked the American fishing industry with demands to allow them to fish in the salmon-rich waters of Bristol Bay.

To the Japanese, fishing rights were their due. T. Takasaki, the managing director of Toyo Seikan Kaisha, Ltd., told American canners that "the spacious colonies held by some powers should be given up to the overcrowded nations in order to make better and fairer distribution of natural resources."[6]

American salmon canners were incensed. A banner headline in *Pacific Fisherman* read, "Japanese Intention To Invade Alaska Salmon Fisheries Is Openly Declared."[7] The rhetoric heated up even further when the Japanese claimed the fish-rich waters of the Bering Sea to be "an extension of the Bay of Tokyo."[8]

Japanese vessels were sighted catching salmon off Ugashik in 1937. Diplomatic efforts thwarted their ultimate plans, but few in the fishing industry were surprised when the Japanese later invaded the Aleutians.

"Encroachment of Japanese expeditions upon the American fisheries of the Aleutian Islands was among the bits of evidence which pointed to the predatory intentions of Nippon," noted the *Pacific Fisherman*. "The fisheries of the Pacific are one of the prizes for which Japan gambled when she precipitated war in the Pacific."[9]

Also aware of the Japanese threat, the U.S. military had begun to prepare well before Pearl Harbor was attacked. Large airstrips were built at King Salmon and Cold Bay in 1941. To mask the buildup, construction equipment was shipped from Seattle under the cover of the "Consolidated Packing Company," a fictitious salmon cannery.[10]

By that time, of course, war was already raging in Europe, creating a strong demand for salmon among our allies. The United States began to stockpile salmon for use in the lend-lease program and for its own purposes. Government purchases of salmon became a significant factor in 1940 and increased to as much as 80 percent of the pack later in the war. In neighboring British Columbia, the entire salmon pack was dedicated to the war effort.

Canned salmon was in demand since it was an excellent source of protein, easily stored and transported and could be served in a variety of forms, even eaten right out of the can.

Salmon, *Pacific Fisherman* touted, "possesses what it takes to satisfy the taste and body demands of vigorous, young men such as we find in the Army."[11]

The 1941 edition of "The Army Cook" contained the following recipe for salmon cakes:

> 20 cans salmon, 1-lb cans
> 30 lbs potatoes, mashed
> 20 eggs
> 2 lbs cracker or bread crumbs
> 2 lbs fat
> Mix well, season to taste with salt and pepper, form in three-inch cakes, roll in flour and fry in deep fat. Serve hot with tomato sauce. (Serves 100)

While fresh fish was also said to be popular with the troops, the trade journal for the Pacific salmon canners noted, somewhat self-servingly, "the canned product lends itself more generally to distribution and use under ... actual combat conditions."[12]

---

[4] *Pacific Fisherman*, 1939 Yearbook, p. 55.

[5] *Pacific Fisherman*, 1939 Yearbook. P. 56. The generic marketing campaign was carried out by Canned Salmon Industry, Inc., which represented producers of 90 percent of the American salmon pack.

[6] *Pacific Fisherman*, March, 1937, p. 9. The magazine notes, however, that "some slight liberties have been taken with the original English translation" of Takasaki's remarks, "in the interest of clearness and idiomatic expression."

[7] Ibid.

[8] *Pacific Fisherman*, May, 1937, p. 19.

[9] *Pacific Fisherman*, 1943 Yearbook, p. 35.

[10] Brian Garfield, *The Thousand-Mile War: World War II in Alaska and the Aleutians* (Garden City, N.Y.: Doubleday, 1969), p. 64.

[11] Quoted in "Fish Dishes are Popular with U.S. Army," *Pacific Fisherman*, 1942 Yearbook, p. 274.

[12] Ibid.

In an advertisement that appeared in *Pacific Fisherman's* 1943 yearbook, the Fish Net & Twine Company of Jersey City, New Jersey, wove together a metaphor of nets, war, and victory. This caption appeared below the ad: " No one likes war. Loved ones are taken from us ... some never to return and others to suffer painful wounds in far off lands across the seas. 'Business as usual' takes a back seat in times like these and nowhere is it any more apparent than in your own affairs. Many of you have turned over your boats to the service and are ashore for the duration, hard at work in war industry ... others, and there are many, are in uniform fighting the good fight on the sea, on the land and in the air. To you who remain on the home front in the fisheries we promise, as we have promised fishermen in other wars, that consistent with the demands of our country's armed forces for our materials, facilities and labor, we will continue to give you fish nets and fittings of top quality. Your catches were never more vital than now. Let us all pull together ... to bring the Victory to which we all look forward. Let's net the conspirators.

By 1941, the financial health of the American canning industry had improved dramatically. Sales were strong and prices high. The wholesale price of canned sockeye salmon jumped 30 percent from the preceding year to $12.48 for a case of forty-eight one-pound cans.[13] When the retail price of a can of salmon also jumped 30 percent, the industry had to answer to charges of profiteering.[14] The industry insisted that even with the price increases, they still were not making money. After a decade of depression, however, the 1940s brought a wel-

---

[13] Average case pack prices were reported annually by the U.S. Department of Commerce, (and later the U.S. Fish and Wildlife Service) in the "Alaska Fisheries and Fur Seal Industries" report (AF&FSI). See year cited. Prices paid fishermen similarly increased. In Bristol Bay, red salmon prices increased from 14.25 cents per fish before the war to 20.33 cents during the war.

[14] *Pacific Fisherman*, 1940 Yearbook, p. 103, in an article by Henry Seaborn, of Skinner and Eddy. The retail price increase from 9 and 10 cents a can to 13 cents is quoted from a letter written by an unnamed irate consumer in California. The species of salmon and can size in question were not identified. The species was obviously not sockeye; probably the unit in question was a half-pound can of a lower cost species such as pink or chum. Still the consumer's anger is noteworthy: "You will learn that the reaction from this graft will not be what you wish. I am not the only one who will drop your product. We do not admire such great patriotism as you are exhibiting. You may call it good business, but we call it absolutely contemptible."

come change in fortune for the canned salmon industry.

"About the only problem that confronts the seller of salmon today is where to obtain the salmon," exclaimed Henry Seaborn of the Skinner and Eddy company.[15] It took a British salmon importer, Colonel Richard Bell-Irving, to remind the American canners of the gravity of the escalating situation:

> As the life of industry in general on this continent is so dependent on the defeat of the evil forces now rampant in Europe and elsewhere, it is desirable for all industrialists to raise their sights and consider the immediate future in its broadest aspects. How many realize that not only our businesses, but our very lives depend on the successful outcome of this conflict?[16]

The industry realized the seriousness of conflict after the bombing of Pearl Harbor. Like other American industries, the fishing industry heartily embraced the war effort. Some fishermen renamed their boats along wartime themes, including *Pearl Harbor, General MacArthur,* and *Victory.* Canners in the Lower 48 packed C-rations and can manufacturers on the West Coast retooled their plants to build everything from ammunition boxes to torpedoes. Industry advertisements frequently featured wartime themes. The Columbia River Packers' Association depicted cannery crews as "war workers on the food front," while the American Can Company, in a fictional letter to a soldier, said, "Write this in your helmet, Bud: Whatever the United Stated asks of it, the American can manufacturing industry will lay on the line."[17]

"The salmon packers now have the opportunity to combine patriotic duty with vastly increased profits," noted federal biologist Frank Hynes, "and with these incentives, it is highly unlikely that anything short of actual enemy invasion will stop them."[18]

Such an invasion came close on June 3, 1942, when the Japanese bombed Dutch Harbor. The bombing occurred as Bristol Bay processors were just gearing up for the salmon season, but that year's effort had already been reduced. Emergency measures put in effect after the bombing of Pearl Harbor had forced many packers, including the largest canning company in the bay, the Alaska Packers Association (APA), to suspend their operations for the season.

The six canneries that operated in Bristol Bay in 1942 comprised the smallest processing effort there since 1898. In order to allocate the limited shipping and manpower, the government imposed the "Cannery Concentration Program" the following season, allowing only about half the canneries in Bristol Bay to operate.

Similar restrictions were also in place in Southeast and central Alaska, but since they were farther away from the conflict, the constraints were less restrictive than in western Alaska.

Wartime conditions had the potential to dramatically alter salmon production in Alaska. Restrictions on the industry could have reduced the pack or, conversely, increased demand and reduced federal oversight of the fisheries, thus bringing about even greater catches. Both instances, in fact, occurred.

The Bristol Bay catch in 1942 was reduced significantly by cannery closures due to the war, with only 6.3 million salmon caught that year.[19] Given excellent escapements reported for the run's parent years, the catch could have exceeded twenty million reds. Fishing operations were also limited that year by wartime restrictions on the Alaska Peninsula and Kodiak. Production from western and central Alaska increased in the latter years of the war as the industry stabilized under the Cannery Concentration Program.

Federal fishery managers, meanwhile, were aware of the potential for over-exploitation of the salmon runs, but took a cautious approach. Ward T. Bower of the U.S. Fish and Wildlife Service summed up their management philosophy during the war:

> Although seasonal ... restrictions were adjusted wherever possible to permit maximum utilization consistent with conservation of the resource, emphasis has been placed on the fact that there will be continuing great need and demand for Alaska fishery products throughout the period of the war and in the post war era ... thus, wherever there was a question as between conservation and exploitation, it was resolved in the favor of conservation.[20]

Indeed, the Egegik River, one of four fishing districts in Bristol Bay, was closed for three years during the war

---

[15] *Pacific Fisherman,* 1941 Yearbook, p. 111.

[16] Ibid, p. 121.

[17] *Pacific Fisherman,* 1943 yearbook, advertising insert, page 160b. The CRPA advertisement is on p. 160e.

[18] U.S. Fish and Wildlife Service, 1942, "Bristol Bay Annual Report," p. 10.

[19] AF&FSI, 1942. Federal fishery managers noted, "as the fishing effort was only about 25 percent of normal, full advantage could not be taken of the runs."

[20] AF&FSI, 1943, p. 2.

in order to restore chronic weak returns. Still, compromises were made, such as in Bristol Bay in 1945 when "government authorities felt that the area should be closed entirely but, since the military need of canned salmon was urgent, it was decided to permit limited operation."[21]

Another instance came in 1941, shortly after the government began its purchases for canned salmon. In July of that year, when it became apparent that the Bristol Bay's catch of red salmon would be unexpectedly weak, prices for canned pink salmon were bid up from $1.65 to $2.00 per dozen. When an exceptionally strong run appeared in Southeast Alaska later that month, fishermen caught a record sixty million pinks.

Although the level of Southeast Alaska pink escapement was termed "adequate," it unquestionably fell far below the 50 percent level mandated by federal law. The eventual production from the record run was the poorest return in more than a decade.

Overall, Alaska salmon production during the war showed a marked reduction from the preceding years. Catches during the war averaged eighty million salmon annually, down from ninety-four million during the four preceding years.

The decline in production cannot be attributed entirely to wartime restriction of the industry. "Although the effects of war contributed to the restricted pack, this was a minor factor," noted *Pacific Fisherman*. "The industry was prepared to produce a normal or better volume, but the fish were simply not available."[22]

However, neither can this decline in run strength be blamed entirely on the war. An overall downward trend in Alaska salmon production was apparent even before the war began. The first notable run failure occurred in Bristol Bay in 1919.

Biologists Charles Gilbert and Henry O'Malley investigated the run collapse and put the blame squarely on a lack of regulation of the industry.

"Unless effective governmental control can be secured to prevent further invasion of a district which already suffers the evil results of unrestricted competition, certain disaster will befall the salmon fisheries of Alaska," they warned.[23]

The White Act, passed in 1924, provided for somewhat greater regulation of the industry, but enforcement was haphazard at best and the industry routinely ignored provisions of the law. Cyclic weaknesses in Bristol Bay run strength were apparent throughout the twenties and thirties. Overall Alaska salmon production continued to decline even after the war.

Whether the war contributed to that biological decline in run strength is debatable. Salmon returns normally fluctuate within a wide range, based on a variety of natural factors over which the industry and government have no control. Certainly, however, the factors blamed for earlier run failures, specifically a lack of management control and fisheries enforcement, were apparent during the war. The number of stream guards, patrol boats and escapement counting weirs were sharply reduced. Wartime conditions exacerbated pre-existing problems bearing on Alaska's salmon runs.

Government demands on the salmon industry were both a help and a hindrance during the war. Government purchases provided a stable market that paid premium prices, but the military also needed much of the fishing industry's fleet. All along the Pacific coast hundreds of fishing vessels were commandeered by the government for use as patrol boats and minesweepers. Many of these "Yippy" boats, so named for their military designation YP, were the large tuna clippers and sardine seiners that fished out of California. In some cases, the vessel's crew was conscripted along with the boat in order that it could be put into immediate use.

In Alaska, 233 vessels were commandeered during the war.[24] Although that included some seiners, most Alaska fishing boats were too small to be of use to the military. Cannery tenders and salmon scows, however, were in demand to move men and matériel in the Aleutian campaign. Some were never returned.[25] Other vessels did not survive the conflict. Pacific American Fisheries' steamer *Clevedon* was destroyed by an explosion and fire on January 12, 1942, while under charter to the army. The SS *Ogontz*, a floating cannery operated by Intercoastal Packing Company in Bristol Bay, was sold for use as a transport ship and was later reported to have been sunk by enemy action.

Meanwhile, salmon packers had to contend with a variety of wartime restrictions, such as restricted use of radios and limited availability of such essentials as rope. Military shipping lane restrictions interfered with fish

---

[21] *Pacific Fisherman*, 1946 Yearbook, p. 83. Federal biologists noted in AF&FSI, 1945, that "indications are that the ... pack was made at the expense of the escapement."

[22] *Pacific Fisherman*, 1944 Yearbook, p. 39.

[23] Charles Gilbert and Henry O'Malley, 1919, "Special Investigation of Salmon Fishery in Central and Western Alaska," in Alaska Fisheries and Fur Industries report for 1919 to the Commissioner of Fisheries, p. 143.

[24] *Pacific Fisherman*, 1944 Yearbook, p. 93.

[25] A detailed listing of vessels used by the military and their postwar status is contained in the archives of Edward W. Allen, University of Washington, Accession 129, Box 22, under "Alaska Salmon Industry." Some of the vessels were reported to be "adrift in ice (lost)."

trap operations. Limited availability of shipping was a major problem for salmon canners, as was a lack of manpower.

Although salmon was considered an important wartime commodity, the conflict sharply reduced the labor pool as cannery workers were called away to the fighting or other defense industries. Cannery workers of Japanese origin, a group which constituted 20 to 25 percent of the labor force prior to the war, were prohibited from entering the territory.[26] The lack of labor was felt most acutely in western Alaska, thereby affording Native Alaskans more opportunity to work.

Prior to the war, Native hire at Bristol Bay canneries was virtually nonexistent. While canneries bought fish from as many as three hundred Native fishermen—mostly setnetters—fewer than two hundred cannery jobs went to Natives, an average of just 4 percent of the industry's labor needs.

The change brought on by the war was dramatic. In 1942, 57 percent of cannery jobs in Bristol Bay were held by Natives, mostly women. The percentage dropped after manpower levels were stabilized by the War Manpower Commission's "Alaska Canned Salmon Plan" in 1943, but the actual number of Natives hired by the industry continued to grow. Overall Native hire at Bristol Bay canneries more than doubled during the war, and doubled again during the post-war reconstruction of the industry. In terms of real employment, the change created fifteen hundred jobs annually for Natives in western Alaska.

The early years of the war presented an unusual situation in Bristol Bay. With plenty of jobs and high pay, residents of Dillingham and Naknek found themselves with a surplus of cash, but since local merchants could not restock their store shelves, they had nowhere to spend it.

Native-hire patterns elsewhere in Alaska, however, showed a different pattern. In both Southeast and central Alaska, Native employment held fairly steady before and during the war years and actually dropped a few percentage points in following years. In terms of real jobs, however, the overall number of Natives employed in both regions held fairly constant throughout the period.

Several reasons for the difference suggest themselves. Both Southeast and central Alaska Natives had a longer history of contact with non-Natives. Western Alaska packers had long indicated a desire to hire more Alaska Natives but claimed them to be unwilling. The demands

of cannery work likely conflicted with the traditional subsistence lifestyle of most Native residents, especially in Bristol Bay, where the fishing season is very short.

Additionally, there were marked differences within the industry itself in the various regions. While Bristol Bay was dominated by a few large packing companies (principally the APA and Libby, McNeill and Libby), there was a much larger number of smaller operators in central and Southeastern Alaska.

Immediately after the war, a major rebuilding effort took place within the Alaska salmon industry. Millions of dollars were spent rebuilding and modernizing canneries. Some plants that were closed under the cannery concentration program, however, never reopened. In Bristol Bay, the APA's Diamond X and M canneries and the Alaska Salmon Cannery on Wood River were immediate victims of the war. Closure of the CRPA's combined flats cannery and the APA's Diamond J came not long afterward. Benefitting from the improved transportation provided by the new military airport at King Salmon, Naknek area canneries flourished while those along Kvichak river were gradually closed down.

The industry also took immediate advantage of new technology. The use of floating processors was greatly expanded after the war, many built on surplus hulls.[27] Among them was *Pacific Queen*, a 165-foot freezer ship built from a surplus army salvage vessel, and the processing vessel *Neva*, a 328-foot floating cannery and freezer ship built from a converted LST.

Some war surplus vessels remain in use today. The landlocked *Star of Kodiak* in Kodiak and the *Unisea*, recently moved from Dutch Harbor to Saint Paul, are both converted Liberty ships. North Coast Seafoods' *Polar Bear*, a cash buyer that operates in Bristol Bay, is a converted submarine net tender.

The growth of the freezer ship fleet represented a major change for the canned salmon industry and hastened the closure of some shore-based plants.

Neither were fishermen denied the benefits of wartime developments. Immediately after the war, fishermen began taking advantage of such wartime innovations as radar and sonar. Tuna clippers pioneered the use of helicopters for spotting fish. In Bristol Bay, however, fishermen were still working from sailboats. Pressure to allow powered vessels into the bay increased dramatically after the war. The arguments of fishermen often bristled with wartime rhetoric.

"If the Congress continues to countenance our being forced to continue fishing in outmoded sailboats, they

---

[26] From minutes of a meeting of the Alaska Salmon Industry in Seattle, January 19, 1942, Alaska Packers Association Records, Alaska State Library, Ms.9 Box 10.

[27] *Pacific Fisherman*, 1952 yearbook, p. 141. "It is significant that none of the freezerships have been built for the purpose. All have been converted. Two of them were Army FP vessels; two were ART tugs; one was a submarine net-tender; one was a Bureau of Indian Affairs Arctic craft, which also took the last Byrd expedition to the Antarctic."

ought to give the army bows and arrows and the navy dugout canoes instead of the billions they're getting now for the A-bomb," argued Hans Hansen of the Alaska Fishermen's Union.[28] Over the industry's objections, power boats were finally allowed into Bristol Bay beginning in 1951.

The events of the war and the pre-war Japanese incursion into Bristol Bay shocked the American fishing industry into adopting a more global posture. Even before the war had ended, the fishing industry discussed the idea of extending U.S. jurisdiction from three miles offshore to two hundred miles. While the Magnuson Act was years away, revival of the Japanese mothership fishery in the Bering Sea prompted negotiation of the International North Pacific Fisheries Convention in 1952.

The war had major impacts on some smaller Alaska fisheries. The Aleutian herring fishery was closed after the bombing of Dutch Harbor and did not reopen until the late 1970s. Cod fishing in the Bering Sea was suspended in 1943 and was slow to recover. American whaling in the Pacific ended during the war years, although the industry was in decline even before fighting erupted. The American Pacific Whaling Company's plant at Port Hobron near Kodiak last operated in 1937. Their Akutan whaling station was closed in 1939 and was used by the navy during the war.

The change in wartime politics, however, also aided in the development of other fisheries. Prior to the war, salmon canners essentially traded away any rights to Bering Sea crab in exchange for a promise that the Japanese would not fish for salmon.[29] The war voided that "gentleman's agreement," and allowed American expansion into the Bering Sea crab fishery in the late 1940s.

But the end of the war also brought more immediate problems for salmon canners. As *Pacific Fisherman* noted:

> Lifting of wartime controls was not an unmixed benefit, as it ended priorities previously enjoyed by the industry, causing many items of material and equipment to be even harder to get than in 1945; and costs of supplies, as well as labor and raw material, mounted far above wartime levels.[30]

More important for the industry, however, was a continuing decline in salmon production. Catches declined from an average of eighty million salmon during the war to seventy-one million in the four years following. Exacerbated by other factors, specifically the revived Japanese high-seas fleet, Alaska salmon production continued to decline in the 1950s and '60s.

Alaska fishermen individually contributed to the war effort in a variety of ways. Hubert McCallum of Sand Point enlisted in the navy and served on destroyers during the war. Toward the end of the conflict his experience in fishing was called upon by the military and he fished for tuna in the Mariana Islands to provide food for the troops. Fishermen Harvey Samuelsen of Dillingham and Paul Gundersen of Nelson Lagoon were among the hundreds of Native residents who joined the Alaskan Scouts. Dave Carlson, a fisherman and storekeeper in Dillingham, along with his wife Mary Emily, worked as civilian radio operators for the military, helping relay needed weather information.[31] Stories of how the war affected individuals are as numerous as there are individuals themselves.

To the industry as a whole, World War II presented major challenges to Alaska salmon canners, perhaps more than other industries, because of its close proximity to actual fighting. By and large, the industry met those challenges and during the war years continued to be a significant packer of a needed, high quality food source. The war provided a needed but ultimately short-term financial boost to the industry and added to its modernization. But the war also exacerbated existing problems within the industry and left it in a perilous position.

The war years were, as noted earlier, a distinctive epoch in Alaska's salmon history.

*Bob King has been news director for KDLG Radio in Dillingham, Alaska, since 1978. He has written extensively about the fishing industry and the history of southwest Alaska.*

---

[28] Hans Hansen, January, Tollefson. 1950 letter to Congressman Thor Tollefson.

[29] Alaska Representative Anthony Dimond, testifying on HR 8344 before the House Committee on Merchant Marine and Fisheries, February 1938, p. 12.

[30] *Pacific Fisherman*, 1947 Yearbook, p. 83.

[31] All from personal communications.

# The SS *Northwestern*:
# The Final Return of
# "The Ship that Always Came Back"

*Michael Burwell*

## I. Early Service as the SS *Orizaba*

On November 23, 1889, the steamer *Northwestern* was launched by the Delaware River Iron, Shipbuilding, and Engineering Company at Chester, Pennsylvania. Built for the New York and Cuban Mail Steamship Company, she was originally named the *Orizaba*—one of three line ships named for exotic Central American locations. The *Orizaba*, built as a passenger steamer, was 336 feet long and weighed in at 3,496 gross tons. It had two decks with spacious interior accommodations, an observation deck, and a dining salon. Originally built with seventy-five state rooms with berths to serve the 199 first-class passengers (and space for another 219 steerage passengers), the ship's passenger quarters were increased and enlarged in 1909 to accommodate 233 first-class passengers. Quarters for more than eighty crew were located forward off the main deck. The vessel was originally powered by a single screw turned by a triple-expansion steam power plant of twenty-six hundred horsepower, with steam under "160 pounds of working pressure from four single-ended Scotch boilers" that produced an average speed of 12.8 knots. Her top speed was rated at 14 knots. The *Northwestern's* hold could stow ninety-eight thousand cubic feet of cargo.

At the vessel's launching, it slid down the ways and hit a tug: the steamer's reputation as a troubled ship had begun.[1]

The *Orizaba* embarked on its first voyage for the Ward Line on March 1, 1890; her destination was Cuba, a port she would continue to dock at until 1898 when the U.S. Army chartered the vessel for troop transport. By 1902 the *Orizaba* was sailing between New York and Colon for the Panama Railway as a banana freighter; it was not until 1906 that the *Orizaba* saw Pacific duty.[2]

## II. "An Extraordinary Log of Trouble"[3]

In March of 1906, the vessel and her Ward Line sister ships *Saratoga* and *Yucatan* were bought by the Northwestern Steamship Company and brought around the Horn to the West Coast. The syndicate formed by the Guggenheim Brothers and J.P. Morgan was the primary owner of The Northern Steamship Company and had purchased the *Orizaba* to join its growing network of ships serving the West Coast and Alaska. On the first of June, 1906, the *Orizaba*, under Captain J.W. Bogg, completed her voyage to Seattle, and entered the Alaska trade by making her first voyage to Nome. She arrived there June 25 and loaded $750,000 in gold from the Nome placers. On her next return trip from Nome, she

---

[1] Gordon Newell, *The H.W. McCurdy Marine History of the Pacific Northwest* (Seattle: Superior Publishing Company, 1966), p. 121; Linda Cook, National Register of Historic Places Registration Form, Completed by Linda Cook in 1993; Austen Hemion, "The S.S. *Northwestern*: The Ship That Always Came Back, Part One," *Sea Chest*, March 1991, pp. 99, 103; U.S. Treasury Department, *Merchant Vessels of the United States* (Washington, D.C.: Government Printing Office, 1892), p. 235.

[2] Hemion, "The S.S. *Northwestern*, Part One", p. 99.

[3] This heading is from a photo caption from a September 23, 1962, *Seattle Post-Intelligencer* article by Dexter S. Bartlett, ex-radioman on the *Northwestern*, concerning the December 1927 grounding at Cape Mudge, B.C.

raced the steamer *Ohio*, and even though the *Orizaba* left half an hour after the other steamer, she tied up in Seattle first. On August 7, 1906, her name was changed to the *Northwestern*.[4] After two more voyages north, the Northwestern Steamship Company changed the vessel's duty to Southeastern Alaska ports,[5] thus beginning the *Northwestern's* first season on the Inland Passage hauling north freight, mail, coal, livestock, timber, rails, and equipment for railroad and mine construction, and haul-

The SS *Northwestern* plies the waters near Seward, Alaska, ca. 1908. *(Photo No. P-399-22-A, Kodiak Historical Society)*

ing south copper ore and the salmon pack. The *Northwestern* carried passengers in both directions in fine style. Summer and winter, the *Northwestern* would perform her passenger and freighting tasks on these sea routes for the next thirty years.[6] Space allows only a summary of the vessel's more dramatic moments and mishaps over the next three decades.

On a March 1907 voyage, the vessel's first stranding under Northwestern Steamship ownership occurred. On

a return voyage to Seattle from Seward with Captain Truebridge at the helm, she grounded at Latouche on March 19, 1907, when a sudden squall drove her onto a nearby reef in Beatson Bay.

By the end of April, the vessel had been moved to the Latouche dock and refloated by building a false concrete bottom over the hole in the hull and pumping out the forward hold. In convoy, the salvage tug *Salvor* and the *Northwestern* departed southward on May 25, 1907, for repairs at Esquimalt, British Columbia. But almost as soon as the two ships started south, the *Northwestern* sprang a leak and the *Salvor* barely got the steamer into Port Valdez and ashore at Swanport before she had taken on enough water to sink again. After more temporary repairs, the trip south continued and seemed to go without incident until June 4 when, nearing Victoria, B.C., the *Northwestern* and the *Salvor* went aground in heavy fog near the mouth of the Fraser River at Sand Head shoal. The *Northwestern* managed to free herself as well as pull off the *Salvor*, and the pair docked in Victoria on June 5. The vessel immediately went into dry dock.[7]

Ownership of the *Northwestern* was transferred to the Alaska Steamship Company on January 14, 1908.[8] The ship spent the winter on the Westward run carrying large cargoes of freight and equipment to Cordova for the construction of the Copper River and Northwestern Railroad, as well as landing large cargoes at the bur-

---

[4] *The Seattle Post-Intelligencer*, March 9, 1906; Skinner Foundation Manuscript Collection, vol. 13, Northwestern File, Alaska Historical Library, Juneau. National Archives and Records Service, Vessel Information Reply, June 8, 1965. Further citations for this collection, volume, and file are referenced as SFMC; *The Seattle Post-Intelligencer*, March 13, 1906; July 3, 1906; July 5, 1906; and August 6, 1906.

[5] *Seward Weekly Gateway*, October 20, 1906; Hemion, "S.S. *Northwestern*: The Ship That Always Came Back, Part One," p. 99; Newell, *Marine History*, p. 121.

[6] A trip aboard the *Northwestern* was a true part of the Alaska experience, as suggested in Lucile McDonald's article, "The Alaska Steam Story—Part 3," from the December 1974 *Sea Chest*, where she quotes former general passenger agent Robert C. Rose:

   Until after the Second World War there wasn't any way to get to Alaska except by ship. People from Ketchikan, Juneau and Anchorage, aboard for several days, got to know residents of other regions. They danced, played cards, had a drink and dined with those from other sections of Alaska. A great many families resulted from these voyages when boy met girl on the *Northwestern*....

[7] *Seward Weekly Gateway*, March 20, 1907; April 13, May 4, May 25, June 8 and June 15; *The Seattle Post-Intelligencer*, March 23, 1907, April 2, April 10, April 11, April 13 and April 16; Hemion, "S.S. *Northwestern*, Part One," pp. 99-101.

[8] *The Seattle Post-Intelligencer*, August 24 and September 30, 1907; Hemion, "The S.S. *Northwestern*, Part One", pp. 99-101; Newell, p. 145.

geoning settlement of Katalla.

After some minor mishaps earlier in the year, the ship ended 1910 a full-scale casualty. The *Northwestern* sailed from Seattle for Cordova, Valdez, and Seward on the night of December 1. In the early morning hours of December 3, while on her way north to Nanaimo for coal, she went hard aground on Pile Point at the entrance to False Bay. The ship hit with such force that it drove sixty feet onto the rocks, tearing a forty-foot gash in the keel plates; soon the vessel had thirteen feet of water in the forward hold.[9]

By April, 1911, the vessel, under the command of Captain J.C. Hunter, had sufficiently redeemed itself to take part in Cordova's "Copper Day," commemorating the completion of the Copper River and North-western Railroad and the arrival of the inaugural trainload of copper ore from the new Kennicott mines. The *Northwestern* transported the inaugural ore to the smelters at Tacoma.[10]

The *Northwestern* departed Cordova on September 25 on the southward leg of her second Alaska run for that month. Two days later the steamer arrived in Ketchikan, skippered on this run by Captain "Dynamite Johnny" O'Brien. As the *Northwestern* pulled adjacent to her moorings, the signal wire between the bridge and the engine room broke. The pilot telegraphed "STOP" but the broken wire registered "FULL SPEED AHEAD" in the engine room and the engineer quickly responded to the erroneous signal. Before a sailor sent below could reach the engineer and correct the command, the *Northwestern* had hit the bow of the *Glory of the Seas*—a once-famed clipper ship now recycled as a floating salmon cannery. Both vessels sustained minor damage.[11]

There were no calamities in 1912, but 1913 dawned with the *Northwestern's* living up to its legacy of trouble. In January it ran aground at Valdez. In February it collided with the *Skagit Queen*. And on September 12, it tangled with the *H.B. Kennedy*.[12]

After the Alaska Railroad Bill was signed by President Wilson on March 12, 1914, the *Northwestern* had a busy schedule carrying railroad stampeders to Seward. Toward year's end, the *Northwestern* was withdrawn from service in order to convert her coal-burning power plant to oil.[13]

In 1915, the *Northwestern* made the new city of Anchorage a regular stopover on its summer runs. When nearing Ketchikan on October 6, the ship grounded in fog on Potter Rock just south of Pennock Island in Tongass Narrows. The ship was able to kedge off at high tide the next morning. While heading southward on the return voyage from Seward, she lost a propeller blade in Resurrection Bay. The ship managed to limp home by October 25 and was put on the marine railway at Eagle Harbor. The vessel proved too heavy for the Eagle Harbor facility; her weight broke the winch chain of the railway cradle. This last incident capped the *Northwestern's* most accident-prone year to date.[14]

For much of 1916, the *Northwestern* was embroiled in labor disputes and delayed by striking crewmen. One sailing was delayed seven and one-half hours over an underdone piece of meat. The local press reported that one of the firemen eating dinner aboard the *Northwestern* had bitten into an under-cooked mutton chop and complained to the waiter. The waiter was not sympathetic, so the fireman quickly took the chop to the galley where he confronted the cook. After an exchange of harsh

---

[9] Hemion, "The S.S. *Northwestern*, Part One", pp. 103-104; Newell, *Marine History*, p. 178; *The Chitina Leader*, December 3, 1910; *Seward Weekly Gateway*, December 3, 1910; *Cordova Daily Alaskan*, December 10, 1910; *Alaska Daily Record*, December 12, 1910; *Alaska Daily Record*, December 15, 1910; *Alaska Daily Record*, December 21, 1910.

[10] Lone Janson, *The Copper Spike* (Anchorage, Alaska: Alaska Northwest Books, 1975), pp. 100-104. The final spike for the Copper River and Northwestern Railroad was driven on March 29, 1911; the *Northwestern* had a part to play in its disposition:

> The copper spike … was placed in a cabinet bearing the plate, "From E.C. Hawkins to S.W. Eccles, President, Copper River & Northwestern Railway." It was sent to Mr. Eccles in New York, making the journey in the safe aboard the steamer *Northwestern*.

[11] Michael Mjelde, "Glory of the Seas, Chapters I-II," *Sea Chest*, December 1991, pp. 16-20; Basil Lubbock, in his book, *The Down Easters* (New York: Dover Publications. Inc., 1987), p. 66, has this to say of the incident:

> In 1909, whilst lying at Ketchikan, Alaska, she was run into by the steamer *Nord-Western* [sic]. The "Glory" was a tough old vessel and the steamer had to go into Heffernan dry-dock for repairs to her bow. When the Down Easter was dry-docked in July, 1910, she was found to be as sound and strong as ever.

It's unlikely that a steel-hulled steamer hitting a wooden vessel would have gotten the worst of this encounter, but Bob DeArmond, Alaska's reigning authority on maritime matters, had this to say in a February 19, 1994 letter to the author:

> The *GLORY*, remember, had oak frames 12 inches square and set 8 inches apart. Her planking was 8-inch oak, making 20 inches of almost solid oak backed by heavy knees and beams. The *NORTHWESTERN* was *not* a steel ship. Her plates were of wrought iron, riveted together. What happened was that the collision forced the *NORTHWESTERN'S* stem back enough that some of the rivets of the plates around the bow were sheared off....

[12] Hemion, "The S.S. *Northwestern*, Part One," p. 105.

[13] Mary J. Barry, *Seward Alaska: A History of the Gateway City. Pt. 1: Prehistory to 1914* (Anchorage, Alaska: M.J.P. Barry, 1986), p. 145; Hemion, "The S.S. *Northwestern*, Part One", pp. 105-106.

[14] Hemion, "The S.S. *Northwestern*, Part One," p. 106; McDonald, *Alaska Steam*, p. 58.

words, the cook landed a blow on the fireman's nose, and a fight was on. Other firemen came to the aid of their brother and threatened to quit if the cook was not fired. The ship was delayed until the shipping manager and the various union representatives finally decided that the cook had every right to defend the invasion of his galley.[15]

Throughout 1916, the *Northwestern* continued to haul Kennicott copper ore from Cordova. Things proceeded smoothly for the ship until summer when, while crossing the Gulf of Alaska on July 15, the ship dropped a blade of its propeller 240 miles off Cape St. Elias.[16]

At 5:00 A.M. on December 29, 1916, she collided with the *Northland*, a lumber schooner, off Northwest Seal Rock off the southern Oregon coast.[17]

After a quiet year-and-a-half, on August 25, 1918, the *Northwestern* returned to her accident-prone ways when she went ashore at Orca near Cordova. Then, on October 5, while attempting to dock at Seattle's Pier 2, the *Northwestern's* stern was hit by the outbound ferry *West Seattle*. On June 1, 1919, the *Northwestern* stranded in Wrangell Narrows.[18] The next two years passed without incident. The vessel continued to carry copper ore, and survived a national seamen's strike.

Early in 1925 the *Northwestern* underwent her third major interior overhaul. Two-berth staterooms were configured from all three-berth accommodations, and each new stateroom was equipped with hot and cold running water.[19]

For the next five years the Northwestern experienced a long period of good luck and managed to neither collide with another vessel nor run aground, but in 1927 luck ran out. On January 8, the *Northwestern* grounded briefly on Maud Island, B.C., the tides apparently confounding the steering. The *Northwestern* was able to back off without assistance.[20]

As the vessel approached Cape Mudge on the morning of December 11, 1927, a heavy snow was falling and a southeast gale blowing. No land was in sight and the Cape Mudge fog signal could not be heard. Echoes from its own horn were hard to discern, so the ship reduced speed and continually took soundings. Two to three minutes before grounding, land was sighted and the ship was put full astern, but it was too late to stop the grounding. Eventually, the halibut boat *Explorer* heard the ship's bell and was able to take off the passengers. All 118 passengers and their baggage were put in the dark and fragrant fish hold and taken to safety at the Tyee Club's summer resort hotel, Willowaw.

This stranding would prove to be the ship's most serious to date, and for a time the vessel was believed to be a total loss.[21]

Much of 1929 was spent in dry dock at Seattle. The *Northwestern's* 1930 Alaska service continued mishap-free until November 6 when she dropped her stern post and rudder in the Gulf of Alaska, two miles southwest of Cape Spencer.[22]

It was not until two years later that the ship made headlines again. At 2:38 on the morning of July 25, 1933, the ship plowed full speed into a reef off the northwest tip of Sentinel Island despite clear weather, the light burning at Sentinel Island Lighthouse, and the lighthouse keeper's blowing the fog horn.

As it was high water, Captain Livingstone stopped the engines off the spit "to let her own momentum take her on the flats.... I did not want to get her on too far and make it more difficult to get her off when the time came to do so." When the ship came to rest, the 180 passengers were immediately put in lifeboats and lowered over the side. After it was clear that the ship would stay righted, the passengers were brought back aboard. After the temporary cementing of hull leaks, two tugs refloated the vessel and the *Northwestern* was able to make her own way slowly to Juneau. She arrived in Seattle five days later, making the entire journey under her own power. Repairs of $65,000 were needed.[23]

---

[15] McDonald, *Alaska Steam*, pp. 83-84.

[16] Hemion, "The S.S. *Northwestern*, Part One"; M.M. Haugland, *A History of Alaska Steamship Company 1895-1954* (master's thesis, University of Washington, 1968), p. 10.

[17] Gordon Newell, *Pacific Coastal Liners* (Seattle: Superior Publishing Company, 1956), p. 76; Hemion, "The S.S. *Northwestern*, Part One," p. 105; Donald Marshall, *California Shipwrecks* (Seattle: Superior Publishing Company, 1978), p. 146.

[18] Hemion, "The S.S. *Northwestern*, Part One," pp. 107-108; *Daily Alaska Dispatch*, September 12, 1918; Bureau of Marine Inspection and Navigation Files, October 5, 1918; June 1, 1919.

[19] Hemion, "The S.S. *Northwestern*, Part One," p. 105.

[20] Hemion, "The S.S. *Northwestern*: The Ship That Always Came Back, Part Two," *Sea Chest*, June 1991, pp. 157-158; Bureau of Marine Inspection and Navigation Files, January 9, 1927; U.S. Coast Guard Report of Casualty, March 10, 1927.

[21] Dexter Bartlett, "The S.S. *Northwestern*: A Tough Ship In Dangerous Waters," *Seattle Times*, September 23, 1962, p. 4; *The Alaska Weekly*, December 16, 1927.

[22] Hemion, "The S.S. *Northwestern*, Part Two," p. 159; U.S. Coast Guard Report of Casualty, February 17, 1931; Newell, *Marine History*, p. 240.

[23] *Alaska Journal*, Winter 1972, 2:1, p. 64; Hemion, "S.S. *Northwestern*, Part Two", pp. 159-163; Bureau of Marine Navigation and Inspection Files, July 25, 1933; U.S. Coast Guard Report of Casualty, August 4, 1933; Don Holm, "Ghosts of Alaskan Commerce," *The Alaska Sportsman*, September 1941, p. 22; *The Alaska Weekly*, July 28, 1933, August 11, 1933, October 13, 1933.

In March of 1935 the *Northwestern* again came to grief. It hit the SS *Tacoma*, moored at Pier 41 in Seattle.[24] Its next incident that year was on December 1, when, northbound from Seattle and again under Captain Glasscock, the *Northwestern* ran into heavy fog in Seymour Narrows. After she passed the light at Cape Mudge, cold caused the ship's whistle to freeze, forcing the ship to depend on unreliable sound echoes through Discovery Passage. The ship grounded near Orange Point. The vessel was able to kedge off at high water four hours later, and a constant checking of the bilges revealed no leakage.[25]

The *Northwestern's* final voyage for Alaska Steamship Company began on September 22. Her master on this historic trip was Captain H. Anderson. The northbound leg went without incident, but, leaving Ketchikan on October 3 for Vancouver, B.C., the *Northwestern* had a bad day. It was a grand marine pratfall, as the steamer managed to hit the Union Oil Dock, three gas fishing boats, and the oil barge (ex-clipper) *Falls of Clyde*. The *Northwestern* came away from the incident with a small leak, but it had inflicted $10,000 damage to the dock, the other vessels, and the *Falls of Clyde*.[26]

After the *Northwestern* docked in Seattle on October 6, 1937, she was officially laid up—the first time since 1906. She spent the next year idle and was moved on October 1, 1938, to Lake Union. When mining stopped at Kennicott in 1938, important return cargoes of copper ore ceased, and Alaska Steam had to liquidate many assets to stay in operation. This, combined with the *Northwestern's* age and the onslaught of the Depression, proved to be the death knell for the ship's career on the Alaska route.

The *Northwestern* burns in Dutch Harbor after being bombed by the Japanese on June 4, 1942. (*U.S. Navy photograph, courtesy Command Historian's Office, Alaskan Command*)

The ship remained idle for almost two more years, even after its purchase in 1939 by Puget Sound Bridge and Dredging Company, Siems-Spokane Company, and Johnson, Drake, and Piper, Inc.—contractors who had formed a conglomerate in anticipation of American war involvement and wartime construction projects.[27]

On August 21, 1940, the construction combine moved the *Northwestern* to Lake Union Dry dock and fitted her for service as a floating barracks. Interior modifications for 280 personnel were made to house troops stationed at the Naval Operating Base at Dutch Harbor and for civilian workers constructing military facilities and the airfield there. The overhaul enabled the *Northwestern* to make one last northerly voyage under her own power.

On September 30, 1940, the *Northwestern* sailed north from Seattle under Captain Robert Kamdron and arrived early in October.[28]

She voyaged north for the last time after a long and important career spanning thirty-four years of passenger and freight service on the Alaska route. In that time, the vessel managed to come back from more than forty mishaps, including fourteen groundings, ten collisions with other vessels, five dock/port facility collisions, two dropped propellers, one lost rudder, one lost anchor, and five crew/passenger incidents that resulted in injury or death. In defense of the steamer, note that she was run summer and winter for thirty-four years. It was a time when fierce competition among steamship companies dictated running on schedule through bad weather and navigating with few buoys or lights in some of the world's most dangerous waters.

[24] Hemion, "The S.S. *Northwestern*: Part Two," p. 163; Bureau of Marine Inspection and Navigation Files, March 3, 1935.

[25] Bureau of Marine Inspection and Navigation Files, December 1, 1935; Hemion, "The S.S. *Northwestern*, Part Two," p. 163.

[26] Bureau of Marine Inspection and Navigation Files, October 3, 1937; U.S. Coast Guard Report of Casualty, December 21, 1937.

[27] Cook, National Register of Historic Places Registration Form, Sec. 8, p. 3; Lucile McDonald, "The Alaska Steam Story, Part 4," *Sea Chest*, March 1975; Newell, *Marine History* p. 480.

[28] D. Colt Denfeld, *The Defense of Dutch Harbor, Alaska: From Military Construction to Base Cleanup* (Anchorage, Alaska: Alaska District, U.S. Army Corps of Engineers, December 1967); Cook, National Register of Historic Places Registration Form, Sec. 8, p. 3; Hemion, "The S.S. *Northwestern*, Part Two," p. 163; Leon Davis, letter to Bruce Merrell, Loussac Library, March 3, 1993.

The following passage from Austen Hemion's definitive 1991 article on the *Northwestern* puts her career in perspective:

> In this day of advanced radars, satellite navigation, and other electronic marvels, it is much easier now to keep a ship off the beach.... Considering that, during *Northwestern's* whole life from 1890 until 1940, the various Masters of this ship ... had poor charts, no electronics, and nothing but their whistles to attempt to ascertain their positions during periods of poor visibility, it is no wonder that Alaska Steamship Company built only two passenger ships during its period of operations in the Alaska trade.
>
> It is a tribute to those Masters and navigating officers that they were as successful as they were, and remarkable too, that there weren't more ships lost.[29]

## III. Last Days at Dutch Harbor

During its first three months in Dutch Harbor, the *Northwestern* was forced by weather to cast loose twice from the dock and ride out the storms while anchored in the harbor. Once the *Northwestern* was ashore north of the pier, it was decided that the vessel would remain there. A gravel berm was created on the seaward side of the vessel, effectively making the ship a shore structure. Here the vessel continued to serve as a dormitory and power plant, home to 280 men and generating heat, steam, and power from her 200-kilowatt steam-turbo generators.[30]

On February 21, 1941, official records indicate that the navy assumed ownership of the vessel from Siems-Drake—although sources conflict on this point.[31]

It was here, next to shore, that the *Northwestern* remained until 1942, when the greatest casualty of the ship's career befell her. The Japanese attacked Dutch Harbor on the morning of June 3, 1942, pursuing targets based on thirty-year-old maps and obsolete intelligence. The weather was bad and visibility poor, but the enemy planes managed to strafe and bomb the area, inflicting

damage on Fort Meares and Dutch Harbor facilities. The *Northwestern* was not hit until the next day, when Japanese planes returned from the carriers offshore. On the afternoon of June 4, eleven Zeroes and nineteen bombers appeared for what would prove a much deadlier raid. The planes set ablaze five newly constructed and recently filled fuel tanks, hit the air station dock, a partially built hangar, a gun emplacement, the hospital at Unalaska, and the beached *Northwestern*. When the attack started, Siems-Drake workers were eating lunch on board but quickly evacuated the ship. Walter R. Strong was aboard and had this to say of the early moments of the attack when interviewed fifty years later:

> That was the day they got the *Northwestern*, a hotel ship tied to the dock. Some of us were aboard having lunch. It was beautiful big pork chops, and I never got to eat one! We bailed off the ship and took cover where we could outside.[32]

A Val bomber scored a direct hit to the *Northwestern's* forward port deck, piercing the hull with a single 550-pound bomb that exploded below deck, igniting the ship's fuel and setting the entire ship ablaze. Wind spread the flames ashore to a nearby issue warehouse, destroying needed spare parts and hardware. All personal gear of the resident civilian workers living aboard was destroyed in the fire. The inferno continued for the better part of three days. The intense heat melted the ship's paint and exposed the steel hull to even more rapid deterioration. Heroic efforts managed to extinguish the flames and save the ship's boilers. Fire crews quickly flooded the engine room, saving the ship's power plant. In less than a week, the boilers were refired and the ship was again generating electricity and steam.

The attack on the *Northwestern* was a temporary setback to local morale, serving more to fuel "nostalgic regret, especially among Alaskans" for the destruction of a ship long important to Alaska's commerce.[33] The bombing of the *Northwestern* was not a serious military setback even though, on the night after the attack, Tokyo

---

[29] Hemion, "The S.S. *Northwestern*, Part Two," p. 163.

[30] Denfeld, *Defense of Dutch Harbor*, pp. 38-39; John Cloe, *The Aleutian Warriors, Part 1* (Missoula, Montana: Anchorage Chapter—Air Force Association and Pictorial Histories Publishing Company, Inc., 1990), p. 124; Donald Goldstein and Katherine Dillon, *The Williwaw War: The Arkansas National Guard in the Aleutians in World War II* (Fayetteville, Arkansas: The University of Arkansas Press, 1992), p. 44; Brian Garfield, *The Thousand-Mile War* (New York: Doubleday & Company, Inc., 1969), p. 39; Penny Rennick, ed., *"Dutch"* (Anchorage, Alaska: The Alaska Geographic Society, 1991), 18:4, p. 39.

[31] Leon Davis has found official correspondence indicating that the *Northwestern* was navy property before she left Seattle for Dutch Harbor. A letter from the Major General Commandant, U.S. Marine Corps, Washington, to the Commanding General, Fleet Marine Force, Marine Corps Base, San Diego, dated 23 August 1940, states that "Pending completion of barracks ashore about the end of December, the Detachment will be quartered in the SS `NORTHWESTERN' at DUTCH HARBOR. The `NORTHWESTERN' is being fitted out at Seattle for this purpose....'"

[32] Ann Chandonnet, "Tours of Duty: Civilian Recalls Tough Times in the Aleutians," *The Anchorage Times*, May 31, 1992, p. F1.

[33] The quote is from Garfield, *The Thousand-Mile War*, p. 176.

Rose claimed that "Japanese bombers [had] destroyed a warship at the Dutch Harbor pier." As John Cloe aptly states in *The Aleutian Warriors*: "...the material damage was insignificant.... Other than the sentimental impact, the damage sustained by the *Northwestern* did not affect the operations at Dutch Harbor in the least."[34]

After the attack, the *Northwestern* continued to provide power for the installation only until a new, heavily fortified power plant onshore near the airstrip was completed in September 1942. With the *Northwestern's* usefulness over, the ship was eventually removed to an anchorage in Captains Bay.[35]

First, however, a stateside scrap drive got the attention of the local command. Lt. Robert C. Rose was given the task of having *Northwestern* filled with scrap and towed south to aid in the drive. The Seabees "set to and made her seaworthy" for the long tow to Seattle.[36] The ship was taken to the nearby pier and piled with scrap metal, much of it welded to the hull to prevent shifting in heavy seas. In the fall of 1943, the readied ship was towed to Captains Bay to wait for the ocean tow south, but no tug was ever found to take the *Northwestern* to Seattle. A second unsuccessful salvage attempt is reported to have been mounted in 1944.[37]

By 1945, the *Northwestern*, still loaded with its cargo of scrap, was again riding at anchor. Some sources maintain that the ship remained there, forgotten, until 1946 when a storm blew it away from the dock and pushed the hulk southwestward, its bow finally grounding in a quarter-fathom at the southern end of Captains Bay. A more likely scenario has navy tugs later in 1945 towing the *Northwestern* to the head of Captains Bay and pushing its bow into the shallow waters of Port Levashef. Recent site analysis indicates

this latter theory of the *Northwestern's* last voyage as the most likely.[38]

Officially, though, the *Northwestern* had been towed back to Seattle in 1944 by the navy where she yielded twenty-seven hundred tons of scrap. Navy records affirm this and Alaska Steamship Company officials as late as 1959 contended as well that the ship had been scrapped in Seattle.[39] Of course, no one thought to ask the local citizens of Unalaska who had always believed it was the *Northwestern* aground in Captains Bay. Local divers explored the wreck in the 1970s and recovered parts of the ship that indicated it was the *Northwestern*.[40] Maritime historian Austen Hemion heeded the locals and identified the bow as the *Northwestern's* in July 1984. But it was not until 1986 that its identity was officially confirmed, when a U.S. Army Corps of Engineers survey team matched World War II photographs of the ship's wartime bomb damage with present-day scars on the hull in Captains Bay, verified that the ship still contained a cargo of wartime scrap metal, and discerned the faint lettering on the bow spelling out *Northwestern*.[41]

In the end, the ship that "always came back" from collisions, strandings, groundings, and near-wrecks saved herself for posterity by living up to her reputation and grounding this one last time—a final mishap that saved her from a final voyage home and a certain trip to the scrap yard. Instead, the SS *Northwestern* ended up in Alaska where she belonged—a monument to forty difficult and productive years of service in northern waters.

Since the war, the ship's rusting bow has become a familiar local sight, jutting fifty feet out of the shallow waters at the head of Captains Bay; over the years, the

[34] Denfeld, *Defense of Dutch Harbor*, p. 95; Cloe, *The Aleutian Warriors*, Part 1, pp. 114-115, 124, 134; Goldstein and Dillon, *The Williwaw War*, 176-177; Gibbs, *Peril At Sea*, p. 150; *Life Magazine*, August 10, 1942, pp. 24-25; Lael Morgan, ed., *The Aleutians* (Anchorage, Alaska: The Alaska Geographic Society, 1980), 7:3, p. 137; Stan Cohen, *The Forgotten War*, *Vol. Three* (Missoula, Montana: Pictorial Histories Publishing Company, Inc., 1992) pp., 60-61.

[35] Denfeld, *Defense of Dutch Harbor*, pp. 95, 106; Garfield, *The Thousand-Mile War*, p. 39; Cloe, *The Aleutian Warriors*, Part 1, p. 121; Sandra Faulkner and Robert Spude, *Naval Operating Base Dutch Harbor and Fort Meares, Unalaska Island, Alaska* (Anchorage, Alaska: National Park Service, 1987), p. 16; Gibbs, *Peril At Sea*, p. 150.

[36] Faulkner and Spude, p. 19.

[37] Cook, National Register of Historic Places Registration Form, Sec. 8, p. 4; Denfeld, *Defense of Dutch Harbor*, p. 156; Hemion, "The S.S. *Northwestern*, Part Two," p. 165; Hemion has the *Northwestern's* move to Captains Bay occurring on August 7, 1942, based on a Seattle newspaper article. The fact that the new power plant didn't go on line until September suggests that Denfeld's date is more reliable.

[38] Denfeld, *Defense of Dutch Harbor*, p. 156; Cook, National Register of Historic Places registration Form, Sec. 7, p. 3; Cloe, *The Aleutian Warriors*, Part 1, p. 121; Dan Magone, Magone Marine Works, phone call, November 4, 1993.

[39] Newell, *Marine History*, p. 511; Faulkner and Spude, p. 19; U.S. Navy, *Building the Navy's Bases in World War II: History of the Bureau of Yards and Docks and the Civil Engineer Corps, 1940-1946. Vol. II* (Washington, D.C.: U.S. Government Printing Office, 1947), p. 177.

[40] A 1974 dive by Jerry Tilley is described in Cohen, *The Forgotten War*, *Vol. IV*, p. 176; Bob Nelson, phone call, October 28, 1993, also discussed diving on the wreck during the mid 1970's.

[41] Denfeld, *Defense of Dutch Harbor*, p. 173.

[42] Hemion, "The S.S. *Northwestern*, Part Two," p. 165; State of Alaska, Division of Parks and Outdoor Recreation, Office of History and Archaeology Permit Number 92-01.

ship's hull has filled with rain water, and the stern has settled sixty feet to the sea floor.[42] The rusting hulk has taken on a new identity—the most historic and picturesque war relic remaining in the vicinity,  the last surviving physical evidence of the June 1942 attack on Dutch Harbor. In 1991, the City of Unalaska began to take steps to protect the *Northwestern* from vandalism. In March 1991, the city received a permit from the State of Alaska to remove and preserve the ship's four-bladed bronze propeller.[43]

The propeller became the centerpiece of a monument at Unalaska Memorial Park honoring the veterans of the war in the Aleutians, dedicated in a June 1992 ceremony. A memorial plaque beneath the mounted blade reads:

DEDICATED TO THE MEN AND WOMEN
WHO LIVED AND SERVED DURING THE
ALEUTIAN CAMPAIGN
ON JUNE 3, 1992
THE 50TH ANNIVERSARY

*Michael Burwell is a technical writer and editor for Minerals Management Service, Alaska Outer Continental Shelf Region.*

---

[43] For the salvage operation, the City of Unalaska paid $10,000 to Magone Marine Works. Magone divers donated their time during the week it took to salvage the propeller.

# Hollywood, Alaska, and Politics:
# The Impact of World War II
# on Films about the North Country

*Frank Norris*

SINCE THE EARLIEST DAYS OF THE SILVER SCREEN, Hollywood has looked north in its search for movie subjects. Well over two hundred movies have been made about Alaska.[1] A few films have been either critical or financial blockbusters. Charlie Chaplin's *The Gold Rush* was the only one fortunate enough to succeed in both categories. But the vast majority of Alaska movies have been forgotten, perhaps deservedly so.

Most Alaska movies have been westerns or other forms of escapist melodrama that have told little about the land and people.

Only a few have made any attempt to dramatize the realities of twentieth-century Alaska, and fewer still have attempted to dramatize the military or political relationships of the territory's residents. Films that had a military or political theme dwelt on World War II and the postwar period.

I'd like to spend the next few minutes looking a little closer at those movies in order to find out why they were made and what they said about Alaska.

When the Japanese attacked Pearl Harbor in December 1941, it confirmed what Americans had feared for some time—that Japan and the United States would go to war and that the Pacific Ocean, from Burma to Hawaii and from Alaska to Australia, would be the theater of that war. In 1940, in anticipation of an eventual attack, the U.S. took the first tentative steps toward creating a military presence in Alaska. During the next

year or two, troops occupied newly-created naval and air bases throughout the territory.

The troops, once in Alaska, must have been amazed at what they saw. That's because Anchorage, Fairbanks, Kodiak, the Aleutians, and the rest of Alaska just didn't fit people's expectations. They had been led to believe that Alaska was a land of eternal winter populated by shy, smiling Eskimos, hard-bitten desperadoes, hopeful prospectors, and golden-hearted dance hall girls.

And who could blame them? America, during the twenties and thirties, had learned most of what it knew about the world from the movies. A few had read about Alaska in their geography lessons, and a few others had seen Alaska tourist brochures or *National Geographic* magazine, but most got their impressions either from the movies or from books that later became movies.

Hollywood used several themes when Alaska worked its way into a story. But what Hollywood most loved to portray about Alaska was a stereotyped, dime-novel re-creation of the gold rush era.

To put it another way, Alaska was similar to the old west but colder. Never mind the realities of the territory: the fisheries, the big mining corporations, the farmers, the bureaucrats, the missionaries, and a century of Russian history.

Hollywood liked the gold rush period because people knew about the Klondike—after all, many in the audience had read Jack London or memorized Robert Service in their high school English class. Early in the

---

[1] Yukon Territory, Alaska's neighbor, should be included as part of that list, because the two places were almost identical in the minds of American moviegoers.

game, they found that gold rushes made for exciting movies. The first big feature film about Alaska was the 1914 production of *The Spoilers*, based on Rex Beach's novel about the Nome gold rush. That movie opened the floodgates to a torrent of other gold rush films. By 1940, the movie colony had cranked out more than 140 feature films about Alaska and the Yukon. All but a handful showed the north country much as Beach, London, and Service had described. A number of early films, in fact, were adaptations of their books, short stories, and poems.

During 1940 and 1941, when Alaska's troop strength was building up, most Americans remained blissfully ignorant of Alaska's strategic and defense value. But in June 1942 the Japanese bombed Dutch Harbor and occupied Attu and Kiska islands, and Alaska became front-page news.[2] Knowing that the enemy had a foothold on American soil made Americans righteously indignant, even if that foothold was at the far end of a windswept chain of islands that few Alaskans and fewer outsiders had ever visited. People who had only the vaguest notions of Alaska's climate and topography began to recognize that the territory held strategic importance to both sides.

Before the war began, Hollywood was immersed in what it had successfully done for years—entertaining the world with an eclectic blend of comedies, dramas, and musicals. Rarely had they made films with a political or military theme.[3] But as the country stepped closer to war, movie makers and the government gradually began to collaborate, because each recognized the importance of the other in furthering their goals. The government, which was gearing up for war, saw movies as a way to convince the American public to back the cause, or at least not to oppose it. And Hollywood

*Report from the Aleutians*, an Academy Award nominee, was released in 1943. As this scene of tents on a wind-scoured flat unfolds, John Huston, the film's director and narrator, opines that "Adak is worthless in terms of human existence, remote as the moon and hardly more fertile." *(Courtesy of the Academy of Motion Picture Arts and Sciences)*

began to recognize that war and its related themes sold at the box office.

Warner Brothers was the first to stick its neck out in 1939 with *Confessions of a Nazi Spy*. Between then and Pearl Harbor, the various studios released six military preparedness films and another twenty-two Nazi-spy thrillers. Most of the early films were directed against the Germans, but when Japan joined the Axis in August 1940, it became a target of Hollywood as well.[4]

After the Pearl Harbor bombing, Hollywood responded by turning up the output of its war pictures. America had precious little to cheer about early in the war, so the first war movies, such as *Wake Island* (1942) and *Bataan* (1943), tried to raise morale by focusing on the personal struggles of the men who fought the war firsthand.[5] During that period, a lone ray of hope shone when General Doolittle and his men bombed Tokyo.

Doolittle's air raid did little damage to the Japanese war machine, but America, desperate for good news, featured the bombing in no less than four wartime films.[6] American audiences would not be ready for a

[2] *New York Times*, June 4, 1942, p. 1; June 11, 1942, p. 1; June 13, 1942, p. 1.

[3] Barry Norman, *The Story of Hollywood* (New York, New American Library, 1988), pp. 178-79, 205.

[4] Norman, *Hollywood*, pp. 106-07; Bernard F. Dick, *The Star-Spangled Screen; The American World War II Film* (Lexington, Ky: University Press of Kentucky, 1985), pp. 94-97, 101; Jay Robert Nash and Stanley Ralph Ross, *The Motion Picture Guide* (Chicago, Cinebooks, 1985), p. 472.

[5] Brock Garland, *War Movies* (New York: Facts on File Publications, 1987), p. 5; Lawrence Suid, *Guts and Glory; Great American War Movies* (Reading, Mass.: Addison-Wesley, 1978), p. 39; Dick, *Star-Spangled Screen*, p. 125; Norman, *Story of Hollywood*, p. 117.

[6] Suid, *Guts and Glory*, pp. 54, 57; Dick, *Star-Spangled Screen*, p. 128. The films were *Bombardier* (1943), *Destination Tokyo* (1943), *Purple Heart* (1944), and *Thirty Seconds Over Tokyo* (1944).

Errol Flynn is nonplussed and outgunned, at least temporarily, in Warner Brothers' *Northern Pursuit*, released in 1943. Flynn played a Mountie who pretended to side with undercover Nazis in the Canadian North. Critics liked the film, particularly the action sequences. *(Photograph courtesy of the Academy of Motion Picture Arts and Sciences)*

realistic war film until their forces could boast of a few victories of their own.[7]

Documentaries, however, were another matter. Audiences had been following the newsreels from Germany and Japan for years and wanted to keep up on the various theaters of war. The government too, through its Office of War Information, wanted pictures produced to satisfy the demand and to put a favorable spin on wartime events. Some of Hollywood's best directors were therefore brought into the service, including John Ford, Frank Capra, William Wyler, and Darryl Zanuck.[8]

One of the military's first documentary makers was John Huston. Huston's directorial career had debuted in 1941 with *The Maltese Falcon*, and he had directed just two other movies—*In This Our Life* (1942) and *Across the Pacific* (1942)—before he enlisted in the Army Signal Corps.[9] His first few weeks in the military were not auspicious. He was sent to Washington, where he did nothing; he was then sent back to California where he was told to cool his heels and await his first assignment. Finally, in August 1942, he and a crew of six cameramen were flown out to Adak Island in the Aleutians.[10]

By the time Captain Huston arrived, the Japanese had been occupying Attu and Kiska for two months,

[7] Norman, *Story of Hollywood*, p. 117; Garland, *War Movies*, p. 5. In 1943, Capra discovered that the filmgoing public was not yet ready for the graphically realistic *Prelude to War*, the first film in the well-known "Why We Fight" series.

[8] Norman, *Story of Hollywood*, p. 129; Axel Madsen, *John Huston, A Biography* (Garden City, N.Y.: Doubleday, 1978), p. 60.

[9] Gerald Pratley, *The Cinema of John Huston* (South Brunswick, N.J.: A.S. Barnes, 1977), p. 44; Madsen, *John Huston*, p. 60.

[10] Ibid., pp. 60-61. Some sources have suggested that Huston did not return to California after his stint in Washington.

and American forces had been on Adak for just over a month.[11] It was Huston's assignment to make a film about the building of the air base there and to document the bombing missions against the Japanese positions on Attu and Kiska. The army gave him free rein to film the unfolding events as he saw fit. Taking full advantage of that freedom, he flew on fifteen bombing runs and twice narrowly escaped death. Huston stuck it out there for six months; he then headed back to Los Angeles and New York, where he edited the footage he had gathered.[12]

The result of his work was *Report from the Aleutians* which, like many other wartime documentaries, was part documentary and part propaganda. As Huston said later of his Aleutians film, "The only ... false note in it is one of optimism, which the country needed at that moment."[13] It was released in July 1943, less than a month before the combined American and Canadian armies invaded Kiska and completed the liberation of the Aleutian Chain.

Huston's film was acclaimed by critics. The *New York Times* called it "one of the war's outstanding records of what our men are doing," while *Variety* called it "a successful attempt to bring to the American people a picture of the tough conditions under which their boys are fighting."[14]

Huston, meanwhile, used the film as a springboard to continued success as a military movie maker. At the urging of the military brass, he headed off to Europe and compiled a documentary of the Italian campaign, *The Battle of San Pietro* (1945), which has been praised as "probably the best film—whether documentary, pseudo-documentary, or pure fiction—about the experience of men in combat."[15] His last wartime documentary was *Let There Be Light* (1945), a controversial film which was never released to the public.[16] He never returned to Alaska as a filmmaker. Even so, he had fond memories

of his time there. In his autobiography, he noted that "There is a strange beauty about the Aleutians.... You are lost in a gray blanket one moment, and in the next the skies are clear and you are in bright sunshine."[17]

By the time *Report from the Aleutians* was released, Hollywood was producing a steady diet of movies that related to all aspects of the war. Perhaps because it was picturesque, the Pacific Theater seemed to be chosen for a large number of war films. The Alaska campaign, which has been called "the forgotten war," was forgotten by Hollywood, too; *Report from the Aleutians* turned out to be the only feature film to document military action on the Last Frontier.

That is not to say that the north country was ignored by wartime movie makers. Wartime audiences had been watching movies that featured Nazi spies ever since the late 1930s, and in 1942 two movies were released which tailored that familiar story line to the high latitudes. *Yukon Patrol*, released in April, was a Republic production starring Allan Lane, Lita Conway, and Robert Kellard. The plot featured Nazi agents scouring the Yukon for minerals critical to the war effort. Canadian authorities were also looking for the same minerals, but *they* wanted them for their medicinal value. As the movie reached its climax, the enemy found the minerals first, but a Mountie caught them red-handed, and all ended well.[18]

Released the same year was *Riders of the Northland*. It was another Nazi spy movie, but this one had a western twist to it. The Columbia production was directed by William Perked; it starred Charles Starred, along with Shirley Patterson and a very young Lloyd Bridges. The plot took place in Alaska, but the heroes, oddly enough, were Texas Rangers. The plot involved three Rangers who were on the verge of joining the army. Just before they were called up, however, they were sent to Alaska to stop a secret Nazi operation. The Germans, it seems,

---

[11] The first U.S. forces landed on Adak on June 28, and the airfield was built between August 26 and September 10. The public, however, did not hear about the invasion until October. On October 4, newspapers reported that troops had "recently" occupied "positions in the Andreanof group of islands." It hinted that Atka was the island most likely to be occupied. It was not until May 8, 1943, that the navy finally announced that Adak Island was the site of a landing field. Kit C. Carter and Robert Mueller, comp., *Combat Chronology, 1941-1945* (Washington, D.C.: Center for Air Force History, 1991), p. 23; Jim Reardon, *Castner's Cutthroats: Saga of the Alaska Scouts* (Prescott, Ariz.: Wolfe Publishing, 1990), pp. 172, 332, 338; *New York Times*, October 4, 1942, pp. 1, 11; May 8, 1943, pp. 1, 5.

[12] Madsen, *John Huston*, pp. 61-62; Pratley, *Cinema of John Huston*, p. 53; John Huston, *An Open Book* (New York: Alfred A. Knopf, 1980), pp. 96, 98.

[13] Pratley, *Cinema of John Huston*, p. 53. John Ford, who directed *Battle of Midway*, refused to call it a propaganda movie, but he and everybody else knew it was. Norman, *Hollywood*, p. 120.

[14] *New York Times*, July 31, 1943, p. 8; *Variety* July 14, 1943. Also see Stuart Kaminsky, *John Huston, Maker of Magic* (Boston: Houghton Mifflin, 1978), p. 38.

[15] Suid, *Guts and Glory*, pp. 181-82. Gerald Pratley (p. 52) claimed that *Battle of San Pietro* was released in 1944, but Brock Garland (p. 6) noted that the film was "so shockingly realistic that it was not shown to the public until after the war was over."

[16] Kaminsky, *Maker of Magic*, p. 39; Pratley, *Cinema of John Huston*, pp. 52, 54-57; Huston, *An Open Book*, pp. 122-26.

[17] Huston, *An Open Book*, p. 93.

[18] Bernard A. Drew, *Lawmen in Scarlet: An Annotated Guide to the RCMP in Print and Performance* (Metuchen, N.J.: Scarecrow Press, 1990), pp. 215-16.

were running a submarine refueling station along the territory's coastline, and an impenetrable series of barbed wire fences had kept the Americans away. Not to worry, however. Starred, the hero, organized a cattle herd which stampeded through the barbed wire and stopped the operation.

The idea of having German submarines in Alaska and cattle herds on our coastline must have seemed ludicrous to wartime Alaskans. But the movie wasn't made for Alaskans, and critics, by and large, felt the movie was well acted and well directed.[19]

Two big northern events stirred the American public during the first year or two of the war. One, as we've seen, was the Aleutian Campaign; the other was the building of the Alcan Highway. The construction of the road offered a classic study of men battling nature, and the pace of construction—over fifteen hundred miles of road in just eight months—was dizzying by any standard.

The publicity generated by the highway made it ripe for adaptation into a motion picture, and in 1943 two movies featured the highway. Paramount released *Alaska Highway*, a potboiler which featured stock footage of road construction. The film was supposedly set around an Army Corps of Engineers construction camp north of Fort Nelson, and featured two brothers on the construction crew who had fallen in love with the same woman. Richard Arlen, Bill Henry, and Jean Parker were the players in the love triangle. The director tried to spice up the plot with a landslide and a forest fire. But the main story line was called by one reviewer, "typical romance stuff set against the harsh Alaskan tundra."[20]

Another highway picture, *Law of the Northwest*, came out the same year. The movie was released by Columbia, the same production company which had released *Riders of the Northland* in 1942. Both the director and the stars were the same as those in the 1942 movie. Charles Starred, who had been a Texas ranger in *Riders of the Northland*, played a Mountie this time. It was his job to push a road through so the Allies could ship valuable war minerals. A devious group of Nazis, however, worked for the road contractor and were determined to undermine the operation. Starred, who was pledged to complete the road on time, soon found out

who had been behind the work slowdowns. The Mountie straightened them out by showing them some fancy gunplay, and as the last reel concluded, the road was completed with time to spare.[21]

Edward G. Robinson and Francis Lederer chat in the anti-Nazi film, *Confessions of a Nazi Spy* (1939), the first Hollywood film to identify the threat of Hitler's Third Reich. *(Courtesy of the Academy of Motion Picture Arts and Sciences)*

One other northern war movie produced in 1943, *Northern Pursuit*, starred the swashbuckling Errol Flynn. The movie took place somewhere in the Canadian north, west of Hudson's Bay. Flynn, the hero, played a Mountie who found an unconscious man at a remote campsite. Flynn nursed the man back to health, only to find that he was a Nazi pilot who had been dropped off by a passing German submarine. The ever-alert Flynn then convinced the man that despite his Mountie uniform he was really a Nazi[22] sympathizer, and the two headed off to a landing field where they waited to get picked up by a German plane. Flynn, of course, was no turncoat, and his true sympathies finally came to the fore when the plane landed to take them away. The film ended with his triumphing over the downed pilot and everyone in the German plane. Critics liked *Northern*

---

[19] Nash and Ross, 2615, I-2724. Before Starred appeared in *Riders of the Northland*, he already had two northern movies to his credit; *North of the Yukon* (1939) and *The Royal Mounted Patrol* (1941). The staple of his career, however, was westerns; he appeared in over one hundred of them.

[20] Nash and Ross, p. 35; *Variety*, October 27, 1943.

[21] *Variety*, July 7, 1943; Nash and Ross, pp. 16, 32.

[22] In World War II movies, ironically, the spies were almost always Nazis. Japan, of course, had more than its share of spies. But Nazi spy movies had been made ever since 1938, two years before Japan even showed itself as a threat to the United States. The Nazi spy movie had become so well established that the first Japanese spy movie was not released until 1942. Several more movies showing Japanese spies and saboteurs were produced during the war, but they continued to be outnumbered by their German counterparts. In movies made with an Alaska or arctic setting, enemy spies were exclusively Germans. Dick, *Star-Spangled Screen*, pp. 93-96, 102, 105-06.

*Pursuit*, particularly the action sequences. Key men behind its creation were director Raoul Walsh and writers Frank Gruber and Alvah Bessie.[23]

In the last two years of the war, movie audiences were provided an increasingly sophisticated collection of war films. With victories becoming more common, and with Hollywood fully geared up to making movies which furthered the aims of the war, patriotic films were a staple at the box office. Alaska, however, was the scene of little wartime action once Attu and Kiska were safely in American hands, and the movie studios ignored the realities of Alaska and the Yukon for the remainder of the war.

In August 1945 the U.S. celebrated the end of the hostilities. For a few short months the world underwent a relatively peaceful reconstruction. But the USSR, which had been a wartime ally, soon emerged as a rival, and by March 1946 Winston Churchill was proclaiming that an "iron curtain" had descended over eastern Europe. Americans had never really trusted the Soviets, even during the war years, and before long the country was swept up in a virulent tide of anti-Communism.[24]

The causes and consequences of the Cold War are far too complex to be discussed here. Suffice it to say, however, that the emergence of the Communist threat resulted not only in the creation of a huge defense establishment, but also in a thorough search for real or imagined sympathizers in positions of influence. Some felt that key operatives in the State Department were Communists—Alger Hiss, for instance. Others felt that influential Communists had infiltrated the Hollywood film community. Hollywood, after all, had long been a haven for liberal thinkers, and it was an open secret that some of its writers were card-carrying members of the Communist Party.[25]

The effort to ferret out Communist sympathizers from Hollywood began shortly after the Republicans took over Congress in the 1946 elections. The chairman of the House Un-American Activities Committee, J. Parnell Thomas, a Republican from New Jersey, arrived in Los Angeles in April 1947 and set up a hearing that fall in which he asked ten prominent writers—the so-called "Hollywood Ten"—whether they were Communist Party members.[26] Some of the ten, as it turned out, were

Communists, and some weren't; a few admitted it, while most refused to provide testimony. Most of the studio heads did not really care whether their employees were Communists, but outside pressures became so great that the studios instituted a blacklist, not only of the "Hollywood Ten," but of anyone else suspected of leaning to the left. It was a dark period in Hollywood's history. Loyalty oaths became the norm, and actors and writers were rewarded for uncovering the real or imagined sins of their fellow workers.[27]

In order to show America that Hollywood had not become a tool of the Red Menace, the studio heads created a film genre which trumpeted patriotism and anti-Communism above all else. By today's standards, most of those movies are painfully dated and artistically deplorable, but their purpose was political, not aesthetic. Some of the better-known films included *I Married a Communist*, *I Was a Communist for the FBI*, *The Whip Hand*, *My Son John*, and *Iron Curtain*. Some movies extolled the virtues of Americans who trod the straight and narrow; others exposed Communist spies among the ranks.[28]

One of the first movies Hollywood produced of that ilk was produced shortly after the October 1947 hearings which exposed the "Hollywood Ten." The waters off Alaska were the setting. *Alaska Patrol*, released by Burwood Pictures, featured a naval intelligence officer, played by Richard Travis, who posed as an enemy agent in order to break up a ring of spies. Most of the action took place on a freighter off the coast of Alaska. Critics liked it; they called it "a tight little yarn ... which bristles with thrills ... and sock suspense."[29]

Many observers, both in and out of the film colony, hoped that the anti-Communist fervor would quietly fade away once the hubbub surrounding the Hollywood Ten trial had dissipated. But Congress was not yet through with its investigations. Four years later it returned, seemingly stronger than ever. Hearings continued off and on for another three years.[30]

During the early 1950s, in response to renewed congressional pressure, Hollywood released another spate of anti-Communist movies. Two were set in the north country. In June 1952, Columbia released *Red Snow*, which was produced and directed by Boris Petroll and

[23] Nash and Ross, pp. 21, 94; *Variety*, October 20, 1943; Dick, *Star-Spangled Screen*, p. 220.

[24] Norman, *Story of Hollywood*, p. 189; *New York Times*, March 6, 1946, p. 4.

[25] Ibid., pp. 180-81.

[26] Ibid., pp. 190-92, 201. Barry Norman's account of Communism in the film industry is relatively brief. For a more detailed study, see Larry Ceplair and Steven Englund, *Inquisition in Hollywood* (Garden City, N.Y.: Anchor Press/Doubleday, 1980).

[27] Ibid., pp. 201-03.

[28] Ibid., pp. 205-06.

[29] *Variety*, January 19, 1949; Nash and Ross, p. 35.

[30] Norman, *Story of Hollywood*, p. 206.

starred Guy Madison, Carole Mathews, and Native Alaskan Ray Mala. The story focused on a group of Eskimo soldiers who were sent off to eastern Siberia in order to investigate Soviet military activities on the other side of the Bering Strait. The Eskimo unit discovered the Soviets in the midst of developing a secret weapon, and the film closed with the defection of a Soviet pilot to the U.S. side. The film's action wasn't much to brag about: one reviewer noted that the "performances are as frozen as the landscape." Critics, however, liked the skillful use of stock footage of Eskimo life. Also notable was the Eskimo military unit, which may have been patterned after the real-life Eskimo scouts organized by Major M.R. "Muktuk" Marston.[31]

In September 1952, with anti-Communist fervor still running high, Monogram Pictures released one more spy movie, *Arctic Flight*. This B-rated feature starred a bush pilot, played by Wayne Morris, who agreed to take a businessman, played by Alan Hale, out to hunt polar bear. The bush pilot, however, soon suspected that the businessman was really a Communist spy intent on photographing western Alaska for intelligence purposes. The pilot's suspicions proved correct, but the spy somehow eluded his grasp after the two had landed. Eventually, both ended up on Little Diomede Island. The spy's goal was to make the three-mile trek west over the ice to Soviet-held Big Diomede, but the pilot confronted him and the two fought it out. The spy got away, but his identification papers were lost in the scuffle. He made it to Big Diomede, but as the curtain closed the Soviets accused him of being an impostor and he was shot. The film was anti-Communist drivel at its worst; its strongest point was the scenery, because it was filmed in western Alaska.[32]

The congressional hearings continued until 1954. That December, however, the censure of Senator Joseph McCarthy made red-baiting less fashionable. Thereafter, the intensity of anti-Communist rhetoric aimed at Hollywood figures began to decline. But some writers continued to be blacklisted, and studios shied away from political or controversial films for years afterward.[33] That rule, perhaps coincidentally, also applied to films about Alaska. Since the mid-1950s, virtually nothing of a political nature has been produced. Some might argue that *Ice Palace*, the 1960 film based on the Edna Ferber novel, was political. It was, but only marginally; development issues, by their very nature, cannot be separated from politics.[34] Otherwise, recently produced Alaska movies have featured the same nature movies, gold rush stories, and generic dramas that characterized northern movies before World War II appeared on the horizon.

*Frank Norris is a historian for the National Park Service, Alaska Regional Office. He is the president of the Alaska Association for Historic Preservation.*

---

[31] The few Alaskans who saw this movie were doubtless pleased that one of their own was starring in the film. Ray Mala, an Eskimo from Candle, had been a movie star for over twenty years. His first starring roles had been *Igloo* and *Eskimo* in the early 1930s. Since then, he had acted in numerous films and had also written several film scripts. Nash and Ross, pp. 25, 69-70; *Variety*, June 25, 1952, Susan Hackley Johnson, "When Hollywood Looks North," *Alaska Journal* 9 (Winter, 1979), pp. 16-18; Ann Fienup Riordan, "Freeze Frame: Alaska Eskimos in the Movies" (ms., February 1992), pp. 20-23, 39-47.

[32] Nash and Ross, p. 89; *Variety*, July 30, 1952.

[33] Norman, *Story of Hollywood*, pp. 206-15.

[34] References to *Ice Palace* are included in the following sources: Johnson, "When Hollywood Looks North," pp. 21-22; Elizabeth Tower, *Mining, Media, Movies: Cap Lathrop's Keys for Alaska Riches* (Anchorage: Elizabeth Tower, 1991), preface, p. 104; *Variety*, June 15, 1960; *New York Times*, June 30, 1960; Nash and Ross, pp. 13, 51-52; Riordan, "Freeze Frame," pp. 54, 55, 59.

# The Civilian Conservation Corps in Alaska (1933-1942) and Military Preparedness

*W. Conner Sorensen*

MY DISCUSSION OF THE CIVILIAN CONSERVATION Corps (CCC) in Alaska and its relationship to military preparedness will address three topics: the special features of the CCC in Alaska; the changing rationale and program of the Alaska CCC as the nation moved from the Great Depression to war; and an assessment of the historical significance of the Alaska CCC with respect to military preparedness.

The CCC in Alaska had several unique features. In "the states," young men between the ages of eighteen and twenty-five lived in camps run by the U.S. Army and worked on projects directed by federal and state conservation agencies.[1] In Alaska, the entire program was administered by the U.S. Forest Service, the army's role being limited to issuing payroll checks through the paymaster of Chilkoot Barracks. Age restrictions were waived for Alaska, so that all men eighteen and over could enroll.[2] In 1937, the Alaska CCC enrollment was opened to Alaska Native men and 50 percent of the enrollees were to be Indians and Eskimos, to reflect the composition of the territorial population.[3] The total enrollment was doubled from 325 to more than 600 and the program was extended to areas outside the national forests. Native crews consisting of both married and unmarried men were organized in so-called "per diem camps." They lived at home, rather than in CCC camps, and were paid an extra dollar per day for housing and food which they provided themselves. In contrast to the states, where enrollment usually peaked in the summer, the Alaska CCC was most active in the winter, when seasonal employment in the fisheries and other employment was slack.

At its peak in 1938, the Alaska CCC had more than a thousand enrollees among a territorial population of just over sixty thousand.[4] Most of the CCC activity was concentrated in Southeast Alaska, which had the most population, and the two largest towns, Juneau and Ketchikan.[5]

The CCC was a highly visible feature of Alaska life in the 1930s. Virtually every town and village in Southeast Alaska, as well as many towns and villages in other regions, had CCC camps. In the villages, all able-bodied men from age eighteen up to those in their seventies worked on CCC projects in the winter months. CCC crews took part in every conceivable activity, including building roads and trails, cabins, and recreation facilities; restoring totem poles and building clan houses; stocking trout in lakes, feeding deer, and trapping

---

[1] For background on the goals and organization of the CCC, see John A. Salmond, *The Civilian Conservation Corps, 1933-1942: A New Deal Case Study* (Durham, North Carolina: Duke University Press, 1967), chaps. 1, 2.

[2] *Daily Alaska Empire* (hereafter *DAE*), 3 April 1937.

[3] This topic is discussed in a paper entitled "A New Deal for Alaskan Natives: The Civilian Conservation Corps Comes to Alaska Villages," presented at a meeting of the Forest History Society, Vancouver, B.C., October 1986.

[4] *DAE*, 1 February and 31 March 1938. The ratio of enrollees to population in Alaska (1 to 60) was about the same as in the nation as a whole. In 1938, there were 260,000 enrollees nationwide among a population of about 131 million. *DAE*, 9 March 1938.

[5] *DAE*, 2 February 1940.

Companies 927 and 2928 stand for retreat on Annette Island, June 1941. *(Photograph courtesy of U.S. Forest Service, Juneau)*

wolves; and organizing search and rescue missions and disaster relief following landslides and fire. In western Alaska, Eskimo crews built community houses, poisoned predators, constructed reindeer corrals, and excavated underground caches in the permafrost to store meat over the summer.[6]

With this overview in mind, we turn to the question: How did the Alaska CCC change in emphasis from unemployment relief to war preparations? In Alaska, as elsewhere, the CCC was perhaps the most popular New Deal program. But in Alaska the emphasis was placed on community improvement and economic development of the territory, rather than on unemployment relief, the rejuvenation of American youth, or the conservation of natural resources. Each year, at the "Open House" anniversary of the CCC held at CCC camps in Juneau and Ketchikan, Forest Service officials and newspaper editors proudly pointed out the value of CCC projects to the communities and to the territory.[7] In 1937, Regional Forester Frank Heintzleman forecast economic recovery for Alaska, pointing to three projects already underway: plans for pulp mills in Southeast Alaska, enlargement of the CCC, and the promotion of

tourism through the production of an Alaska wildlife film.[8] The editor of the *Juneau Empire* headlined its coverage, "The Forest Service Has Part [in] Much [of] Alaska Growth," citing CCC projects like trout stocking and construction of a Bureau of Fisheries lab at Port Walter.[9]

Other benefits of the CCC were noted by Alaska CCC boosters. The *Empire* editor applauded the national CCC program for lifting young men out of city slums and providing them with "healthful, gainful, and productive employment" in a "fresh, stimulating outdoor environment."[10] His description restated Jeffersonian agrarian ideals inherent in the philosophy of the CCC from its founding. However, when describing the Alaska CCC, editors and Forest Service spokesmen more often emphasized the economic and community benefits of the program. The regenerating effect on enrollees was, after all, limited, in a program that included men of all ages.

As the likelihood of war increased, with fascist parties coming to power in Europe and the Japanese moving aggressively in Asia, the relationship of the CCC to national defense was reassessed in the nation and in Alaska. The question was: could a peacetime program

---

[6] Projects are listed in Conner Sorensen, "Civilian Conservation Corps in Southeast Alaskan Newspapers: An Index," *Alaska Historical Commission Studies in History*, No. 173 (June 1985), copies in Alaska State Libraries. For western Alaska, see Alva Blackerby, "We Built a Lot of Happy Houses," *Alaska Life* (December 1941), pp. 14, 28, 30-31.

[7] See, for example, *DAE*, 3 April 1937.

[8] *DAE*, 4 May 1937.

[9] *DAE*, 31 July 1937. See also "Steps on the Road to Alaska Development" [on the expansion of the CCC], *DAE*, 29 April 1937.

[10] "The Worthy CCC," *DAE*, 29 October 1934.

designed to meet the crisis of industrial unemployment among American youth be successfully revamped to meet the coming crisis of war? The question took on special urgency with the outbreak of war in Europe in 1939. In Alaska, the attempt to restructure the CCC proceeded along three lines: (1) redefining the rationale of the CCC program and projects in terms of their defense value; (2) revamping training programs to provide non-combat military training for enrollees and the transfer of trained personnel to defense positions; and (3) the deployment of CCC crews for the construction of defense installations in Alaska.

The re-definition of existing CCC projects in terms of their defense value was relatively simple. Virtually any project that helped improve transportation or communications in Alaska could be interpreted as having defense value, and these included the majority of projects. In 1940, C.M. Archbold, district ranger in Ketchikan, pointed out that many CCC projects completed in the territory that year contributed to national defense. As examples he listed the construction of two emergency airfields, forty miles of roads and trails, fifty bridges, eighteen buildings, two dams, and two water systems. Archbold pointed to the rifle range at Ketchikan as a CCC project that fit directly into national defense (though the range was originally conceived as a community recre-

An air hammer operator on Annette Island, February 1941. *(Photograph courtesy of U.S. Forest Service, Juneau)*

ation activity). He noted that the range would be used by the Coast Guard, the National Guard, and army troops, as well as a soon-to-be-established home guard for Ketchikan.[11] The work of CCC crews doing construction on the naval base at Japonski Island in the Sitka harbor was also obviously related to defense.

Providing military training for CCC enrollees was more involved than reinterpreting projects in terms of their defense value and, in the long run, more important. At the founding of the CCC, the intention of training enrollees for combat duty had been explicitly rejected by President Franklin D. Roosevelt, CCC Director Robert Fechner, and the U.S. Army command. In the early 1930s, the majority of Americans agreed that military training in civilian programs too closely resembled Hitler's work camps and youth organizations.[12]

However, as the international situation deteriorated, Americans came to favor some form of military training for the CCC. In 1936, polls indicated a majority was still opposed, but by 1938, 75 percent were in favor of military training. And at the outbreak of war in 1939, this rose to over 90 percent.[13] CCC officials and Congress quickly responded to the new situation at home and abroad. In 1937, Fechner announced that the CCC camps had molded CCC boys to the point that they were 85 percent

[11] *Ketchikan Alaska Chronicle* (hereafter *KAC*), 15 July 1940. The rifle ranges in Ketchikan and Juneau were often used by troops from Chilkoot Barracks, visiting navy ships' personnel, and regular army troops, as well as by local gun clubs. There is no record of CCC enrollees participating in shooting competition, which was in line with an early ruling by the national director forbidding shooting as a CCC camp sport. "[Navy] Rifle Squad goes out to Mendenhall," *DAE*, 24 July 1936; "Navy Shooters on Rifle Range," *DAE*, 12 July 1937; "Guardsmen Shoot a Rifle Range," *DAE*, 24 February 1941; John A. Salmond, *The Civilian Conservation Corps*, p. 117.

[12] Salmond, *The Civilian Conservation Corps*, pp. 113-116. Incidentally, the charge from Communist and socialist quarters and American peace groups that the CCC would train men for reserve army duty found no echo in Alaska. Opposition to the CCC in Alaska was restricted to complaints from organized labor in Anchorage and Fairbanks, protesting competition from low-paid CCC crews; see Salmond, *The Civilian Conservation Corps*, pp. 14-20; *KAC*, 17 December 1938 and 8 July 1939.

[13] Salmond, *The Civilian Conservation Corps*, pp. 120, 193-195.

prepared for the military, and that additional training could turn them into "first-class fighting men at almost an instant's notice."[14] In 1940, Congress passed the Byrnes Amendment to the CCC appropriation bill. The rider provided for non-combat training for all CCC enrollees, and for the transfer of promising trainees to full-time defense work.[15] By 1940, the relationship of the CCC to the American military was the reverse of 1933. Whereas the army had reluctantly taken responsibility for CCC camps in order to retain influence in a depression-inspired program, by 1940 CCC officials eagerly sought defense functions in order to retain support for a program whose relief function was seriously questioned in a recovering economy.[16]

In Alaska, Forest Service and other leaders eagerly embraced the provision for non-combat training for the CCC. Although Fechner's 1937 military preparedness speech was denounced in a number of newspapers around the country, in Alaska it was reported with apparent approval.[17] In 1940, following passage of the Byrnes Amendment, District Ranger Archbold compared the work of the CCC to non-combat duty performed by army engineers:

> Work of the CCC is generally classed along with similar work performed by regular army engineer troops, during emergency or war time.... They work on roads, trails, bridges, construction of buildings, airfields, seaplane ramps, water and sewage systems and like projects.[18]

The editor of the *Juneau Empire*, following a release likely provided by the Forest Service, pointed out that much of the CCC program up to that time had contributed toward training enrollees in skills appropriate to national defense. "Alaska CCC is Being Trained in War Skills," proclaimed the headline:

> CCC enrollees in Alaska have in reality been getting training in most of the elements of the

"school of the soldier" with the exception that they get no drill, manual of arms, nor target practice. They have been doing work which fits them for real service during any national emergency—fire, flood, or war.[19]

The re-definition of the CCC in terms of defense preparedness coincided with a new emphasis on training in Alaska CCC camps. In December 1939, Alva W. Blackerby was appointed training officer for the Forest Service in Alaska, and he instituted a standardized training program in the CCC camps.[20] Blackerby at first talked about training "future Alaska workers," and encouraging young men to follow "a wholesome way of living," in terms reminiscent of early justifications of the CCC.[21] But, by 1940, the Forest Service was proudly announcing that the "Alaska CCC is Being Trained in War Skills."[22]

Just as CCC projects could be reinterpreted in terms of defense, the skills already being learned by enrollees could be interpreted as preparing them for defense roles. Archbold pointed out that skills such as the operation and repair of trucks, tractors, and loaders; the operation of telephones and radio transmitters; and even such skills as cooking and baking were in demand in the military.[23] Under Blackerby's direction, CCC training was expanded to include training by officials in the U.S. Bureau of Mines and the U.S. Coast Guard. Courses were offered in first aid, navigation, surveying, blueprint reading, office clerking, drafting, use of explosives, use and care of tools, and leadership training.[24]

Forest Service officials in charge of the Alaska CCC did more than reinterpret ongoing CCC projects in terms of their defense value and revise CCC training programs to provide non-combat training for CCC enrollees. They also undertook a major defense project with CCC labor: the Annette Air Field. The project apparently was conceived in response to a suggestion by Fechner, who, while touring the Alaska CCC camps in 1939, expressed the wish that the Alaska CCC undertake a specific defense-related project.[25] The armed forces

---

[14] Ibid., p. 193.

[15] Ibid., pp. 196-197.

[16] Ibid., pp. 9, 208.

[17] *DAE*, 22 December 1937.

[18] *KAC*, 27 November 1940.

[19] *DAE*, 10 July 1940.

[20] *DAE*, 7 December 1939 and 15 February 1941.

[21] *KAC*, 7 December 1939.

[22] *DAE*, 10 July 1940.

[23] *KAC*, 15 July 1940.

[24] Ibid.

[25] Lawrence W. Rakestraw, *A History of the United States Forest Service in Alaska* (Anchorage, Alaska: Alaska Historical Commission; Department of Education, State of Alaska; and the Alaska Region, United States Forest Service, Department of Agriculture; with the assistance of the Alaska Historical Society, 1981), p. 108.

command in Alaska wanted to improve air service between the states and Alaska. In order to shift from amphibious planes to larger and faster wheeled aircraft they needed a runway and refueling station between air bases in Seattle and Anchorage. Annette Island, a flat, boggy island of about ten square miles, located twenty-five miles south of Ketchikan, was chosen as the site of a ten-thousand-foot runway and refueling station.[26]

This was a larger project than the Alaska CCC could undertake with existing crews, so two CCC companies of two hundred enrollees each were recruited from camps in California and Oregon. These four hundred CCC enrollees were to accompany four hundred troops of the Army Corps of Engineers, bringing the total to eight hundred, or about the same number as the total CCC in Alaska.[27]

In August 1940, a twenty-man CCC crew from Ketchikan prepared quarters on Annette for the advance crew of army engineers. The main body of CCC enrollees and army engineers arrived on the army transport *Leonard Wood* later that month.[28] The Ward Lake CCC camp outside Ketchikan served as one of the staging areas for the CCC and engineer troops, their one hundred trucks, five thousand tons of cargo, and one hundred pre-fabricated houses bound for Annette Island. Construction on the island involved the erection of a camp to accommodate twelve hundred men (four hundred additional engineers came later), and the construction of a five-mile truck road to haul rock from a quarry as well as a pipeline (partly below sea level) to bring water to the camp.[29] Bogs and lakes were filled with rock to provide a solid base for the runway itself. The Annette Island base was completed within a year. The first plane landed on a not-quite-completed runway in September 1941.[30]

By that time, the CCC was losing personnel steadily as men moved into defense-related jobs, joined the army, or were drafted.[31] Events moved quickly as the CCC was submerged in war mobilization. By December 1941, America was at war. In April 1942, the CCC cele-brated its ninth and final birthday without an open house because of reductions in personnel. In June 1942 came the attack on Dutch Harbor and Japanese occupation of two Aleutian islands. On July 1, 1942, the CCC was demobilized nationwide, and in August 1942, Aleut families which had been evacuated from their island homes began settling in the former CCC camp at Ward Lake.[32] Alaskans said a fond goodbye to the CCC, regarding it as a worthy program that had accomplished much good for the territory.[33]

In conclusion, the Alaska CCC and its relation to military preparedness were significant in three ways:

First, the CCC mobilized a sizeable number of Alaskans and trained them in skills appropriate to military service. The majority of the Alaska CCC enrollees of military age entered the armed forces, either as enlisted men or as draftees. To varying extents, their CCC experience trained them in the rudiments of military organization.[34] In the CCC, they learned to work in units and to give and to take orders. Many CCC enrollees also acquired specific skills, such as the operation of heavy equipment, first aid, and blueprint reading, which proved valuable to the military. It is estimated, for example, that half of the CCC crew on Annette Island transferred into the Army Corps of Engineers for work on other projects in Alaska.[35]

Second, the CCC built airfields, roads, trails, and communications installations that contributed to Alaska's admittedly meager military preparedness for the Pacific conflict. Annette Island Air Base is the outstanding example of direct military facilities constructed by the CCC. CCC crews also worked at the Sitka Naval Operating Base on Japonski Island and elsewhere.[36] When the Japanese attacked Dutch Harbor, raising fears of an invasion of the mainland of Alaska, the network of trails constructed by CCC crews took on added military significance. In 1942, additional "escape trails" were constructed around the larger towns, including one from Juneau to the Canadian border.[37]

[26] Art Glover, "Art Glover's Experiences as Regional Engineer in Alaska, 1940-46," *Timberlines* (June 1960), p. 26.

[27] Fred H. Bock, "The Civilian Expeditionary Corps? Cos. 927 and 2928, Annette Island, Alaska," in *Yearbook of the National Association of CCC Alumni Convention* (San Luis Obispo, California, 1987), p. 39. The somewhat longer typed transcript of the article accompanies the copy in the possession of the author.

[28] *KAC*, 9 August 1940, 20 August 1940.

[29] Glover, "Experiences," p. 26.

[30] Bock, "Civilian Expeditionary Corps," p. 39.

[31] *KAC*, 21 April 1941, 3 April 1942, 21 April 1942.

[32] *KAC*, 3 April, 1942, 1 July 1942, 15 July 1942, 18 August 1942.

[33] *KAC*, "The CCC Leaves its Imprint," 2 July 1942; *KAC*, "CCC Working Alaska is Reviewed," 15 July 1942.

[34] Information taken from taped interviews with former CCC enrollees by the author, 1983-1986. Tapes and transcripts of the interviews are on file with the Alaska Region, USDA Forest Service, Juneau, Alaska.

[35] Glover, "Experiences," p. 27; *KAC*, 3 April 1942.

[36] *DAE*, 28 March 1938.

[37] *KAC*, 18 March 1942; Glover, "Experiences," p. 24.

Third, the CCC contributed significantly to the integration of Alaska and Alaskans into the fabric of modern America. The process of "Americanization" was particularly important among the 50 percent of the population who were Native Alaskans. It is symbolic that the first Alaskan draftee was Archie Klaney, a Tlingit CCC enrollee from Klukwan.[38] The transition from CCC per diem camp to the military was typical of Alaska Native men in the 1930s and '40s. In many instances, the CCC provided the first meaningful contact of Alaska Native people with the federal government, and for the overwhelming majority the CCC was viewed in positive terms by the participants and their families.[39] The CCC thus contributed to attitudes and morale, which were of importance during the war and later. The overall effect of participation of Native men in the CCC in the 1930s and the U.S. Armed Forces in the 1940s was a massive process of integration of Alaska Native people into the mainstream of American society. The results of this process may be viewed as positive or negative, depending on our value systems and point of reference, but the integration itself can hardly be disputed.

In the course of this conference we will no doubt hear that the integration of Alaska into the mainstream of American life came about through World War II. This is correct, but we should remember that a prior step was taken in this process through the Forest Service administration of the Civilian Conservation Corps in Alaska.

*With support from the U.S. Forest Service, the Alaska Historical Commission, and Sealaska Heritage Foundation, W. Conner Sorensen has been researching the CCC in Alaska and hopes the work will lead to a book on the topic.*

---

[38] *DAE*, 24 October 1941.

[39] This conclusion is based on interviews of former CCC enrollees by the author in the years 1983-1986. Tapes and transcripts are on file with the USDA Forest Service, Alaska Region, Juneau, Alaska.

# My Alaska War Years - 1941 to 1946

*Helen A. Butcher*

SITKA WAS IN THE MIDST OF A CONSTRUCTION BOOM when I arrived in July 1941 for three months. My stay has now stretched to more than fifty-two years. I accompanied Margaret Dunham, who had marriage in mind as she headed north.

Japonski Island, across the Sitka Channel, had been chosen as a naval reserve in the 1890s. In 1940, with the threatening world situation, it started building up as a base for PBY planes to patrol the Pacific. Fort Ray was built to protect the naval operation.

Siems Drake was the major contractor. In the fall the ammunition dump blew up, digging a crater in solid rock about twenty to twenty-five feet deep and seventy-five feet across. The explosion killed six people, including one by a flying rock a half-mile away. Margaret's future husband was Bob Wahl, a United Press correspondent. I was caught up by the drama as he reported the events via Alaska Communications System, Sitka's only direct outside link since 1906. Operated by the U.S. Army, it was generally referred to as the ACS.

At seventy-five cents an hour, my first work as a bookkeeping freelancer was for Marshall Crutcher, one of two CPAs in Alaska at that time. He lived in Ketchikan, but traveled to Sitka and Kodiak, where his main clientele were fish canneries and lumber companies. At that time I worked on the city's purchase of the utility system.

The *Sitka Sentinel* had been approved for official notices in May. On July 25, 1941, this ad appeared: "Final notice that the Alaska School Tax is due. It will be necessary to institute criminal action against non-paying male residents of the territory." In 1978, when the law was repealed, the tax was still ten dollars.

The 1941 Labor Day parade of about five hundred people was led by a band that disembarked from an army transport an hour before. A sergeant on the base wanted to invite Margaret and me over for dinner, but couldn't get permission until the new soldiers coming in every week got settled down. As the troops hadn't been around girls for so long, his advice was to wear lots of rouge and lipstick because we were liable to be blushing most of the time. In September, several Russian VP2 bombers flew in on a mission to observe American aircraft plants. The planes stopped over because of bad weather in Seattle. I saw some of the Russians strolling on the street.

Not far from our house was Sitka National Cemetery, so named in the 1920s by President Coolidge. Site selection had been made by Brigadier General Jefferson C. Davis right after the 1867 purchase of Alaska. A Spanish-American War gun rested on the top of the promontory. Until World War II, it was the only national cemetery outside the forty-eight states. Originally under army supervision, then under the Veterans Administration, it became officially a responsibility of the National Park Service in 1949.

Totem Pole Park was a popular place to visit. It was the dream of Governor John Brady, who thought deteriorating totems needed to be preserved. He solicited donations from villages. The first one came in 1901 from Kasaan, as Sitka's Tlingits were not carvers. Alaska's 1904 St. Louis World's Fair exhibit displayed the donated totems, which were subsequently returned to Sitka. Near the outlet of Indian River, a replica of a Russian blockhouse was built by the Alaska Historical Society and Sitka Commercial Club in 1926. Sitka National Historical Park now has an interpretative center, cultural exhibits, workshops and gift shop, together with well maintained trails and totems. The 1941 sign is still there.

I wandered around in another part of town and found Princess Matsoukov's grave overgrown with weeds. The wife of the Russian commander in 1867, she did not favor Alaska's transfer.

My freelancing came to an end in the fall when I was asked to work for the Navy Ship's Service "to keep the records straight." It operated a restaurant, store, laundry, and tailor shop. The restaurant needed a large inventory, and so the eggs were turned every month to keep the yokes from settling. The navy provided the shore boats for transportation across the channel. I heard Joe E. Brown at the USO, but not Bob Hope. After the declaration of war, dependents of servicemen and some civilians were hastily sent Outside.

I met my husband, Owen, through a couple of marines operating the Ship's Service Store. Our wedding was scheduled for 7 P.M.. April 3, 1942, at the commissioner's office. Owen's brother, Earl, worked for Siems Drake, and was Owen's best man. After a stop at one of the town's bars, Earl had dressed at my house in Finn Alley. With blackouts from 5:30 P.M.. until 9 A.M., as he walked to the office he missed the turn to the right and tumbled over the sea wall onto the rocks below. Earl finally arrived at about 8 o'clock, just as Commissioner W.W. Knight started the delayed ceremony. His brand new suit had holes ripped in the knees. Executive naval officers knew I was married, so after a couple of months I changed my name, for we had been concerned that I might be sent out as a dependent.

Whenever a boat came in, we hurried to Ganty's Grocery as soon as possible for the choice of vegetables, which sometimes were not in the best condition. Prices in the Sitka Sentinel that year were: Arrow shirts, $2.00; all wool slacks, $7.95; Florsheim shoes, $8.95 to $10.00. Cigarettes were $1.10 and $1.60 a carton, while a No. 1 can of Hills Bros. coffee cost 34¢. Pot roast beef was 32¢, but a leg of pork would set one back 35¢ a pound. Sitka Cold Storage offered fishermen $7.60 per hundred pounds of first-quality halibut and $6.00 for seconds. On Berry Island, a fisherman recycled the entrails from his fish-smoking operation to grow a luscious garden. His peas grew six to eight feet high. For 50¢ we bought a gunnysack-full of vegetables.

In February 1942, as Singapore fell, the War Production Board froze all sales, delivery, and rental of new and used tires. Nationwide rationing was expected. Except for some shortages, however, in Sitka we never had to handle ration coupons as was done in the Lower 48. Three pairs of shoes was a ration limit. Silk and nylon hose were salvaged and nylon was also used for a secret military purpose.

If Alaskans traveling Outside attempted to take out rationed food, it was confiscated, as a ration card was easy to acquire. In early 1943, Earl's wife Thelma and he had to apply to the Civilian Travel Control Office for a permit. Later when we flew to Seattle, landing at Boeing Field, we had to check through Traffic Control, too. We were far removed from completion of the Alaska Highway, until a 1944 visit to Fairbanks, where we also learned about the ongoing Russian lend-lease program.

In January 1943, Sitka experienced its coldest winter in a long time. Neither of us had seen saltwater ice before. My family reported that a letter had been censored; we later determined that a couple inches of snowfall had been blacked out. A picture of Sitka, Japonski Island, and Mt. Edgecumbe, taken from halfway up Mount Verstovia, had this notation: "This picture forbidden to be circulated by Navy orders. Return this." "Return" didn't happen until fifty years later, in September 1993.

Owen was a Montana hunter and fisherman. His only condition to getting married was, come fall he was going hunting. Loving the outdoors, I went along on many of his trips. In early spring we hunted around Goddard Hot Springs. The grassy terrain, with clumps of trees in the lawn-like green muskeg, was a beautiful natural landscaping job. I wandered off exploring. Owen panicked as we were in brown bear country and he couldn't find me. Reprimanded, I was told not to get too far away again.

The Russians discovered the springs in the early 1800s, sixteen miles from Sitka, although it had been used by the Natives previously. The Pacific Coast Steamship Company initiated tours in 1884. In a few years, as many as five thousand tourists were traveling to see Alaska's wonders. Doctor Goddard, a Treadwell Mine physician, acquired the hot springs in 1905, hoping to establish a health-care facility. He had been superintendent of the Steilacoom sanatorium near Tacoma in 1892, where Alaskans with mental illness were sent. He was never able to reach his goal, what with title problems and the bureaucracy, but eventually he built it into a plush resort. Movie stars and other famous people often anchored their yachts in its harbor.

Men over sixty-five who had lived in the territory for at least fifteen years were admitted to the first Alaska pioneer home at Sitka. The three-story Goddard Building was purchased by the territory in 1934 for $20,000. It was a place where pioneer home residents could move out to relax and soak in the hot baths. In 1950 the Goddard buildings were dilapidated and so were torn down. The springs are now owned by the city and local users help maintain "Sitka Hot Tubs."

St. Michael's Russian Orthodox Church was built in 1848. It burned in 1966 but most icons and treasures were saved. It was rebuilt of fireproof concrete, and reopened ten years later. It is still in the center of Lincoln Street, keeping it a short one-way street two ways.

We had many fishing adventures on Owen's days off. We climbed the mountain to Blue Lake above where the pulp mill is now. We used a raft hammered together when the boat on the lake was in use. I caught a nice rainbow one day. Two hungry men laced it on a willow stick by an open fire. Alas, it was too late for what would have been a contest-winning fish. We both won prizes later.

After the Japanese attacked, Ship's Service officer Dr. Oliver commented that our man in Tokyo was right on: he knew Alaska was to be attacked, but not where it would be hit. A heavy alert had been on for more than two weeks before. One of the fines was five dollars if a person was caught violating the blackout rules.

Owen and two friends flew to Juneau to check out a twenty-six foot home-built cabin cruiser. It was a rainy, stormy day when he was due back. His boss had called to advise that Owen would be out of a job if he didn't get back for his shift. I was worried until I heard the drone of the float plane. The pilot had skimmed the water passages to find his way through the low clouds and fog.

The first weekend we boated north to the Girl Scout cabin. Anchored in the bay was a fifty-foot fishing boat. "Say didn't we see you a few days ago? It was so stormy and rough, we turned back to Juneau." Already in open waters, Walt Wilson and Mel Race had no choice but to continue on. Fortunately only a wash tub was lost overboard, as the untried boat performed beautifully.

Katlean was an area that the Russians used for growing hay for their livestock. A horse had been left to fend on its own and my note on the slide said that it had been there eight years. On one hunting trip near Katlean, Leo Higley shot a deer, missed, then shot when it jumped up again. He was surprised to find two deer behind the fallen log. Four of us had to come down the long sloping mountain over the windfalls and game trails while it got dark.

A sixty-five-pound halibut was landed and deposited in the shower of a friend, as doors were not locked in those days. Once in a while Owen would bring home a bucketful of halibut cheeks from the cannery. I cooked red snapper to be used like tuna fish.

A southeaster blew up while we were duck hunting in Nakwasina Pass. We hurried to a nearby fish trap anchored for the winter. Traps were strategically placed with wires, sometimes hanging down as deep as sixty feet. Migrating salmon swam into the traps with no way out. A watchman was needed to keep fish pirates away until cannery tenders came to dip them out. After a fish duck stew, we listened during the night to the howling wind driving the rain against the shack. Upon awakening the next morning, we were relieved to see the anchors had held, with the two boats gently rocking in the becalmed waters.

In late November 1942 Salmon Lake at the head of Silver Bay was frozen over. As we headed back in the dory, before Leo could finish a warning, we were in water up to our waists. I took one stroke and dropped my shotgun. Leo swam alongside me. Just as I got to shore, my knee boots, tight with heavy socks, started filling with ice water. I didn't feel cold, but was told to swing my arms and stamp my feet to avoid hypothermia, about which I knew nothing. Ted Harris and Owen stayed with the dory, which we needed to get to the cruiser anchored out in deep water. Back on the boat, I stripped and slithered into a sleeping bag. The men wrung their clothes out, while a quart of whiskey disappeared immediately. That experience ended duck hunting for that year. Our guns were recovered at low tide later, with one sporting a wrinkled barrel, as it went off underwater.

Pregnant, I quit my job in April or May in 1943. Later that year, most of the servicemen had been shipped out to other destinations. Not long afterward the store was closed.

Bob was sent to Chilkoot Barracks in Haines in the first draft call, and Margaret followed as soon as housing was available. Owen's draft number had been called so our boat was sold in the summer of 1943. Regulations changed. All draftees were sent to Fort Richardson. Owen was allowed to stay until daughter Merle was born in Juneau in October 1943. The next day he left and the flight was so rough that even the pilot got sick. After the ninety-day basic training, it was okay for his family to join him. We followed in February 1944. I worked for Henry Cole, manager of Northern Commercial's credit department, which distributed checks for Anchorage winners of the Nenana Ice Pool.

Our log cabin at Ninth Avenue and F Street in Anchorage had three rooms, with a hot-water storage tank and plumbing in a small dirt basement underneath the bathroom. Nephew Gary, who was living with us until school was out, hadn't closed the door tightly during a cold, windy day. No water came from the tap when I started the coal stove that evening. Owen and another serviceman were immediately released for the emergency. What to do? Owen packed a dishpan of snow around the intake line in the dirt hole. By the time the line thawed and water started gurgling in, the valve and cracked frozen pipes had been replaced.

Our one Anchorage fishing trip, with other Montanans, was to Wolverine Lake. We overnighted in a horse barn along the straight stretch on the Old Palmer Highway.

The War Department was concerned with the Alaska coal situation. Civilian miners from the Lower 48 who did not accept Alaska conditions were free to leave. A confidential memo was issued in November 1943 authorizing a hundred enlisted men to be discharged to mine coal.

Owen saw a notice for a power-plant worker at the Jonesville mine, which had been his job for the navy in Sitka. I always said he was sent to Jonesville so fast that I didn't have time to acquire groceries at the commissary. His orders from Alaskan Department Headquarters, Office of Commanding General, May 17, 1944, stated:

> Your request for release to enlisted Reserve Corps for the purpose of mining coal in Alaska is approved. Certain responsibilities will rest upon you, and failure to fulfill any one of them will automatically subject you to immediate recall to active duty. You must remain employed with the mine in which you are originally hired and changes are not permitted without specific authority of these headquarters.
>
> You are authorized to wear your uniform to home or authorized place of employment, thereafter it is not authorized.

A lengthy paragraph dealt with possession of other clothing. "ID tags will be retained by you. Within 5 days after your release, you must report to Selective Service Local Board #9, Palmer. Changes in employment are not permitted without specific authority. By command of Lt. General Buckner."

At Jonesville, we lived as civilians, with normal activities. We traveled to Palmer or Anchorage in the coal train caboose. A potbellied stove was fired up when needed. The road was a mile down the track at Sutton. We flew to Seattle where Ann, our second daughter, was born. Owen trapped that winter, with his partner, Bob Tucker. The harvest was lost when the SS *Yukon* broke up on the rocks out of Seward in February 1946, sinking with all their pelts aboard.

V-E Day was celebrated at the Palmer bars by those not on shift. After Owen had walked the mile up the railroad track at 6 A.M., I toweled his wet, snow-covered head. But he got little sympathy for his condition.

In March 1946, Owen was recalled to active duty. Owen's honorable discharge showed service in the Enlisted Reserve Corps, one year, nine months, twenty-seven days. In June, we moved to Fairbanks to join his brother Earl in the construction business, beginning another phase of our lives.

*Helen A. Butcher wrote her autobiography when she enrolled in a creative writing program at the Anchorage Senior Center. Through the years she has been an accountant, realtor, and bank director.*

# The Home Front:
# The Civilians of Seldovia

*Gaye L. Goerig*

IN MANY WAYS, SELDOVIA WAS TYPICAL OF ISOLATED Alaska communities before World War II. The only way to reach them was by airplane or boat and in those days boats were used more than airplanes. Seldovia's location in lower Cook Inlet, however, made it an important port, for it was boats that brought the mail, the supplies, and the people to Anchorage in upper Cook Inlet and out to the Aleutians and Bristol Bay.[1] It's also where the fishermen of Kachemak Bay congregated and where the salmon canneries were located.[2]

When the United States became involved in World War II, the people of Cook Inlet became involved. Arthur English, Niles Kaho, Harry Leman, and Lowell Thorsness were young Alaska men who were typical of the contribution that Alaska made to the war. They went from being "home boys" to manning the "front line." And, because of the war, George Mooney, from Boston, Massachusetts, and Dorothy Pankey, from Potlatch, Idaho, met and fell in love. All this happened in Seldovia between 1942 and 1945.

In 1942, Arthur English was ten years old and lived in a coal-heated log house with his parents. His mother ran the post office that was in the same building as his house and every morning his father got up early and walked up the hill to turn on the power plant. At about ten in the evening the power would be turned off. Seldovia had electricity but no telephones. A man named Adam Lipke had a radio station in his house—not a commercial station that played music but Morse Code that kept them aware of emergencies and weather reports. When Seldovians wanted to send a telegram they went to Adam Lipke's house.[3]

The people of Seldovia took their boats across Kachemak Bay to Homer where there was a hill with thousands of tons of coal that fell down on the beach. They filled up their boats and hauled it to their two- or three-room houses where they burned it in cook stoves that had a firebox in the back, an oven in the front, and a dust pan underneath. They shook the grates to get the ashes down and keep the draft going through the stove so the fire would burn. It burned well, but made a lot of ash.[4]

Canned goods, flour, sugar, powdered milk, clothing, and hardware were shipped on the Alaska Steam Ship Line from Seattle and sold in the general stores. The entire town was built up on pilings and a boardwalk ran from one end to the other connecting the stores, restaurants and bars, the canneries, and the churches. Art's family also ordered from the Sears Roebuck and Montgomery Ward catalogues, and in those days there was no Department of Fish and Game, so hunting for moose meat and fishing was year round.[5]

There was one school building, with grades one through twelve, and it was common to have two grades

---

[1] Arthur English, telephone interview, September 10, 1993.

[2] Janet Klein, *A History of Kachemak Bay; the Country, the Communities,* (Homer, Alaska), p. 69.

[3] English, telephone interview.

[4] Niles Kaho, personal interview, September 8, 1993.

[5] English, personal interview.

in the same classroom. If the weather permitted, the children played baseball; otherwise they played in the gymnasium. After the fall freeze they would go ice skating on Lake Susan, named for Art's mother. It was traditional for the local police chief to go out and test the ice first to make sure it was safe. And in winter they did a little skiing.[6]

It was May 1942, and school got out early as usual so the kids could start fishing with their parents and working on the boats. The year before, when Art was nine, his father had bought him a little boat which he and his friend Norman Erskin took salmon fishing in Seldovia Bay. They did quite well and sold their fish to one of the canneries.[7]

When the fishing season began and the canneries opened, the population swelled to nearly three times the normal two hundred year-round residents. At that time the Cook Inlet Packing Company only hired local people but the other canneries had to bring in Filipino workers to fill out their crews because they were available and dependable.[8] Pay was very low—twenty-five cents an hour for a cannery worker.

The cannery owners and crew were an integral part of the community during the fishing season. When Gene Mason ran the Cook Inlet Packing Company tender *Westward* over to Ninilchik for a load of fish from the fish traps, he would also pick up villagers and take them back to Seldovia for a shopping trip.[9]

Harry Leman was one of the villagers who had grown up across Cook Inlet in the self-sufficient, farm-like community of Ninilchik. On this side of Cook Inlet people raised hogs, chickens, vegetables, hay, and grain; and in Bear Cove his family had a successful fox farm. In Cooper Landing, named for Harry's grandfather, his family mined for gold that brought thirty-five dollars an ounce. Harry and his family would fish all season and sell their catch to the canneries for about twenty-five cents per fish—not per pound. His mother and other women from Ninilchik would also work in the Seldovia canneries. In the fall, Harry—who had just graduated from Ninilchik High School—would ride down to Seattle on the *Westward*. He would stay with friends and study with a favorite teacher.[10]

Niles Kaho was born in Seldovia and grew up in Cordova. His father was the winter watchman for New England Fish Company and the family lived across Orca Bay. When he was seven or eight years old his father first checked him out on a twelve-horse engine and he took his little gill-netter boat across the bay to Cordova for school in the mornings and back home again at night.[11]

In 1942 he worked all winter at the base camp of the Red Mountain Chrome Mine in Seldovia. In the spring he fished Prince William Sound, and in the fall, seventeen-year-old Niles went to Seattle for his first time away from home. He stayed in a downtown hotel and found a job as a longshoreman on the docks.

Thomas Munson was born in Akutan out on the Aleutian Chain, not far from Dutch Harbor. As a very young child he fished Cook Inlet with his father, working for the Cook Inlet Packing Company in Seldovia. In those days they didn't have power in their seine skiffs; two men would row the twenty-five-foot-long skiff, pulling the twenty-foot seine net around the fish to make the set. There was only a little power boat to pull the skiffs.[12]

When Tommy was five or six years old his parents died and he went to an orphanage in Seward where he lived until he was eighteen years old. In 1942, he had just graduated from high school and wanted to join the navy, so he traveled to Southeastern Alaska to spend six weeks on a naval base.[13]

Life was going along pretty much as usual when, in June, the Japanese bombed Dutch Harbor and invaded Kiska and Attu. Under cover of fog they crept ashore on Attu and killed the schoolteacher, C. Foster Jones, who was attempting to wire news of the invasion to the American authorities. His wife and all of the Attuans were taken to Japan.[14] First shock, then fear spread through Alaska communities. Seldovia began arming itself and there were enforced blackouts.[15]

Major Marvin "Muktuk" Marston was commissioned by Governor Gruening to organize the Alaska Territorial Guard—the home defense force which included about twenty-seven hundred Eskimos, Aleuts, and Indians, as well as non-Natives from communities around western

---

[6] Ibid.

[7] Ibid.

[8] Pedersen, personal interview.

[9] Harry Leman, personal interview, September 7, 1993.

[10] Ibid.

[11] Kaho, personal interview.

[12] Thomas Munson, personal interview, September 13, 1993.

[13] Ibid.

[14] Ted Bank II, *Readings in Anthropology, People of the Bering Sea*, (New York: 1971).

[15] Lowell Thorsness, personal interview, September 3, 1993.

Alaska.[16] Major Marston visited Seldovia and handed out World War I Springfield and Enfield rifles and they organized their "home guard."[17] The men built shacks out on the points and held day and night patrols along the outside beach to watch for Japanese submarines because they felt they were in danger of being invaded.

This was somewhat confusing to Art and the other children, who weren't sure why their parents were so concerned. They walked to school by the oil storage tanks up on the hill that the men said they were guarding, but the guard shack was down by the boardwalk.[18]

Art's family started growing a victory garden of potatoes and carrots. By fall, although there was no rationing in Alaska, some items were hard to get. Enforced blackouts had become a regular part of life.[19]

In November, Lowell Thorsness began working for the Red Mountain Chrome Mine in Seldovia as a bulldozer operator. Thorsness was waiting for a ruling on his army status appeal to the Juneau Draft Board. In 1939 he had left his Midwest home and begun working as a civilian Cat skinner for the navy base at Dutch Harbor. He lived on the old ship *Northwestern* that was no longer fit for sea duty but had been parked ashore with gravel built up all around it. The ship had an engine room to make steam and electricity for the buildings and had staterooms and a galley for board and room. On June 4, when the Japanese bombed Dutch Harbor, Tokyo Rose said that the Japanese had sunk a huge merchant ship in the harbor. But although the ship was hit, it couldn't have been sunk since it was parked on the beach.[20]

On the 19th of June, Thorsness was in the hospital at Dutch Harbor with an attack of appendicitis but, because he was a civilian, the navy doctors wouldn't operate. The

facilities were standing by in case there was another bombing. He took an old freighter to Kodiak, then to Anchorage where he had his appendix out. Bulldozer operators were hard to find and the navy wanted him back to continue working as a civilian at Dutch Harbor, but the draft board wanted him in the army. He

Dorothy Pankey, left, and Ethelyn Estus, childhood friends in Potlatch, Idaho, hoist a Seldovian denizen between them, ca. 1943. The women had come to Alaska for the fishing season and, like others traveling north at the time, first had to obtain travel permits. *(Photograph from the author's collection)*

appealed to the Juneau Draft Board but after recovering from his surgery was told that the Dutch Harbor job had been turned over to the navy. That was why he went to Seldovia to work in the Red Mountain Mine.[21]

On November 14, his papers came through and twenty-four-year-old Lowell Thorsness, along with Harry Leman, Niles Kaho, and Thomas Munson, were in the army. The men from the home front were now manning the front line.[22]

In 1943 the war's impact grew. Alaskans who were Outside when the war started had to obtain travel per-

---

[16] Michael Carey, "Legacies of War," *We Alaskans, The Anchorage Daily News Magazine,* December 1, 1991, p. 14.

[17] Thorsness, personal interview.

[18] English, personal interview.

[19] Ibid.

[20] Thorsness, personal interview.

[21] Ibid.

[22] Ibid.

mits to get back home. People still traveled on the Alaska Steam Ship Company ships, but it was under blackout conditions in a war zone with freighters being sunk out in the Gulf of Alaska by Japanese submarines. There was a German prisoners' camp at Excursion Inlet that was not too far from Juneau. And the mail was censored, even the magazines with whole pages taken out.[23]

In May of 1943, the American effort to take back Attu and Kiska began. Seldovia cannery owner Carl "Squeaky" Anderson was a navy commander in Dutch Harbor and the success of this operation boosted the spirits of Seldovia residents. The dark and lonely winter gave way even before the annual spring arrival of the fishing boats and cannery workers. Two gunboats of the Tenth Emergency Rescue Boat Squadron had come to Seldovia Bay.[24]

The Tenth Emergency Rescue Boat Squadron actually began in Ketchikan in the winter of 1941-42. From Annette Island, by Ketchikan, to Attu at the tip of the Aleutians, boats were standing by to rescue downed fighter pilots. It provided a great psychological boost to young, inexperienced pilots who knew that anywhere on their mission, rescue boats were there for them. Two "crash boats" were stationed in Cook Inlet, one at Anchorage and the other at Seldovia. They were made of wood and in the winter, when the upper inlet filled with ice, the boats would stay in the lower inlet at Seldovia.[25]

It hadn't taken long for the news to get around that the army had started a crash boat unit and was looking for men with experience in Alaska waters. Niles was seventeen and had to get his parents' consent. He was assigned to the P-215, stationed in Southeastern Alaska, and given the rank of corporal. Less than eighteen months later he was the executive officer, taking care of the ship's logs, sending in monthly reports, and supervising the deck crew. The P-215 had the youngest crew in the squadron.[26]

Harry came back to Alaska and enlisted. After completing boot camp he was assigned to the P-215 in Anchorage. When the boat docked in Seldovia he was transferred to the P-217, but the only position open was radio operator and he didn't know a thing about radios. The executive officer, Wayne Webb, was a good radio operator and a willing teacher. During the winter, when the men from the boat went ashore, he and the exec stayed aboard. Harry conscientiously studied Morse code and Wayne rigged up a way for them to send messages back and forth so he could take over the radio by himself.[27]

They stood by that radio on what was called the Homer beam station twenty-four hours a day, 365 days a year and waited for any messages or emergencies. When the call to P-217 came (or Foxtail-17 if they were in the Aleutian Islands) they had to be ready to go out on a rescue mission. The skipper of the boat—the man who was responsible for keeping the equipment and men ready—was Lowell Thorsness.[28]

The 104-foot P-217 was completely self-sufficient, with crew's quarters, full galley, a complete dispensary, and doctor. It had four big Keller machine guns, a 20-millimeter on the stern, rifles, carbines, Thompson submachine guns, and .45's. In Seldovia, there was no other military around except harbor MPs who left them alone. There was no commanding officer, no base commander, no adjutant, no inspectors. Even when they were out in Adak they worked off the base and stood no formations. There was nothing like "KP." There were two cooks who worked twenty-four-hour shifts from noon to noon. They did all the dishes and kitchen work and Lowell observed "that they did more work than anybody on the boat."[29] One of those cooks was Tommy Munson. The navy didn't work out for him and when he was asked if he wanted to get on a crash boat and make corporal right away he said, "Yes!" The only position open at that time was cook and he couldn't even make coffee, but on the P-217 he learned from the first cook, who had been a chef before the war.[30]

The boat had freezers for chicken, pork, beef, and an occasional moose. The cooks had citrus fruits; only fresh vegetables were hard to get. They were allotted a ration-and-a-half per person from the navy base, so they had plenty of everything to work with, including the army old standby, Spam, which nobody ate and which sat on the shelf until the boat was decommissioned after the war.[31]

In Adak, Tommy saw, cooked, and ate his first king crab. Using oil drums on shore, the cooks boiled the crab in salt water. After it was peeled, the crab was taken

[23] Elsa and Walt Pedersen, personal interview, September 9, 1993.

[24] Thorsness, personal interview.

[25] Ibid.

[26] Kaho, personal interview.

[27] Leman, personal interview.

[28] Thorsness, personal interview.

[29] Ibid.

[30] Munson, personal interview.

[31] Ibid.

aboard and served plain, in sauces, or dipped in butter and lemon. Most of the time they cooked with the boat tied to the dock, and out in rough weather they made sandwiches.[32]

Every crash boat had at least two or three Alaska men on it and every Alaska town or village had sons who went to war. Seldovia, like all Alaska communities, opened up its homes and hearts to the men of the crash boats. And of course Harry, Niles, Tommy, and Lowell were right at home. They were given cakes on special occasions and there were dances every weekend. And the GIs had chewing gum for kids like Art, and took them for rides on the crash boat, which seemed really fast compared to their fishing boats. If there was a storm or if the P-217 had been across the inlet in Halibut Cove, they would take the mail or supplies to Seldovia from Homer.[33]

It was the same for Niles and the other men on the P-215 in Southeastern Alaska, especially after the Americans took back the Aleutian Islands. The men got to Wrangell and the town was theirs. They were treated like they had won the war single-handed. And at Christmas a photography studio in Seward took head shots of the whole crew and made Christmas cards for them.[34]

But their main purpose was to stand by for emergencies. These often included rescue of civilians like the mill worker who nearly cut himself in half with a saw in Kodiak, and the halibut fisherman in Sand Point who had appendicitis and had to be taken to Cold Bay. When the P-217 arrived to pick the fisherman up, everybody in the village got sick. Although the men of the P-217 knew that at least half of the villagers were lying, they ran the boat back and forth all day and all night taking the villagers between Sand Point and Cold Bay.[35]

At that time Seldovia and Seward had the only hospitals on the Kenai Peninsula. Once the P-217 received an emergency call that the Homer school superintendent's wife had suffered a stroke and was unconscious. When the crash boat with doctor aboard crossed Kachemak Bay, they saw that a storm had washed a hole right through the gravel spit—making landing at the dock impossible. They laid off shore and the necessary crew and doctor washed up on the beach in a skiff. The woman was unconscious and needed to be taken to the hospital in Seldovia. She was wrapped in army blankets and secured in a wire basket called a Stokes litter,

instead of a flat stretcher.

Because the litter wouldn't fit lengthwise in the boat, they put her across the stern with her head and her feet sticking out over the sides. The weather was what Lowell referred to as "kinda sloppy, but not rough," and as they rowed her out to the crash boat, her head would go down in the water on one side, then her feet would go down in the water on the other side. When they got to the boat, they attached lines to the Stokes litter and she was lifted on board and put in the dispensary with the doctor who stayed with her until they arrived in Seldovia. The tide was out and the only way they could get her from the boat to the shore was by hoisting her up by hand. She was taken to the hospital and twenty-seven days later she woke up and asked, "Where am I and how'd I get here?" No one wanted to tell her.[36]

In the spring of 1944, the Estus family prepared for the annual trip from Seattle to Seldovia to open the Cook Inlet Packing Company. The 104-foot tender *Westward* and 90-foot tender *Adriatic* had been outfitted with supplies and were ready. Sanger Estus and his wife Ethelyn would go on the *Adriatic*, while Sanger's parents and his brother-in-law Gene Mason would go on the *Westward*. Gene's wife, Margaret, would join them later in the summer. And this year they would be taking Ethelyn's young cousin Dorothy Pankey with them on the *Westward*.[37]

Ethelyn and Dottie had grown up together in Potlatch, Idaho. Dottie was twelve years younger than Ethelyn and attended elementary school in a two-room schoolhouse, loved to read, played basketball in high school, and fished in the local lakes. Ethelyn's mother, Addie, was Dottie's favorite aunt and Dottie spent much of her childhood at their house. At sixteen years old, Dottie left Potlatch and went to Spokane to finish school. She graduated from Lewis and Clark High School, attended Cheney Normal for a year, then took classes at Lewiston Normal School while working in a department store.[38]

When the war started, she moved to Seattle and worked in the personnel office of the Boeing plant. She lived in a boarding house with other young people. She was working as a secretary and Teletype operator for Webster Brinkley, a plant that manufactured steering gears and windlasses for the navy, when Ethelyn invited her to go to Alaska for the fishing season. Like others

---

[32] Ibid.

[33] English, personal interview.

[34] Kaho, personal interview.

[35] Thorsness, personal interview.

[36] Ibid.

[37] Dorothy Pankey-Mooney, personal interview, September 2, 1993.

[38] Ibid.

traveling at that time she first had to obtain a passport and travel permits.[39]

The *Westward* and *Adriatic* traveled together in constant radio contact. On the *Westward* Dottie occupied the top bunk in the cabin she shared with Mrs. Estus. Next to their cabin was the head and on the other side of that deck were two cabins for Gene and Margaret, and Mr. Estus and the cannery engineer. In the deck above was the pilothouse, and below were the galley, crew quarters, and the hold. Sanger and Ethelyn were the only ones traveling on the *Adriatic*.[40]

They traveled up the Inland Passage, stopping first at Ketchikan, where the boat was boarded and their passports were checked, and at Wrangell, where Gene had been born and raised. When they crossed the Gulf of Alaska they had to be on the lookout for mines. After eight days they arrived in Seldovia and Dottie was surprised to see so many people at the dock to greet them.41

The first thing she noticed was that the whole town was built on pilings. On the land side of the boardwalk was a building with apartments for Gene and his wife Margaret, Ethelyn and Sanger, and one for the cannery engineer. Across the boardwalk facing the sea was the Cook Inlet Packing Company where Dottie lived in a room just inside the entrance. Her room, opposite Mr. Estus' office, had a bed, a table and chair, and a pot-belly stove which Sanger would light while she was out. Down the hall were the Estus living quarters and the dining room for family and crew. She took her showers at Ethelyn and Sanger's apartment. For the fishermen and cannery employees, there was a bathhouse adjacent to the cannery.[42]

Dottie walked along the boardwalk from one end to the other looking at the cannery, the general stores, the liquor store, the post office, the hotel, the restaurant, the bars, and the Methodist and Russian Orthodox churches. She and Ethelyn would sit on the boardwalk in nice weather and watch with fascination the town and people of Seldovia. Once a small motor boat arrived with a hair dresser who set up a beauty shop in one of the

A wartime romance blossoms in Seldovia, Alaska. George Mooney hailed from Boston, Massachusetts, and Dorothy Pankey from Potlatch, Idaho. *(Photograph from the author's collection)*

homes. All day long, local women arrived to have their hair cut and receive a permanent wave. At the end of the day the hair dresser packed up her bags, got into the little boat and left. The boardwalk was also a favorite place for Dottie to read. And it was while sitting in the sun reading a book that she looked up to see a stranger who would change her life.[43]

George Mooney grew up in Boston and joined the marines when he was seventeen years old. His sea duty from 1934 to 1936 was as a captain's orderly aboard the "floating White House," the USS *Houston*. This included a trip to Alaska to familiarize the navy with Alaska waters. His obligation completed, he served in the reserves and worked as a guard at the Boston Navy Yard.[44]

When the war started he was working as a policeman in the new final assembly department of the plant that made superchargers for B-17s in Everett, Massachusetts. George took a discharge from the marines so he could enlist in the army air corps as a member of the ground crew. After completing officers' training school in Arkansas and a technical course at Casey Jones Aeronautical School in Newark, New Jersey, he was assigned to the Seventh Quartermaster Rescue Boat Squadron in Florida. When a request came in for a chief engineer, arctic service, he put in for it, thinking he would be assigned to the north of England or Scotland. Instead he was assigned to the P-217 of the Tenth Emergency Rescue Boat Squadron in Seldovia, Alaska. It was an anxious farewell from his family, because three years earlier, his sister Ollie's brother-in-law, tail gunner Frank William Peter Gabler, was killed when his B-25 went down in Kiska. The plane and bodies weren't recovered until the following spring.[45]

39 Ibid.

40 Ibid.

41 Ibid.

42 Ibid.

43 Ibid.

44 George Mooney, personal interview, April 10, 1990.

45 Ibid.

George traveled to Fort Lewis, Washington, by train, then to Elmendorf Air Force Base by plane where he picked up a few cans of a special motor oil. He was flown to Homer and met by the P-217. They had just docked in Seldovia when he went ashore to see the engineer of the Cook Inlet Packing Company. The valve spring on a motor was broken, and he wanted to see if the cannery had the equipment to wind the valve. If the cannery had an engineer and equipment to do the job, it would take less time than sending it to Kodiak to be fixed.[46]

But that day he never made it to the cannery. One look at Dottie reading a book on the boardwalk and he stopped looking for the engineer. The first thing George said to the skipper when he got back to the boat was, "Did you see Sanger's cousin? What a dish! I never expected to find a gal like that up here in a little town in Alaska!"[47] And, to the amusement of the crew, he began spending a lot of time visiting the cannery, getting to know Sanger and talking about motors. But Lowell noticed that when he was talking to Sanger he was looking at Dottie. And Sanger was overheard saying, "There can't be that much wrong with the damn boat!"[48]

Throughout the summer, George and Dottie took walks on the beach, danced at the dance hall, and made plans for their future. In the fall, the canneries closed, the boats headed south, and Dottie began working as a secretary for Henry Disston's in Seattle. But the crash boats were still there and the war wasn't over yet. Now it became a long-distance romance.[49]

Dottie's birthday fell on December 16 and the P-217 was in Adak. George decided to send Dottie a dozen roses for her birthday, so he wrote a letter and sent money to Sanger's office in Seattle. Except Dottie never got the roses. What she got was a Parker pen-and-pencil set. He told her, "George wanted you to have roses, but they'll be dead in three days; these won't be dead, they'll last."[50]

George made another try at sending roses and this time it worked. One of his buddies was in Seattle and diligently followed all of George's orders regarding the flowers, including the length of the stems. When they were delivered, Dottie noticed that the roses were beautiful, but the stems were nearly three feet long. In January George was transferred to Seattle and he and Dottie were married.[51]

In the spring of 1945, the fishing boats came back to Seldovia, the canneries opened, and the season began as usual. The crash boats were gone, but Lowell, Harry, Niles, and Tommy would soon be back, once again living and working in the Cook Inlet communities where they still live today.[52] Art would spend the last two years of high school in Montana living with his uncle, then he would also return.[53] George and Dottie would only come back to Seldovia to visit; they would make their home in Spokane, Washington.[54]

The war that made Anchorage the largest city in Alaska turned Seldovia from an important port into a charming but small community. In 1945, Seldovia was incorporated as a second-class city[55] but people and goods began being transported by plane or by auto on the newly built Alaska and Sterling highways. When the Alaska Steam Ship Company stopped running, the canneries had no way to ship their products and the canneries closed for good.[56] In 1962, Seldovia became a first-class city with a stable population of around 450.[57]

*Gaye L. Goerig is a freelance writer. Her parents inspired in her a lifelong interest in Alaska history and World War II.*

---

[46] Ibid.

[47] Ibid.

[48] Pankey-Mooney, personal interview.

[49] Ibid.

[50] Thorsness, personal interview.

[51] Pankey-Mooney, personal interview.

[52] Thorsness, personal interview.

[53] English, personal interview.

[54] Pankey-Mooney, personal interview.

[55] Klein, *Kachemak Bay,* p. 87.

[56] Pedersen, personal interview.

[57] Klein, *Kachemak Bay,* p. 87.

# World War II through
## *The Alaska Sportsman* Magazine

*Timothy Rawson*

A SUBSCRIPTION TO *ALASKA* MAGAZINE IS A FAVORITE Christmas gift from Alaskans to relatives in other states. Although residents of the Last Frontier see the magazine's masthead at every grocery store checkout line, its carefully edited perspective on Alaska receives wider readership Outside than in the state. *Alaska* is currently published in Anchorage. Its folksy blend of articles on environmental issues, history, and local culture gives little clue to the magazine's origins. In a modest frame house in Ketchikan, the magazine began its successful life in 1935 as *The Alaska Sportsman*, which historian Morgan Sherwood called the "single most important private, institutional influence in the history of game animals and people in the Territory."[1] The purpose of its founder, Emery Tobin, was "To hold a mirror to life on the Last Frontier," with a focus on items of interest to those who sought Alaska's animals and fish. The magazine acts as a mirror for the modern reader on life in Alaska during the 1940s, especially for the reactions of the hunting and fishing fraternity to the changes induced by the war: the tension between sourdough nostalgia and Alaska's development, the controversy over resident hunting licenses, the effects on sportsmen and their prey, media censorship, and the dawning of a new era in Alaska's growth.

Tobin's youthful fascination with Alaska was understandable, for the Boston boy's father had been there since Emery was two. August Tobin, a Swedish immigrant, stampeded north in '97, drifted around the Koyukuk for twenty-two years, and finally returned to Boston. Emery grew up in his father's absence and served in France during World War I. Following the war, he became a newspaperman for the *Boston Ledger*, where his supervisor was Ernest Gruening—later to become governor of the Alaska territory. Emery and his father moved to Alaska in 1920 and found a home in the mountains and bays of the Panhandle, settling in Ketchikan. He married a schoolteacher, Clara Willard, in 1926, worked as business manager for the Ketchikan newspaper, and then helped launch *The Alaska Sportsman* in 1935.[2]

The magazine's contents reflected a dual audience. Tobin recognized the allure of Alaska to nonresidents and used the magazine to promote Alaska to potential settlers, writing in the inaugural issue that it was a magazine "by Alaskans for everyone," to give a "true idea of the country." The editorial column "Main Trails and Bypaths" repeatedly extolled the virtues of Alaska's natural resources and its people, and feature articles provided instruction on the territory's geography and "gee-whiz" lessons on the size of Alaska potatoes and bears. For local residents, the Sportsman published how-to articles on trapping, making pemmican, salmon fishing, and the like.

---

[1] Morgan Sherwood, *Big Game in Alaska: A History of Wildlife and People* (New Haven: Yale University Press, 1981), p. 57.

[2] Biographic information from Ethel Dassow, "The Voice of the Last Frontier," *Alaska* (October 1984), pp. 15-21, 85-89, 92-93. Tobin was not the initial editor, but assumed the title with the December 1935 issue. Dassow began her long-time employment with the magazine during World War II and became assistant editor, rewriting manuscripts to give a balance between good grammar and colloquial expression.

While Tobin sought population growth and economic development for Alaska, the magazine carried a complementary theme for residents, "advising intelligent conservation" of animal resources. The magazine served as the mouthpiece for the Alaska Sportsman's Association, whose motto was "Help keep Alaska the Sportsman's Paradise. Protect and propagate wild life."[3] Editorials cited the destruction of game resources that had accompanied European expansion across the continent, while at the same time reveling in the bounty of fauna still available in Alaska. The Sportsman's Association promoted conservation ideals it hoped would sustain fish and game populations, urging Alaskans to follow the regulations of the ten-year-old Alaska Game Commission. The war provided unexpected challenges to the sporting life, yet did not significantly alter the magazine's contents or objectives.

As the conflict in Europe gained intensity, and as the belated recognition of Alaska's strategic value became manifest in construction projects, Tobin began 1940 with an optimistic editorial praising developments in mining, transportation, defense projects, farming, and the salmon industry. He also welcomed to Alaska his former boss, the newly-appointed governor Ernest Gruening.[4] Tourist revenues declined that year as the number of steamers available for passenger use decreased, yet this was offset by the influx of new money and material. The peacetime benefits of the newly-constructed airfields and ports were considered critical to developing the territory's infrastructure, and "the work is setting loose forces which will result in great immediate development of the Territory in an industrial way if war and invasion do not interfere." Tobin echoed this hope five months before the attack on Pearl Harbor, confidently stating that "Far from the centers of world conflict in Asia and Europe, most Alaskans are not excited over the possibility of invasion of this great Territory."[5]

Economic development depended on population growth, and while *The Alaska Sportsman* promoted immigration, it did so selectively. Alaska's population totaled 72,524 in October 1939—slightly over half non-Native—and Tobin stated editorially that "Alaska needs population, wants population."[6] However, a proposal by Interi-

*The Alaska Sportsman* editor, Emory Tobin, founded the periodical in 1935. The magazine's mission, according to Tobin, was "To hold a mirror to life on the Last Frontier." *(Photograph No. 01-3735, Early Prints Collection, Alaska State Library, Juneau)*

or Secretary Harold Ickes in 1939 to resettle in Alaska up to fifty thousand European refugees, presumably Jewish, was met with near-unanimous criticism in Alaska. Newspapers called for settlers "schooled in American traditions," and the resettlement plan was sarcastically said to be "a brilliant idea to help the dictators of Europe."[7] Comparisons of Alaska to Scandinavia had long been common, along with interest in promoting Anglo-Saxon and Nordic settlement. Scandinavian farmers from the upper Midwest comprised the majority of settlers for the Matanuska Valley colony in 1935,

---

[3] "Main Trails and Bypaths;" "The Alaska Sportsmen's Association," January 1935, p. 24. The Sportsmen's Association dissolved in 1938, but not its objectives.

[4] "Main Trails...," January 1940. The relationship between Tobin and Gruening would sour: an August 1949 "Main Trails..." called Gruening "leftish" and "New-Dealing," opposed to outside capital and industrial development. Gruening responded to a friend that "arguing with him [Tobin] is hopeless ... I cannot escape the conclusion that his intellectual honesty is not above reproach." Gruening to Louis Huber, 29 August 1949, Alaska State Archives, RG 101, Box 471, Juneau.

[5] "Main Trails...," July 1940; November 1940; June 1941.

[6] "Main Trails...," October 1939. Population statistics in this paper are from George W. Rogers and Richard A. Cooley, *Alaska's Population and Economy* (College, Alaska: University of Alaska, 1963), tables P-3, P-4.

[7] Quoted in Orlando Miller, *The Frontier in Alaska and the Matanuska Colony* (New Haven: Yale University, 1975), p. 168; Jim Scott, "What Risk Colonization?", *Alaska Life* (October 1940), 3:10, p. 3.

chosen for supposed hardiness and natural aptitude for living in a frontier area with harsh winters. The apparent lack of success of the colony in developing sustainable agriculture provided arguments against refugees, for if Scandinavian farmers had not been successful, what chance had the penniless of Europe's ghettos?[8] Ernest Gruening opposed the plan, much to Ickes' displeasure, and Emery Tobin came down firmly in favor of Scandinavian immigration, but not refugees.[9]

Alaska became part of the Pacific Theater with the Japanese attack on the Aleutians in 1942, and by 1943 the territory hosted 152,000 military personnel. Immigrants in uniform were welcomed, but as early as 1941 a note of concern over their potential effects on fish and game became evident in *The Alaska Sportsman*. "We are glad to see an ever increasing number of them now," but soldiers equipped with automatic rifles presented a "real threat to the game resources of Alaska."[10]

The issue of resident hunting-license eligibility for military personnel was a campaign of the commander of Alaska's defense forces, General Simon B. Buckner. He considered it "manifestly unjust" that soldiers be treated differently because they were not previously residents of Alaska, and predicted the ensuing ill will would "encourage violation of game regulation by individuals who feel that they are discriminated against." To make his point, Buckner personally sought and was denied a resident license by the Alaska Game Commission, despite Buckner's ownership of a local house and land and having lived in Alaska more than the twelve months required by statute.[11] Buckner also issued a dispatch to post commanders announcing the opening of Mount McKinley National Park for hunting trips to soldiers on furlough.[12]

Tobin had editorially urged that "no relaxation of present regulations" should be made before Buckner's case went to court, yet after a federal judge overruled the game commission, Tobin relented by saying it was "manifestly unfair" to deny soldiers hunting privileges when they had met the same statutory obligations as had civilians. National Park Service Director Newton Drury worked effectively in Washington to cooperate with the War Department in opening parks to military recreation while protecting essential park values, and the hunting ban remained in effect in McKinley Park.[13] The predicted effects of thousands of hunting soldiers in legal areas, though, were restrictive seasons and bag limits. With "old-timers" no longer able to fill their pots, Tobin wrote, "The day of easy hunting and long seasons is passing."[14]

The actual effects of the war on Alaska's game resources are difficult to determine. Tobin wrote that Alaskans "have not felt very heavily the mailed fist of Mars," but identified the "illegal slaughter" of animals to be the "most serious permanent disadvantage of present activities."[15] *The Alaska Sportsman* occasionally printed brief mentions of killings by military personnel, such as whales or moose being used as target practice by aerial gunners, but there were no efforts to discredit the military, merely repeated urgings of everyone to obey the game regulations. Less trapping occurred, as men left the villages for active duty or construction work, and wolf numbers reportedly increased. Soldiers received permission to fire at wolves along the Alaska Highway, and military helicopters flew to the reindeer villages of Norton Sound to hunt wolves in the winter of 1943-44.[16]

By 1943, with able-bodied men in short supply, the Alaska Game Commission could dispatch only eight wildlife agents in the territory to deal with the increased numbers of civilian shooters who "required

---

[8] Miller, *The Frontier in Alaska*, p. 167. The so-called Slattery plan received favorable opinion outside Alaska, but did not pass Congress. Miller effectively summarizes this and other resettlement schemes in chap. 9, "Promoting the Last Frontier: The Closed Safety Valve," *The Frontier in Alaska*.

[9] Gruening was a Jew, and his opposition took some by surprise; *Many Battles: The Autobiography of Ernest Gruening* (New York: Liveright, 1973), pp. 268-269; "Main Trails...," December 1939.

[10] "Main Trails...," February 1942; July 1941.

[11] This case and its implications form the backbone of Sherwood's *Big Game in Alaska*. The Buckner quotes are from a letter to Frank Dufresne of the Alaska Game Commission, 19 June 1941, Alaska State Archives, RG 101, Box 470, Juneau.

[12] Buckner to Post Commanders, 2 September 1943, Wildlife Reports 1930-50, Box 2, Denali National Park and Preserve Archives.

[13] "Main Trails...," July 1941; November 1941; William E. Brown, *A History of the Denali-Mount McKinley Region, Alaska* (GPO: National Park Service, 1991), p. 204. Brown describes the various other ways in which McKinley Park became a central recreational facility for Alaska's military use. Sport hunting was only one of many threats to national parks during the war. Their timber, grazing, game, and watercourses received many development proposals spurred by "patriotic" motives.

[14] "Main Trails...," June 1942; November 1941.

[15] "Main Trails...," November 1942. In a letter to Gov. Gruening on 4 October 46, Lt. Col. J.P. Williams of the Alaska National Guard admitted "considerable truth" to reports of shooting safaris by soldiers in the Fairbanks area; Alaska State Archives, RG 101, Box 470, Juneau.

[16] "From Ketchikan to Barrow," *The Alaska Sportsman*, May 1943, December 1943. The helicopter was an unsophisticated machine in 1943, and I have not confirmed this report of whirlybird wolfing.

A wartime anti-Japanese cartoon in *The Alaska Sportsman*. In part, the caption reads, "Japanese taken in the Aleutians may be shot in the back or kicked in the pants." *(The Alaska Sportsman Magazine Collection, Box 11, University of Alaska Fairbanks Archives)*

orientation in the rudiments of good sportsmanship."[17] New facilities and roads—particularly the Alaska Highway—brought hunters into previously undisturbed haunts, and game populations declined, punctuated by a "dark and grisly" free-for-all at the war's end by military and civilians alike.[18]

Industrial production in the 1940s centered on wartime priorities, and *The Alaska Sportsman*'s advertising reflected the effects of material shortages upon the hunting and fishing fraternity. Arms and ammunition

manufacturers turned their entire production to meet the needs of the Allies. Readers of the magazine in 1940 perused advertisements for full lines of ammo and could mail-order a Springfield .30-06 for seventy-one dollars, yet for the next six years only second-hand guns could be ordered from private dealers in the classified ads. Arms manufacturers maintained their consumer links with a memorable genre of print advertising, mingling patriotism with the myth of the civilian sharpshooter. Evinrude Motors used similar ads to keep its name in

---

[17] Fifth Annual Report of the Alaska Game Commission to the Department of the Interior, July 1943-June 1944; Rasmuson Library, Fairbanks. The sudden decline of the Fortymile caribou herd, which had fed Interior Alaskans since the gold rush, provoked considerable concern. Olaus Murie, a biologist with considerable Alaska experience, estimated this herd in 1920 at over a half-million strong, but it reached a population nadir in the 1940s; see Ronald O. Skoog, "Range, Movements, Population, and Food Habits of the Steese-Fortymile Caribou Herd," (M.S. thesis, University of Alaska, 1956), p. 56.

[18] Robert G. McCandless, *Yukon Wildlife: A Social History* (Edmonton: University of Alberta Press, 1985), p. 86; Sherwood, *Big Game in Alaska*, p. 142.

the public eye during the years of unavailability. Metal shortages curtailed the production lines of the Oneida Trap Company, though it continued making the New-house No. 114, the standard Alaska wolf trap.[19] The Victor Trap Company, an Oneida subsidiary, used *The Alaska Sportsman* to advertise a free booklet on the care, repair, and rebuilding of traps, since "A little trap care adds a lot to trap life." Wartime materials research and development offered civilian benefits, and for the hunter, the H & R Arms Company noted that after the war their guns would have the "additional benefit of all the new know-how and ... materials—steels and alloys and plastics." Softwear, too, underwent development, and following the war the clothing and paraphernalia of Alaska's outdoorsmen gained functionality and a certain style through the new army-navy surplus stores. The advertisements reflected the inevitability of American victory with the promise of better days to come.

*The Alaska Sportsman* made no pretense at covering the war as a news magazine, and its feature articles barely recognized that a war raged across the globe. It stayed with familiar themes: hunting and fishing tales, homesteading stories, gold rush reminiscences, and portraits of happy Eskimo families. Only one article appeared about soldiers, from a Sitka resident who opened her house to the "good selection of America's young manhood."[20] The magazine likely served as a haven of escapism from the realities of wartime rationing and casualty lists, its pages filled with images of salmon and moose and hardy independent people. (Letters to the editor were not published until 1960, and during the Vietnam War letters from servicemen certainly conveyed an appreciation for the glimpse of a clean, cold world untainted by the discipline and fear of wartime).

While cartoons could put a humorous edge on the presence of the military in Alaska, some of the advertising had a more aggressive tone, such as the "License to hunt Japs! ... this hunting license gives you the right to hunt the 'black-livered Japanese' in Alaska without restrictions as to limit or season. It authorizes the payment of bounty for any Japanese shot in the Aleutians...." A souvenir plaque was available with the Alaska flag, totem poles, huskies, and an Eskimo, reading "United we stand, Divided we fall, We fight for liberty, one and all, No matter what branch of the Service we're in, We will do plenty to Tokio [sic] & Berlin." This latter

reference was virtually the only one in the pages of *The Alaska Sportsman* to the European theater; the eyes of Alaska were firmly fixed at the enemy across the Pacific.

Meanwhile, the eyes of military censors were upon the printed materials leaving Alaska. Controls were imposed by the Alaska Defense Command in July 1942, and included the mails of military personnel and civilians, media production, and elimination of the freedom to travel without authorization.[21] Emery Tobin agreeably noted that "no fifth-columnists, saboteurs, and spies" were wanted in the territory. But as frustrations mounted as people were unable to return to their homes and as mail stopped coming through because of censors in Minneapolis and Seattle, he decried the censorship as a "wasteful expenditure." Tobin also wondered—creatively, if not logically—whether Georgia would be considered a combat zone if some islands off the coast of California were invaded, since the distance from Ketchikan to Kiska was no less.[22]

A photographic article of the changing face of Anchorage appeared in the August 1941 issue, showing streets and buildings, but no further photos of Alaska towns would be seen in *The Alaska Sportsman* until the end of war. In spite of the censorship on material relating to Alaska's topography, the magazine ran four articles in 1943 about the Aleutians; while they did not discuss the fighting, all the articles included photographs.

As the war drew to a close, the pages of *The Alaska Sportsman* reflected both the tragedy and promise of the coming resolution. The only war photograph published in the magazine was in a 1945 issue, showing an American corpse with the caption, "This American is not expected to buy an extra War Bond in the 5th WAR LOAN." The outdoor product manufacturers were anxious for the GIs to return home on furlough or after discharge and get back in the woods for some recreation, and ads appeared showing soldiers discussing their post-war hunting and fishing plans.

Two years before the war's end, Tobin anticipated a "new land rush" to the territory, much as the nation had settled the West after the Civil War, and in 1945 commented that "The Gold Rush was a minor event compared to the war migration!"[23] To aid the expected migrants, a six-part article ran in 1945 on "What to Expect in Alaska," covering, in a how-to way, such topics as trapping, homesteading, farming, mining, logging,

---

[19] Richard Gerstell, *The Steel Trap in North America* (Harrisburg, Pennsylvania: Stackpole, 1985), p. 209. This fascinating book focuses on the history of America's largest trap-making company, part of the utopian Oneida Community of upstate New York.

[20] Esther Hoyt Goddard, "Comrades of the New Frontier," April 1942.

[21] See Otis E. Hays, "The Silent Years in Alaska," *Alaska Journal* 16 (Limited Edition Collection, 1986), pp. 140-147; Claus-M. Naske, "Governor Gruening and the Alaska War Council," *Alaska Journal* 16, pp. 48-54.

[22] "Main Trails...," September 1942; February 1943.

[23] "Main Trails...," May 1943. The civilian population in 1940 was 74,000; in 1950 it was 112,000.

and commercial fishing. With travel restrictions lifted, steamer companies revived to offer their passages north, alongside advertisements from their new competitors, the fledgling commercial airline companies. While a trip to Alaska prior to the war had been the province of those with adequate leisure and capital for an extended vacation, improved transportation options would lead to the democratization of tourist travel to Alaska, much as Emery Tobin predicted at the war's beginning.

Tobin was a frontier booster in the tradition of those who had promoted the settlement of the American West. The tourist industry showed rapid growth, and *The Alaska Sportsman* evolved less into the voice of the sportsman than to being the source of exported information about Alaska to the increasing number of people who could afford the trip. The tension between the forces for development and those of conservation re-mained, yet the editorial voice of Emery Tobin was convinced that Alaska could sustain development and still remain the sportsman's paradise.

During the 1940s, *The Alaska Sportsman* provided its readership with a consistent product: an Alaska which rewarded the traditional virtues of individual effort, thrift, and persistence—all in a setting of incomparable beauty, opportunity, and imminent adventure. Even then this may have been a vision divorced from reality, but despite the magazine's changes in ownership and name, it remains a vision that effectively sells magazines and inspires many to take their passage north.[24]

*Timothy Rawson received his M.A. degree in northern studies from the University of Alaska Fairbanks. His thesis was entitled "Parks, Politics, and Public Opinion: The Wolf Controversy in Mount McKinley National Park, 1930-1953."*

---

[24] Tobin was editor until a change of ownership on March 1, 1958, when Robert A. Henning and Robert N. DeArmond brought the magazine into their Alaska Northwest Publishing Company. Indicative of changing readership tastes, the "Sportsman" was dropped from the title with the September 1969 issue: "... we're just giving the magazine a title all Alaskans can be proud of without feeling they have to be the outdoors type to join the family." ("Main Trails and Bypaths," pp. 4-5). Today Alaska Northwest no longer owns *Alaska*. The magazine is published by Alaska Publishing Properties Inc., which is presided over by Joseph Meagher.

# For Immediate Sale: Tokyo Bathhouse—How World War II Affected Alaska's Japanese Civilians

*Ronald K. Inouye*

THE CIVILIAN DIMENSION OF WORLD WAR II IN Alaska is largely faceless. The purpose of this paper is to provide Japanese and Japanese-American accounts of World War II from newspaper accounts and oral interviews acquired during the 1991-1992 Alaska's Japanese Pioneers Research Project.[1]

Japanese in Alaska have never been numerous. The names of Jujiro Wada and Frank Yasuda have become historically better known, and in more contemporary times business enterprises of Alaska's Japanese are familiar: Harry Kawabe in Seward; the Kimuras in Anchorage; the Fukuyamas' Juneau Laundry and Sam Taguchi's City Cafe; and, in Ketchikan, the Ohashis' store, the Tatsudas' grocery, Shimizu's New York Cafe, etc.

As the predominance of pre-World War II Alaska Japanese arrivals were single males, many married Alaska Native women and began families. Such Japanese names continue in Alaska communities after two or more generations of non-Japanese contact. In Deering, George "Yamamoto" became George "Moto"; in Cordova, the "Fujis" become "Foode"; and, in Sitka, the name "O-za-wa" took on a more lyrical pronunciation: "Os-awa."

In larger communities like Ketchikan, Petersburg, and Juneau, an identifiable Japanese business and social community developed. Restaurants served American and Oriental food; grocery stores catered to the general public but also stocked rice, *shoyu* (soy sauce), and other Japanese goods; in Ketchikan a Japanese language school began.

With the outbreak of World War II, Alaska Japanese were treated like their counterparts on the United States West Coast. The Issei, first generation immigrants barred from U.S. citizenship by the alien laws of the time, were prime suspects of sabotage. Their children, the second generation born in Alaska and U.S. citizens, or Nisei, were also suspect.

After President Franklin D. Roosevelt signed Executive Order 9066 on February 19, 1942, the army designated geographic "military areas" from which certain individuals could be evacuated. Japanese and Japanese-Americans were the primary designees of that executive order, and Alaska was included in the evacuation regions administered by the War Relocation Authority.

Japanese-American men, women, and children totalling 112,000 were evacuated from the West Coast states and interned in ten isolated, inland camps ranging in size from 7,300 in Granada, Colorado, to 18,789 in Tule Lake, California.

It is ironic that World War II introduced intra-Alaska evacuations: Alaska's Japanese-Americans were moved to the Lower 48, and the Aleuts were transported from the Aleutian and Pribilof Islands to Southeast when the Japanese invasion of the Aleutian Islands occurred.

Immediately after the Pearl Harbor bombing, the ninety-two evacuated Japanese aliens were first assembled regionally, then transported to Immigration

---

[1] Copies of the project are available at the Alaska State Library in Juneau, the Consortium Library archives in Anchorage, and the University of Alaska-Fairbanks Rasmuson Library archives.

Department facilities in Crystal City, Texas, initially, then to Lordsburg and Santa Fe, New Mexico. These Issei men were given less than twenty-four hours notice of evacuation, leaving personal and family relations as well as business and financial affairs in turmoil. It was approximately three years before these Alaska residents were reunited with any family members.

Harry Kawabe's removal from Seward on December 7, 1941, was poignantly described by Otis E. Hays Jr.:

Sometime after five o'clock there was a telephone call from the Alaska Defense Command headquarters at Fort Richardson... there came orders for me to detain the laundry proprietor, Harry Kawabe.

I dreaded the task. Accompanied by men from the provost marshal's office, I arrived at the laundry building in the early evening darkness. I found the proprietor who was in the boiler room stoking the fire. He was alone. We stood in semi-darkness, the only light being the reflection from the firebox. I told him what had to be done. He sighed, hesitated, and then asked to go upstairs.

Tomo Kawabe, wide-eyed, met us at the top of the stairs. Her husband looked at her wordlessly and began collecting a few personal belongings. She turned and rushed to the kitchen. In an apparent state of shock, she hastily opened and heated cans of food and began to set the dining table. Catching my eye, she kept motioning to the table with her hands. "You must eat," she seemed to be pleading.

I asked her to stop. Tight-throated, I could not have swallowed the food—any food—at that time. Nevertheless, she continued almost frantically to motion to the laden table. I had to turn my back to her.

It was finally time to go. Her stoical husband walked down the stairs without a backward glance. Tomo Kawabe, one hand over her mouth, looked after him through the dim stair light.

"Don't worry," I remember saying helplessly, "you'll see him soon." I had no idea that she really would. Whether she believed me, I did not know. She just stood there and gave no sign that she even heard me.

It was now eight o'clock.[2]

Evacuation possibilities also produced apprehension in Yakutat for Fhoki Kayamori, a bachelor cannery worker and watchman for Libby McNeil. Beginning in 1912, Mr. Kayamori took many amateur photographs of Yakutat: people, buildings, festivities, and countryside. Those familiar with the classic Fredericka de Laguna study, *Under Mount Saint Elias: The History and Culture of the Yakutat Tlingit*, will remember his photographs in the third volume of that study, published by the Smithsonian Institution. His visual documentation now resides in the Alaska State Historical Library in Juneau.

Elaine Abraham remembered Kayamori: "He took pictures of every event in the village. We were at a Christmas play put on by the Church, and Mr. Kayamori was up there in front with a camera, you know the kind that goes POOF in front of you—POOF!"

When news of the Pearl Harbor bombing shocked Yakutat, a community meeting was called.

And somebody said, "Where's Mr. Kayamori?" He was the only one that wasn't there. It was already evening; it was about seven o'clock in the evening; and you know it's dark, very dark.

Several of the men took lanterns up to his house, and they found that he had committed suicide (Territorial Death Certificate). He did not leave a note.

What precipitated his suicide? Was he a Japanese informant as some in Yakutat claimed? Or was he a victim of war circumstances?

The families of these Issei aliens were also evacuated in April, taken by ship to Washington state, and settled into the Western Washington Fair Grounds at Puyallup. The assembly center was ironically called "Camp Harmony." For several months rudimentary shelters with temporary provisioning served as home for the Alaskans and Washingtonians awaiting the construction of ten permanent camps inland. The Alaskans designated their camp street as "Alaska Way." In the fall, the 130 Alaska Japanese were among the 9,397 people moved by railroad and interned at the more permanent Minidoka, Idaho, internment camp.[3]

Social relations among the camp residents varied. Although the camp and assembly center conditions were less than ideal, several individuals spoke favorably of being interned. For the first time in many years, they were relieved of the daily chores of hunting, hauling water, and preparing meals because the congregate living provided these services. However,

---

[2] Otis E. Hays Jr., "When War Came to Seward," *Alaska Journal*, Autumn 1983, p. 111.

[3] Roger Daniels, Sandra C. Taylor, and Harry H.L. Kitano, eds., *Japanese Americans from Relocation to Redress*, rev. ed. (Seattle, Washington: University of Washington Press, 1986), p. xxi.

These Alaskan Issei were separated from their families and detained in a New Mexico War Relocation Authority camp. Upon America's declaration of war on the Japanese, the men were removed from their homes in Petersburg, Ketchikan, Anchorage, Seward, Beaver, and other sites, and held in military camps at Fort Richardson and Annette Island before being shipped out of Alaska. Several non-Alaskans are included in the photograph. *(Acc. No. 81-185-DIN, Ronald Inouye Collection, Rasmuson Library, University of Alaska Fairbanks)*

although housed together in cramped, poorly constructed quarters, the families lost their previous unity as the children and young adults spent considerable amounts of time away from family and outside parental guidance and supervision.

Life in the camps was difficult for most evacuees, and particularly for the Alaskans, some of whom had never seen other Japanese or lived in such close conditions. The social ostracism of Alaskans by the non-Alaskans was keenly felt, although many had relatives from the Pacific Coast states in the camps.

The sympathetic reactions of some Alaskans to the Japanese evacuations are documented:

Sponsored by co-workers at the Alaska Glacier Sea Food Company, where many of the adults have been employed, a farewell party was held on Wednesday evening at the Presbyterian Church for the Japanese women and young people soon to leave Petersburg.

About 60 friends were present at the party which was featured by short talks expressing the regret of their friends that conditions have made this move necessary, and voicing the hope that they will be happy in the south, and soon can return....

A delightful dinner was served from a table which was made bright with flowers.[4]

Two merit badges were awarded at a special Boy Scout court of honor last night to Howard Suzuki, who was among the Japanese evacuated from Ketchikan today. He is said by scout officials

---

[4] Ronald K. Inouye, *The World War II Evacuation of Japanese-Americans from the Territory of Alaska* (Fairbanks: 1973), p. 110.

to be the highest ranking Boy Scout in Alaska from the stand point of having won all the badges here.[5]

Alaska Japanese had varied feelings about the situation. As a member of the Alaska National Guard serving at the Chilkoot Barracks in Haines with Charlie and Jimmy Tatsuda and Bob Urata, Pat Hagiwara remembered how they encountered an "awkward and difficult" period as people "suspected their motives and allegiance."

As the military prepared to evacuate Southeast Issei aliens, Pat was placed in the unenviable position of dispatching National Guardsmen to Juneau to pick up Mr. Fukuyama, whose home he had just visited the previous month.[6] And later, with the help of a chaplain, he surreptitiously visited his father and other Ketchikan Issei detained in a tent on Annette Island[7] on the way to his new military assignment at Fort Sheridan, Illinois.

The evacuation of all males over the age of sixteen with mixed Alaska Native and Japanese parentage was of concern from the beginning. Alice Stuart of Fairbanks queried Governor Gruening on April 24, 1942:

I am writing to you about one of the boys who lives in the "Arctic Village" which you visited with his former employer, the late Robert Marshall in the summer of 1938.

[He] is a half-breed Eskimo boy who was adopted as a small baby by an Indian and an Eskimo. He has never seen his father, who was Japanese. His mother was Eskimo.

He has never been below the Arctic circle until the other day when he was sent into Fairbanks to register because he is of Japanese descent. He has never even seen a Jap, nor does he wish to.

He has spent all of his life in the hills, or around Wiseman where he went to school and completed the seventh grade. He is a fine healthy seventeen year old boy who respects and helps his native parents. He accepts responsibility nicely and had enough getup and go to him to obtain a job freighting.

He loves the rivers and mountains of his native home and has no desire to leave it. He is the main support of his family and if he should have to stay away it will work an undue hardship on them as well as upon himself.

Would it not perhaps be possible to find some way that he might return to the Arctic instead of being shipped out to California as I understand they plan to do with him next Monday?[8]

The young man was evacuated.

Life was difficult for remaining family members when the breadwinner was evacuated. Several accounts of the wives and children tell of the social ostracism they experienced in Native villages, and the difficulty of providing for daily subsistence and seasonal financial needs. Territorial relief records noted families requiring assistance when the men were evacuated. In several instances the wives became alcoholics, perhaps due to the dislocation of previously stable family relationships.

However, life settled into a routine at the Minidoka Internment Camp, and became as normal as it could be under the circumstances. Schools were established for the children, the adults gardened, a newspaper began publishing, and the internees created as comfortable a life as was possible within the confines of barbed wire fences.

Seasonally farmers and ranchers from the region solicited evacuees to work and harvest crops. Military-age men volunteered to join the 442nd to fight in Europe or were recruited to work for the Military Intelligence Service in the Far East. In several instances young women of college age were placed in Midwestern and East Coast universities through the efforts of religious organizations. However, for the majority of internees, camp life was as boringly routine as the climate and weather were harsh.

At war's end, in March 1945, those Alaskans who wished to return north were allowed to do so. After three years away from Alaska, some wondered whether they should. Would property and businesses hurriedly left—mostly under verbal agreement and in the care of acquaintances, colleagues, and friends—still be there? Would they be welcome?

These questions were raised in a letter sent to the Ketchikan Chamber of Commerce on June 11, 1945, and reprinted in the *Alaska Fishing News*.

Dear President, Chamber of Commerce:

Due to the Army order of evacuation of all persons of Japanese ancestry, we the undersigned have been evacuated on April, 1942.

Now that this evacuation ban has been lifted, as of January, 1945, and a relocation of the center resi-

---

[5] Ibid., p. 11.

[6] Patrick K. Hagiwara, recorded on May 17, 1991, in Bellevue, Washington, in *Alaska's Japanese Pioneers Research Project*, p. 22.

[7] Ibid., p. 32.

[8] Inouye, *Evacuation*, pp. 107-197.

dents is now in progress, and liquidation of this and other centers is now imminent, we would like to know if we would be able to resume our residence in our former town once again.

We would like to know if we will be able to join the cannery union and be given jobs as others, and to resume our former businesses and be taken into the community again without any prejudices and hard feelings.

Our children also feel, that inasmuch as they have been born and raised in Ketchikan, they would like to continue their school there, like they have been doing prior to evacuation.

We do not believe that everyone of the people who were evacuated will return, as some have relocated elsewhere in the U.S.

Would you kindly tell us what your feelings and others in Ketchikan would be if we were to return?

If, at some time, the Chamber of Commerce meets could you mention this letter and let us now what the sentiment and reaction will be.

We are very anxious to resume our normal way of living, as we have been in a relocation center for three years now and we desire to back there, inasmuch as it is our former home.

If you and the others do not feel that it is the right time to return, we would like to know fully the reasons for and against our return.

Yours truly,
Mr. and Mrs. James Tanino
Mr. and Mrs. James Tatsuda
Mr. and Mrs. G. H. Ohashi
Mr. and Mrs. George Shimizu

While no official action was taken by the chamber, it was suggested that the letter be printed in the press and clippings of the people's reaction be mailed to former Ketchikan Japanese who planned to return.[9]

Of the 193 Alaska Japanese removed from the territory, eighty, along with two children born in relocation centers, returned to Alaska in 1945; 106 chose to relocate elsewhere in the United States; six died in the center; one was interned by the Department of Justice.[10]

The fight for redress through the documentation and recommendations of the Commission on Wartime Relocation and Internment of Civilians was late but successful. In 1988, President Ronald Reagan signed Public Law 100-383, providing a letter of apology and a per-capita monetary payment to Aleuts and Japanese-Americans. Payments totalling $1,926,667 have been made to Japanese-Americans. Ninety-seven evacuees currently reside in Alaska.[11] When payments were issued, each qualified recipient also received a letter from President George Bush:

A monetary sum and words alone cannot restore lost years or erase painful memories; neither can they fully convey our Nation's resolve to rectify injustice and to uphold the rights of individuals. We can never fully right the wrongs of the past. But we can take a clear stand for justice and recognize that serious injustices were done to Japanese Americans during World War II.

In enacting a law calling for restitution and offering a sincere apology, your fellow Americans have, in a very real sense, renewed their traditional commitment to the ideals of freedom, equality, and justice. You and your family have our best wishes for the future.[12]

*Ronald K. Inouye is the editor of the Bibliography of Alaska and Polar Regions at the Rasmuson Library, University of Alaska Fairbanks.*

---

[9] Ibid., pp. 184-85.

[10] Jacobus Ten Brock, Edward N. Barnhart, and Floyd W. Matson, *Prejudice, War and the Constitution* (Berkeley: University of California Press, 1968), p. 135.

[11] "Checks in the mail...," *Pacific Citizen*, Oct. 8-14, 1993, (Los Angeles: Japanese American Citizens League), p. 1.

[12] Daniels, et al., *Relocation*, pp. 221-22.

# Childhood Memories of the War:
# Sitka

*Nancy Yaw Davis*

THE BLACKOUTS, AIR RAID SIRENS, FEAR OF BEING bombed, frightened scurrying to the woods, imaginary submarines, soldier strangers, and Fibber McGee and Molly—remnants of memories from a child's perspective.[1]

I was four-and-a-half years old in December 1941, and I do not recall the war's beginning. But I was nine and peddling *The Sitka Sentinel* in 1945, and clearly recall the war's end. Those years in between are marked by a few specific memories, some good, some bad, and some just interesting, in retrospect, as a child's view of events.

Sitka's population in 1940 was almost two thousand, the fifth largest city in Alaska.[2] I was the youngest of six members of the Yaw family. My father, W. Leslie Yaw, had come to Sitka from Iowa in 1923 to be coach and teacher at Sheldon Jackson School, then part of the Presbyterian National Missions. My mother, Caroline Witzigman Yaw, arrived from Iowa in 1924, also to teach—and to raise a family. They had met in high school and married after Dad graduated from Cornell College. Mother had another semester to graduation, so she remained in Iowa, and then traveled alone to Sitka. Certainly, she was a courageous woman.

My three older siblings were Robert Edgecumbe, Helen Ruth, and Betty Jo. On Christmas Eve, 1942, my younger brother, Charles Stuart, was born. I was supposed to be pleased with this wartime Christmas present, but I puzzled over the Sears Roebuck and Monkey Wards catalogs quite some time, trying to figure out how my parents picked *him* out of all those babies to choose from. For a while there were seven members of the Yaw Family.[3]

The good memories about the war include being taught how to figure-skate on Swan Lake by a soldier named Quinten, a friend of the family. It was a great day when the ice was declared safe and school was closed for a half day so we could race to get our skates. I recall my former skill executing fancy figure eights as I skate now much more cautiously on Westchester Lagoon in Anchorage. When I was six years old, it was okay to talk with Quinten, my teacher, but not to other soldiers.

Admittedly, there was an element of excitement when the air raid sirens screeched their warning hoots, and adults accompanied us home from school down the back street, not Lincoln street, our regular route along Sitka Sound. There is the good memory about special candy bars in the brown, double-handled shopping bag

---

[1] The November 25, 1991, *Newsweek* feature, "Remembering Pearl Harbor," startled me into recalling some of these memories. The conference on "Alaska at War" provided the opportunity to share and to write about some of them.

[2] In 1993, Sitka is still the fifth largest city, with eighty-five hundred residents, which was Juneau's size in 1940, when Juneau was the largest city in the territory. In 1940, Alaska had 72,500 people in it. For a summary of the building and activities of the military on Japonski Island, see the National Historic Preservation Registration Form (1984). Although Sitka was not the major base in Alaska, it seemed to me to be the center of all the defense effort.

[3] My brother Bob joined the army in 1944 and was assigned to a hospital ship. In January 1946 the ship returned to San Francisco Bay, but Bob did not get off. Three weeks later his body was found in the bay. He is buried in the Sitka National Cemetery.

stored in the pantry. I was assigned to carry it to the woods during the air raids at the beginning of the war. Later that special bag was stored in our home's shelter, the former coal room in the cement basement of Pittsburg Cottage on the corner of Jeff Davis Street and Lincoln Street. We stayed there and waited for the all-clear signal. I'm still addicted to candy bars.

And then the bad memories. The fierce reprimand by Dad when he caught me peeking out the upstairs window during a blackout. If we got bombed, it would be all my fault. Also, the terror I sensed in the adults around me as we ran behind the Sheldon Jackson School campus to an assigned location along Indian River. Maybe the bombs would really fall this time. And I cried. Also, I remember being puzzled about the strict instruction never to talk to soldiers, except Quinten. Then, in 1943, an experience and the realization why. It must have been difficult for Mother to raise three daughters in Sitka during the war years.

The Yaw family enjoys a picnic on Sitka, August 1943. *(Photograph from the author's collection)*

Other memories from a child's perspective are a bit humorous. We all had to be super quiet and never speak while The News was on. For years I thought that if we talked our voices could be picked up by the radio and transmitted out to everyone listening, a kind of a worldwide 1940's CB. But, when "Fibber McGee and Molly" came on, we gathered around the radio in the corner of the living room, and we could laugh. I probably did not understand the jokes, but it was all right to laugh when "Fibber McGee and Molly" were on. And I liked the program partly because I thought I could hear people all around the world laughing.

But we dared not laugh, or talk, or even move, when The News was on. Everyone in the house was quiet. No noises tolerated. Just the voice out of the magic box giving the latest news. I sensed the tension; I thought the war was going on right out there just beyond the islands we could see from the front window. And I thought the whole world was listening, not moving, not talking, during The News. That is why you could not hear any background noise. If anyone even whispered, that whisper would be picked up on the radio and all the people of the world could hear the whisper, and not be able to

A pre-war, postcard view of Sitka. Government censors regularly culled photographs of Alaska cities from mail addressed to recipients outside the territory, with the result that few photographs of wartime Sitka are to be found. *(From the author's collection)*

hear The News, the critical news about The War. As a child in the Yaw family in Sitka I was always glad when The News was over and "Fibber McGee and Molly" came on. Or "The Lone Ranger." And we could talk, and eat Iowa popcorn, and play with the dog again.

Then there was a time when the tide was low, and I saw a submarine, right out there, just beyond the islands. I ran home, and called my mother to the front window. She looked carefully with the binoculars and quietly tried to convince me it was just an exposed rock out past the islands in the sound. We were always on the lookout for subs. After the war, from the highest hemlock tree behind the Presbyterian manse, I continued to scan the ocean to the west, looking for the mysterious submarines. Until we studied geography in fifth grade I also expected to see Japan right out there, real close. A child's perspective.

I wonder now what my classmates remember. Do they also recall the sudden, wonderful freedom after the war to explore the woods, climb the mountains, and picnic on the causeway that had been built to connect seven small islands? The fun of sneaking up on the fake airplane in the swamp, and exploring the scary, damp, dark concrete bunkers on The Island (Japonski, now called Mount Edgecumbe). When they climbed the rickety lookout on top of Harbor Mountain, did they also still wonder what the war was all about?

Today when I walk along Lincoln Street past Sheldon Jackson College and out toward the National Park and Monument, I find myself trying to identify that imaginary sub out between the islands. Sometimes it is there. At low tide.[4]

*Nancy Yaw Davis has taught anthropology at Alaska Methodist University and at the University of Alaska-Anchorage. She is writing a book tentatively entitled "Links Across the Pacific." The book addresses evidence of Japanese admixture in language, genetics, and culture in North America between the ninth and thirteenth centuries, A.D.*

---

[4] For information about the civilian experience in Sitka, see W. Leslie Yaw, chap. 4, "The War Years and After," in *Sixty Years in Sitka*.

# Minorities in Alaska's Military

A well-integrated crowd of soldiers watches teams from Shemya and Amchitka
in the Aleutian softball championships at Adak in September 1945.
*(Photo No. SC 215113, National Archives, College Park, Md.)*

# Minority Troops and the Alaskan Advantage During World War II

*Lael Morgan*

IT HAS BEEN ARGUED THAT BLACK SOLDIERS SERVING IN the Far North during World War II were much more affected as a minority by their military careers than Alaska's indigenous Eskimos, Indians, and Aleuts, and cursory investigation would show no room for argument. Negro soldiers, the majority of whom were from the deep South, were shipped north to Alaska and Canada in 1942, thousands of miles from their homes, to serve on a strategic road-building detail with the Army Corps of Engineers through the worst winter on record.[1] They served in segregated units under white commanders, few of whom had much more experience in the North than their troops, and they were given the assignment in the face of vehement objections of General Simon Bolivar Buckner, the all-powerful head of the Alaska Command and a man who was blatantly racist.[2]

Many of these black soldiers could not read or write. More than a few spoke a French patois and understood little English.[3] Practically none had building experience and those who succeeded in getting some good basic training were often deprived of the heavy equipment they had been schooled to operate, and were relegated to backbreaking work with picks, shovels, and axes.[4]

By contrast, the assignment of the Natives[5] who volunteered for the Alaska Territorial Guard (often referred to as "scout battalions") was to remain in their villages and prepare to defend their families. They were already among the world's best marksmen and trackers by virtue of having lived off their cold, harsh lands for centuries, so they needed little training or comprehension of English as preparation for civil defense. The isolation of their remote villages generally shielded them from the discrimination from which black soldiers often suffered. The general lot of these indigenous Alaskans was improved by the provision of military weapons (better than those they had previously used for hunting) and other military equipment. And, since Native guardsmen received no pay, they were not required to abide by military regulations that other minorities found restricting, nor did General Buckner concern himself with them.

The experience of Natives who entered regular federal military service was closer to that of black troops. However, Native Alaskans were not forced into segregated units singled out for discriminatory treatment (as was the case with Alaska-based black units who were banned from towns and confined to tough wilderness assignments). Like their black counterparts, the majority of Native military men served far from their homes, but

---

[1] Kenneth J. Deacon, "Alcan: The Story of Black Engineers and the Road They Made Reality," *Engineer Update*, April 1986, p. 4.

[2] Everett Louis Overstreet, *Black on a Background of White: A Chronicle of Afro-American Involvement in America's Last Frontier, Alaska* (Anchorage: Alaska Black Caucus, 1988), pp. 42-43; Heath Twichell, *Northwest Epic: The Building of the Alaska Highway* (New York: St. Martin's Press, 1992), pp. 144-45.

[3] Robert Platt Boyd, *Me and Company C* (Alburn, Alabama: Platt Boyd, 1992), p. 6.

[4] Twichell, *Northwest Epic*, pp. 130-31, 177, 179.

[5] Native with a capital "N" is used to describe Alaska's indigenous people, while native with a small "n" is reserved for others born in Alaska (*A.P. Stylebook for Alaska*).

Men from Alaska Highway Construction crews take a break. *(Photograph courtesy of the Rev. Edward G. Carroll)*

few found alien climates as life-threatening as the Far North was to blacks.

However, a closer look will show that World War II military experience had far greater impact on Alaskans than on blacks who served there and more greatly affected the state as a whole because of some unexpected advantages it offered to those of the Far North.

Like many of his company, Joseph Prejean, a member of the Ninety-Third from Lafayette, Louisiana, was illiterate when he entered service. But he moved up fast. The young black made excellent money—thirteen hundred dollars on one good night—in the endless rounds of crap games that kept troops from boredom in the North during off hours. Learning to read from a buddy who was going with a school teacher, Prejean got through army cooking school and went on to become a highly paid chef in civilian life.

His parents had worked as tenant farmers for twenty-one years and Prejean recalls that their landlord tried to scare him out of enlisting by predicting he'd be killed.

"I told him I just couldn't make it on $1.50 a week," the well-spoken restaurateur recounted gleefully. "When I got home I had all that money in the bank and he was dead."[6]

After Herbert Tucker of Washington, D.C., narrowly missed passing an entrance exam for officers' training school in the spring of 1942, he found himself crossing the Peace River, British Columbia, with the all-black Ninety-Fifth. He lasted until October when the mercury suddenly plunged to fifty below.

"If I have to pass that test to get out of here, that's what I'm going to do," he decided on the spot. And the next week he was on his way south to become a career officer.[7]

"Sure we knew we were going to freeze to death, so we took precautions," Fred Spencer of Sneads, Florida, recalled, enjoying the irony. "Those northern boys thought they could 'bulldoze' the weather, so they froze their fingers and their toes and their ears."

Spencer, formerly with the Ninety-Third, escaped

---

[6] Joseph Prejean, Lafayette, La., May 1990.
[7] Herbert Tucker, Washington, D.C., May 1990.

with only mild frostbite, saw service in Burma, and came home to land work through his heavy equipment training with the Corps of Engineers.[8]

Although "coloreds" had fought with distinction in early American wars, many of the U.S. high command besides Alaska's General Bucker were uneasy about their enlistment. Negro soldiers had been confined to stateside "housekeeping duties" until they were assigned strategic duty in Alaska due to a shortage of white manpower, but the performance of black troops in the Far North was impressive.

"Yes, there were discrimination problems," recalls the Reverend Edward G. Carroll, now a retired Methodist bishop. He had served as chaplain for the Ninety-Fifth, bucking his white commanding officers to get the best men in his all-black unit into officers' training school. "They said we didn't have the mentality to deal with heavy equipment. The race you don't know is the race you suspect, but our men proved themselves."

Carroll also noted that World War II offered an unprecedented opportunity for his people. Many, for the first time, received the same pay and benefits as white workers and a chance to acquire new skills and to build genuine self-esteem.[9]

Like most of his black counterparts, Athabaskan Richard Frank of Minto enjoyed equal pay with whites for the first time when he enlisted in the army air force. And, although he was equipped with only a fourth-grade education, Frank was astonished to learn he was eligible for specialized military training as an airplane mechanic.

"At first I said, `No.' I was afraid I'd fail and my folks would find out about it. But my commanding officer had faith in me and encouraged me. Passing grade was 2.5 and I came out with 3.9!"

Frank, who saw duty in the South Pacific servicing P-47 fighters for the Sixty-Seventh, later cashed in on his military training as an aircraft mechanic for Wien and Boeing, then went on lucrative assignments on the North Slope.

"Not everyone from my village was that lucky. Some just had routine jobs and then went back to hunting and trapping. But it showed us there was another option. While only four of us from Minto served in World War II, the village now has thirty-one veterans of American military service."[10]

In more than thirty years of interviewing Native veterans throughout Alaska, this writer has heard many stories similar to Frank's from those who served in fed-eral service during World War II, but has encountered no veteran of the Alaska Territorial Guard who cited the experience as a personal highlight or turning point.

"Later, (after the Territorial Guard was organized as a regular National Guard) it became a source of employment. Nominal though it was, it was practically the only source of employment for our villagers," observed Inupiat Eskimo Oliver Leavitt of Barrow—whose father and uncles all served. And yet the ultimate impact went far beyond that, the Native leader noted.[11]

While the black crusade for racial equality was

Athabaskan Richard Frank of Minto enjoyed equal pay with whites for the first time when he enlisted in the army air forces. Although equipped with only a fourth-grade education, Frank nevertheless was trained as an airplane mechanic and later cashed in on his training as an aircraft mechanic for Wien and Boeing. *(Photograph courtesy of Richard Frank)*

already well established at the beginning of World War II, there was no comparable movement among Alaska Natives, who represented five widely varying cultural and linguistic groups with virtually no means of communication. Disenfranchised, with only limited educational and employment opportunities, no legal title to lands they had occupied for centuries, and the highest infant mortality rate in the world, Alaska's Indians, Aleuts and Eskimos had no voice, and most Americans were unaware of their existence.

Even territorial governor Ernest Gruening, who strongly encouraged organization of the Territorial Guard, had little idea where Alaska Natives stood.

"At the time, I knew relatively little about the Eskimos—indeed almost nothing through personal contact," he later confessed. "My reading has informed me that they suffered at the hands of white men through the past.... I wondered whether deep seated resentments might not lurk behind their outwardly friendly appearances....

"My doubts were soon set to rest. Everywhere I

[8] Fred Spencer, Sneads, Florida, May 1990.

[9] The Reverend Edward G. Carroll, Philadelphia, Pa., May 1990.

[10] Richard Frank, Fairbanks, Alaska, November 1993.

[11] Oliver Leavitt, Barrow, Alaska, November 1993.

found only the heartiest response to my pleas for organization in self defense."[12]

Gruening's interest came at a time when Natives throughout Alaska were being hard pressed to assimilate with mainstream Americans. Government school teachers representing the outside world had universally banned the use of Native languages in favor of English, and taught skills that had no practical application in Native villages. Half-a-dozen American churches had joined forces to condemn all Native religions and divided up the state for proselyting. And traders, the only other outsiders to infiltrate the villages, sold acculturation by the yard and the pound, making Natives increasingly dependent on the white man's monetary system.

"By World War II our [Native] leadership was wiped out," observed Inupiat John Schaeffer of Kotzebue. Our villages were controlled by white people; by the government teachers and the missionaries. They'd wiped out our councils and put in their education system."

Initially, it appeared the Alaska Territorial Guard would function the same way, but Major Marvin R. "Muktuk" Marston—a maverick military officer whom General Buckner did not care for and "loaned" to the territory to command the organization—became impressed with the organizational skills of the Natives.

"At first we had white commanders, preachers or teachers, for the first year," recalls Schaeffer, whose father and uncles were early recruits. "But then Muktuk fired most of them and put in Native officers."

Even more important, Marston provided a place for the Native men to meet. Traditionally each village had maintained a "kashim" or "kashgee," a meeting hall where Native men retreated to make their plans, but as outsiders gained control, these had been replaced by schools and churches.

"What Marston did was rebuild the kashgees," Schaeffer explained. "He built village armories which provided a place for our men to meet. This gave our

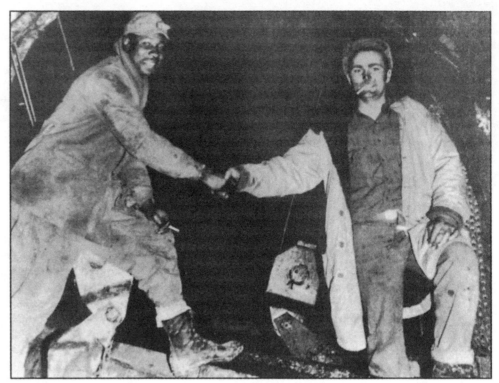

An interregimental competition between the white Eighteenth Engineers and the black Ninety-Seventh brought the separate pieces of the Alaska Highway together near Beaver Creek, twenty miles east of the Canada border. The Ninety-Seventh won the match. Pvt. Alfred Jalufka of the Eighteenth shakes hands with Cpl. Refines Sims Jr. of the Ninety-Seventh. The photo was widely published. *(Army Signal Corps)*

guys a base. They started to take a little more control and there was a political reawakening. The restructured leadership came out of the scouts and the army. For a while there everyone in the Native leadership had also been in the Guard!"[13]

It was the first time since the coming of the white man that Native men had options beyond church- and government-run schools. Many, like Schaeffer, who became a career guardsman and ultimately the Guard's commander, turned to military service for their education and a ticket to see the world outside.

It was military experience, too—both in the Guard and in regular service—that helped many Alaska Natives focus on the problems of discrimination. Richard Frank, now a well respected Native leader and traditional chief of his village, clearly recalled his introduction in flight-mechanics school, at age eighteen, when he failed one phase of his exams for lack of formal education and feared he'd wash out.

"The only person who helped me was a black corporal (ironically his name was White)," Frank noted. "He said, 'We're both minorities. The system that's been cre-

[12] Marvin Marston, *Men of the Tundra* (New York: October House, 1969), p. 4.

[13] John Schaeffer, Kotzebue, Alaska, November 1993.

ated isn't working for us. We've got to work together.'"[14]

It is well documented that both blacks and Native Alaskans performed well above the expectations of military planners who "experimented" with their employment during World War II. The majority of the black builders were decorated for their service in the Far North and "rewarded" by being dispatched to duty in war zones around the world, in the face of an earlier decision that they could not be trusted under fire. Nor should it be lost on the reader that the U.S. Army was the first government agency in America to integrate minorities (during the Korean War), an advancement that might not have taken place had their performance proved less than outstanding during World War II.

However, gains made by Alaska Natives through World War II service are even more spectacular. Impressed by their performance, Alaska's territorial governor Ernest Gruening established Native Guard units as a permanent peacetime fixture. In addition, he campaigned (and won) for Alaska the first anti-discrimination law in America, and also lobbied for more Native participation in government.

"They continue to serve—not only in the Alaska National Guard," he wrote happily in 1969. "They serve in the Alaska Legislature; and it is one of my proudest accomplishments that I persuaded the first Eskimo to run (Percy Ipalook) and to start the inclusion in our territorial and, later, state legislatures of Eskimos to represent areas which are almost wholly inhabited by Eskimo."[15]

However, it was Muktuk Marston, as a delegate to Alaska's Constitutional Convention in 1955, who carefully laid the groundwork for Alaska Natives' biggest economic advancement. Speaking in behalf of a Unalakleet Eskimo who had been divested of his family fish camp by the government because he (as was the case with every other Native in Alaska) had no legal title, Marston successfully pleaded with fellow delegates to recognize the claim of Alaska's Eskimos, Indians, and Aleuts to the lands they had used and occupied for centuries.

Marston's motion that "the state and its people ... disclaim all right or title in or any property including fishing rights held by or for any Indian, Eskimo, or Aleut, or community thereof," found in the general provision of the Alaska Constitution, provided legal backing for the Alaska Native land claims movement that followed.[16]

The Native leadership, originally fostered through the Territorial Guard and other service units during World War II, grew strong enough by 1971 to successfully lobby the U.S. Congress for the largest land claims settlement in American history (a billion dollars and forty million acres of land) and has maintained the political clout with which to manage it.

*Lael Morgan is a member of the Department of Journalism and Broadcasting, University of Alaska Fairbanks. Her most recent book is "Art and Eskimo Power: The Life and Times of Alaskan Howard Rock."*

---

[14] Richard Frank, Fairbanks, Alaska, November 1993.

[15] Marston, *Men of the Tundra*, p. 8.

[16] Gerald Bowkett, *Reaching for a Star: The Final Campaign for Alaska Statehood* (Fairbanks, Alaska: Epicenter Press, 1989), pp. 57-59.

# Race Relations and the Contributions of Minority Troops in Alaska: A Challenge to the Status Quo?

*Charles Hendricks*

NEARLY A MONTH BEFORE THE AFRICAN-AMERICAN soldiers of the Ninety-Seventh Engineer General Service Regiment arrived in Valdez, Alaska, at the end of April 1942, Brigadier General Clarence Sturdevant wrote apologetically to the senior army officer in Alaska, his West Point classmate Major General Simon Bolivar Buckner, "I have heard that you object to having colored troops in Alaska and we have attempted to avoid sending them."

As the assistant chief of engineers charged with overseeing the construction of a military highway to Alaska, Sturdevant had arranged the assignment of the black Ninety-Third and Ninety-Seventh Engineers to the project in mid-March when his planners determined that the four white engineer regiments initially selected to work on the road could not open it unaided in a single year, as desired by the War Department. In mid-April he would seek and obtain a third African-American unit for the project, the Ninety-Fifth Engineers. Sturdevant explained to Buckner that the black troops would be "hard at work in two reliefs on a twenty-hour schedule in out-of-the way places" and that plans called for them to return below the forty-ninth parallel in the fall.[1]

General Buckner, who was already planning to retire in Alaska after the war, seemed, as he responded to Sturdevant, to have some trouble sorting out his professional responsibility for defending American territory from his personal disdain for African-Americans and his vision of Alaska's future:

> I appreciate your consideration of my views concerning negro troops in Alaska. The thing which I have opposed principally has been their establishment as port troops for the unloading of transports at our docks. The very high wages offered to unskilled labor here would attract a large number of them and cause them to remain and settle after the war, with the natural result that they would interbreed with the Indians and Eskimos and produce an astonishingly objectionable race of mongrels which would be a problem here from now on. We have enough racial problems here and elsewhere already.

However, Buckner did not object to employing black troops on the highway "if they are kept far enough away from the settlements and kept busy."[2]

---

[1] Sturdevant to Buckner, 2 April 1942, containing the quotations; Sturdevant to Colonel William Hoge, 3 March 1942; and Sturdevant to Lieutenant General Brehon Somervell, Commander, Services of Supply, 14 March 1942, all in file 611 Alcan Highway, box 14; and annotated copy of Hoge to Sturdevant, 17 April 1942, file 50-15, box 15, all in Accession 72A3173, Office of History, U.S. Army Corps of Engineers, Kingman Building, Fort Belvoir, Virginia; Heath Twichell, *Northwest Epic: The Building of the Alaska Highway* (New York: St. Martin's Press, 1992), p.121; and George W. Cullum, *Biographical Register of the Officers and Graduates of the United States Military Academy*, vol 9 (Boston: 1891-1950), pp. 121-22, 125-26.

[2] Buckner to Lieutenant General John DeWitt, Commander, Western Defense Command, 3 November 1941, and Buckner to Sturdevant, 20 April 1942, copies of both in correspondence of Buckner, Box 14, Records of the Alaskan Department, Record Group 338 (Records of U.S. Army

Buckner's vivid words have been quoted repeatedly since I inserted them, somewhat stretching my topic, in an article on "The Eskimos and the Defense of Alaska" published in 1985, but they do not tell the whole story.[3] In light of the racial attitudes which the Buckner-Sturdevant correspondence evinces, the significant contributions made by African-American troops in Alaska and northwestern Canada during World War II were surprisingly large in my view. Given the stridency with which Buckner expressed his antipathy toward blacks, I find it particularly remarkable that his Alaska Defense Command and its successor, the Alaskan Department, managed, as the war progressed, to provide an atmosphere comparatively conducive to the success of its African-American soldiers.

Buckner was initially unwilling to assume the burden of supplying the Ninety-Seventh through Valdez or Fairbanks. This forced the regiment to haul most of its own supplies and led Sturdevant to instruct his on-site highway commander, Brigadier General William Hoge, to ask "for *white* handling detachments and additional transportation" for the unit. The Ninety-Seventh started slowly as its heavy equipment operators gained experience on road-building machinery that had not been made available to the unit during most of its training in Florida. But it picked up speed as it headed toward the Canadian border. A race for the border developed between the Ninety-Seventh and the Eighteenth Engineers, a white engineer combat regiment building the highway west from Whitehorse. The two regiments met near Beaver Creek, some twenty miles inside Canada, on October 25, 1942. The black troops had won the race.[4]

The Ninety-Third and Ninety-Fifth Engineers, working on Canadian sections of the highway, obtained less

opportunity for such achievement. They built some one hundred miles of road in the southern Yukon by August 10. Despite this rapid early progress, achieved while all Alaska Highway units were still enhancing their speed, the regiment was then assigned follow-up and maintenance duties behind the white 340th Engineers.[5]

The Ninety-Fifth was never given a chance to open new sections of the highway. Upon its arrival at the highway's southern terminus, it was stripped of most its heavy equipment, which was turned over to the white 341st Engineers. The Ninety-Fifth was assigned to build bridges and to widen and improve the roadway—largely by hand—behind the 341st. The black regiment thus took great pride in its construction—in just seventy-two hours—of the three-hundred-foot-long Sikanni Chief River bridge. Similarly handicapped was the 388th Engineer Battalion (Separate), a black unit formed from the Ninety-Third Engineers in Louisiana which began work on the Canadian oil—or Canol—project, in June 1942 without ever obtaining the equipment of a general service regiment. The men of the 388th worked as stevedores on the long river supply route from Waterways, Alberta, to Norman Wells in the Northwest Territories.[6]

Under the War Department's chaplain assignment policies, each of the black units working on the Alaska Highway and Canol projects was assigned a black chaplain, but all of their other officers were white. Brigadier General James O'Connor, who during 1942 took over on-site supervision of both projects, wanted to keep it that way. In January 1943 he rebuffed a War Department offer to provide some secular black officers for the units, arguing that there were no towns with Negro communities along the highway to provide them with social outlets. O'Connor's command also spurned offers made at various times by General Sturdevant for three black

Commands), National Archives (henceforth RG 338, NA), and the undated original of the latter in the Sturdevant file, Office of History, U.S. Army Corps of Engineers. Brigadier General Dwight Eisenhower, then Army Assistant Chief of Staff, War Plans Division, reported that Governor Gruening also opposed assigning black troops to Alaska, arguing, as Eisenhower paraphrased him, "that the mixture of the colored race with the native Indian and Eskimo stock is highly undesirable." See Eisenhower to Army Chief of Staff George Marshall, 25 March 1942, case no 4., file 291.21, Operations Division classified general correspondence, box 472, RG 165 (Records of the Army Staff), NA.

[3] Hendricks, "The Eskimos and the Defense of Alaska," *Pacific Historical Review*, 44 (August 1985), pp. 271-95, with the quotation on p. 280; Everett Louis Overstreet, *Black on a Background of White: A Chronicle of Afro-Americans' Involvement in America's Last Frontier, Alaska* (Fairbanks: That New Publishing Co., 1988), pp. 42-43; Twichell, *Northwest Epic*, pp. 144-45; and Bill Gilford, "The Great Black North," *Washington City Paper*, 13:40 (October 8, 1993), p. 24.

[4] Sturdevant to Hoge, 11 May 1942, containing the quotation, file 50-15, box 15, Accession 72A3173; Twichell, *Northwest Epic*, pp. 122, 211-12, 335; Blanche Coil, Jean Keith, and Herbert Rosenthal, *The Corps of Engineers: Troops and Equipment, United States Army in World War II* (Washington: Army Center of Military History, 1958), pp. 16, 139-40; and Shelby L. Stanton, *Order of Battle: U.S. Army, World War II* (Novato, Calif.: Presidio Press, 1984), pp. 542, 570.

[5] "History of the Whitehorse Sector of the Alcan Highway," 10 June 1943, pp. 6, 9, with the mileage figure taken from John T. Greenwood, "Building the Road to Alaska," in Barry W. Fowle, ed., *Builders and Fighters: U.S. Army Engineers in World War II* (Fort Belvoir, Virginia: Office of History, U.S. Army Corps of Engineers, 1992), p. 134.

[6] Twichell, *Northwest Epic*, pp. 130-32, 143, 188-91; and "The History of the Ninety-Third Engineer Regiment (GS) prior to 1 January 1943," file ENRG-93-O.i, box 19549, World War II Operations Reports, RG 407 (Records of the Adjutant General's Office), NA. While Brigadier General James O'Connor, who assumed command of the southern sector of the highway in May 1942, made the decision to turn the Ninety-Fifth's equipment over to the 341st, Sturdevant and Hoge had already decided in April that the Seventh Regiment, assigned to the project—ultimately the Ninety-Fifth—would be used "in the rear of the 341st." See Hoge to Sturdevant, 17 April 1942.

engineer dump truck companies and up to four black engineer general service regiments to relieve, or, in the case of the companies, to supplement units already on the highway.[7]

As the sole African-American officers in these units, the chaplains bore a heavy morale burden. Captain Edward Carroll, chaplain of the Ninety-Fifth, traveled with a Victrola which he employed both at religious services and in evening relaxation.

Sometimes the chaplains had to step in to protect their men. Chaplain Carroll recalls having done so in the case of a soldier who dated a white woman who had also received the attentions of a white officer. The officer accused the soldier of raping the woman. Reverend Carroll observed that she was a prostitute and assisted the soldier in getting the charges dropped. Chaplain Smith of the Ninety-Seventh was less successful in protecting his soldiers' interests. Fairbanks was placed off limits to the Ninety-Seventh after some white residents became aroused about the black soldiers' open acceptance at the town's restaurants, theaters, bars, and night clubs.[8]

Reverend Carroll, who subsequently became bishop of Boston in the United Methodist Church, was but one of a number of black Alaska Highway veterans to pursue noteworthy careers after the war. Master Sergeant George Owens, who served in the Yukon with the Ninety-Third Engineers, pursued a career in higher education and served as president of Tougaloo College from 1964 to 1984. Sergeant Herbert Tucker of the Ninety-Fifth became head of the District of Columbia's Department of Environmental Services.[9]

While the officers in charge of the Alaska Highway project did not always adequately equip their black regiments or fully utilize their members' talents, they did manage to obtain excellent publicity for their use of black troops. An August 1942 *Time* magazine article on the highway observed that "more than 40 percent of the engineer workers are Negro." The article included a photo of "a cold Alaska river: bridged in two days by U.S. Negro engineers." Newspapers across the United States and Canada published the wire-service photograph of black corporal Refines Sims Jr. shaking hands with white private first class Alfred Jalufka atop their bulldozers at the Beaver Creek meeting of the Ninety-Seventh and Eighteenth Engineers. General O'Connor's aide, Lieutenant Richard Neuberger, a future United States senator, made sure that newspapers serving the African-American community obtained the stories as well. He sent to Walter White, head of the National Association for the Advancement of Colored People, news releases on that final breakthrough and on the formal highway opening ceremony in which two black and two white enlisted men held the ribbon cut by Canadian and Alaska officials.[10]

The army did not meet General Sturdevant's goal of returning the black Alaska Highway regiments to the United States during the fall of 1942. It was able, however, to release the white Eighteenth and black Ninety-Third Engineers to General Buckner's Alaska Defense Command in January 1943. As he began building air bases and troop cantonments west through the Aleutians after the Japanese attack on Dutch Harbor, Buckner became eager to obtain more engineer troops, black or white. He sent the Ninety-Third's first battalion to the important naval and air base at Cold Bay on the Alaska Peninsula, and its second battalion to Fort Glenn on Umnak Island in the Aleutians.[11]

Colonel Walter Hodge, the Ninety-Third's commander, became chief army engineer at Cold Bay, and he was assigned several white infantry and engineer companies to assist the black companies of his First Battalion. At Cold Bay the Ninety-Third built warehouses, installed water and fuel pipelines and a sewage system, expanded the airfield and the base's road network,

[7] Ulysses Lee, *The Employment of Negro Troops, United States Army in World War II* (Washington: Army Center of Military History, 1966), pp. 208-13; and telegram, Colonel Joseph Gorlinski (a Sturdevant subordinate) to O'Connor, 20 August 1942, and letter, Sturdevant to Somervell, 4 February 1943, with 2nd endorsement, Colonel H. A. Montgomery, Commanding, Northwest Service Command, to Somervell, 28 February 1943, all in file 370.5 (Alcan Highway), classified general correspondence, box 130, entry 52A41, RG 77 (Records of the Office of the Chief of Engineers), NA.

[8] Gilford, "The Great Black North," p. 28; Annex 3 (Psychological) to G2 Periodic Report No. 50, 1-8 May 1943, file 91-DC1-2.1, box 7, American Theater, World War II Operations Reports, RG 407, NA; and Lieutenant Colonel J.A. Day, Inspector General, Northwest Service Command, to O'Connor, 29 June 1943, file 333.1 (Ninety-Seventh Engineers), classified general correspondence, box 344, Entry 52A41, RG 77, NA.

[9] Information received by phone from the Information Service of the United Methodist Church and from the Office of the President, Tougaloo College; Twichell, *Northwest Epic*, p. 144; and Gilford, "The Great Black North," pp. 28, 34.

[10] Twichell, *Northwest Epic*, pp. 181, 213-14; *Time*, 40:9, p. 78; Neuberger to White, 4 November 1942 and 26 November 1942, box II-A-642, papers of the National Association for the Advancement of Colored People (NAACP), Manuscript Division, Library of Congress.

[11] Sturdevant to Hoge, 16 August 1942, file 50-15, box 15, Accession 72A3173; Buckner to DeWitt, 25 November 1942, correspondence of Lieutenant General Buckner, box 14, Alaskan Department, RG 338, NA; Unit Diary, Ninety-Third Engineer General Service Regiment, 1943, containing the quotation, in file ENRG 93-0.7, and "History of the Ninety-Third Engineer Regiment (GS) for 1943," file ENRG-93-O.1, both in box 19549, World War II Operations Reports, RG 407, NA; and Stetson Conn, Rose Engelman and Byron Fairchild, *Guarding the United States and its Outposts, United States Army in World War II* (Washington: Army Center of Military History, 1964), p. 284.

The staff of the wartime U.S. Army newspaper *The Adakian* was picked by author Dashiell Hammett, center, the paper's editor. From the left are Alba Morris, Bill Glacken, and Bernard Kalb. Don Miller stands at far right. (*Anchorage Museum of History and Art*)

added an ambulance entrance to the base hospital, built Pacific huts, and relaxed in its own NCO club. Nine of the Ninety-Third's heavy equipment operators were selected in July 1943 to work with white engineer units in Adak, where more men with their skills were needed.

Other members of the unit had trouble at Cold Bay. One private was sent to the station hospital in Anchorage as a "mental case." Another, already a prisoner in the guard house, was charged with assaulting a commissioned officer.[12]

The Second Battalion of the Ninety-Third worked at Fort Glenn along with and sometimes under the direction of the white 802nd Engineer Aviation Battalion. The black battalion surfaced airfield runways and a road and built hangars, warehouses, and Pacific huts to live in. By late April 1943 the battalion's diary was recording considerable satisfaction:

The change in living conditions this organiza-

tion has undergone the past few months is amazing. But four months ago we were living in poorly heated tents in temperatures from 30 degrees to 60 degrees below zero. The present conditions of weatherproof, well-insulated buildings, and electricity seems to be the height of luxury.

Ah, life in the balmy Aleutians.[13]

The black port troops, whose service in Alaska's towns Buckner had earlier dreaded, arrived on the Alaska Peninsula and in the Aleutians soon after the Ninety-Third Engineers. The 383rd Port Battalion sailed to Alaska in April and May 1943, with most of the unit going first to Adak. Company A of the 383rd and detachments from other companies, however, sailed with the Attu task force. Company A landed at Massacre Bay on May 13, D plus two. The black port troops worked eighteen-hour shifts unloading cargo onto beaches initially just a mile behind the combat zone

---

[12] Unit Diary, Engineer General Service Regiment, 1943, and "Diary of Regimental Headquarters, Ninety-Third Engineer Regiment (GS) for Period 1 January 1944 to 22 June 1944," both in file ENRG-93-0.7.

[13] "Diary of Second Battalion, Ninety-Third Engineer Regiment (GS) for Period 1943," file ENRG-93-0.7.

on the island. About a hundred soldiers from these black companies served as litter bearers during the later stages of combat there. Although they came under sniper fire, none were killed or wounded.[14]

Elements of two black port battalions, the 372nd and the 383rd, unloaded ships on most of the western Aleutian Islands for the base-building projects undertaken there in 1943-45. They did their work well. Brigadier General Harry Thompson, who commanded at Adak, reported that his "Negro troops were nearly as efficient in tons per day as the white troops but were definitely more careful in handling cargo." At another island, Thompson observed, "white port troops were removed from ship's work and put on other jobs because of a lack of efficiency compared to the Negro troops." These official reports were a far cry from information the War Department received from Milne Bay, New Guinea, where white officers expressed fears of hostile secret organizations among black port troops and reported substantial quantities of mishandled cargo floating around the bay.[15]

Confrontations between African-American soldiers and white military or civilian authorities occurred frequently during World War II, both in the southern United States and elsewhere. In July 1943 General George Marshall pointed to six "riots of a racial character" that had occurred in "recent weeks" and concluded that "Disaffection among Negro soldiers continues to constitute an immediately serious problem." Sometimes these clashes became violent and claimed the lives of participants. Even if they did not, they could lead to charges of mutiny against black soldiers. For example, seventy-four African-Americans in Hawaii, in Company E, 1320th Engineer General Service Regiment, were tried by court martial for mutiny in 1944 and convicted. The men had failed to report to work after all of their black officers were summarily transferred from the unit.

Thurgood Marshall would participate in the appeals of these cases. Two African-American units that served in Alaska during World War II also experienced mass disobedience, but neither had these problems while in Alaska.[16]

For example, the 483rd Port Battalion came to Excursion Inlet at the northern end of Alaska's Inside Passage in the spring of 1943 after working the previous winter in New Orleans. Assigned not to Buckner's command but to the Seattle Port of Embarkation, the 483rd transshipped lumber and petroleum products to ocean-going vessels heading to the Aleutians. They were a talented group. In their spare time they published a weekly newspaper, improved their living areas, and built a post theater where a number of noted artists, including film star Ingrid Bergman, came to perform. The unit returned to the states in January 1944, and the men were given twenty-day furloughs. When the battalion sailed to England on May 7, 1944, however, it was missing some two hundred men who had gone AWOL shortly before departure.[17]

The unauthorized absences occurred when Lieutenant Colonel Peter Miller, who had commanded the battalion in New Orleans and initially in Alaska, returned to the unit after an absence of several months. Ernest Cain was the first sergeant of one of the battalion's port companies. While subsequently confined in a military stockade, he presented a long list of complaints against Miller, many of which involved charges of racial prejudice. Among these was his refusal to allow any enlisted men to attend officer candidate school; his instructions to a captain in the company "that the only way he could get a promotion was to work the 'niggers' hard and keep them working"; the racially segregated seating he ordered in the theater built by the battalion; and his refusal to allow his soldiers to play softball with teams from white units.[18]

[14] Cards of Headquarters and Headquarters Detachment, 383rd Port Battalion TC, and the 881st and 884th Transportation Corps Stevedore Companies, microfilm box 106, microfilmed unit history cards of the Operations and Directory Section, WDOB [1947]; and former Staff Sergeant Benjamin Woods (of Company A, 383rd Port Battalion) to the Army Center of Military History, 5 May 1988, 383rd Transportation Port Battalion file, all in the Organizational History Branch, U.S. Army Center of Military History, Washington, D.C.; and Brigadier General Harry F. Thompson, Commander, U.S. Troops, Adak, to Lieutenant General Delos Emmons, Commander, Alaskan Department, 28 June 1945, p. 6, file 291.2, box 53, classified general correspondence, Alaska Department, RG 388, NA.

[15] Unit history card of the 372nd Port Battalion, Organizational History Branch, U.S. Army Center of Military History; "Military Strength of the Alaskan Department, 31 December 1943," file 320.2 (Alaskan Dept.) Part I, classified general correspondence, box 126, entry 52A41, RG 77, NA; Thompson to Emmons, 28 June 1945, with the quotations on p. 2; and Major Fred Gustorf, Ninth Service Command, to Somervell, 3 August 1944, case 44, file 322.97 OPD, box 831, Operations Division classified general correspondence, RG 165 , NA.

[16] Lee, *The Employment of Negro Troops*, pp. 348-79; Marshall to Somervell et al., 13 July 1943, containing the quotations, file 291.2, box 2, Northwest Service Command, RG 338, NA; and Court Martial, 1320th Engineers, files, boxes II-B-18 to -20, papers of the NAACP, Manuscript Division, Library of Congress.

[17] History, 483rd Port Battalion, Transportation Corps, 3 April 1944; Historical Report, 656th Port Company, 15 December 1944; Historical Report of Company C, 483rd Port Battalion, now 658th Port Company, 15 December 1944; and Historical Record of the 659th Port Company (Company D), 483rd Port Battalion, all in file TCBN-483-0.1, box 23320, World War II Operations Reports, RG 407, NA; Isadore Zack, "CIC in Zone of Interior: The Case of the Mass AWOL of 483rd Port Battalion," *Golden Sphinx: The Voice of Intelligence*, Fall 1993, pp. 1, 4, 18, copy in 483rd Port Battalion file, Organizational History Branch, U.S. Army Center of Military History.

[18] Zack, "The Case of the Mass AWOL," with the quotation on p. 4.

These grievances came from a unit that served in Alaska, but not under the command of General Buckner or his mid-1944 successor, Lieutenant General Delos Emmons. Respecting the spirit of newly formulated War Department policies opposing discrimination in the use of recreational and other facilities, the Alaskan Department managed to avoid large-scale racial conflict despite the arrival there in February 1944 of the 364th Infantry, an African-American regiment that had been involved in some of the more noteworthy racial clashes of the war.[19]

While stationed near Phoenix, Arizona, in November 1942, some one hundred men of the 364th had engaged in a shooting match with a group of black military policemen in which a soldier and a civilian had been killed and twelve soldiers seriously wounded. Another soldier of the 364th had been killed in 1943 by a local sheriff outside the unit's new station, Camp Van Dorn, Mississippi. Some soldiers involved in the Phoenix disorder had been found to have had tattooed on their bodies the phrase "Double V," standing for victory over both the Axis powers and American racism, a popular slogan in the contemporary black press.[20]

By the time the 364th arrived in Alaska, it had been purged of its most troublesome soldiers and of officers who had failed to demonstrate the ability to lead black troops. More than 250 changes had been made in officer personnel in the year-and-a-half after Colonel John Goodman, a native of Waco, Texas, was given command of the regiment in the aftermath of the Phoenix melee. Goodman issued a policy that "there shall be no discrimination based on race, color, or creed. All officers of the regiment," he explained, "use the same messes, sleeping accommodations, and bath houses." Despite Goodman's policies, some separation of accommodations for white and black officers persisted even in Alaska, and at least one black officer complained to the War Department of discriminatory treatment and sought a transfer to a unit with all black officers.[21]

In response to this complaint, Goodman observed that the mixing of white and black junior officers created unnecessary friction and proposed, with General Buckner's approval, that his junior officers be all of one race. The War Department had just issued a new policy under which black officers would be assigned to army units in company- or battalion-sized groups. In May 1944, the War Department authorized the Alaskan Department to replace the white lieutenants in the 364th with black officers that the department would provide.[22]

The 364th, meanwhile, performed well. In the summer of 1944 it removed pierced-steel plank from runways on Adak "in a highly efficient manner [and] in an exceptionally short period of time," in the words of General Thompson. By June 1945 Goodman, by then a brigadier general and commander of all U.S. troops on Shemya, could see no difference between units with all, some, or no white officers. Goodman expressed his support for racial equality in the army unambiguously: "I am firmly convinced that a man in uniform is a soldier and should be treated the same as any other soldier without regard to color, race, or creed."[23]

The youthful African-American artist Don Miller was among those who benefitted from the racial tolerance which had developed in the Alaskan Department by the end of the war. Miller and black printer Alba Morris joined the ten-man staff of Adak's army daily, *The Adakian*, at the invitation of its editor, mystery writer and, in 1944, corporal Dashiell Hammett. General Thompson, a fan of Hammett's popular detective stories, had placed the author in charge of this paper, apparently unconcerned about Hammett's ties to the Communist Party. Future newsmen Bernard Kalb of NBC and Bill Glackin of the *Sacramento Bee* also served on *The Adakian*. Miller saw his work as a cartoonist on this distinguished staff as a turning point in his very successful career as an artist and illustrator. He would later paint the Martin Luther King Jr. mural in the main

---

[19] Lee, *The Employment of Negro Troops*, pp. 308-09, and Journal, 364th Infantry, March 1941 - May 1946, entries for 14 January - 1 March 1944, file INRG-364-0.7, box 21241, World War II Operations Reports, RG 407, NA.

[20] Ibid., pp. 366-70, and Gustorf to Somervell, 3 August 1944.

[21] Lee, *The Employment of Negro Troops*, p. 222-23, 367; John F. Goodman biography file, Historical Resources Branch, U.S. Army Center of Military History; and Second Lieutenant Robert E. Jackson, Headquarters Company, 2nd Battalion, 364th Infantry, to Major General J.A. Ulio, the Adjutant General, 4 April 1944, with 1st endorsement, Goodman to Ulio, 25 April 1944, containing the quotation; Lieutenant Colonel B. C. Kennon, Commander, 2nd Battalion, 364th Infantry, to Goodman, 21 April 1944; Captain Paul Little, Commander, Company K, 364th Infantry, to Lieutenant Colonel Earl Keiso, Commander, 3rd Battalion, 364th Infantry, 23 April 1944, all in case 40, file 322.97 OPD, box 831, Operations Division Decimal File, RG 165, NA.

[22] 1st endorsement, Goodman to Ulio, 25 April 1944; 3rd endorsement, Buckner to Ulio, 28 April 1944; and telegram, Major General Thomas Handy, War Department Assistant Chief of Staff, G1, to Buckner, 27 May 1944, all in case 40, and Ulio to major army commanders, 7 January 1944, case 27, both in file 322.97 OPD.

[23] Thompson to Emmons, 28 June 1945, pp. 17-18, containing the first quotation, and 1st endorsement, Goodman to Emmons, 30 June 1945, with the second quotation on p. 6, on Lieutenant Colonel W. R. Coleman, Assistant Adjutant General, Alaskan Department, to Goodman, 7 June 1945, all in file 291.2, box 53, classified general correspondence, Alaska Department, RG 388, NA; Journal, 364th Infantry, March 1941 - May 1946, entry for 21 September 1944; and Cullum, *Biographical Register* vol. 9, p. 219.

public library of Washington, D.C.[24]

While other senior commanders in the Aleutians criticized the leadership skills of newly commissioned black officers, all agreed that the policy of equal privileges in athletics, theaters, clubs, stores, and buses had greatly enhanced racial harmony, despite some passive white disapproval. By the end of the war, senior officers in Alaska understood, in the words of the commander of the 383rd Port Battalion, that the "Efficiency of Negro troops reaches a low level under conditions where ignorant, uneducated, and thoughtless white officers use terms such as 'Nigger, black so-and-so, etc.'" That commander recalled a specific instance where delays had followed the use of such terms by navy officers, who likely had had less experience working with black troops.[25]

African-American soldiers performed a wide range of significant work on the Alaska Highway, on the Alaska Peninsula, and in the Aleutians during World War II. Willing workers when given respect, the African-American troops made known their needs as well as their capabilities. Over the course of four years of war, American military leaders in Alaska came increasingly to understand those needs and to provide a surprisingly egalitarian environment for American soldiers, black and white. To a considerable degree, the challenges those military leaders faced in a demanding war led them to implement much more tolerant racial policies than the highly prejudiced statements made just a few years earlier would have led one to predict.

*Charles Hendricks is a historian with the U.S. Army Corps of Engineers at Fort Belvoir, Virginia. He is the author of several chapters of "Builders and Fighters: U.S. Army Engineers in World War II."*

---

[24] Richard Layman, *Shadow Man: The Life of Dashiell Hammett* (New York: Harcourt Brace Jovanovich, 1981), pp. 173-195; Diane Brenner, Anchorage Museum of History and Art, to Hendricks, 2 December 1993; and personal interview with Julia Miller, Don Miller's widow, on 19 April 1994.

[25] Thompson to Emmons, 28 June 1945, pp. 2 (containing the quotation), 4, 5, 8-12, 15; Brigadier General Maxwell O'Brien, Commander, U.S. Troops, Amchitka, to Emmons, 22 June 1945, pp. 2-3; and "Consolidation of Reports: Participation of Negro Troops in the Post-War Military Establishment," pp. 6-8, 10, all in file 291.2, box 53, classified general correspondence, Alaska Department, RG 388, NA.

# I Remember What I Want to Forget

*Sylvia K. Kobayashi*

I REMEMBER ... BUT I WANT TO FORGET. IT HAPPENED OVER fifty years ago. I want to forget the day I lost my country. The day I lost my future. The day all of me was drained, and I felt empty.

I want to forget the day we were herded like cattle into a prison camp.

What did we do wrong? What was our crime?

Who do we pledge allegiance to now?

I can't forget that feeling of total rejection, the feeling of not belonging, the feeling of complete emptiness.

It was April 1942.

We Japanese-Americans were transported from Seattle to the Puyallup fairgrounds ten miles away. There we were assigned one room in a barracks—one room per family. At the time I wasn't aware of my good fortune. I did not have to sleep in a horse stall as some did.

We were immediately ordered to fill sacks with excelsior hay. These were our mattresses, which we set on iron cots.

As reality sank in, I was shocked to find myself among a sea of faces that looked like relatives, so many I could not count.

I quickly learned the meaning of such words as "barracks," "latrine," "mess hall," "community shower," "diarrhea."

In spite of it all, I suddenly realized how much easier it was for me. I was young; I wasn't pregnant; I wasn't a mother; I wasn't elderly. My heart went out to pregnant women who had no choice but to use community showers.

The camp population was composed mainly of the very young, under twenty, and the elderly, over fifty. What was so threatening then to America? The old were past their prime. The young were still too young for serious political views.

Then the army recruiters came. They asked the young men to volunteer, to fight for their country and to prove our loyalty to America—the country that placed them in prison camps.

Lo and behold, volunteers came forward without hesitation. The young men were willing to give their lives to Uncle Sam. But not all went willingly. There were those who felt that injustice had been done. They refused to join until full citizenship rights were restored to them. This, too, took courage. These young men were sent to a federal penitentiary as draft dodgers. They served two years in prison.

Among the volunteers from Minidoka, Idaho, were Alaskans Pete Heyano, Mark Hiratsuka and others. The fathers of these men were Japanese who had married Alaska Native women. They were interned with us. All males over sixteen with one-sixteenth or more of Japanese blood were removed from their homes and imprisoned.

Pete and Mark served in Europe. Pete was put in a service unit and served in France, England, Belgium, etc. He married a young girl from Belgium. The couple made their home in Ekok, Alaska, after the war.

Mark was assigned to the 100th/442nd all-Japanese-American Combat Regiment, the same regiment that Senator Dan Inouye served in.

Mark's life was spared as his comrades on both sides fell. His buddies acted as a shield as he scrambled

Japanese arrive at the Puyallup Assembly Center in Washington, prior to being sent to War Relocation Authority camps elsewhere. From Puyallup many were sent to the internment camp at Minidoka, Idaho. *(Photo No. UW 526, Special Collections Division, University of Washington Libraries)*

between and under their dead bodies as they took the bullets that spared his life.

Recently, Mark's picture appeared on the front cover of the book, *I Can Never Forget*, written by Thelma Chang of Hawaii.

The 100th Battalion showed what Japanese-Americans would do for their country. Starting with volunteers from Hawaii, it was joined with the 442nd Combat Regiment. The men rose from suspicion to acclaim and became known as the "Purple Heart Battalion."

The 100/442nd rescued the lost Texas Battalion who were trapped by the enemy. In the rescue of 222 men, the Japanese-Americans suffered four times that number in casualties.

The Japanese-Americans were among the first to reach Dachau and to free the surviving prisoners.

Then there were the boys from Ketchikan—Charlie Tatsuda and Pat Hagiwara. Charlie and Pat were born and raised in Ketchikan. They were in the original Alaska Guard and were stationed at Chilkoot Barracks when war broke out. They were at Chilkoot when their families were removed and interned.

Pat was in charge of guarding two prominent Juneau businessmen, Mr. Tanaka and Mr. Fukuyama, while his own father was interned at Annette island.

At the time of eviction, Charlie had a sister who was gravely ill at the Ketchikan hospital. She could not be moved and he was not allowed to visit her. He was not allowed to attend her funeral.

Charlie's younger sister, Cherry, begged the authorities for permission to visit her dying sister. After much delay, permission was finally granted. She traveled from the camp in Puyallup, Washington, under armed guard. It was, however, too late; her sister had passed away, alone, without any family members at her side.

Pat Hagiwara joined the regimental combat team in Europe. Charlie Tatsuda was sent to military intelligence school in Minnesota to learn the Japanese language. He graduated as an interpreter and was assigned to the paratroopers.

Charlie served in the Pacific Theater, the Philippines, and Japan. George Kimura was drafted from Anchorage while his wife and family were sent to camp. Due to his skill in the Japanese language, he was sent to Australia and New Guinea.

His first child was born in internment camp but died a few years later due to the deplorable medical facilities.

A little known fact is that forty to fifty Japanese-American GIs served in the Aleutian Campaign. They served as translators, interrogators, and interpreters. So valuable were they that bodyguards were assigned to them. They were in double jeopardy—a target of the enemy and a target of their own men.

Three years ago I met Henry Suyehira, from Emmett, Idaho. Henry graduated from the first language class at the presidio. In May of 1942, Henry was sent to Umnak. He watched the dogfights in the sky between the Zeros and the U.S. aircraft. He was in Umnak when Dutch Harbor was bombed.

Henry was on Attu when the banzai attack came within three hundred yards of headquarters. He was ready to destroy all the documents. Then the engineers came to the rescue and stopped the attack.

Pete Nakao was in on the first assault on Attu. He was assigned a bodyguard, a six-foot-five-inch-tall Scandinavian from Nebraska. Digging a trench for himself was not too bad but it was twice the work for his buddy. They both shared the same trench and foxhole when the banzai attack came roaring down the hill, bayonets thrust forward.

Pete and his buddy scrunched in their trench. They watched in horror as the enemy killed their men and wondered when they would be next.

Roy Matsumoto was assigned to Merrill's Marauders in Burma. The three battalions of nine hundred men were running low on ammunition and supplies and they were surrounded by an enemy regiment of seven thousand men. They were about to be annihilated.

Roy shed all of his clothing as he silently made his way through the jungle to enemy headquarters. Eavesdropping on the enemy, he learned of their plan of a pre-dawn attack. He rushed back to his commanding officer with the news.

The Americans relocated to higher ground, planted booby traps, and waited for the enemy with submachine guns, rifles, etc., poised.

Sure enough, the enemy came. The first assault was completely decimated. As the second assault hesitated, Roy shouted as loud as he could and, in Japanese, gave the command to "Charge!" The enemy obeyed his command and were stopped again.

For this heroic act, after fifty years, Roy Matsumoto, flanked by five generals, was inducted into the Ranger Hall of Fame this year.

The agony of the Japanese-Americans was fighting against the country of their parents and for the country that put them behind barbed wire compounds. The irony was that their parents were denied U.S. citizenship.

The Japanese-American intelligence teams were in most of the campaigns in the Pacific. They were the eyes and ears of every combat command. They were with the army, navy, marines, air force, and were assigned to the forces of Australia, Great Britain, Canada, New Zealand, India, and China.

General MacArthur said, "Never in military history

U.S. Army Lieutenant Charles Tatsuda, a Nisei, was born and raised in Ketchikan, Alaska. He served as a paratrooper and intelligence specialist with the Eleventh Airborne Division. In November 1945, *Collier's* magazine illustrator C.C. Beall found himself wandering around Tokyo with Lt. Tatsuda as interpreter. The portrait Beall painted appeared in *Collier's* November 24, 1945 issue.

did an army know so much about the enemy prior to actual engagement."

The Kobayashi story is somewhat typical of the hardships that were endured by Japanese-Americans. I would like to tell it now.

My husband, Koby, and his three brothers served in the U.S. Army. Two brothers served in the 442nd Combat Regiment in Europe. Number-one son, Mat, volunteered from the internment camp. He was assigned to the antitank company of the 442nd regiment. He participated in the glider invasion of southern France and in the rescue of the lost battalion.

During this period, he met a familiar figure marching up the battlefield. It was his kid brother, Shiro. The brothers embraced. Mat could not utter a word. He thought he would never see Shiro again.

Koby was drafted five days before Pearl Harbor. The army treated the Japanese-American GIs differently from all others. They were removed from the West Coast and transferred inland. They were assigned menial chores such as garbage detail and kitchen detail.

Koby was sent to Camp Robinson, Arkansas. He served as the mail carrier until the captain saw him typing one day. After that he became the company clerk.

He was never allowed to carry weapons so he never participated in bivouac. He was trained to be a member of the cadre but he was not allowed to train new recruits.

Koby was not allowed to visit his parents in the internment camp for a year-and-a-half. The camp was off limits to him. While his buddies went home to visit their families, Koby could not visit his.

Although his knowledge of the Japanese language was very limited, he was sent to military language school in Minnesota. After nine months of intensive studies, he was sent to the Philippines.

When war ended, he landed in Tokyo, September 1945, as part of the advance occupation forces. There he saw people dying of starvation and a country devastated from the effects of war. He returned home as soon as the army would allow, for his main concern was the state of his parents and the family businesses.

When the Kobayashi boys came home from the war, they found their mother and father living in a tent. All their valuable possessions had been stolen and their house set afire.

It is painful for me to remember the past. I want to forget. But, after fifty years, I must remember. I feel compelled to tell the story.

To all of you I say, please remember what I want to forget.

It is part of America's past.

It is part of America's history.

*Sylvia K. Kobayashi works in international public relations and has her own consulting business in Anchorage. During World War II she was interned in camps in Puyallup, Washington, and Minidoka, Idaho.*

# Aleut Relocation
# and Restitution

Pribilof Islands Aleuts look past the cargo nets of the USS *Delarof* during their
evacuation in June 1942.
*(Photo No. 80-G-12163, National Archives, College Park, Md.)*

# "It Only Makes My Heart Want to Cry": How Aleuts Faced the Pain of Evacuation

*Dean Kohlhoff*

As Bill Tcheripanoff, his wife, and four children approached their Akutan home in 1945, a nightmare lay before their eyes. It had begun in 1942 when they were "whipped away" from their home "like dogs—to some strange place," Wrangell, and yet again "to another place wet with constant rain called Ketchikan." They had been Aleut evacuees and now found that all their "possessions were gone or destroyed." A determined Tcheripanoff said, "I knew I had to salvage my house for my family and myself and I worked till my hands bleeding with pain made the wood red." But he concluded, "I cannot go on thinking about my sad experience as it only makes my heart want to cry."

These, too, were the feelings shared by the nearly one thousand Aleuts evacuated to Southeast camps or imprisoned at Otaru City, Hokkaido, Japan, for the duration of the war. By now the grim outlines of this story have been laid out in congressional testimony and video presentation. They reveal a painful episode in Aleut life. Evacuation delivered a succession of traumatic blows to Aleut people. Abruptly taken from their homes, they were subjected to horrible living conditions, saw loved ones die in alarming numbers, and then faced loss of personal property when they were returned home.

Theirs was a tragic World War II odyssey. Remembering the deaths of his sister and both grandmothers at Funter Bay, Anatoly Lekanof of St. George spoke for Aleut evacuees: "This whole story has left a scar in my life."

Indeed, Aleuts from the ten evacuated communities had hanging over them an inescapable funereal reality. Disease was a constant danger in overcrowded camps with dilapidated housing, unhealthy water supplies, and little medical care or equipment. In addition, starvation struck the Aleuts in Japan. All evacuees alike experienced the pain of being ripped from their homes and being treated as outcasts in unfamiliar surroundings. They lacked privacy and had to fight boredom.

But evacuation posed another serious crisis. The move itself and the pathological conditions in the camps threatened deterioration of Aleut morale by eating away in them the conviction that their lives had meaning and significance. Before evacuation, Aleuts were people with strength of purpose. Now they were losing the resolve to meet the challenges ahead.

Despite this threat, Aleuts did not succumb to despair. They maintained a purposeful life while facing the most difficult odds. This success was consonant with the kind of resiliency noticed by William S. Laughlin and other scholars studying their past. Still unexplained, however, is exactly how Aleuts withstood the harsh shocks of evacuation. That they did so is heroic and a tribute to their tradition. But it is a theme about which little has been written, leaving a gap also in the literature of World War II.

What sustained Aleuts consistently in the evacuation was their religion. Adapted over time to Aleut circumstances, Russian Orthodoxy eventually had been transformed into Aleut Orthodoxy and embraced as a distinguishing characteristic. It became a prominent marker in Aleut identity. That identity was put to use in the very first Aleut-Japanese war encounter. When Japanese

291

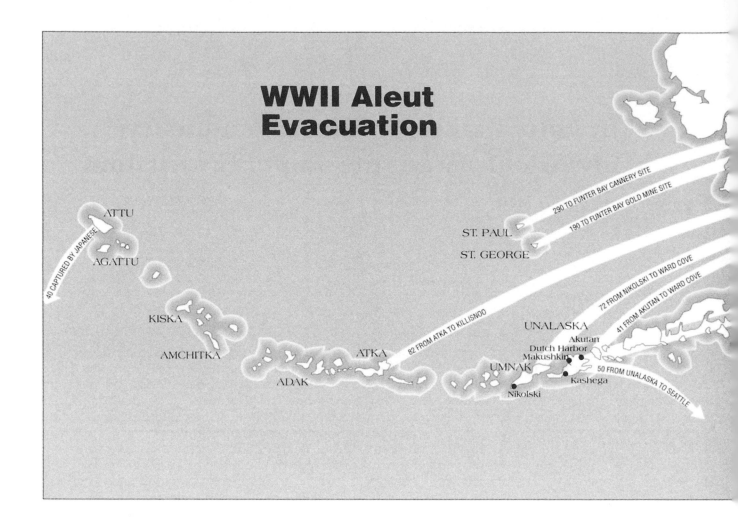

# WWII Aleut Evacuation

ATTU

40 CAPTURED BY JAPANESE

AGATTU

KISKA

AMCHITKA

ADAK

ATKA

82 FROM ATKA TO KILLISNOO

ST. PAUL

ST. GEORGE

290 TO FUNTER BAY CANNERY SITE

190 TO FUNTER BAY GOLD MINE SITE

72 FROM NIKOLSKI TO WARD COVE

41 FROM AKUTAN TO WARD COVE

UNALASKA

Akutan
Dutch Harbor
Makushkin

UMNAK

Kashega

Nikolski

50 FROM UNALASKA TO SEATTLE

troops invaded Attu in early June 1942, the young Aleuts were ready to take up arms and dispatch the enemy. Elders argued, however, that they were hopelessly outnumbered and it would be better for them to contemplate Providence and "think of our God." While in Otaru they argued about religion with their guards, promoting the benefits of Aleut spirituality. Aleut religion also served evacuees partly because the traditions of laymen-as-clergy and community worship lent themselves to a people deprived of home. They gained strength from their religious practice. The church calendar was observed even in Japan. Religious ceremony helped cushion the pain of separation in all evacuation camps.

Yet how religion worked during the evacuation went well beyond identity and solace, important as these were. Aleuts had always been emotionally tied to their island homes. Unlike many visitors to the Aleutian area who hated its treelessness and foggy weather, Aleuts loved the islands, the terrain, sea life, birds, and climate. This was home; and part of the complex of meaning associated with home was their church, the most impor-

tant institution and building in each village. Church and home were one. It was this, of course, that in evacuation they missed the most. But their religious life in camp—an extremely valuable transplant—kept alive the memory of home, gave the evacuees community cohesion and tangible connection to the past. It also kept alive a future, the hope of returning home some day. Without that hope the Aleut will to continue would have been considerably diminished.

This intimate connection between church and home was vividly played out as departing evacuees carried along church articles, such as icons and Bibles, despite a military limitation of only one hand-held package for each Aleut. Deprived like no other evacuees, Atkans at Killisnoo and Attuans at Otaru had been prevented from taking such special reminders of home (although Mike Lokanin kept a "little holy picture" in Japan reminiscent of the Attu church).

In contrast, Luke Shellikoff of Akutan was pleased that his village enjoyed liturgical items at the Ward Lake camp. These had been brought along also to save them

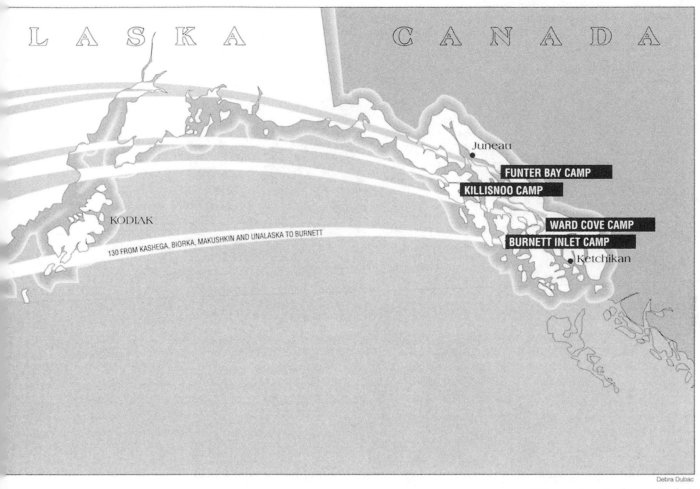

ALASKA CANADA

Juneau

**FUNTER BAY CAMP**

**KILLISNOO CAMP**

**WARD COVE CAMP**

**BURNETT INLET CAMP**

Ketchikan

KODIAK

130 FROM KASHEGA, BIORKA, MAKUSHKIN AND UNALASKA TO BURNETT

Debra Dubac

*Map courtesy Anchorage Daily News*

from possible thievery at their vacated village. Anfesia Shapniskoff, the famous basket weaver, lovingly packed ecclesiastical treasures from Unalaska for the Burnett Inlet church. It was symbolically named after their abandoned house of worship, the Church of the Ascension.

So strong was this attachment to church that Aleuts wished the sight of it to be their first when returning home. The two were one. But herein lies one of the many cruel tragedies of evacuation. After leaving the camps, some Aleuts were deprived of both church and home. In anticipation of return, Alex Prossoff, church treasurer of Attu, had faithfully shepherded $388.22 of church funds through the Japanese years. He had buried it next to his house when the Japanese invaded, hid it under a blanket on the evacuation ship and buried it again near the Otaru internment house.

Yet the Attuans were not allowed to return home. Their village had been destroyed in battle and the U.S. Department of the Interior refused to rebuild it. The Atkans were allowed to return home, but faced bare ground where once their church graced the village. It

had been burned by the U.S. Navy. Besides the Attuans, Aleuts of Biorka, Kashega and Makushin were required to live in other villages for lack of U.S. government support of their ancestral homes. Nevertheless, as testimony to the continuing importance of church and home, the majority of Aleut depositions filed in the reparations process of the early 1980s suggested that funds be used to restore churches as a way of healing evacuated Aleut communities.

While religion was primary, self-sufficiency and cooperation also helped Aleuts in the camps. These were old practical values in the Aleut village tradition. They were put to good use because all Southeast camps needed major repairs or additional housing. Aleuts pitched in with considerable carpentry, mechanical and electrician skills to refurbish and expand these "duration villages," as government officials called them. Aleuts who could find jobs also worked for wages outside the camps. Had there been more jobs, the Alaska Indian Service and U.S. Fish and Wildlife Service goals of total self-support for evacuation camps would have been met. As it was, some Funter Bay evacuees worked in a defense project at Excursion Inlet; both men and women found jobs in Juneau; Atkan men and women worked in nearby canneries; and Burnett Inlet and Ward Lake evacuees were employed in cannery and construction labor in Ketchikan. Like Sophie Pletnikoff, Aleuts who rented apartments and worked in Ketchikan helped relieve the Ward Lake camp's overcrowding.

Within the camps, the cooperative principal at work was succinctly stated by John Nevzaroff of Atka: "We all work together." They used funds from their pre-evacuation store to support a widow with six children in camp and established a successful cooperative store at Killisnoo. When their leader was drowned in an accident, they elected William Dirks to take his place, perpetuating a practice of self-governance. The five Aleut groups at Ward Lake did the same by electing as spokesman Mark Pettikoff of Akutan in a show of cooperation. Women contributed mightily to making camp life more tolerable. With many of the men working else-

Six-year-old Anna Philemenoff stands by her mother, Agnes Lekanof, aboard the *Delarof.* *(Photo No. 80-G-12162, National Archives, College Park, Md.)*

Aleuts line the rail of the USS *Delarof* while being evacuated from the Pribilof Islands in June 1942. *(Photo No. 80-G-12161, National Archives, College Park, Md.)*

where, additional burdens like gathering wood and carrying water fell on women.

The severest testing of self-help came when disease plagued the camps. The two non-Aleut physicians for the Pribilof Islands resigned before the occupancy of Funter Bay. Only a nurse stayed on and she was aided by two Aleuts, Peter Kochergin and Anne McGlashen of St. George. Gertrude Svarney remembered that at Burnett Inlet her mother mended the injured and cared for the sick. She was the only help they had.

As it now seems clear, in relying on church and community, Aleuts were far from passive in facing the pain of evacuation. Yet another characteristic helped them: the innate toughness which long ago had made them survivors. This disposition was expressed in their determination to fight through to the end of camp experience and to see the restoration of their homes. They never conceded defeat. Nor did they consent to camp conditions. Instead they raised their voices in a protest that was a healthy response to adversity, for it directed energies and released emotions. It was an exercise of strength.

These protests from a feisty people took various forms. After about a week at Burnett Inlet, the leader of the Unalaskans, William Zaharoff, wired a request for a "better place to live." The whole Aleut community, he informed the Alaska Indian Service general superintendent, was behind this demand. Martha Newell of Unalaska had her husband write congressional delegate Anthony Dimond in Washington, D.C., to complain about camp policy. The Burnett Inlet evacuees also petitioned territorial governor Ernest Gruening, asking for protection of their homes and belongings when they heard rumors that military vandalism was rife at Unalaska. The Atka women at Killisnoo protested abusive treatment they experienced from a government physician whose physical examinations were repulsive and accusations of venereal disease insulting. Mark Pettikoff of Akutan indignantly countered charges at Ketchikan that Aleuts should be held accountable for pollution of Ward Lake and an epidemic of syphilis. Forty-nine women at Funter Bay, led by the St. Paul group, sent a petition to the Fish and Wildlife Service superintendent protesting camp conditions and asking for better accommodations.

Contrary to the wishes of government officials, Aleuts did not compliantly accept their treatment. Funter Bay evacuees from the start defied authorities and left camp for good-paying jobs. Instead of acting like the "wards" Fish and Wildlife Service officers had called them, Aleuts voted against Bob Bartlett for territorial delegate because he was a political ally of Governor Gruening. A Tlingit Indian political activist, William Paul, had urged them to vote this way—against the political establishment.

Some Pribilovian men, skilled sealers, refused to leave their families in camp to return for sealing in 1943; and those who did demanded and received a wage increase for their seal harvesting work. Aleut school children exhibited a similar rebellious spirit. They plotted an escape from the hated Wrangell Institute Native School by stowing away on a ship, but were foiled when the plan was discovered.

The Attuan prisoners at Otaru also demonstrated their mettle, which helped them through the most troublesome of evacuation circumstances. They mocked their Japanese captors, calling the "rising sun" flag the "meatball" or the "target." Alex Prossoff advised the Japanese military to store their supplies at a spot on the beach of Attu, knowing it would be hit by a storm. When it was, the Japanese threatened to take his life if he ever deceived them again. However, he was the Aleut who hid church funds throughout the captivity. Another Aleut stole the American flag in Attu and hid it for safekeeping.

In Japan, some, like Innokenty Golodoff, weakened by hunger, refused to work. Others threatened to quit working if not paid more than the pittance they received. They gained a tiny increase. Julia Golodoff openly blamed the Japanese for the death of her daughter and was punished for it, but survived. The Attuans used stony silence as defiance when Japanese officials approached them. Some were able to sneak out of their internment house to grub for "fish heads and guts." They once killed two dogs and ate them. They dug "in the hog boxes" when guards were not looking. Only Mike Lokanin and Alex Prossoft were designated spokesmen but consistently gave Japanese interrogators false information and affirmed their allegiance to the United States. They criticized the Japanese government for ruining their Attu homes and imprisoning their people.

What emerges from these and many other evacuation episodes is a portrait of a competent people whose religion, community values and inner strength brought them through the nightmare of evacuation. These characteristics also explain how Aleuts put together a meaningful life for themselves in extremely difficult times after the war. As the history of World War II continues to unfold, what stands out along with strategies, battlefield heroics, victories and defeats, is the effect of the war on civilians like these Aleut evacuees. It is clear that their response to it ennobles them and is a tribute to all Aleuts. And we, too, in the light of their sacrifice and success can in turn be very proud of them and their survival tradition.

*Dean Kohlhoff has taught history at Valparaiso University since 1973. He is currently researching nuclear testing on Amchitka Island.*

# A Matter Very Close to the Aleut Heart: The Politics of Restitution

*Dean Kohlhoff*

DURING WORLD WAR II, ENTERTAINMENT IN THE Pribilof Islands was, as one would expect, extremely rare. But the eight hundred soldiers stationed on St. Paul Island were lucky to have an Aleut phonograph and record collection to break the monotony of foul weather and the noise of northern seals. The most popular spot on the island was an evacuated Aleut house where this valuable musical find became the only source of recreation. "We played the records over so much, we practically wore them out," claimed the radio operator. Their favorite song was Ella Fitzgerald's, "It Ain't What You Do, It's the Way You Do It."

The war, of course, had its own way of "doing it" to Aleuts, their communities, churches, and homes. Evacuation had meant there was no Aleut caretaking available, no protection of property. Military quartering of troops in Aleut dwellings raised the rate of use and breakage of personal property. Nearby military posts and visiting ships meant stealing and vandalism. The extremes of loss, however, were dramatically played out in Atka where the U.S. Navy burned to the ground the Aleut church, and in Attu, where the whole village was destroyed in the battle to retake it from the Japanese.

The damage and loss inflicted on evacuated Aleuts were particularly hard for them to take after the deprivations they had experienced in camps, including the death of loved ones. The sight of their homes upon return was etched into Aleut memory. Mary Bourdukofsky of St. Paul remembered that "all our furniture and personal belongings were gone." Her family's house had been used as a military recreation center. The walls were "full of dart point holes," and hundreds of cigarette craters were burned into the floor. Natalie Misikian recalled that her "mom cried, oh, where's my furniture and everything we left?" Natalie's Shirley Temple doll was missing. She "started crying.... We didn't have anything." Anne McGlashen of St. George said "what hurt most" was that "our artifacts were broken" and religious icons were stolen. Anatoly Lekanof Jr. had to throw away mildewed clothing and also suffered the loss of musical instruments, "radios, fishing gear and hunting guns." His father's chickens and pigs were gone. Dories and outboard motors were missing or "no longer seaworthy."

These lost items, of course, had considerable monetary value. But lost religious items and heirlooms were priceless. Michael Lestenkof of St. George found, half-buried in dirt, the charred form of a pincushion dresser doll he had given his wife for Christmas. Lestenkof was never able to understand why soldiers had insulted him by burning this gift next to his porch.

On the Aleutian Chain, the pattern of loss was similar. Luke Shelikoff of Akutan almost cried when he saw the inside of his house. It looked like "a chicken" coop, "dirty ... looking all over, wallpaper" hanging down to the floor. Guns given to him by his father and godfather had been stolen. Outboard motors, his dory and skiff were gone. The Aleut section of Unalaska city was also a shocking sight. Windows had been broken out, doors bashed in. Philemon Tutiakoff's family never got their house back. It fell to a bulldozer and was replaced by "a couple of cabanas."

The Nikolski people were also dismayed at the sight of their village. "Doors were torn, windows broken," a witness recalled. Personal belongings were "scattered, lost, damaged." The Nikolski church windows were broken out and the interior had been left to deteriorate. The returning Atka people had to be settled in Quonset huts while they built new houses. They had lost all belongings because the navy had refused to allow anything to be carried along in evacuation. The Atka people remember vividly what they lost. Alice Snigaroff Petrivelli still misses "all the pictures of my mother and three brothers, who were deceased ... our beautiful church, our icons, everything."

That these losses occurred nobody has ever denied. Official military investigations and reports closely documented the damage and vandalism. Both services took full responsibility for the evacuations and the resettlement of Aleut communities. The Interior Department, however, refused to support rebuilding of Attu and resettling of Biorka, Kashega, and Makushin. Hence the Aleuts of these four communities lost forever their home villages.

Immediately after the war, non-Aleuts were the first to file claims for evacuation-related losses. The Fish and Wildlife Service was paid for a cottage on St. Paul taken by the Army Weather Bureau. The owner of the Aleutian Livestock Company ranch at Nikolski received monetary restitution for his losses. The owners of southwest evacuation camp sites had been paid rent or had their properties improved as compensation.

But Aleut restitution for damage and loss stood largely unpaid, and seemed closed off by the early 1950s. President Franklin D. Roosevelt authorized only $25,000 to settle Aleut claims covering 881 people evacuated by the U.S. government. Pribilovians, who numbered about one-half of these, remember receiving approximately twelve dollars each. Aleuts of the chain got nothing because according to Fred Geeslin, Alaska Indian Service assistant superintendent, and Deputy U.S. Marshal Verne Robinson, requisitions for replacement items went unfilled. A snafu developed at the region's Seattle supply center. It was never unravelled.

But a type of restitution took a somewhat different twist for Attu people. In October 1945, Interior Department officials filed claims "against the Japanese Government" through the State Department. Attuans felt they deserved to have a rebuilt church and be paid $74,425 for loss of income during imprisonment and destruction of their fox-breeding stock. They also calculated loss of life damages at $220,000, for a total claim of $294,425. The War Claims Commission determined that they were indeed eligible. Attuans had paid a heavy toll as victims of "violations of well-established principles of international law." While only "3.5 percent of internees detained by the German Government" died, the death rate in Japan was more than double, "7.1 percent." The

Aleuts, however, suffered a forty-four percent death rate. Attuans were eventually awarded only $32,000, paid from enemy property retained in the United States by the Department of Justice.

Would justice to the Aleuts ever be fulfilled? How were Aleuts really to be paid for their losses? Was restitution even possible? It seemed not, based on the example of Aleut friends in the Southeast, the Tlingits. They had suffered a bombardment, burning, and pillaging of Angoon village in 1882, by order of U.S. Navy commander E.C. Merriman. Six children had been killed. Ninety-one years later, in 1973, the Tlingit people won a monetary judgment from the government. But the apology they demanded was not forthcoming.

Many Aleuts believed, too, that their wartime suffering was a sacrifice to be forgotten. The less said about it, the better. Aleuts breaking camp at Ward Lake burned the temporary church altar and buried the ashes at home. They and the Atkans brought back trees to plant in the Aleutians. Were not these symbolic acts enough?

They weren't—not to an emerging group of Aleut leaders. They pushed for restitution and won. Forty-three years after evacuation, Aleuts had in hand in 1988 Public Law 100-383, a bill compensating evacuees which included an apology from Congress and the president on behalf of the people of the United States. This victory was gained by older Aleuts like Flore Lekanof and Philemon Tutiakoff from the ranks of evacuees, and younger leaders like Patrick Pletnikoff, Agafon Krukof Jr., and Dimitri Philemenof, who refused to let the past remain silent. In the tradition of American justice they wanted a wrong to be recognized and to be set right. They wanted restitution and the story of what had happened to their people to be known by future generations.

The restitution process began slowly in 1977. Patrick Pletnikoff, executive director of the Aleutian/Pribilof Islands Association, planned legal action against the Japanese and American governments. He sought funding for this from the Interior Department. They refused. Undaunted, Pletnikoff in January 1978 retained the Washington, D.C., law firm of Cook and Henderson.

Then, while Pletnikoff worked with Senator Mike Gravel on projects for cleaning up World War II debris in the Aleutians, Gravel told Pletnikoff that Aleuts might be included in a bill granting civil service retirement benefits to Japanese-Americans interned in World War II. This was the first suggestion of a linkage between the two groups. By the time of his replacement by Greg Brelesford in 1979, Pletnikoff had also contacted the Japanese consulate in Anchorage for restitution. He was sent an icy reply and a quote from the peace accords concerning the "Allied Power waiver of all reparations claims" arising from the war.

Yet Pletnikoff had taken important first steps. One of

the most fortunate, as it turned out, was at this time unforeseen. A young attorney in the Cook and Henderson firm, John C. Kirtland, began research into the "historical context" of evacuation and to compile data on "human suffering" and "property loss." A graduate of the U.S. Naval Academy and a military veteran, Kirtland later on proved an effective practitioner of jurisprudence in guiding the restitution bill through Congress. Fortunately, too, Japanese-Americans and Aleuts joined hands for "Repairing America" in the words of one of their leaders. This alliance helped both groups increase their political influence and allowed "self-conscious Japanese-Americans" to say, "See! We're not just for ourselves."

The Alaska congressional delegation was also most effective in helping the cause. A special Commission on Wartime Relocation and Internment of Civilians had been created by Congress and its mission amended to include Aleut evacuation. Senator Ted Stevens was successful in getting Father Ishmael V. Gromoff of St. Paul appointed to the commission. Kirtland was insistent that any restitution bill must have the full support of Senators Stevens and Murkowski and Representative Young. They worked with Aleuts as a team.

The task of documenting Aleut losses for the commission was extremely difficult, and funding for it had to be found. The Alaska State Legislature and Governor Hammond approved a $165,000 appropriation bill which supported a Kirtland memorandum in equity law and the compiling of Aleut depositions. This research formed the basis for the Aleut section of the commission's report, Personal Justice Denied.

To organize Aleut testimony, the Aleutian/Pribilof Islands Association appointed a three-member leadership "World War II Task Force," chaired by Philemon Tutiakoff. The project to obtain data was coordinated by Alfred Stepetin. Commission hearings were held in 1981 at Anchorage, Unalaska, and St. Paul. Anna Lekanof of St. Paul, Susie Merculief of St. George, Alice Petrivelli of Atka, and Father Merculief of St. George, among others, helped in the preparation of testimony. Fifty-three Aleuts spoke and 136 depositions were presented. This was an impressive record, given that strong hesitancy existed against the probing of painful old wounds.

After the hearings, restitution legislation was introduced by Representative Don Young. Measures by other congressmen were also put into the hopper. No action was taken on them between 1983 and 1985. Problems loomed. The Japanese-Americans were split. Budgetary constraint was the mood expressed in the Gramm-Rudman-Hollings proposals. Furthermore, the Justice Department opposed restitution because, it was argued, victims of war were not necessarily deserving of "special compensation." Also, the restitution bill did not provide for Executive Branch administration, and church restoration under it would violate the First Amendment separation of church and state.

Kirtland, the Alaska politicians, and Aleut leaders addressed these problems skillfully in the American political tradition: they compromised and tailored a revised bill to meet the objections. In 1987, Agafon Krukof Jr., chairman of the Aleut Corporation, and Dimitri Philemenof, executive director of the Aleutian/Pribilof Islands Association, submitted supporting statements and testified at congressional hearings on the newly revised bill. One year later, the end was at hand. On July 22, 1988, the Senate approved the conference report. The House agreed on August 4 by a margin of 257 to 156. President Ronald Reagan's signature sealed the restitution bill on August 10, 1988. Redress was won.

This act was based on human rights. Title II was named "Aleutian and Pribilof Islands Restitution" and designated the association as administrator. A trust was established for $5 million to benefit Attu people and their descendants, plus the communities of Akutan, Atka, Nikolski, St. George, St. Paul, Unalaska, and eligible Aleuts not living in these places. For damaged and destroyed church property, $1.4 million was provided. Individual Aleut evacuees were awarded $12,000 each as "damages for human suffering." About half of those eligible, including leaders like Philemon Tutiakoff, died before receiving payment. Finally, for land on Attu Island which was placed into the National Wilderness Preservation system, the Aleut Corporation was to be paid not more than $15 million.

Significant as these figures are, the process of redress had drawn Aleuts into the political process in unprecedented numbers. It provided training for a new cadre of leaders. One of them, Dimitri Philemenof, not eligible for payment because he was born six months after his parents returned to St. George from Funter Bay, nevertheless felt the restitution issue "very close to my heart." And other Aleut leaders looked beyond restitution to a brighter future. "Compensation," Philemenof predicted, "will assist in the rebuilding process." It would benefit "elderly, disabled or seriously ill" Aleuts and "students in need of scholarships." The trust fund "would help remind" everyone "of the sufferings caused by the severe dislocations" of the war years. Its earnings could be used to promote Aleut culture and train new leaders. Restitution would further Aleut community development. Aleuts always held dear their island homes. Dimitri Philemenof framed the restitution story in that perspective.

There is hope in the Aleut heart.

*Dean Kohlhoff has taught history at Valparaiso University since 1973. He is currently researching nuclear testing on Amchitka Island.*

# Aleuts in Japan, 1942-1945

*Henry Stewart*

## Introduction

IN THIS REPORT, I WILL PRESENT DATA CONCERNING THE internment of the Attuan Aleuts in Japan from September 1942 until September 1945, a period of three years.

Data were gathered from the following sources: interviews with Aleut survivors at Atka and Anchorage; Japanese civilians and army veterans; published war records of the Japanese War History Research Staff; published and unpublished English reports and articles.

Because of the time limits, it will not be possible to present here a detailed discussion of the events or related background studies. Only a brief outline of events and a short discussion of discrepancies between Japanese and American data will be taken up today.

Names of the Aleuts mentioned in this report are those used by informants. Because of the frequent practice of adoption in Aleut society, and marriage/re-marriage of the women, surnames may disagree with other records.

## 1. Occupation of Attu by the Japanese Army

On June 8, 1942, Japanese forces invaded Attu from Holtz Bay at about 1:00 A.M., and effectively occupied the island by about 7:00 A.M. During the invasion, half of the forty-two Aleuts living in Chichagof Village fled into the surrounding mountains. However, responding to the claim by Mike Hodakof (first chief at the time) that no harm would be done by the Japanese Army, all returned to the village by about 9:00 A.M. of the same day.

The Japanese Army set up camp on the flanks of the village, within several hundred meters of the Aleut houses. It is not clear whether this position was planned, or merely a fortuitous decision, but because of the proximity of the Aleut village, the Japanese Army suffered almost no damage or casualties from bombing by American aircraft.

A single strand of barbed wire was placed around the Aleut village. The purpose of this fence was to keep Japanese soldiers out of the village, not to curtail the movement of the Aleuts. With the exception of the requirement to get permission to put out boats, the Aleuts were allowed almost complete freedom of movement, including the use of firearms for hunting.

## 2. Relations between Aleuts and the Japanese Army on Attu

I have not been able to find data showing cruelty by the army toward the Aleuts. Rather, the data show that relations were amicable and relaxed. For example, youngsters often accompanied soldiers and the civilian news cameramen on excursions around the islands.

One exception was that Anacia Golodoff was wounded by a stray bullet fired by the army as it approached the village early the first morning. As a result of this wound, she died—probably in early September—on the ship to Otaru between Attu and Kiska, and was buried at sea near Agattu Island.

### Foster and Etta Jones

Foster Jones, a communications technician, and his wife, Etta, a Native-schools teacher, were the only non-Natives on Attu at the time of occupation. In the American literature, particularly newspapers published immediately following the end of the war, it is generally claimed that Foster was killed when the Japanese Army occupied Chichagof. However, according to an American naval document (Thirteenth Naval District, Document A-16-3(2)), and all Aleut and Japanese accounts, Foster was not killed, but took his own life.

Foster and Etta were put into an abandoned Aleut semisubterranean house (barabara) under armed guard. During interrogation and when being forced into the house, both suffered severe beating and kicking, but were not critically injured.

However, at 6:00 A.M. the following morning, medical officer Akira Ihozumi was called out by the guard. Foster and Etta had cut their wrists, probably in an attempt to commit suicide. Foster's wounds were deep and as a result he died soon after of excessive bleeding. He was buried in the church cemetery.

Etta's wounds were superficial, and she survived to be interned at Yokohama until the end of the war.

Mike Hodakof, chief of the Aleuts on Attu, is shown aboard the USS Casco in May 1942—in one of the few photographs of him known to exist. On the right is Lt. Cdr. Charles "Squeaky" Anderson, along for his local knowledge of the Aleutians. *(James S. Russell Collection, Command Historian's Office. Alaskan Command)*

## 4. Evacuation of Attu in August 1942

The Imperial Headquarters in Tokyo ordered the Japanese forces on Attu to move to Kiska by August 25 to support Japanese forces there. Because no directives were issued as to the disposition of the Aleuts, repeated meetings concerning the disposition of the Aleuts were held by the officers on Attu. In early August the Imperial Headquarters gave permission to remove the Aleuts to Hokkaido.

All the property of the Aleuts, including boats, outboard motors, ovens, stoves, etc., were loaded onto the freighter *Yoko-maru*. Forty-one Aleuts (one old man died of natural causes during the occupation) with their personal effects were boarded onto the coal freighter *Osada-maru*. No soldiers accompanied the Aleuts on their journey to Hokkaido.

I have not been able to ascertain the exact date of departure from Attu, but the army evacuated on August 25, and it is reasonably certain that the *Osada-maru* left on about this date.

At the time of evacuation, all the buildings of the village, including the church, were razed and burned.

## 5. Aleuts arrive at Otaru, Hokkaido

One of the forty-one Aleuts evacuated from Attu, Anacia Golodoff, died of wounds mentioned above and was buried at sea sometime early in September. Thus, it was only forty Aleuts who disembarked the *Osada-maru* at Otaru sometime in the middle of the night of September 26. Otaru was at the time an important commercial and military port on the west coast of Hokkaido.

The Aleuts were taken not to a prisoner-of-war camp but to a vacant railroad employee dormitory at Wakatake-cho, about one kilometer from the piers.

The forty Aleuts were housed in four 3.6 by 3.6 meter rooms (142 square feet, total 568 square feet) on the second floor of the dormitory at about 1:00 A.M., September 26.

No notice was given to the neighborhood in advance concerning the arrival of the Aleuts, and it was not until daybreak that the local residents became aware of their presence.

No guards or other military personnel accompanied the Aleuts. Two local policemen stood watch on the ground floor of the dormitory. At the rear were stashed all of their bulky belongings brought on the *Yoko-maru*.

Contrary to most English reports, all local informants agree that the Aleuts were allowed much freedom of movement. This information is corroborated by Aleut recollections. Local residents recall that within a week or so, the Aleuts walked unaccompanied around the neighborhood, and that the children frequented the local sweet shop. Adults bought food at the butcher and fish shops.

No informants are able to recollect how payment was made for these purchases, but most assume that the charges were sent to the City Office and paid from there. No one recalls instances in which purchases were not reimbursed, although they do not remember whence the reimbursements came.

According to police officer Takeshiro Shikanai, who lived with the Aleuts from April 1944 until their return in September 1945, there were several instances of violence done to the internees. In particular, police officer E., a guard during the period of 1943-1944, mistreated the Aleuts. He took rations allotted to the Aleuts and severely beat Angelena Hodikoff for not doing work at the dormitory. The wounds she received at the police officer's hand did not heal properly until 1946, one year after she returned to the United States.

## 6. Living conditions

The diet of the Aleuts during their internment at Otaru was not very good, particularly as compared to life on Attu, where virtually unlimited amounts of fish and sea mammal were available. However, in contrast to American newspaper and magazine articles about near-starvation conditions, local Japanese informants and the Aleuts themselves state that although there was never enough food, it was not a starvation diet.

It must be borne in mind that by this stage of the war, most food items such as rice, fish, and particularly meat were strictly rationed, even to the Japanese. Japanese accounts of the Aleut diet vary, some informants being of the opinion that the Aleut diet was inferior to that of most Japanese civilians. Other informants stated that the Aleuts received special rations, in addition to the standard rations.

Police officer Shikanai recalls that because Aleuts shared their special rations, he ate better than most other officers.

A Japanese soldier who was with the Aleuts on Attu from June to August came to visit them in the fall of 1942. He saw baked bread, rice, meat, and fresh vegetables in the kitchen on the ground floor where the Aleuts cooked for themselves. It was his opinion that they were eating better than most Japanese civilians.

One favorite food of the Aleuts was herring preserved in lard. Herring was relatively plentiful at Otaru, a fishing port. The Japanese turned up their noses at this concoction.

One Japanese custom that sorely distressed the Aleuts was bathing. Twice a week the Aleuts were taken to the local bathhouse. They firmly believe that this practice was detrimental to their health, and claim that two persons died as a direct result of being bathed. However, in spite of their protests, the Aleuts were obliged to bath regularly.

## 7. Forced labor

I was unable to find any documentation of alleged forced labor as reported in American sources. Volunteers were paid one yen per eight-hour day to dig dolomite from an open pit a short distance from the dormitory. Japanese workers at the same pit, who had to buy their food, were paid one and a half yen per day for the same labor. Both Japanese and Aleut informants state that this labor was voluntary. Most days only four to six Aleuts went to the pits during their first year of internment. The Aleuts did not work after 1944, when they were moved to another house further from the pits. It is my opinion that deteriorating health conditions was another reason that labor was not made available after 1944.

This voluntary labor stands in sharp contrast to forced labor levied upon the Koreans and Chinese, who were daily marched to and from the piers and shipyards.

Japanese yen earned by the Aleuts, said to amount to about seven hundred American dollars (1945 exchange rate) were sent with them upon their return to the United States in 1945. However, according to Aleut informants, this money was taken for safekeeping by officials when they arrived in Seattle and never returned.

## 8. Health conditions

During internment, sixteen of the forty landed Aleuts, and four of the five born at Otaru died. The main cause of death was tuberculosis. One death was reported to have resulted from "dyspnoea (breathing difficulty) from infantile paralysis," although this person also suffered acute tuberculosis.

Dr. Satoru Nogushi, who examined the Aleuts soon after their arrival at Otaru, states that twenty of the forty were suffering from acute tuberculosis. Their condition, in his opinion, was acerbated by the Otaru diet, which was lacking in protein and calories.

Particularly acute cases were hospitalized at the sanitorium. At any one given time, ten to fifteen of the Aleuts were in the hospital. When the surviving Aleuts were moved to a house at Shimizu-cho in April 1944, only twenty-nine of the original forty remained.

The house at Shimizu-cho was much larger than the Wakatake-cho dormitory. Partitions were set up to make individual family quarters.

## 9. Return to the United States

Following the armistice, a Red Cross representative

visited the Aleuts on September 3. Soon after, an American military aircraft dropped food and other supplies near the Shimizu-cho house. On September 17, the surviving twenty-five Aleuts were taken to Chitose, an airport about seventy kilometers (forty-five miles) to the southeast. Of the forty who were interned at Otaru in 1942, only twenty-four survived, in addition to little Alfred Prokopeuff, the sole surviving baby born at Otaru.

According to Officer Shikanai, the remains of the twenty who died at Otaru (including four babies) were taken along. However, I have not been able to corroborate this observation by other data.

Because of weather conditions, it was not until three days later at 2:00 P.M. of the twentieth that the DC-3 transport departed for Atsugi, outside Tokyo.

At 6:45 P.M., the Aleuts, accompanied by Officer Shikanai, arrived at Atsugi. There the Aleuts were undressed and sprayed with an insecticide. It was then that they were told that only one piece of baggage per person would be allowed. All other belongings were disposed of.

The next morning, at 8:00 A.M., the Aleuts departed for Okinawa. Two weeks later, aboard a freighter, they departed by way of Manila, San Francisco, and Seattle to Alaska.

## 10. Topics for further consideration

A. Why were the Aleuts given preferential treatment during their internment? Civilians from China (including Taiwan) and Korea put under the protection of the Japanese Army were treated more harshly.

B. How may the glaring discrepancies between reports in the American media and publications, and statements by the Aleuts themselves, and Japanese informants and documents be reconciled? I do not believe that the favorable statements by Japanese informants in this case are only an effort to cover up wartime atrocities. Rather, it seems to me that American media reports were consciously biased. More research is needed in this area.

*Henry Stewart is a professor at Mejiro Women's College and a lecturer at Waseda University in Japan. He is a student of the ethnology of North American arctic and subarctic peoples.*

# An Alaskan Who Was Interned Introduces Senator Ted Stevens

## Marie Matsuno Nash

MY NAME IS MARIE MATSUNO NASH, AND I'M HERE primarily to bring you a message from my boss, Senator Ted Stevens.

But, before I do that, I want to share with you my special connection with the subject of this session—the internment of our Aleut people during World War II.

As some of you know, I am half Aleut. And, as some of you may also know, today is my birthday: I was born exactly fifty years ago today during my family's internment at a relocation camp in Idaho, after they were uprooted from their home in Ugashik.

My mother was Aleut, but my parents and older brother were sent there because my Hawaiian-born father was of Japanese heritage.

While I was too small to remember what Camp Minidoka was like, I first really understood what happened to my family and many others in high school history class in Haines.

As many of you know, the people who were interned rarely talked about the hardships they suffered when they were sent to camps in Alaska and the Lower 48.

In later years, I felt I helped to make up for some of the injustices they suffered when I testified in Juneau at the time state legislation was being considered to help our Aleuts. And I was especially proud to be a member of Senator Stevens' staff when he introduced legislation in Congress to include my people in the reparations.

I am pleased to be a part of today's conference, and happy to bring you now a few words from my boss, Senator Ted Stevens.

## Congressional Action on Restitution Begins in the 1980s

## Senator Ted Stevens

THERE WERE NO PRESS ACCOUNTS DURING WORLD WAR II of the terrible hardships endured by Alaskans from the Aleutian and Pribilof Islands. Those of us serving overseas in the military, and most Americans in the rest of the nation, knew nothing of their fellow Americans who were taken from their homes and interned in crowded, often squalid, camps. The main reason we didn't know was because correspondence and news reports between Alaska and the Lower 48 were censored during World War II.

I learned about the relocation of the people of the Aleut and Pribilof Islands when I was in Fairbanks as U.S. Attorney in the early 1950s. Not long after that, when I became solicitor of the Department of the Interior during the Eisenhower administration I heard more disturbing stories about the Aleuts' relocation. The department had responsibility for Aleut interests, but had developed no real plan to care for Alaska's Aleut people when they were transported from their island homes to live in abandoned canneries and gold mines in Alaska. Their treatment, we know now, clearly failed to meet the government's responsibility to those under its care.

As a U.S. senator, I welcomed the opportunity to work toward Congress's establishment of the bipartisan Commission on Wartime Relocation and Internment of Civilians. At my request Congress expanded the mandate of the commission to include an examination of the federal government's treatment of our Aleut people during the war, because at first the legislation included only the Japanese-Americans who were relocated to camps in the Lower 48.

Establishing the commission was a major positive step in righting some of the wrongs suffered by American citizens who were, in effect, denied the rights of their American citizenship because of their ancestry.

In the process of its research for a report which was mandated by Congress, the commission held hearings in Anchorage, St. Paul, and Unalaska, as well as in a number of cities in the Lower 48.

The report—completed in 1983 and entitled "Personal Justice Denied"—included recommendations for financial compensation, but admitted "no amount of money can fully compensate the excluded people for their losses and sufferings."

In November 1983, I joined with the late Senator Spark Matsunaga in introducing legislation to authorize the implementation of the commission's recommendations.

The specific measures of restitution are called for in the Aleutian and Pribilof Islands Restitution Act of 1988:

A $5 million trust established for the beneficial use of the six surviving Aleut villages which were relocated, and for the beneficial use of surviving Aleuts and their descendants;
per capita payments of $12,000 for each surviving Aleut evacuee;
the rehabilitation of churches and restoration of church property damaged or destroyed by U.S. forces in Alaska;
the cleanup of wartime debris left on populated islands of the Aleutians; and
$15 million to the Aleut Corporation for the loss of Attu Island.

As most of you participating in this conference know, in 1988 Congress passed that measure authorizing the funds to carry out the recommendations. In 1990 and 1991, Congress appropriated the money, and restitution payments began.

In addition, in the 1988 bill, $1.4 million was authorized for the rehabilitation of Aleutian and Pribilof churches and church property destroyed during World War II. The measure called for an administrator to assess and inventory the costs of repair or replacement of church property. The assessment, completed recently, indicated that the $1.4 million would not begin to cover the losses.

For that reason, in mid-September, I introduced an amendment to the Aleutian and Pribilof Islands Act to increase to $4.7 million the authorization for the restoration and repair of the churches. The amendment has been referred to the Senate Governmental Affairs Committee for consideration.

That, briefly, is the history of the legislation. It attempts to remedy some of the wrongs and provide some measure of redress.

As the commission's report said,

History cannot be undone; anything we do now must inevitably be an expression of regret and an affirmation of our better value as a nation, not an accounting which balances or erases the events of the war.
... Among our strengths as a nation is our willingness to acknowledge imperfection, as well as the struggle for a more just society.

I am confident that we all pray that our nation will never forget the lesson we learned at the expense of Alaska's Aleuts. I'll continue to work to assure the restoration of the churches, to help close one of the final chapters of this tragic story.

*Marie Matsuno Nash was born at a relocation camp in Idaho. Her mother was Aleut and her Hawaiian-born father was of Japanese ancestry. She is a member of Senator Stevens' staff.*

*U.S. Senator Ted Stevens worked for the establishment of the Commission on Wartime Relocation and Internment of Civilians that would examine the federal government's treatment of Japanese-Americans and Aleuts moved to camps during World War II.*

# Aleut Evacuation:
# Effects on the People

*Flore Lekanof Sr.*

## Introduction

JUST SIX MONTHS AFTER THE BOMBING OF PEARL HARBOR on December 7, 1941, Unalaska and Dutch Harbor were bombed on June 3 and 4, 1942, by the Japanese.

## Immediate Effects

I was drafted into the U.S. government work force in May 1942, after the elementary school was closed for the summer. As long as I lived on St. George Island, I would never return to the classroom for schooling. This was the normal practice of the U.S. federal government on the Pribilof Islands since the purchase of Alaska by the U.S. in 1867 from the Russian government.

It was while a handful of U.S. work force was repairing the landing dock that a messenger brought word of the Dutch Harbor bombing. It was about lunch time. We were told to stop working and go to our homes. People all over the village were scared to death. On that foggy day, some of us heard airplanes flying over the island. The fog was so thick that we could not see whether they were American or Japanese planes. I heard my grandmother say it was time for the Creator (God) to come back.

A few days later, my family and others attended the local Russian Orthodox church, where my father was a reader. After church on that beautiful Sunday afternoon, we had our usual Sunday brunch of coffee and bread. While we were gathered around the kitchen table, shocking news was delivered to our home. At once we were to prepare to board a ship. The village was to be evacuated. Every person was to leave on the ship.

Where we were to be taken, we did not know. We were instructed for each person to take the clothing they wore and a sack of personal clothing and effects to the ship. Domestic animals, such as cows and pigs, were disposed of by shooting. After much commotion, we were on the U.S. Army transport ship *Delarof*. The St. Paul people were already on that ship.

Although there were pleasantries exchanged by the St. Paul and St. George people as they met, one could see anxiety on their faces.

In later years, my Uncle Gabriel Stepetin told me that my maternal grandmother on St. Paul Island went into her bedroom to take her own life. She did not want to leave her home. My uncle was able to stop her, but she died in Funter Bay that winter.

## Intermediate Effects

Much illness, physical and mental, was experienced by the Aleut people at Funter Bay, where we were taken. St. Paul people were put on one side of the bay at an old dilapidated cannery site, while the St. George people were put two miles across the bay at an old gold mining camp. Ten percent of the Pribilof people died at the camp during the two years of encampment. Most of these were the elderly and the very young. Many of the deaths were caused by unhealthy living conditions and by pneumonia, tuberculosis, measles, and general mental depression. I lost both of my grandmothers and a sister at Funter Bay. My father suffered from pneumonia and I contracted tuberculosis of the lungs and spent three-and-a-half years in a sanitarium where I nearly died.

## Long-term Effects

Because of the evacuation from their homelands, the Aleut people suffered not only the loss of their loved ones, but their ethnic culture was shaken by exposure to a strange environment. For three years, the elders were not able to guide their people in their customary manner. The government took charge for three years. The usual caring nature of the Aleut people for their own was halted. This was to take away the practice of my people always looking after the interest of everyone living in a village.

Today, one has to pay cash for services—such as fish and a ride to the local store for groceries. Young people are inducted into the American mainstream culture through media and schools to the point that the respect for elders, once held sacred, is almost nonexistent. People are indoctrinated into the concept of cash economy as opposed to subsistence economy. Rendition of some kind, usually cash, is expected and given for services rendered.

## Making Amends

(a) Reparation and an apology from the U.S. government for the evacuation experience.

(b) World War II trust fund established for cultural preservation, among other things.

(c) Establishment of the church restoration fund.

(d) Improved educational opportunities.

(e) Better transportation systems, including airplane services.

(f) Good medical programs by Indian Health Service.

(g) Opportunity for self-government under the Indian Self-Determination Act.

(h) Recognition of the Aleut people as full citizens of the United States of America, with all of the rights in the federal and state constitutions, including the right to vote. Even today, we must still work to take advantage of these rights.

(i) Lastly, the Alaska Native Claims Settlement Act, although not perfect, is in the spirit of good faith to help the indigenous peoples of Alaska, including the Aleut people who were evacuated from their homelands during World War II.

I am an example of what can result from taking advantage of the open doors of opportunity and recently learned human rights and freedoms written into the Constitution of the United States of America and the State of Alaska. These are the freedoms that our brave young men and women fought for during the unforgettable World War II and the Alaska war fifty years ago.

*Flore Lekanof Sr. is the Aleutian/Pribilof Islands Association's Tribal Operations Coordinator for twelve tribes in the Aleutian Islands.*

# Lend-Lease

U.S. and Soviet pilots pose in front of a lend-lease plane, Ladd Field, cir. 1943.
*(Soviet photo courtesy of Command Historian's Office, Alaskan Command)*

# The Bradley Mission:
# The Evolution of the Alaska-Siberia Air Route

*Baker B. Beard*

ALTHOUGH MOST MILITARY HISTORIANS ACKNOWLEDGE the vital role that American aircraft played in the eventual defeat of the *Luftwaffe* in the skies above the Eastern Front, the volumes of historical documentation devoted to preserving the events and experiences of World War II mention little in regard to the tremendous effort involved in the establishment of the Alaska-Siberia air route for the delivery of U.S.-manufactured lend-lease aircraft to the Soviet Union. When an analysis is made of the Alaska-Siberia air route, several questions arise. What events led to the evolution of an Alaska-Siberia airway? Did Major General Follett Bradley play an important role in the negotiations with Stalin for the route? What were some of the operational problems which emerged in the establishment of the route? And, finally, was the Alaska-Siberia air route a decisive factor in the ultimate defeat of the German armies on the Eastern Front?

Although it is agreed by most Western scholars that the battle of Kursk was the turning point at which the initiative in both the air and ground war shifted in favor of the Soviets, the vital role of American P-39s, P-40s, A-20s, and B-25s in gaining air superiority and conducting tactical interdiction missions over the battlefield is often overshadowed by the great tank battle that took place. However, with the P-39s carrying out the role of aerial artillery and the B-25s destroying supply depots and fuel storage facilities, air power proved to be a decisive factor in turning the ground campaign at Kursk into a Soviet victory.

It should thus not be forgotten that a great many of the aircraft that contributed to the Soviet victory on the Eastern Front were American lend-lease aircraft that were ferried to the Soviet Union along the Alaska-Siberia airway. In order to meet the needs of a Soviet Army desperately trying to establish a defensive line against the invading German armies, General Follett Bradley negotiated and implemented an Alaska-Siberia air supply route to ferry crucial lend-lease supplies and aircraft to Soviet forces engaged on the Eastern Front.

As the "somber shadow of the Nazi swastika lengthened across Europe," the Western democracies of Europe urgently scrambled to find some diplomatic means to stem the clouds of war that were gathering.[1] Unlike the Western European states, which were resisting German aggression, the Soviet Union chose to concede to German expansion in Eastern Europe and signed a nonaggression pact with Hitler in August of 1939.[2] In the accord, Hitler and Stalin agreed to respect each other's spheres of expansion and to split Poland between themselves.

On the morning of September 1, 1939, Hitler launched a blitzkrieg on Poland and, within a year, the German war machine had overwhelmed and enslaved Denmark, Norway, Holland, Belgium, Luxembourg, and France.[3] By the end of July 1940 "the bloodthirsty little gutter-

---

[1] Robert Huhn Jones, *The Roads to Russia* (Norman, Oklahoma: University of Oklahoma Press, 1969), p. 3.

[2] Peter Maslowski and Allan R. Millett, *For the Common Defense* (New York: Free Press, 1984), p. 394.

[3] Jones, *The Roads to Russia*, p. 4.

snipe" reigned supreme in fortress Europe.[4] Meanwhile, as the attention of an astonished world was fixed on the collapse of France, the Soviet Union overran and absorbed the independent nations of Lithuania, Latvia, and Estonia and forced Romania to cede Bessarabia and northern Bukovina.[5]

As Great Britain stood alone as the last bastion of democracy in Europe, Winston Churchill looked to the United States for assistance against the seemingly invincible German Army. However, President Roosevelt's hands were tied by both the Neutrality Act as amended in November 1939, and an isolationist Congress that feared being drawn into another European war.

U.S. Army Chief of Staff, General George C. Marshall, along with other American planners, was convinced that any British attempt to resist the imminent German invasion of the British Isles was hopeless. He believed that unless England negotiated a peace with Hitler, that country would promptly become the next *Wehrmacht* victim.[6] However, by the end of September American army tacticians hastily revised their estimates of the situation in England in light of the RAF's victory over the *Luftwaffe* in the skies above Britain. With the RAF's success, American planners came up with the cautious notion that England might hold out for at least six months and conceded that aid to Britain might possibly be considered as "a long-term investment in American security."[7]

In a lengthy memorandum dispatched to President Roosevelt on December 8, 1940, Winston Churchill told the president that he did not believe the people of the United States wanted to see Britain "stripped to the bone." Churchill asked Roosevelt to consider his letter not as an appeal but a "statement of minimum action necessary to achieve our common purpose."[8]

Roosevelt received Churchill's letter on board the USS *Tuscaloosa* where, between December 12 and 16, 1940, he formulated his lend-lease idea (although his chief advisor, Harry Hopkins, didn't know how it might be accomplished legally).[9] Roosevelt's idea hinged upon the revolutionary concept of "[getting] away from the dollar sign" and lending U.S. allies the items needed to defend themselves from the aggressive exploits of the German war machine.[10] Roosevelt did not want to define help "in terms of dollars or loans." He stated, "We will give you the guns and the ships you need, provided that when the war is over you will return to us in kind the guns and ships we have loaned to you."[11]

President Roosevelt impressed upon the American people the gravity of the stakes involved if the country were to isolate itself from a war that could eventually be waged on America's very soil. The American public became well aware that its national security was in question. Even though Americans opposed entry into the war, public opinion swung in overwhelming support to Roosevelt's lend-lease plan. Although the debate in Congress raged for nearly two months, the bill, H.R. 1776, passed in the House 260-165, and in the Senate 60-31.[12] On March 11, 1941, Roosevelt signed the bill inaugurating the Lend-Lease Act into law.[13]

The sweeping delegation of power contained in Lend-Lease may be summarized as follows with regard to its outstanding provisions. The president, "in the interest of national defense," could authorize such agents in the executive branch as he might designate to "manufacture ... or otherwise procure ... any defense article for the government of any country whose defense the president deems vital to the defense of the United States."[14]

Realizing that the collaboration between Nazi Germany and the Soviet Union was only a temporary arrangement, Roosevelt and Churchill moved to try rapprochement in order to neutralize the Soviet Union or even to ally her with the West.[15]

"As Hitler subjugated the European continent and posed a growing threat to the British Isles and U.S. commerce, continued isolation of the USSR seemed increasingly less desirable, and tentative steps were taken to improve relations."[16] On January 9, 1941, Roosevelt formally announced the removal of the 1939 moral embar-

---

[4] Ibid., p. 5.

[5] Ibid.

[6] Ibid., p. 6.

[7] Ibid., p. 8.

[8] Ibid., p. 11.

[9] Ibid.

[10] Ibid., p. 12.

[11] Ibid.

[12] Ibid., pp. 14-16.

[13] Ibid., p. 16.

[14] Raymond H. Dawson, *The Decision to Aid Russia, 1941* (Chapel Hills, North Carolina: The University of North Carolina Press, 1959) p. 9.

[15] Jones, *The Roads to Russia*, p. 26.

[16] Leon Martel, *Lend-Lease, Loans, and the Coming of the Cold War* (Boulder, Colorado: Westview Press, 1979), p. 26.

go on shipments of aircraft, aircraft-construction material, and aviation-gasoline patent processes to the Soviet Union and tried unsuccessfully to secure a partial release of machine tools.[17]

But just as the American public was starting to soften to the idea of aid to the Soviets if Hitler were to declare war against the Soviet Union, the USSR concluded a formal treaty of neutrality with Japan.[18]

The *Washington Post* reflected the sentiments of the American public toward this perceived alliance with Japan by promptly proclaiming the treaty a repeat performance of the Nazi-Soviet pact.[19] On the other hand, while the pact could be construed as releasing Japan for aggressive steps in the Far East, the *New York Herald-Tribune* commented that it could be said "with as much justice" that it released Russia to conduct "a more aggressive anti-German policy."[20]

Just as congressmen such as Pennsylvania Democrat Samuel Weiss began to gather support for legislation which would "place Russia in the same category as her Axis partners and deny her any aid whatsoever under H.R. 1776," the Germans invaded the Soviet Union.

On June 22, 1941, Hitler's panzers crashed through Soviet lines, initiating a surprise attack that was to open Operation Barbarossa against the Soviet Union.[21]

In the days following the German invasion, President Roosevelt declined to issue a proclamation of neutrality in the Russo-German conflict, thus effectively leaving Soviet ports open to U.S. shipping.[22] Furthermore, Acting Secretary of State Sumner Welles was instructed to reassure Soviet Ambassador Constantin Oumansky concerning his requests for assistance. In addition, Secretary Welles was ordered by President Roosevelt to set up a special State Department committee to expedite purchasing operations and export clearances for the Soviet embassy and Amtorg, the Soviet state trading corporation in the United States.[23] In response to President Roosevelt's generous overtures, Oumansky hastily submitted a general list of urgent war matériel "that showed by its emphasis on plant equipment a Soviet determination to fight on, certainly through the coming winter."[24]

Although the Soviets were not asking to be included in the Lend-Lease Act, Oumansky did propose that the United States government grant the Soviet Union a five-year credit of payment for war orders placed in the United States.[25] In order to get around the political difficulties in the way of large credits to meet the immediate needs of the Red Army, Roosevelt, acting on the sugges-

Helen Roberts, a civilian employee of the U.S. military in Helena, Montana, paints the Red Star of the Soviet Union on a lend-lease air transport. *(Acc. No. 91-098-863N, Kay Kennedy Collection, Rasmuson Library, University of Alaska Fairbanks)*

---

[17] Jones, *The Roads to Russia*, p. 27.

[18] Dawson, *Decision*, p. 52.

[19] Ibid.

[20] Ibid., p. 53.

[21] Ibid.

[22] Martel, *Cold War*, p. 27.

[23] Ibid., p. 28.

[24] Ibid.

[25] Jones, *The Roads to Russia*, p. 51.

tion of Harry Hopkins, directed Jesse Jones, secretary of Commerce and federal loan administrator, to purchase from Amtorg up to $100 million worth of manganese, chromite, asbestos, platinum, and other materials and to advance Amtorg $50 million against the purchase to cover more than $140 million in war orders.[26]

When the Harriman mission arrived in Moscow at the end of September, the Russians had their backs to the wall. Leningrad was encircled, the Ukraine had been overrun, and the battle for Moscow was about to begin. Nonetheless, the Russians were holding on, and they conveyed to the members of the mission every sign of willingness to continue the fight.[27] In a series of meetings with Stalin, the Harriman mission negotiated the First Protocol to Russia on October 1, 1941, promising the Russians about 1.5 million tons of supplies through June 30, 1942, under lend-lease provisions.[28]

Although American industry was still in the process of gearing up to meet wartime production orders, the problem with meeting lend-lease orders to the Soviet Union did not lie with industry, but with the greater problem of transporting the war aid to Russia. While the route of choice for the delivery of lend-lease aid to Russia was the North-Russian sea lane to Murmansk, Hitler's U-boats and coastal air patrols, operating from bases in northern Norway and Finland, minimized the route's effectiveness by decimating any Allied convoy bold enough to attempt the run.[29] By sinking nearly 30 to 40 percent of the North-Russian lend-lease convoys, Hitler had, in effect, shut down the route.[30] To Roosevelt's and Churchill's complaints about the perils of the route, Stalin curtly replied, "According to our naval experts, the necessity of stopping the delivery of war supplies to the northern harbors of the USSR is untenable.... No major task can be carried out in wartime without risk of loss."[31]

On April 23, 1942, the Americans suggested to Stalin the possibility of establishing an Alaska-Siberia air route to ferry lend-lease aircraft to Russia for immediate use on the Eastern Front.[32] Fearing the Japanese reaction to such an arrangement, Stalin asked if the U.S. would, instead, consider an air route via Canada-Iceland-Murmansk to Moscow.[33] The suggestion was turned down

and Stalin conceded to the Alaska-Siberia route—known as ALSIB—commenting, "I'm afraid our friends, the Japanese, won't like the Alaska-Siberia route."[34]

In May 1941, Harry Hopkins discussed the feasibility of the Alaska-Siberia delivery route with Brigadier Gen-

Major General Iakov, of the Soviet Air Force, prepares to fly a P-39 out of Ladd Field, near Fairbanks, during World War II. *(Command Historian's Office, Alaskan Command)*

eral Dwight D. Eisenhower and other prominent army tacticians.[35] In response, the War Department came up with a practical and simple delivery plan for the operation of an Alaska-Siberia air route.[36] Agreeing in principle to the plan, the Soviet ambassador to the United States, Maxim Litvinov, visited Harry Hopkins on July

---

[26] Ibid., p. 52.

[27] Martel, *Cold War*, p. 30.

[28] George C. Herring, Jr., *Aid to Russia 1941-1946* (New York: Columbia University Press, 1973), p. 17.

[29] Jones, *The Roads to Russia* p. 99.

[30] Ibid., p. 106.

[31] Ibid.

[32] Ibid., p. 111.

[33] Ibid.

[34] Ibid.

[35] Ibid.

[36] Ibid.

9, 1941, to inform him that Russia had agreed to use the route.[37] Cabling Stalin on June 17 and June 23, 1941, Roosevelt requested that there be an immediate establishment of the route and suggested that Russian pilots ferry the aircraft to Russia.[38]

On July 3, 1942, the United States military attache to the Soviet Union, Colonel Joseph A. Michela, notified President Roosevelt that Stalin had finally accepted the U.S.-sponsored proposal.[39] In immediate response to Stalin's change of heart, President Roosevelt selected Major General Follett Bradley to go to Washington to work out the details of the proposed route with Soviet Ambassador Belyaev.[40]

As senior representative of the American delegation, General Bradley was tasked with accomplishing three objectives: to arrange for the delivery via Alaska of war-aid airplanes to a mutually acceptable point of delivery in the Soviet Union; to arrange for U.S. survey flights to obtain detailed information pertaining to existing airdromes in Siberia; and to furnish to the Soviet government information concerning the availability of aircraft in accordance with the Russian protocols and contemplated deliveries via the Siberian route.[41]

In order to get the ALSIB ferry route operational before the harsh Siberian winter freeze occurred, General Bradley pushed the members of the conference to accept the route developed a year earlier by U.S. Army tacticians. That included an initial departure from Nome, Alaska, to Velkal, Semcham, Yakutsk, Kirensk, Krasnoyarsk, Novo-Sibirsk, Omsk, Sverdlovsk, Kesan, and Moscow.[42] However, General Bradley decided to extend the eastern terminal of the ALSIB route to Fairbanks, Alaska, since recent Japanese footholds in the Aleutians had made Nome more difficult to supply and vulnerable to attack.[43]

Bradley organized a party headed by Colonel Alva L. Harvey and eight other experts to make a detailed survey of the ALSIB route and the Soviet airdromes along the route.[44] Colonel Harvey and his party left Fairbanks, Alaska, on 22 August, 1942. While they were en route to Moscow, a rift emerged between the Soviet government and the War Department that threatened the ALSIB project altogether.

The point of dispute was over the number of transports that would be necessary for the purpose of carrying ALSIB ferry pilots from Moscow to Fairbanks. The Soviets insisted that a minimum of forty-three transport planes of the DC-3 type were necessary to ferry pilots along the route, and they demanded that these transports be handed over to Soviet pilots without delay, as the success of the ALSIB route depended upon the effectiveness of the transport role.[45] In response to the Soviet request, General Bradley requested that the Soviet delegation inform him of the basis for their calculations for forty-three transports.

The Soviets presented their calculations to General Bradley on August 11, 1942. They were based upon the fact that the transports would have to operate from Fairbanks to Moscow, with each transport carrying sixteen passengers. With a ferry schedule that consisted of twenty-five B-25s, one hundred A-20s and one hundred U.S. fighters, there would be 620 crew members to ferry per month. Making allowances for bad weather, short hours of daylight, and maintenance, the round trip would require an average of twenty-six days.[46] General Bradley suggested that by using two-man crews in A-20s and three-man crews in B-25s and by cutting out administration transports along the route, twenty transports could adequately handle all ALSIB ferry requirements.[47]

The Russians bitterly protested. But instead of arguing over relatively minor points, General Bradley recommended that the War Department let the United States delegation in Moscow negotiate the operational arrangements for the ALSIB route free from outside interference in order to get the route operational before the winter freeze.[48]

On August 16, 1942, Bradley informed Soviet delegate Major General Sterligov that the United States could spare only ten transports for ALSIB operations;

[37] Ibid.

[38] Ibid.

[39] Ibid., p. 156.

[40] Ibid.

[41] Maj. General Bradley's Letter of Instruction, USAF Academy Library, Special Collections Branch, Bradley Papers, 20 July 1942.

[42] Proceedings of the Joint United States-Russian Military Mission, Convened in Moscow, USSR, 1942 (hereafter cited as Joint U.S.-USSR Proceedings), p. 1.

[43] Ibid.

[44] Marshall to Bradley, 15 August 1942, Special Collections Branch, USAF Academy Library, MS# 1, Bradley Papers (hereafter cited as Bradley Papers).

[45] Michela to Milid, 6 August 1942, Bradley Papers.

[46] Joint U.S.-USSR Proceedings, pp. 6-7.

[47] Bradley to War Department, 13 August 1942, Bradley Papers.

[48] Joint U.S.-USSR Proceedings, p. 11.

however, he did recommend a plan that could meet the projected delivery schedule with only ten transports.[49] In view of the constraints, General Bradley recommended that the projected delivery figures could be met if the Soviets excluded navigators and engineers from bomber ferry crews; if the Soviets made full use of formation flights for both bombers and fighters to reduce the need for navigators except in lead ships; if the Russians provided additional transports; and if the end of the ferry run were changed to Krasnoyarsk.[50] Despite the allocation of only ten transports by the War Department, General Bradley was able to convince the War Department to allow the transports to be operated by Soviet pilots on temporary loan.[51]

As Bradley worked to find a middle ground between the demands of the War Department and those of the Soviet delegation, the Soviets, on August 25, 1942, suddenly decided that they would be unable to open air operations along the ALSIB route.[52] They felt that ten transports were too few to insure delivery of enough aircraft to make the operation of this route worthwhile.[53] In response to the Soviet decision to close the ALSIB route, General Bradley informed the Soviets that the United States would be glad to take over control of operations and supply of ALSIB. As Bradley had hoped, his statement—implying that Americans could get the job done in spite of any hardship—spurred the Soviets to reconsider their decision to close ALSIB operations. Sterligov informed General Bradley that they had decided to accept the ten transports offered by the United States and operate them with Soviet crews in an attempt to deliver via ALSIB the maximum number of combat aircraft per month that transport facilities would permit.[54]

On August 31, 1942, the Harvey survey party arrived in Moscow. Colonel Harvey reported to Bradley that he considered all fields west of Krasnoyarsk excellent, though those east of Krasnoyarsk, while suitable for operations, still required some improvements to insure operations throughout the winter.[55] Harvey praised the Soviet Air Force personnel as being extremely skilled and competent.[56] He also commented on the good air-ground radio communications along the route.[57] With the approval of the route, the release of the transports, and Soviet pilots en route to Fairbanks, it seemed as if the ALSIB route would be operational within a few weeks.

Then, on September 21, 1942, the War Department notified General Bradley that General Belyaev, head of the Soviet Supply Mission to the United States, had informed the War Department that the Soviet Union would accept delivery via ALSIB of only the planes now at Fairbanks, after which ALSIB would be closed for further operations.[58] With this news the War Department stopped all planes en route to Alaska and retained possession of the ten transports on temporary loan to the Soviets, since these would now be needed on the southern route.[59] Due to the diplomatic and political snags in his attempts to work out the details of operations along ALSIB, Bradley suggested that if the Soviets should definitely decide to abandon ALSIB, everything should be done to prepare the route for the next spring.[60]

Once again, the Soviets decided to keep ALSIB open. On October 4, 1942, the Soviets told General Bradley that they earnestly desired to continue the operational development of the ALSIB route.[61] However, the War Department had already decided, on October 6, 1942, to cancel ALSIB due to the continual Soviet indecision.[62] General Bradley urged the War Department to reconsider its decision to cancel ALSIB by representing the Soviet period of indecision as a prudent course of action on their part in deciding whether ALSIB or the southern air route was more satisfactory.[63] On that same day, in a last effort to get the ALSIB route operational, General Bradley met with Stalin and found that he urgently desired the opening of ALSIB.[64] On October 8, 1942, the

---

[49] Marshall to Bradley, 15 August 1942, Bradley Papers.

[50] Joint U.S.-USSR Proceedings, p. 8.

[51] Ibid., p. 10.

[52] Bradley to War Department, 25 August 1942, Bradley Papers.

[53] Joint U.S.-USSR Proceedings, p. 8.

[54] Ibid., p. 9.

[55] Ibid. p. 5.

[56] Ibid.

[57] Marshall to Bradley, 15 August 1942, Bradley Papers.

[58] Marshall to Bradley, 21 September 1942, Bradley Papers.

[59] Marshall to Bradley, 23 September 1942, Bradley Papers.

[60] Bradley to War Department, 25 September 1942, Bradley Papers.

[61] Joint U.S.-USSR Proceedings, p. 10.

[62] Marshall to Bradley, 6 october 1942, Bradley Papers.

[63] Marshall to Bradley, 12 August 1942, Bradley Papers.

[64] Bradley to War Department, 6 October 1942, Bradley Papers.

War Department decided to proceed with the original plan of operations for ALSIB after a long conference with the Russian Mission in Washington.[65] By Oct 25, 1942, all Soviet crews were in Fairbanks; all ten of the transports were released to Soviet pilots; and Velkal was now frozen and ready for use by fighters.[66]

As General Bradley was dealing with the political problems that emerged between the War Department and the Soviet Union, operational problems arose as ALSIB became active. One problem that nearly broke into political debate was the placement of radio compasses in all aircraft ferried along the ALSIB route. The Soviets expressed their view of the necessity for installation of radio compasses, since the extremely hazardous flight conditions due to unpredictable weather and the lack of navigational checkpoints made navigation exceedingly difficult.[67] General Bradley assured the Soviets that the B-25s and the transports would have radio compasses, but that the A-20s and fighters probably would not have them.[68] The Soviets argued that the compasses were absolutely necessary to keep aircraft losses at a minimum and that Soviet pilots relied on them to return to their proper airdromes during combat operations.[69]

General Bradley felt that it was impractical to install radio compasses in fighters when these planes were going to be flown across Siberia in formations led by bombers with radio compasses anyway, due to the reduced crews for ferry operations. However, against his own notions on the subject, Bradley echoed Harvey's recommendation that compasses were needed and requested radio compasses for all aircraft flown along the ALSIB route.[670] The Air Service Command, however, recommended that compass loops be eliminated from all fighters because these planes were already overloaded, lacked space, and the cost of installation would be excessive.[71] By October 24, 1942, to the Soviets' dismay, the United States ordered all radio compasses removed from aircraft immediately upon arrival at their Russian destination and shipped back to the United States for installation on other planes to be delivered.[72]

By late November 1942, the ALSIB ferry route was near full capacity in its delivery of the projected 212 planes per month—the rate that would meet the supply schedule agreed upon in the Second Protocol. Though the aircraft deliveries were far behind the protocol schedules, the aircraft were now steadily being ferried via ALSIB and arriving on the Eastern Front at an increasing rate. By early 1943, significant numbers of American P-39s, A-20s, and B-25s were beginning to appear on the Eastern Front in time to give the Soviets a distinct edge over the *Luftwaffe* in the closely contested air campaigns over Stalingrad, Kuban, and Kursk. These campaigns would determine the winner of air superiority over the Eastern Front for the remainder of the war.

The timely arrival of lend-lease A-20 and B-25 medium range bombers, and the P-39 Airacobra greatly increased the odds against the qualitatively superior *Luftwaffe* in the later months of 1942 through the summer of 1943.[73] With the steady arrival of American A-20s and B-25s from the ALSIB corridor to the front, the Soviet Air Force was able to quickly expand its obsolete bomber force and transform it into a credible offensive asset against the *Luftwaffe*.[74] Since the *Luftwaffe* lacked effective night interceptors, the Soviet Air Force was able to capitalize upon the A-20's and B-25's ability to operate at night to cripple the *Luftwaffe* in night interdiction strikes.[75]

But over the Eastern Front it was the role of the fighter that finally wrested air superiority from the *Luftwaffe*. Although the P-39 Airacobra was considered obsolete by most Allied air forces, the aircraft and their Soviet pilots became a deadly combination. The plane outperformed the British Spitfire and the American P-40 in nearly every category of combat performance, and Soviet pilots expressed great affection for the P-39 as being "an excellent, powerfully armed fighter-bomber."[76] In addition to being a great ground support aircraft, it also proved to be a superior interceptor. Soviet airmen such as Aleksandr I. Pokryshkin—who scored twenty kills against the *Luftwaffe* at Kuban while flying an American

[65] Joint U.S.-USSR Proceedings, p. 11.
[66] Bradley to War Department, 15 October 1942, Bradley Papers.
[67] Joint U.S.-USSR Proceedings, p. 18.
[68] Ibid., p. 16.
[69] Bradley to War Department, 20 September 1942, Bradley Papers.
[70] Joint U.S.-USSR Proceedings, p. 16.
[71] Arnold to Bradley, 2 September 1942, Bradley Papers.
[72] Bradley to War Department, 25 October 1942, Bradley Papers.
[73] Von Hardesty, *Red Phoenix* (Washington, D.C.: Smithsonian, 1982), p. 141.
[74] Ibid., p. 139.
[75] Ibid., p. 159.
[76] Ibid., p. 141.

P-39—exemplified the lethality of a skillfully piloted Airacobra.[77]

As the defense of Stalingrad drew to a close, the Soviet Air Force rebounded to display an augmented strength in modern aircraft able to battle the *Messerschmitt* 109 on an even par. Due primarily to the steady deliveries of American aircraft over ALSIB, the Soviet Air Force was able to commit fourteen hundred combat aircraft to Stalingrad, three-quarters of which were of modern design.[78]

In conclusion, the efforts of Major General Follett Bradley in negotiating and implementing the Alaska-Siberia air supply route to ferry crucial lend-lease aircraft to Soviet forces on the Eastern Front proved to be a decisive factor in the air war on the Eastern Front. Nearly eight thousand lend-lease combat aircraft were delivered via ALSIB during the course of the war. The aircraft were decisive in that they provided the Soviet Air Force with a steady supply of capable, modern aircraft able to fight the *Luftwaffe's* best on an even par. The technological force provided by American lend-lease aircraft not only provided the power for the Soviet Air Force to gain eventual air superiority on the Eastern Front, but also allowed the Soviets sufficient time to build huge aircraft factories east of the Ural Mountains. As American aid complemented the Soviets' production of modern aircraft, the *Luftwaffe* was forced to opt for defensive operations. After gaining air superiority at Kursk, the Soviet Air Force continued to bleed the *Luftwaffe* of resources and men, as it continued to gain strength in both men and aircraft. The importance of the Bradley Mission in implementing the Alaska-Siberia air route cannot be overemphasized. Without it, it is quite possible that the Soviets could have lost the hotly contested air victories at Stalingrad, Kuban, and Kursk, which would drastically have altered the course of the war on the Eastern Front.

*Baker B. Beard is a graduate of the U.S. Air Force Academy. His paper is based upon primary documentation obtained from the Follett Bradley Papers in the Gimble Collection at the academy's library.*

---

[77] Ibid., p. 121.

[78] Ibid., p. 104.

# The Northwest Ferry Route

*Daniel L. Haulman*

ALASKA PLAYED A MORE PROMINENT PART IN WORLD War II than many persons realize. Not only was it the site of the only Japanese invasion of North America, but it also harbored airfields in the Aleutian Islands from which the Eleventh Air Force could raid Japanese bases in the Kurile Islands. Most important, it provided a route through which thousands of American warplanes went to Russia to fight the Germans on the Eastern Front in Europe. Thus, Alaska contributed to the Allied victory, not only against Japan in the Pacific, but also against Germany in Europe.

Even before Japanese aircraft attacked Pearl Harbor on December 7, 1941, American military authorities considered the strategic value of Alaska for air power. As early as 1934, Lieutenant Colonel Henry H. "Hap" Arnold, later to become commanding general of the army air forces in World War II, led a flight of ten bombers from Washington, D.C., to Fairbanks, Alaska, via Edmonton, Canada.[1] Later in the 1930s, American and Canadian pilots explored routes between Alaska and the northwestern United States.[2] The attack on Hawaii magnified concern over the vulnerability of the Pacific coast of the United States and the Alaska territory. Alaska could also furnish bases from which to strike back at the Japanese empire. For both defensive and offensive military operations, the United States needed an air route to Alaska.

In June of 1941, Adolf Hitler had scrapped his non-aggression pact with Joseph Stalin and invaded the Soviet Union. Three million Axis troops advanced quickly along a eighteen-hundred-mile front. Within a month, German troops captured 700,000 square miles of territory and seized or destroyed hundreds of Soviet aircraft. Before the end of the year, German forces approached Leningrad and Moscow, and the Soviet Union appeared ready to collapse.[3] Such an event would have left Britain and the United States to face a vastly strengthened Germany. President Franklin D. Roosevelt authorized the shipment of lend-lease supplies—including desperately needed airplanes—to Joseph Stalin. The United States needed the Alaska air route for ferrying airplanes to the Union of Soviet Socialist Republics.

Each of the routes by which the airplanes were first delivered seemed inadequate. Ice and submarines threatened a sea route to Murmansk and Archangel around German-occupied Norway. Another sea route to the Persian Gulf stretched for thousands of miles and consumed enormous amounts of time. After arrival by ship the planes still had to cross the deserts of Iran to reach the Soviet Union.[4] There was an air route, but it was also impractical, reaching thirteen thousand miles

---

[1] AFHRA, Alaska Division, Air Transport Command History, 19391942, vol. II, p. 258.

[2] Ibid., vol. I, pp. 33, 78-79; vol. II, pp. 72-73; Stanley W. Dziuban, *Military Relations Between the United States and Canada, 1939-1945* (Washington, D.C., 1959), pp. 200-202.

[3] Robert Goralski, *World War II Almanac: 1931-1945* (New York, 1981), pp. 164-168.

[4] Robert W. Coakley and Richard M. Leighton, *Global Logistics and Strategy* (Washington, D.C.: 1955), p. 349.

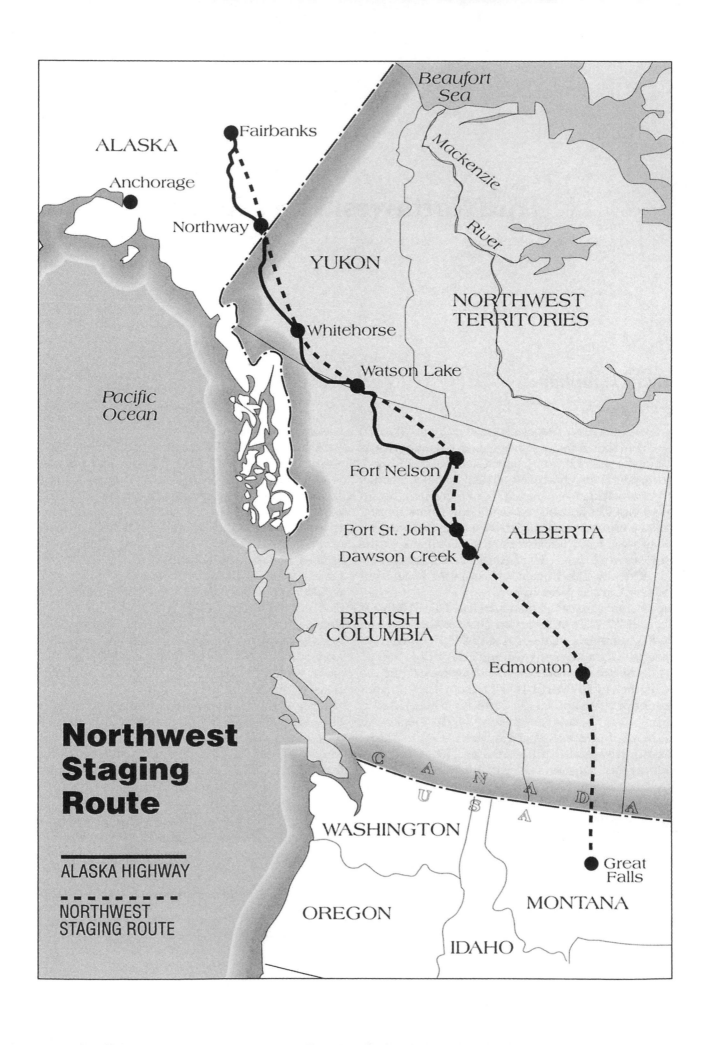

Beaufort
Sea

Mackenzie
River

ALASKA

Fairbanks

Anchorage

Northway

YUKON

NORTHWEST
TERRITORIES

Whitehorse

Pacific
Ocean

Watson Lake

Fort Nelson

Fort St. John

ALBERTA

Dawson Creek

BRITISH
COLUMBIA

Edmonton

C A N A D A
U S A

WASHINGTON

Great
Falls

MONTANA

OREGON

IDAHO

# Northwest
# Staging
# Route

ALASKA HIGHWAY

- - - - - - -
NORTHWEST
STAGING ROUTE

from Florida to South America and Africa, to Iraq, Iran, and, finally, to the Soviet Union. Distance was not the only problem. The desert sands of northern Africa and the Middle East took their toll on the airplanes.[5] A shorter air route for lend-lease aircraft from the United States to Siberia via western Canada and Alaska would solve many problems.

When Japanese military forces attacked Attu, Kiska, and Dutch Harbor in Alaska's Aleutian Islands in June 1942, a rudimentary air route across western Canada had already been laid out by the Canadian Department of Transport and United Transport of Canada, later called Yukon Southern Air Transport.[6] The army air forces had already flown P-40 fighters of the Eleventh Pursuit Squadron and B-26 bombers of the Seventy-Seventh Bombardment Squadron to Alaska for the Eleventh Air Force.[7] At the news of the Japanese attacks, the U.S. government asked eleven domestic airlines to fly all available planes to Edmonton for emergency deliveries of troops and military cargo to Alaska. By the third week in June, forty-six planes were available. Between June 14 and 30, they flew two hundred special missions through the Alberta capital.[8]

Although the Northwest Staging Route, as the northern air path across western Canada and Alaska came to be called, found its first use in the defense of Alaska, it eventually became primarily a lend-lease conduit. The Soviet government at first resisted plans for such a route because it did not want American bases in Siberia.

Stalin feared not only excessive foreign influence in Soviet internal military affairs, but also premature war with Japan. He did not want to fight the Germans and Japanese at the same time, and Tokyo might interpret American bases in Siberia as a prelude to bombing operations against Japan from the north. When the Army Air Forces Ferrying Command's General Harold L. George proposed an Alaska-Siberia route to the Soviet ambassador in Washington in June, 1942, he was turned down.[9]

In July, Major General Follett Bradley went to Moscow on a special mission to persuade the Soviet leadership to open the northern air route for lend-lease deliveries. Stalin agreed on condition that the planes be turned over to Soviet air crews within Alaska rather than Siberia.[10]

During the next month, August 1942, two members of the Soviet Purchasing Commission flew from Washington, D.C., to Fairbanks to arrange for the movement of United States airplanes to the Union of Soviet Socialist Republics through Ladd Field.[11] The project was called the "Alsib Movement" because the aircraft would fly from Alaska (Al) to Siberia (sib). The Soviet commissioners were joined at Ladd Field (now Fort Wainwright) on September 4 by permanent members of the USSR military mission in Alaska, led by Colonel Mikhail G. Machin.[12] His party flew from Siberia on a camouflaged C-53, accompanied by a B25 with Red Air Force markings.[13] One day earlier, the first lend-lease combat airplanes—a flight of five A-20s led by Captain Edmund Averman—had arrived at Ladd from Great Falls, Montana. A second flight of five A-20s followed shortly afterwards.[14] On September 11, another group of lend-lease planes arrived from the southeast, a flight of twenty-two P-40s.

Soviet ferry pilots landed at Ladd Field on September 24 after a week-long delay at Welkal, Siberia, because of bad weather. They included fourteen A-20 crews, twenty-eight pursuit crews, and seven cargo crews. After five days of transition training, Lieutenant Colonel Paul Nedosekin of the Red Air Force led the first flight of lend-lease aircraft—twelve A-20s—from Ladd Field to Siberia. Captain Vladimir Finogenov led the first flight of P-40s from Alaska to Siberia on October 9. The ferry route was at last operational.[15]

At Ladd Field, five American officers taught Soviet crews how to fly the lend-lease planes. Of these officers, only one spoke Russian. The others depended on interpreters and sign language for communication. After

---

[5] AFHRA, *Impact* (periodical published by the Office of the Assistant Chief of Air Staff, Intelligence, Washington, D.C.), vol. I, No. 7 (Oct 1943), p. 35; AFHRA, History of the Caribbean Division, Air Transport Command, part II, the South American Sector, Jan-Jun 1942.

[6] Dziuban, *Military Relations*, pp. 200-201; AFHRA, Alaskan Division, ATC History, vol. II, pp. 72-73.

[7] Dziuban, *Military Relations*, pp. 202-203.

[8] AFHRA, Alaskan Division, ATC History, 1939-1942, vol. II, pp. 24, 155, 164; Dziuban, *Military Relations*, p. 204.

[9] AFHRA, Alaskan Division, ATC History, 1939-1942, vol. II, pp. 19-22, 240-241, 244-245; Wesley Frank Craven and James Lea Cate, *The Army Air Forces in World War II*, vol. 7 (Chicago, 1958), p. 154.

[10] Coakley and Leighton, *Global Logistics*, p. 565; Dziuban, *Military Relations*, p. 216.

[11] AFHRA, Alaskan Division, ATC History, 1939-1942, vol. II, p. 269.

[12] Ibid.

[13] AFHRA, Ladd Field History (BU-1466-HI) Fall 1938-31, Jan 1944, microfilm roll A0177.

[14] AFHRA, 7th Ferrying Group History, Jan 1942-Dec 1944, pp. 72-90; Craven, *AAF in WWII*, vol. 7, p. 155; AFHRA, Alaskan Division, ATC History, 1939-1942, vol. II, p. 266.

[15] AFHRA, Ladd Field History (BU-1466-HI) Fall 1938-31-Jan 1944 (microfilm roll A0177).

about a hundred Soviet crewmen were trained, they trained other Soviet pilots.[16]

Until October 1942, Colonel LeRoy Ponton de Acre, commander of the Seventh Ferrying Group at Great Falls, supervised the Northwest Staging Route, which was also called the Northwest Ferrying Route.[17]

During that month, the Air Transport Command activated the Alaskan Wing under Colonel Thomas L. Mosley to take charge of the route.[18] His headquarters was located at Edmonton, Alberta.

To accommodate the thousands of aircraft flying the Northwest Staging Route, the United States and Canadian governments constructed a series of fifteen air bases between Great Falls, Montana, and Nome, Alaska. They included Lethbridge, Calgary, Edmonton, and Grande Prairie in Alberta; Fort St. John and Fort Nelson in British Columbia; Watson Lake and Whitehorse in the Yukon; and Northway, Tanacross, Big Delta, Fairbanks, and Galena in Alaska.[19] A U.S.-Canadian committee called the Permanent Joint Board on Defense set policy for the route and its construction in a series of recommendations subject to approval in Ottawa and Washington. Board co-chairmen were Colonel O.M. Biggar of Canada, and Fiorello H. LaGuardia, mayor of New York.[20] At first, Americans built the bases in Montana and Alaska while Canadians worked on the facilities on Canadian territory. But the unusually severe winter of 1942-1943 delayed construction.[21] The United States, with a more abundant labor supply, persuaded Canada to allow American construction personnel to work on the Canadian bases during the rest of 1943.[22]

Of the fifteen route bases, four were especially important: Great Falls, Edmonton, Whitehorse, and Fairbanks. Great Falls was the starting point, and eventually embraced two airfields: Gore Field and East Base. Ferrying command pilots flew new airplanes from factories across the United States to Great Falls, the home of the Seventh Ferrying Group. Its pilots flew the lend-lease planes—after they were winterized and modified—up the air base chain to the Soviet crews at Fairbanks.[23]

Largest of the Canadian bases on the Northwest Staging Route, Edmonton served as headquarters of the Alaskan Wing, later Alaskan Division, of the Air Transport Command. Edmonton contained aircraft modification facilities, and it was constructed more by Canadian labor than any of the other bases on the route.[24] When Colonel Mosley was transferred to North Africa in May 1943, Colonel Dale V. Gaffney, who had commanded Ladd Field at Fairbanks, replaced him as head of the Alaskan Wing at Edmonton. Gaffney became a brigadier general when the wing became a division, and under his leadership the ferrying route grew tremendously in size and efficiency. His determination to improve the air highway earned him the nickname "Screaming Eagle of the Yukon."[25]

Whitehorse in the Yukon was another important Canadian base on the Northwest Staging Route. About midway between Edmonton and Fairbanks, Whitehorse was also a significant location for two other World War II construction projects in western Canada: the Alaska Highway and the Canol (or Canadian oil) pipeline. The Alaska Highway followed the staging route so that planes and ground vehicles going to and from Alaska could support each other. To furnish gasoline for the highway and the ferrying route, a Canadian oil pipeline was built from Norman Wells to Whitehorse. Americans constructed an oil refinery at Whitehorse to process crude oil from northwestern Canada.[26]

Unquestionably the most important of the six Alaska bases on the route was Ladd Field. In fact, it was the most significant base of the northern lend-lease ferry route, primarily because it was the transfer point where the Americans turned over the lend-lease airplanes to Soviet personnel. Ladd Field contained seven large hangars to shelter the many planes in bad weather. If the aircraft passed inspection, they were flown by Soviet pilots westward through Galena to Nome and Siberia. Occasionally Soviet inspectors rejected planes in need of repair, modification, or winterization. Fairbanks was chosen over Nome and Galena as the transfer point because it was less vulnerable to Japanese attack, had a better climate, was larger, and was easier to supply. Ladd Field was located only about three miles from the center of Fairbanks, which, during the war, doubled its

[16] AFHRA, Alaskan Division, ATC History, 1939-1942, Vol. II, p. 278.

[17] Ibid. pp. 25-26, 197, 263, 286-287; 7th Ferrying Group History, Jan 1942-Dec 1944, p. 11; Craven, *AAF in WWII*, vol. 7, p. 156.

[18] Ibid., p. 157; AFHRA, "Highlights of the Air Transport Command," Personnel Narratives Division Studies, Study No. 5, p. 5.

[19] Craven, *AAF in WWII*, vol. 7, pp. 152, 164, 232. AFHRA, *Impact*, Aug 1944, vol. II, No. 8, pp. 30-33.

[20] AFHRA, Alaskan Division, ATC History, 1939-1942, vol. I, pp. 44-45; Dziuban, *Military Relations*, p. 201; Craven, *AAF in WWII*, vol. 7, p. 157.

[21] Ibid., pp. 152-155; Dziuban, *Military Relations*, p. 205.

[22] Ibid., pp. 207-210; Craven, *AAF in WWII*, vol. 7, pp. 162-163.

[23] AFHRA, HQ, 1455 AAF Base Unit Historical Report, Jan 1944-Apr 1945, vol. II, pp. 1, 2, 6, 12, 33-34, 36; Craven, *AAF in WWII*, vol. 7, p. 164.

[24] Ibid., pp. 152, 155, 166-167.

[25] Ibid., pp. 161-163. Dziuban, *Military Relations*, p. 204.

[26] Karl C. Dod, *The Corps of Engineers: The War Against Japan* (Washington, D.C., 1987), pp. 299-300, 318-320.

Soviet officers gather in the briefing room at Ladd Field, ca. 1943. Americans considered Soviet personnel polite, well-behaved, and disciplined, and admired the fact that many of the Russians had flown on the front lines in Europe. *(Acc. No. 91-098-842, Kay Kennedy Collection, Rasmuson Library University of Alaska Fairbanks)*

1940 population of 3,445 people. It was also important as an Eleventh Air Force base, and it sheltered a cold weather testing detachment throughout World War II. Some bombers from these organizations occasionally bombed ice jams on the Yukon River when these caused flooding of the ATC base at Galena.[27]

The Soviet personnel at Ladd Field generally got along well with the Americans. Colonel Machin remained commander of the Soviet military mission in Alaska until May 1944, when he was replaced by Colonel Peter Kisilev. Kisilev was succeeded by Major General Ivan A. Obrazkov in December 1944. Ladd Field was also home to a detachment of the First Aviation Ferrying Regiment of the Soviet Air Force, commanded by Colonel N. S. Vasin.

Soviet officers were allowed to use the officers' club and officers' open mess at Ladd Field, where they grew to enjoy the slot machines and pool tables. Russian officers and enlisted men alike relished the American movies shown at Ladd, and the frequent dances. They loved buying American consumer goods from local stores, including cigarettes and other items not abundant in Russia during the war. The Russians liked strong, unmixed alcoholic beverages, but did not usually get drunk or disorderly. Americans described the Soviet personnel as polite, pleasant, well-behaved, and disciplined, and admired the fact that many of the Russian ferry pilots had flown on the front lines in Europe. Soviet transports brought Russian ferry pilots periodically back to Ladd Field after they had delivered their planes to Welkal, in Siberia. The transport planes returned to Siberia with other lend-lease cargo.[28]

Occasionally the Soviet personnel at Ladd entertained their American hosts. On "Red Army Day" on February

---

[27] Craven, *AAF in WWII*, vol. 7, pp. 155-165; AFHRA, Ladd Field History (BU-1466-HI), microfilm roll A0177.

[28] AFHRA, Ladd Field History (BU-I466-HI), microfilm roll A0177.

23, 1943, the Russians had a party open to Americans. To celebrate two years of ferrying aircraft from Alaska to Russia, the Soviet military mission in Alaska gave a party for aircraft maintenance personnel on September 30, 1944.[29]

However, friction developed between Soviet and American personnel at Ladd over the failure of some of the lend-lease aircraft to arrive on time. At one point, a Soviet officer flew to Edmonton to see what was causing delays. He returned satisfied with the route organization and methods.[30]

Although the Alaskan Wing of the Air Transport Command maintained the Northwest Staging Route bases, it did not control the aircrews which ferried the planes northwestward. They remained under the Seventh Ferrying Group, which served General William H. Tunner's Ferrying Division. Generals Gaffney and Tunner sometimes disagreed over issues such as who should control the air crews and how they should be employed. Gaffney failed to persuade Tunner to permanently assign pilots to various bases along the route, so that they could develop expertise over short segments of the airway instead of having to fly all the way from Great Falls to Fairbanks.[31] After delivering their planes to Ladd Field, the ferrying division pilots would return to Montana as passengers on chartered commercial airliners, usually those of Northwest Airlines. Military aircrews did not always get along well with the civilian pilots, who earned more money and had better accommodations and work schedules. Some of the military pilots also felt they were treated like luggage.[32]

Great hazards faced all pilots who flew the Northwest Staging Route. It covered a distance of more than two thousand miles, and because of en-route delays sometimes required two weeks or more to traverse. Cold temperatures as low as seventy degrees below zero Fahrenheit and winter storms with hurricane-force winds threatened men and machines alike, as did fog and clouds that often obscured very high mountains. Seemingly endless forests and snowfields with few landmarks enticed flyers to get lost, despite a well-planned string of radio stations.[33]

Despite problems of organization, climate, distance, and terrain, the army air forces orchestrated a crescendo of aircraft deliveries from the United States to the Soviet Union along the Northwest Staging Route between September 1942 and the summer of 1945. In 1942, 150 lend-lease planes went through Canada and Alaska to Siberia. In 1943, the number jumped to 2,662, and in 1944 to 3,164. On September 10, 1944, Ladd Field celebrated the 5,000th lend-lease aircraft delivery after the route had been in service for less than two years. In just six months of 1945, 2,009 planes went to Russia through Alaska.[34] More than 7,900 airplanes flew to Siberia along the northwest route during World War II. This was more than all the airplanes sent by the U.S. to the USSR by all the other routes combined. Only 993 went by the southern air route through South America and Africa. About 5,100 went by the sea routes.[35]

Of the aircraft delivered through Alaska, more than five thousand were fighters—mostly P-39s and P-63s. More than thirteen hundred were A-20 light bombers, and there were about seven hundred each of B-25 medium bombers and C-47 transports.[36] The Soviets did not want heavy bombers, partly because, as mentioned earlier, they did not want to antagonize Tokyo with the threat that they might be used against Japan from Siberia, and partly because they preferred to let the British and Americans handle the strategic bombing of Germany from the west. Russian forces depended more on fighter and light bomber aircraft than heavy bombers to support their ground offensives.

In addition to the more than seventy-nine hundred lend-lease planes, the United States also flew along the Northwest Staging Route about 716 aircraft for the defense of Alaska. Thus, more than ten times as many planes went for the defense of Russia as for the defense of Alaska, reflecting the Roosevelt administration's belief that Germany posed a greater threat to the Allies than Japan did to Alaska.

Thus, a total of more than eighty-six hundred airplanes flew the Northwest Staging Route during World War II.[37]

Important visitors flew the Northwest Ferrying Route during World War II. Among them was Vice President Henry A. Wallace, who flew through Ladd Field on the

---

[29] Ibid., p. 83.

[30] Ibid., p. 86.

[31] Craven, *AAF in WWII*, vol. 7, p. 169.

[32] Ibid., p. 168.

[33] Ibid.

[34] Ibid., pp. 159, 165.

[35] Von Hardesty, *Red Phoenix: The Rise of Soviet Air Power, 1941-1945* (Washington, D.C., 1982); appendices 9-10; AFHRA, "Highlights of the Air Transport Command," Study No. 5, pp. 4-12; Craven, *AAF in WWII*, vol. 6, p. 405, vol. 7, p. 153.

[36] AFHRA, HQ, 1455 AAF Base Unit Historical Report, Jan 1944-Apr 1945, vol. II, p. 37; Craven, *AAF in WWII*, vol. 7, p. 165.

[37] Dziuban, *Military Relations*, p. 216.

way to and from Asia on a trip to Allied nations there between May and July 1944.[38] In August of that year, the Soviet delegation to the Dumbarton Oaks Conference on post-war security in Washington, D.C., flew through Ladd Field. Among the delegates was Andrei Gromyko, Soviet ambassador to the United States and later Soviet foreign minister during much of the Cold War.[39]

The experience of building and operating the northwest air route proved that three allied nations, the United States, Canada, and the Soviet Union, could cooperate successfully against a common enemy. It also proved the ability of a host of engineers and pilots, communications and logistics personnel, both military and civilian, to overcome problems of terrain, weather, distance, and fatigue. Although the need to deliver lend-lease planes to Russia or to defend Alaska from Japan evaporated with the end of World War II, the route left a heritage in the Alaska Highway, in continuing commercial air routes between Alaska and the Lower 48, and in the experienced air crews who contributed to what became the Military Airlift Command. The thousands of warplanes delivered to and through Alaska between 1942 and 1945 contributed in no small measure to the survival of Russia, the defeat of Hitler, and the defense of North America during the greatest of all wars.

*Daniel L. Haulman is with the Air Force Historical Research Agency, Maxwell Air Force Base, Alabama. He has written the pamphlet, "The Army Air Corps in the Asiatic-Pacific Theater in World War II."*

---

[38] AFHRA, Gaffney personal papers, Report on ATC Special Mission No. 52.

[39] AFHRA, Ladd Field History (BU-I466-HI), microfilm roll A0177.

# The Construction and Use
# of the Fairbanks-Krasnoiarsk Air Route

*Tat'iana Kosheleva*
*Translated by Katerina Solovjova*

ON JUNE 22 OF 1941, THE TROOPS OF FASCIST Germany invaded the territory of the Soviet Union. Thus began the Great Patriotic War in Russia.

During the first months of the war the success of Hitler's troops forced the Soviet government to evacuate a considerable number of aviation factories. On the home front, factories continued to work at full capacity. Nevertheless, there was a lack of battle machinery at the fronts. The fronts lacked modern airplanes, and that is why air superiority belonged to the German fascists.

The Allies—the United States and England—promised to help with that and to provide the aircraft. On the third day of the Great Patriotic War, June 23, 1941, President Roosevelt made a statement about the support of the Soviet Union in the war against the fascist aggression. The lend-lease law that was passed by the Congress on March 11, 1941, included the USSR as a target for aid.

In June of 1941, during the visit to Moscow of presidential assistant Harry Hopkins, it was decided to organize immediate war aid for the USSR. At the same time they discussed the issue of the creation of the unique air bridge that would allow the Allies to transfer airplanes from the United States to the USSR along a route that would be inaccessible to the fascists.

It was very hard to transport the battle machinery to the snowed-in fields of Russia. One of the routes led from American ports through the Pacific and Indian oceans, the Arabian Sea, and the Persian Gulf to the port of Basra. From Basra, part of the machinery was transported through Iran via railroad. The other part of it was assembled in Maghil and Shaibah, in the territory of Iraq, and transported on aircraft. Transportation of goods along this route would take more than two months.

The second route was over the North Atlantic, and it went via Iceland through the North, Norway, and Barentsovo seas to Arhangel'sk and Murmansk. Based on the shores of occupied Norway, Hitler's naval and air forces actively tried to stop the passing vessels. Thus, in June of 1942, only twelve vessels out of the convoy PQ-17, which comprised thirty-five ships, were able to reach Murmansk. The rest were sunk. The sunken ships carried 210 airplanes, 430 tanks, 3,350 trucks, and 100,000 items of other military cargo.[1]

Starting in December 1941, until June 1942, Germans sank forty-five cargo vessels, including eleven Soviet ships. The total value of all cargo was $121.8 million.[2]

It was necessary to find a safe route for cargo and machinery transportation to Russia. On October 9, 1941, the Russian State Committee of Defense passed Decree No. 739-s concerning the establishment of an air route with the United States via East Siberia. The decree implied that it would be possible to organize the transportation of the planes by flying them to the Soviet-German front.

---

[1] F. Al'berti, "Trassa 50 Let Spustya" (The Route 50 Years Later), *Vozdushnyi Transport* (Air Transport), No. 44, 1992, p. 7.

[2] S. Gribanov, *Vozdushnyi Transport*, No. 6, 1993, pp. 40-46.

Soviet aircraft specialists suggested three variants of the route. The first variant was along the Northern Sea. It was not approved due to the long winter season, bad weather, and the impossibility of providing the quick supply of airplane fuel, the necessary machinery, and additional airport supplies. The second route suggested was supposed to go from Alaska to Komsomol'sk-na-Amure. This route was not approved either, due to a number of climatic and geographical matters. The third proposed route went through the central part of the northeast of the Soviet Union. It was recommended and approved by the Soviet State Committee of Defense. The route went from Alaska, across the Bering Strait, the central part of Chukotka, Kolyma, Iakutiia, and Siberia to Krasnoiarsk. The total length of the route was 6,450 kilometers. The advantages of this route were the stable anticyclone weather and the existence of big towns— Anadyr', Magadan, Iakutsk, Kirensk, Krasnoiarsk—that divided the route into equal segments. All sections of the route were explored and studied by polar pilots in advance. These pilots were Molokov, Liapidevskii, Levanevskii, Mazuruk and others. Some of the airports along the route needed reconstruction.

Due to the necessity of the construction of the new airports and the reconstruction of the old ones, the Soviet State Committee of Defense obliged the central directorate of the Civil Air Fleet, the local economic organization of East Siberia and the Far East, to provide everything—on a short-term basis—for the construction of the long air route.

On June 17, 1942, Roosevelt wrote to Stalin: "Ambassador Litvinov informed me that you approved the transfer of the American airplanes via Alaska and Siberia to the East Front."[3]

In his next letter, written June 23, 1942, Roosevelt suggested: "I am ready to order American crews that are occupied in the airplane transfer to deliver airplanes to Lake Baikal."[4]

Stalin answered: "Soviet Government already gave necessary orders to finish in the nearest future all works in Siberia related to the receiving of the airplanes.... As far as whose pilots are going to deliver airplanes from Alaska, I think that we can entrust it to the Soviet pilots."[5]

At the end of 1941, the route of the future airway was completely approved with the help of the legendary polar pilots Liapidevskii, Mazuruk, and others.

Noted in Russia as an extraordinary polar pilot, Mazuruk was appointed to be the chief of the air route.

The air route went through the little Siberian town of Kirensk, lost on the vast taiga of the Irkutsk region. Kirensk is located on an island between two rivers: the Lena and the Kirenga, the latter of which flows into the Lena. Before the war there had been only an airport for float planes, and the planes would land on the Kirenga River.

The construction of the airfield for the big planes started in October of 1941. Every day more than seven hundred mobilized local people worked on the construction. The work conditions were very hard. According to the evidence given by the workers, there wasn't enough machinery. At first they had only one tractor, and so horses were used very often.

Almost all of the towns participated in the construction. The workers would mix tar and gravel by hand, then manually spread it at the airstrip. The area was very swampy, and so it was necessary to make drainage wells. Then the workers would put down a layer of gravel and pour tar on top.

Very often the runway would sink, potholes would appear, the surface would freeze, and the work would have to start all over. The living conditions for the airport builders were very poor: people lived in dug-out mud huts. The authorities would let them go home— some four kilometers away—only one or two times a month, and then only with a special pass.

Nevertheless, people understood that during wartime every citizen of the country needed to put as much effort into the work as possible.

On June 18, 1942, the special committee of the Soviet State Air Force approved the operation and use of the airport in Kirensk, and, starting at the beginning of 1943, the airport was completely transferred in the authority of the air route management. On September 25, 1942, Mazuruk, the chief of the air route, officially reported to the government that the air route was open.[6] The special inspection of the military air force checked the readiness of the route. The inspectors flew from Moscow to Fairbanks and back. At the same time (August 26-31, 1942), the American committee, led by General Bradley, inspected the route. Both the Soviets and their American colleagues confirmed the readiness of the route for airplane transfer.[7] The American airplane transfer along the main route—Fairbanks-Nome-

[3] *Chairman Stalin Correspondence*, p. 24; *Correspondence of the Chairman of USSR Council of Ministers with United States President and Prime Minister of Great Britain during the Great Patriotic War, 1941-1945*, vol. 2 (Moscow, 1957), p. 26.

[4] Ibid., p. 25.

[5] Ibid., p. 26.

[6] E.V. Altunin, *Ocherki Po Istorii Grazhdanskoi Aviatsii* (Essays on the History of Civil Aviation), p. 210.

[7] Collections of Irkutsk Museum of Regional Studies, No. VS 6082-4.

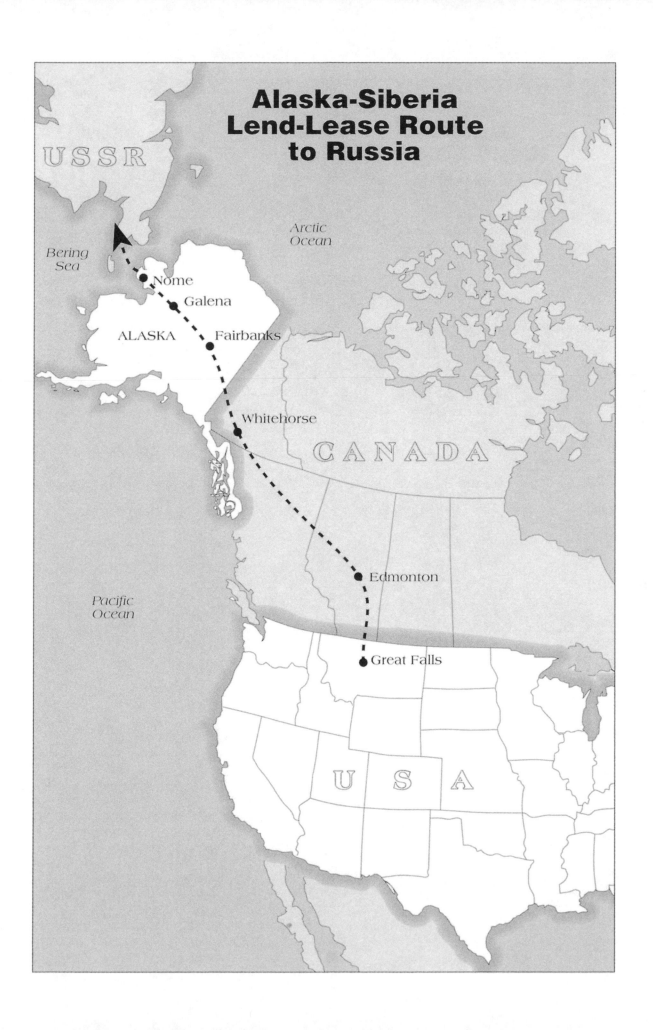

# Alaska-Siberia
# Lend-Lease Route
# to Russia

USSR

Arctic
Ocean

Bering
Sea

Nome

Galena

ALASKA    Fairbanks

Whitehorse

CANADA

Pacific
Ocean

Edmonton

Great Falls

U S A

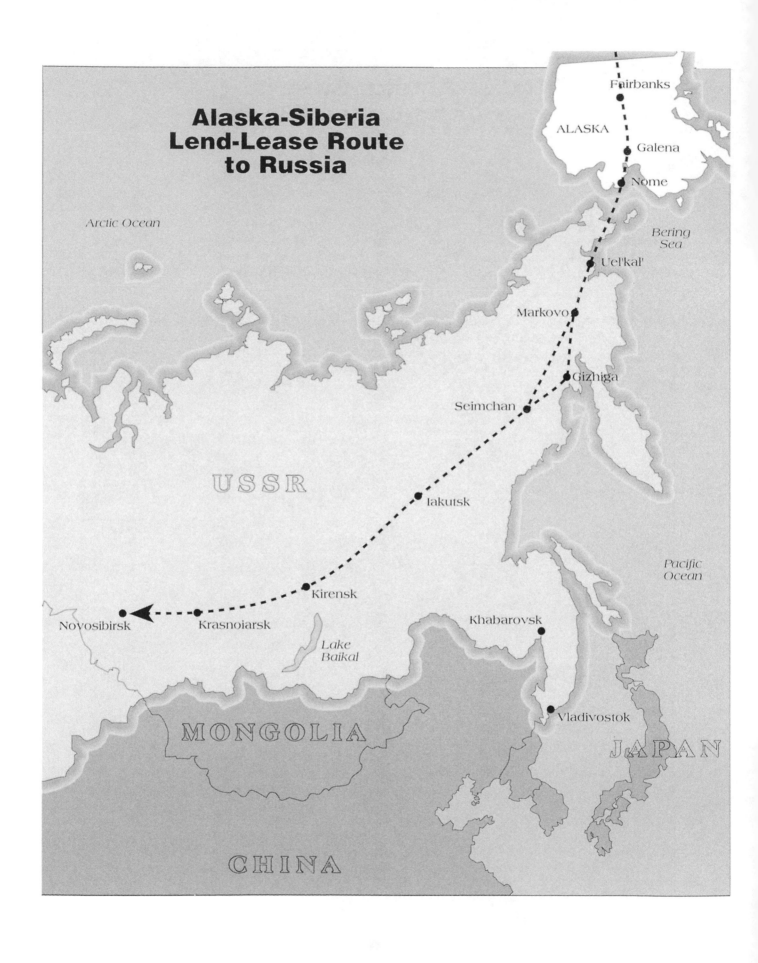

# Alaska-Siberia
# Lend-Lease Route
# to Russia

Arctic Ocean

ALASKA

Fairbanks

Galena

Nome

Bering
Sea

Uel'kal'

USSR

Markovo

Gizhiga

Seimchan

Pacific
Ocean

Iakutsk

Kirensk

Khabarovsk

Novosibirsk    Krasnoiarsk

Lake
Baikal

Vladivostok

MONGOLIA

JAPAN

CHINA

Uel'kal'-Seimchan-Iakutsk-Kirensk-Krasnoiarsk—started October 7, 1942.[8]

Lieutenant Prokushev, a one-time junior technician (now a war veteran), came to Kirensk to service airplanes in August of 1942. Prior to that he studied battle machinery and English at the specialized courses in the town of Chkalovsk. On the Kirensk-Iakutsk part of the route he was the leading specialist-instructor. He remembers that the first group of A-20 bombers left Fairbanks on October 7, arrived in Iakutsk on November 7, and in Krasnoiarsk on November 11.

Former pilot Klimkin, who now lives in Kirensk, transported more than ten Airacobras along the route. According to his reminiscences the participants of the transfer flew in unheated airplanes at very low temperatures. They had to land on a runway covered with ice. The oil would harden in the engines at minus sixty to minus seventy degrees Celsius, and all rubber parts and hoses would break.

The entire route was divided into five parts: Fairbanks to Uel'kal' (1,560 kilometers), Uel'kal' to Seimchan (1,450 kilometers), Seimchan to Iakutsk (1,200 kilometers), Iakutsk to Kirensk (1,400 kilometers), and Kirensk to Krasnoiarsk (920 kilometers).

The Soviet military mission which would technically inspect the airplanes started its work in Fairbanks even before the route was open. Colonel Manin was the head of the mission. Very soon the first Soviet squadron, under the command of Colonel Nedosekin, was stationed at the American air base, Ladd Field. Here Americans established a study center for Russian pilots. Among the American instructors was Nikolai De Tolli, a descendant of Barklai De Tolli, the famous Russian general of the 1812 war against Napoleon.

According to the reminiscences of David Sherl', the navigator of the transfer division, the first Soviet airport in Uel'kal' had a runway made of wooden planks. The spaces between the planks were filled with gravel and dirt. Several *yurtas* (nomad tents) served as offices, and the canteen or dining area was built of boards. There also was a barrel-like metal structure where pilots would rest. The fact is that before the war there had been almost no airports in northeast Siberia. There were only a few unpaved airstrips for light airplanes such as the Po-2.

The Second Squadron of the transfer division was stationed in Uel'kal'. It was under the command of Colonel Mel'nikov. From Uel'kal', airplanes were transferred to the settlement of Seimchan, on the Kolyma River. Here the route went above the uninhabited central part of Chukotka and the Kolymskii Range.

The Third Squadron, under the command of Lieutenant Colonel Tverdohlebov, was stationed in Seimchan. Pilots flew their airplanes to Iakutsk through the Oimiakon—said to be the coldest spot in the Northern Hemisphere—through the huge mountain ranges of Cherskii and Verhoianskii. It seems that this segment was the most difficult one. Pilots flew at very high elevations through the mountains and used oxygen masks. It was especially difficult for the fighter-pilots, since they were accustomed to spending not more than an hour in the air during battle. The total air time on this part of the route was four hours.

The Fourth Squadron, under the command of Hero of the Soviet Union Major Vlasov, was based in Iakutsk. Later, Lieutenant Colonel Smeliakov replaced Major Vlasov in this position. The Eighth Transport Squadron (C-47) and its airplanes were also stationed in Iakutsk. The pilots of this squadron would fly the crews to their stations after they delivered airplanes to the next point on the route.

The Fifth Squadron, under the command of Colonel Matiushkin, was based in Kirensk. The last section of the route was the shortest one—920 kilometers. The route went above the taiga between the Lena and Enisei rivers. There were no large settlements, and so rivers were the main reference points for navigators. Sometimes fog and bad weather would force pilots to fly blind for a long time, by instruments only.

In Krasnoiarsk the airplanes were inspected by the special committee of the Military Air Force. The bombers would continue to fly to the front, another forty-five hundred kilometers away. The fighter planes—with detached wings—were transported to the west of the country via railroad. The entire route, from the American factories through Canada and Alaska to the front, was fourteen thousand kilometers. During the war years, 8,094 airplanes were transported along the Krasnoiarsk-Uel'kal' route. More than 250 fighting squadrons were armed with these airplanes.[9]

The November 5, 1944, decree of the Presidium of the Supreme Soviet of the USSR and the November 25, 1944, order of the Peoples Committee for the Defense of the USSR awarded the transfer division the Red Banner Award.

For the first time in the history of aviation, the large-scale transfer of airplanes was accomplished. It was a long-distance transfer accomplished under conditions of extreme low temperatures and across sparsely populated areas.

---

[8] TsGNNKH, collection 9527, register 1, file 1888, p. 24.
[9] Al'berti, "Trassa 50 Let Spustya," *Vosdushnyi Transport.*

Number of airplanes transferred

| | | | |
|---|---|---|---|
| 1942 | 114 | 1942 | 131 |
| 1943 | 2,456 | 1943 | 2,464[10] |
| 1944 | 3,033 | | |
| 1945 | 2,482  (in 9 months) | | |

During the whole period of transfer, seventy-three airplanes were lost, not a large percentage of the total number of aircraft involved. The most difficult loss was that of 114 people.

In recent years, the search groups or "Poisk" (which means "search") were organized in Magadan, Irkutsk, and Kirensk. Thus, during the fall of 1987, young Kirensk pilots found on the Lena taiga the remains of lost pilots and pieces of the "Boston," an A-20 bomber that had crashed. The tragedy happened in March of 1943, near the Sosnovka River, twenty-eight kilometers away from town in deep taiga. Parts of the fuselage were scatted over an area with a radius of 150 meters. The search group was able to find two fragments of the aluminum layer from the fuselage and to determine the identifying number of the crashed bomber. The number was 13587, and with the help of this number we were able to find in the central archive of the Soviet Army the names of the lost pilots.

On September 1, 1988, we organized the burial cere-mony of the remains in Kirensk Central Park. The pilots' relatives—who did not know for forty-five years about the fate of their loved ones—were very thankful to the search group Poisk, and supported them in their honorable mission.

During the years of the Great Patriotic War the people of Siberia and the Siberian Far North—under difficult conditions of permafrost, lack of roads, sparse population and material resources—were able to accomplish a heroic deed. They made their contribution to victory. The heroes were the participants in the construction of a unique route and the pilots who delivered the aircraft so necessary on the front against the Germans.

The American allies also made a great contribution to the victory. American airplanes bombed Germans on the Volga; America's famous canned meat saved people from hunger; and veterans still remember American yellow shoes.

Russians remember and value American help in the war.

*Tat'iana Kosheleva is a curator in the History Department of the Irkutsk Regional Studies Museum in Russia. The museum contains more than one hundred items relating to the lend-lease program.*

---

[10] Collections of Irkutsk Museum of Regional Studies. No. 6082-9.

# The Alaska-Siberia Lend-Lease Program

*Alexander B. Dolitsky*

## Acknowledgement

*I would like to acknowledge the Fiftieth Anniversary of World War II Commemoration Committee of the U.S. Department of Defense for sponsoring this project and providing excellent resources on World War II. I am especially thankful to the staff of the National History Day Institute, University of Maryland, College Park, for organizing the seminar, "Conflict and Compromise: The Special Topics of World War II," and the participants in the Alaska-Siberia lend-lease program—Boris Dolitsky, Bill Schoeppe, Randy Acord, Gerald J. Dorsher, and Charles Binkley—who contributed their personal insights to the success of this research. My colleague at the University Museum of the University of Pennsylvania, Dr. Henry Michael, kindly reviewed this paper and made suggestions for its improvement.*

*This research is dedicated to my father, Boris A. Dolitsky, Soviet Army officer from 1939 to 1947.*

## Objectives

THE AIM OF THIS PROJECT IS TWOFOLD. FIRST IS TO record oral history by interviewing North American and Russian participants in the Alaska-Siberia lend-lease period. Most historians relied heavily on written records as a source of information for describing World War II in Alaska. Oral history of this period is virtually absent. Such testimony is urgently needed to provide an adequate interpretation of Soviet-American relations during World War II and to analyze the behavioral psychology of Russians in a conflict setting and in a hostile, foreign environment. Many Alaskans assisted Russians during the war. Their insights are critical for a better understanding of the Russian people and culture during a conflict when cooperation between allies is required. Oral testimony, employed as a method of inquiry in the project, sought to preserve the memories of those who participated in the Alaska-Siberia lend-lease program.

Second is to demonstrate, by using oral testimony, primary and secondary sources from the Alaska-Siberia lend-lease period, that the domestic needs of the United States, not purely patriotic and ideological motives, determine its foreign policies and external interests. Only after sixteen years did the United States recognize the USSR. Although on November 16, 1933, the United States and the Soviet Union confirmed their first diplomatic agreement, hostility toward each other continued.[1] Despite political tensions between the two nations, in the summer of 1941 the United States offered the USSR a generous lend-lease program that expressed the American desire for close collaboration with the USSR against their common enemies, Germany and its allies. Why did the United States offer such firm support to its former ideological and political enemy? Is history between nations with different economic and political structures always a static phenomenon, with little or no change in their relations? Or is it in constant flux, based on immediate needs and distribution of forces?

---

[1] A.P. Zatsarinsky, *Ekonomicheskiye otnosheniya SSSR s Zarubezhnymi stranami, 1917-1967* (Economic relationships of the USSR with foreign countries, 1917-1967) (Moscow: Mezhdunarodnyye otnosheniya 1967).

## The Beginning of the Great Patriotic War of the Soviet People

On June 22, 1941, fascist Germany launched a massive attack against the Soviet Union. One hundred and fifty-three German divisions crossed the Soviet border along a wide front and German planes carried out heavy bombing of border points, airfields, railway stations, and towns. At the same time, Romania, Hungary, and Finland sent a combined total of thirty-seven divisions against the Soviet Union. Along the Soviet borders were concentrated 190 divisions, comprising 5.5 million men, 3,712 tanks, 4,950 planes, 47,260 guns and mortars, and 193 military ships.[2] Fascist Italy also declared war on the Soviet Union, and Germany was further aided by Spain and Bulgaria. At the same time, Japan kept a million soldiers of the well-trained Kwantung Army ready for action along the Soviet Far East borders.

The situation at the front at the beginning of the war was extremely unfavorable for the Soviet Army. The Soviets were outnumbered nearly two to one. They suffered devastating damage from enemy air attacks that destroyed almost the entire Soviet Air Force in the first two weeks of the war. By early July 1941, Germans occupied Lithuania, a large part of Latvia, and the western territories of Belorussia and the Ukraine. German forces were approaching the Western Dvina and the upper reaches of the Dnieper. Thousands of Soviet soldiers performed unparalleled acts of bravery and, by mid-July 1941, the enemy was halted near Kiev for seventy-three days. The *Wehrmacht* killed or captured more than 660,000 Russians—about one-third of the Red Army—in the battles of Kiev. These encounters, along with the Battle of Uman, were the greatest defeats in the Russian people's history.[3] As a result of the defeat, the north, center, and the south were wide open to rapid German advance.

By November of 1941, the Germans occupied the Baltic states, Belorussia, Moldavia, most of the Ukraine, the Crimea, and a large part of Karelia, the former republic east of Finland. They had also seized a considerable territory around Leningrad and Moscow. Before the war, those parts of the country that were occupied by November 1941 had contained 40 percent of the total population of the Soviet Union and produced 63 percent of the nation's coal, 58 percent of its steel, and 38 percent of its grain. Human losses were enormous and the Soviet people's independence was at stake once again.[4]

## To Help or Not to Help, This is the Question

After the German invasion of the Soviet Union, the governments of Britain and the United States declared their support for the USSR in its struggle against fascist aggression. On June 23, 1941, president Franklin Roosevelt told the media, "Hitler's armies are today the chief dangers to the Americas." This statement contained no clear promise of Russian aid but only reflected the State Department's policy. On the next day, however, Roosevelt announced at a press conference that the United States would give all possible help to the Soviet people in their struggle against Germany and its allies; preliminary discussions with Soviet officials began on June 26, 1941.[5]

Conservatives argued nevertheless that America's aid ought to be restricted to proven friends, such as Great Britain and China. In late July and August, Congress debated this subject. Isolationists insisted that aid to Russia was aid to Communism—even that which existed in this country. At the same time, others thought the Russian front might be America's salvation. In July 1941, a public opinion poll indicated that 54 percent of Americans opposed Russian aid but, by September, those opposed declined to 44 percent, while those who favored helping Russia rose to 49 percent.[6] Consequently, based on the metamorphosis of public opinion, Roosevelt's approach to aiding the Soviets was cautious but intuitively optimistic. He distrusted them but did not think they, in contrast to the Germans, intended to conquer Europe. Roosevelt calculated that Russians would resist the German assault longer than anyone anticipated, which would help the British and perhaps preclude America's involvement.[7] Roosevelt relied heavily on the assessment of senior advisors Harry Hopkins and Averell Harriman, who urged Roosevelt to bring Russia in under lend-lease. Roosevelt still held back, however.

In July 1941, Roosevelt appointed Hopkins, Oumansky, and Purvis as an intergovernmental committee on Russian aid, and granted Hopkins' request to go to Russia on July 26. Hopkins met with Stalin and other

---

[2] A.M. Soskin, *Istoriya KPSS* (History of the Communist Party of the Soviet Union) (Moscow: Politizdat 1972).

[3] Brian Catchpole, *A Map History of Russia* (London: Butler and Tanner Ltd. 1990).

[4] B.D. Datsyuk, *Istoriya SSSR*, vol 2 (History of the USSR) (Moscow: Mysl' 1970); M.R. Kim, *History of the USSR: The Era of Socialism* (Moscow: Progress Publisher 1982).

[5] Robert H. Jones, *Roads to Russia* (Oklahoma: Oklahoma University Press, 1969).

[6] Raymond H. Dawson, *The Decision to Aid Russia, 1941* (Chapel Hill: University of North Carolina Press, 1959); Jones, *Roads to Russia*.

[7] Arnold A. Offner, *The Origins of the Second World War* (Florida: Robert E. Krieger Publishing Co., Inc. 1986).

Soviet authorities and came to the conclusion that the Russians would withstand the German attack; he cabled Washington his confidence that Russia would not collapse. In early September of 1941, Roosevelt sent Averell Harriman to Moscow as special advisor for lend-lease. Harriman—a large investor in the Soviet economy since 1918—was to work out a temporary-aid program with British representatives.

## U.S.-Soviet Lend-Lease Negotiations

On July 7, 1941, a Soviet delegation flew from Vladivostok to Nome and then on to Kodiak and Seattle for secret talks with American officials regarding aircraft deliveries to the USSR and the feasibility of Pacific supply routes. The Soviet and American delegations discussed several possible routes for shipping planes and war materials to the USSR. The first route was the sea route across the North Atlantic and around the North Cape to the ice-free arctic ports of Murmansk and Archangelsk. This route was shorter but by far the more dangerous route because the German Navy and its allies patrolled these areas very thoroughly. The second route was by ship across the Atlantic Ocean, around South Africa's Cape of Good Hope, and then north to the Iraqi port of Basra, where supplies would be loaded onto trains and transported to Soviet Central Asia via Iran. Either way, goods took too long to reach the USSR, and the desert sands of Iran ruined aircraft engines.[8]

From September 29 to October 1, 1941, representatives from Britain, the Soviet Union, and the United States attended a conference held in Moscow. This conference drew up a plan for deliveries of armaments, equipment, and foodstuffs to the Soviet Union, while the USSR in its turn agreed to provide strategic raw materials for Britain and the United States.[9] During the conference Harriman for the first time suggested delivery of United States aircraft to Russia via Alaska and Siberia using American crews. However, Stalin rejected this idea unconditionally, perhaps to avoid provoking Japan. Despite some political tension at the Moscow conference, on October 30 Roosevelt approved and on November 4, 1941, Stalin accepted $1 billion in aid to be repaid in ten years, interest free.[10]

Although the Soviet government was pleased with the aid, they complained that no serious military action had been taken by the Allies against Germany and that the Soviet Union was bearing the brunt of the war alone. Russians suggested that the British and U.S. open a second front in France or the Balkans or send troops through Iran—which the Russians and British had jointly occupied in August in order to preclude German influence there—to attack the Ukraine from the south. The Soviet government continued to insist that opening a second front in Europe would relieve pressure from enemy attacks on the Eastern Front. The Allies, however, were reluctant to initiate this plan at that time because of lack of the forces for a second front and their involvement in the Pacific and North African theaters. Churchill, Stalin, and Roosevelt understood that there was yet no agreement on joint war or peace aims, so the Allies made a commitment only to provide lend-lease support to Russia.[11]

In December 1941, the United States and the USSR signed the first lend-lease protocol to provide aid to the Soviet Union. The USSR accepted most of the lend-lease terms, but specific details had not yet been worked out. On May 29, 1942, Vyacheslav Molotov, a Soviet foreign commissar and Joseph Stalin's right hand on foreign affairs, arrived in the United States to discuss the lend-lease matters. This was the first official visit of the Soviet dignitary to American soil. Being cautious and uncertain in a formerly hostile country, he carried in his luggage some sausages, a piece of black bread, and a pistol for survival if need be.[12] The provisions show just how strained relationships were between the eastern and western allies. Nevertheless, during Molotov's visit President Roosevelt suggested that (1) American aircraft be flown to the USSR via Alaska and Siberia and (2) that Russian ships pick up lend-lease supplies from America's West Coast ports for ferrying across the Pacific to Vladivostok and other Russian Far East ports. This was in addition to two other routes (the northern run to Murmansk and the Iran route) proposed in July. In this way, lend-lease supplies could more quickly and safely reach the Ural industrial complex around Magnitogorsk via the Trans-Siberian Railway.

After careful consideration of various proposals, the best route for planes seemed to be via Alaska and

---

[8] Stan Cohen, *The Forgotten War: A Pictorial History of World War II in Alaska and Northwestern Canada* (Missoula: Pictorial Histories Publishing Company, 1981); Cohen, *The Forgotten War*, second edition, 1988.

[9] M.R. Kim, *History of the USSR*.

[10] Offner, *The Origins of the Second World War*.

[11] Ibid.; P.N. Pospelov, *Istoriya Kommunisticheskoy Partii: 1938-1945*, vol. 5, part 1 (History of the Communist Party of the Soviet Union: 1938-1945), (Moscow: Politicheskaya Literatura 1970).

[12] Robert Francaviglia, "The Alaska-Siberia Aircraft Ferry Project (1942-1945)," manuscript (Juneau: Alaska State Library 1973); Burns J. MacGregor, *Roosevelt, the Soldier of Freedom (1940-1945)* (New York: 1970).

Siberia. Although great distances were involved and the worst possible weather conditions would be encountered, the planes would be delivered in flying condition and the possibility of enemy interference was remote. American support for the Alaska-Siberia route was also based on the hope that, eventually, Siberia's air bases would be used for bombing raids on Japan.[13] The Soviets, however, were hesitant to use this route. They thought that the Alaska-Siberia route was too dangerous and impractical, that Siberian cities were not prepared to accommodate the heavy air traffic, and that the presence of Americans in the Soviet Far East would be unwanted. The Soviets were also afraid that the Pacific supply routes, and the Alaska-Siberia route in particular, would provoke Japanese military action against Russia. Nevertheless, with losses mounting on the sea run to Murmansk and the great distances involved in the Middle East, the Soviets finally agreed to open the Alaska-Siberia air route on Aug. 3, 1942.[14] The final lend-lease agreement was signed in Washington, D.C., on June 11, 1942, entitled "Agreement between governments of the USSR and USA on principles employed to the mutual assistance in fighting a war against the aggression."[15]

The Alaska-Siberia delivery route finally became a reality in August 1942. The air route connected Great Falls, Montana, Edmonton and Whitehorse, Canada, Fairbanks, Galena, and Nome, Alaska. A major field was built in Nome, the last stopping point for the planes before they left for Siberia. In Siberia airplanes continued their long trip from Uel'em through Markovo, Iakutsk, Kirensk, Krasnoiarsk, and, finally, to Novosibirsk. In the thirty-one months of the program, nearly eight thousand aircraft were sent through Great Falls for transfer to Russia.

## The Russians are Coming

On August 26, 1942, the first Soviet envoys, Col. Piskunov and Alexis A. Anisimov, members of the Soviet Purchasing Commission, arrived in Nome. On September 4, 1942, the first Russian aircraft arrived in Alaska bringing more mission members to set up permanent command stations at Ladd Field, in Fairbanks, and in Nome. By the summer of 1943, there were many Russians stationed at Fairbanks, Nome, Galena, Edmonton, and Great Falls; at the height of the program there were anywhere from 150 to 600 Soviet pilots and other personnel at Ladd Field alone.[16] Those Soviets who were assigned to work on American soil were ideologically drilled to maintain loyalty to their motherland and psychologically threatened about the possible consequences if they did not. Separate facilities were built in Fairbanks and Nome for Russian officers and other staff. The Russian government also preferred to use its own interpreters, predominantly women in uniform who had passed classified clearance procedures in the Soviet Union before coming to the United States.[17]

Although the Russian airmen who were sent to Alaska to pick up the lend-lease aircraft were guests in Alaska and the Alaska mission was regarded as a rest from combat, they tended to remain aloof from the Americans. Sometimes Soviets socialized with Americans and expressed their ideological views, but reluctantly and with great caution. For the most part, the Soviets and Americans were cordial towards one another and some of them became good acquaintances afterwards, leaving a lasting mark of a good memory and compassion for each other.[18] However, Soviet insistence that the planes be in perfect condition before being flown to Siberia caused constant delays and some antagonism between the two commands.

There were many crashes by both the Russian and American pilots, caused mainly by weather conditions but also by poor maintenance and overloading, lack of fuel, and, incidentally, a large consumption of hard liquor by Russian pilots the day before a long and dangerous journey. Bill Schoeppe remembers that the winter of 1942-43 was extremely cold in Alaska and planes had to be winterized before they could be flown out in very difficult conditions.[19] From September 1942 to September 1945, 133 planes were lost to weather conditions or pilot error—only 1.6 percent of the 7,983 planes that were delivered to the Russians.[20]

---

[13] Hubert Van Tuyll, *Feeding the Bear: American aid to the Soviet Union: 1941-1945* (New York: Greenwood Press, 1989).

[14] Cohen, *The Forgotten War* (1981); Cohen, second edition (1988); Jay H. Moor, "World War II in Alaska: The Northwest Route; A Bibliography and Guide to Primary Sources," *Alaska Historical Commission Studies in History*, No. 175 (Anchorage, Alaska: Alaska Historical Commission, 1985).

[15] Zatsarinsky, *Ekonomicheskiye otnosheniya SSSR s Zarubezhnymi stranami.*

[16] Cohen, *The Forgotten War* (1981); Cohen, second edition (1988); Moor, "World War II in Alaska: The Northwest Route; A Bibliography and Guide to Primary Sources."

[17] Randy Acord and Bill Schoeppe: personal communication, 1993.

[18] Bill Schoeppe, Randy Acord, and Charles Binkley: personal communication, 1993.

[19] Bill Schoeppe: personal communication, 1993.

[20] Oleg Chechin, "Rescue of a Soviet Navigator," *Soviet Life*, 1989, 11:39-42; Cohen, *The Forgotten War* (1981); Cohen, second edition (1988); E.F. Furler Jr., "Beneath the Midnight Sun," *Air Classics*, 1984, 20:3: pp. 25-34.

## Trust but Verify

In four years of war, the United States supplied nearly fifteen thousand aircraft to the Soviet Union. More than half were flown over the northwest route through Alaska. Looking back, some American military experts questioned whether the Russians needed all these aircraft. By 1943, the USSR was building a great number of planes in factories in the Ural Mountains and already had technical military superiority over the enemy.[21] In 1943, Soviet industry produced thirty-five thousand airplanes and twenty-four thousand tanks and self-propelled guns, compared to twenty-five thousand airplanes and eighteen thousand tanks produced by Germany.[22] In sum, despite their smaller industrial capacity and a reduced base of strategic raw materials, the Soviet Union still produced more military equipment than Germany with a claimed total output during war of 137,000 aircraft, 104,000 tanks and self-propelled guns, and 488,000 artillery pieces.[23]

According to some military analysts and to some American participants in the program, the Soviet Union was stockpiling lend-lease equipment for post-war use and probably used the air route for espionage.[24] American soldiers of the Korean War (1950-53) were puzzled to see so much American equipment captured by American troops during that conflict.[25] Evidently the Chinese and Soviets provided military aid to Korea using the very same supplies they had themselves received from the United States several years earlier. American analysts were not prepared to explain the extent and intention of Soviet secrecy during World War II—ranging from combat operations to agricultural production. Information would often have to come directly from Stalin, which led some officials to conclude that "... Stalin apparently was the only individual in the Soviet Union who had the authority to give some information".[26]

Some American experts also argue that some uranium was shipped through Great Falls to the Soviet Union and that, in May 1944, U.S. Treasury banknote plates had gone up the air route.[27] Of course, opposing views deny any such Russian conspiracy.[28]

Much information remains that speaks of the helpful U.S. attitude toward the USSR and vice versa during the war. Hints that post-war evaluation of the Soviet lend-lease program may uncover some embarrassing facts are engendered more by the context of the Cold War and by global foreign affairs policies that began during the Truman presidency than by any wrongdoing during the war. It is not surprising that the House of Representatives' hearing during the McCarthy era in the late 1940s and early 1950s exaggerated and fabricated much in order to persecute liberal thinkers, radical socialists, and those sympathetic to the Soviet Union.[29]

## Feeding the Russian Bear

From 1941 to 1945, about $12.5 billion in war materials and other supplies was shipped to the Soviet Union over four major routes.[30] In addition to military equipment, the USSR received such non-military items as cigarette cases, records, women's compacts, fishing tackle, dolls, playground equipment, cosmetics, foods, and even 13,328 sets of false teeth. The Soviet requests for food emphasized canned meat (Tushonka), fats, dried peas and beans, potato chips, powdered soups and eggs, dehydrated fruits and vegetables, and other packaged food items. Although dehydration solved shipping problems to Russia, such requests also resulted in the rapid expansion of American dehydrating facilities, which eventually influenced the domestic market and diet of the American people from the post-war period until the present.

Lend-lease accounts show that in 1945 alone, about 5.1 million tons of foodstuffs left for the Soviet Union from the United States, while their own 1945 total agriculture output reached approximately 53.5 million tons.[31] If the twelve-million-member Soviet Army received all of the foodstuffs that arrived in Russia through lend-lease from the United States, then each man and woman would have been supplied with more than a half pound of concentrated food per day for the duration of the war. Undoubtedly lend-lease food proved vital to the maintenance of adequate nutrition

---

[21] George Racey Jordan, *Major Jordan's Diaries* (New York: Harcourt Brace Jovanovich, 1952).

[22] Soskin, *Istoriya KPSS.*

[23] Kim, *History of the USSR.*

[24] Randy Acord: personal communication, 1993.

[25] Gerald Dorsher, a veteran of the Korean War: personal communication, 1993.

[26] Van Tuyll, *Feeding the Bear: American aid to the Soviet Union: 1941-1945.*

[27] Jordan, *Major Jordan's Diaries;* Jordan, *From Major Jordan's Diaries,* manuscript (Alaska State Historical Library, 1965).

[28] Bill Schoeppe: personal communication, 1993.

[29] Jay H. Moor, "World War II in Alaska: The Northwest Route; A Bibliography and Guide to Primary Sources."

[30] Van Tuyll, *Feeding the Bear: American aid to the Soviet Union: 1941-1945.*

[31] Jones, *Roads to Russia.*

levels for Soviets and other lend-lease beneficiaries. For example, in 1944, 2 percent of the United States food supply was exported to the Soviet Union, 4 percent to other lend-lease recipients, 1 percent in commercial export, and 13 percent to the United States military. This aid was only possible due to the sacrifices made by the American people and the enormous increase in American agricultural and industrial production—up 280 percent by 1944 over the 1935-1939 average.[32]

Although the Soviet government tried to minimize the importance of the lend-lease support by arguing that the United States supplies to Russia represented only 4 to 10 percent of the total Soviet Union production during the war, the aid items were essential for the survival of the Soviet Union. For example, while Soviet production of steel was about nine million tons in 1942, under lend-lease the Soviet Union received about three million tons of steel. The Soviet T-34 tank engine and Soviet aircraft made use of lend-lease aluminum. Copper shipments (about four million tons) equaled three-quarters of the entire Soviet copper production for the years 1941-1944. About 800,000 tons of non-ferrous metals (e.g. magnesium, nickel, zinc, lead, tin), a million miles of field telegraph wire, 2,120 miles of marine cable and 1,140 miles of submarine cable formed an impressive figure, especially when compared to Soviet production.[33]

In addition to non-military items, the Soviet Union also received under the lend-lease agreement: 15,000 airplanes—equivalent to 12 percent of those produced in Soviet plants; 9,000 tanks and self-propelled guns, or 10 percent of Soviet production; 362,000 lend-lease trucks and 47,000 jeeps—compared to 130,000 trucks manufactured in the Soviet Union. All this equipment greatly contributed to the mobility and survival of the Red Army. Unfortunately, many of these materials deteriorated because they were poorly maintained or wastefully stockpiled due to Soviet carelessness and the inefficient state infrastructure. However, most of the materials were widely used and often admired by Red Army soldiers. In fact, the legendary Soviet air ace and three-time Hero of the Soviet Union, Alexander Pokryshkin, used a lend-lease Airacobra to shoot down forty-eight of the fifty-nine Nazi planes credited to him.[34]

Many non-military and military items were funnelled through Great Falls. The United States received payment from Russia for only a small fraction of these items. However, Bill Schoeppe, a resident of Juneau and then an airplane mechanic at Ladd Field, Fairbanks, remembers that two airplanes loaded with ten thousand pounds of gold—valued at about $5.6 million in 1943—traveled from Siberia to the Lower 48 in 1943. No written record has been found so far of that transaction or of other transactions of a similar nature. The records of the Foreign Economic Administration's (FEA) Division of Soviet Supply (DSS) have disappeared. The National Archives does not have them and neither does the Department of State. In the early 1970s many of the FEA records were inadvertently shredded, and DSS records may have been among those that were destroyed.[35]

## Thanks, but No Thanks

Undoubtedly, the Alaska-Siberia lend-lease agreement is a focal point in modern history. Many Alaskans worked together with Russians on the cooperative program. Although the two nations still faced possible invasion by the Japanese, the northwest route was a vehicle for hope. Just a few months after the tide of war turned in favor of the Allies, however, expectations of continued post-war cooperation shifted to mutual suspicion and antagonism.

Franklin D. Roosevelt was most instrumental in holding the Allies together against their enemies during the war and was responsible for implementation of the lend-lease program to the Soviet Union. Roosevelt gambled four times on strategic planning: He predicted Britain's survival and he won. He believed that Russia would withstand German attack and he won again. He was confident that Germany and Japan would eventually be defeated and he was right a third time. And he further speculated that by not attaching a dollar sign or political strings to Russian aid, he could secure their friendship and cooperation after the war. But this time he lost. He lost because he naively believed that sincerity and good intentions would change Communist objectives against capitalist countries. Roosevelt held the illusion that lend-lease was a channel of communication with the Soviet people that would eventually bring about democracy in the Soviet Union and cause partnership with the West to flourish. In reality it was only a channel of communication with one Soviet—Joseph Stalin. In fact, few Soviets knew much about the magnitude of American aid to Russia and the sacrifices connected with the program.[36]

---

[32] Ibid.; Van Tuyll, *Feeding the Bear: American aid to the Soviet Union: 1941-1945.*

[33] Jones, *Roads to Russia*; Van Tuyll, *Feeding the Bear: American aid to the Soviet Union: 1941-1945.*

[34] Jones, *Roads to Russia*; personal communication with Pokryshkin's son, 1991.

[35] Moor, "World War II in Alaska: The Northwest Route; A Bibliography and Guide to Primary Sources."

[36] Boris Dolitsky, Soviet Army officer from 1939 to 1947: personal communication, 1993.

Relying on unwritten rules of political reciprocity, Roosevelt was often puzzled that the Soviet government refused to permit Western allies to send military observers and technicians to the Eastern Front. He was also puzzled by the Soviets' vigorous insistence on the opening of a second front in Europe early in the war, this when the U.S. was already involved in military activities in the Pacific and North African theaters, as well as with lend-lease convoys to Europe. These Allied activities diverted significant enemy forces from the Eastern Front. Sometimes Roosevelt was irritated that the Soviets could not understand the complexity of the lend-lease delivery to the Soviet Union and its logistics; further, the U.S. Congress and 49 percent of the American people were consistently reluctant to support Soviet aid. The American administration often quarreled with the Soviets about delivery schedules. The Soviets even refused to open the Alaska-Siberia lend-lease route until August of 1942, when they realized that they might not have other alternatives. In addition, Soviet authorities insisted upon more rigid specifications for the war equipment than did, for instance, the war offices of Britain. As a result of all these complications and miscommunication, American officials were unable to adequately observe the use made of Western equipment. They had to rely largely on rather vague and general reports made by Soviet authorities that great quantities of American equipment, for example, were being used in the 1945 offensive.

But what was most astonishing to American representatives was Soviet reluctance to acknowledge, either in the press or in public, the support they received from the United States. At the end of the war, the Soviet government regarded lend-lease as an insignificant 4 percent of the total industrial production of Soviet enterprises. The production of Soviet industry, of course, has always been exaggerated to demonstrate the accomplishments and advantages of the Soviet socialist state. On June 19, 1962, Soviet General Secretary Nikita Khruschev asserted that "... during World War II American monopolists made billions of dollars on war deliveries. They fattened themselves on the blood of people lost during two world wars."[37] The aid program was pictured by Soviet historians as an effort to expand American imperialism and to use Soviet resistance for their own mobilization.

Soviets efforts to minimize the role of lend-lease may have been motivated by considerations of national prestige and image. Only recently have Soviet scholars been admitting that lend-lease actually contributed to the war effort. Although during the war the Soviet government gave decorations to a number of Westerners, and it recently honored seamen who had served on the Murmansk run, they still emphasize the small size of lend-lease in relation to Soviet production and the heroism of the Soviet people in delivering lend-lease supplies.[38]

*Alexander B. Dolitsky teaches Russian studies at the University of Alaska in Juneau.*

---

[37] Nikita Khruschev, cited in Jones, *Roads to Russia*.

[38] Pyotr Petrov, "When We Were Allies", *Soviet Life*, 1991a, March issue, part 1, pp. 42-4; "When We Were allies", *Soviet Life*, 1991b, May issue, part 2: pp. 18-19.

# The Alaska-Siberia Friendship Route

*David S. Raisman*
*Translated by Katerina Solovjova*

THE BRIDGE OF FRIENDSHIP BETWEEN ASIA AND America is a result of the establishment of the famous air route between Alaska and Siberia. The State Committee of Defense formed an air force division that consisted of civilian specialists and servicemen. According to the lend-lease agreement, the division would transfer American fighter planes from the U.S. via Alaska, Chukotka, Kolyma, Siberia, and farther to the Eastern Front.

Professor Jacobs correctly noted that the U.S. and Russia had special relations during World War II. For the Russian government this was against Hitler's Germany as well as against the Russian people. This was an effort to save the totalitarian regime. It is well known that you cannot preserve the peace by force. You can achieve peace only through understanding. The peace is born with the help of joint efforts of diplomats, state officials, and friendship. A good example of this was the air route between Alaska and Siberia.

Papanin, the famous polar pilot and Hero of the Soviet Union, remembers: "We decided to use a relay-race method of transfer. Each of all five squadrons worked only on its part of the route and got very familiar with it. The most difficult part was between Seimchan and Iakutsk, twelve hundred kilometers in length. Here the airplanes flew over the Cherskii and Verkhoianskii ranges near the pole of cold [the geographical point thought to be the coldest in the Northern Hemisphere—ed.]. "

The route went over the taiga and tundra. Pilots were able to observe not only the beauty of nature, but also the remains of economic activity of the Northeast Direc-

torate of Corrective Labor Camps of the Peoples' Committee of Internal Affairs. It was one of the Gulag branches. The pilots saw the camp structures, the dumps near mountain mines, scattered fishing, hunting, and reindeer herding settlements, and the car convoys that were going down Kolyma roads.

After the beginning of the war, the Dal'stroi Construction Department got fewer of the prisoner-convicts that had provided cheap labor. This immediately adversely affected the volume of gold mining.

| Year | Number of Prisoners | Volume of Gold Mined |
|------|--------------------|--------------------|
| 1940 | 176,685 | 80.02 tons |
| 1941 | 148,301 | 75.8 tons |

As a result, people who had worked on contract with the Dal'stroi Construction Department were not allowed to move back to the central regions of the country. Many prisoners who were the victims of the Stalin repression received an arbitrary extension of their sentence. That caused the increase in the number of civilian workers in the Dal'stroi Construction Department.

| Year | Number of Prisoners | Percent who were civilian |
|------|--------------------|--------------------------|
| 1941 | 148,301 | 62.4 |
| 1942 | 126,044 | 76.4 |

Later in the war the number of prisoners in Kolyma and Chukotka decreased. In 1944 only ninety-one thousand prisoners worked in the Dal'stroi enterprises and continued to mine strategic metals—gold and tin—for

A work crew near Susuman, Magadan, in Siberia, takes a break while building a memorial in 1972. A lend-lease A-20 bomber had crashed at the site thirty years before. *(Photo courtesy of the author)*

the country. Prisoner labor was used during construction of airports and runways at Seimchan, Omolon, and Chaibuha. U.S. vice president Henry Wallace visited sites in Kolyma in May of 1944. Russian officials showed him Magadan, settlements, mines, and camps that had been cleaned ahead of time and had thereby acquired a civilized look for the occasion.

The lend-lease aid that came from the United States helped a lot of people of Kolyma and Chukotka. Northeast Russia would regularly receive supplies of food, medicine, transport, and tools. Of course, the real help to the front was the transfer of American fighter planes by Russian pilots.

For a long time the Alaska-Siberia route was considered to be the secret mission of the Allies. The number of transferred airplanes and personnel losses during this operation were kept secret—although the Soviet press did publish some figures.

A work group of the editorial board of "The Motherland Defenders" Memory Book for the region organized a search for the residents of Kolyma and Chukotka who had been called up for military service and who had been killed, declared missing, or who had died of illness or of their wounds. Through their search the group was able to uncover information that lends more accuracy to the biographies of the specialists of this air force division.

The analysis of the losses of division personnel (the book is currently in the Iakutsk Archive) shows us that forty-one airmen were killed on the route between Fairbanks and Iakutsk, including seventeen crew: twenty-five officers, four technicians, five sergeants, and seven civilians. The first losses occurred in 1942 when two airplanes crashed near Markovo and two airmen were declared missing.

Most of the air crashes occurred in the May-to-June period, but, in reality, machines and people were lost every month. In 1943, ten crews wrecked; in 1945, there was only one. By that time pilots had become more experienced in flying foreign fighting machines. Also, by then the aircraft were equipped with the necessary navigation instruments. Among the crashed airplanes were four C-47s and four A-20s.

According to official documents, 115 people were killed during the entire time the air route was in use. There are several graves in the area of Kolyma and Chukotka: six people in Markovo, seven in Seimchan, and nineteen in Uel'kal'. One crew of three crashed in the Bering Sea on May 30, 1944. The three were declared missing.

There are graves of only four crews comprising eight people in Uel'kal': Purim—February 1943; Spiridonov, Konsuhov, Pehota—May 29, 1943; Sengenio—December 24, 1944; Zotov, Zverono, Iashkin—February 29, 1944. The last crew died in Nome, but was buried in Chukotka. Nine people died in Fairbanks: Kisel'nikov, Korev, Savenko, Nureev, Murav'iov, Zaremba, Moiseev, Skarednov, and Shchepochihin. In 1946, nine Soviet specialists who had died in Alaska were reburied at Fort Richardson near Anchorage. There are another five Soviets buried there, although how they came to die is not known: Aksuka, Kal'ia, Diskov, Gustavson, and an unknown soldier.

In total, there were fourteen Soviet citizens buried in Alaska. The relatives of these people were told that they had been in Chukotka. Thus, we were able to discover that our losses in Kolyma, Chukotka and Alaska were bigger—around fifty people.

We continue to search for the people who transferred airplanes to the front and others who built them. For example, we look for the school girls from Buffalo who collected money to build a fighter plane and gave that aircraft to one of the best pilots of the squadron, Vladimir Suvorov. We have tried to find the name of the American aircraft mechanic who died along with Russian engineer Major Kisel'nikov during the test flight of a bomber in December of 1942.

The communities, students, and other local organizations expended much effort and established memorials at the sites of aircraft wrecks: five in Kolyma and two in Chukotka. In 1990 the workers of the Northeast Zoloto Union and Bering Straits Native Corporation organized a meeting of war veterans who labored over the air route between Alaska and Siberia.

At present we are preparing a textbook, *Our Region in the War Years*, and an educational program on Alaska for the students of the Magadan region. We plan to introduce all the materials and facts related to the contribution of the Allies to victory. The youth should know the true history of the Asian-Pacific region.

I would like to invite American and Japanese authors to help us write a joint textbook on the war in the Pacific from 1939 to 1945. This textbook will be used by school students. We invite historians to express their different points of view. The most important thing for us is to understand the problems of civilization. Submissions for the textbook should be sent to:

Upravlenie obrazovaniia administratsii
goroda Magadana Ul. Gor'kogo 2,
Magadan 685000
Nachal'nik Upravleniia
Maksimova G.V.

Maksimova G.V.
Directorate Chief
Magadan Directorate of Education Administration
2 Gor'kogo Street,
Magadan 685000

*David S. Raisman is a journalist and teacher in the Siberian city of Magadan. He is also a docent of the Department of Education of the International Pedagogical University in the same city.*

# The Hula Operation:
# The Top Secret Soviet-American Naval Lend-Lease Operation in Alaska in 1945

*Richard A. Russell*

## Introduction

FOR SIX MONTHS IN THE SPRING AND SUMMER OF 1945, the U.S. Navy trained Soviet Navy combat crews—about 12,400 men—in the operation of 149 American naval vessels planned for transfer to the Soviet Pacific Ocean Fleet under lend-lease. Based at Cold Bay, Alaska, Operation HULA placed American and Russian sailors side by side in the largest and most difficult transfer program of World War II.[1] Yet, in spite of its unique purpose to both equip and train Soviet amphibious forces for the climactic fight against Japan, the particulars of this transaction have escaped serious scrutiny.[2]

The purpose of this paper is to provide an overview of the operation's genesis and execution.

In the 1930s, the potential for Washington and Moscow to cooperate in restraining Tokyo—which, after all, was one of the unspoken objectives of American recognition of the Soviet Union in 1933—was not realized beyond wistful ideas and the few hollow gestures they produced. Two examples are Stalin's pledge to station a battleship in the Far East if permitted to contract for its construction in the United States, and the brief visit to Vladivostok by an American squadron in 1937.

This period is familiar enough so that it need not be repeated here. Suffice it to say that by the time of Japan's attack on Pearl Harbor in December 1941, the staggering success of the German attack on the Soviet Union and the acquiescence of Japan to the movement of American lend-lease goods to the Soviet Far East via the North Pacific left Stalin with few means and little desire to open the two-front war that Franklin D. Roosevelt want-

---

[1] Soviet naval personnel trained at several U.S. locations during the war, including: the Washington Navy Yard, for diving school; Elizabeth City, North Carolina, for pilot training; and Miami, Florida, at the Submarine Chaser Training Center. See RG 19, Bureau of Ships, General Correspondence, 1940-1945, in various files, from twenty boxes of Soviet-related lend-lease materials, beginning with Box 495, at the Washington National Records Center, Suitland, Maryland. Unfortunately, the files are not arranged in chronological or subject order.

[2] See Edward Pinkowski's "Soviet Trainees in U.S.A. in World War II," *Russian Review* vol. 6, No. 1 (Autumn 1946), pp. 11-16. Though pertinent navy records remained classified until the early 1970s, Pinkowski's is a reasonably accurate description of the operation. Major works by American and Soviet historians fail to mention Cold Bay; see Samuel E. Morison, *History of United States Naval Operations in World War II*, vol. 14, *Victory in the Pacific, 1945* (Boston: Little, Brown and Company, 1960); G. M. Gelfond, *Sovetskii Flot v Voine s Yapone* (Moscow: Voennoe Izdaltelstvo Ministerstva Oboroni Soiuza SSR, 1958); and E. Zakharov, et al., *Tikhookeanskii Flor* (Moscow: Voennoe Izdaltelstvo, Ministerstva Oboroni SSR, 1966). D. Colt Denfeld, in *Cold Bay in World War II: Fort Randall and Russia, Naval Lend-Lease* (Alaska District: U.S. Army Corps of Engineers, 1988): pp. 28-36, reprinted large portions of the navy's Naval Administration for his booklet on Cold Bay and environs, which began as an environmental impact study; CINCPOA, "Administrative history of the North Pacific Area," vol. 156, *United States Naval Administration in World War II* (Washington: Department of the Navy, 1945): pp. 264-278, on which Denfeld relies, reprinted large sections of the final report submitted by the commanding officer of HULA-2, which is found in Top Secret (declass) *War Diary of Cold Bay, Naval Detachment*, "September 1945," WWII War Diaries, Box 462, Operational Archives, Naval Historical Center, Washington, D.C. (hereafter "NHC" is Operational Archives, etc.). An earlier version was presented in brief at the Conference of Soviet and American Military Historians held at the National Defense University in Washington, D.C., in April 1990.

ed.[3] This situation prevailed until 1944, with a regular ebb and flow of hope and frustration on the American side, which sought basing rights for its aircraft in Siberia and suffered concern for the security of the lend-lease route.[4]

# I

In October 1944, at a meeting which included Prime Minister Churchill, Ambassador W. Averell Harriman, and General John R. Deane, head of the U.S. Military Mission in Moscow, Stalin revived Allied hopes for collaboration against Japan with a pledge to commence offensive operations against Japan three months after the defeat of Germany. One of the requirements for Soviet participation, according to Stalin, was a buildup of a reserve of supplies in the Soviet Far East.[5]

Accordingly, Soviet representatives later presented General Deane with a list of supplies required to support their entry into the Pacific War, which they wanted considered apart from the lend-lease supplies already allocated to them under the annual agreement, in this case the Fourth Protocol. Deane treated this requisition as a military project, working through the Office of the Joint Chiefs of Staff (JCS) rather than the Soviet Protocol Committee.[6] The Joint Logistics Committee (JLC) of the JCS approved the request, now codenamed "MILE-POST," with the proviso that its fulfillment not adversely affect existing or anticipated operations in Europe or the Pacific. The JLC also recommended the exclusion of items that could not be delivered in 1945. The initial request for small naval vessels was eliminated on this basis.[7]

The original MILEPOST list was under consideration by a subcommittee of the JLC when, on December 5, 1944, Admiral V.A. Alafusov, chief of staff of the Soviet Navy, presented to Rear Admiral Clarence E. Olsen, head of the navy division of the U.S. Military Mission in

Moscow, a list of ships and equipment necessary to expand the Soviet Pacific Fleet, preparatory to entering the war against Japan. According to Alafusov, he intended that the naval requirements outlined in MILE-POST be superseded by the new list. In Washington, the staff of Admiral King, Commander in Chief of the U.S. Fleet and Chief of Naval Operations, established priorities on naval vessels and equipment which did not appear on both of the Fourth Protocol and MILEPOST lists.[8] Olsen insisted, then, that the MILEPOST list be coordinated with the new Soviet Navy list into one final request before it was transmitted to the authorities in Washington.[9] On December 20 Olsen and Alafusov agreed to a single request for vessels, aircraft, and equipment. The revised request listed seventeen different types of surface ships, including frigates and minesweepers, two types of aircraft, including three hundred torpedo-carrying A-26 light bombers, and a variety of port equipment and electronic components.[10] Eventually, the JCS asked the Protocol Committee to administer MILEPOST, which, as Annex III, became part of the Fourth Soviet Protocol in April 1945.[11]

# II

The distinguishing feature of the proposed transfer was, of course, the commitment in considerable time and resources to train Soviet naval personnel on board the lend-lease vessels. In December 1944, General Deane reported that "[Rear Admiral] Olsen considers it urgent that a program for training of personnel and for delivery of some of each type ship should be set up at once" to instruct the Soviet crews in the operation of their ships before the Soviet Union entered the war. Deane and Olsen both agreed that the Soviet needs were worthwhile and felt that it was undesirable "to withdraw any ships from active combat longer than required for turnover," but expressed concern for the inexperience of

---

[3] For a comprehensive treatment of Soviet-Japanese relations in the 1930s, featuring a climactic military denouement, see Alvin D. Coox, *Nomonhan: Japan Against Russia, 1939*, 2 vols. (Stanford, Calif.: Stanford University Press, 1985); see also George Alexander Lensen, *The Strange Neutrality: Soviet-Japanese Relations during the Second World War, 1941-1945* (Tallahassee, Fla.: The Diplomatic Press, 1972), pp. 123-127; on FDR's inquiry about Soviet intentions in the Pacific War, see Hugh Phillips, "Mission to America: Maksim M. Litvinov in the United States, 1941-43," *Diplomatic History* vol. 12, No. 3 (Summer 1988): pp. 262-264. An overall treatment of Soviet-American relations during this period, which includes the aborted battleship deal, is Thomas R. Maddux, *Years of Estrangement: American Relations with the Soviet Union, 1933-1941* (Tallahassee, Fla.: University Presses of Florida, 1908).

[4] See Grace Person Hayes, *The History of the Joint Chiefs of Staff in World War II: The War Against Japan* (Annapolis, Md.: Naval Institute Press, 1982), pp. 130-135, 272-277.

[5] Ibid., pp. 245-247.

[6] Ibid., p. 248.

[7] Coakley and Leighton, *Global Logistics*, pp. 690-691; Deane, *Strange Alliance*, pp. 226-239; and Top Secret (declassified) Memorandum, DeLany to King, dated October 22, 1944, which contains the list of naval vessels and port equipment requested by the USSR.

[8] Top Secret (declassified) Memorandum, DeLany to King, "Naval Vessels and Port Facilities for Russia", n.d., Strategic Plans Division Records, Pacific Section, 1940-1946 (Series XII), File R-3 (1), Box 172, Operational Archives, NHC (hereafter SPDR).

[9] Top Secret (declassified) Dispatch, Deane to War Department, dated December 13, 1944, SPDR.

[10] Top Secret (declassified) Dispatch, Deane to War Department, dated December 20, 1944, SPDR

[11] Coakley and Leighton, *Global Logistics*, p. 691.

their potential ally in the types to be transferred.[12]

In early January 1945, Fleet Admiral N.G. Kuznetsov, People's Commissar for the Soviet Navy (its commander in chief), inquired as to the feasibility of receiving the MILEPOST vessels in the Aleutians or Dutch Harbor "in order to better preserve security of turnover and to eliminate need of great numbers of Soviets having to traverse whole of US."[13] The latter referred to Kuznetsov's desire to move approximately three thousand Soviet sailors destined for Alaska by ship from Murmansk to the U.S. East Coast. As the admiral later explained his plan, trains could carry the sailors across the United States to the West Coast, and ships could carry them from the West Coast to Alaska.[14] The extant documentation is not precise, but over the next four weeks just prior to the Yalta Conference, it seems the only decision reached was to rule out Dutch Harbor as a training and transfer site.[15]

During the Yalta Conference, at a meeting of the American and Soviet chiefs of staff on February 8, Admiral Kuznetsov stated that Kodiak was the Soviet government's second preference after Dutch Harbor for a transfer site, but was informed by Admiral King that Cold Bay already had been selected. Though not familiar with Cold Bay, Kuznetsov accepted once its location on the map was pointed out to him. With respect to transporting Soviet sailors across the Atlantic Ocean and U.S., King suggested that Soviet crews could be moved in empty convoy ships on their return leg to North America. But King informed Kuznetsov that the poor shipping situation in the Pacific would present great difficulties in moving the crews from the U.S. West Coast to Alaska. The Soviet admiral did not offer to ship them in Soviet vessels, and the matter was deferred.[16] A directive issued by Admiral King about one week after the end of the Yalta Conference officially established the transfer program.[17]

Under the original scheme, the navy planned to train crews for 180 vessels at Cold Bay. The vessels included thirty frigates (PFs), twenty-four minesweepers (AMs), thirty-six wooden-hulled minesweepers (YMSs), fifty-six subchasers (SCs), thirty large infantry landing craft (LCI[L])s, and four floating repair shops (YRs).[18] After the completion of training, the vessels would be transferred to Soviet custody, and then steam in convoy part of the way under American escort, to their prospective home port—usually Vladivostok via Petropavlovsk.

## III

Remote Cold Bay, lying to the extreme southwest tip of the Alaska Peninsula, satisfied the deep concern for secrecy that both sides desired. Secrecy was especially precious to the Soviet government, which was not at this point prepared to compromise its status as a neutral in the Pacific War.[19] Moreover, it was expected that the military establishment there—Fort Randall and the recently decommissioned naval air auxiliary facility—could be quickly rehabilitated to provide adequate housing and support, but would not otherwise require significant expansion because most training was scheduled to take place aboard ship. The limited repair facilities at Cold Bay meant that most ships would have to be repaired and outfitted on the U.S. West Coast.[20]

Captain William S. Maxwell, commander of Naval Detachment 3294 (HULA-2), recommissioned Cold Bay when he arrived on March 19, 1945. Contrary to reports he had obtained in Washington, the base was in no condition to receive Soviet trainees. Miserable weather and the general layout of the base, the facilities of which were spread across seven miles of territory, presented serious problems in the effort to rapidly rehabilitate the base.[21]

The commanding officer and his staff loosely interpreted his instructions to adapt training to the conditions at Cold Bay. Maxwell believed thorough shore-based training on equipment and procedures would help to prevent casualties among the Soviet personnel—and damage to the vessels once shipboard exercises began. But a contingent of nine representatives of the Soviet Purchasing Commission, which arrived on March 23, asserted a different view. They expressed disappointment with what they considered to be the excessive amount of shore-based training outlined in the tentative plan presented by Maxwell's staff. To reach an accom-

---

[12] Ibid.

[13] Top Secret (declassified) Dispatch, U.S. Naval Attache (Moscow) to King, dated January 9, 1945, SPDR.

[14] U.S. Department of State, *FRUS: The Conferences at Malta and Yalta, 1945* (Washington, D.C.: Government Printing Office, 1955), pp. 760-762.

[15] Top Secret (declassified) Memorandum, COMINCH [King] to COMNORPAC [Fletcher], dated January 18, 1945, and Secret (declassified) Letter, Yakimov to King, dated January 30, 1945, SPDR.

[16] *FRUS, Malta and Yalta, 1945*, pp. 760-762.

[17] See references in Top Secret (declassified) Memorandum, Bieri to VCNO, dated March 2, 1945, SPDR.

[18] Ibid. Cold Bay was one of three locations from which MILEPOST vessels were transferred. Several vessels sailed directly from West Coast ports to the Soviet Union and other, smaller craft, such as patrol torpedo boats, were shipped on Soviet cargo vessels.

[19] See Lensen, *The Stranqe Neutrality*, pp. 123-127.

[20] Ibid.

[21] Diary, Cold Bay, pp. 4-5.

modation, the American and Soviet personnel worked day and night over the next week to design a program for the first training cycle. The new plan was agreeable to both sides and served as model for all training cycles.[22]

Training was planned by ship types, with a set number of days allotted for shipboard and shore-based training. Captain Maxwell believed that deviations from this fixed schedule might undermine the speed with which the American team delivered fighting ships to the Soviet Navy. This proved to be the case when the prospective crews of twelve Admirable-class minesweepers, six wooden-hulled minesweepers, and twenty subchasers—220 officers and 1,895 enlisted men—began the first shore-based training program on April 16. Soviet personnel, it was found, knew almost nothing about radar and sonar and very little about working the engineering plants, and so training in these areas was especially intense. For training, personnel were divided by ship types and then by prospective crews for individual ships. Among each crew a nucleus of sailors was identified who were familiar with basic ship handling, but even they required instruction with regard to the special characteristics of their ship type.[23]

Unforseen delays in installing and removing equipment from the transfer vessels upset the initial schedule. A total of six minesweepers arrived with electronic equipment that was not authorized for transfer to the Soviet Navy. In some ships the unauthorized equipment was removed. Another minesweeper and nine subchasers required major repairs at Dutch Harbor. Round trips of nearly four hundred miles to Dutch Harbor delayed the subchaser program by eight days. These unfortunate circumstances were somewhat ameliorated by representatives of the Bureau of Ships who exercised their authority to amend equipment lists and improve the coordination between Cold Bay and the West Coast shipyards.[24]

The most efficient training program conducted at Cold Bay concerned the transfer of thirty large infantry landing craft in two fifteen-ship programs. During this phase, HULA-2 instructors trained one hundred Soviet naval officers and eight hundred enlisted men in general ship operation and in amphibious warfare, such as attack formations and beaching. The second group of landing craft completed their shakedowns one week ahead of schedule and were transferred at the end of July 1945.[25]

In terms of size, armament, and cost, the thirty Tacoma-class frigates were the most significant vessels transferred at Cold Bay. They mounted three 3-inch dual-purpose guns and two twin 40-ram antiaircraft guns, measured 304 feet in length, displaced 2,100 tons, and possessed a design speed of approximately twenty knots.[26] Many of the vessels scheduled for transfer to the Soviet Navy were veterans of escort duty in the southwest Pacific Theater.[27]

Navy Detachment 3294 scheduled the first frigate training cycle to begin on June 14 and to last twenty-five days. A group of nine frigates arrived from the West Coast on the 14th of June and, following a material inspection by American and Soviet personnel, began to receive the Soviet crews.

The transfer experience of *Coronado* (PF-38) was typical of the program at Cold Bay. Soviet officers and enlisted men reported on board in small groups beginning June 18. Shipboard training began in earnest on the 26th, although *Coronado* did not get underway until two days later, when Soviet gunners fired the ship's guns for the first time. The prospective commanding officer came aboard five days before his crew took over control of the ship on June 30. Their performance earned high marks from the American captain who praised their ability to handle the warship and their "amazing" cooperation in spite of the language barrier.[28] By July 1, the complete Soviet crew of twelve officers and 178 enlisted men was embarked.[29] Simultaneously, most of the American crew departed, so that by July 7 a nucleus of only four officers and forty-four enlisted men remained to decommission the ship.[30] American and Soviet crews trained every day, so that the task of training the prospective crews of ten frigates—approximately two thousand officers and

[22] Ibid., p. 4.

[23] Ibid., pp. 6-7.

[24] Ibid., pp. 8-13.

[25] Ibid., pp. 14-15. The tabbed section for "May 1945" contains a copy of the syllabus used for the shakedown exercises of the LCI(L)s, including diagrams of various maneuvers and approaches to a beach.

[26] U.S. Navy Department, Bureau of Ships, *Ship's Data: U.S. Naval Vessels*, vol. 2, *Mine Vessels (Less CM & DM), Patrol Vessels, Landing Ships and Craft* (NAVSHIPS 250-011 April 15, 1945) (Washington: Government Printing Office, 1946), pp. 106-113.

[27] Individual ship histories are found in *Dictionary of American Fighting Ships*, 8 vols. (Washington: Naval Historical Center, 1959-1981); Top Secret (declassified) Memorandum, DeLany to King, dated October 22, 1944, notes that the "Frigates have been found unsuited for tropical service in the Pacific."

[28] Secret (declassified) War Diary of USS *Coronado* (PF-38), "June 1945," pp. 3-4, Box 760, WWII War Diaries, NHC.

[29] Diary, Cold Bay, pp. 15-16.

[30] *Coronado*, "July 1945," pp. 1-2.

enlisted men—was completed as scheduled on July 8.[31] Most of the next three days was spent fueling the ships, taking on provisions, and otherwise preparing them for transfer to the Soviet Navy. The formal transfer ceremony took place on the afternoon of the 12th.[32] Three days later the first ten frigates steamed out of Cold Bay and set course for Petropavlovsk on the Kamchatka Peninsula.[33]

The HULA-2 unit transferred a second increment of minesweepers ahead of schedule, so that by the end of July, 100 vessels out of the original 180 were in Soviet hands. Less successful, the subchaser program continued to be trouble-plagued and threatened to upset Captain Maxwell's October 1 transfer deadline. Shoddy repair work and supply shortages in Seattle were the major causes of difficulty. By highlighting the importance of Soviet-American cooperation, Maxwell was able to substitute subchasers on duty with the Thirteenth Naval District for the unsatisfactory vessels originally intended for transfer.[34]

The Soviet-American team accelerated their efforts to transfer the remaining vessels when they received the news that the Soviet Union had entered the war against Japan at midnight, August 8/9, 1945. The commanding officer noted that the Soviet personnel seemed genuinely pleased with their new status as allies of the Americans. Navy Detachment 3294 completed the final shore-based training of 3,700 Soviet officers and enlisted men on August 25, raising the total of Soviet naval personnel trained at Cold Bay to about 12,400. In late August and early September, training was limited to that instruction needed by the Soviets to navigate their ships home. This effort to transfer as many ships as possible was aided by the Soviet Navy, which returned sailors previously trained at Cold Bay to serve as nucleus crews for the remaining vessels.[35]

Two frigates were transferred on September 2 and four more on September 4. The program ended the following day, when Maxwell received a directive to cease all lend-lease activities. By this time, 149 ships had been transferred to the Soviet Navy—142 days after the start of the program. Vessels still en route to Cold Bay were ordered to return to Seattle. The four frigates transferred on the 4th remained for further training and shakedown until the 17th, when they departed for Petropavlovsk. Maxwell then decommissioned the base.

## IV

One writer called the vessels transferred at Cold Bay "part of the price to secure Soviet intervention in the Pacific war against Japan."[36] Indeed, as part of MILEPOST, the vessels leased to the Soviet Union were intended for use against the Japanese armed forces. Yet, the U.S. Navy's success in eradicating Japanese seapower, the strategic bombing of Japan, and the success of the atomic bomb rendered invalid much of the original concept of U.S. and Soviet operations in northeast Asia. Nonetheless, at Cold Bay, Maxwell learned from the senior Soviet officer, Rear Admiral B.D. Popov, that the landing craft trained by Navy Detachment 3294 in July led the attack against Paramushiro in the Kurile Islands, just ten days after their arrival in Petropavlovsk. Others participated in operations against Japanese positions in North Korea and on Sakhalin Island.

The lend-lease operation at Cold Bay was successful in spite of the language barrier, the constant impediment of bad weather, and the poor condition of many of the prospective transfer vessels. In this respect HULA-2 stands as a rare example of successful Soviet-American collaboration in the closing months of the war. At a time of increasingly uncertain relations, Soviet and American personnel at Cold Bay escaped the distrust which came to characterize relations between Washington and Moscow. It stands as one of the many minor issues which, if fully examined, contribute to the historiography of Soviet-American relations and a greater understanding of the onset of the Cold War.[37]

*Since 1989, Richard A. Russell has been a historian at the Naval Historical Center, Washington Navy Yard.*

---

[31] *Coronado*, "July 1945," p. 1. This war diary and the war diary of Cold Bay report that ten frigates were transferred from this cycle, which contradicts *Department of the Navy, Ship's data: U.S. Naval Vessels*, vol. 2, Secret (declassified) NAVSHIPS 250-012 dated 1 January 1949 (Washington: Bureau of Ships, 1949), which reported that eleven were transferred on July 13. A Confidential (declassified) "List of Lend-Lease Craft transferred by the United States Government to the Government of the Union of Soviet Socialist Republics..." found in the Reference Files, NHC confirms the transfer of ten frigates on July 12, 1945.

[32] Ibid., p. 1.

[33] Ibid., p. 1.

[34] Diary, Cold Bay, p. 19.

[35] Ibid., pp. 22-23.

[36] Jurg Meister, *Soviet Warships of the Second World War* (York: Arco Publishing Company, Inc., 1977), p. 145.

[37] The story of the fate of the naval lend-lease vessels following the end of the war may warrant study in its own right, inasmuch as the Soviet government was not inclined to return the transferred vessels in accordance with the lend-lease agreement and in spite of repeated requests for their return by Washington. Protracted and somewhat acrimonious negotiations were conducted during the Truman and Eisenhower Administrations with the result that some of the vessels were returned, such as the frigates in 1949; some were written off by the Soviets as unsea-

worthy and sunk in view of American observers; and a few were purchased. An overall settlement on lend-lease aid to the Soviet Union was not made until 1972. See, for example, U.S. Department of State, *Foreign Relations of the United States, 1949*, vol. 5, *Eastern Europe; The Soviet Union* (Washington, D.C.: Government Printing Office, 1976), pp. 689-690; and George C. Herring, Jr., *Aid to Russia, 1941-1946: Strategy, Diplomacy, the Origins of the Cold War* (New York: Columbia University Press, 1973), pp. 296-301.

# Historic Preservation

The Henderson River bridge on Attu.
*(Photograph by Charles E. Diters, U.S. Fish and Wildlife Service)*

# Recent Archeological Investigations
## of World War II Material
## in Kiska Harbor, Aleutian Islands

*Larry E. Murphy*
*and Daniel J. Lenihan*

IN 1985, AS PART OF THE WORLD WAR II PACIFIC THEME Study, the secretary of the Interior designated Attu Battlefield and Airfields a National Historic Landmark (NHL), and Kiska Island a National Historic Landmark to commemorate the Allied-Japanese campaigns of 1942-43. National Historic Landmark designation is the highest level of official recognition accorded historic sites of national significance.

The original NHL studies needed further documentation, particularly for underwater sites, and so in September 1989 a joint archaeological project was conducted to investigate World War II remains in the Aleutian Islands. Three agencies participated in these investigations: the U.S. Navy, the National Park Service, and the U.S. Fish and Wildlife Service, the last of which has jurisdictional responsibility for the Aleutian sites. Park Service and navy participation were under the auspices of Project SeaMark. The project is an ongoing cooperative agreement which has been in effect since 1985 and which utilizes U.S. Navy assets to document shipwrecks of national significance, under the supervision of National Park Service underwater archaeologists. Naval participation is viewed by them as training and mobilization opportunities. Project SeaMark has documented U.S. and Japanese shipwrecks in Hawaii, Guam, Palau, Marshall Islands, Bikini Atoll, and other areas.

Aleutian Island archaeological project objectives were to systematically survey, locate, and nondestructively evaluate submerged World War II remains in the Aleutians (those not addressed in the original NHL designation studies) and to conduct additional inventory and documentation of terrestrial sites within the two

landmarks. Documentation of submerged Aleutian campaign materials was especially important. Historical documents indicated that numerous submerged sites associated with combat operations were probable, including complete vessels, boats, aircraft, and refuse areas of archaeological importance. The cold, protected waters of Kiska Harbor, combined with its inaccessibility, promised high levels of preservation. Consequently, Kiska Harbor was the primary target, with offshore areas of Attu a close second.

A research plan was developed that went beyond simply augmenting historical documents through examination of material remains. A principal object of inquiry from an archaeological perspective was the nature of maritime-supported combat, and explanations for variable cultural behavior in conflict. Combat situations that control for geography, such as consecutive Japanese and U.S. occupations in an isolated area, are particularly important to developing anthropological perspectives on warfare from a comparative basis. One important variable between the U.S. and Japanese occupations is that the Japanese effort was solely a maritime endeavor and much more isolated than the U.S. occupation, which soon developed airplane support.

Some archaeological assumptions that were utilized and which affected data collection and interpretation during the project are: 1) Japanese and Allied occupation settlement patterns and activity areas will vary, be distinguishable, and reflect aspects of different cultural systems, military strategies, and active combat levels; and 2) isolated groups in conflict will salvage, reuse, recycle, and stockpile used materials in relationship to

*Above*, Japanese Class A midget submarine, Kiska. *(Photograph by Michael Eng, National Park Service, Southwest Region, Santa Fe, N.M.)*

*Right*, Dan Lenihan video-tapes the interior of a midget submarine as Larry Murphy looks on. The two men have just returned from a dive and are still wearing their dry-suits. *(Photograph by Michael Eng, National Park Service, Southwest Region, Santa Fe, N.M.)*

levels of isolation and stress. For instance, Japanese remains should reflect more defensive recycling than U.S. remains.

Comparative examination of refuse should provide data otherwise unavailable from documentary sources.

Some research questions were specific to underwater sites: How did the characteristics of refuse differ from anchorage sites? How did Allied and Japanese occupations vary in location and composition? How can vessels wrecked by bombing be differentiated from those torpedoed or scuttled? And how did salvage activities vary among sites between Allied and Japanese occupations? Can Japanese salvage activities be distinguished from Allied operations, especially what was removed by Japanese salvors vs. material removed by Allies? Finally, can signatures for Japanese and Allied salvage activities be developed for use in interpretation of site formation processes to account for how the sites appear today, both in the Aleutians and elsewhere?

The principal naval asset for the project was ARS 50 *Safeguard*, a 250-foot salvage vessel that sailed from Honolulu to Kiska.

*Safeguard* docked at Adak and picked up a team of navy divers from Mobile Diving and Salvage Unit 1, stationed at Honolulu, and a team of terrestrial archaeologists led by Susan Morton, of the Alaska Region National Park Service; Chuck Diters, of the Fish and Wildlife Service; and historians Stan Cohen and John Cloe. *Safeguard* was deployed in Kiska and served as base for operations.

The survey strategy was to conduct a high-resolution side-scan sonar survey of Kiska Harbor in a manner capable of systematically locating historical-period cultural remains above the sea floor. Side-scan sonar uses microsecond pulses of sound emitted multiple times a second to develop a topographic rendition of the seabed and any materials on or above it.

The sensor was towed behind the survey vessel, a thirty-five-foot work boat carried aboard *Safeguard*. The work vessel was outfitted with a radar reflector and sonar. High-resolution bridge radar was used for positioning. One-hundred-yard survey transacts were plotted north and south throughout the harbor to provide 200 percent sonar coverage.

*Safeguard's* bridge navigation team provided positioning that guided the survey boat by radio along the preplotted transects, and fixes were taken along the survey lane so targets could be easily relocated. Plots were positioned in ten to fifteen seconds and radioed to the survey vessel allowing pilot corrections. The combination of sonar records and navigation fixes provides a permanent record that allows determination of sonar coverage level and relocation of targets of interest. When a target was located, a buoy was positioned at the site and a

team of divers deployed. Divers dressed in dry suits to protect against the thirty-six-degree water. In addition to divers, a remotely operated vehicle (ROV) carrying a TV camera was used. The use of this cable-tethered device for target location greatly increased efficiency because diver time could be used for site documentation rather than target search. Hand-held underwater video and still cameras were also used. Numerous sites underwater and on land were investigated during nine operational days in Kiska harbor.

The first site investigated by Park Service divers was the *Nissan Maru*, a 427-foot, 6,800-ton merchant vessel that was carrying fuel and other supplies when sunk by U.S. bombers on June 19, 1942. The ship is important because it is the only vessel representative of the original occupying Japanese force remaining in Kiska Harbor. The vessel was sunk by a high-altitude bombing mission, and its loss was confirmed by the first U.S. photographic reconnaissance of the Japanese occupation on June 21.

Although the vessel burned after being hit amidships, evidence of its cargo still remains. The vessel had six hatches, and three sets of kingposts still standing, with the principal damage in the bridge area aft of amidships. Indications are that at least one large bomb, possibly a thousand-pounder, exploded in the number-four cargo hold; about fifty feet of hull port and starboard are missing from an internal explosion in this area. The vessel was armed with a 3-inch gun on elevated mounts forward and aft. The ten-sided gun mount is typical of Japanese practice and is common on Japanese armed merchantmen throughout the Pacific. Ready ammunition boxes are present with lids still closed, perhaps reflecting a sudden attack or a state of unreadiness. The aft deck has an engine-order telegraph in place, but the binnacle has been removed, probably by souvenir-hunting divers.

An inverted vessel with a sharp clipper-type bow was found. The vessel was heavily damaged and machinery, including the forward-deck capstan, was lying outside the hull. It is believed this vessel was a mine-layer or sub-chaser, although no records so far examined indicate any presence of minelayers. Still, a mine field was recorded in the U.S. Strategic Bombing Survey of 1946. The U.S. sub *Grunion* was reported to have sunk two subchasers near Kiska Harbor. Period subchasers had sharp bows, and this vessel fits the basic dimensions of a 167-foot length and 22-foot beam. Other possibilities are net-layer or minesweeper; both types of vessels are recorded sunk in the area in the Strategic Bombing Survey records.

One of the most interesting finds was a 250-foot-long Japanese submarine, whose measurements indicate it was most probably *RO-65*. *RO-65* was likely sunk by an

American bomber September 28, 1942, although the Japanese claim the sub was lost by accident while diving to escape an airstrike. The diving planes were horizontal, rather than pointed downward as would be expected if the sub were diving, and the screw was fouled with cable, perhaps from later salvage attempts. The submersible deck gear was in place. A debris field lies to the south of the hull, which was facing east toward the harbor mouth. The debris field contained most of the sail-related equipment. The forward torpedo loading hatch was open and a Park Service archaeologist entered to video the sub's interior. A 21-inch torpedo was in place on the port side. Material evidence on this site points to sinking by bombing. There was external structural damage to the pressure hull and the entirety of the sail material lay off the hull side. Some salvage is evident: hatches are open, deck guns are missing. It is not clear at present when this was done or by whom, whether contemporary Japanese, Americans, or later souvenir hunting divers.

In addition to the sunken sites, there were exposed vessels along the shore. One appears to be the *Nozama Maru*, sunk by air attack on the northwest side of the harbor. This vessel carried a load of mines. Modern sal-

*Left*, Dan Lenihan ascends with video camera in hand after a dive on the Nissan Maru in Kiska Harbor. *(Photograph by Larry Murphy, National Park Service, Southwest Region, Santa Fe, N.M.)*

*Above*, deck gun on the Nissan Maru, Kiska Harbor. *(Photograph by Larry Murphy, National Park Service, Southwest Region, Santa Fe, N.M.)*

vagers have removed about half this vessel. The *Uragio Maru* faces west, with starboard side against the shore.

Farther up on shore a two-man, type-A midget submarine remains on its launching blocks in the subpens. This is the same type of midget sub involved in the December 7, 1941, attack on Pearl Harbor, and which were the world's first successful midget submarines. The sub is well preserved considering internal demolition charges and fifty years of exposure to weather and souvenir hunters. Originally there were three midgets when the Allies returned. Only the one on the blocks and portions of another in the surf zone remain visible from the surface today. The sail is in good shape, and much remains of the interior spaces and propulsion machinery.

Kiska Island, around the harbor, is one of the best-preserved historical battle scenes anywhere. The slow erosion processes on the tundra have had little effect on the bomb craters still visible on the hills surrounding the harbor. The view, overall, contributes to a distinct sense of recent abandonment. Dumps of U.S. and Japanese material are numerous. Right-hand drive Japanese truck frames are piled up, along with Zero engines and other evidence of Japanese occupation. It is clear that the Japanese intended a long occupation: extensive support structures are in place, such as a water hydrant, from which a rubbing of the Japanese characters was taken for translation. Some of the most dramatic remains are the numerous tunnels from the extensive Japanese underground system, some concrete reinforced. Many are still sound and contain Japanese material. Japanese gun emplacements, disabled by U.S. troops, remain pointing skyward, as they were when abandoned. Evidence of U.S. troop occupation remains in both standing structures and collapsed ones.

In conclusion: twenty-five side-scan targets were located. Fewer than half were dived upon. Additional sites located included landing craft, likely both Japanese and U.S.; dump sites containing numerous 3-inch shells and other debris; and aircraft wreckage, one of which may be a B-17. Much additional survey and documentation work needs to be done. Ideally this will be accomplished before additional losses are suffered to this important National Historical Landmark commemorating the "forgotten war" of the Aleutian Campaign.

*Daniel Lenihan is Chief of the National Park Service, Submerged Cultural Resources Unit. Larry E. Murphy is a research archaeologist with the unit. Both have been in their positions for more than twenty years.*

# Attu and Kiska, 2043:
# How Much of the Past Can the Present Save for the Future?

## Charles E. Diters

*The recent centennial of the American Civil War and the bicentennial of the Revolutionary War successively focused attention on the diminishing physical reminders of those conflicts. The fiftieth anniversary of the Second World War comes at an opportune moment, when we still have time to consider and treat the historical properties. However, much of what remains from World War II is far from centers of current civilian population. This is especially true at the Attu and Kiska National Historic Landmarks. These areas are distant and difficult of access for the public, and almost as prohibitively so for the agency managing them. Consequently, treatment options (such as the recovery of a P-38 Lightning aircraft from Attu) which might not be appropriate in other parts of the country, should at least be given full consideration. Several questions will be addressed: What can we preserve in place? What should we recover and preserve or restore? How can we interpret these National Historic Landmarks?*

D URING THE 1960S THE UNITED STATES OBSERVED THE centennial of the Civil War; in the 1970s we focused our attention on the nation's bicentennial, including the Revolutionary War. Today, commemorating the fiftieth anniversary of the Second World War, we are blessed with several advantages over our situation in the previous two cases. First, we still have with us a large number of the veterans of that conflict, both those whose contributions we have heard this week and others who could not be with us at this symposium.

Second, we have a much fuller documentary record of this war than of the earlier ones, both in written form and in extensive archives of still- and motion-picture photography; indeed, in some cases we can actually hear the war's rumble. Third, and this is the focus of my paper today, we still have around us a tremendous material resource resulting from the war, which we can observe, appreciate, and maintain with an eye to preservation for future generations.

I will address, briefly,
 • first, the condition of the historic fabric today;
 • second, the threats to these resources; and
 • third, what alternate uses we may make of these resources, and what parts we may actually be able to save.

While I will focus my attention primarily on the national historic landmarks on Attu and Kiska islands, which are managed by the U.S. Fish and Wildlife Service as part of the Aleutian Islands unit of the Alaska Maritime National Wildlife Refuge, I will also be drawing some examples from elsewhere in Alaska to the extent that they bear directly on the question at hand: What is it that we, in the late twentieth century, actually *can* preserve for the future? I do not ask the more philosophical question of what *should* be preserved, in the best of all possible worlds. We do not live in that world.

Attu and Kiska islands are extremely remote and difficult to access. Only Attu has an airfield, and it is served regularly only by U.S. Coast Guard aircraft providing logistical support to the Loran station. Charter aircraft service is possible, as was used for this year's observances of the anniversary of the recapture of the island. Kiska, while not as distant from the U.S. mainland, lacks an airfield, and is accessible only by boat.

On Attu, where the National Historic Landmark

The hulk of the *Nozima Maru* on a beach at Kiska. *(Photograph by Charles E. Diters, U.S. Fish and Wildlife Service)*

includes both the battlefield and the later U.S. operating bases, the United States presence has obscured many of the traces of the Japanese occupation. Not only was the island a site of major military development during the latter phases of the war, but it has been occupied much of the time since then. Significant elements include:

• a chapel, only recently a victim to wind and weather (a similar chapel at Amchitka Island has gone the same way);

• the remains of public and industrial buildings, such as theaters, laundries, warehouses, and fuel storage and distribution systems;

• examples of engineering activities, including roads, bridges, and construction machinery and debris;

• various domestic structures, from the common to the specifically military (I also include other residential structures in this group, although, as in the case of the brig, I suspect the residents were less than pleased to be there); and

• specifically military installations, such as the airfield itself, radar installations, magazine areas, and so on.

Already, in areas where buildings were removed after the war, some of the traces are hard to find. Nonetheless, old roads and compacted areas are still obvious from elevated positions, if only due to changes in vegetation.

On Kiska, the situation is almost completely reversed. There is some evidence of the Allied presence after the

A Japanese 75-millimeter gun on Kiska. *(Photograph by Charles E. Diters, U.S. Fish and Wildlife Service)*

reoccupation in 1943, such as the Canadian masonry or the remains of the runway that was completed in only a few days during August of that year. But the primary material evidence is predominantly, even overwhelmingly, Japanese.

As at Attu, there are religious structures, as well as evidence of occupation sites, though often without structural elements remaining. There are also quantities of portable materials, such as discarded barracks stoves, personal protective equipment, and many examples of discarded munitions, both for small arms and for larger weapons.

There is evidence of mundane engineering, which may be only photographed, or may be recorded differently. There are remains of more military engineering as well, including positions defended with gravel or soil-filled fuel drums, and large numbers of accesses to underground facilities that have yet to be fully explored.

There are maritime remains at Kiska (in addition to the ones that the Park Service and the navy have documented on the bottom of the harbor), including several wrecked freighters such as the *Nozima Maru*. Also included are the remains of at least three two-man submarines, of the same type as those used at Pearl Harbor, that were to be used for the coastal defense of Kiska.

However, by far the most striking collection of material from the Japanese occupation has to be the artillery. While most small arms—up to and including heavy machine guns—were either taken off the island by the Japanese troops during their evacuation, or were dumped into the ocean, the great majority of the Japanese artillery pieces remain in place, such as the one at North Head. Most guns were in open positions, but some had shields that would protect at least against shell fragments. The largest guns were 6-inch rifles of British manufacture; it is a common story that these were taken by the Japanese at the capture of Singapore, but documentation of this seems to be lacking. Least common of the sizes on the island were the 76-millimeter guns installed in concealed positions near the marine railway at the sub base. Also found are the protected fire-control structures for the artillery, such as the one near the airfield.

The most common pieces were the 75-millimeter dual-purpose guns. These were originally designed as antiaircraft weapons, but were used extensively against ground forces on Attu, and would no doubt have been used similarly on Kiska. Most often, they were removed from their wheels and mounted in fixed positions, but they could be relocated quickly and fired while still on their tires.

Surprisingly, the tires on one piece—a 75-millimeter gun—still hold air after nearly fifty years.

As on Attu, time is beginning to obscure some of the features of the scene on Kiska, but vegetation changes over built-up areas and the scars of combat will no doubt be visible for years to come.

If we could freeze things as they are today, we would clearly have a tremendously exciting snapshot of the war in the North Pacific. As you all certainly know, this cannot be done. Time and weather alone will, inexorably and despite our best efforts, remove all traces of the war except perhaps for earthworks that may be visible centuries, or even millennia, hence. Unfortunately, natural

forces are only one part of the threat to these tangible reminders of World War II on Alaska soil.

Among the most critical risks are vandalism and theft. Many of the "portable" pieces that still exist at both Attu and Kiska are obviously almost fair game for

The remains of a P-38 Lightning that crashed on Attu in 1944. *(1991 photograph by Debbie Corbett, courtesy U.S. Fish and Wildlife Service)*

the collector. Evidence of vandalism may actually be easier to detect after the fact than by the simple removal of an artifact. One monument to the casualties from Task Force 9 has been defaced by someone who scratched his or her name into the surface. And this is not a one-time thing: a stainless-steel pipe "time capsule," affixed to the boulder on which a plaque is mounted, was removed from the island by a party or parties unknown at some time between 1989 and a visit I made this summer [1993].

The location of these sites in the western Aleutians is a two-edged sword; while it reduces the annual visitation to a very low level, it also makes patrol or enforcement exceedingly difficult, if not impossible. On the other hand, while proximity to population centers makes patrol of historic sites easier, it also exposes them to far more risk from casual vandalism.

Second among the risks is that which comes from simple use or re-use of these properties. Such continued use is a mixed blessing. On Attu, for example, much of the effort to keep roads open beyond the Coast Guard's immediate needs stems from the need for access to the air force's remote seismic monitoring station on the island. On the other hand, the need for this access nearly resulted in the loss of the Henderson River Bridge, which is a contributing element within the National Historic Landmark.

At Adak, the old Bering Hill chapel was about to be sacrificed as a fire department training exercise in 1989. The exterior and the interior were both in serious need of repair, and a grass-roots effort served to save the structure in time for it to be used for services commemorating the reoccupation of Attu and Kiska in June of 1993. This serves to illustrate another point, that nothing is static in the Aleutians. The Bering Hill chapel is still in need of a new roof, and efforts were underway to find ways to fund this work when the down-sizing of the naval air station at Adak began. When Adak was a community as well as a military base, such preservation efforts were possible. It is not at all certain that they will be in the future.

The line between creative re-use and vandalism is also sometimes hard to define. As illustration, a map was saved by Coast Guard personnel, and is now protected from the weather in a warehouse. But one structure, the recreation building on the island, contains pieces—such as a Japanese post and a chapel railing—less appropriately re-used.

We must also ask what will ultimately happen to all of these resources when the military presence vanishes completely. We may see this presaged in ongoing efforts, under the auspices of the Army Corps of Engineers, to "clean up debris" left by earlier generations of military occupation. Structures like the Izembek Quonset huts which were photographed in 1968 at Cold Bay are long gone today. Other structures, such as an observation post overlooking Cold Bay, were spared due to a combination of remote location and a condition that could best be described as being "environmentally benign." Other structures, such as the fuel pumping station on Attu, may prove impossible to save, even with the best of intentions, due to petroleum or other hazardous waste contamination.

With sufficiently large budgets and staffs, and particularly with the addition of supportive local populations that simply do not now exist, it might be possible to resist many, if not all, of these threats. Unfortunately, the budgets and the constituencies are small in comparison to the problems. To date we have had to content ourselves with small-scale visitation and commemoration, often tied to specific anniversaries and parties to the conflict:

- 1981 Memorial at Attu
- 1993 Memorial at Attu
- 1993 Aleut Memorial at Attu
- Japanese Memorial at Attu
- Colonel Yamasaki Monument below Engineer Hill
- Titanium Memorial, dedicated to World Peace
- Text of Japanese Titanium Memorial

These are all moving and significant, and each, in its own way, serves to commemorate the lives and deaths of the many men and women who lost their lives in the conflicts of the North Pacific. However, these, like the islands themselves, are seldom visited, and, like the battles themselves, are often forgotten.

Like the Civil War earthworks I saw at Harpers Ferry only recently, the earthworks on Attu and Kiska and the other islands in the Aleutians will be there for centuries to come, barring any direct action on our part to obliterate them; those who have the opportunity to visit them will benefit, but their numbers will never be large. A better, at least partial, solution may be seen in the National Park Service's plans for an interpretive center at Unalaska, which is both a National Historic Landmark and a place more convenient and congenial for visitors than those islands farther to the west.

Should we, then, continue to try and maintain the more portable items on these islands as they exist today? Certainly, the guidance provided to us in the general philosophy of historic preservation is that preservation in place is regarded as the highest and best use, all other things being equal. In this case, however, it may be that all things are not equal.

I will cite only one case in point, that of historic aircraft. These wrecks, scattered throughout the state and representing all services and parts of the war, are a valuable resource both for public use and for the private collector. Some of the remains, such as those at Amchitka, have already been the target of illegal collecting. Fortunately, in that case, our attention was called to the problem in time to prevent the material from leaving public hands, and the remains were subsequently collected by a museum with appropriate permissions and stipulations in place.

Some of the aircraft are listed on the National Register of Historic Places. One on Attu was so listed as an individual object a number of years ago, and subsequently included as a contributing element in the National Historic Landmark description for Attu.

Others have been deemed ineligible by the U.S. Fish and Wildlife Service, in consultation with the Alaska State Historic Preservation officer. Some of these aircraft were scheduled to be collected by the U.S. Air Force (during the summer of 1994, if paperwork and weather cooperated) for restoration and interpretation for the public benefit at Elmendorf Air Force Base in Anchorage and at the Hill Air Force Base Museum in Utah.

If we do preserve other aircraft or other items such as artillery in place, we will indeed provide a substantial benefit for a few. I, for one, have taken great delight in being able to see and experience such amazing resources in this fashion. The U.S. Fish and Wildlife Service biologists who have been conducting work on Buldir for many years have even taken a proprietary interest in "their" P-38, as have the Coast Guardsmen on Attu. But, ultimately, aren't we verging on selfishness if we maintain preservation in place for these items as the *only* acceptable outcome? Far more of the public will be able to benefit from these resources if they are wisely and thoughtfully recovered.

Finally, it is good that the fiftieth anniversary of the Second World War has given us the opportunity to address this issue now, while there is still enough time for us to make this and similar difficult decisions before we are left dealing only with the shards and fragments of the past.

*Charles E. Diters is the Regional Archaeologist and Regional Historic Preservation Officer for the U.S. Fish and Wildlife Service, Alaska Regional Office.*

# The Landscape of a Landmark:
# National Historic Landmark Preservation
# in the Aleutian Islands

*Linda Cook*

IN THE WORDS OF ROGER KENNEDY, DIRECTOR OF THE National Park Service, "Historic preservation is about keeping care of physical instances of shared values."[1] Physical instances or cultural resources provide a window into the events of the past; they mark a point of reference for public historians and they interpret human life and social process. In 1986 and 1987 the secretary of the Interior, through the National Park Service, designated five locations in the Aleutian Islands in southwestern Alaska as National Historic Landmarks (NHLs) for their role in the events of the Aleutian Campaign and the war in the Pacific from 1941 to 1945. These landmarks provide firsthand contact with the physical evidence of history and are unparalleled sources of discovery and insight. Preservation of these resources is more than a one-time endeavor: "Preservation is not a once for all event; it is an ongoing process in which each generation reinforces, revises, or expands its cultural memory through interaction with the artifacts and landscapes of its past."[2]

This paper proposes that the World War II landmarks in the Aleutians are more than isolated ruins and obsolete infrastructure. Rather they are landscapes transformed by human endeavor that should and can remain intact if they are given an even chance early in the planning stage to contribute to design in development and environmental reclamation.

The NHLs associated with the World War II Aleutian campaign are:

• Dutch Harbor Naval Operating Base and Fort Mears, U.S. Army;

• Cape Field, at Fort Glenn on Umnak Island;

• Adak Army Base and Adak Naval Operating Base;

• the Japanese Occupation Site on Kiska Island; and

• Attu Battlefield and U.S. Army and Navy airfields on Attu.

As NHLs, there is no question that these properties rank among the nation's elite cultural resources. Administered by the National Park Service, NHLs constitute the nation's most treasured resources deemed worthy of preservation even though there is federally appropriated funding to support this stance. Of the approximately two thousand NHLs nationwide, forty-four are in Alaska.

The designation "National Historic Landmark" carries a certain mystic quality that all too often leads one on a quest for bronze plaques and granite obelisk monuments. The landmarks in the Aleutians are real places where real people lived through real events. They are not arbitrary locations so designated to mark an associated event, nor are they frozen in time. Designation of properties as NHLs is primarily commemorative and nonrestrictive to private ownership. On the federal level, however, sections 106 and 110 of the National Historic

---

[1] These words are excerpted from Kennedy's address at the National Conference of State Historic Preservation Officers Board of Directors meeting, July 25-26, 1993.

[2] Reuben M. Rainey, "The Memory of War: Reflections on Battlefield Preservation," in *The Yearbook of Landscape Architecture: Historic Preservation* (New York: Van Nostand Reinhold Company, 1983), p. 70.

Preservation Act of 1966, as amended, require federal agencies to review properties relating to projects and to activities that could affect them. To date there is no enforced directive that requires these agencies to unequivocally retain and preserve historic properties, but if a property is on, or "eligible" for inclusion on, the National Register of Historic Places, it must be documented, nominated, and mitigated.

Despite its limited ability to prescribe mandatory preservation of NHLs, the NHL program encourages shared stewardship and the exchange of educational and technical information between the National Park Service and local, state, and federal agencies, property owners, developers, and interested organizations and individuals. The Aleutian Islands, like many locations in Alaska, are an interesting overlay of federal designations, state and private lands, and individual interests that inspire partnership projects.

Given the size and location of these five landmarks, all the contributing resources have yet to be completely understood, documented, and mapped. Trying to preserve the number of severely weathered structures and ruins located on vast tracts of mostly uninhabited land is intimidating. Trying to document thousands of individual buildings is an ongoing challenge, given Alaska's short field seasons and the cost of operating seasonal crews in the Aleutian Islands. Furthermore, buildings are but one aspect of these landmarks. Comprised of roads, bridges, culverts, paths, trenches, runways, battlefields, dams, revetments, quarries, docks, bomb-blast marks, and other objects, these landmarks constitute unique visual experiences or cultural landscapes that tell the story of how airstrips were built in a matter of days and how men and women lived, fought, and coped with the isolation of being stationed on these remote islands.

Any discussion of the preservation of these landmarks

Reinforced concrete foundation, with a Pacific hut in the background, at Alexai Point, Attu, 1976. *(RG 77, National Archives—Alaska Region)*

requires an understanding that all these components interact and complement one another. The deliberate removal of a central feature, such as an airplane hangar, bridge, or battery lookout, may directly or indirectly jeopardize the historic integrity and interpretation of a surrounding valley or mountain vista. The related histories of how, why, and who built the structures are also gone. In most cases, except for the resource base on Unalaska and Adak Islands, there has been little intentional change to the layout of these military encampments. They remain cohesive landscapes that interact with each other and, in so doing, choreograph a sequence of nationally historic events. While the loss of Quonset huts blown apart by hurricane force winds can be anticipated, and is telling in itself, the intentional demolition of historic buildings, structures, and features is a land management decision that has long been overlooked in site planning.

Historic landscapes are defined as geographical areas that historically have been used by people, or shaped or modified by human activity, occupancy, or intervention, and that possess a significant concentration, linkage, or continuity of areas of land use, vegetation, buildings, and structures, roads and waterways, and natural features.[3] Add to this definition that they are places that

---

[3] Kennedy address, National Conference.

Remains of a wooden dock at Chichagof Harbor, Attu, 1976. *(RB 77, National Archives—Alaska Region)*

possess visual cohesiveness and character-defining features. Keeping in mind these two ideas—what the image of a place as a whole looks like and what the features are that most strongly transmit the information—the following discussion gives a brief overview of landscape preservation strategies for World War II landmarks on Umnak, Attu, and Unalaska islands.

## Cape Field at Fort Glenn, Umnak

Fort Glenn on Umnak Island is located approximately sixty miles west of the City of Unalaska and is the site of thousands of World War II-related buildings, structures, and objects. Built as a support airfield for the defense harbor at Unalaska, the sprawling four-runway army air base and naval air facility served more than ten thousand troops. Transferred to the state of Alaska under the Omnibus Act of 1966, today Fort Glenn is a virtual ghost town—except for a family of cattle ranchers who have renovated several World War II buildings and who call the fort home. The expanse and undisturbed quality of the resource make Fort Glenn an outstanding conceptual model for landscape preservation.

In 1991, National Park Service historians visited the

site and conducted a boundary review of the landmark to include all landscape features as part of the landmark. The original NHL nomination, completed in 1986, only recognized the runways, gun emplacements, and a few structures as contributing resources to the designation. Despite their overwhelming number, architectural integrity, and contents, all Quonset, Pacific, Yakutat, and Cowin huts, frame buildings, hangars, and other buildings were considered non-contributing as were all structures and infrastructure.

Research compiled in the boundary review indicated that the land area transferred to the state was considerably smaller than the original boundaries of the historic fort. The reduced acreage was the result of the efforts of a diligent sheep-ranching operation on the site in the late 1950s and early 1960s. The ranchers strongly petitioned the Department of the Interior to reduce the acreage of the federal airport parcel from more than nine thousand to seventy-five hundred acres in order to preserve prime winter lambing areas. In 1986, the reduced seventy-five-hundred-acre parcel's boundaries also became the boundaries for the NHL. The boundary review determined that despite the unusual rationale, the NHL size was appropriate. The review only amended the description of contributing resources to include all World War II-related construction, infrastructure, landscape, and objects.

The generosity and hospitality of the ranchers allowed NPS staff to visit and interpret the fort in depth in just a few days, a task that otherwise would have been impossible. This exchange has led to an ongoing discussion on the condition and long-term use of the site. Also, in the event of an environmental cleanup under Public Law 98-212, passed in 1983, the new boundaries are a mechanism to address and coordinate the cleanup with the integrity of the landmark, keeping in mind the visual quality and architectural cohesiveness of the fort. Any environmental cleanup should be designed to remove loose cables, transformers, hazardous material, toxic waste, and ordinance. Nontoxic World War II-related objects such as empty barrels could be left in place; full barrels would be, of course, another issue. All other buildings, structures, and infrastructure—no matter how "unsightly"—should be left intact and preserved: in this case preservation can simply mean avoidance and the acceptance that these buildings and structures have a definite place within the landscape. When one is forced to think of the outcome of an unmonitored environmental cleanup on Umnak—with no respect for the integrity of resource—the insightful comment of an NPS employee immediately comes to mind: "What if there had been a Corps of Engineers to go in and clean up after Gettysburg?"[4]

## Attu Battlefield and U.S. Army and Navy Airfields, Attu

A pivotal issue of landscape preservation on Attu Island concerns a trestle bridge which has been identified as an important component to interpreting the landmark. In 1990-91 the Department of the Air Force determined that removal and replacement of the Henderson River Bridge at Attu Battlefield and U.S. Army and Navy Airfields on Attu would not affect the landmark. The air force maintains one of a chain of seismological sensing stations on the island. The station monitors Russia's nuclear-treaty compliance and to arrive at the sensing station requires crossing the Henderson River. The air force proposed replacing this timber trestle bridge with a series of six eight-foot culverts and associated fill. In stating that the removal of the bridge would have no effect on the landmark, the air force made the determination that the bridge failed to contribute to the property's location, setting, materials, workmanship, feeling, or association. As part of the Attu

Battlefield Landmark, the bridge had even more to convey.

As defined:

> Battlefields are an important type of cultural landscape. They are places that have been profoundly marked by human endeavor. While the significance of many battlefields derives from a brief and extraordinarily violent moment in time, the basic principles for identifying, evaluating, documenting, registering, and protecting can be applied more broadly, particularly to significant historic rural landscapes. The characteristics that define a broad range of rural landscapes—natural features, land uses, vegetation, historic building types—also define many battlefields.[5]

In a series of meetings between the air force, the State Historic Preservation Office, the National Park Service and others, a second proposal took shape to establish either an alternative route or build a new bridge near the historic one. In 1993 the air force applied for Department of Defense Legacy funds to conduct a preservation and rehabilitation study of the bridge for foot traffic only. The air force plans to replace two smaller World War II bridges upstream for vehicular traffic.

## Dutch Harbor Naval Operating Base and Fort Mears, U.S. Army, Unalaska

Perhaps the best-documented landmark in the Aleutians, Dutch Harbor Naval Operating Base and Fort Mears National Historic Landmark, has been the subject of repeated study and debate. Unalaska is the principal port of the Bering Sea bottom-fish industry and over the last six years there has been a dramatic increase in the demand for available dock and shoreline on which to build. After the Army Corps of Engineers cleanup in the late 1980s, many buildings were razed, but the imprint of construction, the sites where lives were lost, and the techniques used to camouflage and integrate military construction within the landscape remained. Four projects within the privately-owned landmark illustrate the two sides to resource preservation in Unalaska.

Completed in 1992, the Grand Aleutian Hotel stands on the site of the World War II Margaret Bay cantonment on Amaknak Island. The target of Japanese bombs in June 1942, subsequently left to ruin after the army decommissioned the base, and then demolished by the Corps in 1986-1987, the dozens of two-story army barracks were only one component of this landscape. Along

---

[4] Lael Morgan, "Aleutians Legacy From World War II: Clean it up but save the Battlefields!" *Alaska* magazine (May 1980), p. 77.

[5] "Guidelines for Identifying, Evaluating, and Registering America's Historic Battlefields," *National Register Bulletin*, 40, 1992, p. iii.

the shoreline, twenty-four concrete pillboxes remained, as did World War II roads and the man-made configuration of Margaret Bay.

To make way for the hotel complex, the project developer slated the pillboxes for removal. In consultation with the Corps of Engineers to obtain a permit, the developer learned that most of the pillboxes retained integrity and association with the site. Determined to proceed as planned, the owner sought redesignation of the landmark. In order to address the effects of their actions under Section 106 of the Historic Preservation Act of 1966, as amended, the Corps of Engineers—as lead federal agency—continued to meet with the developer, the State Historic Preservation Office, and the National Park Service to try to incorporate the pillboxes into the hotel design. A final design plan left nineteen of the original twenty-four pillboxes in place. A boundary review has since recommended the exclusion of this section of the landmark.

Built in 1942, the Aerology Operations building served as the Naval Air Transport Terminal. Located near the airport runways, the building remained in use through the early 1980s. In 1992, the MarkAir vice president of properties directed a historically sensitive rehabilitation of the terminal, based on historic photographs. The building now serves as the VIP lounge and offices for the airlines, and as offices for the U.S. Coast Guard. The National Park Service recognized this project as well as the Grand Aleutian Hotel with certificates of appreciation in 1992, awarded for preserving endangered National Historic Landmarks.[6]

In the late 1980s one of the aircraft bays in the double-pen blast hangar near the Unalaska airport runway began to show significant structural deterioration. A design for new construction was adopted that was compatible with the original, both in scale and roof design. And so the hangar retains a sense of association. Although the color and material are different, there is no doubt of the success of the addition when one considers possible alternatives that could have included a larger addition, certain to have completely overshadowed the historic component.

To the disappointment of many, the Hill 400 concrete battery command station at the southern end of Amaknak Island has become the recipient of a noisy pulsating antenna. While retaining integrity of design and location, the station has lost a sense of association that interpreted one's feelings of isolation and control as one looked out over Unalaska Bay in anticipation of enemy aircraft or ships. During the planning stages for the installation of the antenna, the owners failed to realize that this station is one of the most striking World War II structures on the island. Locally known as Bunker Hill, this lofty retreat is a popular place to get away from it all. Although removable, the antenna has degraded the structure. A local historic preservation ordinance could have permitted installation of the antenna near but not directly through this key historic structure.

Some degree of preservation needs to be above the whims of short-sighted construction. How do you convey a sense of place if in each stage of development one erases all evidence of earlier actions and endeavors? All too often the excuses of limited public accessibility and visibility have directed land-use decisions in the Aleutians. Many argue that because of the remote location, there is little need to preserve or maintain features. Many have asked, "Who is going to see them anyway?" These same voices have claimed that demolition is the only safe, prudent, and practical alternative to a resource that is economically obsolete and potentially dangerous. This stance is less than supportive of the thousands of troops deployed to the Aleutians more than fifty years ago and highly insensitive to the Aleut interests in the region and the returning families of fallen Japanese soldiers.

The Aleutians merit resource protection and should achieve that protection through the National Battlefield program, the National Historic Landmark program, interagency agreements, the Department of Defense, local historic preservation organizations, veteran's organizations, Alaska Native organizations and corporations, and local planning incentives that support historic resources and preservation.

*Linda Cook is a historian for the National Park Service. She has a degree from the Graduate School of Architecture, Planning, and Historic Preservation, Columbia University. She has worked with the City of Unalaska on local preservation projects.*

---

[6] The Preservation Assistance Division of the National Park Service in Washington, D.C., requests nominations for these certificates from regional office staff. The National Park Service awards certificates to individuals or organizations that have successfully preserved an endangered landmark. Dutch Harbor Naval Operating Base and Fort Mears, U.S. Army NHL has been identified as a Priority 1 endangered landmark to Congress.

# Making It Right:
# Restitution for Aleut Churches Damaged and Lost During the Aleut Relocation in World War II

*Barbara Sweetland Smith*

A T A TIME WHEN PROSPECTS FOR HISTORIC RESTORA-tion projects are particularly low nationwide, there is a bright spot in the Aleutian Islands. One feature of the Aleut Restitution Act of 1988 was to set aside money for repair and restoration of Aleut churches damaged by the U.S. military occupation of the villages during World War II. The Aleutian/Pribilof Islands Association (A/PIA) has recently completed a two-year study of the condition of the churches in six of the villages which were occupied by the U.S. military during World War II and made its recommendations to the secretary of Interior and to Congress. On the basis of this report, Senator Ted Stevens and Congressman Don Young have introduced an amendment to the Aleut Restitution Act to increase the amount authorized for church repair and restoration from $1.4 million to $4.7 million. At the same time, the Aleutian/Pribilof Island Trust has begun to develop an overall plan to spend the moneys that are approved. The seven-member Aleut board is consulting with architects and contractors. Included in their thinking is a modern conservation laboratory for the repair and treatment of artifacts to be based at Unalaska.

It now seems clear that there will be funds available for major restoration of six of Alaska's most important historic buildings. Each of the churches in the villages evacuated during World War II is on the National Register of Historic Places and three of them are National Historic Landmarks. One, the Church of the Holy Ascension at Unalaska, has been designated by the National Trust for Historic Preservation and the National Park Service as the most endangered historic church in America.

An Orthodox church is more than a sacred building to its owners. It is a repository for an exceptional body of religious art. Even the most modest chapel in the smallest village has on its walls scores of paintings, on canvas or wood, and possesses fine textiles and silver or brass utensils. Each of these items is blessed when it enters church service and may not be removed from the church without appropriate ceremony. Thus, through-out the Aleutian region, ancient works of art glow behind candles which themselves are placed in fine old candlestands or *lampadas*.

The Aleut people accepted Christianity in the eigh-teenth century. The churches of the region have their origin in the first decades of the nineteenth century. The oldest inventories of our subject churches date from the 1830s and reveal that significant numbers of materials from those first years still are venerated—honored—by the Aleut faithful. (In all, the A/PIA project in 1992 doc-umented 1,606 church furnishings.) It is this astonishing artistic and cultural legacy—so deeply entwined with Aleut culture as to have become part of it—that the Aleuts were forced either to leave behind in 1942 or to hurriedly pack and take with them into the deplorable conditions of the internment camps.

The six churches covered by the Aleut Restitution Act are in the towns of Akutan, Atka, Nikolski, and Unalas-ka, in the Aleutian Islands, and St. George and St. Paul in the Pribilofs. Not directly acknowledged in the act but certainly in the minds of the Aleut planners are four additional churches which were lost to the people because of the war—the chapels at Attu and in three small villages on or near Unalaska Island: Biorka,

Kashega, and Makushin. The residents of these four communities were compelled to live elsewhere. Their villages are gone now, and they intend that their losses will not be forgotten in the restoration plans.

Although much of the emphasis in the A/PIA study is on the poor condition of the historic churches today and the link to events from 1942 to 1945, it is nonetheless true that the very survival of five of the six churches is testimony to the remarkable skill of Aleut builders and craftsmen. The youngest of the churches built before World War II, at St. George, is fifty-seven years old, a venerable age indeed for a wooden structure in the Aleutians. The oldest, at Unalaska, will be one hundred years old in 1995. Each church reflects both excellent initial construction and devoted maintenance over many years. Still, the condition of the buildings today is poor and has been aggravated by several factors related to the wartime evacuation, which include:

1) Vandalism to the buildings by the troops garrisoned in the villages. This allowed water to invade the superstructure and to continue to rot the foundation and wall supports.

2) A two- to three-year break in the critical annual maintenance cycle, so that damage from wind and rain, not to mention bullets and vandals, could not be repaired, thereby allowing wind-driven water deep into the structure.

3) The necessity, after the war, for the villagers to make repairs with green lumber salvaged from military installations, which was the only material available to them.

4) Adverse conditions during the evacuation for packing, shipping, and storing outstanding works of religious art.

5) Inexpert efforts to repair the works of art damaged by the shipping.

6) The cumulative effect of inadequate repairs at the time, both to building and objects, which has hastened deterioration.

7) The war-induced devastation of the region's natural resources, which introduced the Aleuts for the first time to real poverty, from which they have never completely recovered.

The fate of the churches and their furnishings during World War II depended a good deal on the degree of warning the people had about evacuation and on the military commanders in charge thereafter. The first to feel the panic of war were the Attuans. Their island was invaded on June 7 by the Japanese and they were taken prisoner. When the forty-one Attuans left the island in September for Japan, their church was intact and they thoroughly expected to return; they even concealed their

Church of the Holy Ascension, Unalaska, ca. 1948-53. *(Photograph courtesy Anchorage Museum of History and Art)*

church treasury in Japan throughout their imprisonment, with the intention of putting it to use to make repairs to the church building. Their hopes were tragically in vain. The church, the only building standing in Attu village, was obliterated by a U.S. B-24 on October 15, 1942.

In the meantime, the Atkans, too, had lost everything. The men of the USS *Gillis* came ashore at Atka on June 12 and torched the entire village, destroying all but three houses, the possessions of the Aleuts, and their church, which contained a quite remarkable collection of fine religious art. The eighty-one Atkans, who saw the fire from nearby fish camps to which they had been ordered, left on ships with only the clothes on their backs.

The Pribilofs were next to be evacuated, a few days later. Given only a few hours' notice, the communities of St. George and St. Paul had no time to secure the churches or pack away the furnishings; they were able to take from the church only a few items. The doors were locked and the people sailed away. The Pribilof churches were used as chapels by the occupying forces and as a result someone among the officers took responsibility for looking after them. Very little appears to have been lost or stolen from the churches on the Pribilofs. The buildings, however, suffered as all the churches did from the absence of the faithful and critical maintenance by the home caretakers.

The forty-seven residents of the tiny Unalaska Island communities of Biorka, Kashega, and Makushin also had no warning, but they were not so fortunate as the Pribilovians. Their loss was total: they were evacuated without notice, forced to sail away from their homes and church and at the end of the war, told they could not return to their ancestral home; they were forcibly relocated, mostly to Unalaska and Akutan. Their relatively new chapels stood abandoned, with the icons still on the walls.

The villages of Akutan, Nikolski, and Unalaska had some warning as they were not evacuated until July. Consequently they were able to pack the church furnishings, and Akutan and Unalaska made plans to bury the crates for the war's duration. Instead they were allowed to take the furnishings with them. Still, the trauma of hasty packing—especially of objects already almost a hundred years old—and storage in unheated and leaky warehouses in Southeast Alaska took its toll on these

Chapel of the Dormition of the Mother of God, Attu, ca. 1941. American bombers destroyed the church, along with the rest of the village, after the Japanese occupied the island.

Site of the St. Nicholas Church, burned by the U.S. Navy in 1942. Atka, 1945. *(Photo No. RG 75-CCF-AK-123-7469-1A, National Archives, College Park, Md.)*

fine art objects. Many canvases were torn, metal objects were dented, exquisite enamels were crushed. And, in the terrible storage conditions of Southeast Alaska, mold thrived on sacred paintings.

The Unalaska church was used by the military encamped at Fort Mears as a chapel and, because of its size, also as a warehouse. This use helped to curtail vandalism, but maintenance of the building was poor and bullet holes in the roof went unrepaired until the Aleuts returned. The chapels at Nikolski and Akutan fared the worst from outright vandalism, as the military made no use of the buildings. At Nikolski, U.S. troops spent the war in Aleut homes; they used the distinctive cupola of the church for target practice. At Akutan, U.S. troops hacked at the door of the chapel with an axe and, from the inside, broke windows which were boarded on the outside.

Forty-six years after the Aleuts returned to their shattered villages, the Aleutian/Pribilof Islands Association evaluated the damage to the churches and estimated the cost of making repairs. An architect examined each of the churches. A distinguished iconologist and conservator visited five of the communities to examine 440 ancient and fragile works of art. Elders contributed their recollections about care of the church before the war and repair efforts afterwards. The result is an eleven-hundred-page document, *Making It Right: Restitution for Churches Damaged and Lost During the Aleut Evacuation of World War II.* (A bit of serendipity: The icon expert discovered a number of icons which may have been painted by Aleuts. They are of an extremely high quality artistically but are distinctive in their Aleutian-style background and the absence of tell-tale Cyrillic superscripts as identifiers on the paintings.)

Two of the churches present unique situations. The church at Atka is a post-war building, constructed on the site of the church burned in 1942. Of the six churches, it is in the worst condition, reflecting the extremely poor building materials available to the community after the war. The community wants to replace this building entirely with another which would at the same time commemorate the losses of the displaced Attuans who now live among them. Included in these plans also is commemoration of a chapel on Amchitka Island, destroyed by U.S. bulldozers in the buildup to retake Kiska in 1943. Amchitka had for generations been the Atkans' traditional fox-trapping site and a seasonal residence. Replacement of the exceptional collection of liturgical art at Atka itself will be quite impossible. Its value, based on a pre-war inventory, is $196,000. Among the remarkable furnishings were gilded silver icons on the *iconostas*, or icon screen, across the front of the nave. Besides Atka, only the cathedral in Sitka possessed such a wealth of liturgical display.

Another unique situation exists at Unalaska. The Unalaska church is often called "the cathedral." It has three altars, or chapels, and in the late nineteenth and early twentieth centuries served as the seat of the bishop of Alaska for many months at a time. Its grand scale reflects the important role of Unalaska in the maritime economy of the region in the late nineteenth century. The church was built in 1895, and is the latest incarnation of the Church of the Holy Ascension founded in 1824 by the priest Ioann Veniaminov, who is now venerated by Orthodox worldwide as St. Innocent. The side chapels of the church contain evidence of St. Innocent's woodworking skill in the design of the *iconostas* in the St. Innocent Chapel, and the Royal Doors in the St. Sergius Chapel. They also have become a magnet for the artistry of Aleuts throughout the region, whose icons hang throughout the cathedral.

The Unalaskan community has already undertaken the Herculean task of restoring this historic landmark. It has raised half a million dollars toward the $1.58 million estimated to replace the roof and the foundation, insulate and plumb the building, and bring the electrical system to safe levels. These sums, however, do not include funds for restoring the extraordinary collection of religious art in the cathedral. Two conservators visited Unalaska and estimated the cost of cleaning and repairing damaged works of art to be $188,000.

Almost four dozen of the principal icons at Unalaska present a unique conservation problem. The Unalaskans were able to take some of the church furnishings with them. They took many of the icons, which they removed from their frames. At Burnet Inlet internment camp, they put most of the icons in storage. The Unalaskans soon noticed mold on them and attempted to clean the canvas icons with "3-in-1" oil, the only lubricant available to them. This treatment occurred several times over the three years of internment. When they returned to Unalaska they noted some of the paint beginning to flake off the paintings. The church warden applied shellac to the painted surface in an effort to secure the paint. The result has been a chemical reaction between the oil and the shellac which has made the canvases extremely dark and very brittle. A/PIA arranged to clean and repair one of these icons in a trial conservation effort. It proved very successful and has quite stunned the congregation with its renewed brightness. It proved more costly than estimated, but reveals what the church must once have looked like.

Restoration and repair of the historic Aleut churches of the Aleutian and Pribilof islands and of their furnishings now seems a reasonable prospect. Both the conservator and the architect agree that the first priority must be to stabilize the environment of the buildings, which includes repair of the superstructure to prevent leaks and shoring up of the foundation. To be done correctly, each of the buildings must be insulated so as to control the wide fluctuations of temperature and humidity which result from sporadic heating of the buildings; and more efficient heating systems should be installed. Ideally, humidity controls should be introduced to protect the exceptional artistic legacy; this would involve plumbing the building. The consulting architect has advised the community on how to protect the exterior finish from the abrasive Aleutian weather.

Once the buildings are secure, the community may then turn its attention to the cleaning and repair of its interior furnishings. Vera B. Espinola, the distinguished icon expert and conservator who consulted on the church condition assessment, proposed to the Historical Commission that Unalaska establish a conservation laboratory. She observed that many tasks, such as cleaning, re-stretching, re-framing, and repairing could be done in the community, and would work in well with the high school and community college. The Aleut Restitution Trust also is interested in this idea.

The goal of the Aleut Restitution Act was to make a just restitution for the "injustices and unreasonable hardships" suffered by the Aleut people because of U.S. policy during World War II. In testimony before the Commission on War-Time Relocation of Civilians, Aleut elders stated repeatedly their number-one plea for restitution: "Restore our churches."

It now appears that the time may be at hand when this dream is realized. And Americans also may rejoice that we have helped to preserve an outstanding historical and cultural link with our Russian heritage.[1]

*From 1991 to 1993, Barbara Sweetland Smith was director of the Aleut Church Restitution Project of the Aleutian/Pribilof Islands Association. She has authored several resource books on Russian America and the Orthodox Church in Alaska. Her most recent book, based on the Aleut restitution program, is "A Sure Foundation: Aleut Churches in World War II."*

---

[1] In 1994, Congress approved and President Clinton signed an amendment to the Aleut Restitution Act increasing the amount of money for church restitution to a total of $4.7 million. The increase was based on the findings of the project described in this paper.

# Turning the Forgotten into the Remembered: The Making of Caines Head State Recreation Area

*Jack E. Sinclair*

A YEAR BEFORE THE INVASION OF ATTU, TROOPS WERE delivered to the shores of a strategic headland facing the violent, cold waters of the Gulf of Alaska. Their mission was to construct the beginnings of a fortification to guard the only all-Alaska, ice-free access to the central population of Alaska. What soon developed was a complex harbor defense system. Between 1945 and 1971, few visitors explored the forests that grew up around the former fortifications at Caines Head, on Resurrection Bay near Seward. Although it was designated a state park in 1971, it was not until 1984 that the first trail opened along the former army roads to uncover uniquely preserved wartime structures. The story of Caines Head, its buildings, the men who were stationed there, and the part they played in the harbor defenses of Seward are revealed through the creation of this maritime state park.

Here are snippets from anecdotes of the time:

• The Baldwin Cold Storage Company no longer makes doors for the meat locker in town; due to the wartime economy, they're making structural steel, gas-proof doors for the plotting and spotting room for Pacific Coast fortifications.

• A war contractor wants $250,000 to pull a two-inch communications cable from salt water, over a peninsula mountain pass, and back down to salt water. The chief army engineer decides that's too expensive and will do it with local GIs. Brute strength gets the job done in a day.

• An orphan mountain goat becomes the camp mascot; "Sgt. Billy" lives for five years with the men, even after returning to civilization.

• A USO troupe of six makes the rounds in December 1942—even to the wilds of Alaska—and wows the boys of "The Beach." The recreation hall is decorated with evergreen boughs and balloons; ladies are provided boat transportation from town; and actress Ingrid Bergman lunches at a Seward cafe with the HQ Battery intelligence officer.

• A pack of Lucky Strikes accompanies every place setting at the Christmas dinner. "Please pass the sidearms" means pass the salt and pepper.

These are only glimpses of the stories within stories utilized at Caines Head State Recreation Area in an attempt to instill in the visitor a spirit of the times.

The dynamic classroom that a military installation set in the northern rain forest of Alaska provides takes on many dimensions. The natural and historical resources that exist on this windy headland south of Seward create a vivid and exciting adventure for all that make the effort to reach its shores.

The waters of Resurrection Bay are a branch of the cold and violent seas of the Gulf of Alaska. If not for the sheltering islands and headlands at the mouth of this bay, Seward would not be what it has become today. These protective, physical barriers allowed this deep-water port to become—for a brief period of the wartime 1940s—the busiest waterfront on the West Coast of North America.

By 1940, Seward was known for, among many things, its direct rail to the Interior of Alaska, its deep, year-round, ice-free port, and the ring of steeply rising mountains and islands surrounding it. It was the terminus of the rail supply route for the greater population of Alas-

One of the four 155-millimeter guns at Rocky Point in Resurrection Bay. These were on fixed Panama mounts and capable of hurling a ninety-five-pound projectile some ten miles. Camouflage netting covered everything not obscured by trees. Caines Head is at the right in the photo. *(Photograph by Henry Mazinski, courtesy of Alaska Division of Parks and Outdoor Recreation)*

ka, year-round, and thus was a vital link to civilian and military interests as the U.S. and Alaska's involvement in World War II intensified.

By June 30, 1941, the first troops arrived in Seward. Their mission was to set up advance preparations for the construction of fortifications to protect the city of Seward, the harbor facilities, and the rail terminus. The earliest constructed military features of the recreation area began on July 31, 1941, at South Beach and Caines Head. These were mostly log structures and tents supporting the 227 men of A Battery of the 250th Coast Artillery Regiment from Camp McQuaide, Watsonville, California. They brought with them four tractor-drawn 155-millimeter guns, protected by their own antiaircraft guns.

Lacking supplies and materials, this scrappy outfit nevertheless built defense facilities out of native timber. A log spotting and plotting room was built into the ground; a communications shack resembled a classic log cabin with one exception: the walls were double thickness, with a two-foot-thick layer of cobbles between the walls.

Log base end stations coordinating the guns were located atop the two-hundred-foot bluff east of the South Beach shoreline and another three hundred feet up the craggy face of the Caines Head headland, all of which were reached by crude log ladders. A pile-driven pier was constructed at South Beach, only to be removed upon completion of onshore developments. This battery interacted with the garrison at Fort Raymond in Seward—manned by 20 officers and 455 enlisted men— to defend the railroad terminus and Port of Seward.

Eventually, permanent, fixed harbor defenses were constructed on the north slope bordering the bay and on the islands at its mouth. The installations included 6-inch batteries at Caines Head and Rugged Island, together with searchlight positions and supporting fire-control facilities and necessary housing at Rocky Point, Topeka Point, Carol Cove, Chamberlin Point, Barwell Island, and Alma Point. The West Construction Company was employed to build these fortifications and support facilities. In less than two years all but a small percentage of these facilities were accepted as complete.

An appreciation of the difficulties facing these first construction crews can be gleaned from the *Narrative Report of Alaska Construction, 1941-1944*, by the Army Corps of Engineers' Lieutenant Colonel James D. Bush Jr. Bush wrote of Seward Harbor defenses:

Barwell Island, Rugged Island, Topeka Point, Rocky Point and Caines Head, all in the vicinity of Seward on the southern coast of the Alaska mainland, are predominantly granite, rising abruptly out of deep water and terminating in precipitous points and escarpments. This is typical of the entire coastline near Seward on Resurrection Bay. In fact, it is so rugged and formidable as to preclude the possibility of landing and sustaining troops in any force, without very elaborate preparations, equipment and supply lines. It is even difficult and hazardous to land a survey party except during calm weather and during certain stages of the tide. The places where such landings can be made are few.

By July 1942 the standardized sixty-three-man barracks, Quonset huts, Pacific huts, and other support structures common throughout the Pacific Theater had arrived unassembled from Seattle, and the South Beach Cantonment—capable of sustaining more than five hundred troops—was created.

Five-and-a-half miles of road was built at Caines Head, none of which connected to the town of Seward. Services and supplies arrived by boats docking at the North Beach Pier, or were lightered ashore at South Beach by smaller "J-boats."

The A Battery of the 250th Coastal Artillery (C.A.), after completing the bulk of the initial work, welcomed the young, new, selective-service personnel of the 267th Separate Coast Artillery Regiment, many of whom were fresh off the farms or from the cities of Pennsylvania.

In 1943, the 250th was redesignated and merged with the 267th C.A. as C Battery. They settled into a rustic wilderness camp life underneath the northern rain forest canopy at Caines Head. The men spent their time detailed to the same work that was most probably happening in a thousand other areas of the Pacific: digging trenches, marching, drilling with large and small ordinance, fixing and repairing tools and equipment. Their play took on a similar role as well: hiking, fishing, badminton, trips to the movie house in Seward, ice skating, or gambling away another month's pay with cards or dice in the barracks.

By March 25, 1943, the installations at Caines Head were designated as Fort McGilvray (named for an army officer who commanded Fort Kenay in 1869). On May 11, 1943, American forces had landed on Attu; by May 30 the occupation of Attu was complete; and by August 15 the American occupation of Kiska was complete. Thus, on March 29, 1944, instructions were sent from Alaskan Department headquarters for the entire harbor defenses of Seward to be dismantled. Within a few short months the installations of Caines Head were dismantled, the guns shipped to locations in South Dakota and San Diego, California, and the buildings left to nature.

As with most towns abandoned by the war but left with the debris, the residents of Seward scavenged

The earliest military construction on what is now the recreation area began on July 31, 1941, at South Beach and Caines Head. This structure, the plotting and spotting room, is probably one of the earliest built at South Beach. *(Photograph by Henry Mazinski, courtesy of Alaska Division of Parks and Outdoor Recreation)*

building materials from Caines Head. Weather conditions, however, were not always suitable for transport of the material. The economy of the town entered a postwar decline, and relied once again on fishing and stevedoring to sustain itself. Caines Head was largely forgotten, and slowly the army roads began to be reclaimed by the surrounding forest.

In 1971 the newly created Division of Parks received authorization and jurisdiction over park lands near many Alaska communities where available outdoor recreation opportunities were seen as a vital part of each community's future development. Approximately eighteen hundred acres were initially selected at Caines Head, creating Caines Head State Recreation Area (SRA). In 1974 this park area was expanded to include more than four thousand additional acres, contributing to its present-day size of 5,961 acres.

By 1984, the interest in Alaska's recreational resource potential was in full force. The recent creation of the Kenai Fjords National Park nearby had brought new attention to the Seward area by way of potential tourism and a flood of outdoor recreation enthusiasts.

A handful of state park staff visited Caines Head in

the Fall of 1984 to do preliminary clearing of the old army roads. After ten days of clearing mile after mile of dog-hair thickets of spruce, they realized they had uncovered a buried treasure. The concrete fortress atop Caines Head, Fort McGilvray, looked like it had been freshly broken out of its forms, window panes were still intact in many casings, doors were functional, old *Life* magazines littered rooms. This park would prove, according to many military and engineering experts, to be one of the most well-preserved batteries in Alaska.

By 1985 the first park ranger was appointed to Caines Head SRA. The hidden remains of a time gone by slowly started to reveal themselves. From the military archives, the recorded as-builts were recovered and from these the actual complexity of the installation hidden among the alder and spruce was discovered.

In 1985, one of the many remarkable veterans of the 267th CA, Jack Turnbull, was visiting Seward and was surprised to find a park now enclosing the former haunts of his war years. Enthused by the recollection of those days, in 1987 Mr. Turnbull helped to organize the first reunion in forty years of the 267th Separate Coast Artillery Battalion. This group, has since met annually, and, through its efforts, donated hundreds of documents, uniforms, military supplies, stories, photographs, and even an M1 Garand rifle. The story behind the story starts to emerge. A spirit of the times surfaces.

In 1991, Seward welcomed these veterans back as thirteen former GIs arrived for a dedication at the park and a celebration hosted by the town. This provided opportunities for recording their recollections on video, with the result to be donated to the University of Alaska Fairbanks' oral history program.

The future of Caines Head, like other military-turned-park areas, is at the mercy of the people who use it. Without public support, through donations of time and money, the lobbying of state representatives, and fostering a love and appreciation for the natural and historical resources of the park, the heritage we've been endowed with will be lost to time and the elements.

Historic preservation measures are minimal at pre-

sent. Due to the costs involved, no restoration of any of the structures has yet been proposed, and only minor efforts have been taken to slow or stop the weathering process. Keeping roots of trees from taking hold and cracking concrete, coating some metal surfaces with oil to prevent corrosion, and maintaining a presence to prevent thefts and vandalism are a few of the measures now being utilized. Perhaps the least the division can

A view out the windows of the Base End Station atop Fort McGilvray. Note the intact window sashes and unbroken panes. Metal shields inside the station could be slid out of the way for operations or locked closed for protection from attack. *(Photo No. 85-023-12-E, Alaska Division of Parks and Outdoor Recreation)*

do—and possibly the most critical—is to document what currently exists and to determine what is important to save.

The challenge for the future is to interpret, to retell the story—and the story within the story—to a generation and generations hereafter that are largely ignorant of the world situation as it existed fifty years ago.

Why is it important to do this? There are many reasons—too many to list. However, much of the hatred we see still simmering throughout the world today of race against race, people against people, strangely resembles the conditions of a world now only remembered by a few.

Caines Head is where people physically, mentally, and emotionally interact with a portion of history. Through the discovery and revelation of the efforts required to build and live in this beautiful, violent, and challenging area of the North Pacific, hopefully something important is imparted: respect and understanding for conditions of a world at war; how and why these fortifications were built and just as quickly abandoned; how the world has changed since the construction; and how the world has changed because of it.

The reasons the army chose the headlands and islands of Resurrection Bay for strategic fortifications are the same reasons that make this park such a stunning and scenic destination. Yet it must also be confessed that the same miserable, cold and wet conditions that those troops endured during those first few months beginning in July 1941 can also be appreciated by today's visitor on any given day.

From J-boats to tour boats, Quonset huts to public-use cabins, military-issue canvas parkas to modern Gore-Tex anoraks, Caines Head is once again occupied, now with a new mission: discovery, understanding, respect, and recreation.

*Jack Sinclair is a Kenai District ranger, Alaska State Parks. For the past several years he has been recording the accounts of World War II veterans stationed in the Seward area.*

# Right before Your Eyes:
# Finding Alaska's World War II Records
# in the National Archives

## R. Bruce Parham

WHEN MOST PEOPLE THINK ABOUT WORLD WAR II in Alaska, they call to mind images of fighting in the Aleutian Islands or construction of the Alaska Highway. Few give thought to the millions of pages of federal, civilian, and military agency records in the National Archives System. In the Pennsylvania Avenue headquarters of the National Archives in Washington, D.C., and at National Archives facilities throughout the country, there are hundreds of thousands of boxes of World War II maps, memorandums, orders, combat reports, telegrams, photographs, films, and more. Such documents are the evidence of the unique issues and events, of the tragedies and triumphs, that make World War II the most significant conflict of the twentieth century. This paper will give an overview of how to find materials on the Aleutian Campaign and Alaska in the archives that are held in the Washington, D.C., area, the National Personnel Records Center in St. Louis, Missouri, and the National Archives - Alaska Region in Anchorage.

Researchers have long relied on the records in the National Archives to document and evaluate the role and impact of the federal government in Alaska. In working on the fringe of the National Archives System of Washington, D.C.-area repositories, presidential libraries, federal records centers, and regional archives, I do not claim to have any magical answers about how researchers can find their way to the Alaska-related World War II holdings in the Washington, D.C., repositories or elsewhere. However, now researchers can refer to a wide variety of guides (many of them issued during the National Archives commemoration of World War II, 1991-1995), catalogs, reference information papers, professional conference proceedings, and general information leaflets to find descriptions of many of the major record groups pertaining to the records of civilian and military agencies in Alaska.[1]

Generally, a record group relates to a single originating department, bureau, or agency of the federal government (for example, Record Group 26, Records of the U.S. Coast Guard).[2]

I would like to talk now about how to chart the twists and turns of a researcher's course on finding World War II records relating to Alaska in the National Archives. I hope that along the way of your research, you can avoid the more obvious rocky shoals and other hazards of navigation through the myriad archival repositories that hold World War II records—principal-

---

[1] Many of these publications are cited in U.S., National Archives and Records Administration, *Select List of Publications of the National Archives and Records Administration*, General Information Leaflet No. 3 (Washington, D.C.: National Archives and Records Administration, 1989); U.S., National Archives and Records Administration, *National Archives 1993 Publications* (Washington, D.C.: National Archives Trust Fund Board for the National Archives, 1993); U.S., National Archives and Records Administration, *World War II Resources from the National Archives and Its National Audiovisual Center* (Washington, D.C.: National Archives Trust Fund Board for the National Archives, 1992); in the "Publications" section of *Prologue: Quarterly of the National Archives*; and in U.S., National Archives and Records Administration, Office of Public Programs, *National Archives News: An Update on the National Archives World War II Commemoration, 1991-1995*.

[2] U.S., National Archives and Records Administration, *Guide to the National Archives of the United States* (Washington, D.C.: National Archives and Records Administration, 1987), p. 6.

ly the National Archives Building in Washington, D.C.; the Washington National Records Center in Suitland, Maryland; the National Personnel Records Center in St. Louis; the ten presidential libraries, especially the Roosevelt, Truman, and Eisenhower presidential libraries; and the thirteen regional archives scattered across the country.

The physical location of World War II textual and non-textual records in the Washington, D.C., area will radically change when the National Archives begins moving to the new National Archives building at College Park, Maryland (informally known as "Archives II").[3] Beginning in November 1993 and continuing through March 1996, the National Archives will begin to move more than one million cubic feet of records from facilities in Suitland, Maryland, and Alexandria, Virginia, and the National Archives Building in Washington, D.C. The move plan will involve transferring all records at the Alexandria, Virginia, facility to College Park, many records now at the National Archives Building and Washington National Records Center in Suitland to College Park, and some records at Suitland to the National Archives Building.

The National Archives at College Park will be located on thirty-three acres of the University of Maryland campus and, with 1.7 million square feet of space, is the largest archives in the world. The National Archives building at College Park will open for research in 1994.[4]

Archives II will augment, not replace, the National Archives Building ("Archives I") in Washington, D.C. Both buildings will operate as archival facilities with different emphases. Records remaining in the National Archives Building in Washington will include those relating to genealogy, selected series of American Indian records, old military (prior to World War II), the navy, the courts, and the Congress. All special media and non-textual records will be moved to College Park as well as military records, except navy records, from World War II to the present, and all executive branch civilian agency records.[5]

Many of the World War II era records, such as those for the "Modern Army", "Air Force", and "Defense" will be moved starting in April 1995 and with a completion date of March 1996.

During this three-year period, entire record groups will be closed for research and reference activities, including requests for information and reproductions. During the move of textual records, most records will be closed and reopened at the record group level. In other words, whole clusters will not be closed during a specific time frame; rather, individual record groups within the cluster will be closed, moved, and then reopened to researchers.

National Archives staff members have prepared a number of finding aids describing the holdings of the National Archives. The contents of every record group are described in a general way in the *Guide to the National Archives of the United States.*[6]

The end of each descriptive guide entry will cite any finding aids for textual and microfilm records for that record group, such as inventories or preliminary inventories, special lists, or descriptive pamphlets for microfilm publications. An inventory or preliminary inventory describes in detail the records in a single record group or part of a record group. The National Archives also produces subject guides and other finding aids as well as microfilm catalogs. A comprehensive list of finding aids in print appears in *Select List of Publications in the National Archives and Records Administration*, General Information Leaflet No. 3 (1989).[7]

There are several guides that are of particular interest to the Aleutian campaign and other theaters of operation. The *List of Logbooks of U.S. Navy Ships, Stations, and Miscellaneous Units, 1801-1947* (Special List 44, 1978) describes approximately seventy-three thousand logbooks of U.S. Navy ships, stations, and miscellaneous units that are held by the National Archives.[8] For instance, there are logbooks for all of the ships in Admiral Charles McMorris's task force that fought the Battle of the Komandorski Islands on March 26, 1943—the *Salt*

---

[3] The *Archives II Researcher Bulletin* contains updates on the move schedule of records. Researchers can contact the Textual Reference Division (NNR), National Archives and Records Administration, 7th and Pennsylvania Avenue, N.W., Washington, D.C. 20408, to obtain copies and to be put on the mailing list. Researchers may also write to that division or contact the Reference Services Branch (NNRS) at the above address or call (202) 501-5400, for more information on the move status of specific records. If researchers are planning a research trip to Washington, D.C., between 1993 and 1996, they should verify with the Textual Reference Division (NNR) the move status of specific records at least several weeks before traveling to Washington, D.C. U.S., National Archives and Records Administration, *Archives II Researcher Bulletin*, No. 5 (Spring 1993), p. 3.

[4] The new address of The National Archives at College Park is 8601 Adelphi Road, College Park, Maryland 20740-6001.

[5] U.S., National Archives and Records Administration, News Release, "National Archives Prepares for Massive Move of Records," 28 August 1992.

[6] *Guide to the National Archives.*

[7] *Select List of Publications of the National Archives.*

[8] U.S., General Services Administration, National Archives and Records Service, *List of Logbooks of U.S. Navy Ships, Stations, and Miscellaneous Units, 1801-1947*, Compiled by Claudia Bradley, Michael Kurtz, Rebecca Livingston, Timothy Mulligan, Muriel Parseghian, Paul Vanderveer, and James Yale, Special List 44 (Washington, D.C.: National Archives and Records Service, 1978).

*Lake City* (CA-25), the *Richmond* (CL-9), the *Bailey* (DD-492), the *Coghlan* (DD-606), the *Monaghan* (DD-354), and the *Dale* (DD-353). Coast Guard vessels are described in the *List of Logs of United States Coast Guard Vessels in the National Archives, 1790-1941* and in *List of Coast Guard Vessel & Shore Unit Logs at United States Coast Guard Headquarters, Washington, D.C., 1942-1944*.[9]

In seeking to find World War II records, the best source still is *Federal Records of World War II* (1950-1951).[10]

This guide is divided into two volumes, one concerned with the activities of the so-called civilian agencies, the other with those of the military agencies. Each of the hundreds of entries contains separate civilian and military agency administrative histories; information on organizational relationships between the various units of an agency; statements on the location, custody, and cubic footage of the records as of 1949; and bibliographic citations for agency administrative histories and other secondary sources. The records described in each volume were selected to demonstrate that federal records can provide researchers with valuable information for understanding both America's participation in the war and the effects of the war upon the United States.

Although not intended to provide a complete description of all World War II records, each volume and the detailed index can be used by researchers to find information on particular subjects within the groups of records, among many, that are likely to contain the desired information. Searches can be further narrowed by using lists or the detailed inventories of the groups of records which may be pertinent.

The volume for *Civilian Agencies* includes descriptive entries for records from field offices located in Seattle, Alaska, or elsewhere that administered Alaska's civilian wartime activities, such as the War Assets Administration, the Office of Price Administration, Division of Territories and Island Possessions (Department of the Interior), Office of Fishery Coordination, the Alaska Spruce Log Program (Forest Service), the Alaskan Highway Office of the Public Roads Administration, and so forth. Since few descriptive finding aids exist for many field office records, *Federal Records of World War II* is

often the only comprehensive source for detailed information about the organization, functions, activities, and records of the government's World War II agencies.

The volume for *Military Agencies* is divided into four parts, "Interallied and Interservice Military Agencies", "The War Department and the Army", "The Naval Establishment", and "Theaters of Operation." Among the index entries for Alaska are those for the Alaskan Air Command, Alaska Communications System, Alaska Defense Command (including the Eleventh Air Force), the Alaska Sector of the Western Defense Command based at Fort Richardson, the Alaska Division of the Air Transport Command, the Alaska Sector of the Northwest Sea Frontier with headquarters in Seattle and later Adak, the Naval Establishment (which served as branch offices of the Navy Department) of the Seventeenth Naval District at Kodiak, and the Alaska Highway. Included in the entry for the Northwest Service Command are descriptions for the headquarters records of the Alaska Highway at Dawson Creek, British Columbia, and information on two other principal projects, the Canol Project and the operation of the White Pass and Yukon Railway.

Other federal archival records on the war in Alaska can be found in George Ulibarri's *Documenting Alaskan History: Guide to Federal Archives Relating to Alaska* (1982), a collaborative effort between the National Archives, the Alaska Historical Commission, and the University of Alaska.[11]

In twelve separate chapters, Ulibarri describes selected records covering a wide range of subjects relating to Alaska. Of particular interest due to the impact of World War II on Alaska, are those chapters on "Alaskan Industries and Trade", "Natural Resources", "Governing Alaska", "Transportation and Communications", and "Military, Naval, and Maritime Activities." Most of the materials described in Ulibarri are held by National Archives facilities in the Washington, D.C., area—not at the National Archives - Alaska Region in Anchorage. This guide can be used in tandem with various National Archives inventories for many of the record groups to identify specific materials of interest on the war on the "home front" in Alaska and on various military aspects.[12]

---

[9] U.S., Coast Guard, *List of Logs of United States Coast Guard Vessels in the National Archives, 1790-1941*, Compiled in the National Archives by Thornton W. Mitchell and Arthur Dyer of the Division of Treasury Department Archives, NAVCG 116 (Washington, D.C.: U.S. Coast Guard, 1944); and U.S., Coast Guard, *List of Coast Guard Vessel & Shore Unit Logs at United States Coast Guard Headquarters, Washington, D.C., 1942-1944* (Washington, D.C.: U.S. Coast Guard, 1944).

[10] U.S., General Services Administration, National Archives and Records Service, *Federal Records of World War II*, vol. 1, *Civilian Agencies* (Washington, D.C.: Government Printing Office, 1950); and U.S., General Services Administration, National Archives and Records Service, *Federal Records of World War II*, vol. 2, *Military Agencies* (Washington, D.C.: Government Printing Office, 1951).

[11] George S. Ulibarri, *Documenting Alaskan History: Guide to Federal Archives Relating to Alaska*, Alaska Historical Commission Studies in History No. 23 (Fairbanks: University of Alaska Press, 1982).

[12] Inventories and preliminary inventories provide researchers with series-level descriptions of the holdings of individual record groups in

I will also call your attention to *World War II: An Account of Its Documents* (1976), which contains the eighteen papers presented at the Conference on Research on the Second World War held in June 1971 at the National Archives.[13] This conference was organized by the National Archives to provide a forum between archivists and historians, the custodians of the records and their principal users. The nine sessions presented at the conference were devoted to Second World War research in the United States and abroad, wartime diplomacy, military biography, access to archival sources, the role of science and technology, the wartime emergency agencies, and official historical programs. Several of the papers provide a good description of the World War II military records now held in the National Archives Building in Washington, D.C., the Washington National Records Center in Suitland, Maryland, and at the Roosevelt, Truman, and Eisenhower presidential libraries.

During the National Archives' fiftieth anniversary commemoration of World War II (1991-1995), several reference information papers have been updated and reissued to provide ready-reference information about federal archival records relating to the war. Topics covered in recent reference information papers include *Audiovisual Records in the National Archives Relating to World War II* (RIP 70 revised); *Records Relating to Personal Participation in World War II: 'The American Soldier' Surveys* (RIP 78); *World War II Records in the Cartographic and Architectural Branch of the National Archives* (RIP 79); and *Records Relating to Personal Participation in World War II: American Prisoners of War and Civilian Internees* (RIP 80).[14] In the reference information paper on cartographic records, there are twenty-four entries on "Alaska", the "Alcan Highway", and the "Aleutian Islands." Some of the items listed include vertical and oblique aerial photographic prints of Attu and the Aleutians; Coast and Geodetic Survey aeronautical charts prepared for the army air forces; architectural drawings of Coast Guard stations in Alaska (including plans of depots, patrol and radar bases, and air stations, as well as plans of lifesaving stations and lighthouses); beach studies of Kiska; "view charts" of the Aleutians and St. Lawrence Island, including perspective views of approaches to aid aviators; more than four thousand published aeronautical charts designed for use by naval aviators, many dating from World War II; and so forth. Although only a few thousand copies of each of these recent papers has been published, you may contact the Fulfillment Center (NEDC) in Capitol Heights, Maryland, to request these and other National Archives publications.[15]

Various National Archives holdings are also now available on-line. The Motion Picture, Sound and Video Branch and the Still Picture Branch have begun to make information about National Archives audiovisual holdings available through the Internet Computer Network. Among a growing number of on-line files is one entitled "Select Audiovisual Records: Pictures of World War II."[16]

The National Archives is also developing a computerized Archival Information System (AIS), which is

---

the National Archives. Each inventory and preliminary inventory also contains an administrative history of the agency that accumulated the records described. Many of these inventories were reproduced on National Archives Microfilm Publication M248 (*Publications of the National Archives, 1935-1968*), which includes most NARS finding aids through 1968. There are unpublished inventories on National Archives Microfilm Publication T1086 ("Finding Aids Issued Primarily for Staff Use in the National Archives," 5 rolls), which is available for research use at many National Archives facilities. See U.S., National Archives and Records Administration, *Select List of Publications of the National Archives and Records Administration*, General Information Leaflet No. 3 (Washington, D.C.: National Archives and Records Administration, 1989), for a comprehensive list of inventories and preliminary inventories, and special lists.

[13] James E. O'Neill and Robert W. Krauskopf, eds., *World War II: An Account of Its Documents*, National Archives Conferences, vol. 8: Papers and Proceedings of the Conference on Research on the Second World War, June 14-15, 1971, National Archives Building, Washington, D.C. (Washington, D.C.: Howard University Press, 1976).

[14] U.S., National Archives and Records Administration, *Audiovisual Records in the National Archives of the United States Relating to World War II*, Reference Information Paper 70 (revised), Compiled by Barbara Berger, William Cunliffe, Jonathan Heller, William T. Murphy, and Les Waffen (Washington, D.C.: National Archives and Records Administration, 1992); U.S., National Archives and Records Administration, *Records Relating to Personal Participation in World War II: "The American Soldier" Surveys*, Reference Information Paper 78, Compiled by Ben DeWhitt and Heidi Ziemer (Washington, D.C.: National Archives and Records Administration, 1991); U.S., National Archives and Records Administration, *World War II Records in the Cartographic and Architectural Branch of the National Archives*, Reference Information Paper 79, Compiled by Daryl Bottoms (Washington, D.C.: National Archives and Records Administration, 1992); and U.S., National Archives and Records Administration, *Records Relating to Personal Participation in World War II: American Prisoners of War and Civilian Internees*, Reference Information Paper 80, Compiled by Ben DeWhitt and Jennifer Davis Heaps (Washington, D.C.: National Archives and Records Administration, 1992).

[15] Address: Fulfillment Center (NEDC), Customer Service Section (NEDCS), National Archives and Records Administration, 8700 Edgeworth Drive, Capitol Heights, Maryland 20743-3701 (telephone: 800-788-6282). This toll-free telephone number can be used to obtain ordering instructions or information on the availability of fee and free publications, microfilm, audiovisual products, and so forth.

[16] U.S., National Archives and Records Administration, *NARA Staff Bulletin*, No. 331, 20 July 1993, p. 2.

designed to streamline the archival description or cataloging process and to facilitate reference. The system will contain data about records in the custody of other federal agencies, the federal records centers, and the National Archives. If all goes well, AIS will be able to track records through their "life cycle," from creation to eventual disposition. For the researcher community, the so-called "reference module" will provide on-line searching capabilities not only about what is available in the National Archives but what will be available in the future.[17]

The paper guides can be supplemented by contacting staff members of the National Archives in the Washington, D.C., area who are responsible for the records. Researchers should contact them for information about the finding aids, records, and possible restrictions on records before they make a visit. There is also a list, "National Archives Primary Reference Contact List," with over 100 subjects with the names, room, and telephone numbers of reference archivists responsible for records relating to specific subjects.[18] This list includes such topics as "Coast Guard", "Defense Plant", "Japanese Internment-Internee Files", "Maps", "Military, 20th Century", "Military Intelligence", "Navy, 20th Century", and "World War II." Although National Archives staff members do not do research for individuals, they will answer telephone or written questions about holdings and will furnish copies of documents for a fee if the request identifies the documents adequately.

Moving past finding aids, I would like to call attention to some significant groups of records in the National Archives held by the National Personnel Records Center in St. Louis and in Anchorage at the National Archives - Alaska Region. While working as an appraisal archivist in the Military Operations Branch in St. Louis in 1989-1990, I became acquainted with the large body of approximately fifty thousand cubic feet of unscheduled army records and another thirty-three thousand cubic feet of Army Air Corps and air force records, also unscheduled, that are held there.

The army and air force records in St. Louis consist of the administrative files of all military organizations below Department or Chief of Staff levels (such as depots, hospitals, and schools). These eighty-three thousand cubic feet of records represent army and air force organizational records that were retired to NPRC and its predecessor repositories between 1948 and 1968.

Afterwards, all non-personnel related field organizational records were sent to the newly opened Washington National Records Center at Suitland, Maryland. The NPRC collection then, is a closed collection, covering generally the period from World War II to Vietnam.[19]

The army records include the combat-type clusters of records, beginning with the numbered and named (or geographical armies), and move through divisions, brigades, corps, groups, and regiments, etc. The support-type groupings include those materials for centers, schools, boards, agencies, districts, services, arsenals, stations, etc.

The air force records that make up the collection represent the total records-keeping activity of the service (exclusive of personnel and pay records) below Headquarters, U.S. Air Force, during the years of its inception, birth, and formative development as an independent branch of the armed forces and a separate military department. The large volumes of World War II army air forces material in St. Louis help document the rapid growth of the air arm brought on by the war, and provide necessary background and context which explain the subsequent emergence of an independent air force. The 266 cubic feet of indexes cover such clusters of records as army air forces, numbered air forces, major commands, airports, army air fields and bases, training bases, depots, flights and groups, troop carrier groups, ports, technical schools, squadrons, wings, groups, and voluminous research and development records. Among the air force records are those of the Air Ferrying Command and the Air Transport Command, including eighty-nine cubic feet of central or functional files, which includes box after box of War Plans Division studies for proposed American bases in Siberia and the ATC's travel plans for President Roosevelt's trip to the Yalta Conference.

The army and air force records held by the National Personnel Records Center are, by and large, unavailable for research by the general public. However, as these materials are appraised, screened, arranged, and transferred to National Archives facilities in the Washington, D.C., area or to the regional archives, important new research opportunities will be opened up.

The National Archives - Alaska Region holds several World War II collections that were identified and transferred to Anchorage after our facility was opened in 1990 or during the process of making the records in our

---

[17] U.S., National Archives and Records Administration, *Archives II Researcher Bulletin*, No. 3 (Winter 1992), pp. 1-2.

[18] The "National Archives Primary Reference Contact List" is available upon request from the Textual Reference Division (NNR), National Archives and Records Administration, Washington, D.C. 20408.

[19] William G. Seibert, "Talk to NN Archivists," 29 October 1990, U.S., National Archives and Records Administration, Office of the National Archives, National Archives Notice NN91-R19, "Briefing on NPRC Army and Air Force Disposition Project," 4 December 1990.

Washington, D.C.-area repositories "move-ready" during the move to the new archives building at College Park. Some examples:

(1) U.S. Fish and Wildlife Service records (Record Group 22), especially the Pribilof Islands Program Records, 1923-1969, contain information related to the operation of the so-called "Funter Bay Evacuation Camp" from 1942 to 1945. There are eyewitness accounts of the June 16, 1942 evacuation from the Pribilof Islands, information about the horrible living conditions, especially the problems brought about by a poor water and sanitation system; the rampant flu and tuberculosis epidemics; the 1943 sealing operations; and the shocking effects of bureaucratic inefficiency and incompetence by federal and Alaska territorial agencies.[20]

(2) Records of the Alaska field office of the Office of Price Administration (OPA) (Record Group 188) contain information of potential value to researchers in the area of local history. To stabilize prices and rents, the OPA set maximum prices for commodities and rents, rationed scarce essential commodities, and authorized subsidies for production of some of these items. There are forty boxes of Price Operation Records which document the wholesale and retail price schedules for hundreds of commodities, such as clothing, hosiery, rubber footwear, food, and dairy products. The OPA apparel files contain retailer's reports for B.M. Behrends Company, Inc., of Juneau, showing the retail price for cotton sheets ($2.50), maximum price ($2.50), the direct cost to the seller ($1.27), and the amount of markup ($1.23).[21] In the dairy products files, the successful petition effort of Creamers' Dairy in Fairbanks to avert an Interior milk shortage reveals the dairy's ongoing business operations over a five-year period.[22] The fur survey files in the same record series detail the kinds of furs sold with the lowest and highest prices received in Alaska from 1941-1945.[23]

(3) There are extensive records of naval districts and shore establishments (Record Group 181) for the Seventeenth Naval District (Alaska) (approximately 414 cubic feet) covering the 1941-1956 period. Included among these records are the central subject files from the district's offices at Kodiak, and of detached units such as naval facilities at Adak, Amchitka, Andreanof Island, Attu, Cold Bay, Dutch Harbor, Kiska, and Sitka. Also included are files created by the Military Sea Transport Service and operational files for individual ship classes. By the end of World War II, the naval districts exercised almost complete administrative control over naval operations within their limits, including naval shipyards, stations, training stations, air installations, and advanced bases.[24]

(4) The Alaska Communications System (ACS) records, which is an incomplete collection of army and air force records dating from 1900-1961, includes annual reports, drafts of the history of the Alaska Communications System's World War II operations, station photograph albums from the 1940s and 1950s, photographs of cableships, and station folders with captioned photographs.[25] ACS achievements in World War II included planning and supervising the Alcan Highway Telephone Line, constructing and operating the Alaska Defense Command radio net, and participating in the Battle of Attu. In 1994, the Alaska Region received an additional seventeen cubic feet of records of the Alaska Communications System, 1909-39, from the records of the Office of the Chief Signal Officer (Record Group 111). This material includes monthly and annual reports, letters, reports, memoranda, telegrams, and other papers relating to the establishment and maintenance of radio stations, radio and cable equipment, the laying and maintenance of cables, and message traffic of the Alaska Communications System.

(5) In 1992, the Alaska Region received more than nine thousand World War II engineer as-built drawings and other cartographic records from the U.S. Army Corps of Engineers' Alaska District at Fort Richardson.

(6) In 1993, the Alaska Region received the field operations records of the War Assets Administration (Record Group 270) from the National Archives in Washington, D.C. The purpose of the WAA was to dispose of all

[20] File "D," Pribilof Islands Program, Records, 1923-1969, Box 33; Records of the Fish and Wildlife Service, Record Group 22; National Archives - Alaska Region, Anchorage, Alaska.

[21] File "Behrends, B.M. (Dry Goods)," Board Files, Board No. 7, Juneau, Alaska, Price Department, Alaska District Office, Region IX (Territorial) Records, 1941-47, Box 158; Records of the Office of Price Administration, Record Group 188; National Archives - Alaska Region.

[22] File "Daries [Dairies] - Fairbanks," Price Operations Records, 1942-1946, Price Department, Alaska District Office, Region IX (Territorial) Records, 1941-47, Box 63, Records of the Office of Price Administration, Record Group 188; National Archives - Alaska Region.

[23] File "Furs & Hides," Price Operations Records, 1942-46, Price Department, Alaska District Office, Region IX (Territorial) Records, 1941-47, Box 66; Records of the Office of Price Administration, Record Group 188; National Archives - Alaska Region.

[24] U.S., National Archives and Records Administration, National Archives - Pacific Northwest Region, "Records of Naval Districts and Shore Establishments in the National Archives - Alaska Region, Part of Record Group 181," comp. by Janusz M. Wilczek (Seattle, Washington: National Archives - Pacific Northwest Region, 1990); and U.S., National Archives and Records Administration, Records of Naval Districts and Shore Establishments in the Regional Archives, Part of Record Group 181, Special List 58 (Fort Worth, Texas: National Archives - Southwest Region, 1991), pp. 51-54.

[25] See Alaska Communications System, Records, 1900-1961, Boxes 1-27 (12 cu. ft.); Records of the United States Air Force Commands, Activities, and Organizations, Record Group 342; National Archives — Alaska Region.

domestic surplus property and arrange for the transfer of such property between government agencies. In Alaska as elsewhere, the WAA disposed of consumer goods, industrial and maritime property, and airports and craft.

*R. Bruce Parham is Assistant Director, National Archives - Alaska Region. He is currently researching Joseph W. Ivey and U.S. Customs enforcement on the Alaska-Yukon frontier during the Klondike gold rush.*

# The War's
# Aftermath

Miss Anchorage (Rita Martin) and a firefighter attach the 49th star to a flag on the Federal Building in Anchorage, June 30, 1958.
*(Photo No. BL79.2.2686, Alaska Railroad Collection, The Anchorage Museum of History and Art)*

# The Legacy of War

*John Haile Cloe*

TWO INFANTRY COMPANIES AT CHILKOOT BARRACKS near Haines guarded Alaska on the eve of World War II. Along with a small seaplane base at Sitka and a contingent of army and navy communications personnel scattered throughout the territory, they provided the only military presence in the sparsely populated territory.

Although the military had considered the defense of Alaska during its pre-World War II planning, the economic realities of the time, higher priorities elsewhere, and a general feeling that Alaska and the North Pacific area were not as strategically important as other areas, resulted in no action other than a number of army and navy surveys during the 1920s and '30s, and the preparation of various staff studies recommending that the territory be defended. Additionally, the 1935 Wilcox Bill, introduced by Republican Senator Mark Wilcox of Florida, called for the construction of a military airfield near Fairbanks as part of a six-field program throughout the United States. Although authorized, it was not funded until April 1939. Construction of Ladd Field (now Fort Wainwright), a cold-weather test facility, began that summer. It was the first major military airfield to be built in Alaska.

However, with the outbreak of hostilities in Europe and the growing threat of the Japanese in the Pacific, the United States began a major rearmament program from which Alaska benefited.

The war planners realized that the territory, because of its size and widely scattered and isolated population centers, was an air theater of operations. As a result, emphasis was on building air bases to protect not only army facilities but those of the navy as well.

Construction began on Fort Richardson and its air base, Elmendorf Field, on 8 June 1940. The first troops, the Fourth Infantry Regiment and its support units, arrived on 27 June 1940.

Colonel (later Lieutenant General) Simon B. Buckner, assumed command of all army ground and air forces in Alaska in July 1940, and the Alaska Defense Command, later Alaskan Department, was formed.

The first air unit, the Eighteenth Pursuit (later Fighter) Squadron, arrived in February 1941. It was equipped with P-36 Hawks. Two bomber squadrons equipped with B-18 twin-engine bombers arrived shortly afterward. By 7 December 1941, there were twenty-three hundred Army Air Corps personnel assigned to Alaska. The three under-strength flying squadrons available for the defense of Alaska were still equipped with obsolete aircraft.

Following the Japanese attack on Pearl Harbor, a fighter squadron and a bomber squadron were rushed to Alaska over the northwest staging route in the dead of winter. Of the twenty-four P-40s deployed, seven were lost to accidents and five of the fourteen medium bombers deployed were destroyed in crashes.

Better procedures were developed, facilities were improved, and the Alaska Highway was built partly in response to a need to provide a year-round surface capability for delivering supplies and equipment to air fields along the route. Later deployments became routine without any alarming incidents.

The Eleventh Air Force was formed in February 1942 to manage the rapidly expanding air forces in Alaska.

Construction of military airfields on Umnak Island in the eastern Aleutians and at Cold Bay on the Alaska Peninsula began in an effort to counter the increasing Japanese threat.

The Japanese, during the first six months of the war, had literally run wild in the Pacific and Far East, inflicting one stunning defeat after another on the surprised and confused Allies. By early April they had achieved virtually every objective.

Overconfident, they decided to push their empire eastward to provide a better defensive line, the objective being to hold a demoralized America at bay while negotiating a favorable truce with an enemy they perceived to be materialistic and morally weak.

Their plan called for finishing off the remainder of the U.S. Pacific Fleet—heavily damaged in the Pearl Harbor attack—and establishing a defensive line that ran from Port Moresby, New Guinea, through the Samoan and the Fiji islands, north to Midway Island and the western Aleutians. Part of the plan was frustrated during the Battle of the Coral Sea when an American carrier task force turned back the Port Moresby invasion force. Despite the setback, the Japanese decided to go ahead with the Midway-Aleutian operations.

The plan developed by the Imperial Navy was complex. It spread the Japanese combined fleet of two hundred ships all over the Pacific.

The Aleutian part of the plan called for a carrier strike against Dutch Harbor on June 3 as a diversion from their main strike against Midway. Additionally, the Japanese planned to occupy Adak, Kiska, and Attu. They also planned to establish a long-range seaplane base at Adak from which patrols could be flown southward towards Midway. Additionally, they wanted to counter a possible American offensive from the Aleutians.

The Japanese struck Dutch Harbor as planned the morning of June 3 with a follow-up attack on the afternoon of June 4. The casualties inflicted on the ground at Dutch Harbor and nearby Fort Mears were minimal. The Americans had been forewarned of the attack though radio communications intercepts and were prepared. Thirty-five men were killed in action and another twenty-eight wounded. Four oil tanks containing twenty thousand gallons were destroyed as were two barracks and three warehouses, one of which contained a crated SCR-271 radar set. Two antiaircraft positions were hit and a 20-millimeter and 37-millimeter gun destroyed. A hangar was slightly damaged and the barracks ship *Northwestern* badly damaged.

Units of the Eleventh Air Force and the navy's Fleet Air Wing Four had been deployed forward to locations near Dutch Harbor prior to the attacks. Fighters and bombers of the Eleventh Air Force operated from Cold Bay and the recently completed air field at Otter Point

on the east side of Umnak Island. Fleet Air Wing Four PBY patrol aircraft operated from Dutch Harbor and bays in the eastern Aleutians and on the Alaska Peninsula.

U.S. Army and Navy air units were active prior to, during and after the attacks. As a result of the intense actions, the Eleventh Air Force lost a four-engine B-17 bomber with its nine-man crew. Two twin-engine B-26s were lost with six men killed in action and one wounded. Two P-40 fighters were shot down with the loss of one pilot and another wounded. Fleet Air Wing Four suffered the heaviest losses in the air, with six PBY Catalinas destroyed, twenty-three men killed, three taken prisoner, ten missing in action, and two wounded.

None of the Japanese ships were harmed. However, the Japanese lost seven aircraft, one of which was a Mitsubishi A6M2 "Zero" fighter. Virtually undamaged, it was recovered more than a month later from Akutan Island by American forces and restored to flying condition. The Japanese Navy fighter was flown against American aircraft to determine its strengths and weaknesses. The information obtained provided a technological breakthrough in the development of American tactics.

The Japanese suffered a crushing defeat at Midway and lost the strategic initiative in the Pacific. The Aleutian phase of the operations was carried out as planned with the occupation of Attu and Kiska. The decision to occupy the two islands provided the Japanese military a convenient excuse to mask their defeat at Midway. The "great Aleutian victory" was made possible by the diversion at Midway.

The Japanese occupation of the western Aleutians placed the Americans in a dilemma. Strategically, they could be ignored since they were such a small force in a location far removed from their base of resupply in the northern Kurile Islands. However, the Joint Chiefs of Staff could not ignore the public and political reality: a piece of the North American continent had been occupied by a hostile nation.

The organizational structure had been created initially to deal with the Japanese. It thrust into the Aleutians and did well. However, with the expulsion of the Japanese, the overwrought structure became convoluted and violated the principle of unity of command. The structure was further weakened by the incompatibility of the two principals—General Buckner, of the Alaskan Defense Command, and Admiral Robert Theobald, commander of the North Pacific area.

The Aleutian campaign was essentially a navy show—because of the geographical nature of the area—and Buckner, while providing forces and support, had little control over operations. Aggressive by temperament, General Buckner frequently clashed with cautious Admiral Theobald, who was described as having one of the best minds and worst dispositions in the navy. The problems were further compounded by General John Dewitt, commander of the Western Defense Command, headquartered in San Francisco. Dewitt, despite the recommendations of Buckner, the suggestions of the Joint Chiefs of Staff, and the urging of General George Marshall (the Army Chief of Staff), refused to relinquish control over Alaska. Since it was within his area of responsibility, he would not allow it to become a separate theater command.

The Aleutians, partly because of the command relations problems and other difficulties—namely the notorious weather and the bleak and rugged terrain—became, in the words of Samuel Elliot Morison, "a theater of military frustration."

Reinforcements were sent to Alaska prior to and following the Dutch Harbor attack. They included another fighter squadron, equipped with P-38s, and three bomber squadrons, two heavy and one medium.

Canada also contributed substantial forces to the effort to protect Alaska and drive the Japanese from the Aleutians. Warships were dispatched north, and the Royal Canadian Air Force made a sizable contribution of two provisional wings. X Wing was headquartered at Elmendorf Field. Two of its squadrons were committed to the Aleutians and the third flew antisubmarine operations out of Nome on the Bering seacoast. Y Wing was located at the RCAF base established on Annette Island in Southeastern Alaska. It provided air defense for the area and nearby Prince Rupert and flew antisubmarine patrols over the Gulf of Alaska. The wartime contribution would later develop into the Cold War commitment of both nations to the common air defense of North America and the formation of the North American Air Defense Command, or NORAD.

The Aleutian campaign was primarily an air war, conducted by bombers and fighters of the Eleventh Air Force against the major Japanese base on Kiska and, to a lesser extent, the more distant Attu Island. The navy also conducted a series of inconclusive naval bombardments against the two islands.

The first phase of the campaign involved the occupation of the uninhabited island of Adak and the construction of a runway there. Troops began going ashore on August 30 and immediately started building a runway in a drained tidal lagoon. The runway was ready within ten days. This put the Eleventh Air Force within 250 miles of Kiska. Prior to that, the bombers had to fly a round-trip distance of thirteen hundred miles without fighter protection.

The next phase, the occupation of Amchitka, occurred on 12 January 1943, as a preliminary for an amphibious assault to retake Kiska in early May. However, when

shipping was withdrawn Admiral Thomas Kinkaid, who had replaced Theobald, convinced the Joint Chiefs of Staff that Kiska could be bypassed and Attu taken instead, with lesser forces. At the time, his intelligence staff told him that the island was lightly defended by a garrison of five hundred second-rate troops.

By then the Japanese garrisons in the Aleutians had been effectively isolated by a combination of sea and air patrols. Their fate was firmly sealed when an escorted convoy of reinforcements and supplies intended for Attu turned back during a naval surface engagement fought off the Komandorski Islands on March 26. On May 11, the Seventh Infantry Division, trained for desert warfare in California but selected for combat on a mountainous, cold, damp, and fog-shrouded island at the tip of the Aleutians, waded ashore at three different locations. The plan called for linkup of forces in Jarmin Pass behind the main Japanese defenses at Holtz Bay and Chichagof Harbor. The trapped Japanese then could be dealt with by aerial and sea bombardment. General Dewitt predicted the whole operation would not last more than three days.

Instead of five hundred Japanese, however, the forces under the command of Major General Albert Brown were faced with more than twenty-three hundred of an enemy who fought with courage and skill. Weather canceled most of the planned air strikes, and so the engagement became an infantryman's war in the truest sense. It took hard-fought, small-unit encounters to dislodge the Japanese from their positions on the high ground.

The battle ended during the early morning hours of May 29, when the surviving Japanese made a suicide charge that almost succeeded in breaking through the American positions along Engineer Ridge. Attu was the third amphibious operation that American forces had participated in. It was the first island assault for the army and as preparations for the assault on the island had progressed, the strength and capabilities of the enemy had been grossly underestimated and the full effects of the weather and the terrain ignored.

The Americans paid the price: 549 Americans died. Another 1,148 were wounded, and some 2,100 were taken out of battle by various causes. Approximately 2,350 Japanese died. Only twenty-nine survived as prisoners.

The final stage in securing the Aleutians was the retaking of Kiska. With the lessons learned from Attu, a considerably larger combined Canadian-U.S. force of thirty-three thousand assault troops was assembled to overcome the estimated five-thousand-man garrison on the island.

When the troops went ashore on August 15, they discovered that the Japanese had evacuated their garrison on July 28. The occupation of Kiska marked the end of the Aleutian campaign.

Approximately 8,500 Japanese had tied down about 144,000 Americans and Canadians during the final phase of the campaign. More than a billion dollars was spent on building and sustaining an infrastructure to support the campaign. Approximately one thousand Americans and Canadians were killed in combat.

Material damages included the loss of 225 aircraft, of which forty-one were lost in combat. The remainder were operational losses. The Aleutian campaign accounted for the highest operational loss of aircraft in any theater that the United States had been engaged in. For every one aircraft lost to combat, four were lost to other causes, notably weather.

Two destroyers, two submarines, one transport and one cable layer were sunk by hostile action. Combat damages were inflicted on a heavy cruiser, two transports and one barracks ship.

The Japanese, too, lost heavily in the Aleutians. In addition to their entire garrison on Attu, they lost approximately five hundred men on Kiska. Another thousand, approximately, lost their lives at sea, and about 150 navy airmen died. Three destroyers, five submarines and nine transports were sunk. Three destroyers and two transports were damaged.

Operations were hampered in the North Pacific by the lack of a unified command system to coordinate joint operations. Finally, the forces used in the Aleutians could have been put to good use elsewhere; a strategy of containment would have worked just as well. The Japanese, because of the distances from their support bases, and the fact that the Americans and their Canadian allies had quickly achieved air and naval superiority, never really posed any substantial threat to the rest of North America.

For a brief period, serious thought was given to using the Aleutians as an invasion route to Japan. Consideration was also given to basing B-29s on the western islands, and a base was built on Shemya for that purpose. However, the idea was quickly dropped in the face of the difficulties posed by weather and terrain.

Instead, airfields built on Shemya and Attu were used to launch bomber raids and reconnaissance missions against Japanese bases in the northern Kurile Islands. They tied down Japanese forces that could have been committed to countering the American drive across the central Pacific. The last mission over the Kuriles was flown on 3 September 1945, by two B-24s from the 404th Bomber Squadron on a high-altitude photo reconnaissance mission to gather intelligence on the Soviet forces which had just occupied the islands. Intercepted by Soviet fighters, they turned back.

The intercept illustrated the underlying tensions that were developing between the Soviet Union and the United States.

Alaska, because of its location, had served as a transshipment point for aircraft and small naval vessels destined for the Soviet Union under the lend-lease program. Almost eight thousand aircraft, mostly fighters and medium bombers, were transferred to Soviet control at Ladd Field and 149 vessels, primarily patrol craft and minesweepers, were turned over to the Soviet Navy at Cold Bay. The transfers were not without tensions.

The wartime relationships between the Soviet Union and the free world rapidly deteriorated following war's end. Winston Churchill's famous "iron curtain" speech at Westminster College in Fulton, Missouri, on 5 March 1946, has been popularly referred to as the beginning of a Cold War that would last until 1989.

The immediate post-war era was marked by organizational changes and the redirection of defense efforts. The Eleventh Air Force was redesignated the Alaskan Air Command on 18 December 1945, and the Alaskan Department was redesignated United States Army, Alaska (USARAL) on 5 November 1947. The naval component, the Alaskan Sea Frontier (ALSEAFRON), had been established on Adak Island on 15 April 1944.

The most significant organizational change occurred on 1 January 1947, when the Alaskan Command (ALCOM) was established as one of the first of three unified commands to be created. Its establishment resulted partly from the lessons learned during World War II. In addition, Alaska's strategic location for offensive and defensive operations, its widespread population centers, and its inadequate communications dictated the establishment of an organization for centralized planning and coordination of training and operations. Its three components were AAC, USARAL and ALSEAFRON.

Lieutenant General Howard A. Craig, U.S. Army Air Forces, served as the first Commander in Chief, Alaskan Command. With the establishment of the U.S. Air Force as a separate service on 18 September 1947, senior military leadership in Alaska passed to the air force, where it has remained ever since.

The mission of the Alaskan Command at the time of its establishment was to provide for the defense of Alaska and to protect the North American continent from attacks across the polar regions. Another, more visible, mission was humanitarian support. Time and again, the military would come to the aid of its civilian neighbors during periods of need—ranging from the 1964 Good Friday earthquake to routine search-and-rescue missions.

With the end of World War II, defense forces were reoriented from defending Alaska against the Japanese threat to meeting the threat of Soviet bomber attacks across the polar regions. Forces were withdrawn from the Aleutians and, except for Adak Naval Station and

Shemya Air Force Base, all bases were closed during the late 1940s.

The military embarked on a massive construction program during the 1950s to develop an air defense system and bases for the ground and sea defense of Alaska. Temporary World War II facilities gave way to the construction of permanent facilities. Defense forces were expanded to counter the Cold War threat posed by the Soviet Union and its satellite nations.

The army relinquished the old Fort Richardson to air force control during the early 1950s and built a new, permanent post nearby to accommodate ground defense forces. In the early 1960s, the army took possession of Ladd Air Force Base, renamed it Fort Wainwright, and expanded facilities there to accommodate the stationing of ground forces north of the Alaska Range.

The navy expanded its facilities on Adak and at Kodiak to counter the Soviet submarine threat in the North Pacific. The air force constructed a series of eighteen aircraft control and warning (AC&W) radar sites throughout Alaska and a distant early warning (DEW) radar system across northern Alaska and Canada, and into the Aleutians. It then linked them with the White Alice long-line communications system.

The construction projects and the influx of personnel to man the defenses had a significant impact on Alaska's economy and social structure, similar to that which the discovery and development of oil would later have. By 1960, Alaska's population had grown to 226,167—up from 128,643 in 1950.

The military helped provide the foundation upon which statehood was developed.

When President Eisenhower signed the proclamation declaring Alaska a state on 3 January 1959, the military presence in Alaska had already started to decline, a direction that would not be reversed until the 1980s. The decline was driven by changes in strategy, technology and the war in southeast Asia.

The Soviets developed an intercontinental ballistic missile capability during the late 1950s. It became their primary nuclear warhead delivery system. With a diminished Soviet bomber force, there was no longer a need for the U.S. to maintain a large air defense system. As a result, the Alaskan Air Command's aircraft control and warning radar sites were reduced from eighteen to thirteen and the Aleutian DEW line was closed. Five of its six fighter interceptor squadrons were inactivated. Ladd Air Force Base was transferred to the army in 1960, and renamed Fort Wainwright. By 1960, the Alaskan Air Command's assigned strength had dropped to 13,049, from a peak of 20,687 in 1957. The figures would continue to decline throughout the 1960s and 1970s.

The command assumed more of a role of supporting other commands, particularly the Military Airlift Command, which began using Elmendorf AFB as a stopover point for its C-141 and C-5 flights to and from southeast Asia. C-141 landings at Elmendorf began in December 1967 and had grown to twelve hundred per month by 1969. When the Combat Pacer flights ceased in mid-1973, C-141s had made approximately forty-six thousand landings and takeoffs at Elmendorf en route to and from the war zone. The flights underscored the importance of Alaska's strategic position as the "Air Crossroads of the World," an importance recognized by General Mitchell and others.

The army and navy in Alaska likewise suffered from the need to support the southeast Asian conflict. Units were taken from Alaska, sent to Vietnam and never returned. Personnel strengths declined and readiness suffered because of more pressing needs elsewhere. Maintenance suffered because of a lack of funds, as did new construction. The only major construction project during the 1960s was the building of the ballistic missile early warning site at Clear to provide early warning against Soviet missile attacks and the construction of a pipeline from Whittier to Anchorage to support the Combat Pacer requirements.

The decline continued into the post-Vietnam era with its emphasis on economies and the reduction of headquarters and headquarters manning. The army inactivated one of its two brigades in Alaska and the navy turned over its base at Kodiak to the U.S. Coast Guard. Both USARAL and ALSEAFRON were disestablished in the early 1970s and, on 1 July 1975, the Alaskan Command was disestablished. In its place, Joint Task Force-Alaska was created as a provisional command that could be activated by the Joint Chiefs of Staff to provide a joint command during war or an emergency. However, the various disestablishment actions left a command relations problem very similar to that of World War II. The defense of Alaska was again split between the army and air force, which had the responsibility for mainland Alaska on the one hand, and the navy, which had responsibility for defending the Aleutians on the other.

The 1980s marked a period of modernization and expansion of military forces in Alaska. The F-15 Eagle replaced the F-4 Phantom in 1982 as AAC's air defense fighter. The A-10 Thunderbolt arrived the same year to support the army's close air support requirements. The old manpower-intensive aircraft control and warning radar system was replaced with minimally attended, contractor-maintained long-range radars. It meant that where each site used to have an average of 120 military personnel, those functions could now be performed with as few as two contract technicians. Air defense command and control was centralized in the regional operations control center on Elmendorf AFB. Finally, the

Sixth Infantry Division was activated.

The Sixth Infantry Division (Light) was activated in 1986, with its headquarters located at Fort Wainwright. A second F-15 squadron was activated on Elmendorf AFB the following year, and a third squadron was activated in 1991. The earlier-model F-15s were replaced with newer ones. The dual-purpose F-16 replaced the A-10 at Eielson Air Force Base, and the A-10s were converted to forward air control aircraft and assigned to another squadron which was activated for that purpose.

A major construction program began during the early 1980s to replace outdated facilities and to build new ones to accommodate the additional forces.

To solve the problem resulting from the 1975 disestablishment of ALCOM, a new Alaskan Command was activated 7 July 1989 as a subordinated unified command under the Pacific Command, with the responsibility for the defense of all of Alaska, thereby heeding the lessons learned during war and peace in Alaska.

The final effort to improve the command structure resulted in the redesignation of the Alaskan Air Command as the Eleventh Air Force in August 1990. It was placed under the Pacific air forces.

While the 1990s and the end of the Cold War saw the reduction of forces in Alaska with the closure of Galena as a forward operations base and the planned inactivation of the Sixth Infantry Division, the early part of the decade also saw increased emphasis being placed on Alaska's importance as a strategic location for basing forces and the training opportunity benefits it offered. Training deployments to other world locations became routine. Units from other locations began using Alaska's range and training areas on an increasing basis.

The end of the Cold War has brought profound changes to the military. However, Alaska's strategic importance is still recognized as it was in 1935 when Gen. Billy Mitchell called it one of the most strategic places in the world for basing aircraft. Already, within recent years, we have seen a doubling of F-15 fighters on Elmendorf from thirty to more than sixty, the addition of an F-16 squadron at Eielson AFB, and the transformation of that base into one of the premier fighter training centers in the air force.

*John Haile Cloe is with the Third Wing History Office, Elmendorf Air Force Base. He is the author of "Top Cover for America: The Air Force in Alaska, 1920-1983" and "The Aleutian Warriors: A History of the 11th Air Force and Fleet Air Wing 4."*

# Northern Sentry, Polar Scout: Alaska's Role in Air Force Reconnaissance Efforts, 1946-1948

*John T. Farquhar, Major, USAF*

ON DECEMBER 21, 1945, THE FIRST JOINT CHIEFS OF Staff study of Alaska's role in post-war U.S. defense planning concluded:

... the probability of trouble developing in the Alaskan Area as a result of conflict between U.S. and USSR policies is fairly remote. The Soviet capability to launch a major operation against the Alaskan Area in the next five years is estimated to be almost nil; ... it does not appear necessary to station air forces or ground force combat troops in the Alaskan Area except for training, acclimatization, experimental purposes, limited reconnaissance and surveillance, and for limited local defense of selected bases.[1]

Yet, two years later, Joint Emergency War Plan PINCHER called for Alaska-based strategic bombers to strike Soviet targets. By 1948, War Plan BROILER envisioned Alaska bases as vital to America's atomic deterrent against superior Soviet conventional forces. This dramatic conceptual shift emphasized the air force effort to establish a strategic air presence in the Arctic. Beginning in August 1946, the U.S. Air Force conducted extensive, covert reconnaissance missions to exploit Alaska's strategic potential. Although the arctic reconnaissance program gathered valuable photographic and electronic intelligence, its primary contribution consist-

ed of practical lessons which transformed war planning theory into operational reality. Strategic reconnaissance missions provided the information to make America's war plans feasible during the initial phase of the Cold War before 1950.

With the rise of the Soviet threat following World War II, the Strategic Air Command (SAC) viewed the vast, uninhabited expanse of the Arctic as a potential avenue for strategic air attack. As the shortest distance between the continental United States and the Soviet Union, planners recognized the advantages of transpolar attack for bombers with limited range.[2] Arctic routes also provided SAC bombers a means to reach their targets without flying over Soviet defenses in Europe.

By 1947, General George C. Kenney, the first commander-in-chief of SAC, identified the atomic bomb as the decisive weapon in future war:

When we consider that 100 atom bombs will release more foot pounds of energy than all the TNT bombs released by all the belligerents of World War II combined ... and that that effort could be put down in a single attack, it is evident that the long drawn out war is out of date. When it is further considered that probably 80 percent of World War II's bombs were wasted, 100 atomic bombs would cause at least four times the destruc-

---

[1] JCS 1295/2, Appendix B: "An Outline Plan for the Military Development of Alaska," 21 Dec 1945, File: CCS 660.2 Alaska, 3-23-45, Record Group 218, National Archives (NA), Washington, D.C.

[2] Anthony Leviero, "The Polar Concept in Air Strategy," *The Army Information Digest* (December 1947): pp. 45-48.

tion... No nation, including our own, could survive such a blow.[3]

Kenney's strategic concept emphasized a short destructive war that would be over in a few days. He considered the bombing of targets that would affect enemy production in a few months to be "meaningless." Kenney's SAC regarded the advantage gained by a surprise attack as "so great that it can be considered decisive. I believe this should be studied, analyzed and discussed far more than we are doing today."[4] As a result, the Strategic Air Command considered Alaska as a vital strategic base for launching the atomic strikes that were the offensive heart of U.S. war plans.

Before SAC bombers could use arctic routes, they faced formidable challenges. Navigators encountered tremendous obstacles in the form of vast, uncharted areas, featureless terrain, magnetic disturbances, and celestial anomalies. These conditions complicated such routine procedures as determining aircraft position and measuring drift caused by crosswinds.[5] Because strategic bombers must first find their targets before dropping bombs, even atomic bombs, SAC realized the need to develop usable polar navigational techniques. Consequently, the Air Staff dispatched the Forty-Sixth Reconnaissance Squadron to Ladd Field, near Fairbanks, Alaska, with orders to explore and map the Arctic.

From August 1946 to September 1948, SAC reconnaissance aircraft systematically tested the feasibility of trans-polar operations. Before the deployment, little was known about flying north of the Arctic Circle except for the perils of a small band of early aviators who braved the elements in open-cockpit planes. Following World War II, the research and development branch of the War Department general staff initiated Project No. 5 to explore the frozen North. Approved by both Chief of the Air Staff General Carl A. Spaatz, and Army Chief of Staff General Dwight D. Eisenhower, the Air Staff instructed SAC to accomplish the photomapping and electronic reconnaissance required.[6]

Under the auspices of Project No. 5 (known as Project Nanook to the air crews), the Forty-Sixth Reconnaissance Squadron solved many of the navigational problems involved with arctic flying. Originally composed of aircraft and aircrews assigned to SAC, the squadron, under the command of Major Maynard E. White, conducted the most ambitious polar photomapping projects to date.[7] In Operation FLOODLIGHT, reconnaissance crews searched uncharted arctic waters for new land masses that might be used for future bases or weather stations. Sorties from Ladd AFB attempted to map Area "A" (between 160 and 180 degrees East longitude and 73 and 77 degrees North latitude), Area "B" (north and east of Area A), Area "C" (the route between Alaska and Iceland), and Area "D" (the area between 85 degrees North latitude and the North Pole, except for a portion of northeast Greenland.)[8] As a result of FLOODLIGHT, the F-13s of the Forty-Sixth Reconnaissance Squadron discovered "Target X," a floating ice mass roughly fourteen by seventeen miles in size, which provided considerable oceanographic information about the Arctic.[9] Reconnaissance crews also established scheduled air service between Ladd Field and Iceland in Operation POLARIS.[10] By May 1947, SAC added Operation EARDRUM, the trimetrogon photomapping of Greenland, to the tasks of aerial reconnaissance.[11]

In each of these projects, reconnaissance crews gathered weather data, searched for potential emergency landing fields, recorded magnetic electronic phenomena, and experimented with various navigational tech-

---

[3] *Strategic Air Command 1947*, vol. 1, p. 138, USAF Historical Research Center (USAFHRC), Maxwell Air Force Base, Alabama.

[4] Ibid. p. 139.

[5] Headquarters Strategic Air Command, Operations Analysis Section, Report No. 9, "Radar in Arctic Regions," 11 March 1947, Papers of Harry S. Borowski, Series 3, Box 3, Folder 10: Arctic, United States Air Force Academy Library Special Collections (USAFA).

[6] Routing and Record Sheet (hereafter abbreviated R & R), HQ USAF - AFOIR-RC to CSGID, Subject: Photography of Floodlight (Project No. 5), Nov 18, 1948, TS Control number: 2-5373, File number: 25600 to 5699, Box 43, Entry 214, Record Group (RG) 341, NA.

[7] Interview with Colonel Maynard E. White, USAF, Retired, and Ken White, USAFA, 6 October 1993. Ken W. White, Major White's son, published a book, *World in Peril: The Origin, Mission & Scientific Findings of the 46th/72nd Reconnaissance Squadron* (Elkhart, Ind.: K.W. White & Associates, 1992), that provides a fascinating account of the human dimension of the reconnaissance effort.

[8] *History Strategic Air Command 1948*, vol. 1, pp. 248-249.

[9] Memorandum for Chief, Air Intelligence Requirements Division, from Carl M. Green, Major, USAF, Reconnaissance Branch, Air Intel Requirements Div, Directorate of Intelligence, Subject: Coordination of Photo and Photo Intelligence Activities, 11 December 1947, TS Control number: 2-682, File number: 2600 to 2-699, Box 40, Entry 214, RG 314, NA; Memorandum for Record, Problem: Coordination and Dissemination of Aerial and Radar Scope Photography by the Alaskan Air Command with HQ AAF, Air Intelligence Div., n.d., n.p., TS Control number 2-450, File number: 2-400 to 2-499, Box 39, Entry 214, RG 341, NA.

[10] Ibid.; *History Strategic Air Command 1948*, vol. 1, p. 248.

[11] Trimetrogon photomapping involved three cameras firing simultaneously to provide horizon to horizon coverage. Letter, Kenneth P. Bergquist, Colonel Air Corps, Deputy Asst. Chief of Air Staff, to Commanding General, Strategic Air Command, Subject: Operation EARDRUM, 3 Mar 1947, in *Strategic Air Command 1947*, vol. 4, Tab 113, USAFHRC.

F-13s undergo maintenance in Hangar No. 4, Ladd Field, in the late 1940s. The aircraft on the left has been partially modified. The one facing it has been more fully modified. *(Photograph courtesy Maynard E. White, Colonel, USAF (Ret.) and Ken White)*

niques.[12] By September 1948, the Forty-Sixth/Seventy-Second Reconnaissance Squadron had flown more than five hundred missions, ten thousand flying hours, including more than one hundred flights to the North Pole, and explored 5.5 million square miles of the Arctic. Unfortunately, the achievements of Project Nanook did not come without cost: the reconnaissance squadron witnessed twelve air aborts, forty-three ground aborts, four crashes, and five fatalities.[13]

Although the arctic exploration of Project No. 5 resulted in great advances in scientific knowledge and navigational techniques, two secret reconnaissance projects sought photographic information on the Soviet threat. In Project 20, aircraft flew semimonthly surveillance missions from Point Barrow to the tip of the Aleutian Chain by way of the Bering Strait. Crews photographed any unusual object or activity.[14] Moreover, Project 23 combined electronic intelligence (ELINT) and photography. For each mission, two aircraft flew along the Siberian coast adjacent to Alaska. One aircraft flew at high altitude "directly over the coastline," while the second plane flew a parallel course several miles out to sea. Although the electronic intelligence mission gathered useful information on available Soviet radars, the oblique photos from K-20 aerial cameras provided poor pictures and little usable information.[15]

---

[12] Letter, Enos L. Cleland, 1st. Lt., Air Corps, Flight "B" Commander to Commanding Officer, 46th Recon Sq (VLR) Photographic, Subject: Progress Report for Flight "B," 30 July 1947, in Historical Section, Strategic Air Command, The Strategic Air Command 1947, Vol. 4: Supporting Data (Operations) ([Offutt AFB, Neb.]: 1 June 1949), Tab 116, File number: 416.01, Vol. 4, 1947, USAFHRC.

[13] On October 13, 1947, the Air Force redesignated the 46th Reconnaissance Squadron as the 72nd Reconnaissance Squadron. Interview with Col. Maynard E. White and Ken White, USAFA, 6 October 1993.

[14] Memorandum for Chief, Air Intel Requirements Div. from Green, Subj: Coordination of Photo, 11 Dec 47, NA.

[15] Oblique aerial photography refers to cameras mounted in the aircraft fuselage at an angle which provided panoramic coverage of the horizon. It is not clear how much electronic intelligence gathering equipment was aboard the aircraft used in this project; Ibid.

Adding to the frustration caused by poor long-range photography, a Project 23 sortie demonstrated the political hazards of aerial reconnaissance. On January 5, 1948, the Soviets issued a sharp diplomatic protest over U.S. Air Force reconnaissance activity in the Arctic. The Soviet note claimed an American airplane violated Soviet air space on December 23, 1947 "for about seven miles along the coast of the Chukotsk Peninsula at a distance two miles from the shore."[16] An Air Staff investigation revealed that Project 23 Mission Number 7 M 263A had violated a State Department restriction calling for no flights closer than twelve miles to Soviet territory. No means existed, however, to determine whether the plane had violated Soviet territory as alleged.[17] Although the Soviet protest resulted in political embarrassment for the United States and the U.S. Air Force, it also revealed unexpected Soviet capability to track peripheral reconnaissance flights.

F-13s of the Forty-Sixth Reconnaissance Squadron at Ladd Field. The tail and outer edges of the wings were painted red, the underside of the plane was painted black, and all remaining areas were unpainted aluminum. *(Photograph courtesy Maynard E. White, Colonel, USAF (Ret.) and Ken White))*

While photomapping sorties produced information necessary to arctic flight operations and occasional glimpses of Soviet equipment and installations, SAC electronic intelligence flights probed Soviet arctic defenses. Nicknamed "Ferrets," special electronic intelligence aircraft carried state-of-the-art equipment to detect, locate, and analyze Soviet radar stations. From the Ferrets' information, analysts determined the operating characteristics of the enemy's radar, which allowed planners to plan routes to avoid detection and engineers to design electronic countermeasures.[18]

The first B-29 Ferret represented a significant technological advance over previous improvised intelligence aircraft. Technicians removed the B-29's guns and converted the rear pressurized section to an electronic intercept station. The conversion also transformed the bomb bay into additional fuel storage tanks.[19] The ELINT B-29 featured a thirteen-man crew, including two pilots, three navigators, six Ravens, a radio operator, and a flight engineer.[20] The Raven crew consisted of three positions that operated search and analysis equipment and three positions dedicated to direction-finding.[21]

Before deploying to Alaska, the ELINT B-29 crew trained at Wright Field, Dayton, Ohio, for Ferret operations. Under the command of Captain Landon Turner, the command pilot, and Captain Robed R. Perry, the senior Raven, the crew flew familiarization sorties over Ohio. The Ravens operated their search receivers to intercept radars and analyze their frequency, pulse repetition frequency (PRF), pulse length, scan rate, and other characteristics. The new Ravens also learned to take direction-finding (D/F) bearings and to plot them with the assistance of the navigators.[22] By March 1947, the crew proceeded to Andrews AFB where the army air force's research and development branch explained that their mission would be to fly long-range Ferret missions north of Siberia.[23] Following the briefing, the ELINT B-29 flew to Ladd AFB in Alaska. Captain Perry explained

---

[16] Soviet Note No. 261, Embassy of the Union of Soviet Socialist Republics, January 5, 1948, TS Control number: 2-934, File 2-900 to 2-999, Box 40, Entry 214, RG 341, NA.

[17] The existing documents present conflicting information regarding the border restriction for Project 23. Documents that resulted from the investigation of the incident confirm that the pilot violated the Department of State limitation of twelve miles from the Soviet coast as shown in Letter, AFOIR-CM to Commander-in-Chief, Alaska, Subject: Violations of Soviet Frontier, n.d., TS Control number: 2-934, File: 2-900 to 2-999, Entry 214, RG 341, NA. Yet, a memo explaining Alaskan photographic efforts stated that the Alaskan Air Command had no boundary restrictions when this sortie was flown. See Memo for Record, Subject: Photographic Coverage—Chukotski Peninsula, n.d., TS Control number: 2-1378, File: 2-1300 to 2-1399 (1948), Box 41, Entry 214, RG 341, NA.

[18] Perhaps the best surveys of electronic warfare may be found in Alfred Price, *Instruments of Darkness* (Los Altos, Ca.: Peninsula Publishing, 1987) and *The History of U.S. Electronic Warfare* 2 vols. (Alexandria, Va.: Association of Old Crows, 1989), by the same author.

[19] Although B-29s modified for photographic or Ferret missions were designated RB-29s in 1948, the first B-29 Ferret was simply referred to as an ELINT B-29 or "the prototype B-29 ferret." In all probability, Project 23 missions were flown by less capable "jury rigged," or hastily improvised aircraft. Interview, Joe Wack, Colonel, USAF (ret.) by Alfred Price, n.d., p, 10, File 11: Col. J. Wack, Association of Old Crows (AOC) archive, Alexandria, Va.

[20] Electronic Warfare Officers on electronic intelligence aircraft were nicknamed "Ravens." Ibid., p. 12.

[21] Letter, H.C. Monjar to Frank Voltaggio, 10 June 1982, File 59: Lt. Col. H. Monjar, AOC.

[22] Voltaggio, "Out in the Cold..." p. 8, File: Voltaggio, AOC; Wack, AOC 11, p. 11.

[23] Wack, AOC 11, p. 11.

that the vagueness of their assigned task complicated mission planning:

> My orders were explicit enough in giving us first priority on fuel, maintenance and support at all USAAF bases world-wide, but vague enough to allow us to file clearance and fly anywhere in the world we wanted to go. Now this may seem funny, but I never got a briefing on what they wanted us specifically to do in Alaska. Maybe somebody else did, but I never got one, and I was the project officer.... Nobody gave me a briefing on what was where or what they wanted or anything. They just said "Go and see what radars are there."[24]

Officially designated "B-29 #812," and nicknamed "Sitting Duck" by its crew, the B-29 Ferret probed the Siberian coast for signs of Soviet radar. From June 11 to August 21, 1947, the "Sitting Duck" flew nine reconnaissance sorties, first along the northern coast of Siberia and then along the southern edge.[25] Before the Ferret flights, the air force had no information on Soviet radars in this area. After the B-29 Ferret exploration, the crew discovered a chain of scattered Soviet RUS-2 early warning radars along the southern periphery of the Soviet Far East and the absence of Soviet radars along the USSR's Arctic Coast.[26] According to Captain Perry, the crew inadvertently drifted over Soviet territory on one sortie:

> On one of those missions we were supposed to make a little dip into Anadyr Bay, which is a big bay maybe 120 miles wide and 120 miles deep ... we were just supposed to make a little "V" into it. All of a sudden I looked at the radar and I called up Kelly (the navigator). I said, "Kelly we're over land!" He says, "I know it." I said, "Why don't we get the hell out of here?" I said, "Flanagan (1st navigator), what the hell are we doing?" Flanagan said, "Well, we've hit a reverse jet stream and we're trying to get out. It's carried us inland about

In 1948, air force analysts calculated that the Soviet Tupolev Tu-4, a B-29-type bomber, could reach targets in the northwest United States on two-way mission and, on a one-way mission, strike as far as Topeka, Kansas. *(Photograph courtesy Maynard E. White, Colonel, USAF (Ret.) and Ken White))*

50 miles and we're making about 20 knots ground speed trying to get out."[27]

Eventually, Headquarters USAF passed instructions to the commanding general of the Alaskan Air Command that prohibited flights closer than fifteen miles to Soviet territory.[28]

The Alaskan reconnaissance sorties demonstrated the value of the B-29 Ferret. The aircraft's long range allowed coverage of the vast distances encountered in the Arctic and northern Pacific and the data gained by the ELINT crew established the initial Electronic Order of Battle (EOB) for the Soviet Far East.[29] The flights also revealed gaps in Soviet radar defenses along the Arctic Circle. As polar flying experiences and advances in navigation technology reduced the uncertainty of arctic operations, Alaska reconnaissance operations confirmed the validity of polar routing for SAC's new long-range B-50 and B-36 bombers.

The Berlin Crisis of 1948 awakened American policy makers to the danger of inadequate strategic intelligence. President Truman viewed the blockade as a test of western resolve and patience. At issue was the western presence in Berlin and the viability of the Marshall

---

[24] Voltaggio, "Out in the Cold..." p. 11, File: Voltaggio, AOC; Perry AOC 31, p. 9.

[25] This total does not reflect training and ferry missions. See AAF Forms 5A, Individual Flight Record attached to Voltaggio, "Out in the Cold..." File: Voltaggio, AOC.

[26] Waco, AOC 11, pp. 12-13.

[27] Voltaggio, "Out in the Cold..." p. 12, File: Voltaggio, AOC.

[28] The documents available do not specifically link the Headquarters, U.S. Air Force action to the Ferret overflight. Instead, the documentary trail stops at an August 16, 1947 request from the Commanding General, Alaskan Air Command, for special instructions regarding boundaries. Staff Summary Sheet for Deputy AC/AS-2, Subject: Reissuance of instructions regarding operation of two 46th Recon Sq A/C now being fitted w/RCM ferret equipment, 20 August 1947, TS Control number: 2-296, File number: 2200 to 2-299 Jul 47-Aug 47, Box 39, Entry 214, RG 341, NA.

[29] The term "Electronic Order of Battle" refers to a list of enemy radars and other electronic equipment that catalogs the location and characteristics of the equipment for intelligence and mission-planning purposes.

Plan. As Truman perceived the crisis, the Soviets tried to convince the people of Europe that the United States would support them only in economic matters and would back away from any military risk. The question remained: How could the United States remain in Berlin without risking all-out war?[30] Although the Berlin Airlift provided the means of facing the challenge without hostilities, President Truman appreciated the gravity of the situation:

> Our position in Berlin was precarious. If we wished to remain there, we would have to make a show of strength. But there was always the risk that the Russian reaction might lead to war. We had to face the possibility that Russia might deliberately choose to make Berlin the pretext for war, but a more immediate danger was the risk that a trigger-happy Russian pilot or hotheaded Communist tank commander might create an incident that could ignite a powder keg.[31]

Thus, the Berlin Crisis resembled the political miscalculation which was expected to launch the war envisioned by the Joint Emergency War Plans. Rather than planning exercises based on hypothetical scenarios, the Berlin Crisis illustrated the distinct possibility of war with the Soviet Union.

Combining with the tension of the Berlin Crisis, reports of Soviet activities in Alaska raised additional worries over potential Soviet attack. On March 25, 1948, a memorandum for W. Stuart Symington, Secretary of the Air Force, from General Carl Spaatz, Air Force Chief of Staff, listed Soviet jamming of reconnaissance flights, Soviet aerial reconnaissance of the Arctic Ocean and Greenland, and construction of airfields on the Chukots-

ki Peninsula as examples of alarming activities.[32] Air force leaders calculated that Soviet bombers could reach targets in the northwest United States on two-way missions, and that Soviet B-29-type bombers could strike as far as Topeka, Kansas, on one-way missions.[33] Considering the impact of America's intelligence failure prior to Pearl Harbor, the prospect of airfields capable of launching long-range bombers prompted U.S. efforts to reconnoiter the areas of Siberia adjacent to Alaska. Symington pushed the program further when he asked General Spaatz why no pictures existed of Soviet airfields on the Chukotski Peninsula.[34]

The effort to photograph Soviet bases on the Chukotski Peninsula illustrated the technological and political constraints present for strategic photographic intelligence. On one hand, vertical air photographs of Soviet airfields risked the loss of a plane and a grave international crisis. On the other, existing aerial cameras proved inadequate for long-range oblique photography.[35] To solve the dilemma, Major General C.P. Cabell, director of air force intelligence, proposed to reduce the State Department's restriction on aerial operations from twelve miles to three miles and to use 40-inch focal-length cameras.

When the air staff finally agreed to send this proposal to the Department of State in May 1948, the Berlin crisis had changed the political climate. Not seeking to further inflame international tensions, General Lauris Norstad preempted the request for reduced restrictions. By May 13, 1948, the Department of State increased the restriction to forty miles to avoid provoking the USSR.[36] Although the actions avoided igniting the volatile political situation, the increased buffer zone left unsolved the operational problem of how to photograph the Chukotski Peninsula.

---

[30] Harry S Truman, *Years of Trial and Hope*, vol.2 of *Memoirs of Harry S Truman* (Garden City, N.Y.: Doubleday and Co., 1956), pp. 123, 125.

[31] Ibid., p. 124.

[32] Directly across the Bering Strait from Alaska, Cape Chukotsk was usually addressed as the "Chukotski Peninsula" by American documents. For the sake of simplicity, I have adopted this transliteration. Memorandum for the Secretary of the Air Force from Cad Spaatz, Chief of Staff, United States Air Force, Subject: Some Reports of Soviet Activities in Alaska and Adjacent Thereto, 25 March 1948, TS Control number: 2-1193, File number: 2-1100 to 2-1199, Box 40, Entry 214, RG 341, NA.

[33] Although officially designated the Tupolev Tu-4, contemporary documents called the aircraft, the "Soviet B-29 type bomber." I have adopted the practice. R & R, Frank P. Sturdevant, Colonel, USAF, Executive, Air Intelligence Division, Directorate of Intelligence, to Industrial Planning Division, Directorate of Procurement and Industrial Planning, Subject: Strategic Consideration Re Boeing Aircraft Production, 12 Aug 1949, TS Control number: 2-8670, File: 2-8600 to 2-8699, Box 45, Entry 214, RG 341, NA.

[34] Memorandum for Spaatz from Symington, 5 April 1948, TS Control number: 2-1378, File number: 2-1300 to 2-1399 (1948), Box 41, Entry 214, RG 341, NA.

[35] The existing photographs originated from short-focal-length coverage made from flights in Project 23 mentioned earlier. Unfortunately, the photographs produced no information of significant intelligence value. R & R, Air Intelligence Requirements Division (AFOIR-RC), Subject: Photographic Coverage-Chukotski Peninsula, n.d., TS Control number 2-1378, File number 2-1300 to 2-1399 (1948), Box 41, Entry 214, RG 341, NA.

[36] R & R, Director of Intelligence to Director of Plans and Operations, Subject: Photographic Coverage—Chukotski Peninsula Airfields, 7 May 1948, TS Control number: 2-1560, File number: 2-1500 to 2-1599, Box 41, Entry 214, RG 341, NA; MFR, "To brief background facts on establishment of 40-mile limit for reconnaissance flights in Pacific Area," TS Control number: 2-3015, File number: 2-3003 to 3099, Box 42, Entry 214, RG 341, NA.

The resolution of the Chukotski airfield dilemma demanded technological innovation. Colonel George W. Goddard provided the breakthrough in the form of 48-, 60-, and 100-inch focal-length cameras at the Air Material Command.[37] In addition, by October 1948, the success of the Berlin Airlift reduced international tensions and permitted air planners to narrow the reconnaissance restricted area to a distance of twenty miles from the Soviet shore.[38] Therefore, during October and November, an Air Force F-13, equipped with an experimental 100-inch camera mounted for oblique photography, completed needed coverage of the Chukotski Peninsula. Further analysis of the photos dispelled fears of substantial bases at the sites favorable to long-range missions against the United States.[39]

Complementing the Chukotski photography campaign, the director of air force intelligence revamped the Alaskan Air Command's (AAC) electronic intelligence effort. Rescinding previous electronic reconnaissance directives, a July 26, 1948, letter established uniform policy, operating procedures, search areas, and defined ELINT objectives. Air force headquarters directed the AAC to concentrate its efforts on discovering radar chains and operating schedules and to determine which signals, if any, belonged to IFF (Identification Friend or Foe) systems.[40] The identification of Soviet ship-borne radar systems also emerged as a priority.[41] In sum, the AAC policy letter resulted in standardized procedures and centralized control for the two RB-29 Ferret aircraft dedicated to the Alaska electronic intelligence program.[42]

By 1949, Air Force reconnaissance aircraft flew sorties against the Soviet coastline as a matter of routine. The early Alaska Ferret missions established the location and operating characteristics of eleven Soviet radar sites.

Equally important, Alaska-based reconnaissance revealed significant gaps in Soviet arctic defenses. This important information enabled war planners to develop routes for strategic bombers to be used in the event of war. Electronic intelligence proved useful in designing electronic warfare devices, including jamming equipment for Soviet radars. On the other hand, photographic reconnaissance aircraft from the Forty-Sixth/Seventy-Second Reconnaissance Squadron defused fears of Soviet air bases in northeast Siberia. Air force intelligence still considered Chukotski facilities as potential staging bases for Soviet B-29s, but worries over imminent use of the fields subsided.

Although the electronic and photographic intelligence provided by Alaska-based strategic reconnaissance proved vital to war planners, perhaps the greatest impact of the program consisted of practical lessons in arctic flying. Before the Forty-Sixth Reconnaissance Squadron's deployment, polar flying remained largely theoretical. But crews learned how to "aviate, navigate, and communicate" in the harshest flying environment. Fortunately, the resourcefulness of the junior officers provided novel solutions, to include the development of grid navigation techniques. Moreover, the program tackled the challenge of maintaining flyable aircraft under arctic conditions. By early 1949, the Forty-Sixth/Seventy-Second Reconnaissance Squadron conquered daunting problems and demonstrated the feasibility of the Joint Emergency War Plans' polar attack schemes.

In the broad view, post-war Alaska reconnaissance demonstrated significant gaps in U.S. intelligence about the Soviet Union. American war planners knew little about their prospective opponent. The Chukotski Peninsula alarm illustrated a tendency to magnify the unknown threat. In addition, USAF analysts tended to

[37] Colonel Goddard pioneered modern aerial photography from the 1920s. Letter, Walter R. Agee, Brigadier General, USAF, Chief, Air Intel. Req. Div., Directorate of Intelligence to Commander-in-Chief, Alaskan Air Command, 15 Dec 1948, TS Control number: 2-5676A, File number: 2-5600 to 2-5699, Box 43, Entry 214, RG 341, NA.

[38] The existing documents fail to mention the exact date of the shift to a twenty-mile buffer. Letter, H.M. Monroe, Colonel, GSC, Chief of Staff, Headquarters Alaskan Command to Chief of Staff, United States Air Force, Subject: Importance of Long-range Photography to the Alaskan Theater, n.d., TS Control number: 2-5676A, File number: 2-5600 to 2-5699, Box 43, Entry 214, RG 341, NA.

[39] Specifically, the flights photographed Soviet facilities located at Uelen, Lavrentiya, Mys Caplina, and Provideniya areas. MFR, Problem: To present recently established Photo Intelligence to supplement the information contained in the article "Chukotsky Peninsula" appearing in the March issue of the Air Intelligence Digest, n.d., TS Control number: 2-6725, File number: 2-6700 to 2-6799 (March 1949), Box 44, Entry 214, RG 341, NA.

[40] "Specific objectives of the electronics reconnaissance mission are as follows: a. To search and report upon the following frequency spreads: (1) 50 Mcs to 1500 Mcs. (2) 1800 Mcs to 2000 Mcs. (3) 2400 Mcs to 3100 Mcs... b. While intense search should be centered on the above spreads, systematic full range searches should not be ignored..." Letter, C.P. Cabell, Major General, USAF, Director of Intelligence, Office of Deputy Chief of Staff, Operations to Commanding General, Alaskan Air command, Subject: RCM Ferret Program—Alaskan Air Command, 26 Jul 1948, TS Control number: 2-3037, File: 2-3003 to 3099 Jul 1948, Box 42, Entry 214, RG 341, NA.

[41] Letter, Cabell to CG, AAC, Subj.: RCM Ferret Program—AAC, 26 Jul 48.

[42] On March 10, 1948, the AAC Ferret program was suspended until new aircraft could be procured. When two RB-29s equipped for Ferret operations appeared, the program resumed on June 10, 1948. MFR, Problem: To provide the Alaskan Air Command with a directive to cover the electronic reconnaissance activities of the ferret aircraft under the control of that command, n.d., TS Control number: 2-3027, File number: 2-3003 to 2-3099 Jul 1948, Box 42, Entry 214, RG 341, NA.

suffer from "reverse-mirror" imaging. For example, air intelligence assumed the Soviets would use northeast Siberian airfields to conduct strategic bombing operations consistent with U.S. air doctrine. Likewise, air force analysts projected Soviet bomber strengths based upon this assumption.

In other words, The U.S. based much of its war planning upon what Americans would do, not upon what the Soviets actually planned to do. In fairness, given the lack of intelligence available on the Soviet Union in the early days of the Cold War, few alternatives existed for war planners. Thus, Alaska-based aerial reconnaissance played a significant role in post-war analysis of the Soviet threat, which in turn influenced war planning and force structure.

*John Farquhar is an assistant professor of history at the U.S. Air Force Academy. He has flown as navigator on RC-135 aircraft, including numerous strategic reconnaissance sorties from Eielson Air Force Base, Alaska.*

# Reeve Aleutian Airways

*Janice Reeve Ogle*

### Introduction

IN NOVEMBER OF 1942, AFTER TEN YEARS OF FLYING IN Valdez and Interior Alaska, Robert C. Reeve signed an exclusive contract with the Alaska Communications System, a branch of the U.S. Army Signal Corps. His assignment was to fly men and materials to newly-established military installations along the Alaska Peninsula and the Aleutian Islands. The men were to install communications and navigational aids at the airfields that had been hastily constructed by the military following the bombing of Dutch Harbor and the occupation of Attu and Kiska Islands by Japanese forces. He spent the next three wartime years flying there as the only civilian authorized in the combat zone.

In 1992, Reeve Aleutian Airways, Inc., had the honor of transporting World War II veterans to Dutch Harbor for the fiftieth anniversary of the bombing of Dutch Harbor. In June of 1993, Reeve Aleutian proudly transported eighty-four people to Adak and Attu Islands for ceremonies commemorating the fiftieth anniversary of the Battle of Attu. In July 1994, Reeve Aleutian proudly transported thirty-seven Japanese veterans and surviving family members to Attu Island for memorial services. And, in August, Reeve Aleutian proudly transported fourteen United States and Japanese veterans to Adak for a commemorative visit to Kiska via Coast Guard cutter.

The existence of Reeve Aleutian Airways, Inc., today is intimately intertwined with the course of World War II in the Aleutians.

### Part One: 1902-1942

Robert Campbell Reeve was born in Waunakee, Wis-consin, on March 27, 1902. In 1917, during World War I, he joined the army infantry and was discharged as a sergeant at the end of the war. After several years roaming around the Orient, RCR—as I shall refer to him—took flying lessons from two barnstormers in Texas. In 1926 he earned his commercial pilot's license and his engine and aircraft maintenance licenses. After a short stint as a flying cadet in the Army Air Corps, RCR joined the Ford Motor Company ferrying Ford Tri-motors to South America for delivery to Pan American Grace Airways. In 1929 he hired on with PANAGRA, flying air mail in a single-engine Fairchild 71 along Foreign Air Mail Route Number 9 between Lima, Peru, and Santiago, Chile, and across the Andes to South America's eastern coast. In 1932 RCR returned to the States and stowed away to Alaska, ending up in Valdez. After repairing an old Eaglerock, he established a living by flying prospectors to gold mines and around Valdez and flying charter flights all over the Territory of Alaska and the Canadian Yukon. For the next ten years, using Fairchild 51 and 71 aircraft, he continued bush flying, including glacier and mudflat takeoffs and landings, using wheels and skis, flying anything, anywhere, anytime, just to make a living.

In 1940, when the Civil Aeronautics Board (CAB) granted certificates and allotted territories to fledgling air services, RCR was aced out of the Valdez area. He spent a year in Fairbanks and then, with World War II getting closer to home, a summer in Nabesna, flying eleven hundred tons of supplies and three hundred workers to Northway for construction of the Northway airfield. Northway was one of a network of airfields from Canada to Nome, vital to the defense of Alaska and the United States. This was followed by contract flying of workers, materials, and supplies into other new airfields in the network: at Big Delta, Tanacross, Galena, Moses Point, and Nome.

In November of 1942, RCR moved to Anchorage and began the most remarkable flying of his career—flying in the Aleutians during World War II under exclusive contract to the Alaska Communications System and flying to the new military air bases along the Alaska Peninsula and the Aleutian Islands in his Fairchild 71 and his Boeing 80-A. Bomber runways had been hastily built at Port Heiden, Cold Bay, Dutch Harbor, Umnak, and Atka, with the ones at Adak and Amchitka still under construction.

This area, the birthplace of the winds, is infamous for its changing and unpredictable weather, violent storms, extremely high and sustained winds, and dense, widespread blankets of fog. RCR made his first flight to Cold Bay in December 1942.

### Part Two: 1943-1945

The Aleutian Campaign; The Thousand-Mile War; the Forgotten War. At this point in my writing I found it virtually impossible to do justice to that three-year period of 1943 to 1945. Imagine my relief upon realizing that I was not dealing with writer's block, but with a dearth of documentation upon which to draw. The great majority of my source material was purely anecdotal.

Between the secrecy involved in the effort, and the urgent and critical nature of his flights, I would assume that this three-year period was as much a blurred passage of time as it seems to be in retrospect. My father spent the better part of three years flying in the Aleutian Islands in a Boeing 80-A and a Fairchild 71. Although the new airfields had radio beacons, he avoided them and preferred to arrive unannounced and unnoticed. Most of his flying was purposely contact—visual—so as not to become involved with the big, fast military planes. He hobnobbed with the bomber pilots, played poker with them, and once temporarily lost his plane to them in a poker game. He ditched his planes several times in the beach surf and dodged Japanese fighter planes as deftly as he dodged military protocol. In short, he became one with the military efforts in the Aleutians. Those three years passed very quickly and ended successfully.

### Part Three: 1946-1980

Prior to and during the war years, the Aleutian Islands were sparsely populated but rich in natural resources: commercial fishing, sheep ranching, the Pribilof fur seal harvest, and the Aleut people themselves. Air transportation had not touched the Aleutians; travel

to, from, and within them was only by boat. Until World War II there were no airport facilities and even after the war no one was interested in using them, probably largely because of the often horrendously inhospitable weather conditions and, to some extent, the sparse revenue base—no one, that is, except RCR.

When the war ended, all of the Alaska territory, with the exception of the Aleutians, had been allotted by CAB certification to, among others, Art Woodley in Southeastern, the Wien brothers in Fairbanks and northern Alaska, Ray Petersen in western Alaska, and Mudhole Smith in the Copper River area.

In the winter of 1945, RCR filed an application with the CAA to operate scheduled service on the 1,783 mile route between Anchorage and Attu.

RCR bought his first surplus C-47 aircraft from the air force in February of 1946. He himself accomplished the conversion to commercial use as a DC-3 in record time. As luck would have it, he was then in a position to operate passenger flights between Seattle and Alaska in April, when a steamship strike halted all surface travel. He and two key friends flew the DC-3 twenty-six round-trips in fifty-three days. With the proceeds he paid off the first DC-3 and bought three more.

During the summer of 1946 he used the DC-3s for once-a-week flights down the "Chain," doing business as Reeve Aleutian Airways. Before the year was over he was operating two round-trips a week and did so for two years before the Civil Aeronautics Board (CAB) awarded Reeve Aleutian a temporary five-year certificate. On March 24, 1947, Reeve Aleutian incorporated to become Reeve Aleutian Airways, Inc. (RAA).

Beginning in 1949 the military started postwar deactivation of one airfield after another, which would have left Reeve Aleutian with few good alternate airports and refueling stops. RCR succeeded in getting Shemya AFB reclassified as militarily desirable, took out a long-term lease on the field at Dutch Harbor, and began himself operating the facilities at Dutch Harbor, Umnak, and Port Heiden. The expense of operating and maintaining those airports put RAA heavily into debt. Federal subsidies to airlines were standard at the time, but sporadic and unpredictable. In 1950 the CAB finally agreed to assume the six-figure estimated cost of runway and navigational aid maintenance, weather reporting, refueling, communications, and overnight accommodations. This helped, but it was still a struggle to stay in business, much less regain financial health.

In 1953, Fort Randall, at Cold Bay, was to be deactivated. RCR obtained a lease on that field, too. The following year Shemya was closed and Cold Bay became vital as a refueling stop for military and commercial flights to the Orient. The C.A.A. later took over authority and responsibility for operating and maintaining the Cold Bay airport facilities.

Small communities without runways were served by the amphibious Reeve Grumman Goose and Sikorsky, which could land in nearby lake, lagoon, bay, sea, or ocean waters and taxi up onto the beach.

By the mid-fifties, Reeve Aleutian was beginning to earn its way and the need for larger, faster planes became evident. In early 1957 the first Reeve Aleutian DC-4 was put into service to the western Aleutians. Acquisition of the DC-4s was accompanied by three dramatic changes: the move from Merrill Field to the new Anchorage International Airport, the first Reeve stewardesses to take care of all those passengers, and the first Reeve flight engineers to take care of all those engines. The DC-4s made two round-trips a week out of Adak, Shemya, and Attu. That year was also the beginning of the banner period for Reeve Aleutian when the United States Air Force commenced construction of its Distant Early Warning network (DEW), including the Aleutian DEWLine sites at Port Heiden, Port Moller, Cold Bay, Cape Sarichef, Driftwood Bay, and Nikolski. Reeve Aleutian added C-46 freighters to its fleet, fantastic performers for large loads into the short, unimproved airstrips all over Alaska that supported DEWLine construction.

In 1961, sixteen years after the end of World War II, I myself began living a part of Reeve Aleutian's history, and began my lifelong love affair with the Aleutian Islands. During my first summer as a Reeve stewardess on DC-4s, I was a fool in paradise, and have been ever since. It took what seemed like forever to get from Anchorage to Shemya and Attu with en-route stops at Kodiak, Port Heiden, Cold Bay, Umnak, Adak, and occasionally Amchitka (to drop off or pick up Sea Otter Jones). It was actually twelve to fifteen hours, weather permitting, and after overnighting at Shemya, we'd retrace our steps back to Anchorage the next day. Because the planes were unpressurized, our maximum flight altitude was eight or ten thousand feet. On good weather days it was much lower. The World War II debris and volcanoes along the way became very familiar, and the remarkable, lovely Aleut people became my special friends.

In 1962 the first Reeve DC-6 arrived to replace the DC-4s. Oh my word, they were pressurized and reduced the en-route time considerably. And then in 1968 they, too, were replaced, by Lockheed Electras. The almost-jet-speed Electras introduced another first for Reeve Aleutian: a round trip out to the end of the Aleutians and back, all in just one day.

Bob Reeve stands next to his son, Richard, at Anchorage's Merrill Field in 1943. In November 1942, under contract to the military, Reeve began flying to the Aleutians in his Boeing 80-A (background) and Fairchild 71 (foreground). *(Courtesy Robert C. Reeve Collection, Reeve Aleutian Airways)*

In the meantime, our DC-3s continued the milk run: Flight 11 from Anchorage to King Salmon, Port Heiden, Port Moller, Sand Point, Cold Bay, Cape Sarichef, Dutch Harbor, Driftwood Bay, Umnak, and Nikolski, a three-day flight fed by and feeding the big planes in Cold Bay. The seventies brought replacements for the DC-3s: NAMCO YS-11s—285 mph with Rolls Royce engines—cut the en-route times in half, and thus also eliminated the need for overnights on the milk run.

In the Spring of 1978, after forty-six years of active leadership, seventy-six-year-old Robert C. Reeve appointed his eldest son, Richard D. Reeve, President and Chief Executive Officer of Reeve Aleutian Airways, Inc.

In 1979, Reeve Aleutian Electras pioneered a direct route from Seattle across the North Pacific Ocean (1,802 miles) to Cold Bay, using Loran C navigation equipment. This provided one-stop service from Seattle to Aleutian communities during the late seventies' commercial fishing boom.

Entering the eighties, we operated a fleet of three Electras and three YS-11s, a fleet small and austere, but flexible and efficient, and most ideally suited to the weather conditions and runway facilities in the unique Aleutian area.

Robert C. Reeve, founder of Reeve Aleutian Airways, died in his sleep on August 25, 1980, at the age of seventy-eight. In the RCR tradition of business as usual, no matter what, the loyal and dedicated and talented people of Reeve Aleutian carried on as an era began to end. In the fall of 1980, Janice M. "Tilly" Reeve was elected Chairman of the Board.

## Part Four: 1980-1993

Reeve Aleutian entered the jet age in early 1984, adding two Boeing 727s to its fleet. The first, N831RV, was named "RCR," and the second, N832RV, was named "Tilly," after Mr. and Mrs. R.C. Reeve. On May 4, 1993, Janice M. "Tilly" Reeve died peacefully at home, and the era ended.

As traffic increased and airport improvements made flying to the Aleutians easier, it became popular for other air carriers to try to cash in on the situation. In some cases the pure-profit motive was their undoing. In other cases, similar motives remain to be judged on a time-will-tell basis.

Fifty years ago, RCR first flew to the Aleutians as a civilian and as a part of the war effort. Since then Reeve Aleutian has become an integral part of Aleutian life. Facing challenges of the turbulent airline industry of the '90s, Reeve Aleutian maintains a solid position in the Aleutians, is no stranger to adversity, and looks forward to many decades of service in the Aleutians and Alaska.

*Janice Reeve Ogle is a vice president, member of the board of directors, and corporate secretary-treasurer of Reeve Aleutian Airways, Inc.*

# The Alaska State Defense Force

*Leo J. Hannan*

W HEN ERNEST GRUENING TOOK OFFICE AS GOVER-nor of the Territory of Alaska in December 1939, there had never been a National Guard in Alaska, although several local home guard units had existed during World War I. Governor Gruening immediately took steps to create an Alaska National Guard. His effort resulted in the organization of the Alaska National Guard's 297th Infantry Battalion.

Hostilities throughout the world and American recognition that the country could soon become involved in a World War resulted in the federalization of the 297th in September 1941.

As a result of this action, the National Guard was not available to the territory to assume the local defense role. With this realization, Governor Gruening decreed that every able-bodied Alaska male not in military service or essential to war work would be enrolled in the territorial guard and kept at home for the defense of Alaska.

In 1941 there were a limited number of federal troops stationed in Alaska under an organization known as the Alaskan Command. Federal officers Major (later Lieutenant Colonel) Marvin "Muktuk" Marston and Captain Carl Schreiber were assigned by the Alaskan Command to assist the territorial governor in the formation of the Alaska Territorial Guard (ATG). To aid in the effort the federal and territorial governments supplied rifles, very limited ammunition, and other limited logistical and administrative support. A comment by an ATG member illustrates how limited the support was: "The ATG members were issued a 1917 Enfield rifle, .30-06 caliber, and 20 rounds of ammunition. The instructions given at the time of issue were to use two rounds to zero the rifle

[in] and save the rest for the momentarily expected Japanese invasion of Alaska."

Alaskans in towns, bush villages, and isolated areas flocked to join the ATG. These men provided security to vital facilities throughout the territory, manned remote outposts, and were the only military reserve available to counter a Japanese attack of Alaska.

The Japanese invasion of the remote Aleutian Islands of Attu and Kiska was primarily a diversion to draw American forces from the Pacific and no further attempt was made to continue the conquest of Alaska.

The militiamen of the ATG saw no combat action during World War II but provided essential security functions which freed federal troops to serve in combat areas. Upon return of the National Guard to territorial control at the end of World War II, the Alaska Territorial Guard was disbanded and gradually faded into history.

When Alaska became the forty-ninth state in 1959, state statutes were established which are still in effect today. The statutes included provisions that all able-bodied citizens of the United States residing in Alaska, between the ages of seventeen and fifty-nine, are members of the state militia. The state militia is divided into the organized militia—consisting of the Alaska National Guard, Alaska Naval Militia, and the Alaska State Defense Force—and the unorganized militia, that is, all other citizens available for militia service.

Although the militia statutes had been enacted in 1959, with the exception of the National Guard the organized militia was not expanded until 1984, when Governor William Sheffield established the Alaska State Guard as an all-volunteer, back-up military reserve. At that time, the Alaska State Guard was authorized to wear the shoulder patch worn by the Alaska Territorial Guard of World War II. In 1987 the organization's name was changed to the Alaska State Defense Force.

Currently the Alaska State Defense Force consists of one regiment in cadre status and headquartered in Anchorage, and battalions headquartered in Juneau, Anchorage, and Fairbanks. Current authorized strength of the regiment consists of 182 cadre personnel, with a full call-up strength of 1,103. Regimental headquarters is based in the Alaska National Guard Armory on Fort Richardson in Anchorage.

*Leo J. Hannan is a retired U.S. Air Force civilian employee. He is currently a lieutenant colonel in the Alaska State Defense Force.*

# A Well-Kept Secret

*Gwynneth Gminder Wilson*

ONCE UPON A TIME, MORE THAN FIFTY YEARS AGO, I was a senior at Goucher College in Baltimore, Maryland. Pearl Harbor occurred, December 7, 1941, in the middle of the academic year. We had hardly recovered from our shocked surprise when the U.S. Navy stepped in to organize a class in cryptology—the breaking of codes and ciphers. It was arranged through a professor of English, who handpicked the students involved.

There has never been a clue as to why we were chosen. We were a diverse group in personality and our selected majors ranged from history through economics to psychology. We were immediately sworn to secrecy, a secrecy which was meant to be observed scrupulously from 1941 to 1991. Because of this long, well-kept secret, details concerning this class remain hidden. What one does not talk about one tends to forget.

However, once the navy lifted its ban, we were able—painstakingly—to reconstruct who was involved and what other colleges had taken part. These were Bryn Mawr, Smith, Vassar, Mount Holyoke, Radcliffe, and Wellesley. At Goucher, approximately eight of my classmates and, the next year, nine, were recruited.

The class met weekly on the top floor of Goucher Hall in a locked room. While Dr. Ola E. Winslow did the teaching, there was occasional assistance from a naval officer from Washington, D.C. We started with simple codes where the most common letters in a language—E for example, in English—were the key to the solution, and worked up to more complex problems.

Upon graduation, I had a choice among several options. I chose to work as a civil servant in Washington, D.C., while most chose to become WAVES (Women Accepted for Voluntary Emergency Service). These were to become the first women commissioned as naval officers in World War II.

I was assigned to the Japanese section. The U.S. had reconstructed the main Japanese diplomatic cipher machine—which was called "Purple"—well before our involvement in the war. Because Japanese is written pictorially, with symbols as letters, it was necessary to improvise for transmitting messages a system based on a western alphabet, which was known as "Kona." Similarities could be noted which could lead to the deciphering of messages. Basically, this is very dull since much time can be spent over many messages seeking a match. One of the frustrations was that finding an apparent match never led to the satisfaction of knowing whether it was important. Some officer would gather it up and walk away.

One of my classmates was fluent in German and so was assigned to the German section. She tells of breaking the code of a radiogram saying that the ship her brother was serving on had been sunk. Because of the secrecy, she could not tell her family. Happily, her brother wrote a letter to say that his battalion had been dropped off in Bermuda prior to the sinking. Many years later she was to find herself as a tourist at Scapa Flow—in the Orkneys off northern Scotland, where the British fleet lay—and knew immediately from the work she had done in the navy exactly where she was.

When the U.S. entered the war, the joint British and American efforts to break the ciphers were known as Ultra. Five of the WAVES from Goucher were assigned to Operation Ultra.

The Germans had a seemingly unbreakable naval code, known as Enigma. Some work had been done on breaking the Enigma code by the Poles, who had given this information to the British. Dr. Frederic O. Musser, of Goucher College, described Enigma encoding as follows:

To encrypt a message, the text was typed letter by letter on a keyboard attached to an Enigma machine. Each typed letter generated a current which passed through a plug board from which it emerged as a different letter. The signal was then directed to a rotor wheel in which alphabetic letters on the rim were interconnected by internal wiring. Thus, from this rotor the already encrypted version of the originally typed letter emerged as yet another letter. This process continued through a sequence of rotor wheels before the final encrypted form of the letter was displayed on a lighted display panel.

Every time the current generated by typing a particular letter passed through the first rotor, the rotor would revolve one space so that if the same letter were repeated, it would exit the wheel as a letter different from its first appearance. When the first wheel reached a certain point in its revolution the second wheel would revolve one space, and each of the following rotors would later do the same. Moreover, the orders of the wheels could be changed as could the plug board settings. Thus, each successive letter typed into the Enigma machine would be encrypted by a different cipher from the one used for the preceding letter. It could require billions of tests to arrive at correct knowledge of all the settings of all the rotors and the plugboard for a given day, and the next day the process could change.

The code-breaking work was accomplished by a fascinating group of brilliant cryptanalysts, aided by an occasional seizing of documents and keys from captured German ships, and the "Bombe," a huge, elaborate machine designed for digesting keys to find links.

The WAVES dealt with processing messages already decrypted and translated. Using these they could track the positions of submarines relating this to the movements of ships and convoys. Also, they monitored neutral shipping, determining when ships were supplying U-boats or other, less-innocent activities.

Because of the groups of U-boats running in "wolf packs," the transporting of troops and materials across the Atlantic was a perilous undertaking. When the German code was broken and the Germans were kept from discovering this, sea lanes were made safe for shipping by avoidance of the wolf packs. Ultimately, the wolf packs themselves were located and destroyed.

While it is questionable that breaking the Enigma code shortened the war, it is undeniable that it saved lives and kept a balance in the war in the Pacific, since men and ships did not need to be deployed to the Atlantic.

My husband once decried that I had done nothing in the war. That too is part of a well-kept secret

*Gwynneth Gminder Wilson has a degree in history and previously worked for the Johns Hopkins University Institute of the History of Medicine.*

# Writing about the War

The following three authors of works about World War II in Alaska were asked to present their perceptions with respect to writing about the war in the Aleutians.

## Writing about the War

*John H. Cloe*

When I became an air force historian on Elmendorf Air Force Base in 1973, I soon learned that there was very little published on the Aleutian Campaign. The only post-World War II book was Brian Garfield's *The Thousand-Mile War*.

In looking through the office files, it became readily apparent to me that there was a wealth of information on that largely ignored and forgotten piece of our Alaska heritage. Later visits to various archives confirmed that impression. I found that most of the information had been declassified years ago, except that which dealt with the North Pacific deception plan code-named "Webblock." I was also fortunate to visit all the principal Aleutian battlegrounds, including Kiska Island, and to have interviewed those who fought there, Japanese included. The experiences left an unforgettable impression on me.

In 1980, I attended the reunion of the Eleventh Air Force Veterans. Several of the forty veterans in attendance commented that they were disappointed by the fact that so little had been written about them. I felt they were the forgotten warriors of "The Forgotten War." While you can stock a small city library with books written about the Eighth Air Force, nothing has

appeared, outside of a few articles, on the Eleventh Air Force.

In 1982, Major Mike Monaghan and I, during a casual hallway conversation, decided to write a book on the history of the air force in Alaska. The result was *Top Cover for America, the Air Force in Alaska, 1920-1983*. The Anchorage chapter of the Air Force Association—and, more particularly, Bill Brooks, one of its members—agreed to provide financial backing. In return, the royalties went into the association's scholarship fund. After approaching more than ten publishers, we accepted Stan Cohen, of Pictorial Histories. Unfortunately, Mike did not live to see the book's publication in 1984. He died of cancer in December 1983. *Top Cover* went through three printings before it became too dated.

Writing *Top Cover* clinched my desire to write a history of the Eleventh Air Force and the lonely and forgotten air war its members fought in the North Pacific.

We tried the same approach we had used for *Top Cover*. Again, Stan agreed to publish it. I might note that Stan has been highly successful with his *Forgotten War* series and his many other publications on Alaska's history—a contribution, I feel, that has not been fully recognized.

I started work on the *The Aleutian Warrior, A History of the Eleventh Air Force and Fleet Air Wing Four*, in September 1988. I decided to include the navy's Fleet Air Wing Four in the history because of the vital role they played in the air war in the North Pacific. Originally I had intended to cover the entire World War II period.

Stan and I agreed on a somewhat unorthodox

approach for publishing the book. As I completed each section, Stan would have it typeset and complete the layout. The result was a project where some parts were in layout, some in typeset, others in my computer, and parts in my head. I do not recommend that approach to publishing a book. Additionally, we did not hire an editor or submit the manuscript to peer review. Instead we relied on friends, including Admiral James Russell, for those responsibilities. Finally, the book differed from Stan's normal publications in that there were end notes, a total of 850.

As the book progressed, Stan and I realized it was getting to be too long, and we decided to cover the Aleutian Campaign as Part One of the history and to publish Part Two later. Part Two would cover the Kurile operations. Unfortunately my wife's terminal cancer and her death left me in a state where I did not want to take on another major writing project.

*The Aleutian Warriors* was published in July 1991, and the first edition immediately sold out. Sales of the second edition were considerably slower, and the third edition is even slower in reaching its depletion. This indicates to me that we are dealing with a niche publication with limited interest.

This is unfortunate, since I still feel that the war in Alaska has not been fully appreciated and understood. There is every chance that the Alaska at War Symposium will generate more interest. Also encouraging is the fact that a number of books are being published about the war and its impact on Alaska and northwest Canada. Hopefully *The Thousand Mile War* will be republished. Despite its errors, it remains the classic.

This leads me to one of the questions posed to writers about the war: why has so little been written about the war in the Aleutians?

First, I believe it was an insignificant campaign that should not have been fought at all. Second, it occurred early in the war and was quickly overshadowed by larger and more strategically oriented campaigns. Third, there was a considerable amount of censorship and secrecy involved at the time. Finally, the principal military leaders did not perform very well, resulting in the loss of resources and personnel that could have been put to better use elsewhere. In short, it was an embarrassment.

Samuel Eliot Morison's comment, "The Aleutians should have been left to the Aleuts," sums it up best. However, this in no comfort to the men and women who fought and endured in the North Pacific during World War II. The Aleuts, I am sure, would have agreed with Morison's assessment, particularly in view of the sad fate they suffered.

If the Aleutian Campaign has been ignored, the Kurile Operations have truly been consigned to the dustbin of history. Little is known about the army air forces and navy air crews that flew the sacrificial missions from the western Aleutians against Japanese military and naval installations in the northern Kurile Islands.

Fortunately, Otis Hays has done yeoman's work in bringing that part of our history to light. His recent book, *Home From Siberia,* is an account of the 291 airmen held captive as internees in the Soviet Union during the war. Two hundred and forty-two came from Aleutian bases. They were forced to divert to Soviet bases after running into difficulty during air strikes against the Kuriles. Otis is currently working on an account of the deception plan, Webblock, which will be published in the next two years. It should shed some much-needed light on the real purpose of the Kurile Operations. And hopefully I will be inspired to complete Part Two of *The Aleutian Warriors.*

While I am on the topic of the Kuriles, I might also add that it was through the efforts of Ralph Bartholomew, President of the Eleventh Air Force Association, and Alaska's congressional delegation that the *Home from Siberia* men were recently accorded POW status for veterans' benefits.

Another topic of interest to writers about the war is the myths that came out of the war in Alaska. War myths will always be with us. The persistent classic of the Aleutian Campaign is that it is the only battle fought on American soil since the War of 1812. The defenders of Bataan, Wake, and Guam might take exception to that statement.

Another is the repeated account that the Japanese Mitsubishi AM6M2 Zero, recovered virtually intact on Akutan Island, was used as the basis for the design of the Grumman F6F Hellcat. In fact, the Hellcat was going into production when the Zero was found. Of course, the Americans exploited the captured Zero for technical intelligence. It was flown against American fighters to determine its strengths and weaknesses. The information was sent to the field, and Captain Ronald Reagan narrated a training film featuring the Zero. The story is well documented in Jim Rearden's book, *Cracking the Zero Mystery.*

There are other myths which I will not go into detail about, such as the possible American plans to use poison gas on the Japanese on Attu, the homosexual issue, the high number of suicides, the sending of a destroyer to recover President Roosevelt's stranded dog on Adak, and so on.

A couple of comments should suffice: Poison gas was routinely carried aboard ships during World War II operations as a hedge against the other side's using it first; Gore Vidal certainly popularized the homosexual issue in the movie *Advise and Consent*; the Aleutians were a terrible place to be assigned to, particular after the campaign ended, and whether the suicide rates exceeded that of other places is debatable; and the Republicans made much of the stranded-dog incident during the 1944 presidential elections, leading Roosevelt to retort, "The Republicans have not been content with attacks on my wife and myself. No, they now include our little dog Fala."

I will leave it to others to exploit those topics.

The true story is of those forgotten warriors who fought in the North Pacific during World War II. They are of a passing generation that came of age during the Great Depression, went off to fight in the greatest war ever inflicted on mankind, and then came home to make America the greatest nation in the world. Some have presented papers at this symposium, and there are others in the audience. I salute you.

*John Haile Cloe was the recipient of the Alaska Historical Society's Alaska Historian of the Year Award in 1992 for his book, "The Aleutian Warriors, A History of the Eleventh Air Force and Fleet Air Wing Four."*

## Remarks for the Alaska at War Conference

*Elmer Freeman*

In addressing the question of why so little had been written about the Aleutian Campaign prior to 1969, several things must be considered. First of all, John Wayne never fought in the Aleutians. By romanticizing Iwo Jima and Guadalcanal, Hollywood stirred writers all over America to jump on the bandwagon and write about the war in the South Pacific. When films of the Battle of Midway were made, there was at best an off-hand reference to the Japanese operation in the Aleutians and perhaps a twenty-second shot of a PBY flying into the fog.

Because of the shortage of reading material, I expected to find our operations in the Aleutians super-classified when I first started to write. What I found was that the Aleutian Campaign was somewhat classified, but mostly officials appeared to ignore it. One is left with the impression that if we had not been there to keep the Japanese stranded at their initial invasion sites of Kiska and Attu, it would have been a complete surprise if the Japanese had taken over Vancouver Island and begun bombing Seattle.

The one attempt I know of where we could have gotten some recognition was the film, *Report on the Aleutians*, which was made at Adak by John Huston and his crew. But it never was widely circulated and, like everything else about the Aleutian Campaign, it was put on the shelf and gathered dust for some forty years

until released on videotape.

The earliest book I have found on the Aleutian Campaign is called *No Tumult, No Shouting: The Story of the PBY*, by Lois and Don Thorburn, a husband-and-wife team. The book came out in 1945 and had an interesting format: chapters alternated between the PBY flights in the Aleutians and the construction of the PBYs at the Consolidated factory in San Diego. The book had a very patriotic flavor and made numerous references to buying war bonds. The book has been out of print for a number of years.

As for access to research materials, there is a fair amount out there if you keep digging. Of course, one of my best and primary sources has been Admiral James S. Russell. Since he was the skipper of our squadron, he can pinpoint people, places, and events in those days as well as anybody alive. I have been the beneficiary of his hospitality at his home, where he made his library of documents available to me and where we also engaged in wonderful conversations about our days in the Aleutians. On some occasions I have written a two-line question to him and very shortly received a three-page answer.

Two important resources for any researcher are the National Archives and the Navy Historical Center. My experience in dealing with the National Archives by mail has been a bit frustrating, mainly because there is an eight-week turnaround on all correspondence. Finally my wife spotted some bargain fares from Spokane to Washington, D.C., and we visited the National Archives in person. That was a great experience. In three days' time we looked through literally thousands of photos and chose over a hundred to order. They cover PBY operations from Seattle to Sitka to Kodiak, and every base from there to Attu. The attendants in the still-photo department where we did our work were very helpful and made our days there very pleasant.

One regret I have was that during our stay in Washington, D.C., we did not have time to visit the Navy Historical Center. All of my dealings with them have been by mail and telephone and have been quite fruitful. The first time I dealt with them I asked if they would send me a sample of available materials. In a couple of weeks I received a hundred pages of the war diary of Patrol Squadron Forty-two. That is some kind of sample. Otherwise, what I have received from the Navy Historical Center has been mainly rolls of microfilm containing official records of the campaign.

Another important primary source of information has been the other participants in the Aleutian Campaign.

One would think that interviews with men who participated in our operations in the Aleutians would answer lots of puzzling questions and add lots of new information. Actually, these interviews are a little tough to handle sometimes. It turns out that if four guys witnessed the same incident, each has a different memory of what happened. So if you can finally get at least two to agree, you have some assurance that you have resolved the conflict. But even then your final draft of the story may be a bit tenuous. The Patrol Wing Four group has had a couple of reunions and some of the informal sessions at these reunions can be quite fruitful for a writer. However, one must remember that any story told and retold by old sailors tends to pick up a few new twists along the way and to become a bit exaggerated here and there.

Several areas of dispute illustrate the problem of accuracy in sources. One never-ending conflict that persists in Patrol Wing Four is who was first to bomb the Kurile Islands from the Aleutians. Our departed shipmate, Carl "Bon" Amme, as skipper of VP-45, claimed that he led a three-plane flight on the first bombing mission to the Kuriles. He admitted that the target was socked in and they dropped their bombs by radar.

Ole Haugen, a crewmember of VP-43, declares that didn't count as the first mission because they didn't see anything. He claims the honor for VP-43 because their planes actually saw their target when they flew their first bombing mission to the Kuriles a few days later.

Also, there is endless discussion about who hit the Japanese Zero which went down on Akutan Island on June 4, 1942. Those of us from VP-42 prefer to think that one of Ensign Albert Mitchell's gunners (preferably our old buddy Rebel Rawls, whose body was recovered a day or so later) fired the shot during the engagement when Mitchell's PBY was shot down in flames near Egg Island, east of Dutch Harbor. But there are those who claim the Zero was hit by ground fire during the bombing raid at Dutch Harbor. Jim Rearden's book, *Cracking The Zero Mystery*, seems to agree with the VP-42 version.

As I have researched the Aleutian Campaign, its conduct, and outcome, I have uncovered one area which appears to me to have been deliberately forgotten.

Some weeks before this conference I attended an author's reading, given by a former B-17 pilot who flew bombing missions over Germany and who had written a book about his experiences. He told of a set of missions when the B-17s flew straight on from Germany and landed in Russia to refuel before flying another mission over Germany on their way back to England. During their three-day stay in Russia they were treated like visiting royalty. I couldn't help but compare that story with the contrasting accounts of our navy airmen who were forced to land in Russia in the Pacific Theater of Operations and who were interned there as a result.

That is one phase of the Aleutian Campaign which is difficult to research, apparently because of the political climate at the time and since. Since the Soviet Union fell apart a couple of years ago there have been reports of Americans from various conflicts held prisoner by the Russians. Our officials in Washington claim to be surprised by this news. My suspicion is that they know much more than they will admit.

One of the microfilms I received from the Navy Historical Center furnished me with a detailed list of the navy crews that landed in Russian territory after sustaining battle damage while bombing the Kurile Islands. Since Russia was our ally in World War II, one would expect that all that needed to be done was send a transport plane or ship over there and retrieve our people. But the politics of the situation condemned those internees to a prison-like existence for many months and, finally, a secret repatriation after a tortuous trip of thousands of miles to the Iranian border. When they finally arrived back in the states they were warned that they were to say nothing about their experience and were even required to sign statements to that effect. Even forty-five years after the fact, the former internees I talked with seemed a bit fearful of discussing their experiences.

To a U.S. Navy aircrew gunner sitting in a cold prison hut and living on short rations, the story that Russia was afraid that any aid given to U.S. airmen would incur the wrath of Japan and cause the Japanese to attack Russia does not hold water. By 1944, when these events were taking place, Japan was backing down on all fronts and Russia was winning its war in Europe. President Roosevelt should have told Joe Stalin to return our people or his supply of B-25s, P-39s, and numerous ships from the U.S. would be cut off. To my way of thinking this whole phase of the U.S. relationship with the Russians in the Pacific was a disgrace.

In addition to researching the Aleutian Campaign and discussing experiences with old shipmates, publishing my book has been a satisfying experience. In trying to get it published I received my share of rejections. But I must say that the rejections were always friendly and encouraging. "Don't give up—keep trying." But when I was dealing with the University of Washington Press and they were seriously considering publishing the book, they were talking about a publication date over two years away. And they didn't like my title. And they argued with me about the facts in some parts of the text. When it was decided that they would not publish my book, I published it myself and was able to meet the deadline of mid-May 1992, in time for the fiftieth anniversary remembrance of the bombing of Dutch Harbor on June 3, 1942. So for three glorious days my book was a best-seller in Unalaska. That was a thrill which will keep me going for a long time.

*Elmer Freeman captained a PBY in Patrol Squadron 42 shortly after World War II began. His latest book, "Those Navy Guys and their PBY's: The Aleutian Solution," was published in 1992.*

## War and History

*Lael Morgan*

I got my first introduction to revisionist history by omission in the Alaska State Archives in the mid-1970s. A researcher for Time/Life Books was working there and something was said about the World War II series her company was producing.

"What are you going to do about the Aleutian Campaign?" the librarian asked eagerly.

"We're going to leave it out," the Time/Life lady said firmly. I don't want to think about that.

Heath Twichell recently remarked he thought Alaska's part in World War II history was often ignored because it isn't particularly important in the overall view. And granted, placed alongside accounts of Guadalcanal and the invasion of Normandy, it does pale. But at risk of sounding like one of those proverbial "we don't care how they do outside, let them freeze in the dark" Alaskans, let me suggest another reason.

Much of Alaska's World War II history is a real embarrassment to military men and Americans in general. The Time/Life lady is not the only one who doesn't want to think about it. For starters, the invasion of the Aleutians by the Japanese was the first time foreigners had ever succeeded in landing on American soil, I believe. Luckily for us they made a tactical error in doing so, but it wasn't so much the American forces as ultimately the weather that dislodged them, like Napoleon in Russia. We so heavily outnumbered the enemy on our invasion of Attu and made so many blunders, like the Battle of the Blips, that it's hard to discuss this confrontation with any braggadocio. Rather we called it a good learning experience, which it was. A lot of big men and a lot of clever people were out there, but it was a tough one.

As to Kiska, that battle cost the lives of twenty-four American and Canadian boys who managed to gun each other down before they noticed the enemy had departed. The U.S. treatment of the Aleuts, evacuated for their own protection, turned out to be as bad or worse than that suffered by those Aleuts captured by the Japanese. And this information is just from the material that's been published.

I've long been bothered by a rumor that the Japanese complained we used mustard gas during the Battle of Attu. My father-in-law died as results of mustard gas from World War I, and I know all too well good reasons why the Geneva Convention banned it. And yet, I found mustard gas on the manifest of the U.S. ships involved in the Aleutian campaign and I was so boggled by the idea, I never used the material. (They say a good reporter knows two-thirds more than they he or she can ever report.)

Likewise the grim, graphic account of the last Japanese to surrender on Attu some months after the invasion. He came out of the hills, skeleton thin and waving a white flag, only to be beaten to death by the picks and shovels of members of the Corps of Engineers, one veteran assured me.

Almost as disquieting is the well-documented account of a Japanese delegation that arrived in Attu in the late 1980s, hiked a day into the hills, and unearthed the remains of several of their dead. If no Japanese escaped the Battle of Attu, as we are led to believe, how did they know where to look? And the blatant racism of General Simon Bolivar Buckner, head of the Alaskan Command, diminishes the stature of a brilliant general.

I got to the National Archives right after World War II records were declassified. I have walked and camped every Aleutian battlefield. I've toured with both Americans and Japanese veterans of that campaign, and I can tell you I wish the Aleutian War, the war in Alaska, was as straightforward to write about as it is fascinating.

As for writing about it, John Cloe gave me fair warning in July that he planned to take the approach that journalists make poor historians and historians make poor journalists; a suggestion I found astonishing because I'd never considered either side. I know historians who make excellent journalists, and I know journalists who make excellent historians. The work of Woodward and Berstein ain't too shabby, and I'd hire Heath Twichell for my newspaper any day because the man has intellectual curiosity and he can write. I also know journalists who make lousy historians, and historians who couldn't do journalism if their Ph.D.'s depended on it. Just like I know a few journalists who are now good journalists and historians who might better have gone into dentistry.

One of the nasty little points that did occur to me was that journalists who do not write well, cannot expect to stay employed, while, alas, the same cannot be said about historians. But that's exactly the petty sniping that Cloe expected to reduce me to and, on further consideration, I think he's done us a favor by bringing up the subject. I assume Cloe's definition of historians is synonymous with that of academicians, who are cautious by nature. Journalists, on the other hand, are freer to gamble. If they get it wrong, they can print a retraction, and it's all on the bottom of the bird cage tomorrow anyway. Historians who blow it face vicious sniping from gleeful fellow academicians, possible failure of tenure if they don't already have it, and the prospect of not being invited to participate in symposiums like this one. Books, which historians are more likely to write than journalists, stay on the shelves forever. Historians are never allowed to forget, while the world is kinder to journalists—except when they make really embarrassing mistakes, such as the headline, "Dewey Wins!"

For this reason, journalists are more often inclined than historians to bring up unexplored areas, like why the blacks who built the Alaska Highway were steadfastly left out of the history books for fifty years, or why the U.S. Navy was packing mustard gas to the Aleutians, one of the windiest areas in the world and certainly the most stupid place to use it ... and what happened to the last Japanese in Attu.

Really, I think there's room in the world for historians to tackle journalism and vice versa. Developing new job skills keeps one from getting old too quickly. And, frankly, you historians can keep us journalists honest while we keep you lively.

*Lael Morgan is a member of the Department of Journalism and Broadcasting, University of Alaska Fairbanks. Her most recent book is "Art and Eskimo Power: The Life and Times of Alaskan Howard Rock."*

# World War II in Alaska, Northwest Canada, and the North Pacific:
# A Selected Bibliography[1]

*Compiled by*
*R. Bruce Parham*

THE LITERATURE ON WORLD WAR II IN ALASKA, northwest Canada, and the north Pacific is voluminous, although not as extensive as that of other sub-theaters of operation. In this selected bibliography are cited only the major English-language works that may be particularly useful for further reading, provide a general introduction to various aspects of the war, are generally subject-specific to the war in the north, are of mostly recent publication, or that appear to me to be of special note. Included are works that are available, biographies, autobiographies, official documents and histories, films, articles, and a few theses and dissertations. No attempt will be made here to list all of the works cited in the other sections of these proceedings. All books and articles referred to in each of these essays have been cited at their first mention in the footnotes.

Except in a few instances, articles from *Life, Time, Collier's*, and other popular magazines written during World War II have been omitted because of their high volume. Many popular magazines of this period are included in military history bibliographies or indexed in various reference sources, such as the *Reader's Guide to Periodical Literature*. For more detailed discussion of the literature, especially of primary sources, the reader may wish to refer to parts one and two of this bibliography.

The bibliography is divided into eleven parts: (1) Archival Guides and Finding Aids; (2) Alaska and Military History Bibliographies; (3) War in the North Pacific; (4) Defending the Territory; (5) The Alaska Highway; (6)

War's Impact on the Home Front; (7) Minorities: Civilian and Military; (8) Aleut Relocation and Restitution; (9) Lend-Lease; (10) Historic Preservation; and (11) The War's Aftermath. Part one lists archival guides, principally from Alaska and other U.S. archival repositories. Part two includes many U.S. military history bibliographies, several of which are subject-specific to Alaska's military history. Parts three through eleven follow the outline of the "Alaska at War" Conference proceedings and the sessions that were presented at the "Alaska at War" Conference. Due to the large number of secondary sources on Alaska, northwest Canada, and the North Pacific, the division into these subject categories may be more useful to the reader than would be any attempt at a long bibliography without the groupings.

On the Aleutian Campaign, it is still best to start with the official American histories, which are separated by military service. The U.S. Army's *U.S. Army in World War II* set is made up of several series, including series of each of the theaters as well as each of the services. Developments relating to Alaska and the fighting in the Aleutians are covered in *The Western Hemisphere: Guarding the United States and Its Outposts; Special, Studies, Military Relations Between the United States and Canada, 1939-1945; The War in the Pacific, Strategy and Command, The First Two Years; The Technical Services, The Corps of Engineers: Troops and Equipment;* and *The Technical Services, The Corps of Engineers: The War Against Japan.* Wesley F. Craven and James L. Cate prepared the seven-volume

---

[1] Special thanks to Carol Burkhart and John Haile Cloe for contributing entries from their World War II bibliographies to this list. I would like to acknowledge the research assistance that Dean Kohlhoff provided on the section on "Aleut Relocation and Restitution."

official air force history, *The Army Air Forces in World War II*. I included two volumes from this series, *The Army Air Forces in World War II, Combat Chronology, 1941-45*, and *The Pacific: Guadalcanal to Saipan, August 1942 to July 1944*. Naval operations in the North Pacific are covered by Samuel Eliot Morison in *History of United States Naval Operations in World War II*, Volume 7, *Aleutians, Gilberts and Marshalls June 1942 - April 1944*. In addition, Brian Garfield, *The Thousand-Mile War: World War II in Alaska and the Aleutians*, provides the best one-volume survey of the campaign.

The existing secondary literature is large and is so greatly varied in quality that it makes a great deal of sense to try not to be even more exhaustive—something a printout from a computerized catalog can do far better. However, it made some sense to give a fuller accounting of these sources because of the less than adequate coverage of Alaska literature over time in the major bibliographic databases and indexes. The best place to begin a search is the University of Alaska Elmer E. Rasmuson Library's *Bibliography of Alaskana* (1979-1992) and on-line *Bibliography of Alaska and Polar Regions* (1993 to the present), which cites books and other monographs and articles about Alaska and the Polar Regions (northern Scandinavia, Canada, Russia, Iceland, Greenland, and Antarctica). The *Bibliography of Alaska* is also available on PolarPac, a CD-ROM database distributed by the Western Library Network (WLN) of Lacey, Washington. Other useful abstracts and indexes are *Academic Abstracts* (1984 to the present) and *America: History and Life* (1964 to the present), and *Historical Abstracts* (1973 to the present). The Western Library Network is an on-line bibliographic utility that provides access to the holdings of member libraries in the Pacific Northwest (including Alaska) and Canada. The University of Washington Allen Library's Special Collections and Preservation Division maintains the Pacific Northwest Regional Newspaper and Periodicals Index, a card file of more than one million subject entries to Pacific Northwest-related articles (including Alaska) in regional newspapers and periodicals, and of pamphlet material.

## PART 1:
## ARCHIVAL GUIDES AND FINDING AIDS

Canada. National Archives of Canada. *Public Records Division Special Publications Series: Sources for the Study of the Second World War*. Ottawa: 1979.

Envirosphere Company. *World War II in Alaska: A Historic and Resources Management Plan*. Volume 1, *A History of World War II in Alaska and Management Plan. Final Report*. Submitted in Partial Fulfillment of National Park Service Contract CX 9700- 5-005 in Cooperation with the U.S. Army Corps of Engineers, Alaska District. Anchorage: U.S. Army Corps of Engineers, Alaska District, 1987.

Envirosphere Company. *World War II in Alaska: A Historic and Resources Management Plan*. Volume 2, *Archival Sources: A Finding Aid. Final Report*. Submitted in Partial Fulfillment of National Park Service Contract CX 9700-5-005 in cooperation with the U.S. Army Corps of Engineers, Alaska District. Anchorage: U.S. Army Corps of Engineers, Alaska District, 1987.

Gray, Paul D. "The Human Record of Conflict: Individual Military Service and Medical Records." Prologue: *The Quarterly of the National Archives* 23 (Fall 1991): 307-313.

Mattison, David. *Catalogues, Guides and Inventories to the Archives of Alberta, British Columbia, Northwest Territories and the Yukon Territory*. Vancouver: Archives Association of British Columbia, 1991.

O'Neill, James E. and Robert W. Krauskopf. *World War II: An Account of its Documents*. National Archives Conferences, Volume 8. Washington, D.C.: Howard University Press for the National Archives Trust Fund Board, 1976.

Stirling, Dale, comp. *The Alaska Records Survey: An Inventory of Archival Resources in Repositories of the United States and Canada*. Second Edition. Alaska Historical Commission Studies in History No. 209. Anchorage: Alaska Historical Commission, May 1986.
Listing of 341 archival collections relating to Alaska at 152 research centers. Available on microfiche from the Environment and Natural Resources Institute, University of Alaska Anchorage, 707 "A" Street, Anchorage, Alaska 99501.

U.S. Army. Army Military Research Collection. *Manuscript Holdings of the Military History Research Collection*. Compiled by Richard J. Sommers. Special Bibliography Series, No. 6, vol. 2. Carlisle Barracks, Pa.: U.S. Army Military History Research Collection, 1975.

U.S. Army. Center for Military History. *Catalog and Index to Historical Manuscripts*. Vol. 1, *Headquarters, War Department and Department of the Army*. Vol. 2, *Army Service Forces*. Compiled by Hannah M. Zeidlik. Washington, D.C.: U.S. Army Center for Military History, 1979.

U.S. National Archives and Records Administration. *American Women and the U.S. Armed Forces: A Guide to the Records of Military Agencies in the National Archives*. Compiled by Charlotte Palmer Seeley. Revised by Virginia C. Purdy and Robert Gruber. Washington, D.C.: National Archives Trust Fund for the National Archives and Records Administration, 1982.

—-. *Audiovisual Records in the National Archives of the United States Relating to World War II*. Reference Information Paper 70 (revised). Compiled by Barbara Berger, William Cunliffe, Jonathan Heller, William T. Murphy, and Les Waffen. Washington, D.C.: National Archives and Records Administration, 1992.

—. *Guide to Federal Records in the National Archives of the United States*. Third Edition. Three Volumes. Washington, D.C.: Government Printing Office, forthcoming 1995).

—. *Guide to the National Archives of the United States*. Washington, D.C.: National Archives and Records Service, 1974; reprint, Washington, D.C.: National Archives and Records Administration, 1987.

—. *Microfilm Resources for Research: A Comprehensive Catalog*. Revised Edition. Washington, D.C.: National Archives and Records Administration, 1990.

—. *Records Relating to Personal Participation in World American Military Casualties and Burials*. Compiled by Benjamin L. DeWhitt. Reference Information Paper 82. Washington, D.C.: National Archives and Records Administration, 1993.

—. *Records Relating to Personal Participation in World War II: American Prisoners of War and Civilian Internees*. Reference Information Paper No. 80. Compiled by Ben DeWhitt and Jennifer Davis Heaps. Washington, D.C.: National Archives and Records Administration, 1992.

—. *Records Relating to World War II: "The American Soldier" Surveys*. Reference Information Paper No. 78. Compiled by Ben DeWhitt and Heidi Ziemer. Washington, D.C.: National Archives and Records Administration, 1991.

Includes Survey Topic No. S-133(15)A/B, "Attitude of troops in Alaska," April-May 1944.

—. Select List of Publications of the National Archives and Records Administration. General Information Leaflet No. 3. Washington, D.C.: National Archives and Records Administration, 1994.

—. *World War II Records in the Cartographic and Architectural Branch of the National Archives*. Reference Information Paper No. 79. Compiled by Daryl Bottoms. Washington, D.C.: National Archives and Records Administration, 1992.

U.S. National Archives and Records Service. *Audiovisual Records in the National Archives of the United States Relating to World War II*. Reference Information Paper No. 70. Compiled by Mayfield S. Bray and William T. Murphy. Washington, D.C.: National Archives and Records Service, 1974.

—. *Federal Records of World War II*. Volume 1, *Civilian Agencies*. National Archives Publication No. 51-7. Washington, D.C.: Government Printing Office, 1950.

—. *Federal Records of World War II*. Volume 2, *Military Agencies*. National Archives Publication No. 51-8. Washington, D.C.: Government Printing Office, 1951.

—. *List of Logbooks of U.S. Navy Ships, Stations, and Miscellaneous Units, 1801-1947*. Compiled by Claudia Bradley. Special List No. 44. Washington, D.C.: National Archives and Records Service, 1978; reprint, Washington, D.C.: Government Printing Office, 1982.

Ulibarri, George S., comp. *Documenting Alaskan History: Guide to Federal Archives Relating to Alaska*. Alaska Historical Commission Studies in History, No. 23. Fairbanks: University of Alaska Press, 1982.

Walle, Dennis F. with Carolyn J. Bowers. *Guide to the Manuscript Collections at the University of Alaska Anchorage*. Fairbanks: University of Alaska Press, 1990.

Zobrist, Benedict K. "Resources of Presidential Libraries for the History of the Second World War." *Military Affairs* 39 (April 1975): 82-85.

## PART 2:
## ALASKA AND MILITARY HISTORY BIBLIOGRAPHIES

Allard, Dean C. *U.S. Naval History Sources in the United States*. Washington, D.C.: Government Printing Office for the Naval History Division, Dept. of the Navy, 1979.

Blewett, Daniel K. *American Military History: A Guide to Reference and Information Sources*. Reference Sources in the Social Sciences Series, No. 7. Littleton, Colo.: Libraries Unlimited, 1994.

Coletta, Paolo E., comp. *A Selected and Annotated Bibliography of American Naval History*. Lanham, Md.: University Press of America, 1988.

Cresswell, Mary Ann and Carl Berger. *United States Air Force History, An Annotated Bibliography*. Washington, D.C.: Office of Air Force History, 1971.

Dornbusch, Charles E. *Histories of American Army Units: World Wars I and II and Korean Conflict with some Earlier Histories*. Washington, D.C.: Dept. of the Army, Office of the Adjutant General, Special Services Division, Library and Service Club Branch, 1956.

—. *Histories, Personal Narratives: United States Army*. Cornwallville, N.Y.: Hope Farm Press, 1967.

Haycox, Stephen W. and Betty Haycox, ed. *Melvin Ricks's Alaska Bibliography: An Introductory Guide to Alaskan Historical Literature*. Alaska Historical Commission Studies in History, No. 4. Anchorage: Alaska Historical Commission, 1977.

Annotated bibliography of Alaska history materials.

Heimdahl, William C. and Edward J. Marcolda, comps. *Guide to United States Administrative Histories of World War II*. Washington, D.C.: Dept. of the Navy, Naval History Division, 1976.

Higham, Robin D.S. *Official Histories: Essays and Bibliographies from around the World*. Manhattan, Kans.:

Kansas State University Library, 1970.

—-. *A Guide to the Sources of United States Military History*. Hamden, Conn.: Archon Books, 1975.

Higham, Robin D.S. and Donald J. Mrozek. *A Guide to the Sources of United States Military History. Supplement I*. Hamden, Conn.: Archon Books, 1981.

—-. *A Guide to the Sources of United States Military History. Supplement II*. Hamden, Conn.: Archon Books, 1986.

—-. *A Guide to the Sources of United States Military History. Supplement III*. Hamden, Conn.: Archon Books, 1993.

Kinnell, Susan K. *Military History of the United States: A Bibliography*. Clio Bibliography Series, No. 23. Santa Barbara, Calif.: ABC-CLIO, 1986.

Lane, Jack C. *America's Military Past: A Guide to Information Sources*. American Government and History Information Guide Series, Vol. 7. Detroit, Mich.: Gale Research Co., 1980.

Moor, Jay H. *World War II in Alaska: The Northwest Route [Ferrying Lend-Lease Aircraft to the Soviet Union]: A Bibliography and Guide to Primary Sources*. Alaska Historical Commission Studies in History, No. 175. Anchorage: Alaska Historical Commission, 1985.
Annotated list of government documents on US/USSR lend-lease aircraft program.

Nielson, Jonathon Macauley. *An Interpretive Survey of Alaska's Military Heritage, 1867-1969*. Alaska Historical Commission Studies in History, No. 37. Anchorage: Alaska Historical Commission, 1980. Microfiche.
Bibliography of role of United States military and naval services in Alaska history. Available on microfiche from the Environment and Natural Resources Institute, University of Alaska Anchorage, 707 A Street, Anchorage, Alaska 99501.

—-. *A Research Guide to Alaska's Military History, 1867-1979*. Alaska Historical Commission Studies in History, No. 38. Anchorage: Alaska Historical Commission, 1980. Microfiche.
Bibliography of published and unpublished sources for study of Alaska military history. Available on microfiche from the Environment and Natural Resources Institute, University of Alaska Anchorage, 707 A Street, Anchorage, Alaska 99501.

—-. *Armed Forces on a Northern Frontier: The Military in Alaska's History, 1867-1987*. Contributions in Military History, No. 74. New York: Greenwood Press, 1988.

Pappas, George S., Elizabeth Snoke, and Alexandra Campbell. *United States Army Unit Histories*. Rev. Ed. U.S. Army Military Institute, No. 4. Carlisle Barracks, Pa.: U.S. Army Military History Institute, 1978.

Sbrega, John L. *The War against Japan: A Bibliography*. New York: Garland, 1969.

U.S. Army. Army Military History Institute. *The Era of World War II*. Vol. 1, *General Reference Works, Biography*. Compiled by Roy Barnard, William Burns, and Duane Ryan. Vol. 2, *Pacific*. Compiled by Duane Ryan. Vol. 3, *Mediterranean and European Theaters of Operations*. Compiled by Louise Arnold. Special Bibliography Series, No. 16. Carlisle Barracks, Pa.: U.S. Army Military History Institute, 1977-1979.

U.S. Library of Congress. Division of Bibliography. *Aleutian Islands: A List of References*. Washington, D.C.: 1943; reprint, Ann Arbor, Mich.: University Microfilms, 1969.

Ziegler, Janet. *World War II: Works in English, 1945-1965*. Stanford, Calif.: Hoover Institution Press, 1971.
In the bibliographic essay in Gerhard L. Weinberg, *A World at Arms: A Global History of World War II* (New York: Cambridge University Press, 1994), Weinberg states that "Arthur L. Funk has prepared sequels to this book, the first covering the years 1965-75 issued by the World War II Studies Association (formerly the American Committee on the History of the Second World War) and the second, entitled *The Second World War: A Select Bibliography of Books in English Since 1975*, published in 1985 by Regina Books of Claremont, California. Current bibliographic coverage is in the Newsletter of the World War II Studies Association."

## PART 3:
## WAR IN THE NORTH PACIFIC

### Official Histories and Government Documents

Bates, Richard W. *The Battle of Midway including the Aleutian Phase, June 3 to June 14, 1942: Strategic and Tactical Analysis*. Newport, Rhode Island: U.S. Naval War College, 1948.

Buckley, Captain Robert J., Jr. Part 5: "The Aleutians—A Battle against Weather." Chap. in *At Close Quarters: PT Boats in the United States Navy*. Washington, D.C.: Dept. of the Navy, Naval History Division, 1962.

Bush, James D. *Narrative Reports on Alaska Construction, 1941-1943*. Anchorage: Anchorage Construction Division Office, 1944; reprint, Anchorage: U.S. Army Corps of Engineers, Alaska District, 1984.
Describes all major construction projects. Includes maps.

Camp Earle (Attu, Alaska). *Short History-Battle of Attu*. 3d ed. Attu: 1945.

Carter, Kit C., and Robert Mueller. *The Army Air Forces in World War II, Combat Chronology, 1941-45*. Washington, D.C.: Center for Air Force History, 1991.

Coll, Blanche D., Jean E. Keith and Herbert H. Rosenthal. *The United States Army in World War II, Technical Services, The Corps of Engineers: Troops and Equipment*.

Washington, D.C.: Dept. of the Army, Office of the Chief of Military History, 1953.

Conn, Stetson, Rose C. Engelman, and Byron Fairchild. *The United States Army in World War II, The Western Hemisphere, Guarding the United States and Its Outposts.* Washington, D.C.: Dept. of the Army, Office of the Chief of Military History, 1964.

Craven, Wesley Frank, and James Lea Cate, eds. *The Army Air Forces in World War II.* Vol. 1, Plans and Early Operations. Washington, D.C.: Office of Air Force History, 1983.

—. *The Army Air Forces in World War II.* Vol. 4, *The Pacific: Guadalcanal to Saipan, August 1942 to July 1944.* Washington, D.C.: Office of Air Force History, 1983.

Dod, Karl C. *The United States Army in World War II, The Technical Services, The Corps of Engineers: The War Against Japan.* Washington D.C.: Dept. of the Army, Office of the Chief of Military History, 1987.

Dziuban, Stanley W. *The United States Army in World War II, Special Studies, Military Relations Between the United States and Canada, 1939-1945.* Washington, D.C.: Dept. of the Army, Office of the Chief of Military History, 1959.

Ferguson, Lt. Arthur B. *AAF, Alaska Air Defense and the Japanese Invasion.* Army Air Force Historical Study, No. 4. Washington, D.C.: Assistant Chief, Intelligence, AAF Historical Division, April 1943.

Huntoon, David H. *The Aleutians: Lessons from a Forgotten Campaign.* Fort Leavenworth, Kans.: School of Advanced Military Studies, U.S. Army Command and General Staff College, 1988.

Japan. Kaijo Hoancho. Suirobu. [*Summer Conditions in the Aleutian Islands and Bering Sea*]. Publication 146 (Oceanographic Memoirs, No. 20). Tokyo: Hydrographic Office, 1943.
Japanese text.

—. [*Northern Seas in Summer Season*]. Publication 146 (Oceanographic Memoirs, No. 3). Tokyo: Hydrographic Office, 1937.
Japanese text.

Morton, Louis. *The United States Army in World War II, The War in the Pacific, Strategy and Command, The First Two Years.* Washington, D.C.: U.S. Government Printing Office, 1962.

Parker, Frederick D. *A Priceless Advantage: U.S. Navy Communications Intelligence and the Battles of Coral Sea, Midway, and the Aleutians.* United States Cryptologic History Series IV, World War II Volume 5. Fort George G. Meade, Md.: National Security Agency, Center for Cryptologic History, 1993.

Stacey, Charles P. *Six Years of War: The Army in Canada, Britain and the Pacific.* Ottawa: Queen's Printer, 1955.

—. *Arms, Men and Government: The War Policies of Canada, 1939-1945.* Ottawa: Queen's Printer, 1970.

—. *Canada and the Age of Conflict.* Vol. 2, *1921-1948, The MacKenzie King Era.* Toronto: University of Toronto Press, 1978.

*Studies on Local Forecasting for Selected Alaskan and Aleutian Stations.* n.p.: s.n., 1944.

Tooke, Lamar. *Infantry Operations in the Aleutians: The Battle for Attu.* U.S. Army War Studies Program Paper. Technical Report No. AU-A223 584. Carlisle Barracks, Pa.: U.S. Army War College, 1990.

U.S. Advanced Intelligence Center. North Pacific Area. Command History, North Pacific Force. Aleutian Campaign (AIC NorPac No. 880): A Brief Historical Outline to and Including the Occupation of Kiska, August 1943, 1944. Two Volumes. n.p.: 14 August 1945.

U.S. Alaska Defense Command. Intelligence Division. *The Enemy on Kiska*, 19 August-1 September 1942. Periodic Report No. 60. Kiska: HQ, U.S. Troops, Office of the Intelligence Officer, 24 November 1943. Description of facilities and equipment abandoned by Japanese on Kiska Island.

U.S. Army. 50th Anniversary of World War II Commemoration Committee. *Fact Sheet: Aleutian Islands Campaign.* Washington, D.C.: The Committee, n.d. Available from the 50th Anniversary of World War II Commemoration Committee, HQDA, SACC; Pentagon, Room 3E524, Washington, D.C. 20310-0107.

U.S. Army Air Forces. *Alaska Air Defense and the Japanese Invasion of the Aleutians.* Army Air Forces Historical Studies, No. 4. Washington, D.C.: Assistant Chief of Air Staff, Intelligence Historical Division, 1944.

U. S. Army. *The U. S. Army in Alaska.* Pamphlet 360-5. APO Seattle: Department of the Army, Headquarters, 172D Infantry Brigade (Alaska), May 1976.
Sixth edition of history of U.S. Army in Alaska prepared by Office of Information, 172nd Infantry Brigade (Alaska). Pages 85-95 cover World War II.

U.S. Army. Center of Military History. *Aleutian Islands.* The U.S. Army Campaigns of World War II Series. Compiled by George L. MacGarrigle. Washington, D.C.: Government Printing Office, 1992.

U.S. Army. Corps of Engineers. Building the Navy's Bases in World War II. Vol. 2, History of the Bureau of Yards and Docks and the Civil Engineer Corps, 1940-1946. Washington, D.C.: Government Printing Office, 1947.

U.S. Army. Office of the Chief of Military History. *Japanese Monographs*: No. 46, "Aleutians Operations Record, June 1942- July 1943"; No. 47, "Northern Area, Monthly Wartime Reports, Jan. 1943-July 1943," incomplete; No. 88, "Aleutian Naval Operation, Mar. 1942-Feb. 1943," and No. 89, "Northern Area Naval Operations, Feb. 1943-Aug. 1945."
Copies are available on microfilm from the Library of

Congress, Washington, D.C.

U.S. Army. Western Defense Command and Fourth Army. *Final Report of Reduction and Occupation of Attu from the Combat Intelligence Point of View*. Intelligence Memorandum No. 8. n.p.: Western Defense Command, Assistant Chief of Staff, G-2, 9 August 1943.
Summary of combat intelligence on Japanese occupation forces, Attu, October 23, 1942-May 31, 1943.

—. *The Battle of the Aleutians: A Graphic History, 1942-1943*. Adak: Produced by the Intelligence Section, Field Forces Headquarters, 1944.
Dashiell Hammett and Robert Colodny are co-authors of this report.

U. S. Coast Guard. Public Information Division. Historical Section. *The Coast Guard at War*. Vol. 3, *Alaska*. Washington, D.C.: Headquarters U.S.C.G., February 1946.

U.S. Far East Command. *The Imperial Japanese Navy in World War II: A Graphic Presentation of the Japanese Naval Organization and List of Combatant and Non-Combatant Vessels Lost or Damaged in the War*. Tokyo: Military History Section, Special Staff, General Headquarters, Far East Command, Feb. 1952.

—. *Aleutian Naval Operations: March 1942-February 1943*. Japanese Monograph No. 88. Tokyo?: The Command, 1953, microfilm (16mm); reprint, Washington, D.C.: Distributed by Office of the Chief of Military History, Department of the Army, 1958.
Japanese account of the planning and conduct of the Aleutian Campaign. Drafted by Commander Jakuo Mikami, former Staff Officer in Charge of Operations, Japanese Navy General Staff. Other Japanese monographs covering the operations of the Japanese armed forces in the Aleutian area are nos. 46 and 47.

—. *Northern Area Naval Operations (February 1943-August 1945)*. Japanese Monograph No. 89. Tokyo?: The Command, 1953. Microfilm (16mm).
Held by Library of Congress, Washington, D.C.

U. S. Joint Army-Navy Assessment Committee. *Japanese Naval and Merchant Shipping Losses During World War II by all Causes*. Washington: U.S. Government Printing Office, 1947.

U.S. Navy. Naval Historical Center. *U. S. Naval Experience in the North Pacific During World War II: Selected Documents*. Washington, D.C.: Naval Historical Center, 1989.

U.S. Navy. Bureau of Yards and Docks. *Federal Owned Real Estate Under the Control of the Navy Department*. Washington, D.C.: U.S. Government Printing Office, 1937.

U.S. Navy. Northern Pacific Intelligence Center. *Aleutian Campaign*. n.p.: 15 December 1944.

U.S. Navy. Office of Naval Intelligence. *The Aleutian Campaign: June 1942-August 1943*. Washington, D.C.: Office of Naval Intelligence, Publication Branch, 1945.
One of a series of combat narratives of U.S. Navy operations during World War II. Contains detailed accounts of the Battle of the Komandorski Islands, and the planning and occupation of Attu and Kiska. Maps, photographs, naval battle tracks, and tasks organizations.

U.S. Office of Assistant Chief of Air Staff, Intelligence. *Air Pilot Manual of the Aleutian Islands*. Washington, D.C.: 1943.

U.S. Strategic Bombing Survey (Pacific). Naval Analysis Division. *The Campaigns of the Pacific War*. Washington, D.C.: Government Printing Office, 1946; reprint, New York: Greenwood Press, 1969.
Includes transcripts of USSBS interrogations of American and Japanese military personnel involved in the Aleutian Campaign. Chapter VI, "The Aleutian Campaign," by Capt. James S. Russell, USN, details Aleutian Campaign Kurile operations. Contains charts, maps, and statistical tables.

U.S. War Department. *The Capture of Attu, As Told by the Men Who Fought There*. Washington, D.C.: Infantry Journal, 1944.

## Books

Agawa, Hiroyuki. *The Reluctant Admiral: Yamamoto and the Imperial Navy*. New York: Kodansha International, 1979.

Alaska. Alaska Historical Commission. *7th Alaska History Symposium: The Military in Alaska's Past*. Alaska Historical Commission Studies in History, No. 156. Anchorage: Alaska Historical Commission, 1984.

*Aleutian Islands View Book: 32 Illustrated Pages of Aleutian Scenes and Activities*. s.n.: 1944.
A copy is held by the Denver Public Library, Denver, Colorado.

Amme, Capt. Carl H., ed. *Aleutian Airdales*. Plains, Mont.: Plainsman Publishing, 1987.

Anastasia, Bernard. *Wind Blown and Dripping: A Book of Aleutian Cartoons*. Adak?: s.n., 1980.

Andrieu d'Albas, Emmanual M. *Death of a Navy: Japanese Naval Action in World War II*. New York: Devin-Adair Co., 195

Antonson, Joan M. and William S. Hanable. *Alaska's Heritage*. Two Volumes. Alaska Historical Commission Studies in History, No. 133. Anchorage: Alaska Historical Society for the Alaska Historical Commission, Department of Education, State of Alaska, 1985.

Benedict, H. Bradley. *Ski Troops in the Mud, Kiska Island Recaptured: A Saga of the North Pacific Campaign in the Aleutian Islands in World War II with Special Emphasis on Its Culmination Led by the Forerunners of the 10th Mountain Division*. Littleton, Colo.: H.B. & J.C. Benedict, 1990.

Berry, P.S. *The Canol Project: An Adventure of the U.S. War Department in Canada's Northwest*. Limited First Edition. Edmonton, Alberta: Published by the author, 1985.
The National Library of Canada holds a legal deposit copy. A reference copy is held by the Library of Congress in Washington, D.C.

Binek, Lynn K. *Drawing the Lines of Battle: Military Art of World War II Alaska*. Anchorage: Anchorage Museum of History and Art, 1989.

Birdsall, Steve. *Log of the Liberators*. Garden City, N.Y.: Doubleday, 1973.

Bishop, John. "Action Off Komandorski." In *The United States Navy in World War II*, comp. and ed., S. E. Smith, 659-669. New York: William Morrow & Co., 1966.

Blair, Clay Jr. *Silent Victory: The U.S. Submarine War Against Japan*. Philadelphia: Lippincott, 1975.

Blum, John Morton. *V Was For Victory: Politics and American Culture during World War II*. New York: Harcourt Brace Jovanovich, 1976.

Bowman, Waldo G., et al. *Bulldozers Come First: The Story of U.S. War Construction in Foreign Lands*. New York: McGraw-Hill, 1944.

Bradley, Charles C. *Aleutian Eagles*. Fairbanks: University of Alaska Press, 1994.

Burhans, Robert D. *The First Special Force: A War History of the North Americans, 1942-1944*. Washington, D.C.: Infantry Journal Press, 1947; reprint, Nashville, Tenn.: Battery Press, 1981.

*The Capture of Attu: Tale of World War II in Alaska, As told by the Men who Fought There*. Anchorage: Alaska Northwest Publishing Co., 1984.
Reprint edition of U.S., War Department, *The Capture of Attu, as Told by the Men who Fought There* (Washington, D.C.: Infantry Journal, 1944). Published simultaneously in the Summer 1984 issue of *Alaska History*, vol. 14, no. 3.

Carison, William Samuel. *No Mean Victory: The Saga of the Army Air Forces in Alaska and the Aleutians*. Three Volumes. s.l.: s.n., 1946.
Typescript of unpublished material.

Carter, Sir Michael, Field Marshall. *The War Lords*. Boston: Little, Brown & Company, 1976.

Casewit, Curtis W. *Mountain Troopers! The Story of the Tenth Mountain Division*. n.p.: Crowell, 1972.

Cloe, John Haile. *The Aleutian Warriors, A History of the 11th Air Force and Fleet Air Wing 4, Part I*. Missoula, Mont.: Pictorial Histories Publishing Company for the Air Force Association, Anchorage Chapter, 1991.

Cloe, John Haile and Michael F. Monaghan. *Top Cover for America, The Air Force in Alaska 1920-1983*. Missoula, Mont.: Pictorial Histories Publishing Co. and Anchorage Chapter, Air Force Association, 1984.

Coates, Ken S. and William R. Morrison. "War and Upheaval, 1939- 1946," Chap. in *Land of the Midnight Sun: A History of the Yukon*. Edmonton: Hurtig Publishers, 1988.

Coffey, Frank. *Always Home: 50 Years of the USO*. New York: Brassey's (US), 1991.

Cohen, Stan. *The Forgotten War, A Pictorial History of World War II in Alaska and Northwestern Canada*. Missoula, Mont.: Pictorial Histories Publishing Co., 1981.

——. *The Forgotten War, A Pictorial History of World War II in Alaska and Northwestern Canada*, Vol. 2. Missoula, Mont.: Pictorial Histories Publishing Co., 1988.

——. *The Forgotten War, A Pictorial History of World War II in Alaska and Northwestern Canada*, Vol. 3. Missoula, Mont.: Pictorial Histories Publishing Co., 1992.

——. *The Forgotten War, A Pictorial History of World War II in Alaska and Northwestern Canada*, Vol. 4. Missoula, Mont.: Pictorial Histories Publishing Co., 1993.

Collins, Henry, Austin H. Clark, and Egbert H. Walker. *The Aleutian Islands: Their People and Natural History*. Smithsonian Institution War Background Studies, No. 21. Washington, D.C.: 1945.

Cuttlefish 5. *The Aleutian Invasion*. Unalaska, Alaska: Unalaska City School District, 1981.

Day, Beth. *Glacier Pilot*. New York: Holt, Rinehart and Winston, 1970.

Doolittle, General James H. "Jimmy." *I Could Never Be So Lucky Again*. New York: Bantam Books, 1991.

Driscoll, Joseph. *War Discovers Alaska*. Philadelphia, Pa.: Lippincott, 1943.
Description of Alaska's sociological and economic conditions during World War II. Contemporary example of racial bias against Japanese.

Dull, Paul S. *A Battle History of the Imperial Japanese Navy (1941-1945)*. Annapolis, Md.: U.S. Naval Institute, 1978.

Ford, Corey. *Short Cut to Tokyo: The Battle for the Aleutians*. New York: C. Scribner's Sons, 1943.

Fowle, Barry W., Editor. *Builders and Fighters: U.S. Army Engineers in World War II*. Fort Belvoir, Va.: U.S. Army Corps of Engineers, 1992.

Freeman, Elmer A. *Those Navy Guys and Their PBYs: The Aleutian Solution*. Spokane: Kedging Publishing Company, 1992.

Fuchida, Mitsuo and Okumiya Masatake. *Midway: The Battle that Doomed Japan*. Annapolis, Md.: Naval Institute Press, 1955.
Masatake was Air Officer aboard the carrier *Ryujo* at the Battle of Dutch Harbor.

Gage, S.R. *A Walk on the Canol Road: Exploring the First Major Northern Pipeline*. Oakville, Ontario: Mosaic Press, 1990.

Garfield, Brian. Bantam edition. *The Thousand-Mile War: World War II in Alaska and the Aleutians*. New York:

Doubleday, 1982.

Gilman, William. *Our Hidden Front*. New York: Reynal & Hitchcock, 1944.

Goldstein, Donald M. and Katherine V. Dillon. *The Williwaw War: The Arkansas National Guard in the Aleutians in World War II*. Fayetteville: University of Arkansas Press, 1992.

Goforth, J. Penelope, ed. *The Aleutian Eagle*, Special WWII Edition. Vol. 1, No. 16. Alaska Historical Commission Studies in History, No. 67. Anchorage: Alaska Historical Commission, 1982. Microfiche.
Historical photographs of World War II in the Aleutian Islands.

Grant, Shelagh D. *Sovereignty or Security?: Government Policy in the Canadian North, 1936-1950*. Vancouver: University of British Columbia Press, 1988.

Griffin, D.F. *First Steps to Tokyo, The Royal Canadian Air Force in the Aleutians*. Toronto: J.M. Dent and Sons, 1944.

Griffin, Harold. *Alaska and the Canadian Northwest: Our New Frontier*. New York: Norton, 1944.

Gruening, Ernest. *The State of Alaska: A Definitive History of America's Northernmost Frontier*. New York: Random House, 1954.

Handleman, Howard. *Bridge to Victory: The Story of the Reconquest of the Aleutians*. New York: Random House, 1943.

Haugen, Jack O., ed. *The Story of VP-43*. San Bruno, Calif.: n.p., 1967.
On the PBY patrol squadron.

Hays, Otis, Jr. *Home From Siberia: The Secret Odysseys of Interned American Airmen in World War II*. College Station: Texas A & M University Press, 1990.

Holmes, W.J. *Double-Edged Secrets: U.S. Naval Intelligence Operations in the Pacific during World War II*. Annapolis, Md.: Naval Institute Press, 1979.

Hoyt, Edwin P. *War in the Pacific*, Number 5: *Aleutians*. New York: Avon Books, 1992.

Hudson, Ray, ed. *The Aleutian Invasion: World War Two in the Aleutian Islands*. Cuttlefish Five. Unalaska: Unalaska City School District, 1981.

—. *People of the Aleutian Islands*. Alaska Historical Commission Studies in History, No. 196. Unalaska: Unalaska City School District, 1986.

Hugh, B., and B. Cave. *We Build, We Fight! The Story of the Seabees*. New York: Harper & Bros., 1944.

Hutchison, Isobel Wylie. *The Aleutian Islands*. Second Edition. London: Blackie & Sons, 1942.
First published in 1937 under the title *Stepping-stones from Alaska to Asia*.

Hutchinson, Kevin D. *World War II in the North Pacific: Chronology and Fact Book*. Westport, Conn.: Greenwood Press, 1994.

Iizuka, Tsutomu. *Kessen Middoue, Attsu*. Tokyo: Gakushu Kenkyusha, 1972.

Iriye, Akira. *Power and Culture: The Japanese-American War, 1941-1945*. Cambridge, Mass.: Harvard University Press, 1981.

Jacobs, William A. *History of the Alaska District, United States Army Corps of Engineers, 1946-1974*. n.p.: Government Printing Office, 1976.
Prepared from a manuscript researched and compiled by Lyman Woodman.

*The Japanese Navy in World War II*. Annapolis, Md.: U.S. Naval Institute, 1969.

Johnson, Robert Erwin. *Bering Sea Escort: Life Aboard a Coast Guard Cutter in World War II*. Annapolis, Md.: Naval Institute Press, 1992.
History and memories of service aboard the cutter *Haida*.

Karig, Walter and Eric Purdon. *Battle Report, Pacific War: Middle Phase*. New York: Rinehart and Co., 1947.

Kasukabe, Karl Kaoru. *The Aleutian Front Graphics, as Told by the American and Japanese Men who Fought in the Aleutions [sic] Front*. Nagoya, Japan: Commercial Art Center, 1987.
Text in English and/or Japanese.

—. *The Way to Join the International Federation of Mountain Soldiers Sparked by Mr. Sherman Smith's Mountaineers' Comradeship: Japan Alpine-Ski Soldiers Association [the Aleutian Front Graphics as Told by the American and Japanese Men who Fought in the Aleutians Front]*. Nagoya, Japan: Commercial Art Center, 1989.

Kostenuk, Samuel and John Griffin. *RCAF Squadron Histories and Aircraft, 1924-1968*. Toronto: Samuel Stevens Hakkert & Company, 1977.

Langsom, Walter, ed. *Historical Documents of World War II*. Princeton, N.J.: Princeton University Press, 1958.

Lorelli, John A. *The Battle of the Komandorski Islands*. Annapolis, Md.: Naval Institute Press, 1984.

*Life's Picture History of World War II*. New York: Time Inc., 1940.

Long, Everett A. and Ivan Y. Neganblya. *Cobras Over the Tundra*. Fairbanks: Arktika Publishing, 1992.

Love, Edmund C. *The Hourglass*. Washington, D.C.: Infantry Journal Press, 1950.

Matthews, Courtland W. *Aleutian Interval*. Seattle: Frank McCaffrey Publishers, 1949.

McCormick, Ken and Hamilton Darby Perry, ed. *Images of War: The Artists' Vision of World War II*. New York: Orion Books, 1990.

Mikesh, Robert C. *Japan's World War II Balloon Bomb Attacks on North America*. Washington, D.C.: Smithsonian Institution Press, 1973.

Mills, Stephen E. *Arctic War Planes—Alaska Aviation in World War II*. New York: Bonanza Books, 1971.

—. *Arctic War Planes: Alaska Aviation of WWII: A Pictorial History of Bush Flying with the Military in the Defense of*

*Alaska and North America.* New York: Bonanza Books, 1978. Originally published as *Arctic War Birds.*

Monday, David and Lewis Nalls. *USAAF at War in the Pacific.* New York: Scribner's, 1980.

Morison, Samuel Eliot. *History of United States Naval Operations in World War II.* Vol. 4, *Coral Sea, Midway and Submarine Actions, May 1942-August 1942.* Boston: Little, Brown & Co., 1951.

—. *History of United States Naval Operations in World War II.* Vol. 7, *Aleutians, Gilberts and Marshalls June 1942-April 1944.* Boston: Little, Brown and Co., 1951.

Morgan, Murray. *Bridge to Russia: Those Amazing Aleutians.* New York: E. P. Dutton & Company, 1947.

Murray, Robert Haynes. *The Only Way Home.* Waycross, Ga.: Robert Haynes Murray, 1986.

Naske, Claus-M. and Herman E. Slotnik. *Alaska: A History of the 49th State.* Second Edition. Norman: University of Oklahoma Press, 1987.

Nishijima, Teruo. *Attsuto gyokusai: jukyu-nichikan no sento kiroku.* Hokkaido: Hokkaido Shinbunsha, 1991. Personal narrative of a Japanese officer regarding the Battle of Attu. Copy held by the Anchorage Museum of History and Art Library.

Paneth, Philip. *Alaska, Backdoor to Japan.* London: Alliance Press, 1943.

Potter, Jean. *Alaska Under Arms.* New York: Macmillan, 1943.

Rawls, Walton. *Disney Dons Dogtags: The Best of Disney Military Insignia from World War II.* New York: Abbeville Publishing Group, 1992.

Rearden, Jim. *Cracking the Zero Mystery: How the U.S. Learned to Beat Japan's Vaunted World War II Fighter Plane.* Harrisburg, Pa.: Stackpole Books, 1990.

Richardson, Harold W. "Alaska and the Aleutians." In *Bulldozers Come First: The Story of U.S. Construction in Foreign Lands.* W. Bowman, ed. New York: McGraw-Hill Book Co., 1944.

Schull, Joseph. *The Far Distant Ships: An Official Account of Canadian Naval Operations in the Second World War.* Ottawa: 1961.

Scrivner, Charles L. *The Empire Express: The Story of the U.S. Navy PV Squadrons' Aerial Strikes against the Japanese during World War II.* Temple City: Historical Aviation Album, 1976.

Smith, Holland M. and Finch, Percy. *Coral and Brass.* Reprint, Washington, D.C.: Zenger, 1979.

Sugiyama, Masami. *On the Trail of the Picture: A Trip to the Aleutians.* Tokyo: Sugiyama Publishing Co., 1987. Text in Japanese. Copy held by the Anchorage Museum of History and Art Library.

Thorburn, Lois M. *No Tumult, No Shouting: The Story of the PBY.* New York: H. Holt & Company, 1945.

Tizuka, Tsutomu. *Kessen Middoue, Attsu.* Tokyo: Gakushu Kenkyusha, 1972.

*U.S.S. Richmond in the Pacific War.* Philadelphia: Allen, Lane & Scott, 1945.

Watts, Anthony J. *Japanese Warships of World War II.* Garden City, N.Y.: Doubleday, 1967.

Webber, Bert. *Aleutian Headache: Deadly World War II Battles on American Soil.* Medford, Oreg.: Webb Research Group, 1993.

—. *Retaliation: Japanese Attack and Allied Countermeasures on the Pacific Coast in World War II.* Corvallis: Oregon State University Press, 1975.

—. *Silent Siege: Japanese Attacks Against North America in World War II.* Fairfield, Wash.: Ye Galleon Press, 1984.

—. *Silent Siege-II: Japanese Attacks Against North America in World War II.* Medford, Oreg.: Webb Research Group, 1988.

—. *Silent Siege-III: Japanese Attacks on North America in World War II—Ships Sunk, Air Raids, Bombs Dropped, Civilians Killed—Documentary.* Medford, Oreg.: Webb Research Group, 1992.

Wheeler, Keith. *The Pacific is My Beat.* n.p.: Books, Inc., 1943.

Will, Anne M. *A History of the City of Kodiak.* Alaska Historical Commission Studies in History, No. 15. Anchorage: Alaska Historical Commission, 1981. Microfiche. A history of the City of Kodiak from the Russian period through World War II.

Winton, John. *Ultra in the Pacific: How Breaking Japanese Codes and Cyphers Affected Naval Operations Against Japan.* London: Leo Cooper, 1993.

## Fiction

Griese, Arnold A. *The Wind is not a River.* New York: Crowell, 1978.

Oland, John. *Gods of War.* Garden City, N.Y.: Doubleday, 1985. Epics of courage and honor in the Pacific by Americans and Japanese.

Vidal, Gore. *Williwaw.* New York: E.P. Dutton and Co., 1946.

## Films

Alaska. Alaska Historical Commission. *Alaska at War.* Directed by Laurence A. Goldin. 60 min. Anchorage: Alaska Video Publishing, Inc. for the Alaska Historical Commission, 1987. Videocassette. An account of World War II as it was experienced in Alaska, from war preparedness to the bombing of Dutch Harbor on Unalaska Island, the occupation of Kiska and Attu by Japanese forces, and their eventual evacuation of Kiska. Also discusses the ferrying of lend-lease airplanes to the Soviet Union, the fate of the Aleuts during the war, and the impact World War II had on Alaska economically and socially.

Films, Inc. and CBS News. *The Frozen War.* Produced by Berton Benjamin and narrated by Walter Cronkite. 30 min. Wilmette, Ill.: Films, Inc., 1969. 16mm film.

Describes the invasion of the Aleutian Islands by American troops from May to August of 1943, showing the difficulties presented by a hard-fighting enemy and a hostile climate. Telecast on "The Twentieth Century," a CBS TV documentary program.

KYUK, Bethel Broadcasting, Inc. *Bethel: The War Years.* Written and Produced by Richard Goldstein. 11 min. Bethel, Alaska: Bethel Broadcasting, Inc., 1987. Videocassette.

This short video was made for the local television program, "Delta Review."

Lucerne Films, Inc. *Victory at Sea: The Magnetic North.* Produced by Lucerne Films and the National Broadcasting Company, Inc. 27 min. New York: National Broadcasting Co., 1953. 16mm film.

U.S. War Department. Army Air Forces. *Army Air Forces: Pacific. Combat Film Report, No. 504.* 18 min. n.p.: Army Air Forces for the Treasury Department, 1944. 35 mm.

U.S. Army Air Forces (AAF) in the North Pacific. Reproductions are available from the Motion Picture, Sound, and Video Branch (NNSM), National Archives and Records Administration, College Park, Maryland 20740-6001.

U.S. War Department. Army Pictorial Service. *Operations Against Kiska.* 15 min. Washington, D.C.: War Department, 1943. 16mm film.

Reproductions are available from the Motion Picture, Sound, and Video Branch (NNSM), National Archives at College Park, 8601 Adelphi Road, College Park, Md. 20740-6001.

United States. War Department. Army Pictorial Service. *Report from the Aleutians.* Directed by John Huston. 47 min. Washington, D.C.: War Department, 1943. 16mm film.

U.S. forces establish a military installation with an airfield on Adak Island and conduct bombing raids against Japanese positions on Kiska Island. Flying long hours, without benefit of adequate visibility, landing strips, or fuel, many flyers die. Japanese fail to take Dutch Harbor and Midway but occupy Attu, Agattu, and Kiska. Army Service Forces (ASF) ships supply Adak. Broadcast and non-broadcast quality reproductions are available from the Motion Picture, Sound, and Video Branch (NNSM), National Archives and Records Administration, College Park, Md. 20740-6001.

## Articles

Arnold, Maj. Gen. Henry H. "Our Air Frontier in Alaska." *National Geographic,* October 1940, 487-504.

"Battle of Alaska, Profit and Loss." *Time,* 27 July 1942.

Baudot, Marcel, Henri Bernard, Hendrik Brugmans, and Michael R. D. Foot, eds. *Historical Encyclopedia of World War II.* New York: Greenwich House, 1977. S.v. "Aleutian Islands," by Alvin D. Coox.

Brown, Frederick A. "U.S. Navy Weather Stations in Siberia." *U.S. Navy Institute Proceedings* 88 (July 1962): 76-83.

Buckner, Brig. Gen. Simon, Jr. "Cannery That Wasn't There." *Scholastic,* April 12, 1943.

Personal account of the deception used in the construction of airfields at Cold Bay and Umnak to mislead the Japanese.

"Buck's Battle." *Time,* 16 April 1944. Cover story of Lt. Gen. Simon B. Buckner Jr.

Clemmens, William. "Report on the Aleutians." *Reader's Digest,* March 1943, 76-100.

Cloe, John Haile. "Fifty Years Ago This Month, Attack on Attu." *VFW Magazine,* May 1993, 26-28.

—. "Aleutian Tigers Prowled the Bering Sea, The 11th Air Force in the North Pacific." *VFW Magazine,* May 1993, 30.

—. "Komandorskis: Naval Duel in the North Pacific." *VFW Magazine,* May 1993, 32.

Coates, Kenneth S. and William R. Morrison. "War Comes to the Yukon." *The Beaver* (October/November 1989): 29-34.

—. "The American Rampant: Reflections on the Impact of the U.S. Armed Forces Overseas during World War II." *Journal of World History* 2 (Fall 1991): 201-221.

—. "Soldier-Workers: The U.S. Army Corps of Engineers and the Northwest Defense Projects, 1942-1946." *Pacific Historical Review* 62 (August 1993): 273-304.

Colley, David P. "Time Capsule in the Aleutians." *VFW Magazine,* May 1993, 22-23.

Corral, Roy. "The Aleutians: Pearls of the High Seas." *Alaska,* November 1991, 35-42.

Cressman, Robert J. "Desperate Battle of Unalga Pass." *Naval History* 4 (Fall 1990): 31-41.

An account of the PBY flown by Ensign Albert Mitchell at Dutch Harbor and shot down by the Japanese.

Davison, Lonnelle. "Bizarre Battleground—the Lonely Aleutians." *National Geographic Magazine,* August 1943, 316-317.

Denfeld, D. Colt. "Fort Mears Was No Second Pearl Harbor!" *Periodical: Journal of the Council on America's Military Past* 14 (March 1986): 3-12.

Diubaldo, Richard. "The Canol Project in Canadian-American Relations." Canadian Historical Association, *Historical Papers* (1977).

"Dutch Harbor, U.S. Gets Look at Its Destruction." *Life,* 10 August 1942, 24-25.

Egan, Robert S. "Erie Class Gunboats." *Warship International*, vol. 6, no. 2, 1969, 115-123.

Ellis, Dan. "Springfield Rifles and Forgotten Men." *Alaska Journal* 10 (Autumn 1980): 54-59.

Firsthand account of Ellis's year on Attu, 1943, after its recapture from the Japanese.

"Extracts from a Diary Found on the Body of a Japanese Officer on the Island of Attu." *Explorers Journal* (Spring 1944): 2-5.

Eyre, James K., Jr. "Alaska and the Aleutians: Cockpit of the North Pacific." *U.S. Navy Institute Proceedings* 69 (October 1963): 1287-1297.

Ford, Corey. "Alaska Gets Hot." *Collier's*, 29 November 1941, 46-48.

A pre-Japanese invasion account of the strategic importance of the three Alaska bases—Sitka, Kodiak, and Dutch Harbor.

Fradkin, Philip L. "The First and Forgotten Pipeline." *Audubon: The Magazine of the National Audubon Society*, November 1977, 58-79.

Franklin, William M. "Alaska, Outpost of American Defense." *Foreign Affairs* 19 (October 1940): 245-250.

Frisbee, John L. "The Forgotten Front." *Air Force Magazine*, February 1984.

An account of the air war in the Aleutians.

Fuichida, Mitsuo and Masatake Okumiya. "Prelude to Midway." *U.S. Navy Institute Proceedings* 81 (May 1955): 505-513.

Furler, E.F., Jr. "Beneath the Midnight Sun (Part I)." *Air Classics* 20 (February 1984): 28-34.

—. "Beneath the Midnight Sun (Part II)." *Air Classics* 20 (March 1984): 25-29.

Gay, James T. "Incident at Saint Paul Harbor." *Alaska Journal* 9 (Spring 1979): 54-55.

"German Prisoners of War in Alaska: The POW Camp at Excursion Inlet." *Alaska Journal* 14 (1984): 16-20.

Glines, Carroll V. "The Forgotten War in the Aleutians." *Air Force Magazine*, March 1968, 75-84.

—. "America's War Below Zero." *Frontier* (January 1983): 44-46.

Brief description of the war in the Aleutians with an emphasis on the role of severe weather.

Gruening, Ernest. "Strategic Look Ahead." *National Geographic Magazine*, August 1943, 281-315.

Hammond, Lieutenant Colonel David B. "Aleutian Water Transportation Problems." *Military Engineer* 36 (November 1944): 373-375.

Handleman, Howard. "Kiska Japs Goodbye Again." *Alaska Life*, October 1943, 14-18.

—. "Kiska Story." *Alaska Life*, November 1943, 44-48.

Hardin, Lieutenant Colonel John R. "Engineers Rush Alaskan Defenses." *Military Engineer* 34 (January 1942): 1-4.

Hartman, Douglas R. "Nebraska's Lost Battalion." *Nebraska History* 73 (Summer 1992): 82-90.

Hatch, Fred John. "Allies in the Aleutians." *Aerospace Historian* 21 (Summer/June 1974): 70-78.

Royal Canadian Air Force operations in support of the Aleutian Campaign. Includes maps and photographs.

Hays, Jr., Otis E. "The Silent Years in Alaska: The Military Blackout during World War II." *The Alaska Journal* 16 (1986): 140-147.

An account of censorship in Alaska during World War II.

Hill, Robin Mackey. "The Aleutians." *Alaska Business Monthly*, October 1992, 20-32.

Describes geography, climate, history, economy, demographics, commercial centers, transportation and communication, tourism, local government, land ownership, and contacts for the entire Aleutian chain.

Hutchinson, H.B. "One Way is through Alaska." *United States Naval Institute Proceedings* 65 (January 1944): 1-9.

Hutchison, Isobel Wylie. "Riddle of the Aleutians." *National Geographic Magazine*, August 1942, 769-792.

Kilralfy, Theodore J. "Japan's Alaska Strategy." *New Republic*, 29 June 1942.

Karamanski, Theodore J. "The Canol Project: A Poorly Planned Pipeline." *Alaska Journal* 9 (Autumn 1979): 17-22.

Kilralfy, Alexander. "Japan's Alaska Strategy." *New Republic*, 29 July 1942.

Laidlaw, Lansing S. "Aleutian Experience of the `Mad M'." *Oregon Historical Quarterly* 80 (Spring 1979): 30-49.

March, G. Patrick. "Yanks in Siberia: U.S. Navy Weather Stations in Soviet East Asia, 1945." *Pacific Historical Review* 57 (1988): 327-342.

May, Ronald V. "Battle at Attu—the Japanese side." *Journal of the Council on America's Military Past* 13 (December 1985): 3-8.

"Mail Call." *Periodical: Journal of the Council on America's Military Past* 14 (March 1986): 13-16.

Letters concerning Paul Nobuo Tatsuguchi's diary found on Attu.

McGara, Ken. "Aleutian Islands Shrouded with Mystery, War Memories." *Sunday Oklahoman*, 27 July 1986.

McCandless, Bruce. "The Battle of the Pips." *U.S. Navy Institute Proceedings* 84 (February 1958): 49-56.

McKay Robert S. "Unforgiving Struggle for Attu." *World War II*, September 1986, 16-25.

Merritt, Sgt. Allan. "Crash Boat to the Rescue." *Alaska Life*, September 1944, 3-7.

Millsap, Ralph H. "Skill or Luck?" *U.S. Navy Institute Proceedings Historical Supplement* 111 (March 1985): 79-97.

Admiral Charles H. "Soc" McMorris and the Battle of the Komandorski Islands.

Morgan, Lael. "An Artist's War in the Aleutians." *Alaska Journal* 10 (Summer 1980): 34-39.

Morgan, Lael, ed. "The Aleutians." *Alaska Geographic*, vol. 7, no. 3. Anchorage: Alaska Geographic Society, 1980.
See Chapter 13, "World War II," 113-162 and Chapter 14, "Post War," 162-189.

Naske, Claus-M. "Governor Gruening and the Alaska War Council." *The Alaska Journal* 16 (1986): 48-54.

O'Brien, Charles F. "The Canol Project: A Study in Emergency Military Planning." *Pacific Northwest Quearterly* 61 (April 1970): 101-108.

Orr, Capt. Robert D. "Operations in the Aleutians." *Military Review*, January 1943.
Describes the logistical efforts to support operations.

Patty, Stanton H. "Alaska Sprouts Wings." *Aerospace Historian* 14 (Spring 1967): 15-21.

Perras, Galen R. "Canada as a Military Partner: Alliance Politics and the Campaign to Recapture the Island of Kiska." *Journal of Military History* 56 (July 1992): 423-454.

Pinney, Charles. "A Military Bush Pilot on the Forgotten Front." *Aerospace Historian* 22 (Summer/June 1975): 1-5.

Politzer, Geneva B. "Rising Sun Over Alaska." *American History Illustrated* 25 (May-June 1990): 36-39.

Ponko, Vincent, Jr. "The Navy and the Aleutians before World War II." *Alaska Journal* 13 (Spring 1983): 128-131.

Pratt, Fletcher. "Campaign without Glory: The Navy in the Aleutians, 1942-1943." *Harper's*, November 1944, 558-569.

Rearden, Jim. "Kiska: One Island's Moment in History." *Alaska*, September 1986, 18-21 and 49-51.

—. "The Akutan Zero, Part I," *Alaska*, September 1987, 46-49, 55-59.

—. "The Akutan Zero, Part II," *Alaska*, October 1987, 33-35, 63-65.

Reeve, Robert C. "My Friend Squeaky Anderson." *Cook Inlet Historical Society Newsletter* 2 (February 1966): 1-2.

—. "I Should have Stayed in Bed." *Aerospace Historian* 22 (Summer/June 1975): 77-79.

—. "Islands of the Seals: The Pribilofs." *Alaska Geographic*, vol. 9, no. 3. Anchorage: Alaska Geographic Society, 1982.

—. "Unalaska/Dutch Harbor." *Alaska Geographic*, vol. 18, no. 4. Anchorage: Alaska Geographical Society, 1991.

—. "Kodiak." *Alaska Geographic*, vol. 19, no. 3. Anchorage: Alaska Geographic Society, 1992.
Includes an article by L.J. Campbell on the "Military Buildup on Kodiak," pp. 44-47.

Roy, R.H. "Western Canada during the Second World War." *Journal of the West* 32 (1993): 54-61.

Schel, Pierre. "Kiska—A Fine Invasion." *Yankee Magazine*, November 1978, 137-143, and 265-281.

Stokesbury, James. "Battle of Attu." *American History Illustrated* 14 (April 1979): 30-38.

Sutherland, Mason. "A Navy Artist Paints the Aleutians." *National Geographic Magazine* (August 1943): 157-177.

Sweetman, Jack. "50 Years Ago ... Clash off the Komandorskis." *U.S. Navy Institute Proceedings* 119 (March 1993): 12-13.

Talley, Benjamin B. "Amchitka: The Aleutians in Mid-December 1942." *Alaskana*, vol. 6. no. 4, 1978, 48.

Taylor, Griffith. "Arctic Survey, IV: A Yukon Doomsday: 1944." *Canadian Journal of Economics and Political Science* 14 (August 1945).

Thompson, Erdwin N. "North Star Defense: Alaska World War II Military Bases." *Council on America's Military Past* 14 (September 1986): 26-44.

Woodman, Lyman L. "An Alaskan Military History." *Alaska Sportsman*, February 1969, 17-21, 49-52.

—. "An Alaskan Military History." *Alaska Sportsman*, March 1969, 22-26, 52-53.

—. "The Trans-Canada, Alaska and Western Railways, Proposals during World War II for Better Transportation in the North." *Alaska Journal* 4 (1974): 194-202.

—. "Japanese Threat and Alaska German POWS." *Journal of the Council on America's Military Past* 13 (1985): 18-26.

—. "Back to Attu." *The Alaska Journal* 16 (1986): 180-181.

Woodring, Jeannie. "Northern Passage." *Sky*, March 1992, 56-62.
Magazine published by Halsey Publishing Co., Fort Lauderdale, Florida, for Delta Air Lines passengers.

## Theses and Dissertations

Bowen, B.L. "The Economic Impact of the Military on Alaska." M.A. thesis, University of Alaska, 1970.

Bowen, Jerold E. "Where Eagles Roost: A History of Army Air Fields before World War II." Ph.D. dissertation, Duke University, 1977.

Lorelli, John A. "The Battle of the Komandorski Islands." M.A. thesis., California State University, Chico, 1978.

O'Brien, Charles F. "Canadian-American Cooperation in Alaska and the Canadian Northwest, 1939-1946." M.A. thesis, University of Wyoming, 1962.

Willson, Roger E. "The Truman Committee." Ph.D. dissertation, Harvard University, 1966.
Assesses the Canol Project.

## Part 4:
## Defending the Territory
### Official Histories
### and Government Documents

Howard, Richard A. *Down in the North: An Analysis of Survival Experiences in the Arctic Areas.* Maxwell Air Force Base, Alabama: U.S. Arctic, Desert, and Tropic Information Center, 1951.

### Books

Lenz, Mary and James Barker. *Bethel: The First 100 Years, 1885-1985, Photographs and History of a Western Alaska Town.* Bethel: City of Bethel, 1985.

Marston, Muktuk. *Men of the Tundra: Alaska Eskimos at War.* New York: October House, 1969.

Salisbury, C.A. *Soldiers of the Mists: Minutemen of the Alaska Frontier.* Missoula, Mont.: Pictorial Histories Publishing, 1992.

History and even pre-history of those who have defended Alaska, including the National Guard and the Alaska Territorial Guard, with more than 150 photographs.

### Fiction

Rearden, Jim. *Castner's Cutthroats, Saga of the Alaska Scouts.* Prescott, Ariz.: Wolfe Publishing, 1990.

### Articles

Dimond, Anthony J. "Is Our Neck Out?" *American Magazine*, August 1940, 43.

Hendricks, Charles. "The Eskimos and the Defense of Alaska." *Pacific Historical Review* 1 (1985): 271-295.

Meyers, George N. "The Alaska Scouts." *Yank*, November 8, 1943, 7-9.

## Part 5:
## The Alaska Highway

### Official Histories
### and Government Documents

Huntley, Theodore A. and R. E. Royall. *Construction of the Alaska Highway.* Washington, D.C.: Government Printing Office, 1945.

U.S. Army Service Forces. *The Alaska Highway.* Two Volumes. Washington, D.C.: 1945.
Filmed by the Library of Congress (No. 51360).

U.S. Congress. House. 79C, 2S. *The Alaska Highway* (An Interim Report from the Committee on Roads Pursuant to H.Res. 255), H. Rept. No. 1705. Washington, D.C.: Government Printing Office, 1946.

### Books

Bennett, Gordon. *Yukon Transportation: A History.* Ottawa: Department of Indian and Northern Affairs, 1978.

Brebner, Phyllis Lee. *The Alaska Highway: A Personal and Historical Account of the Building of the Alaska Highway.* Erin, Ontario: Boston Mills Press, 1985.

Coates, Ken. *North to Alaska! Fifty Years on the World's Most Remarkable Highway.* Fairbanks: University of Alaska Press, 1991.

Coates, Kenneth, ed. *The Alaska Highway: Papers of the 40th Anniversary Symposium.* Vancouver: University of British Columbia Press, 1985.

Coates, K. S. and W. R. Morrison. *The Alaska Highway in World War II: The U.S. Army of Occupation in Canada's Northwest.* Tulsa: University of Oklahoma Press, 1992.

Coe, Douglas, pseud. *Road to Alaska: The Story of the Alaska Highway.* n.p.: J. Messner, 1943.

Cohen, Stan. *Alcan and Canol: A Pictorial History of Two Great World War II Construction Projects.* Missoula, Mont.: Pictorial Histories Publishing Company, 1992.

—. *The Trail of '42.* Missoula, Mont.: Pictorial Histories Publishing Company, 1979.

Cole, Terrence M., Jane G. Haigh, Lael Morgan, and William E. Simeone. *Alaska or Bust: Promise of the Road North.* Fairbanks: University of Alaska Museum, 1992. Catalog for the "Alaska or Bust" exhibit commemorating the fiftieth anniversary of the Alaska Highway.

Deer, Cathy. "—And Where Will You Build This `Alcan Highway'?" Whitehorse, Yukon: Black Horse Publishing, 1992.

Hunt, William R. *Passage to the North: A Traveler's Companion to the Historic Sites & Frontier Legends along the Alaska Highway.* Harrisburg, Pa.: Stackpole Books, 1992.

Menzies, Don. *The Alaska Highway: A Saga of the North.* Edmonton, Alberta: Douglas, 1943.

Morrison, William R. and Kenneth A. Coates. *Working the North: Labor and the Northwest Defense Projects, 1942-1946.* Fairbanks: University of Alaska Press, 1993.
The story of the "uncommon efforts of the common people" who worked on the Alaska Highway and other World War II construction projects.

Naske, Claus-M. *Paving Alaska's Trails: The Work of the Alaska Road Commission.* New York: University Press of America, 1986.

Rimley, David. *Crooked Road: The Story of the Alaska Highway.* New York: McGraw Hill Book Company, 1976.

Twichell, Heath. *Northwest Epic: The Building of the Alaska Highway.* New York: St. Martin's Press, 1992.

### Articles

Alaska Geographic Society. "Adventure Roads North: The Story of the Alaska Highway and other Roads in *The Milepost*." *Alaska Geographic*, vol. 10, no. 1. Anchorage: Alaska Geographic Society, 1983.

"Alaska Highway." *Truck Tracks* (Army Service Forces, Northwest Service Command Headquarters), Special Souvenir Edition, vol. 2, no. 8, 16 February 1944.

Coates, Kenneth and Judith Powell. "Whitehorse and the Building of the Alaska Highway, 1942-1946." *Alaska History* 4 (Spring 1989): 1-26.

Coates, Ken S. and William R. Morrison. "The Army of Occupation: Americans in the Canadian Northwest during World War II." *Journal of the West* 32 (October 1993): 9-18.

Honigman, J.J. "On the Alaska Highway." *Dalhousie Review* (January 1944).

Krakauer, Jon. "Ice, Mosquitoes and Muskeg—Building the Road to Alaska." *Smithsonian*, July 1992, 102-112.

Lane, Colonel Albert L. "The Alcan Highway." *Military Engineer* 34 (October 1943): 492-499.

McMillion, Major Shelby A. "The Strategic Route to Alaska." *Military Engineer* 34 (November 1942): 546-553.

Morgan, Lael. "Forgotten Pioneers." *Alaska*, February 1992.

——. "Miles & Miles." *Fairbanks (Alaska) Daily News-Miner* Heartland Magazine, 9 February 1992, H8-H13.

——. "Writing Minorities Out of History: Black Builders of the Alcan Highway." *Alaska History* 7 (Fall 1992): 1-13.

——. "Rewriting a Little Alcan History." *Frame of Reference: A Publication of the Alaska Humanities Forum* 4 (May 1993): 8-10.

Neuberger, Richard. "Alcan Epic." *Yank Magazine*, 10 February 1943.

Olsenius, Richard. "Alaska Highway: Wilderness Escape Route." *National Geographic*, October 1991, 68-99.

Pratt, Henry. "Building the Road to Alaska." *California Highway Patrolman*, November 1992, 50-53.

Rainey, Froelich. "Alaskan Highway: An Engineering Epic." *National Geographic Magazine*, February 1943, 143-168.

Richardson, Harold W. "Alcan—America's Glory Road." Part I: "Strategy and Location." *Engineering Newsrecord* (December 1942).

Schreiner, John. "Highway to Alaska." *Canadian Geographic*, March-April 1992, 80-88.

Sturdevant, Brigadier General Clarence L. "The Military Road to Alaska: Organization and Administrative Problems." *Military Engineer* 35 (April 1943): 173-180.

Williams, Griffin H. "Alaska's Connection: The Alcan Highway." *Pacific Northwest Quarterly* 76 (1985): 61-68.

Woodman, Lyman. "Building the Alaska Highway: A Saga of the Northland." *Northern Engineer* 8 (Summer 1976): 11-15.

Wright, William P. "The Alaska Highway, How We

May Put Peace to Work, an Investigation Sponsor by the Great Falls Tribune, Great Falls, Montana." *Great Falls Tribune*, 26 September- October 7, 1945. Microform.

## Films

Canada. National Film Board of Canada. *Pincers on Japan*. 19 min. Toronto: The Board, 1944; reprint, 1991. Videocassette.

Documents Canada's place in defending the Pacific coast during World War II. Ship convoys carrying secret war matériel steam out of Canadian ports while patrol boats and lookouts keep a constant vigil. The close cooperation between the United States and Canada is illustrated by scenes along the Alaska Highway.

Profile Concepts, Inc. The Alaska Highway ... the First 50 Years. Produced by Garry N. Chaloner and Len Braumberger. 30 min. Vancouver, B.C.: Public Works Canada, 1991. Videocassette.

KAKM TV, Alaska Public Television, Inc. *The Alaska Highway*. Written and Produced by Tom Morgan. 58 min. Anchorage, Alaska: Alaska Public Television, Inc., 1992. Videocassette.

# PART 6:
# WAR'S IMPACT ON THE HOME FRONT

## Official Histories
## and Government Documents

U.S. Office of Fishery Coordination. *A Review of the Consolidation Program for the Alaska Salmon Industry*. n.p.: n.p., 194-.

## Books

Naske, Claus-M. "The War Years," chap. in *Paving Alaska's Trails: The Work of the Alaska Road Commission*. New York: University Press of America, 1986.

## Articles

Gruening, Ernest H. "Strategic Alaska Looks Ahead." *National Geographic Magazine*, September 1942, 281-315.

Description of Alaska by its territorial governor.

Hays, Jr., Otis E. "When War Came to Seward." *Alaska Journal* 13 (Autumn 1980): 107-114.

Lawler, Pat. "Buckner and his Boys Invade Alaska—Taking the Territory by Storm." *Alaska Journal* 2 (1981): 84-99.

Naske, Claus-M. "The Battle of Alaska had Ended and ... the Japs Won It." *Military Affairs* 59 (July 1985): 144-151.

Walsh, James. "When the Cows Come to Nome." *Alaska Journal* 14 (1984): 30-32.

Story of Walsh Brothers Dairy, Inc., suppliers of fresh milk to the City of Nome.

# PART 7:
## MINORITIES: CIVILIAN AND MILITARY

### Books

Daniels, Roger, Sandra C. Taylor, and Harry H.L. Kitano, ed. *Japanese Americans from Relocation to Redress*. Revised Edition. Seattle: University of Washington Press, 1986.

Overstreet, Everett Louis. *Black on a Background of White: A Chronicle of Afro-Americans' Involvement in America's Last Frontier, Alaska*. Fairbanks: That New Publishing Company for the Alaska Black Caucus, Anchorage, 1988.

### Articles

Inouye, Ronald K. "Harry Sotaro Kawabe: Issei Businessman of Seward and Seattle." *Alaska History* 5 (Spring 1990): 34-43.

Naske, Claus-M. "The Relocation of Alaska's Japanese Residents." *Pacific Northwest Quarterly* 74 (July 1983): 124-132.

# PART 8:
## ALEUT RELOCATION AND RESTITUTION

### Official Histories and Government Documents

*Aleutian and Pribilof Islands Restitution Act. Statutes at Large*. 102 (1988).

Public Law 100-383, 102 Stat. 903-916, is divided into two sections: (1) Title I, "Civil Liberties Act of 1988," pp. 904-911, which pertains to Japanese Americans evacuated, relocated, and interned during World War II; and (2) Title II, "Aleutian and Pribilof Islands Restitution Act," 102 Stat. 911-917, which relates to Aleut residents of the Pribilof Islands and the Aleutian Islands west of Unimak Island who were forcibly evacuated, relocated, and interned.

*Aleutian and Pribilof Restitution Act. U.S. Code*. Vol. 50, secs. 1989c (1989), 917.

U.S. Congress. House. *A Bill to Provide for Payments to Certain Individuals of Japanese Ancestry who were Interned, Detained, or Forcibly Relocated by the United States during World Warr II*. 96th Cong., 2d sess., H.R. 5977.

U.S. Congress. House. Judiciary Committee. Subcommittee on Administrative Law and Governmental Relations. *Commission on Wartime Relocation and Internment of Civilians: Hearings before the Subcommittee on Administrative Law and Governmental Relations, House Judiciary Committee*. 96th Cong., 2d sess., 2 June 1980. CIS, CIS1581:H521-15.

The Congressional Information Service Index provides current comprehensive coverage of committee hearings, House and Senate reports and documents, and Senate executive reports. CIS references (CIS1581:H521-15) refer to information that may be accessed through printed serial volumes and microfiche sets available at U.S. government depository libraries or through several large computer services.

U.S. Congress. House. *A Bill to Accept the Findings and to Implement the Recommendations of the Commission on Wartime Relocation and Interment of Civilians*. 98th Cong., 1st sess., H.R. 4110.

U.S. Congress. House. *A Bill to Authorize payments to Certain Aleut Citizens of the United States for Personal Property Losses and Unreasonable Physical Hardship Suffered while Interned, Detained, or Relocated in Temporary Camps during World War II, to Make Restitution to the Aleut People for Certain Community Property Losses Suffered during World War II, to Protect Residents of the Aleutian Islands by Removing Abandoned Ammunition and other Hazardous Debris from Populated Areas, and for other Purposes*, 98th Cong., 1st sess., 1983. H.R. 4322.

U.S. Congress. House. Committee on the Judiciary. Subcommittee on Administrative Law and Governmental Relations. *Japanese-American and Aleutian Wartime Relocation: Hearings before the Subcommittee on Administrative Law and Governmental Relations of the Committee on the Judiciary, June 20, 21, 27, Sept. 12, 1984*. 98th Cong., 2d. sess., 1985. CIS, CIS85:H521-36.

U.S. Congress. Senate. *A Bill to Authorize Redress Payments to Certain Residents of the United States of Japanese-American, Aleut, or other Ancestry who were Interned, Detained, or Forcibly Relocated by the United States during World War II, and for other Purposes*. 98th Cong., 1st sess., S. 1520.

U.S. Congress. Senate. *A Bill to Accept the Findings and to Implement the Recommendations of the Commission on Wartime Relocation and Internment of Civilians*, 98th Cong., 1st sess., 1983. S. 2116.

U.S. Congress. Senate. Governmental Affairs Committee. Subcommittee on Civil Service, Post Office, and General Services. *Recommendations of the Commission on Wartime Internment and Relocation of Citizens: Hearings before the Subcommittee on Civil Service, Post Office, and General Services, Senate Governmental Affairs Committee, Aug. 16, 29, 1984*. 98th Cong., 2d sess., 1984. CIS, CIS86:S401-41.

Hearings were held in Los Angeles, Calif. on Aug. 16, and in Anchorage, Alaska, on Aug. 29.

U.S. Congress. House. *A Bill to Implement the Recommendations of the Commission on Wartime Relocation and*

*Internment of Civilians*, 99th Cong., 1st sess., 1985. H.R. 442.

U.S. Congress. Senate. *A Bill to Accept the Findings and to Implement the Recommendations of the Commission on Wartime Relocation and Internment of Civilians*, 99th Cong., 1st sess., 1985. S. 1053.

U.S. Congress. House. *A Bill to Accept the Findings and Implement the Recommendations of the Commission on Wartime Relocation and Internment of Civilians with Respect to the Aleut People*, 99th Cong., 1st sess., 1985. H.R. 2415.

U.S. Congress. House. Judiciary Committee. Subcommittee on Administrative Law and Governmental Relations. *Civil Liberties Act of 1985 and the Aleutian and Pribilof Islands Restitution Act, Part 2: Hearings before the Subcommittee on Administrative Law and Governmental Relations, House Judiciary Committee, April 28, July 23, 1986*. 99th Cong., 2d sess., 1986. CIS, CIS87:H521-23.

U.S. Congress. House. *A Bill to Accept the Findings and Implement the Recommendations of the Commission on Wartime and Internment of Civilians with Respect to the Aleut People*, 100th Cong., 1st sess., 1987. H.R. 1631.

U.S. Congress. House. Judiciary Committee. Subcommittee on Administrative Law and Governmental Relations. *Legislation to Implement the Recommendations of the Commission on Wartime Relocation and Internment of Civilians: Hearings before the Subcommittee on Administrative Law and Governmental Relations, House Judiciary Committee, Apr. 29, 1987*. 100th Cong., 1st sess., 1987. CIS, CIS88:H521-15.

U.S. Congress. House. House Consideration and Passage of H.R. 442. 100th Cong., 1st sess. *Congressional Record*, vol. 133 (17 September 1987), H7555.

U.S. Congress. House. H. Rpt. 100-372 on H.R. 1631, *Aleutian and Pribilof Islands Restitution Act*, 15 October 1987. 100th Cong., 1st sess., 1987. CIS, CIS87:H523-16.

U.S. Congress. House. "Civil Liberties Act of 1987." H.Res. 263. 100th Cong., 1st sess. *Congressional Record* (17 September 1987), vol. 133, no. 141.

U.S. Congress. Senate. *S. Rpt. 100-202 on S. 1009, Accepting the Findings and Implementing the Recommendations of the Commission on Wartime Relocation and Internment of Civilians*, October 15. 1987. 100th Cong., 1st sess., 1987. CIS, CIS87:S403-8.

U.S. Congress. House. Committee on the Judiciary. *Aleutian and Pribilof Islands Restitution Act Report (to Accompany H.R. 1631) (including Cost Estimate of the Congressional Budget Office)*. 100th Cong., 1st sess., 1987, H.R. 372.

U.S. Congress. Senate. Governmental Affairs Committee. Subcommittee on Federal Services, Post Office, and Civil Service. *To Accept the Findings and to Implement the Recommendations of the Commission on Wartime*

*Relocation and Internment of Civilians: Hearings before the Subcommittee on Federal Service, Post Office, and Civil Service, Senate Governmental Affairs Committee, June 17, 1987*. 100th Cong., 1st sess. CIS, CIS88:S401-6.

U.S. Congress. Senate. *A Bill to Accept the Findings and to Implement the Recommendations of the Commission on Wartime Relocation and Internment of Civilians*. 100th Cong., 2d sess., 1988. S. 1009.

U.S. Congress. Senate. Senate Consideration of S. 1009. 100th Cong., 2d sess. *Congressional Record* (15 April 1988), vol. 134, S4095.

U.S. Congress. Senate. Senate Consideration of S. 1009. 100th Cong., 2d sess. *Congressional Record* (19 April 1988), vol. 134, S4267.

U.S. Congress. Senate. Senate Consideration of S. 1009, Consideration and Passage of H.R. 442 with Amendments, and Indefinite Postponement of S. 1009. 100th Cong., 1st sess. *Congressional Record* (20 April 1988), vol. 134, S.4322, S4386.

U.S. Congress. House. House Disagreement to the Senate Amendments to H.R. 442, Request for a Conference, and Appointment of Conferees. 100th Cong., 1st sess. *Congressional Record* (27 April 1988), vol. 134, H2621.

U.S. Congress. Senate. Senate Insistence on its Amendments to H.R. 442, Agreement to a Conference, and Appointment of Conferees. 100th Cong., 1st sess. *Congressional Record* (11 May 1988), vol. 134, S5486.

U.S. Congress. House. Submission in the House of the Conference Report on H.R. 442. 100th Cong., 1st sess. *Congressional Record* (26 July 1988), vol. 134, H5796.

U.S. Congress. House. H. Rpt. 100-785, Civil Liberties Act, Conference Report on H.R. 442, July 26, 1988. 100th Cong., 1st sess., 1988. CIS, CIS88:H523-22.

U.S. Congress. Senate. Senate Agreement to the Conference Report on H.R. 442. 100th Cong., 1st sess. *Congressional Record* (27 July 1988), vol. 134, S10151.

U.S. Congress. House. House Consideration of the Conference Report on H.R. 442. 100th Cong., 1st sess. *Congressional Record* (3 August 1988), vol. 134, H6261.

U.S. Congress. House. House Agreement to the Conference Report on H.R. 442. 100th Cong., 1st sess. *Congressional Record* (4 August 1988), vol. 134, H6307.

U.S. President. Commission on Wartime Relocation and Internment of Civilians. *Personal Justice Denied: Report of the Commission on Wartime Relocation and Internment of Civilians*. Washington, D.C.: Government Printing Office, December 1982.
For Aleuts, see pp. 18-23, 315-359.

U.S. President. Commission on Wartime Relocation and Internment of Civilians. *Personal Justice Denied. Part 2: Recommendations*. Washington, D.C.: Government Printing Office, June 1983.

U.S. President. "Presidential Remarks." *Weekly Compila-*

*tion of Presidential Documents* (10 August 1988), vol. 24.

*United States Code Congressional and Administrative News, 100th Congress, Second Session, 1988.* Volume 4, Legislative History: Public Laws 100-293 to 100-418. St. Paul, Minn.: West Publishing Co., 1988.

Gives legislative history of Public Law 100-383 regarding the wartime relocation of civilians (pp. 1135-1164), including the Aleutian and Pribilof Islands Restitution Act.

## Books

Aleutian/Pribilof Islands Association. *The Aleut Relocation and Internment during World War II: A Preliminary Examination.* Funded by the Legislature of the State of Alaska. Administered by the Department of Community and Regional Affairs, Contract LG 21-72-3-481. Anchorage: Aleutian/Pribilof Islands Association, Summer 1981.

Aleutian/Pribilof Islands Association. *The Treatment of the Aleuts: A World War II Tragedy.* Anchorage: Aleutian/Pribilof Islands Association, Inc., 1981?

Inouye, Ron L. *Alaska Materials of Committee on Wartime Relocation.* Alaska Historical Commission Studies in History, No. 79. Anchorage: Alaska Historical Commission, 1983. Microfiche.

Copies of testimonies before the committee. Sets of records are at the Department of Archives and Manuscripts at the Consortium Library, University of Alaska Anchorage; the Alaska and Polar Regions Department, Elmer E. Rasmuson Library, University of Alaska Fairbanks; and at the Historical Section of the Alaska State Library, Juneau.

Johnson, Susan Hackley. *The Pribilof Islands: A Guide to St. Paul, Alaska.* St. Paul: Tanadgusix Corp., 1978.

John C. Kirkland, in *The Aleut Relocation and Internment during World War II: A Preliminary Examination,* describes this publication as a "highly informative guide [that] provides an overview of the past and present of St. Paul Island and its residents. The section entitled `Exile' contains several pages on the World War II evacuation and relocation of St. Paul residents in June 1941 [1942] from the Pribilofs to Funter Bay in Southeastern Alaska."

Jones, Dorothy Knee. *A Century of Servitude: Pribilof Islands under U.S. Rule.* Lanham, Md.: University Press of America, 1980.

Kirtland, John C. *The Relocation and Internment of the Aleut People during World War II: A Case in Law and Equity for Compensation.* Anchorage: Aleutian/Pribilof Islands Association, 1981.

Kirtland, John C. and David F. Coffin, Jr., comp. *The Relocation and Internment of the Aleuts during World War II.* Eight Volumes. Funded by Alaska State Legislative Grant No. 21-72-3-727. Anchorage: Aleutian/Pribilof Islands Association, Inc., 15 September 1981.

Consists of eight volumes and a master index: (1) *Index to Evidence,* Volume 1: *The Military Situation;* (2) *Index to Evidence,* Volume 2: *The Evacuation;* (3) *Index to Evidence,* Volume 3: *Conditions at the Camps;* (4) *Index to Evidence,* Volume 4: *Repatriation and Resettlement;* (5) *Index to Evidence,* Volume 5: *Sealing Operations;* (6) *Index to Depositions,* Volume 6: *Depositions of Persons Evacuated from Atka, Unalaska and Nikolski;* (7) *Index to Depositions,* Volume 7: *Depositions of Persons from St. George Island;* (8) *Index to Depositions,* Volume 8: *Depositions of Persons from St. Paul Island;* and (9) *Master Index: Evidence and Depositions, Volumes I-VIII.*

Kohlhoff, Dean. *The Wind was a River: Aleut Evacuation in World War II.* Seattle: University of Washington Press, 1995.

Milan, Leda Chase. *Ethnohistory of Disease and Medical Care Among the Aleut.* Anthropological Papers of the University of Alaska Fairbanks. Fairbanks: University of Alaska Fairbanks, 1974.

Oliver, Ethel Ross. *Journal of an Aleutian Year.* Seattle: University of Washington Press, 1988.

Oliver's *Journal of an Aleutian Year* covers the year June 1946 through June 1947. This is a poignant presentation of the return of the Atkans to Atka Island after they were hastily evacuated to Southeast Alaska for the duration of World War II. Also includes an account of the people of Attu Island who were evacuated to Japan in 1942 and later resettled at Atka. Includes three appendices, two relating personal histories of Mike E. Lokanin and Alex Prossoff recounting their experiences as civilian internees in Japan. The third appendix is a compilation of all people living on Attu at the time of the Japanese invasion, June 7, 1942, and what happened to them.

Rogers, George W. *An Economic Analysis of the Pribilof Islands, 1870-1946.* Fairbanks: Institute of Social, Economic, and Government Research, University of Alaska Fairbanks, 1976.

Smith, Barbara Sweetland. *Making it Right: Restitution for Churches Damaged and Lost during the Aleut Relocation in World War II.* Vol. 1, *A Just Restitution.* Vol. 2, pts. 1-2, *Documents.* Anchorage: Aleutian/Pribilof Islands Association, 1993.

"A report to the Secretary of the Interior Pursuant to P.L. 100-383."

Smith, Barbara Sweetland and Patricia J. Petrivelli. *A Sure Foundation: Aleut Churches in World War II.* Anchorage: Aleutian/Pribilof Islands Association, 1994.

Stein, Gary C. "Uprooted: Native Casualties of the Aleutian Campaign of World War II." Fairbanks: University of Alaska Fairbanks, n.d.

According to John C. Kirkland in *The Aleut Relocation and Internment During World War II: A Preliminary Examination*, "this extensively documented paper relates the story of the Attu military campaign and the taking of Attu inhabitants as prisoners of war by the Japanese. Their experience in Japan as prisoners are described as are repatriation efforts to return Attuans and Aleuts to their home communities after the war." Unpublished manuscript.

—. "A Transportation Dilemma: Evacuation of the Aleuts in World War II." In *Transportation in Alaska's Past,* edited by Michael S. Kennedy. Alaska Department of Natural Resources, State Division of Parks, Office of History & Archaeology Publication No. 30. Anchorage: Alaska Historical Society, 1982.

Stewart, Henry. "Preliminary Report Concerning the 1942 Japanese Invasion and Occupation of Attu and the Subsequent Removal of Attuans to Japan, 1942-1945." In *The Relocation and Internment of the Aleuts during World War II.* Volume 1: *The Military Situation,* comp. John C. Kirkland and David F. Coffin Jr., 95-163.

Unalaska City School District. Unalaska City School. "Four Villages Abandoned in the Aleutian Islands during the Twentieth Century." *Cuttlefish 2.* Unalaska: Unalaska City School, 1978.

## Articles

"APIA World War II Project." Cook Inlet Native Association *Trail Blazer,* December 1980-February 1981, 1.

Argel, Greg. "Justice Denied: Aleut Relocation and Internment in World War II." *Indian Affairs* 106 (May 1984).

Beach, Mary L. "Refugees from the Pribilofs." *Alaska Life* 7 (August 1944): 18-21.

Berikoff, Emil. "Aleuts, Veterans Remembered." *Senior Voice,* 8.

Brelsford, Gregg. "From the Executive Director." *Aang Angagin Aang Angaginas,* November-December 1981, 2.

Brown, Tricia. "Untold War Story." *Anchorage Daily News,* 23 May 1992, 1(F) and 3(F).

Duncan, Roy. "The Aleuts Go Home." *Yank,* May 18, 1945, 7.

"Funter Bay Remembered." *Aang Angagin Aang Angaginas,* June 1992, 1.

George, Marilyn E. "Evacuation Wreaks Havoc on Aleutian Population." *Senior Voice,* November 1990, B15-B19.

Golodoff, Innokenty. "The Last Days of Attu Village." *Alaska Sportsman,* December 1966, 8-9.

Innokenty Golodoff, one of the few survivors of Attu, tells the story of the Japanese WWII occupation of

Attu and his subsequent internment in Japan.

Hattis, Ruth. "Forgotten Internees." *The Progressive* 56 (May 1992): 16.

Jones, Howard. "Etta Jones ... POW." *Alaska Life,* December 1945.

Kobayashi, Sylvia. "Aleuts in Japan." National Japanese American Historical Society, *Nikkei Heritage* 4 (Winter 1992): 9-10.

Madden, Ryan. "The Forgotten People: The Relocation and Internment of Aleuts during World War II." *American Indian Culture and Research Journal* 16 (Fall 1992): 55-76.

"More to Come." *Aang Angagin Aang Angaginas,* November-December 1981, 10.

Petrivelli, Alice. "A View from the Aleutian Islands." *Inuktitut,* no. 73 (1974): 14-29.

Philemonof, Dimitri. "The Aleuts." National Japanese American Historical Society, *Nikkei Heritage* 4 (Winter 1992): 8-9.

—. "Executive Update." *Aang Angagin Aang Angaginas,* June 1992, 3.

"Related Hearing Activities." *Aang Angagin Aang Angaginas,* November-December 1981, 10.

"Relocated Aleuts will Receive Compensation." *Council,* February 1990, 3.

Rose, Frances H. "Akutan: Forging a New Formula for Survival." *Alaska Journal* 13 (1982): 26-32.

Scigliano, Eric. "The Aleuts' Last Stand." (Seattle) *Weekly,* 16 September-22 September 1981, 15-25.

—. "Adrift in the Bering Sea.: (Seattle) *Weekly,* 9 November-15 November 1983, 32-35.

"World War II Hearings." *Aang Angagin Aang Angaginas,* November- December 1981, 6.

"World War II Reparation Trust Board." *Aang Angagin Aang Angaginas,* April 1992, 1.

## Films

Aleutian/Pribilof Islands Association, Inc. *Aleut Evacuation: The Untold Story.* Directed by Michael and Mary Jo Thill. 60 min. Girdwood, Alaska: Gaff Rigged Productions for the Aleutian/Pribilof Islands Association, Inc., 1992. Videocassette.

## Microforms

U.S. National Archives and Records Administration. National Archives Microfilm Publication M1293, *Public Hearings of the Commission on Wartime Relocation and Internment of Civilians.* Records of Temporary Committees, Commissions, and Boards. Record Group 220, National Archives, Washington, D.C. 6 rolls (35mm). Washington, D.C.: 1983.

Microfilm copy located at National Archives - Alaska Region, Anchorage, Alaska.

U.S. National Archives and Records Service. Federal

Archives and Records Center (Seattle). Microfilm A3303, *Pribilof Island Logbooks, 1872- 1961*. Records of the Fish and Wildlife Service. Record Group 22, National Archives-Alaska Region, Anchorage, Alaska. 19 rolls (35mm). Seattle: 1967.

Microfilm copies of daily logbooks of the fur seal fishery in the Pribilof Islands, 1870-1961, concerning fishery operations and statistics, weather ship movements, island activities, and other related matters. Also recorded is information on the Aleut evacuation and relocation from the Pribilof Islands to Southeastern Alaska, 1942-1945.

# PART 9: LEND-LEASE

## Official Histories and Government Documents

Denfeld, D. Colt. *Cold Bay in World War II: Fort Randall and Russian Naval Lend-Lease*. Anchorage: U.S. Army Corps of Engineers, 1993.

## Books

Herring, George C., Jr. *Aid to Russia: Strategy, Diplomacy, The Origins of the Cold War*. New York: Columbia University Press, 1973.

Jones, Robert H. *The Roads to Russia: United States Lend-Lease to the Soviet Union*. Norman: University of Oklahoma Press, 1969.

Jordan, George Racy. *Major Jordan's Diaries*. New York: Harcourt Brace Jovanovich, 1952.

Long, Everett A. and Ivan Y. Neganblya. *Cobras Over the Tundra*. Fairbanks, Alaska: Arktika Publishing, 1992.

Lukas, Richard C. *Eagles East: The Army Air Forces and the Soviet Union, 1941-1945*. Tallahassee: Florida State University Press, 1970.

Ringgold, Herbert. "Life Line to the USSR." In *Air Force Diary: 111 Stories from the Official Service Journal of the USAAF*, ed. James H. Straubel. New York: Simon & Schuster, 1947.

Van Tuyll, Hubert P. *Feeding the Bear: American Aid to the Soviet Union, 1941-1945*. New York: Greenwood Press, 1989.

## Articles

Brandon, Dean. "ALSIB: The Northwest Ferrying Command" (Parts 1 and 2). *Journal of the Aviation Historical Society* (Spring- Summer 1975).

Brandon, Dean R. "War Planes to Russia." *Alaska*, May 1976, 14-17.

Furler, E.F., Jr. "Beneath the Midnight Sun (Part I)." *Air Classics* 28 (February 1984): 28-34.

——. "Beneath the Midnight Sun (Part II)." *Air Classics* 20 (March 1984): 25-29.

Hays, Otis E., Jr. "White Star, Red Star." *Alaska Journal* 12 (1982): 9-17.

Lake, Gretchen. "Photo Essay: The Russians are Coming, The Russians are Coming, Fifty Years Ago, the Russians were Coming." *Alaska History* 8 (Spring 1993): 33-41.

Pstygo, Ivan Ivanovich. "Samolety Nad Markova I Vel'kalem" [Airplanes over Markova and Uelkal]. *Voprosy Istoril* [Russia] 10: 153-156.

## Theses and Dissertations

Carr, Edwin Remmen. "Great Falls to Nome: The Inland Air Route to Alaska, 1940-1945." Ph.D. diss., University of Minnesota, 1946.

# PART 10: HISTORIC PRESERVATION

## Official Histories and Government Documents

Alaska. Legislature. Special Committee on Veterans Affairs. *The Historical Remains of the "Battle of Alaska": Report of the Special Committee on Veterans Affairs to the Alaska State Legislature*. Prepared by Frank P. Lee. Juneau: The Committee, 1982.

Butowsky, Dr. Harry A. *Warships Associated with World War II in the Pacific, National Historic Landmark Theme Study*. Washington, D.C.: U.S. Government Printing Office, 1985.

Goforth, J. Penelope. *Aleutian/Pribilof Islands Photograph Project*. Alaska Historical Commission Studies in History, No. 99. Anchorage: Alaska Historical Commission, 1983. Microfiche.

Consists of numbered description of photographs, not the photographs themselves. Available on microfiche from the Arctic Environmental Information and Data Center, University of Alaska Anchorage, 707 A Street, Anchorage, Alaska 99501.

U.S. National Park Service. Alaska Regional Office. *Naval Operating Base Dutch Harbor and Fort Mears*. Compiled by Sandra McDermott Faulkner and Robert L. S. Spude. Anchorage: Historic American Buildings Survey Recording Project Report, National Park Service, 1987.

——. *National Register of Historic Places: Alaska*. Teaneck, N.J.: Chadwyck-Healey, 1984. Text-fiche.

Consists of more than 300 National Register of Historic Places Inventory-Nomination Forms for districts, sites, buildings, structures, and other objects significant in American history and located in Alaska. Includes Edwin T. Thompson, "National Register of Historic Places Inventory-Nomination Form" for Dutch Harbor Naval Operating Base and Fort Mears. Available on microfiche (32 fiche) at the Z.J. Loussac

Library, Anchorage Municipal Libraries, Anchorage, Alaska.

——. *Unalaska Preservation Plan.* Compiled by Linda Cook. Anchorage: Alaska Regional Office, National Park Service, October 1990.

——. *World War II in the Aleutians: Alternatives for Preservation and Interpretation of Historic Resources at Dutch Harbor Naval Operating Base and Fort Mears, U.S. Army, National Historic Landmark, Unalaska, Alaska.* Anchorage: Alaska Regional Office, National Park Service, May 1992.

——. *World War II National Historic Landmarks: The Aleutian Campaign.* Compiled by Carol Burkhart and Linda Cook. Washington, D.C.: Government Printing Office, 1993.

### Articles

Auer, Michael J. "World War II: Aleutian Reminders." *CRM*, vol. 14, no. 8 (1991): 15-17.
Published by the National Park Service to promote and maintain high standards for preserving and maintaining cultural resources.

Brown, William E. "Forgotten Chapters of a War." *CRM*, vol. 14, no. 8 (1991).

Denfeld, D. Colt. "Coastal Defenses in Alaska: A Brief History and Status Report." *Coastal Defense Study Group News*, July 1986.

Faulkner, Sandra M. "Naval Operating Base, Dutch Harbor and Fort Mears." *Public Historian* 11 (Spring 1989): 92-94.

——. "Public History in the Aleutians." *Arctic Research of the United States* 6 (Fall 1992): 71-73.

Lenihan, Daniel J. "Aleutian Affair: Archeologists Return to Japan's World War II Beachhead in Alaska." *Natural History*, June 1992, 51-61.

Metcalf, Faye. "Attu: North American Battleground of World War II (Special Series: Teaching with Historic Places)." *Social Education* 57 (April-May 1993): 1-12.
A group of lesson plans produced by the National Park Service and the National Trust for Historic Preservation on the island of Attu, which could be used to teach students the realities of war. It covers topics such as Japanese occupation, the complexity of military operations, the valor of troops in battle, and information on historic sites.

Morgan, Lael. "The Aleutian Legacy from World War II: Clean it up, but Save the Battlefields." *Alaska*, May 1980, 6-8, 76-77, 79-80.

——. "The Attu-Kiska Battleground: National Monument Forgotten." *Alaska*, July 1979, 6-8, 56-65.
Visits Atka, Attu and Kiska and reviews events of World War II and repercussions of war.

Sterling, Dale A. "Historic Preservation in the Aleutians." *Journal of the Council on America's Military Past*

13 (1984): 3-7.

"Time Capsule in the Aleutians." *Compressed Air Magazine* (October/November 1992): 16-21.
An account of Kiska Harbor survey, Kiska and Attu National Historic Landmarks, and a proposal for a World War II park.

## PART 11:
## THE WAR'S AFTERMATH

### Official Histories and Government Documents

U.S. Army Corps of Engineers. Alaska District. *The Defense of Dutch Harbor, Alaska, from Military Construction to Base Cleanup.* Compiled by D. Colt Denfeld. Anchorage: Defense Environmental Restoration Program, Alaska District, U.S. Army Corps of Engineers, December 1987.

U.S. Army. Corps of Engineers. Alaska District. Tetra Tech, Inc. *Draft Environmental Impact Statement for World War II Debris Removal and Cleanup, Aleutian Islands and Lower Alaska Peninsula, AK.* Anchorage: Department of the Army, Corps of Engineers, Alaska District, 1979.

U.S. Army. Corps of Engineers. Alaska District. *Debris Removal and Cleanup Study, Aleutian Islands and Lower Alaska Peninsula, Alaska.* Compiled by Thomas Dowell. Anchorage: Department of the Army, Corps of Engineers, Alaska District, 1976.
U.S. Army Corps of Engineers directed study of World War II debris left in the Aleutians. Inventory of facilities, structures, and weapons. Includes maps and photographs.

### Books

Fradkin, Philip L. *Wanderings of an Environmental Journalist: In Alaska and the American West.* Albuquerque: University of New Mexico Press, 1993.
Includes a chapter, "War on the Refuge" (the Alaska Maritime National Wildlife Refuge), which discusses the effect of the war on the Aleutian environment. Also included is a chapter on "The First Pipeline" (the Canol pipeline).

Rogers, George W. *The Future of Alaska: Economic Consequences of Statehood.* Baltimore: The Johns Hopkins Press, 1962.

### Articles

Berman, Gerald S. "Reaction to the Resettlement of World War II Refugees in Alaska." *Jewish Social Studies* 44 (1982): 124- 132.

——. "From Neustadt to Alaska, 1939: A Failed Attempt of Community Resettlement." *Immigrants & Minorities* [Great Britain] 6 (1987): 66-83.

Denfeld, D. Colt. "Alaska World War II Bases - Today." *Journal of the Council on America's Military Past* 15 (1987): 11-31.

Levi, Steven C. "Attu: Island of Agony." *Alaska*, February 1990, 26-29, 59-63.
    Brief history of Attu, description of visit to the island, documentation of Japanese and American photographs, documents, and ashes left at monuments on Engineer Hill.

Woodman, Lyman. "CANOL: Pipeline of Brief Glory." *Northern Engineer* 9 (Summer 1977): 14-28.

—-. "Cleaning up after a War." *Northern Engineer* 11 (Winter 1979): 16.

# Index

1st Aviation Ferrying Regiment (Soviet Air Force), 323
5th Fleet, Japanese, 33, 34, 37, 45, 67–68, 72
6th Infantry Division (Light), 398
7th Ferrying Group, 150
7th Motorized Division, 64
8th Bomber-Reconnaissance (BR) Squadron (RCAF), 19, 22–23, 24, 25
10th Army, 9
11th Air Force, 23, 25, 73, 150, 323, 393–394, 395, 398, 415
11th Air Force Service Command, 153
11th Army Air Force, 9, 21, 73. *See also* Tenth Emergency Rescue Boat Squadron
11th Fighter Squadron, 24
11th Pursuit Squadron, 321
12th Air Fleet, Japanese, 71, 72
13th Infantry Brigade, Canadian (Greenlight Force), 88, 97–102
13th Naval District, 5
17th Naval District, 111
18th Engineers, 278, 279
18th Pursuit Squadron, 393
30th Infantry Brigade Greenlight Force, 97–102
46th/72nd Reconnaissance Squadron, 400, 401, 405
77th Bombardment Squadron (USAAF), 321
87th Mountain Infantry, 55, 91, 105–107
93rd Engineer Gen. Service Regiment, 277, 278, 279–280
95th Engineers, 278
97th Engineer Gen. Service Regiment, 277, 278, 279
100th/442nd (all-Japanese-American) Combat Regiment, 285, 286
184th Infantry Regiment, 91
195th Port Battalion, 135–136
250th Coast Artillery Regiment, 379

267th Separate Coast Artillery Regiment, 379, 380
297th Infantry Battalion (Alaska National Guard), 155, 411
340th Engineers, 185, 278
341st Engineers, 179–184, 278
364th Engineers, 282
372nd Port Battalion, 281
383rd Air Base Squadron, 151
383rd Port Battalion, 280–281, 283
388th Engineer Battalion (Separate), 278
404th Bomber Squadron, 396
442nd Combat Regiment, 287–288
447th Quartermaster, 182
483rd Port Battalion, 281
924th QM Boat Squadron, 131
1320th Engineer General Service Regiment, 281

## A

A-20 aircraft, 150, 311, 317, 321, 324, 332, 342
A Battery, 250th Coast Artillery Regiment, 378, 379
ABC-22. *See* Joint Canadian-United States Basic Defense Plan–2
*Abner Read* destroyer, 9
Abraham, Elaine, 260
*Abukuma* light cruiser, 71
Acord, Randy, 141
*Across the Pacific* (film), 229
Adak
　airfield construction on, 62
　Alaskan Scouts on, 44–45
　alcohol consumption on, 138–139
　attack on Japanese on, 24
　food on, 137
　health issues on, 138–139
　housing on, 136, 138
　Liberty ships at, 137–138

　life on, 1942–1944, 135–140
　personal hygiene on, 137
　Seabees on, 137
　strategic location of, 4
　weather on, 136, 138
　*See also* Aleutian Campaign
Adak-Attu Occupation Force, 68
*Adakian, The* (Adak army daily), 280, 282
Adak Naval Station, 396
Adams (Col.), 89, 91
*Adriatic* tender, 249, 250
*Advise and Consent* (film), 416
Aerology Operations building, 369
African-American soldiers
　chaplains, 278–279
　confrontations with authorities, 281
　discrimination against, 136, 279, 281–282, 283
　officers, 278–279
　work at naval/air bases, 279–280
　work on Alaska Highway, 277, 278–279
　work on Canol pipeline, 277
Agattu, 40
air-borne search radar (ASV), 74
Air Corps Marine Rescue Service, 131
aircraft control and warning (AC&W) radar sites, 397
airfield construction
　on Adak, 62
　on Aleutian Chain, 59–65
　on Amchitka Island, 62, 64
　on Attu, 62, 136–137
　at Cold Bay, 212, 394
　at Elmendorf Air Force Base, 62, 393
　at Juneau, 63–64
　at Ladd Field, 393
　on Umnak Island, 61–62, 394
　at Yakutat, 59–60
airfields, building of. *See specific locations*

Air Force Document Center, Maxwell Air
    Force Base, 131
Air Transport Command (ATC), 149, 322, 324
Aishihik, 194
*Akagane Maru,* 70
Akehurst, Jack (Maj.), 92
Akutan Island
    Aleut population, 1940, 161
    whaling industry at, 217
Alafusov, V. A. (Adm.), 346
Alaska
    consequences of war, 203
    defense priority after Pearl Harbor attack, 21
    military installations, numbers of, 203
    personnel, numbers of, 203
    population, 1940, 265n2
    statehood, 209, 397
    strategic location of, 3–4
    troops, numbers of, 203
Alaska at War Conference, and writing about
    war, x, 417–419
Alaska Canned Salmon Plan, 216
Alaska Coastal Airlines, 59
Alaska Communications System, 193, 241,
    388, 407
Alaska Defense Command, 257
    Canadian defense of Alaska and, 23
    search dogs and, 152
    supplying aircraft to, 150
Alaska Department Headquarters, 244
Alaska Department (later USARAL), 396
Alaska Fishermen's Union, 217
Alaska Game Commission, 254, 255–256
Alaska gold rush, 219
Alaska Highway
    roadside facilities, 189, 191
    bridge-building, 186–187
    construction of, 150
    corridor, 20, 167, 322
    cost of, 167, 171, 177
    earliest travelers along, 190
    economic development along, 189, 191
    film about, 231
    length of, 177
    map of, 168
    Native settlements along, 189, 193–194
    proposed routes, 20, 173–175
    roadside development, 189–194
    travel conditions, 190, 193
    working/living conditions along, 179–185
Alaska Historical Society, 242
Alaska Indian Service, 298
Alaska International Highway Commission,
    173
*Alaska* magazine (formerly *The Alaska
    Sportsman*), 253
Alaska Maritime National Wildlife Refuge, 359
Alaskan Air Command, 396, 397, 405
    *See also* 11th Air Force
Alaska National Guard, 155, 160, 411

Alaska Native Claims Settlement Act (1972),
    308
Alaska native settlements along
    Alaska Highway, 189, 193–194
Alaska Naval Militia, 411
Alaskan Command (ALCOM), 396, 411
Alaskan Indians, 194
Alaskan Scouts
    on Kiska, 45, 90, 92
    leaders of, 43
    memoir about, 43–46
    Native fishermen as, 217
    training of, 43–44
Alaskan Sea Frontier (ALSEAFRON), 396, 397
Alaskan Territorial Guard (ATG), 411
Alaska Packers Association (APA), 214
*Alaska Patrol* (film), 232
Alaska Peninsula, 280, 347
Alaska Railroad, 60, 63, 203–204
Alaska Railroad Bill, 221
Alaska Road Commission, 167, 175, 177
    *See also* Alaska Highway
Alaska School Tax, 241
Alaska Scouts, 163
Alaska-Siberia (ALSIB) air route, 16, 169–171,
    311–318, 336
    Churchill and, 312
    as friendship route, 341–343
    Roosevelt and, 312–314
    *See also* Alaska-Siberia lend-lease program
Alaska-Siberia lend-lease program, 334–338
    *See also* lend-lease
*The Alaska Sportsman Magazine,* 253–258
Alaska Sportsman's Association, 254
Alaska Spruce Program, 130
Alaska State Archives, 419
Alaska State Defense Force, 411–412
Alaska Steamship Company, 139, 220, 223, 224
Alaska Steam Ship Line, 245, 248, 251
Alaska Territorial Guard (ATG), 155–160,
    247–248, 271, 411
    formation of, 156–157
    local accounts of, 157–158
    racial issues, 159–160
    reconnaissance/reporting by, 159
    social/political aspects of, 159–160
    training for, 158–159
    weapons/ammunition/supplies for, 158
Alcan (GI name for Alaska Highway). *See*
    Alaska Highway
Alcan Highway Telephone Line, 388
alcohol, difficulties with, 128, 139, 180
ALCOM (Alaskan Command), 396, 411
Aleut Church Restitution Project, 375
Aleut Evacuation of World War II, 374
Aleutian and Pribilof Islands Restitution,
    297–299
    for church property, 299, 371–375
    report documenting Aleut losses, 299, 306
    Senator Stevens on, 305–306

Aleutian Campaign, 67–74
    casualties, 396
    expulsion of Japanese, 70–72
    intangible results of, 73–74
    Japanese-Americans in, 285–287
    material damages, 396
    occupation by Japanese, 68–69
    preliminary events/planning, 67–68
    pressure on Kuriles, 72
    strategic relation to Midway operations, 67
    tangible results of, 72–73
    weather effect on, 68, 69, 74
Aleutian Chain
    airfield construction on, 59–65
    base closures, 396–397
    deception activities in, 16–17
    historical remains on, 366
    Japanese attack as diversion, 37, 42
    Japanese proposed attack on, 21
    original area covered by, 67
    strategic location of, 3, 13
    *See also individual islands*
Aleutian Islands. *See* Aleutian Chain
Aleutian Livestock Company, 298
Aleutian/Pribilof Islands Association (A/PIA),
    371, 372, 374
Aleutian Solution (hooch made of fruit juice),
    136, 139
*The Aleutian Warriors* (Cloe), 29, 225, 415–416
Aleut Memorial at Attu (1993), 362
Aleut people, 161
    on Attu, internment in Japan, 301–304
    Attu population evacuated to Otaru,
        302–304
    death rates, 298
    disease/illness and, 291, 295, 307
    evacuation effects, 307–308
    evacuation to camps in Southeast, 162, 259,
        290–295, 298, 302, 307
    fox trapping by, 162, 374
    identity of, 291–292
    induction of into U.S. forces, 163
    population in 1940, 161
    redress for evacuation of, 263, 308
    religion and, 291–293
    support of war effort by, 161–164
    villages in 1940, 161
    women in evacuation camps, 295
    *See also* Aleutian and Pribilof Islands
        Restitution; Aleutian Campaign
Aleut Restitution Act, 371
Alexandria, Egypt, 24, 28
A-25 light bomber, 346
A-26 light bomber, 346
All-America City, Anchorage as, 209
Allard, Dean C., 13–14
Allied Combined Chiefs of Staff (ACCS), 15, 99
Alma Point, 378
AL Operation. *See* Aleutian Chain
Alps, 54, 107

ALSIB. *See* Alaska-Siberia (ALSIB) air route
Amaknak Island, Hill 400 concrete battery command station, 369
Amchitka Island, 24–25, 41, 45
    airfield construction on, 62, 64
American Can Company, 214
American Civil War, 185, 358
American fishing industry, 211
Americanization, 240
American Western Defense Command, 20, 64, 97
Ames, Albert, 146
Amme, Carl "Bon," 418
Amphibious Training Force Nine, 88
Amtorg, 313, 314, 328
Anadyr', 328
Anchorage, AK, 203–204
    as All-American City, 209
    consequences of war on, 203–209
    as defense priority, 21, 23
    financial/social elite in, 206–208
    first annexation by, 208
    housing shortage, 206–207
    juvenile delinquency and, 208
    Korean War effect on, 208
    population, 1940, 59
    railroad at, 60
    selection as army headquarters, 204, 206
Anchorage International Airport, 409
Anchorage Museum of History and Art, xvi
Anderson, Carl "Squeaky" (Cmdr.), 135, 163, 248
Anderson, H. (Capt.), 223
Andreanof Islands, 43
    *See also* Attu
Andrews, Frank (Signalman), 117
Angoon, Tlingit village, 125
Anisimov, Alexis A., 336
Annette (community near Ketchikan), 239
Annette Island, 20–21, 22, 26
    airfield at, 60–61, 131, 239
Annex F, 78
Annex III (Fourth Soviet Protocol), 346
Anthony Dimond collection, 190
anti-discrimination laws, 275
Anvil lead-zinc mine, 192
Anzio, 94
Apennines, 54, 106
archaeological research, on Attu/Kiska, 353–357, 359–363
    significant historical elements on Attu, 360–361
Archangel'sk (ice-free arctic port), 15, 149, 319, 327
Archbold, C. M., 237, 238
Archival Information System (AIS), 386
Arctic
    mapping, 400
    serial reconnaissance activity in, 399–406

*Arctic Flight* (film), 233
Arctic search and rescue, 149–153
Arctic Slope Regional Corporation, 158
Army Corps of Engineers, 59, 60, 62, 63–64, 225
    African American soldiers and, 271, 273
    Aleut construction workers and, 162
    CCC and, 239
Army Signal Corps, 229
Army Transport Service, 63
Arnold, Henry H. "Hap" (Gen.), 42, 61, 171, 319
ARS 50 *Safeguard* salvage vessel, 355
*Arthur Middleton*, 48, 129
artist, combat, 47–55
asbestos, 314
assimilation, of Native Alaskans, 274
ASV equipment, 74
ATG. *See* Alaska Territorial Guard
A-10 Thunderbolt aircraft, 397, 398
Atka, 62, 161
atlas, of Aleut territory, 162
Atlin, 173, 176
atomic bomb, 29, 399
Attu
    airfield construction on, 62, 136–137
    Alaskan Scouts on, 46
    Aleut-Japanese Army relationship on, 301
    Aleut population, 1940, 161
    Aleut evacuated to Otaru, 302–304
    Attu Battlefield, historic, 368
    casualties on, 122
    Japanese evacuation of, 302
    Japanese seizure of, 7, 37, 164, 301, 395
    Japanese treatment of non-natives on, 301–302
    last Japanese survivor, 419
    placed into National Wildlife Preservation system, 299
    recapture of, 81–85
    restitution for churches damaged on, 371, 372
    strategic location of, 3, 7, 13
    submarines and, 111
    U.S. Army/Navy Airfields, historic, 368
    U.S. assault on Japanese on, 7–8, 25, 41
    weather effects, 81, 85
    *See also* Aleutian Campaign; archaeological research, on Attu/Kiska
Attu, Battle of, 27, 28, 61, 64, 81, 287
Attu Battlefield and Airfields National Historical Landmark, 353
Attungana, Patrick, 156–157, 158
Atwood, Evangeline, 209
Australia, 21, 34, 36, 286
Averman, Edmund, 321
AWOL, 281
Axis powers, 14, 16, 19, 319
*Aylwin* (DD-335), 119

**B**

B-26, 45, 68, 76, 321
B-38, 76
*Bailey* destroyer, 114, 115, 116, 117
B-26 aircraft, 45, 68, 76, 321, 394
B-29 aircraft, 13, 404
B-38 aircraft, 76
Baker, Ancil D. "Red" (Maj.), 141–142
Baldwin Cold Storage Company, 377
Bamboo Bay, Kiska, 92
Bane, Frank, 201
BarBee Shipyard, WA, 133
Barnaby, Joseph, 211
Barrow, AK, 158–159
Bart, Billy, 43
Bartholomew, Ralph M., 416
Bartlett, Bob, 199
Barwell Island, 378
Basra (Iraqi port), 327, 335
*Bataan* (film), 228
Bates, Sam, 43
battlefields, defined, 368
Battle of Midway, 32, 103
*The Battle of San Pietro* (documentary film), 230
Battle of the Coral Sea, 394
Battle of the Komandorski Islands, 8, 41, 114–119, 206
Battle of the Pips, 9, 30–32, 42, 104, 119
Battle of Tsushima, 36
Battle of Uman, 334
Baum, John W. (Col.), 60
B-10 bombers, 171
B-24D 41-23853 (aircraft that crashed), 141–142
B-24D 41-23873 (aircraft that crashed), 142
B-24D 42-40910 (aircraft that crashed), 143–146
Beach, Rex, 228
Beach Blue, Attu, 81, 91
Beach Green, Attu, 92
Beach Red, Attu, 81, 92
Beach Scarlet, Attu, 81, 91
Beach Yellow, Attu, 81, 91
Beard, Baker B., 318
Beaver Creek, 192, 278, 279
Belgium, 311
Bell-Irving, Richard (Col.), 214
Belorussia, 334
Bereskin, Chester, 163
Bergman, Ingrid, 281, 377
Bering Sea, 15, 24, 49, 68, 212, 217, 368
    cod fishing in, 217
Bering Strait, 150, 401
Bering Straits Native Corporation, 343
Berlin Airlift, 404, 405
Berlin Crisis (1948), 403–404, 404
Bert and Mary's, 189
Bessie, Alvah, 232
Bethel, AK, 46

Bezeau, M. V., 26
B-29 Ferret, 9, 13, 42, 396, 403
B-17 Flying Fortress aircraft, 9, 45, 68, 69, 76, 357, 394, 418
*B-17 Flying Fortress* Jablonski, 27
Big Delta, AK, 143, 169, 322
Biggar, O. M. (Col.), 322
Bikini Atoll, 353
Bilcoe, Griffith, 47
Binkley, Charles, 333
Biorka (evacuated/never rebuilt), 161, 371
Bismarck Archipelago, 67
Blackerby, Alva W., 238
blackouts, 199, 242, 247, 248
blast hangar (near Unalaska airport), 369
B-24 Liberator, 9, 45, 69, 76, 134
B-24 Liberator aircraft, 9, 45, 69, 76, 134
blitzkrieg, 169
B-25 medium range bomber, 36, 150, 250, 311, 317, 324
Boca de Quadra, 128
Boeing 80A, 408
Boeing Field, 242
Bogg, J. W. (Capt.; skipper of *Orizaba*), 219
Bolingbroke, 23, 25, 129
Bonin Islands, 33
Boomer, K. A., 24
Boothia Peninsula, sled trip to, 152
Bourdukofsky, Mary, 297
Bower, Ward T., 214
Bradley, Follett (Maj. Gen.), 315, 321
Bradley Mission, 315–318
Brady, John, 241
Brail, Phil, 145
B Rations, 137
Brelesford, Greg, 298
Bridges, Lloyd, 230
Bristol Bay, AK, 68, 211–212, 214–216
British Columbia, Canada, 19
   Prince Rupert port, 20, 21, 22
British Far Eastern Fleet, 34
Broad Beach, Kiska, 92
BROILER War Plan, 399
Brooks, Bill, 415
Brown, Albert E. (Maj. Gen.), 28–29, 64, 81
Brown, Joe E., 157, 242
Buckinghorse River, 180, 184
Buckner, Simon Bolivar (Gen.), 7, 8, 9, 61, 64, 140, 393
   Alaska defense planning and, 126–127
   at Anchorage, 206, 207
   death of, 206
   discrimination and, 159
   hunting privileges, 255
   Kiska and, 100–101
   racism of, 271, 273, 277, 278, 279, 419
   relationship with Theobald, 76, 77, 394–395
Buffalo Junction (former Delta Junction), 193
Building 1001, Ladd Field, 146
Bukhti Point, 118

Bukovina, 312
Bulgaria, 334
Bunker Hill, 369
Burhans, R. D., 94
Burma, 14, 67, 287
Burnett Inlet (Aleut evacuation camp), 293, 294, 295
Burns, Ralph "Stormy" (Lt.), 129
Burwash Landing, 189
Burwell, Michael, 226
Bush, George, 263
Bush, James D., Jr. (Lt. Col.), 64, 378–379
Bush, Norman, 184
bush pilot, 408
Butcher, Helen A., 241–244
Butler, William O. (Brig. Gen.), 61–62, 64, 76, 77, 79
Byrnes Amendment (CCC appropriation bill), 238

**C**

Cabell, C. P. (Maj. Gen.), 404
CA (Coast Artillery), 140
Cain, Ernest (First Sgt.), 281
Cain, Frank "Killer" (Boilermaker), 115–116
Caines Head, strategic headland, 377, 378, 379
Caines Head State Recreation Area (CHSRA), 379–381
C-5 aircraft, 397
C-141 aircraft, 397
Calgary, Alberta, 322
California, 23, 62, 64, 114, 140, 215
   Camp McDowell, Angel Island, 88
   Presidio, San Francisco, 132
   shipbuilding in, 132, 134
   Stockton Air Base, 132
   Treasure Island, 132
Camp Field, Umnak Island, 365
Camp Hahn, CA, 140
Camp Hale, CO, 54
Camp Harmony assembly center, 260
Camp McDowell, Angel Island, CA, 88
Camp McQuaide, CA, 378
Camp Minidoka, ID, internment camp, 305
Camp Stoneman, CA, 93
Canada, and defense of Alaska, 19–26, 42, 72, 87–95, 98, 99, 322
Canadian-American Permanent Joint Board on Defense, 150
Canadian Department of Transportation, 321
Canadian Fusiliers, 100
Canadian Joint Staff Mission, 98
Canadian Pacific Railroad, 173
Canadian Sector Search and Rescue Unit, 151
Candelaria, Gary, 119
Candelaria, Joseph J. "Candy," Jr., 113, 114–116, 117, 118, 119
cannery, 216
   safeguarding, 127
Cannery Concentration Program, 214

Canol (Canadian oil) pipeline, 153, 167, 169, 192, 278
Cape Field, Umnak Island, 367–368
Cape Mudge, 222, 223
Cape of Good Hope, 15
Cape Sarichef, 409
Cape St. Elias, 222
Capra, Frank, 229
Captains Bay, Unalaska Island, 225
Carcross, BC, 192
caribou, 256n17
Carlson, Dave, 217
Carlson, Mary Emily, 217
Carmacks, BC, 192
Carol Cove, 378
Carroll, Edward (Capt.), 273, 279
Casablanca Conference (Jan. 1943), 98
Casco Cove PT base, Attu, 134
*Casco* seaplane tender, 62–63, 63n8
*Case* destroyer, 77
Castillon, France, 94
Castner, Lawrence (Col.), 43, 44
Caucasus Mountains, 15, 34
*Cavanaugh* (appropriated yacht), 44
CCC (Civilian Conservation Corps), 131, 204, 235–240
censorship, 30, 201, 242, 248, 257, 266
Central Pacific Theater, 4, 16, 36
Ceylon, 34, 36
Chamberlin Point, 378
Chandonnet, Fern, xvi, 81
Chang, Thelma, 286
chaplain, African-American, 278–279
Chaplin, Charlie, 227
Charley River, 143–146
Charlie Lake, BC, 179
Chennault, John (Maj.), 24
Chernofsky Harbor (Unalaska Island), 61, 133
Chichagof Harbor, Attu, 81, 84–85, 395
Chichagof Village, Attu, 301
Chief Signal Officer, 388
childhood memories of Sitka, 265–267
Chilkoot Barracks, Haines (formerly Fort Seward), 199, 235, 243, 262, 286, 393
chromite, 314
Chukotka, 342, 343
   photographing, 402, 404–406
Church, Norbert, 46
Church, Robert, 44
Churchill, Winston, 15, 232, 312, 335, 346, 396
Church of the Holy Ascension, Unalaska, 49, 161, 371
   *See also* Russian Orthodox Church
CINCPAC, 40
City of Unalaska, 226, 337
Civil Aeronautics Administration (CAA), 59, 204
Civilian Conservation Corps (CCC), 131, 204, 235–240
Civilian Travel Control Office, 242

Civil War, American, 185, 358
Clear, AK, 397
*Clevedon* fisheries steamer, 215
Cloe, John Haile, 8, 28, 29, 225, 355, 419
clothing, 88, 93
coal, 4, 136, 204, 221, 244, 245
Coast Artillery (CA), 140
Coast Guard, U.S., 125–130
*Coast Pilot* (navigator's bible), 104
*Cobrushka* (Russian nickname for P-39), 171
Cochran, Grady, 48, 49
code-breaking, 413–414
cod fishing, 217
*Coghlan* destroyer, 114, 116
Cohen, Stan, 29, 355, 415–416
*Col. Joseph C. Morrow* (HA-2), 133–14, 133–134
cold, 43, 61, 144, 150, 183, 186, 187
    *See also* weather
Cold Bay, AK, 3
    African American soldiers at, 279–280
    airfield construction at, 212, 394
    Operation HULA at, 345–350
Cold War
    Alaska and, 397
    beginnings of, 396
    reconnaissance in Arctic during, 399–406
cold weather testing station, 59, 141, 153
Cold Weather Test Lab, 141, 142
Cole, Henry, 243
Colombo, Ceylon, raid on, 36
Colonel Yamasaki Monument, 362
Columbia River Packers' Association, 214
Combat Pacer, 397
Combined Chiefs of Staff
    Kiska assault and, 25
    on North Pacific as defensive theater, 24
Combined Fleet Command (IJN), 33, 34, 36, 37, 40
Commission on Wartime Relocation and
    Internment of Civilians, 263, 299, 305–306
communism, films about, 232
Communist Party, 232, 282
Company D, 341st Engineers Regiment, 179, 180, 182, 184
Conference on Research on the Second World
    War (June 1971), 386
*Confessions of a Nazi Spy* (film), 228
Consolidated Packing Company (ficticious
    name), 212
Constitutional Convention, Alaska (1955), 275
construction difficulties, airfield, 61, 62, 63
Construction Quartermaster, US Army, 59
Contact Creek, 185
Cook, Linda, 369
Cook and Henderson (law firm), 298
Cook Inlet Packing Company, 246, 249, 250, 251
Cooper Landing, 246
Coos Bay, OR, 133

Coox, Alvin D., 46
copper, 221, 222, 223
Copper Creek, 46
Copper River and Northwestern Railroad, 220–221
Coral Sea, 113, 393, 394
Cordova, AK, 22, 246
Corlett, Charles H. (Maj. Gen.), 42, 88
*Coronado* (PF-38), 348
*Corwin* cutter, 125
court martial actions, 92, 93, 281
Cowin huts, 367
crab fishery, Bering Sea, 217
*Cracking the Zero Mystery* (Rearden), 416, 418
Craig, Howard A. (Lt. Gen.), 396
Crane, Leon (First Lt.), 143, 144–146
crash boats, 133, 134, 248, 249, 251
crashes, aircraft, 141–146, 150
C Rations, 137, 180
Creamers' Dairy, Fairbanks, 388
Crimea, 334
Crompton, Wilson G. (Warrant Officer), 131
*The Cruise of the "Ada"* (Poor), 157
Crutcher, Marshall, 241
cryptology, 413–414
Crystal City, TX, 260
C-46 transport, 409
C-47 transport, 140, 170, 324, 342, 408

## D

*Dale* destroyer, 114, 116, 117
Dall, William Healy, 162
Dal'stroi Construction Department (USSR), 341–342
Davis, Jefferson C. (Brig. Gen.), 131, 241
Davis, Nancy Yaw, 267
Dawson Creek, BC, 173, 175, 177, 179, 183, 184
DC-3 aircraft, 150, 408, 410
DC-4 aircraft, 409
de Acre, LeRoy Ponton (Col.), 322
Deane, John R. (Gen.), 346
deception activities, 16
Decree No. 739-s (establishment of U.S.–
    Siberia air route), 327
DE (destroyer escort), 48
defenses, Alaska, ix, 59–65
    during Cold War, 397–398
    post-WWII, 396–397
    pre-WWII, 59–62, 393
    during 1980s and 1990s, 397–398
    during WWII, 62–65, 393–396
    *See also* Aleutian Campaign
de Laguna, Frederica, 260
*Delarof* transport ship, 307
Delkettie, Buck, 46
DeLong, Leon B. "Slim" (Col.), 62
Delta Junction, 191, 193
Denmark, 311
*Dent* destroyer, 77
Department of Defense Legacy funds, 368

DeSomery, Don (Sgt.), 133
DeTillio, James "Ditto," 139
De Tolli, Nikolai, 331
The Devil's Brigade (First Special Service
    Force nickname), 87
*The Devil's Brigade* (Adelman & Walton), 87
DeWitt, John L. (Lt. Gen.), 41, 61, 395
    Canadian support of Alaska and, 20, 22, 24
    recapture of Kiska and, 98
DEWline (Distant Early Warning), 208, 397, 409
Dieppe, 97, 102
Dillingham, AK, 216
Dimond, Anthony J. "Tony," 190, 199, 295
Dirks, William, 294
Discovery Passage, 223
discrimination
    against African-American soldiers, 273, 279, 281–282, 283
    against Native Alaskans, 159, 274
disenfranchisement, 273
Distant Early Warning (DEW) radar net, 409
Diters, Charles E. "Chuck", 355
Dixon's Entrance, 127, 129
Dnieper River, 334
dog, sled, 146, 151, 152
Dole, Bob, 113
Dole, "Minnie" (National Ski Patrol founder), 53
Dolitsky, Alexander B, 339
Dolitsky, Boris, 333
Donley, Gordon R. (Capt.), 131–132, 134
do-nothing affair (Japanese pun on Doolittle's
    raid), 36
Doolittle, Jimmy (Gen.), ix, 29, 36, 68
Doolittle raid on Japan (1942), ix, 29, 36, 37, 39, 43, 67, 228
Dorsher, Gerald J., 333
Draper, William, 53, 54, 55
Driscoll, Joe, 203
Drury, Newton, 255
Duerden, Frank, 192
Duggan, Bill, 46
Dumbarton Oaks Conference (Aug. 1944), 325
Dunham, Margaret, 241
Dunn, Beverly C. (Brig. Gen.), 60
dusky shearwaters/fulmars (sea birds), 31
Dutch East Indies, 33, 43
Dutch Harbor (Aleutian fishing port), 4, 5
    Coast Guard at, 128–129
    as defense priority, 21
    as floating barracks, 223
    historical landmarks on, 365
    Japanese attack on, 23, 29, 37, 40, 394
    role of weather on attacks on, 7
    *See also* Aleutian Campaign
Dutch Harbor Naval Operating Base,
    historical, 368–369
Dvina River, 334
Dyer, Tom, 200

## E

Eagle, aircraft, 397
Eagle Harbor, 221
Eagle River, AK, 44
EARDRUM, Operation, 400
Eareckson, William O. (Col.), 27, 64
Eareckson Air Force Station, 64
Earle, George, 55, 107
East Base, MT, 322
Eastern Front, 6, 311, 317, 318
Edmonton, BC
    Alaska Highway and, 175
    strategic position of, 169, 321, 322
    telephone lines at, 153
Egan, Bill, 158
Egegik River, 214
Eielson Air Force Base, 143, 398
Eight Bomber-Reconnaissance (BR) Squadron
        (RCAF), 19, 22–23, 24, 25
Eighty-Seventh Mountain Infantry, 55, 91,
        105–107
Eisenhower, Dwight D. (Brig. Gen.), 397, 400
Eklutna Indian School, 204
Eklutna Lake, 44
Eklutna power project, 175
Electra (Lockheed aircraft), 128, 409
electronic intelligence, 401–405
Electronic Order of Battle (EOB), 403
ELINT (electronic intelligence), 401, 403, 405
Elmendorf Air Force Base (CA), 23, 60–62,
        250, 363, 393, 397, 398
Elsa, AK, 192
Emmons, Delos (Lt. Gen.), 159, 282
Emoto (Lt. Cmdr.), 111
Engineer Hill, Attu, 64, 85, 111, 395
England. See Great Britain
English, Arthur, 245
English Channel, 131, 187
Enigma Code, 414
Enlisted Reserve Corps, 244
epidemics, 153, 156
Eskimos, stereotypes of, 155
    See also Inuit people; Yup'ik people
Espinola, Vera B., 375
Esquimalt, BC, 220
Estonia, 312
Estus, Ethelyn, 249–250, 251
Estus, Sanger, 249
Etorofu (Iturup), 33, 72
Europe-first policy, 15
Ewart, Grainger, 137
Executive Order 9066, 259

## F

Fairbanks, AK
    minority soldiers in, 279
    population, 1940, 59
    telephone lines at, 153
    See also Fairbanks-Krasnoiarsk Air Route

Fairbanks-Krasnoiarsk Air Route, 327–332
    construction of, 328, 331
    transfer operations, 331–332
    weather effects on, 331
Fairchild 71 aircraft, 407
F-13 aircraft, 405
Fairview, section of Anchorage, 208
Fallon, (Capt.), 151–152
Falls of Clyde clipper ship/oil barge, 223
False Bay, 221
Far East, 262, 312, 328, 334, 345
farming, 246, 254, 257
Faro, YT, 192
Farquhar, John T. (Maj.)
Farragut destroyer, 113
Farrington, Hank (Sgt.), 43
F-15 Eagle aircraft, 397
Fechner, Robert, 237–238
Federal Aviation Administration (FAA), 208
Ferber, Edna, 233
Ferret (electronic intelligence aircraft
        nickname), 402
F4F fighters, 76
Field General Courts-Martial, 93
Fifth Fleet, Japanese, 33, 34, 37, 67–68, 72
Fiji, 36, 43, 67
film, Alaska and North Country, 227–233
Finland, 334
Finnish War, 53
Finogenov, Vladimir (Capt.), 321
First Air Division, 71
First Protocol to Russia, 314
The First Special Service Force (Burhans), 87
First Special Service Force (FSSF; joint
        Canadian-U.S.), 25, 87–95
Fish and Wildlife Service, U.S., 214
    relationship with Aleuts, 162, 163
fishing industry, 211–217
    Coast Guard and, 127
    competition in, 156
fishing rights, Japanese, 212
Fleet Air Wing Four (USN), 9, 74, 394, 415
Fletcher, Frank Jack (Adm.), 10–11
FLOODLIGHT, Operation, 400
Florence, Italy, 54, 107
Flying Dragon (aircraft, Japan), 121
Flynn, Errol, 140, 229
fog, 7–9, 23, 43, 46, 48, 69, 71, 89, 113, 221
    See also weather
food shortage, Territory of Alaska, 128
Ford, John, 229
Foremost (F/V), 129
Forester Island, 127
Forest Service, 207, 235, 236, 238, 240
Forgotten War (Aleutian Campaign
        nickname), 230, 357
Fort Devens, MS, 53, 54
Fort Dix, NJ, 184
Fort Ethan Allen, VT, 88, 93
Fort Glenn, Umnak Island, 280, 365, 367–368

Fort Lawton, WA, 132
Fort Lewis, WA, 53
Fort McDowell, 88
Fort McGilvray, Caines Head, 379, 380
Fort Meares, AK, 163, 224, 365, 368, 374, 394
Fort Nelson, BC
    Alaska Highway and, 173, 183, 184
    Northwest Ferry Route and, 322
    rescue dogs at, 150, 151, 152
Fort Randall, Cold Bay, 347, 408
Fort Ray, AK, 241
Fort Raymond, Seward, Alaska, 378
Fort Richardson, 60, 61, 243, 393, 397, 412
    rescue dog training at, 152
Fort Seward (later Chilkoot Barracks), 198
Fort St. John, BC, 179, 185, 189, 192, 322
Fort Wainwright (formerly Ladd Field), 142,
        393, 397, 398
Fourteen (Fighter) Squadron, 25
Fourth Soviet Protocol, 346
Fox, George, 163
Fox (Lt.), 136
fox trapping, by Aleut people, 162, 374
F-4 Phantom aircraft, 397
France, 14, 19, 94, 288
Frank, Richard, 273
Freddy's Freighters, 92
Freeman, Charles S. (Adm.), 79
friendly fire casualties, 105–106
Friesen, Russel, 115, 116, 117, 118, 119
FS Operation, 36
Fukuyama family, 262, 286
Fulton, George, 31
Funk, Wilford, 106
Funston Park, CA, 132
Funter Bay Evacuation Camp, 132, 163–164,
        291, 294, 295, 307, 388
fur prices, 1941–1945, records, 388
fur seals, 125, 156

## G

Gabler, Frank William Peter, 251
Gaffney, Dale V. (Brig. Gen.), 150, 153, 322
Galena, base at, 206, 322, 398
Galena (Yukon River village), 46, 206, 322, 398
Gardiner, Ted, 199
Gardner, George E. (Col.), 150
Gardner, John, 162–163
Garfield, Brian, 8, 27–32, 415
Gastineau Channel, 127, 128
Geeslin, Fred, 298
Gehres, Leslie E. (Capt.), 62, 76, 77, 79
Geist, Otto, 156
Geneva Convention, 419
George, Harold L. (Gen.), 321
Germany, 334, 418
Gerow, Leonard T. (Gen.), 61
Gertrude Cove, 118
Gilbert, Charles, 215
Gilbert destroyer, 77

Gillam, Harold (bush pilot), 128
Glackin, Bill, 282
Glasscock (Capt.; *Northwestern*), 223
Gleim (Col.), 139
Glenhawk, 46
*Glory of the Seas* clipper ship, 221
Glyn, Martin A. (Capt.), 137
Goddard, George W. (Col.), 405
Goddard Hot Springs, 242
Goddard (Treadwell Mine physician), 242
Goerig, Gaye L., 251
gold
    mining in Siberia, 341–342
    shipped to U.S. from USSR, 338
gold rush theme, in film, 227–228, 233
*The Gold Rush* (film), 227
Golodoff, Anacia, 301, 302
Golodoff, Innokenty, 295
Golodoff, John, 162
Golodoff, Julia, 295
Good Friday Earthquake (1964), 396
Goodman, John, 282
*Good Morning Captain* (Fulton), 31–32
Good News Bay, AK, 46
Goose Bay, 151
Gore Field, MT, 322
Governmental Affairs Committee, Senate, 306
Grahek, Judy, 197
Gramm-Rudman-Hollings proposal, 299
Granada, CO (Japanese internment camp), 259
Grand Alliance, 14
Grande Prairie, AB, 169, 322
Gravel, Mike, 298
Gray, Maggie Panigeo "Magee", 157, 158–159,
    160
Great Britain, 14, 17, 34
Great Depression, 185, 235, 417
Great Falls, MT
    lend-lease program and, 170, 171, 324, 338
    search and rescue and, 151, 152
Great Patriotic War, 327, 332, 334
Great Slave Lake, 151
Greenland, photomapping, 400, 404
Greenlight Force (30th Infantry Brigade,
    Canada), 97–102
*Gridley* destroyer, 77
Gromoff, Ishmael V., 299
Gromyko, Andrei, 171, 325
Gruber, Frank, 232
Gruening, Ernest L., 28, 59, 253, 254
    Alaska Highway and, 167, 171, 190
    Alaska Territorial Guard and, 155, 158
    diaries of, 197–201
    immigration and, 255
    knowledge of Alaska Natives, 273–274
    National Guard and, 275, 411
    reaction to discrimination against Native
        Alaskans, 159
Grumman F6F Hellcat aircraft, 416
*Grunion* submarine, 355

Guadalcanal, 40, 42
Guam, 47, 353
Guggenheim Brothers, 219
Gulag, 341–342
Gulf of Alaska, 377
Gulkana, AK, airfield, 206
Gunderson, Paul, 163, 217

**H**

Hagiwara, Pat, 262, 286
*Haida* cutter, 128
Haigh, Jane, 194
Haines, AK, 127
Haines Road Junction, 191
Hajduckovich, John, 194
Hale, Alan, 232
Hales, David A., 201
Hall Scott factory (Berkeley, CA), 132, 134
Haman, Ray, 193
Hamill, Ralph, 106
Hammel, Sam, 48
Hammett, Dashiell, 29, 206, 282
Hammond, Jay, 299
Hanable, William S., 80
Hanabusa (Capt.), 111
Hannan, Leo J., 412
Hansen, Hans, 217
Harriman, Averell, 314, 335, 346
Harrington, Frank, 46
Harris, Ted, 243
Harvey, Alva L. (Col.), 315, 316, 317
Hatcher Pass, 204
Haugen, Ole, 418
Haulman, Daniel L., 325, 331
Hawaii, 6, 9, 21, 34, 281, 353
    strategic location of, 3–4
Haycox, Stephen, 209
Hays, Otis, 260, 416
*H.B. Kennedy*, 221
Healy, Johnny, 176
Hedlun, Nels, 46
Heintzleman, Frank, 236
Heitt (Maj.), 183, 184
helicopter, 149, 216, 255
Hemion, Austen, 224, 225
Henderson River Bridge, 362
Hendricks, Charles, 283
Hepburn, Arthur J. (Adm.), 5
Herdum, Vincent, 43
herring fishery, Aleutian, 217
Heyano, Pete, 285
Hickel, Walter J., 176, 178, 208
Hickerson, John, 98
Highland, John, 43
Higuchi, Kiichiro (Gen.), 42, 110, 111–112
Hill, Clarence (First Lt.), 45, 142
Hill, Ken, 45
Hill 400 concrete battery command station,
    Amaknak Island, 369
Hiratsuka, Mark, 285

Hirohito, Emperor, 110, 111
Hiroshima, 29
Hiss, Alger, 232
historian, definition of, 419, 420
Historic Preservation Act, 369
history, writing about, and war, 419–420
Hitler, Adolf, 112, 311–312, 313, 314, 319
Hodakof, Mike (first chief of Chichagof
    Village), 301, 302
Hodge, Walter (Col.), 191, 279–280
Hodge, Walter Mrs., 191–192
Hodikoff, Angelena, 303
Hoge, William (Brig. Gen.), 278
*Hokkai* Detachment (Japanese Army), 39, 40
Holland, 311
Hollywood Ten, 232
Holtz Bay, 45, 70, 81, 395
Holzhauser, Norton, 43
*Home from Siberia* (Hays), 416
Home War Establishment squadrons
    (Canada), 23
homosexuality, 416
Hong Kong, Canadian battalions loss at,
    99n16, 100
*Honolulu* light cruiser, 77
Hook, Arthur (Coast Guard Chief
    Boatswain), 128
Hoover Institution on War, Revolution and
    Peace, 75
Hope, Bill, 163
Hope, Harry, 312
Hope, Herbert, 163
Hopkins, Harry, 312, 314–315, 327, 334–335
Hopson, Eddie, 158
Horn, Peter H. (Lt. Cmdr,), 114, 115
Hoskins, Harold E. "Hos" (Second Lt.), 143,
    144, 146
Hosogaya, Boshiro (Adm.), 6, 33, 37, 39, 40, 41
    Aleutian Campaign and, 69, 114
    failure in mission of supporting Attu, 8
    raids on Dutch Harbor and, 7
housing
    Cowin huts, 367
    Nissen hut, 184
    Pacific huts, 367, 379
    Quonset hut, 136, 137, 138, 362, 366, 379
    Yakutat huts, 367
Hozumi, Matsutoshi (Maj.), 39
H.R. 1776 (Lend-Lease Act), 312
Hudson, Ray, 49
HULA. *See* Operation HULA
Hull, Cordell, 21, 118
*Humphreys* (destroyer), 77, 79
Hungary, 334
Hunt, William "Bill," 178
Hunter, J. C., 221
hunting in Alaska, 161, 255–256
    licenses, for military personnel, 255
Huston, John, 228, 229–230, 417
Hynes, Frank, 214

## I

Iakutsk, 341
ice-free port
  Archangel'sk, 15, 149, 319, 327
  Murmansk, 15, 149, 170, 314, 319, 327
  Seward, AK, 377–378
Iceland, 149, 400
*Ice Palace* (film), 233
Ickes, Harold, 197, 198, 294, 295
I-class submarine (Japan), 42
icons, religious, 374, 375
IFF (Identification Friend or Foe) systems, 405
Igagik, 45
IGHQ (Imperial General Headquarters,
    Japan), 37, 40, 41, 42, 72
Ihozumi, Akira, 302
IJN (Imperial Japanese Navy), 33–34
Ile de Port-Cros, 94
Ile Du Levant, 94
Iliamna, Old, 44
*I Married a Communist* (film), 232
Imperial Japan. *See* Japan
*Indianapolis* heavy cruiser, 70, 77
Indian Health Service, 308
Indians, Alaskan, 194
Indian Self-Determination Act, 308
infant mortality, 273
Inglagusaq (Aleut warrior), 161
Inouye, Dan, 285
Inouye, Ronald K., 263
Inside Passage, navigation along, 127
International North Pacific Fisheries
    Convention (1952), 217
*In This Our Life* (film), 229
Inupiaq people, 155–156
    *See also* Alaska Territorial Guard (ATG);
      Yup'ik people
Ipalook, Fred, 157
Ipalook, Percy, 275
Iran, 149, 327, 335
Iron Curtain, 232, 396
*Iron Curtain* (film), 232
Irwin, David (Lt.), 151–152, 153
Irwin, Zachary T., 153
Iseda (Sgt.; Japanese POW), 111
isolationism, 312
Issei, 259, 260, 261–262
Italy
  documentary film on, 230
  Tenth Mountain Division in, 106–107
Itchadag (Aleut warrior), 161
Iturup, 33, 72
*I Was a Communist for the FBI* (film), 232
Iwo Jima, 8

## J

Jacobs, William A., 153
Jacobson, Jake, 43
Jalufka, Alfred (Pvt. 1st class), 279

Jamison, Mitchell, 47
JANFU (joint army-navy foul-up), 106
Japan
  attack on Dutch Harbor, 23, 29, 37, 40
  plan to neutralize Australia, 36
Japanese-Americans
  in Aleutian Campaign, 285–287
  internment camps, 285
  service in World War II, 262, 285–286, 288
  in U.S. military, 262, 285, 288
Japanese Campaign in Alaska, strategic
    perspective on, 33–38
Japanese civilians, in Alaska, 259–263
Japanese Imperial General Headquarters
    (IGHQ), 21, 34, 37, 39, 43–46, 67, 70, 72
Japanese Northeast Fleet, 72
Japanese Pioneers Research Project, Alaska
    1991–1992, 259
Japanese prisoner of war, 41, 111
Japan-Soviet Neutrality Pact, 15
Japan-USSR Neutrality Pact, 13, 14
Japonski Island, naval base on, 241
Jarmin Pass (Attu), 81, 84
Java, 67
J-boats, 379
Jews, 112, 254
*John B. Floyd* (liberty ship), 88
John Hart Highway, BC, 192
Johnson, Robert Erwin, 128
Joint Board, 16, 20, 21–22
    *See also* Joint Chiefs of Staff
Joint Canadian-United States Basic Defense
    Plan–1940, 19
Joint Canadian-United States Basic Defense
    Plan–2 (ABC-22), 19–20, 21
Joint Chiefs of Staff (JCS)
  Alaska defense planning and, 126–127
  attack on Attu and, 41, 394
  Greenlight Force and, 102
  lend-lease program and, 346
  southern Pacific and, 24
Joint Defense Board, and Alaska Highway, 173
Joint Emergency War Plan PINCHER, 399, 404
Joint Security Control, 16
Joint Task Force-Alaska, 397
Jones, C. Foster, 246, 301–302
Jones, Etta, 301–302
Jones, Jesse, 314
Jonesville, 244
Juneau, AK, 59, 199, 243, 259
  airfield construction at, 63–64
Juneau Draft Board, 247
*Juneau Empire*, 236, 238
*Junyo* carrier, 37, 40, 68, 79

## K

Kadin, Mikhail, 162
Kaho, Niles, 245, 246, 247, 249, 251
Kaktovik, Barter Island, 157
Kakuta, Kakuji (Vice Adm.), 37, 39–40

Kalb, Bernard, 282
Kalekta Bay trail, 162
Kamchatka Peninsula, 3, 9, 33, 68
Kamdron, Robert (Capt.), 223
*Kane* destroyer, 90
*Kant* destroyer, 77
Karelia, 334
Kasaan, AK, 241
Kashega (evacuated/never rebuilt), 161
Kasukabe, Karl Kaoru, 123
Katalla, AK, 221
Katlean, AK, 243
Kawabe, Harry, 260
Kawabe, Torno, 259
Kawase, Ohiro (Vice Adm.), 41
Kayamori, Fhoki, 260
Kelly, Joe, 44
Kenai Fjords National Park, 379
Kendrick, Philip, 43
Kennedy, Roger, 365
Kenney, George C. (Gen.), 399–400
Kennicott copper mines, 221, 223
Keno, AK, 192
Kesan, Russia, 315
Ketchikan, AK, 69, 259
Ketchikan Chamber of Commerce, 262–263
Keystone Canyon, 177
Khlerekoper, Fred (Rev.), 156, 158
Khruschev, Nikita, 339
Kiev, 334
Killisnoo (Aleut resettlement camp), 292, 294,
    295
*Kimiknwa Maru*, 68
Kimura, George, 286
Kimura, Masatomi (Rear Adm.), 42
King, Bob, 217
King, Ernest J. (Adm.), 5–9, 36, 75
  lend-lease program and, 346
  Theobald relieved from duty and, 8, 79
King, William Lyon Mackenzie
  Kiska and, 97, 99, 102
  meets with Roosevelt, 19
Kingfisher Bay, 139
King Salmon, AK, airstrip at, 212
Kinkaid, Thomas C. (Rear Adm.), 8, 9, 40–41,
    395
KINY radio, 199
Kirensk, Siberia (lend-lease route stop), 328, 332
KIRO radio, 199
Kirtland, John C., 299
Kisel'nikov (Maj.), 343
Kisilev, Peter (Col.), 323
Kiska Garrison Force, 72
Kiska Harbor, 24
Kiska Island
  Alaskan Scouts on, 45, 90, 92
  casualties on, 105–106
  geography of, 104
  invasion of, 87–95, 97–102, 100

Japanese evacuation of, 8, 30–31, 41–42, 44, 46, 71, 72, 104–105, 111–112, 119, 121–123, 395
Japanese occupation site on, 365
Japanese seizure of, 7, 37
lack of secrecy of battle plans for, 103–104
as National Historical Landmark, 353, 357
positive results of, 103
strategic location of, 4, 7, 13
submarines and, 118
U.S. assault against Japanese on, 7–8, 25, 41
U.S.-Canada, occupation of, 395
weather on, 9, 89, 104, 105, 121
*See also* Aleutian Campaign; archaeological research, on Attu/Kiska
Kiska Occupation Force, 68
*Kiso* light cruiser, 68
Kittyhawk (Canadian term for P-40), 23, 25
Klaney, Archie, 240
Klimkin (pilot on lend-lease route), 331
Klondike gold rush, 125
in film, 227
Kluane Lake, NT, 189, 192
Knight, W. W., 242
Kobayashi, Koby, 287–288
Kobayashi, Mat, 288
Kobayashi, Shiro, 288
Kochergin, Peter, 295
Kodiak, AK, 44, 200
as defense priority, 21
strategic location of, 5
Kodiak Naval Base, 24, 59, 73, 76
Koga, Mineichi (Adm.), 41
Kohlhoff, Dean, 295, 299
Kolyma, AK, 342
Kolyma River, 341
Komandorski Islands, 8, 70–71
Korea, 13
Korean War (1950–1953), 275, 337
Kosheleva, Tat'iana, 327
Koyuk, village of, 157, 159
Krasnoiarsk (site on lend-lease route), 331
Kresky (Pharmacist Mate), 114
*Kriegsmarine*, 15
Krukof, Agafon, Jr., 298, 299
Kurile Islands, 67
Aleutian Campaign and, 71, 72
attacks against Japanese by US on, 9–10
Soviet occupation of, 10
strategic location of, 3, 102
Kursk, battle of, 311, 318
Kuznetsov, N. G. (Fleet Adm.), 347
Kvichak River, 216
Kwantung Army, 33

## L

Labrador, 150
Ladd Field (later, Fort Wainwright), 61, 142, 143, 146, 397
Building 1001, 146

construction of, 393
lend-lease and, 150, 170, 321–324
rescue dog training at, 152
strategic position of, 169
LaGuardia, Fiorello H., 322
Lakard, Arnold "Arnie", 43, 44
Lake Baikal, 328
Lake Laberge, 194
Lame Hill Ridge, Kiska, 91
land claims, by Native peoples, 160, 275
Landing Craft, Infantry (LCI), 89, 347
Landrum, Eugene M. (Gen.), 28–29, 111, 135
land titles, 273
Lane (Reg. Cmdr.), 179, 182
*Lansdowne*, 118
La Perouse Strait, 15
Larry Hill, Kiska, 91
Lasso Hill, Kiska, 91
Latouche, 220
Laughlin, William S., 291
*Law of the Northwest* (film), 231
Lawson Hills, 91
LB-30, 76
LCI (Landing Craft, Infantry), 89, 347
lead mining, 192
Leahy, M. Joseph, 130
Leary (Vice Adm.), 79
Leavitt, Oliver, 273
Lederer, Francis, 231
Lee, John C. H. (LTG.), 60
Lekanof, Anatoly, 291
Lekanof, Anna, 299
Lekanof, Flore, Sr. (Aleut leader), 298
Leman, Harry, 245, 246, 247, 249, 251
lend-lease (aircraft from U.S. to Soviet Union)
aircraft, 16, 150, 169–170, 317
aircraft numbers, 6, 16, 170, 171, 317, 324, 332, 337, 338
aircraft/personnel losses, 170, 332, 336, 342–343
Alaska-Siberia Air Route, 311–318, 341–343
aluminum shipments, 338
arms, 338
copper shipments, 338
evolution of air route, 311–318
Fairbanks-Krasnoiarsk Air Route, 327–332
foodstuffs, 15–16, 17, 337–338, 342
Liberty ship, 138
medicine, 342
non-military shipments, 15–16, 17, 337–338
North Russian sea land to Murmansk, 314
Northwest Ferry Route, 319–325
obstacles to, 15, 16
Operation HULA, 345–350
petroleum, 15–16, 17
post-war effects, 337, 339
raw materials, 17, 338
significance of, 13–14, 15–16, 17
Soviet complaints about, 170–171, 315–316, 317

steel, 338
suggested routes, 319, 321, 327, 328
sunken cargo, 327
tanks, 338
tonnage, 15
tools, 342
transport, 338, 342
vessels, 15, 346, 347, 349
Leningrad (USSR), 15
*Leonard Wood*, 239
Le Regiment de Hull, 100, 102
Lestenkof, Michael, 297
Lethbridge Air Base, AB, 322
*Let There Be Light* (documentary film), 230
Levanevskii (Russian pilot), 328
Levelock, AK, 46
Leveque, Rene (missionary), 153
Liapidevskii (Russian pilot), 328
Libby, McNeil, Libby Cannery (Yakutat), 59
Liberty ships, 88, 89
at Adak, 137–138
Lighthouse Service, 126
Lilly Creek, 91
Limpid Creek, 91
Link Hills, Kiska, 91
Lipke, Adam, 245
liquor shipments, 128
Lithuania, 312, 334
Little Kiska Island, 24
Litvinov, Maxim, 314–315
Livingstone (Capt.), 222
logbooks, USN, 384–385
Lokanin, Mike, 295
LORAN (long-range navigation) construction, 130
*Louisville* heavy cruiser, 77
Lucas, Harry, 199
Lucas, Stell, 199
*Luftwaffe*, 15, 170, 311, 317, 318
Luxembourg, 311
Lytle and Green Co., 189–190

## M

MacArthur, Douglas (Gen.), 9, 287
on Aleutians, 42
meeting with Hirohito, 111
MacDonald, Donald, 167, 173, 175–178
MacDonald, Thomas, 177
Machin, Mikhail G. (Col.), 321, 323
Mackenzie River system, 151
Madison, Guy, 232
Magadan, Siberia, 328, 332, 342, 343
Magma, Chichi (Vice Adm.), 40
Magnitogorsk industrial complex, 335
Magnuson Act, 217
Mahan, Alfred Thayer, 4
Maine, 158
*Making It Right: Restitution for Churches Damaged and Lost During the Aleut Evacuation of World War II*, 374

Makushin (evacuated/never rebuilt), 161
Makushin Bay, 40, 79
Mala, Ray, 233, 233n31
Malaya, 67
Mallard, Wimpy (*Dale* crewman), 118
*Maltese Falcon* (film), 229
Manchuria, 13, 33, 112
manganese, 314, 342
mapping, photomapping Greenland, 400, 404
Marcus Island, 67
Mare Island Naval Shipyard, CA, 114
Margaret Bay cantonment, 368–369
Markovo, 342
Marmion Island, 127
Marshall, A. C. (Col.), 90
Marshall, George C. (Gen.), 42, 61, 79, 312, 395
    on African-American soldiers, 281
    recapture of Kiska and, 97–98
Marshall, Thurgood, 281
Marshall Islands, 34, 36, 67, 353
Marshall Plan, 403–404
Marsh Lake Lodge, 191
Marston, Marvin "Muktuk" (Lt. Col.), 155,
    157–160, 208, 233, 246–247, 274, 275, 411
Marston mat, 61, 63
Martz, Mike, 160
*Maru* (merchant-cruiser transport), 41, 355,
    356–357
Mason, Gene, 246, 249
Mason, Margaret, 249
Massacre Bay (Attu), 41, 64, 81, 111, 280–281
Matanuska Colony, 204, 254–255
Matsumoto, Roy, 287
Matsunaga, "Spark", 306
Matua, 33
Maxwell, William S. (Capt.), 347, 349
Maxwell Air Force Base, AL, historical
    documents at, 131
May, Joseph, life on Adak, 135–140
*Maya* (heavy cruiser, IJN), 37, 115, 117
Mayo, AK, 192
Mazuruk (Russian pilot), 328
*McCall* destroyer, 77
McCallum, Hubert, 217
McCarthy, Joseph, 233
McCarthy era, 232
McCloy, John J., 90
McCrane, Joseph C. "Mother", 113, 116
McDonald, Thomas, 117
McDougall, Morris, 190
McGlashen, Anne, 295
McGregor, G. R. (Wing Cmdr.), 23–24
McKinnon, Capt., 48
*McLane* (cutter), 129
McMorris, Charles Horatio "Soc" (Socrates;
    (Rear Adm.), 8, 40–41, 114, 118, 384–385
McNaughton, Andrew (Gen.), 98
medical care, emergency, 249
memorial
    Attu Battlefield, 368

Attu Battlefield and Airfields National
    Historical Landmark, 353
    Colonel Yamasaki Monument, 362
    First Special Service Force, 94
    Memorial at Attu, 362
    monument fashioned from *Northwestern*
        propeller, 226
    Titanium Memorial, 362
    Unalaska Memorial Park, 226
Memorial Tenth Mountain Division Highway,
    106
Mendoza, Harry, 140
*Men of the Tundra* (Marston), 155, 157
Mentasta Lake, 194
Merculief, Father, 299
Merculief, Susie, 299
Merriam, Al, 47
Merriman, E. C., 298
Metcalf, Frank, 199
Methodist Church, 250
Michael, Henry, 333
Michela, Joseph A. (Col.), 315
midget submarine, Japanese, 69
Midway Island
    Japanese attack on, 21, 36
    Japanese defeat at, 6–7, 23, 394
    strategic relation to Aleutians operations,
        37–38, 67
MILEPOST (codename for HULA Operation),
    346
*Milepost Guide*, 192
Military Airlift Command, 397
military construction
    in Alaska during WWII, 59
    post-war, Native peoples and, 160
    *See also* airfield construction; Alaska
        Highway
Military Members, 100
Military Sea Transport Service, files of, 388
Miller, Don, 282
Miller, Edward, 10
Miller, Glenn, 182
Miller, Peter (Lt. Col.), 281
Minami-Tori Jima, 34
mineral exploration, Native peoples and, 156
Minidoka, ID (internment camp for Alaskan
    Japanese), 262, 285, 286
mining, 254
    Anvil lead-zinc mine, 192
    copper, 221, 223
    gold, in Siberia, 341–342
Minoki, Junichiro (Maj. Gen.), 40
minority troops in Alaska, 271–275
    black soldiers, 271, 272–275
    discrimination and, 273, 274
    Native Alaskan soldiers, 271–272, 273
    race relations, 277–283
Minto (Athabaskan village), 273
MI Operation. *See* Midway Island
Misikian, Natalie, 297

missionaries, Christian, 156
Mitchell, Albert (Ensign), 418
Mitchell, Billy (Gen.), 4, 9, 397, 398
Mitsubishi Nagoya Aircraft Works, 141
Miyo, Tatsukichi (Cmdr.), 36
Mobile Diving and Salvage Unit 1, 355
Mogg, Billy, 157
Moldavia, 334
Molokov (Russian pilot), 328
Molotov, Vyacheslav, 171, 335
Monaghan, Mike (Maj.), 415
*Monaghan* destroyer, 114, 115
Mooney, George, 250–251
*Moonlight Maid* (yacht appropriated for
    service), 44, 62, 62n7
Moore, George W. (First Lt.), 125
Moore, Pat, 46
Moore Ridge (Attu), 81, 84
Morgan, J. P., 219
Morgan, Lael, 275, 420
Morison, Samuel Eliot, 8, 9, 10, 42, 109, 395, 416
Morris, Alba, 282
Morrisette, Stephen M., 142, 146
Morrison-Knudsen Company (M-K), 63–64, 128
Morse Code, 43
Morton, Susan, 355
Moscow, 15
Moses Point, 46
Mosley, Thomas L. (Col.), 150, 322
mountain troops, 53–55
Mount Katmai, eruption of, 1912, 125
Mount McKinley National Park, 255
Mt. Edgecumbe, 242
Muncho Lake, 192
Munson, Thomas, 246, 247, 248–249, 251
Murchie, J. C. (Vice Chief Maj.-Gen.), 100
Murmansk (ice-free arctic port), 15, 149, 170,
    314, 319, 327
Murphy, Larry E., 357
Museum of Western History (Denver), 56
Muskwa River, BC, 181, 182
mutiny charges, 281
*My Son John* (film), 232

**N**

*Nachi* (heavy cruiser), 37, 115, 117
Nagasaski, 29
Nagumo (Adm.), 33, 36
Nakao, Pete, 287
Nakazawa, Tasuku (Capt.), 37
Naknek, AK, 216
Nakwasina Pass, 243
Nanaimo, 221
*Narrative Report of Alaska Construction* (Bush),
    378–379
Nash, Gerald, 203
Nash, Marie Matsuno, 305–306
*Nashville* light cruiser, 77, 79
*Nathaniel Wyeth* liberty ship, 88
National Archives, 338, 383–389, 417, 419

Alaska Region, 387–389
Archives I, 384
Archives II, 384
finding aids, 384–386
online records, 386–387
National Association for the Advancement of
Colored People (NAACP), 279
National Battlefield program, 369
National Defence Headquarters (NDHQ), 98
*National Geographic*, 30, 48, 227
National Historical Landmarks (NHLs)
Attu Battlefield and Airfields, 353, 359–360
Kiska Island, 353
National Historic Landmarks, 353, 359, 362,
365–369
National Historic Preservation Act (1966),
365–366
National Park Service, 207, 365, 367, 368, 369
National Personnel Records Center, 387
National Register of Historic Places, 366, 371
National Ski Patrol, 53, 54
National Trust for Historic Preservation, 371
Native land claims, 275
Native religions, condemnation of, 274
natural resources, 192, 221, 223, 254
natural resources, Alaska, 4, 253
Naval Detachment 3294 (HULA-2), 348, 349
Naval Historical Center, 417
Naval Intelligence (USN), 76
naval lend-lease operation. *See* HULA
Operation
Naval Patrol Wing Four, 76, 418
navy bases in Alaska. *See specific locations*
Navy Historical Center, 417, 418
Nazi Germany, 311–313
Nedosekin, Paul (Lt. Col.), 321, 331
Neely, Alastair, 95
*Nemeha* cutter, 129
Nenana Ice Pool, 243
Neuberger, Richard (Lt.), 279
Neutrality Act, 126, 312
Neutrality Pact, Japan-USSR, 15
*Neva*, 216
Nevzaroff, John, 163, 294
New Caledonia, 67
Newell, Martha, 295
New England Fish Company, 131
New Guinea, 281, 286
New York and Cuban Mail Steamship
Company, 131, 246
*New York* (battleship), 75
*New York Herald- Tribune*, 316
Nielson, John, 157, 203
Nikolski (Aleut village), 161, 297–298
Nimitz, Chester W. (Adm.)
Midway Island and, 6–7, 37, 40
recapture of Kiska and, 97–98
replaces Theobald with Kincaid, 8
Theobald and, 8, 76
Ninety-Fifth, 272–273

Ninilchik, 246
Nisei, 259
Nishijima, Teruo, 112
*Nissan Maru* (Japanese freighter), 355
Nissen hut, 184
No. 115 (Fighter) Squadron (Canada), 20
Nogushi, Satoru, 303
Nolan, Mary, 191
Nolan, Mike, 191
Nold, George J. (Maj. Gen.), 60
Nome, AK, 23, 24
airfield at, 206, 336
ALSIB ferry route and, 315
gold rush at, 228
rescue dog training at, 152
nonaggression pact, 6, 149
Normandy, invasion of, 419
Norris, Frank, 233
Norstad, Lauris (Gen.), 404
North American Air Defense Command
(NORAD), 395
North Bend (OR), 134
North Coast Seafoods, 216
Northeast Area Fleet (Japanese), 72
Northeast Zoloto Union, 343
Northern Army (Japan), 42
Northern Commercial Co., 243
Northern Pacific Railroad, 132
*Northern Pursuit* (film), 229, 231–232
The Northern Steamship Company, 219–220
*Northland*, 222
North Pacific
geography effect on strategy, 13
prewar preparations in, 3–6
significance for European theater, 13–17
as vital lead-lease route, 10
North Pacific deception plan, 16
North Pacific Force (USN), 7–8
North Pacific Theater, 4, 6, 9, 10
North Pole, 400, 401
North Slope, 273
Northway (Athabascan village), 194
North-West Air Route, 19
*Northwestern*, 247
Northwest Ferry Route, 319–325
Northwest Sea Frontier, 78–79
Northwest Staging Route, 167, 194, 320, 322
North-West Staging Route, 20, 21, 24, 169
Norton Sound, 24, 157, 255
Norway, 87, 149, 311, 314
*No Tumult, No Shouting: The Story of the PBY*
(Thorburn & Thorburn), 417
Novo-Siberia, 315
Novosibirsk (lend-lease route site), 336
*Nozima Maru* (Japanese freighter), 356–357,
360, 361
NRMA, 99
Nulato, AK, 46
Numata (Capt.), 111
Nunivak Island, 46

**O**
Obrazkov, Ivan A. (Maj. Gen.), 323
O'Brien, "Dynamite Johnny" (steamship
captain), 221
O'Connor, James (Brig. Gen.), 278–279
Oenga, Andrew, 158
Office of Price Administration (OPA), 388
Office of War Information, 229
Ogasawara Islands, 67
Ogdensburg Declaration, 19
O'Geara (battery commander, Adak), 139–140
Ogle, Janis Reeve, 410
*Ogontz*, SS (floating cannery), 215
Ohashi, G. H., family, 263
Ohlsen, Otto F., 60, 61
*Oimiakon*, 331
Okinawa, 206
Old Palmer Highway, AK, 244
Oliver, Simeon, 163
Olsen, Clarence E. (Rear Adm.), 60, 346
O'Malley, Henry, 215
Omnibus Act (1966), 367
Omori, Sentaro (Rear Adm.), 39
Omsk, 315
*Onandaga* cutter, 128–129
One Percent for Art Program, 49
Onishi, Takijiro (Vice Adm.), 42
Ono, Takeji (Capt.), 39
Operation AL, 39
Operation AOB, 39
Operation AQ, 39
Operation Barbarossa, 17, 170, 313
Operation EARDRUM, 400
Operation FLOODLIGHT, 400
Operation HULA, 345–350
Operation Husky (code-name for invasion of
Sicily), 88
Operation Landcrab, 41
Operation MI (Japanese offensive against
Midway), 43, 44
Operation Plough, 87
Operation POLARIS, 400
Operation Ultra, 413–414
Operation Uranus, 17
optical Aleutian (effect of constant Aleutian
fog on soldiers' eyes), 106
Orange war plan, xi
Otaru, Hokkaido, 302–304
forced labor, 303
freedom of movement for Aleuts, 302–303
health conditions, 303
living conditions, 302, 303
return to U.S., 303–304
Otaru, Japan (site where Attuans interned),
291, 293, 295, 302
Otrick, Philip, 45
Oumansky, Constantin, 313
Our Glory Road to Tokyo (Alaska Highway
nickname), 169

Outside (Alaskan slang for contiguous U. S.), 209, 242
Owens, George (Master Sgt.), 279

**P**

Pacific Coast Steamship Company, 242
Pacific Command, 102
*Pacific Fisherman* (trade journal), 212, 215, 217
Pacific huts, 367, 379
*Pacific Queen,* 216
Page, Woodrow, 43
P-38 aircraft, 45, 71, 363
P-39 Airacobra, 171, 317–318, 331, 338
P-39 aircraft, 150, 311, 324
P-40 aircraft, 24, 40, 45, 76, 79, 150, 311, 317, 321, 393, 394
P-63 aircraft, 324
Palau, 353
Paloff Harbor, AK, 200
Panama Canal, strategic location of, 3–4
Panama Railway, 219
Pankey, Dorothy, 249–250, 251
Papanin (Soviet pilot), 341
parachute rescue squad, 128
Paramushiro, 71
    Japanese airstrips on, 33
    U.S. raids on, 10, 30, 134
Parham, R. Bruce, ix, 390
Park, Richard (Col.), 62
Parker, Andrew "Red", 115, 117
Parker, Ralph C. (Capt.), 62, 79
    Alaska defense planning and, 126–127
Parks, George A., 199
Patrol Squadron Forty-two, 417
Patrol Wing Four, 78, 418
Paul, William, 295
PBY aircraft, 45, 62, 68, 69, 79, 121, 129, 394, 417
P-30 cabin cruiser, 131
P-31 cabin cruiser, 131
P-749 crash boat, 134
P-756 crash boat, 134
Peace River, BC, 272
Pearkes, George (Maj. Gen.), 98, 100, 101, 102
Pearl Harbor, 21, 33, 221
Permanent Joint Board on Defense (PJBD), US-Canadian committee, 19, 21, 22, 98, 99, 322
Perras, Galen Roger, 102
Perry, Robed R. (Capt.), 402–403
*Perseus* cutter, 161, 200
Persian Gulf route, lend-lease program, 17, 319
*Personal Justice Denied* (report documenting Aleut losses), 299, 306
Peters, Liv, 45
Petersen, Ray, 408
Petrivelli, Alice Snigaroff, 298, 299
petroleum, 4, 15, 17, 281
Petropavlovsk, 349
    U.S. weather station at, 10
Pettikoff, Mark, 294, 295

phantom flotilla. *See* Battle of the Pips
P-36 Hawks, 393
Philemenof, Dimitri, 299
Philippines, 3, 14, 33, 43, 288
Pile Point, 221
pillboxes, preservation of, 369
PINCHER (Joint Emergency War Plan), 399
pioneer home, 242
Pips, Battle of the, 9, 30–32, 42, 104, 119
Piskunov (Col.), 336
P-40K, 23, 24
platinum, 314
Pleissner, Ogden, 55
Pletnikoff, Patrick, 298–299
Pletnikoff, Simeon, 163
P-38 Lightning, 359
Po-2 aircraft, 331
Point Lay, 158
Poisk (search groups), 332
poison gas, 416, 419
Pokryshkin, Aleksandr I. (Soviet ace), 317–318, 338
*Polar Bear,* 216
POLARIS, Operation, 400
Pompeo, Richard (Master Sgt.), 143, 144, 146
Pontoon Joe, (Japanese bomber pilot nickname), 48–49
Pope, Maurice (Gen.), 98
Popov, B. D. (Rear Adm.), 349
population
    Alaska, 1960, 397
    Aleut, 1940, 161
    Sitka, 1993, 265n2
    territorial, 254
Port Angeles, WA, 132
Port Heiden, AK, 408, 409
Port Hobron, AK, 217
Port Levashef, 225
Port Moller, 44
Port Moresby, 34, 67, 394
Port Valdez, 220
Potter Rock, 221
POW (prisoner of war), 41, 111, 395, 416
Prejean, Joseph, 272
preservation, historic, 351, 353
Presidio, San Francisco, 132
Presque Isle, ME, 152
PRF (pulse repetition frequency), 402
Pribilof Islands, 125
    Aleuts on, 161, 163–164
    churches damaged on, 371, 372
    *See also* Aleutian and Pribilof Islands Restitution
Price Administration, Office of (OPA), 388
price controls, 201, 207
Price Operation Records, 388
*Prince of Wales* battleship, 104
Prince Rupert, BC, 20, 21, 22
prisoner of war, 41, 111, 395, 416
Project 20, 401

Project 23, 401
Project NO. 5 (AKA Project Nanook), 400, 401
Project SeaMark, 353
Prokopeuff, Alfred, 304
Prokopeuff, Ralph, 163
Prokushev (Lt.), 331
propellers, 47, 226
Prossoff, Alex, 293, 295
PT boat, 45, 134
Public Law 98-212 (environmental cleanup), 368
Public Law 100-383 (restitution to Aleuts and Japanese-Americans), 263, 298
Puget Sound, 223
pulse repetition frequency (PRF), 402
Purple Heart Battalion, 286
Pustoi Bay, Umnak Island, 61
Puyallup Assembly Center, WA, 260, 285, 286
P-26 vessel, 76
P-114 vessel, 132, 133
P-115 vessel, 132–133
P-141 vessel, 133
P-142 vessel, 133
P-146 vessel, 133
P-214 vessel, 134
P-215 vessel, 249
P-217 vessel, 134, 248, 249, 250, 251
P-219 vessel, 134
P-220 vessel, 134
PV-I Venturas aircraft, 9
PV-2 Harpoons aircraft, 9
Pyramid Mountain (Kodiak)

**Q**

Quebec (First) Conference (Aug. 1943), 93
Quisling Cove, Kiska, 91
Quonset hut, 136, 137, 138, 366, 379

**R**

Race, Mel, 243
race relations, 277–283
radar, 405
    ASV equipment, 74
    Distant Early Warning (DEW) radar net, 409
    Soviet RUS-2 early warning, 403
    use in Aleutian Campaign, 74
    White Alice troposphere communications system, 208, 397
Radford, James, 43, 44
Radio Tokyo, 90
railroad
    Alaska Railroad, 59, 60, 63, 203–204
    Canadian Pacific Railroad, 173
    Copper River and Northwestern Railroad, 220–221
    legislation concerning, 221
    Northern Pacific Railroad, 132
    trans-Alaska-Bering Strait-Siberian Railroad, 176

Rainbow Creek, Kiska, 92
Rainbow war plan, xi
Raisman, David S., 343
Ranger Hall of Fame, 287
Ranger Hill, Kiska, 92
Rankin, Jeannette, 199
rationing, 242, 248
Rat Islands, 43
Ravens (electronic warfare officers), 402
Rawson, Timothy, 258
RB-29 Ferret aircraft, 405
Reagan, Ronald, 263, 416
Rearden, Jim, 416, 418
records, World War II
    at Hoover Institution, 75
    at Pentagon, 28–29
    at University of Oregon, 29
    See also National Archives
Red Army Day, 323–324
Red Banner Award, 331
Red Menace, 232
Red Mountain Chrome Mine, 246, 247
Red Snow (film), 232–233
Reeve, Janice M. "Tilly", 410
Reeve, Richard D., 409
Reeve, Robert Campbell, 407–410
Reeve Aleutian Airways, 407–410
Reid destroyer, 76, 77
reindeer herding, 156
Reliance cutter, 125
Reneke, Larry, 29
Report from the Aleutians (documentary film),
    228, 230, 416
restitution
    to Aleuts, 297–299, 305–306, 371–375
    to Japanese-Americans, 263
Resurrection Bay, 221, 377, 378
Rexford, Herman, 157
Reynard Cove, 68
Reynolds, Georgeie, 32
R-7 half-track tractor, 152
R-6 helicopter, 149
Rice, Bob, 146
Richardson, John (Chief Petty Officer), 116
Richardson Highway, oldest highway in
    Alaska, 193
Richmond cruiser, 114, 115, 117
Riders of the Northland (film), 230, 231
Rika's Roadhouse, 189
Riot Hill, Kiska, 92
Rising Sun (Japanese flag), 109
Riva Ridge, Italy, 106–107
Robber Hill, Kiska, 92
Robert Campbell Highway, 192
Roberts, Helen, 313
Robinson, Edward G., 231
Robinson, Verne, 298
Rockwell, Francis W. (Rear Adm.), 8, 41, 42
Rocky Mountain Rangers, 100
Rocky Point, 378

Roll, Finn W. (First Lt.), 90
Romania, 334
Roosevelt, Franklin D.
    at Adak, 140
    Alaska Highway and, 173
    Aleut restitution and, 298
    appoints Gruening governor of Alaska, 198
    Canadian defense of Alaska and, 19, 21
    Japanese/Japanese-American internment
        and, 259
    lend-lease program and, 169, 312–314, 315,
        319, 327, 328, 334–335, 338–339
    recovery of dog of, 416, 417
Rose, Robert C. (Lt.), 225
Rose Hill (Kiska), 92
Rosenhauer, Joseph, 46
Ross River, 192
Routes A–D (Alaska Highway), 173
Royal Air Force (RAF), 131, 312
Royal Canadian Air Force (RCAP), 395
Royal Canadian Artillery, 100
Royal Canadian Engineers, 100
Royal Canadian Mounted Police, 153
Royal Canadian Navy, 24
Ruby, AK, 200
Rufes (seaplane version of Japanese Zero
    fighter), 24
Russell, James (Adm.), 29, 30, 417
Russell, Richard A., 10
Russia, 3
    See also Soviet Union
Russian-German War, 6, 313
Russian Orthodox Church, 250, 291
    faith among Aleuts, 291–292, 371
    restoration of/restitution for churches,
        371–372
Russo-Japanese War, 34, 36
Ryuho (carrier bombed by Doolittle), 29
Ryujo (carrier, IJN), 29, 37, 40, 68, 79

S
SAC (Strategic Air Command), 399–400
Safeguard salvage vessel, 355
SAF (Soviet Air Force), 316, 317, 328, 334
Sagstad Shipyards, WA, 134
Saint John Fusiliers, 100
Saipan, 47
Sakhalin Island, 15
salmon industry, in Alaska during World War
    II, 211–217, 254
    canneries, 246
    Japanese and, 212, 216
Salt Lake City cruiser, 8, 114–115, 116, 117
salvage, 225, 355
Samoa, 67
Samuelsen, Harvey, 217
Sands destroyer, 77
Sarana Bay, 45
Saratoga, 219
Scammon, Charles M. (Capt.), 125

Scandinavian immigrants, 254–255
Schaeffer, John, 274
Schneider, Joe, 179–181, 182
Schoeppe, Bill, 338
schools, Native peoples and, 156, 274
Schreiber, Carl, 411
Schuler, Dolph, 185, 187
scientific exploration, and Native peoples, 156
S class submarine, 77
Screaming Eagle of the Yukon. See Gaffney,
    Dale
Seabees (USN construction battalions), 9, 48,
    133, 137, 140
Seaborn, Henry, 214
seal harvesting, 162, 164, 295
Sea of Okhotsk, attacks against Japanese by
    U.S., 10
seaplane base, 5, 20
search and rescue, Arctic, 150–153
Sea Scouts, 131
Seattle, WA, 60
Second Attu Invasion Force (Japan), 69
Second Mobile Force (Japan), 67, 68, 69, 73, 74
Second Protocol, 317
Second Strike Force (Japan), 37
Segal Island (north of Kiska), 92
Seibert, James B. (First Lt.), 143, 144, 146
Seims-Drake Construction Company, 161, 162
Seldovia, AK, 153
    civilians of, 245–251
Semcham, 315
Semichi Group, 37–38, 46, 70
Sentinel Island, 222
Service, Robert, 227
Seventh Ferrying Group, 150, 322
Seventh Infantry Division, 8, 41, 81–85, 395
Seventh Motorized Division, 64
Seventh Scout Company, 81
Seventy-Second Reconnaissance Squadron,
    401, 405
Sevetlee, Johnny, 46
Seward, AK (ice-free port), 377–378
    See also Caines Head State Recreation Area
Sgt. Billy, camp mascot, 377
Shag Village, 46
Shaishnikoff, Vasilii, 162
Shapsniskoff, Anfesia, 293
Shauna salmon trawler, 134
Sheffield, William "Bill", 411
Shellikoff, Luke, 163, 292–293, 297
Shemya Air Force Base, 62, 396, 397
Shepler, Dwight, 47
Sherl', David, 331
Sherwood, Morgan, 253
Shikanai, Takeshiro, 303, 304
Shimada, Shigetaro, 34
Shimizu, George, family, 263
Shimizu's New York Cafe, 259
Shimushu, 72
Shubrick (Coast Guard), 125

Siberia
    gold mining in, 341–342
    railroads, 176, 335
    U.S. Army operations in, 4
    U.S. weather station in, 10
    See also Alaska-Siberia Air Route; Alaska-
        Siberia lend-lease program
Siberian Railway, 15
Siberian Yupik people, 156
Sicily, First Canadian Division in, 97
Siems-Drake (Fort Ray contractor), 224, 241,
    242
Sikanni Chief River bridge, 278
Silver City, Northwest Territories, 189
Sims, Refines, Jr., 279
Sinclair, Jack E., 381
Sitka
    childhood memories of, 265–267
    population, 1940, 265
    population, 1993, 265n2
    strategic location of, 5
Sitka Commercial Club, 242
Sitka National Cemetery, 241
Sitka National Historical Park, 242
Sitka Naval Operating Base, 239
Sitka Sentinel, 241, 242, 265
Sitting Duck (nickname for B-29 Ferret), 403
Skagit Queen, 221
Skagway, 192
Skinner and Eddy, 214
ski troops. See mountain troops
sled dogs, 151
Smith, Barbara Sweetland, 375
Smith, "Mudhole" (bush pilot), 408
Smith, Sherman, 123
Smith, W. W. (Rear Adm.), 40
Smokejumper School, 128
SNAFU, 106
Snag, 191
Snedden, C. W., 197
snow, 39, 43, 54, 87, 144, 187, 222
snow weasel track vehicle, 54
Solomons Campaign (South Pacific, 1942-
    1943), 7
Sorensen, W. Conner, 240
South Addition, Anchorage's first annexation,
    208
South Beach, Seward, AK, 378, 379
South Pacific, 7, 79, 110, 169
Soviet Air Force (SAF), 316, 317, 328, 334
Soviet Purchasing Commission, 321, 347–348
Soviet State Committee of Defense, 327–328
Soviet Supply Mission, 316
Soviet Union
    Cold War and, 397
    enters war against Japan, 10
    Germany invades, 327, 334
    offensive against Germany, 17
    See also lend-lease

Spaatz, Carl (Gen.), 400, 404
Spain, 334
Spalding, Arnold, 43
Special Services Force (Canada), 25, 105
Spencer, Fred, 272–273
Spitfire, British fighter plane, 317
Spitzbergen, 149
The Spoilers (film), 228
SS Aleutian, 128
SS Bell, 93
SS Heywood, 93
SS Northwestern (passenger steamer), 219–226
SS Ogontz (floating cannery), 215
SS Tacoma, 223
SS Yukon, 244
St. George, Pribilof Islands, 307
    Aleut population, 1940, 161
    restoration of church on, 372
St. Innocent Chapel, 374
St. Louis light cruiser, 77
St. Michael's Russian Orthodox Church ,
    Sitka, 243
St. Paul, Aleut village in Pribilofs, 161, 298,
    307
Stacey, C. P., 97
Stahlberg, Ernest (Machinist Mate), 116–117,
    118
Stalin, Joseph, 6
    lend-lease program and, 171, 311, 314, 315,
        316, 319, 321, 328, 334–335
Stalingrad counter-offensive. See Operation
    Uranus
Standard Oil Company, 132, 200
Star of Kodiak, 216
Stars and Stripes, 206
State Historic Preservation Office, 369
Statehood, Alaska (1959), 209, 397
Steese Highway, 175
Stefansson, Vilhjalmar, 173
Stepetin, Alfred, 299
Stepetin, Gabriel, 307
Stephens Brothers shipyard, CA, 132, 134
Sterligov (Maj. Gen.), 315–316
Stevens, Ted, 299, 305–306, 371
Stewart, Henry, 304
Stimson, Henry L., 99
Stockton Air Base, CA, 132
Strategic Air Command (SAC), 399–400
Stuart, Alice, 262
Stuart (Gen., Canada), 98–99, 100, 101, 102
Sturdevant, Clarence (Brig. Gen.), 159, 277,
    278–279
submarine, 355
    Coast Guard and, 129
    I-class, 42
    midget submarine, Japanese, 69
    RO-65, 355–356
    S-class, 77
    type-A, 357

suicide, 416, 417
    Japanese, 41, 85, 111, 112, 260
    Native Alaskan, 159
Sumatra, 67
Summit Lake, 192
Suvorov, Vladimir, 343
Suyehira, Henry, 287
Suzuki, Howard, 261
Svarney, Gertrude, 49, 295
Sverdlovsk, 315
Swanport, 220
Swanson, Henry, 162–163
Sweeper's Cove, Adak, 135
Symington, W. Stuart, 404

T

Tacoma, WA, 221, 242
Tacoma Air Force terminal, 133–134
Tacoma-class frigate, 348
Taguchi, Sam, 259
Takahashi, Hisashi, 6
Takao heavy cruiser, 37
Takasaki, T., 212
Talbot destroyer, 77
Talley, Benjamin B. (Col.), 9, 30, 59–64
Talley, Virginia M., 59
Tanacross, AK, 194, 206
Tanaga, 62
Tanino, James, family, 263
Target X, 400
Tartarski Strait, 15
Task Force Eight (later, North Pacific Force), 40
Task Force Fifty-One, USN, 76, 118
Task Force Nine, 361
Task Group 16.6, 114
Tate, J. R. (Cmdr.), 199
Tatsuda, Charlie, 262, 286, 287
Tatsuda, Cherry, 286
Tatsuda, James "Jimmy," 262, 263
Taylor, Ike, 192
Taylor Highway, 193
T-boats, 133
Tcheripanoff, Bill, 291
Teben'kov, M. D., 162
Teheran Conference (1944), 171
Telegraph Trail, 173, 176
Tenth Emergency Rescue Boat Squadron,
    131–134, 153, 248, 250
Tenth Mountain Division, 54, 106–107, 123
Terent'ev, Koz'ma, 162
Terrace, BC, 140
Teslin Lake, 192
Texas Battalion, 286
Texas Rangers, 230
Theobald, Robert A. (Rear Adm.), 75–80
    army-navy relations and, 7, 8
    operation plan of, 77–79
    relationship with Buckner, 76, 77, 394–395
    relieved of command, 8, 41, 79–80
    retrospective assessment of, 7, 80

Third Judicial District, 204

Thirteenth Infantry Brigade Group (Canada), 25, 89

Thirteenth Naval District, 5

Thomas, J. Parnell, 232

Thompson, Bob (Capt.), 43, 45

Thompson, Harry (Brig. Gen.), 281, 282

Thomsen, Niels P. (Lt.), 129

Thorburn, Don, 417

Thorburn, Lois, 417

Thorsness, Lowell, 245, 247, 248, 249, 251

*Those Navy Guys and their PBY's: The Aleutian Solution* (Freeman), 419

*Thousand Mile War, The* (Garfield), 27–32, 416

Tilden, Mel, 43

Timor, 67

tin can (destroyer), 113, 119

tin mining, in Siberia, 341–342

Titanium Memorial, 362

Tlingit people, 295, 298

T-15/M-29 ("snow weasel" track vehicle), 54

Tobin, August, 253

Tobin, Emery, 253–254, 255, 257, 258

Tojo, Hideki (Gen.), 112

Tok Junction, 191, 193

Tokyo, 29, 34, 45, 73, 228

Tokyo Base, 71

Tokyo Rose, 104, 224–225

Tomioka, Sadatoshi (Capt.), 34

Tongass Narrows, 221

Toovak, Kenneth, 160

*Top Cover for America* (Monaghan & Cloe), 415

Topeka Point, 378

torpedo boat, 45, 120

Torres (Capt.), 152

Totem Pole Park (Sitka), 241

totem poles, 241–242

tourism, 254, 258

Toyo Seikan Kaisha, Ltd., 212

TP-92 vessel, 133, 134

trans-Alaska-Bering Strait-Siberian Railroad, 176

Trans-Siberian Railway, 335

Treasure Island, CA, 132

Treaty of Portsmouth, 15

TRIDENT Conference (May 1943), 25, 87

Trincomalee, Ceylon, 36

*Triton* (submarine), 44

troops, minority. *See* minority troops in Alaska

Troy, John, 197

Truman, Harry S.
  Alaska Highway and, 167–168
  Berlin Crisis and, 403–404

tuberculosis, 303, 307

Tucker, Herbert (Sgt.), 272, 279

Tule Lake, CA, internment camp, 259

*Tuna,* submarine (USN), 44

tundra, 8, 49, 89

Tundra Army. *See* Alaska Territorial Guard

Tunner, William H. (Gen.), 324

Turnbull, Jack, 380

Turner, Landon (Capt.), 324, 402

*Tuscaloosa,* 312

Tutiakoff, Martha, 162

Tutiakoff, Philemon, 297, 298, 299

Tutiakoff, Vincent, 163

Tverdohlebov (Lt. Col.), 331

Twenty-Fourth Field Company, 100

Twichell, Heath, 190, 419

Typhoon Cobra (Dec. 1944), 119

**U**

U-boats, 314

Uel'em, 336

Uel'kal', Siberia (lend-lease route town), 331, 336, 342, 343

Ugaki, Matome (Rear Adm.), 34

Ugashik, 44, 212

Ukraine, 334, 335, 341

Ulibarri, George, 385

Umnak Island, 48, 69, 408
  airfield construction on, 61–62, 394
  as defense priority, 21
  Fort Glenn, 280, 365, 367–368
  historical landmarks on, 365

Unalakleet, 43, 46

Unalaska, 69
  Aleut population, 1940, 161
  bombing on hospital at, 224
  removal of Aleut from, 161
  restoration of/restitution for churches damaged on, 371–372, 373–374
  trail systems on, 162
  *See also* Dutch Harbor

Unalaska Memorial Park, 226

unemployment, 236, 237

*Unisea,* 216

United States Army, Alaska (USARAL), 396, 397

United Transport of Canada, 321

University of Oregon, repository, 29

Upickson, Arthur, 43, 45

*Uragio Maru,* 357

Urata, Bob, 262

U.S. Army, reasons to defend Alaska, 3–4

U.S. Army Air Forces, 7, 9, 40, 46, 73, 131, 158

U.S. Army Corps of Engineers. *See* Alaska Highway; Army Corps of Engineers

U.S. Army Signal Corps., 407

U.S. Bureau of Mines, 238

U.S. Forest Service, 235, 236, 238, 240

U.S. Navy, forces in Alaska, December 1941, 6

U.S. Pacific Fleet, 394

U.S. Revenue Marine. *See* Coast Guard, U.S.

U.S. Strategic Bombing Survey of 1946, 355

USAAF (US Army Air Force), 45, 170

USARAL (United States Army Alaska), 396, 397

USO, 130, 140, 377

USS *Hornet,* 36

USS *Houston* ("floating White House"), 250

USS *Monaghan* (DD-354), 113–119

U.S.–Soviet relationship, 341, 418
  *See also* lend-lease

**V**

vandalism, of Aleut villages, 295, 296, 298, 372, 374

Van Stone, James, 158

Vasin, N. S. (Col.), 323

Vaughn, Norman (Lt. Col.), 151, 153

Vega Point, Japanese outpost on Kiska, 121

Velkal, 315, 317

Veniaminov, Ioann (St. Innocent), 374

Verbeck, William (Col.), 43, 200

Verkhoianskii Range, 341

Verlakelum (Lt.), 43

Veterans Administration, 241

Victor Trap Company, 257

victory disease, 33

victory garden, 247

Vidal, Gore, 206, 416

Vietnam, 397

Vietnam War, 257

Vladivostok, 3, 4, 14, 15

**W**

Wada, Jujiro, 259

Wahl, Bob, 241

Wainwright, village of, 157

Wakatake-cho, 32

Wake Island, 67

*Wake Island* (film), 228

Walker, Edgar, 43, 44

Wallace, Henry A., 171, 324–325, 342

Walsh, Raoul, 232

war bonds, 257, 417

War Claims Commission, 298

War Committee (Canada), 88, 98–99, 102

Ward Lake, 131, 239, 298

War Labor Board, 207

War Manpower Commission, 216

Warnick, Lucian, 29–30

War Plan BROILER, 399

War Plans Division studies, 387

War Production Board, 242

War Relocation Authority, 259

Washington Conference (Dec. 1941), 15

Wasley, Pvt., 179

Watson Lake, YT, 151, 173

WAVES (Women Accepted for Voluntary Emergency Service), 413–414

*Wayanda* cutter, 125

weather
  cold, 39
  difficulties caused by, 13
  effects on Alaska-Siberia lend-lease program, 336

weather (*continued*)
  effects on search and rescue, 150
    fog, 7–9, 23, 39, 43, 46, 48, 69, 71, 89, 113, 221
    snow, 39, 43, 54, 87, 144, 187, 222
    williwaw winds, 16, 136, 140
Webb, Wayne, 248
Webblock (North Pacific deception plan code
    name), 415
*Wehrmacht*, 334
Welles, Sumner, 313
Wenz, Ralph (Sgt.), 143, 144, 146
Wertzel, Ruben, 184
Westall, Billy, 43, 45
West Construction Company, 63, 378
Western Air Command, Canadian, 21, 22, 23
Western Defense Command (WDC), 97
Western Washington Fair Grounds at
    Puyallup, internment camp, 260
Westover, Joseph (Maj.), 151, 153
*Westward* (tender), 246, 249, 250
whaling, 156, 217
*The Whip Hand* (film), 232
White, John Wesley (Capt.), 125
White, Maynard E. (Maj.), 400
White, Walter, 279
White Act (1924), 215
White Alice troposphere communications
    radar system, 208, 397
Whitehorse, NT, 153, 173, 176, 190, 192, 322
Whitesel, Carlin (Col.), 61, 64
Whittier, AK
  pipeline to Anchorage, 397
  railroad at, 63
Wien brothers, 408
Wilcox, Mark, 393
Wilcox Bill, 393
Willard, Clara, 253
*Williwaw* (Vidal), 206
williwaw winds (strong winds), 16, 136, 140
Wilson, Gwynneth Gminder, 413–414
Wilson, Walt, 243
Wilson, Woodrow, signs Alaska Railroad Bill,
    221
Winnipeg Grenadiers, 100
Wiseman, 262
Wishbone Hill, 204
WLW radio station (Cincinnati), 199
wolf hunting, 255
Wolper, David L., 87
Wolverine Lake, 243–244
woman
  Aleut, in evacuation camp, 295
  memoirs of, 241–244
Woodchopper, AK, 145, 146
Woodley, Art, 408
Woodley Airways, Old, 44
Wood River Buttes, 141–142
Wooley, Chris, 156
World's Fair, St. Louis (1904), 241
World War II, strategy in, 14–15

World War II Pacific Theme Study, 353
Wrangell Institute Native School, 295
Wrangell Narrows, 127, 222
Wright, Laura Beltz (first Alaska territorial
    guardswoman), 157
writing about war, perspectives on, 415–420
Wyler, William, 229

**X**

XI Fighter Command (Canada), 24

**Y**

Yakutat
  airfield construction at, 59–60
  as defense priority, 21, 22–23
Yakutat and Southern Railway, 59–60
Yakutat huts, 367
Yakutsk, Siberia, 315
Yalta Conference (Feb. 1945), 10, 347
Yamamoto, George, 259
Yamamoto, Isoroku (Adm.), 6, 34, 35–36, 39,
    40, 69
  death of, 110
  failures of, 109
Yamazaki, Yasuyo (Col.), 41, 71, 110, 111
Yarnell, Harry (Adm.), 4
Yasuda, Frank, 259
Yaw family, 265–267
Yippy boats, 215
Yokohama, Japan, 302
Yoneyama (Lt. Col.), 110
Yost, Harry, 187
Young, Dale, 193
Young, Don, 299, 371
YP ("Yippy") boats, 215
*Yucatan*, 219
Yukon Indian Agency, 193–194
Yukon Indians, 194
Yukon-Kuskokwim Delta, 156
*Yukon Patrol* (film), 230
Yukon Southern Air Transport, 321
Yup'ik people, 155–156

**Z**

Zaharoff, William, 295
Zanuck, Darryl, 229
Zero (Mitsubishi A6M2), Japanese fighter, 40,
    44, 45, 121, 129, 224, 357, 394, 416, 418
Zeusler, Fredrick A., 126–127, 128
zinc mining, 192
*Zuiho* carrier, 69
*Zuikaku* carrier, 69